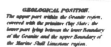

GEOLOGICAL POSITION.
The upper part within the Granite region,
covered with the primitive Clay Slate ; the
lower part lying between the lower Boundary
of the Granite and the upper Boundary of
the Marine Shell Limestone region.

COLUMBIA.
The Capital of South Carolina
Latitude North. 33°.57'.30".
Meridian of the State passing through
the Observatory of the College.

R S H A W

O R A N G E B U R G H

Columbia and Richland County

Columbia and Richland County

A SOUTH CAROLINA COMMUNITY, 1740–1990

JOHN HAMMOND MOORE

University of South Carolina Press

Published in cooperation with the
Richland County History Commission

Copyright © 1993 University of South Carolina

Published in Columbia, South Carolina, by the
University of South Carolina Press

Printed in Canada

Library of Congress Cataloging-in-Publication Data

Moore, John Hammond.
   Columbia and Richland County : a South Carolina community,
1740–1990 / John Hammond Moore.
      p.   cm.
   Includes bibliographical references and index.
   ISBN 0–87249–827–1
   1. Columbia (S.C.)—History.   2. Richland County (S.C.)—History.
I. Title.
F279.C7M67   1993
975.7'71—dc20   92-18919

Ascend, at dusk, the hills of Lexington
And view the twinkling city far below,
Skirting the margin of the Congaree
And mounting along the noble ridge
That leads to fragrant woods of pine beyond.
Where else in all the land are mingled thus
The sweeping reaches of the coastal plain,
The rugged Piedmont's serried fields of flint,
The pleasant pageantry of sand-hill scrub
Flaming in autumn with a Gypsy's gold?

The singing mother of tall, gallant sons
And soft-eyed daughters, wonderfully fair.
The spirit of youth is in her and the heart
That beats in those whose joy is work well done.
She speaks the language of a high-born dame,
Yet wears the easy grace of country folk
Whose priceless heritage is happiness.

From Chapman J. Milling's
"Sesqui-Centennial Ode," published in
his *Singing Arrows* (Columbia, 1938).

Contents

Illustrations

Unless other sources are cited, all photographs were made by staff photographer Charles Gay from materials at the South Caroliniana Library.

Tables

Preface

Telling the story of a region is a task like few others, for the scope of the undertaking is far from clear. The tale, unlike biography, lacks beginning and end. In addition, a domain such as Richland County had no boundaries until the 1790s, and two centuries later urban sprawl has, to a large degree, obliterated frontiers once thought sacrosanct. Development of Columbia, both county seat and state capital, and the growth of the Midlands have obscured waves of change experienced by any emerging metropolis and its hinterland. Yet one must be realistic, and for purposes at hand a period of 250 years has been selected: from the onset of European settlement on the east bank of the Congaree to the final decade of the 20th century.

This era encompasses several wars, one of them bringing profound consequences in its wake, as well as flush times of high cotton and harsh seasons when crops withered and died. Columbia—a two-mile grid of wide streets laid out in the wilderness to welcome a functioning bureaucracy—indeed had a unique birth, but the ensuing annals of city and county recount events common to most American communities, with one notable exception. And that is the element of compromise that permeates the local scene. Richland's capital was born in compromise in 1786 and has spent much of its lifetime tempering the clashing views of upcountry and low. It is no accident that the Midlands usually seeks the *middle* way when political seas get rough.

In recent decades, this attitude has been enhanced by a perception that Columbia speaks (in racial matters, for example) for the state as a whole. Thus this community, whether playing the role of referee or peacemaker, must pick and choose its path with great care. At the same time, rival population centers within South Carolina frequently view Columbia as the "fair-haired child" of state government that gets more than its share of goodies. Clearly, the heart of the Midlands is not immune to outside forces, be they a hundred miles away or a thousand, and it never was. Thus regional history becomes both the local story and that of the world outside, at least insofar as that world impinges upon day-to-day events.

Sorting out these various threads—city, county, regional, state, national, and even international—would have been impossible without the help of the South Caroliniana Library and its staff, specifically assistance provided by Herbert Hartsook, Thomas Johnson, Eleanor Richardson, and Allen Stokes. Virtually all of the material cited in the pages that follow, published and unpublished items, can be found in that splendid research center. The only exceptions would be personal interviews and census data and official records deposited at the South Carolina Department of Archives and History.

Three other local residents deserve a vote of thanks, each for different reasons. Ronald Bridwell first launched a history of Columbia in 1984 as part of this city's bicentennial celebration under the sponsorship of the State-Record Publishing Company, and I am indebted to him for extensive research in the antebellum period. Theodore J. Hopkins, Jr., has displayed unusual interest in this undertaking and, together with his aunt, Laura Jervey Hopkins, and mother, Jane McDowell Hopkins, has opened numerous fruitful avenues of inquiry. Augustus T. Graydon—lawyer, raconteur, repository of much knowledge concerning Columbia, Richland County, and South Carolina—was instrumental in resuscitating this project as it lay dormant and all but forgotten.

In the mid-1980s, perhaps stirred by Columbia's birthday party, county officials formed a commission to develop a county flag. This group, urged on by County Councilman John Monroe and others, in time turned its attention to the need for a county history and appointed the Richland County History Commission in 1987. Meanwhile, the bicentennial year came to a close, the State-Record Company changed hands, and Graydon made funding available for the writing of a joint city-county history. The Richland County History Commission, headed by C. David Warren, director of the Richland County Public Library, provided the framework for *Columbia and Richland County: A South Carolina Community, 1740–1990*.

Warren has been ably assisted by a group of interested individuals who have furnished timely encouragement and advice, among them, Nancy E. Bailey, Justine Bond Culler, James L. Lancaster, Robert J. Moore, and Milton Davenport. Rex B. Jarrell, Jr., also served on this commission for a time, as did the late Henry Lumpkin. I am deeply indebted to all of those cited here and scores more who are not. Family papers, reminiscences, institutional histories, census returns, documents official and unofficial, and the files of local newspapers are the stuff from which the Columbia-Richland story has been fashioned, aided, to no small degree, by personal interviews, random recollections, and casual conversation. As always, the voice breathes new life into the printed word.

Columbia and Richland County

PART I

Foundations,
1740–1800

Much of this period actually can be classified as the "pre-history" of the region between the Congaree and Wateree rivers; for it was not until the mid–1780s that Richland County and Columbia became realities. In fact, only in the last twelve months of the 18th century did Richland achieve true independent status with the little community of Columbia as its seat of local government. By that time, some residents, a few of whom had lived here a half century or more, had seen frontier give way to settlement, and chaos and warfare supplanted by peace and order.

Yet the land that became Richland County was, in many ways, an atypical frontier. Largely a colony of ex-Virginians, for several decades it was merely a necklace of farms and plantations strung out along the banks of two rivers without any real nucleus or market place of its own. Boundaries were vague and unclear; the future uncertain. Nevertheless, protected by a band of sand hills to the north and water to the south, east, and west, these pioneers, eager to grow tobacco on virgin soil, had little reason to fear the depredations of intruders. Indians and outlaws, who wandered into the Midlands from time to time, gravitated instead to more attractive targets such as Fort Congaree to the west and Pine Tree Hill (Camden) to the east. In short, this inland peninsula was an isolated pocket of humanity and might have remained so except for two unforeseen developments.

One was the concept of centrality that gripped South Carolinians and many other young Americans of the 1780s, the belief that authority exerted from a *central* location could somehow more effectively express the will of the electorate. This may well have been a mix of pragmatic reasoning, wishful thinking, and disdain for older cities tainted by pre-1776 associations, but it was nonetheless real. The other was the truly remarkable influence a handful of individuals had upon the land between the Congaree and Wateree. These men, eager to develop and exploit their

1

holdings in the Midlands, used persuasion and the powers of high office to create Richland County and the town of Columbia and, within a brief time, catapult them into the forefront of South Carolina's political, economic, and cultural life.

In 1785, there was nothing in the region but pine forests and a few cleared fields. Fifteen years later there was a county and a county seat that also was the capital of the state, an ambitious little town that was preparing to build, of all things, a college. This institution, it was hoped, would meld together upcountry, lowcountry, and Midlands. Thus from seeming obscurity had sprung a unique community, the first in American history to take on the difficult task of transferring the machinery of a functioning bureaucracy to a wilderness setting and making that experiment work.

Of Land
and People

CHAPTER ONE

The region that became Richland County in the closing years of the 18th century and soon gained special prominence as the new seat of state government is shaped somewhat like an arrowhead, an inland peninsula pointed, perhaps prophetically, in a southeasterly direction toward the original capital, Charleston. It consists of 771 square miles and includes several tracts of land on its western and northern borders that once belonged to neighboring counties. A large slice of Lexington's Dutch Fork community and a triangular portion of Fairfield County, both acquired in the early 20th century, are the most important of these territorial changes. Originally the Broad and Congaree rivers were Richland's western boundary, but the first of these acquisitions added several towns and villages located between the Saluda and Broad, an area now served by I–26, and also gave county residents direct access to Newberry County. Then the northern frontier, long virtually two straight lines marking the Fairfield-Kershaw border, was redrawn so that the community of Blythewood and its environs are in Richland County, not Fairfield. However, the Wateree to the east and the Congaree to the south and west, with their bewildering twists and turns and swamps and marshes, continue to delineate Richland's boundaries with Sumter, Calhoun, and Lexington counties.

Although geographers Charles Kovacik and John Winberry remind us in their fine study of South Carolina that the local landscape has been altered over many centuries by weather, erosion, fire, and man, it remains basically a rolling countryside, which they designate as part of this state's *inner* coastal plain.[1] Elevation above sea level varies from 80 feet where the Congaree meets the Wateree to 550 feet in northern sections. The county's most obvious physical features are sand hills (a narrow, disjointed band of usually gentle slopes that mark the fall line zone) and various streams and rivers that eventually form the Santee en route to the

3

Atlantic Ocean. The sand hills tend to define the Midlands, a region separating the coastal plain (lowcountry) from the Piedmont (upcountry). The term "Midlands," used infrequently in the late 19th century, was given new prominence by Columbia newsman Henry Cauthen in the 1950s.[2] Both sand hills and Midlands are synonymous with fall line zone, the region where the first cataracts, shoals, or falls are encountered as one proceeds inland from the coast. With the exception of the Congaree and Wateree, both of which often were called the "Santee" in colonial days, most of the local waterways were named for or by early settlers—names such as Gill, Raglin, Carter, Cedar, and Cane (or Crane) that have persisted to the present day.

And, although South Carolina's rivers and creeks are capricious entities—often too high and too swift or sluggish, shallow, and useless for commercial purposes—the traditional fall line still has significance; for it is at this point that goods often were loaded or unloaded, trade developed, and settlements appeared. Some historians have discounted the importance of the fall line in South Carolina, stressing that goods and people usually moved to and from the lowcountry by wagon, pack-horse, or on foot, not by boat. Nevertheless, cheap and easy water transport always was an attractive, if elusive, alternative and, in some seasons, feasible. Thus one can easily trace the fall line across the state through Cheraw, Camden, and Columbia to Augusta on the west bank of the Savannah River.

The Richland County landscape can be divided into three major areas. Lower Richland, an east-west band of coastal plain stretching from the Congaree Swamp north to the Sumter Highway, is by far the best farmland. Not surprisingly, here were the first settlements and it was here that large-scale agriculture and substantial estates developed during the opening decades of the 19th century. By drawing a line from Columbia to the northeast corner of the county, the upper two-thirds can be divided into two triangles: sand hills and Piedmont. The former, the lower side of which abuts the Sumter Highway, conforms in a general way to Fort Jackson's domain. The soil, less fertile than that found in the other two areas and never farmed extensively, has produced lumber and forest products. This expanse of sand and pine has, through the years, been both blessing and curse. Since few people lived there, it did not attract Indians, outlaws, and others bent on mayhem and long served as a protective barrier of sorts for those living in lower Richland. At the same time, the absence of community life for many decades tended to limit population growth within the county as a whole. The Piedmont triangle, bordering the Congaree-Broad-Saluda rivers on the west and Fairfield County on the north—traditionally a region of small farms—is now becoming more and more a maze of suburban homes, shopping malls, office buildings, and industrial parks.

Except for swamps and outcroppings of pine barrens, both of which at times have had their admirers, the environment of central South Carolina is conducive to human habitation. Natural resources, even if not overly abundant, have been plentiful enough to satisfy the needs of local residents for thousands of years. The climate, classified by experts as "humid subtropical," is characterized by hot summers and mild winters, although the Richland County area occasionally experiences snow, ice, and below-freezing temperatures. According to state authorities, the average January reading is 44°; the average July temperature, 81°.[3] The region has an annual rainfall of about 46 inches and a 220-day growing season.

It is impossible, of course, to say when Indians first settled here, but archeological remains indicate various groups of people have lived in central South Carolina for some 10,000–15,000 years. Of those tribes only a handful play any role in the Richland County story. The most important of these are the Congaree, Wateree, Catawba, Cherokee, and Saluda. The Congaree and Wateree, relatives of the Catawba, with whom they subsequently merged in the opening decades of the 18th century, were Siouan speakers living in the eastern part of the state close by the region that eventually became Richland County. The powerful Cherokee, an Iroquoian-speaking tribe and arch-enemies of the Catawba, dominated northwestern South Carolina and flowed over into the mountains of North Carolina and Tennessee. The Saluda, an Algonquian-speaking group apparently drawn south from Pennsylvania in the 1600s by the lure of Spanish trade, dallied briefly in the Saluda County area, at least long enough to get their name into colonial records and bestow it upon the river that joins the Broad to form the Congaree. However, during the early 1700s these original carpetbaggers packed up and headed north. The Congaree, the native Americans most closely associated with Richland County, oddly enough, may never actually have lived within its borders.

Soon after the English got a toehold at Charleston in 1670, a few intrepid souls, a strange, reckless breed of men who mixed easily with the natives, headed inland in search of furs, pelts, deer skins, and anything else of value that Indians were willing to exchange for beads, axes, guns, strong drink, and blankets. Few of these daredevils left records, for few of them could write. But in December 1700, John Lawson, an explorer hired by the lords proprietors, set out from Charleston on a fifty-nine-day jaunt that took him up the Santee and Wateree into North Carolina, where he subsequently helped to found both Bath and New Bern.

Lawson's story of this trip, *A New Voyage to Carolina*, provides solid proof of white penetration of the interior, as well as a rare glimpse of the Congaree.[4] He and his friends—the original party included six Englishmen, three Indian males, and a squaw—began their journey in a large canoe, stopping at various islands and battling "Swarms of Musketoes" as they made their way up the coast to the Santee. Moving inland, they often lodged at night in houses built for the Indian trade, making themselves comfortable even if the owners were away. According to Lawson, this was an accepted practice, providing one replaced food eaten with gifts of tobacco, paint, beads, or similar items. Just south of a great swamp (Lake Marion?) the travelers tarried at an Indian hut where they were served boiled goose, venison, racoon, and ground nuts. In this region, Lawson wrote, there were large savannahs filled with cattle and great flocks of cranes, geese, and turkeys.

Near the juncture of what are now the Congaree and Wateree rivers, the Lawson party came upon an Indian settlement consisting of about a dozen houses. Only women were present, the men having gone "a Hunting for a Feast." Nevertheless, they were well received and immediately offered food.

These people, the Congaree, were, according to Lawson, "kind and affable to the *English*." He noted that they had "stragling [sic] Plantations up and down the Country" in a land that, in his opinion, certainly could provide forage for many cattle and hogs. Their ranks were dwindling, however, as a result of disease. This explorer was especially intrigued by storks and cranes that the Congaree captured when young and kept as pets. Two other aspects of native life puzzled Lawson: the great differences between various neighboring tribes and their sexual practices . . . although he actually managed to explain intimate relations between English traders and Indian maidens quite satisfactorily.

Altho' their Tribes or Nations border one upon another, yet you may discern as great an Alteration in their Features and Dispositions, as you can in their Speech, which generally proves quite different from each other, though their Nations be not more than 10 or 20 Miles in Distance. The Women here being as handsome as most I have met withal, being several fine-fingered Brounetto's [fine-figured brunettes?] amongst them. These Lasses stick not upon Hand long, for they marry when they are young, as at 12 or 14 Years of Age. The *English* traders are seldom without an *Indian* Female for his Bedfellow, alledging [sic] these Reasons as sufficient to allow for such Familiarity. First, They being remote from any white People, that it preserves their Friendship with the Heathens, they esteeming the white Man's Child much above one of their own getting, the *Indian* mistress even securing her white Friend Provisions whilst he stays amongst them. And lastly, This Correspondence makes them learn the *Indian* tongue much the sooner, they being of the *French*-man's Opinion, how that an *English* wife teaches her Husband more *English* in one Night, than a School-master can in a Week.[5]

Some historians, among them Hugh Lefler, editor of a recent edition of Lawson's journal, conclude that "Congaree Town" was located on the northern bank of the Congaree River, placing it within present-day Richland County. Others are not so sure. Since Lawson and his friends now were on foot and he says nothing about crossing the Santee—only that this town was "seated upon a small branch of *Santee* River"—it is quite possible that the Indian village was on some small stream flowing into the Santee from the east, not the west. Also, according to some sources, at this time the region between the Santee-Wateree and the Congaree-Broad was a sort of no-man's-land separating the Catawba and their allies from the Cherokee. If true, one would expect the small band of Congaree to prefer the safety of the Santee's east bank, land now in Sumter County, not Richland.

In any case, within a decade or so remnants of this tribe (probably less than one hundred men, women, and children) were living in present-day Lexington County. They apparently had been nudged westward by the Wateree, a tall people, according to Lawson, much given to pilfering, who, in turn, had felt pressure from still other Indian tribes. The new home of the Congaree on the west bank of the river that bears their name was strategically important because of its location on the trade route from Charleston to both the Cherokee and the Catawba. Just south of the junction of the Saluda and the Broad, that trail split, with one branch leading northward over the Congaree toward the Catawba Nation and the other running along the south bank of the Saluda into Cherokee country.

However, the Congaree had hardly unpacked their belongings when the entire South Carolina frontier was set ablaze by the Yemassee War (1715–1716). This last great effort to oust white intruders of course failed, but before it was over some fifteen tribes joined in this bloody assault, among them, the Congaree. But the Cherokee, who displayed only spasmodic interest in these goings-on or cheered from the sidelines, at length rejected overtures from the Creeks (the ringleaders of this affair, despite top billing given to the Yemassee) and came to the aid of the English.

One immediate result of this turmoil, in addition to the deaths of four hundred settlers and an impoverished and disheartened colony, was a new Indian policy. Instead of currying favor with all factions, colonial leaders henceforth would exploit inter-tribal rivalries to their advantage and also try to regulate the activities of those trading with the Indians, a prime cause of the Yemassee uprising. To implement this strategy, a government-operated trading "factory," as well as a small garrison, was established at "the Congarees" five miles south of the juncture of the Saluda and Broad rivers near present-day Cayce. For a few years some fifteen to twenty men were stationed at a crude earthen fort erected there, but by the early 1720s the Indian trade once more was back in private hands and these facilities were abandoned.

The impact of these events was at least two-fold. In the midst of the Yemassee War—or perhaps on the eve of hostilities—the Congaree departed for Catawba territory and joined forces with that tribe, never to return. Secondly, the enhanced prestige of the Cherokee in English eyes greatly increased commercial activity along the path leading from Charleston to their inland empire, which indirectly was of some benefit to the region destined to become Richland County.

The Wateree, who had joined in the general assault upon white settlers during the Yemassee War, tended to follow the example set by the Congaree. Although they apparently did not move *en masse,* by 1740 the people who gave their name to the river on Richland's eastern boundary were living among the Catawba. In short, both the Congaree and Wateree, their ranks much diminished, had chosen the losing side in the Yemassee War and paid the price exacted by faulty judgment. By the time restless English settlers pushing inland from the coast and south from the interior of North Carolina and Virginia began to think about carving farms and fields out of the wilderness between the Congaree and Wateree, the native Indians had departed. Their legacy, somewhat indistinct today, included the utilization of crops such as corn and squash, certain agricultural techniques, and a handful of lyrical words such as Saluda, Santee, Wateree, and, of course, Congaree.

And the term "the Congarees" lingered on in colonial decades with at least three meanings—settlement developing in and around forts that appeared from time to time on the west bank of the Congaree River, plantations and farms in the region between that waterway and the Wateree, or the general area drained by the Congaree and its tributaries. In other words, "the Congarees" might mean a specific point of settlement (perhaps where the community of Granby would appear in the 1770s) or it could refer, with a broad wave of the hand, to a large segment of South Carolina's Midlands frontier.

During the decades following the Yemassee War, Indian-white relations were far from smooth. To some extent, the complicating factors were both international and regional as the French, Spanish, and English sparred with each other and Virginia, Georgia, and South Carolina vied for the lucrative Indian trade. However, the basic causes of discontent were much the same as before: sharp, even dishonest, trading practices, mistreatment of natives (and mistreatment of traders by Indians as well, it should be noted), and unease among various tribes as pioneer farmers encroached upon their lands and threatened their way of life. None of these developments had any immediate impact upon the Richland County area; but, as settlers became more numerous in the Midlands, their ranks created a somewhat safer milieu, as well as competition for land.

Although records are scanty, the first white men to live in this region undoubtedly were Indian traders and cowboys. Lawson indicated that by 1700 those looking for furs and deerskins had penetrated deep into the Piedmont and reported he saw large herds of cattle grazing fifty miles from the coast. Neither trader nor cowboy—the first wave of white migration so prominent in the fabled West of 19th century America— cleared land or settled, but during the early 1700s both were seen more frequently along the banks of the Congaree, Wateree, and Broad. In their wake, or perhaps intermingled with them, were occasional squatters, dirt-poor pioneers, who scratched out a living as best they could. This roving, shiftless class secured no title to land, cleared but little of it, and soon moved on, often forced out; or, willing to accept some small pittance from legal owners for their pioneering effort, they departed with a smile, ready to try their luck elsewhere, perhaps in the sand hills.

According to Edwin Green's *History of Richland County* (1932), no one acquired title to land between the Congaree and Wateree and then proceeded to cut down trees, clear fields, and build a home until 1740.[6] However, in May of 1732 several speculators laid claim to property at the mouth of Gill's Creek on the east bank of the Congaree nearly opposite the old fort. In all, Dr. Daniel Gibson, Henry Gigniliatt, Jacob Satur, and Thomas Stitsmith, acting in concert, acquired 1,800 acres just south of the point where the Southeast Beltway crosses the Congaree River. Whatever plans Gignillatt, a Charleston vintner, and his friends may have had, they did not include living in the Midlands.

Three years later, Thomas Brown, a licensed trader with the Catawbas who resided near the old fort, apparently purchased property in the southeastern corner of Richland County from the Wateree Indians, but in 1739 the government banned such land transactions, both past and future. Subsequent appeals by Brown that he be reimbursed were turned aside by colonial authorities.

In 1738, John Cartwright, agent for one John Selwyn, petitioned the crown for a grant of 200,000 acres in this area, land on which a thousand Protestants would settle within ten years. Nothing came of this scheme. And Robert Mills writes in his famous *Statistics of South Carolina* (1826) that Benjamin Singleton was Richland County's first settler, having established "cowpens" near Cane Creek on the Broad River "about the year 1740." But Green rejected this claim since he found no proof that Singleton ever was a county resident.

Beginning in 1740, however, a group of pioneers appeared along several creeks in lower Richland firmly intent upon creating farms and building homesteads. What attracted them (and some speculators as well) was rich bottom land frequently inundated by the waters of the Congaree . . . land on which at least one of these individuals planned to grow rice.[7] Among the first to establish a home there was Philip Jackson who had 250 acres surveyed at Green Hill in 1740 and for a time gave his name to what later became Gill's Creek. A few miles down river, Philip Raiford, who migrated from North Carolina, acquired nearly 1,300 acres in 1742–1743. The waterway near his property, now called Mill Creek, at first was known as "Raiford's Creek." John Pearson, who married Raiford's daughter in 1742 and settled nearby, subsequently became a surveyor and an active promoter of upcountry real estate. Still another surveyor, John Fairchild, also bought land along "Raiford's Creek," as did Thomas Howell, whose family had moved south from Maryland.

Fairchild gained special prominence in 1751 when he raised a company of rangers to protect settlers from Indian outrages. In May of that year he told the governor that he and his neighbors had few arms and needed help. Many were newcomers to the area and knew little of Indian ways, he added, yet all of the men were full of spirit and ready to defend their homes and country. Fairchild also wrote of a fort then being constructed as a safe haven for women and children. Where this facility was located is not known; however, it probably was similar to several "private" forts that had appeared on the west side of the Congaree River for precisely the same reasons.

Among Fairchild's neighbors was blacksmith Thomas Wallexellson, who built a home on the banks of the Congaree in 1741 and began to ply his trade. Four years later, having failed to have his land surveyed and properly registered, he hurried to Charleston where he successfully rebuffed an attempt by Gilbert Gibson, "contrary to law and the intent of an hospitable Neighbour," to seize much of his timber.

Meanwhile, other settlers began to clear farms on the eastern shore of the Congaree north of Green Hill, land now part of the city of Columbia, while still others created a similar band of homesteads to the east on the banks of the Wateree. In 1741 Mary Russell acquired property in the extreme southeastern corner of the county washed by both the Congaree and Wateree. The following year, Joseph Hasford, a former Cherokee trader living in Orangeburg, had 200 acres surveyed ten miles up the Wateree where the river was choked by a "raft" of trees. Other early landowners along the Wateree included George Brown, Ann Dungworth, Joseph Jackson, Joseph Joyner, Mary Raney, Martin Sallom, Richard Singleton, and Thomas Smith.

Edwin Green wrote that soon settlers came "from all directions," but this confident assertion is somewhat misleading. According to his research, between 1740 and 1746 only thirty-nine individuals acquired land between the Congaree and Wateree rivers. The truth is, the center of regional activity was not here but on the other side of the Congaree in present-day Lexington County, as it had been for some time and would continue to be throughout much of the 18th century. After all, the major trading route into Cherokee-Catawba lands went up the *west* bank of the Congaree, a fort had been built there, and yet another would appear in 1748 when South Carolinians once more were alarmed by Indian warfare.

A second trade route followed the *eastern* bank of the Santee-Wateree, the path Lawson apparently took in 1701. Although not the main gateway to the Catawba realm, within a few years considerable backcountry commerce would move along this route to and from the northern colonies and give birth to a formidable rival to "the Congarees"—the community of Pine Tree Hill (Camden). Significantly, both of these commercial thoroughfares bypassed land lying within the pincers created by the Congaree and the Wateree rivers.

According to historian Robert L. Meriwether, the total population of what might be called the Jackson-Raiford settlement was only about 200 souls in 1747. Green Hill, he noted, was that region's outlet for wheat, cattle, and other produce, but that site, in his opinion, was badly hand-icapped, hemmed in as it was by swamps and mud much of each year. Meriwether also suggests that Indians perhaps constituted still another obstacle to settlement, since the Catawba and Wateree probably contin-ued to hunt from time to time in forests they knew well.

Of special significance to the Midlands region was the creation in 1733 of ten inland townships by order of the governor and council, one of them to be located along the west bank of the Congaree south of the Sa-luda River and another about forty miles to the northeast on the east bank of the Wateree. Following the marriage of Frederick, Prince of Wales, in April of 1736 to Princess Augusta of Saxe-Gotha, the Congaree settlement assumed the name of the bride's north German duchy, the other being named Fredericksburg for the groom.

These communities, patterned after New England models, had a dual purpose: protect lowcountry plantations from Indian incursions and offset a burgeoning slave population that was causing much more official concern than the activities of aboriginal Americans. To attract settlers, the government offered the head of a family 50 acres of land for each person, white and black, that he took to the frontier, including himself. In time, a few of these pioneers even were provided with tools and provisions at government expense. Meriwether describes in detail how some of these townships prospered, while others did not. Fredericksburg apparently was settled in some fashion in 1737, but then nothing much happened for a decade or so. After 1750, however, warrants and surveys increased and Fredericksburg was transformed into Pine Tree Hill, which eventually became Camden. Saxe-Gotha, as we shall see shortly, enjoyed an initial burst of activity followed by rather slow growth, a pattern dictated to a marked degree by what was happening in Europe, not America. Open warfare from 1739 to 1748 made trans-Atlantic travel risky; but with peace, immigrants once more appeared in Charleston seeking free land on the South Carolina frontier.[8]

In the early 1730s, just as these townships were taking shape, some of the same speculators who bought property on the east bank of the Con-garee were busy acquiring land close by the region that soon would be-come Saxe-Gotha. Among them was Catawba trader Thomas Brown, an ambitious go-getter who also laid claim to 250 acres near Ninety Six, fifty miles inland along the Cherokee Path. However, the first group of new-comers to be granted homesteads under the township plan was a small band of German-speaking Swiss who arrived in Charleston in February 1735. In their midst were several who, unable to pay for their passage, sought help from the government. Colonial authorities eventually complied with this request—even though the township fund was temporarily in the red—and ordered the men and their families to go to "the Congarees."

Meriwether's research indicates that not all of them reached their destination, some apparently going to other townships. But Jacob Gallman selected a homesite below the old fort, and Martin Fridig acquired 250 acres two miles above the first falls of the Congaree where he someday would operate a ferry. Colonial records, Meriwether noted, reveal that an Anglicizing process already was under way. Jacob Gallman soon was John Coleman, and Fridig was transformed into Friday. He also writes that at least six more German-Swiss families came to "the Congarees" at that time, but fails to identify them. In May 1735, a Charleston merchant reported that these people were "industrious and settling apace."[9]

During the next few years more German families—whether Swiss or not is not always clear—arrived in Charleston and were transported to Saxe-Gotha at the expense of the township fund. At the same time, numerous English names such as Lang, Baker, Berry, and Myrick begin to appear on local plats. And, at length, some of these individuals, Myrick for one, moved across the Congaree to the Richland County side, and still others began to clear fields on the north bank of the Saluda, land that eventually would become part of the county as well.

Of particular interest are Stephen and Joseph Crell, who arrived in Saxe-Gotha Township in 1736 and received 750 acres near the mouth of Tom's [Thom's/Thames] Creek just below Congaree Creek. At his death in 1763, Stephen, who became a justice of peace and sold goods as Stephen Crell and Company, owned a herd of cattle and various books, including a Hebrew Bible and a Greek testament. Three years after Joseph came to the frontier, he so impressed colonial officials with plans to erect a water mill—a facility, he emphasized, that would greatly benefit those growing wheat—that they contributed £22 toward completion of the structure. However, this would-be miller quickly tired of the project and decided to sell his property. The advertisement he placed in the *South-Carolina Gazette* (1 September 1739) provides an excellent description of the type of substantial frontier establishment one might find along the banks of the Congaree at that time.

To Be Sold

A Plantation containing 500 Acres of choice land on *Santee* River on both sides of Thames Creek in Saxe Gotha Township alias the Congrees, upon the Trading Road, compleatly scituated to keep a Store, and a Stock of Cattle and Mares, with new fram'd Dwelling House and other Buildings thereupon, *viz* a Large Cornfield, Potatoes, Peas, Beans, &c. as also Wheat and Hemp already gather'd, and put up for working; moreover about 8 Bushels of Hemp Seed (the Produce of a Quarter of an Acre) 20 Acres of the Land being in Good Fence all high dry Swamp rich Land fit for to raise Hemp without requiring any dunging, and will bring two Crops between the Times of the Freshe[t]s, there may be raised the next Summer a large Crop of Hemp.

As likewise to be sold three choice healthy Slaves that have had the Small Pox and aquainted to manage the Hemp and to dress Deer Skins, Household Stuffs, Plantation Utensils, a Waggon, a Plough, a Brewkettle, Brass Kettles, Grind Stones, Hoes, Axes, Carpenter's Tools &c sundry other Necessaries.

As also choice Cows, Horses and Hoggs.

Any Person inclinable to purchase paying Four Hundred Pounds down may have Credit for the Remainder until the first of March next giving Security and may apply to me at Saxe Gotha.

Joseph Crell.

Since no mill is mentioned, Meriwether concluded that Philip Puhl (or Poole), who bought this plantation, probably carried out Crell's plans; for, in 1748 Puhl owned a corn mill and was eager to erect a saw mill nearby. Meanwhile, Martin Friday had built a mill near his ferry and at the time of his death in the late 1750s owned yet another on Twelve Mile Creek . . . as well as a tan-yard, a wind mill, nine blacks, a glass window worth three shillings, and "a small sett of House Organs."

At about this time, according to Green, lower Richland also could boast of a mill. William Hay, who moved south from Virginia, in 1748 appealed to Charleston authorities to assist him in completing his "gris mill." Council records indicate this mill was in operation by September of 1749, so Hay presumably got the help he sought. The structure probably was located about a mile below Bluff Road on "Raiford Creek," soon to be known as "Hay's Mill Creek," and finally as Mill Creek.

Just as Saxe-Gotha was about to experience new growth it lost two of its most important citizens—Catawba trader Thomas Brown and surveyor George Haig, who, to his regret, also got involved in Indian affairs. Brown died in 1747 leaving both an impressive estate and equally impressive debts. The decline of the Catawbas had, it seems, brought personal disaster in its wake. Nevertheless, Brown's possessions included two silver watches, a sun dial, a coffee mill, a trading boat valued at £21, 250 bushels of wheat, 43 head of cattle, 185 horses, and 22 slaves, some of whom had experience handling river craft.

Haig, a man Meriwether salutes as "among the most interesting" found on the South Carolina frontier, was a Charleston gentleman who was appointed a deputy surveyor for the colony in 1733. In this capacity he surveyed much of Saxe-Gotha and Orangeburg townships, bought 1,140 acres of land (some of it along the Congaree River), carried on trade with the Indians, and headed up a local militia company. Constantly in correspondence with the governor concerning Indian affairs, in 1746 he helped negotiate the purchase of the Ninety Six region from the Cherokee. During that same outing he angered a group of Iroquois when he seized some of their captives. Two years later, while on a trip into Catawba territory with Thomas Brown's half-breed son, the pair were taken prisoner by Iroquois braves and carried northward through various Cherokee towns. White traders along the way tried unsuccessfully to get the Cherokee to intercede in Haig's behalf, and Elizabeth, his wife, sent a spirited plea to the governor through her husband's Charleston factor. Appended to this appeal was a practical postscript: "Please to send me something for a Gown that is light & Coarse for every day's Wear & very Grave, if Callico let there be but White in it or Stamped Linen."[10]

A year later Pennsylvania authorities informed the South Carolina council that Haig was dead. Conrad Weiser, an Indian agent, reported that Haig, worn out by travel and despairing of his fate, had forced his captors to kill him. His companion, however, was ransomed by Weiser and eventually returned to South Carolina. An inventory of Haig's personal estate, worth about seven hundred and fifty pounds, listed two silver watches, five candlesticks, fifteen pack-horses, forty-four other horses, eighteen slaves, and forty-two gallons of rum.

It is not known whether the widow Haig got her dress goods, but incidents such as her husband's murder led to the re-establishment of a garrison at Saxe-Gotha late in 1748. And Elizabeth subsequently married Lieutenant Peter Mercier, one of the commanders of that post. Mercier, in turn, was killed on the Virginia frontier in 1754, leaving Elizabeth to fend for herself once more.

During these years, three events—one in Europe and two in America—had considerable impact upon life in the Midlands. The British-Spanish-French fracas that began when a Spanish captain cut off the ear of Robert Jenkins, master of the brig *Rebecca*, and then turned into a dynastic free-for-all, ceased in 1748. With peace, German-Swiss immigrants again made their way to Charleston and up the Congaree to Saxe-Gotha. On this side of the Atlantic, the purchase of land near Ninety Six by the ill-fated Haig and his associates tended to transfer the nucleus of Indian trade activity from Saxe-Gotha to that region. And the defeat of British forces near Pittsburgh in 1754 in yet another war convinced many restless frontier families living in Virginia and North Carolina to head south, not west.

Most of the newcomers to Saxe-Gotha Township were, according to Meriwether, German, not English. Between 1749 and 1759 the latter recorded 130 headrights; the Germans, 250. Of the German immigrants, perhaps one-fifth of them settled east of the Congaree. Among the English moving into the area was John Taylor of Amelia County, Virginia, whose son, Thomas, would play a prominent role in the history of both Columbia and Richland County. In 1756 Taylor purchased the property of Wallexellson the blacksmith, the same man who once rushed to Charleston to prevent a neighbor from seizing his woodlands.

Henry Christopher Beudeker, a Westphalian brewer and linenmaker, like Joseph Crell before him, arrived in 1748 brimming with grand schemes. Having tasted Philadelphia and New York beer ("the best of which he reckoned bad"), Beudeker secured a seventy-one-pound loan from the township fund with which to start a brewery, perhaps because he conjured up visions of kegs of beer floating down river to Charleston. The following year, citing the loss of his barley crop, he sought still more money. This appeal was turned down, and apparently no one ever drank any "Beudeker Beer."

Soon Martin Friday was feeding travelers and carrying them across the shoals of the Congaree on his ferry. Friday's Ferry, established by an act passed on 11 May 1754, would assume special significance in the 1780s when South Carolinians were seeking a new site for a state capital. Friday was to keep two men (one of them white) in attendance at the ferry at all times. Ordained ministers, those going to and from church, Indians, and public servants were to be carried across the Congaree free of charge. All others had to pay 1 shilling, 3 pence.

The success of this enterprise inspired Jacob Geiger, Robert Steill, and Elizabeth Haig Mercier to seek similar privileges from colonial authorities, but Friday was able to withstand these challenges and maintain his monopoly. Downstream near Green Hill, "Raiford's Creek" folk had to use a private ferry until 1756 when Thomas Howell built a road thirty miles long leading from a ferry farther south on the river and connecting with another highway that took travelers to Friday's Ferry. This new roadway soon was handling traffic bound northward to the Catawbas, thus diverting some trade to the east bank of the Congaree.

A year later colonial authorities established St. Mark's Parish (which included the Richland County area) as a back-country election district. This huge expanse of territory, about one-third of the province, extended from the Santee to the North Carolina line. Its original nucleus was an Anglican church in Williamsburg Township, far from the Congaree settlement. The entire region was to have two representatives in the Assembly . . . not much of a concession on the part of the lowcountry grandees, true, but a beginning.

By 1760 the banks of the Congaree were home to perhaps 800 or 900 people. But the best lands were taken, and some settlers (both old and new) were moving inland, up the Saluda and Broad. And to the east, frontier families along the Wateree were looking to Pine Tree Hill, not "the Congarees," for leadership. Although there were obvious strains among such a diverse group of people from varied backgrounds, the presence of farms, ferries, roads, mills, stores, and even plans for a brewery reveal that a relatively stable society was developing. The township scheme, at least at Saxe-Gotha—and eventually in Camden—was a success, and credit for establishing such outposts must go to the colonial government. Yet, as the next two decades would reveal all too clearly, this stability was deceptive. Just over the horizon lay a generation of chaos and destruction that would affect virtually every household in the area, bring tragedy to many of them, and give birth to a new nation, a new county, a new seat of state government, and—some would say—a new society as well.

Notes

1. Charles F. Kovacik and John J. Winberry, *South Carolina, A Geography* (Boulder, Colo., 1987), pp. 18–20.
2. *Ibid.*, p. 7. The fifty-five-mile Carolina Midland Railroad, for example, that served Aiken and Barnwell counties in the 1890s subsequently became part of the Southern Railway System.
3. *Ibid.*, pp. 33–36. Few will be surprised to learn that Richland County summers are one degree warmer than those in surrounding counties. See map in Kovacik and Winberry (p. 36).

4. Although numerous versions of this work exist, see especially Hugh Talmage Lefler (editor), *A New Voyage to Carolina by John Lawson* (Chapel Hill, 1967).
5. *Ibid.*, pp. 35–36.
6. See Green's Chapter IV, "Early Settlers," pp. 23–32. These properties lay in Craven County, a creation of the 1680s that never developed into an election district as planned and had little significance other than for the recording of deeds.
7. Robert L. Meriwether, *The Expansion of South Carolina, 1729–1765* (Kingsport, Tenn., 1940), pp. 59–61.
8. Green's summary of plats in the Richland County area reflects these trends. Between 1748 and 1752, 102 were recorded, compared with only 42 prior to that time. It should be noted that, since some fees were required to establish title, this frontier land was not actually "free."
9. Quoted in Meriwether, p. 54.
10. *Ibid.*, pp. 58–59.

Regulators and Rebels

CHAPTER TWO

The principal themes of life in the Midlands from the late 1750s to the 1780s—growth and disorder—are not unrelated. In 1765, some 12,000 people were living in or near the fall line zone, with another 10,000 residing farther inland in the Piedmont. Within a decade their ranks increased nearly four-fold, giving South Carolina a greater upland population than any other southern colony, an estimated 83,000.[1] That figure represented half of all South Carolinians and 79 percent of the white population in the province. Yet these people had virtually no local government, no courts, no jails, and, for all practical purposes, only two representatives to speak for their interests at the seat of all authority, Charleston. And, while settlement of the upcountry was growing by leaps and bounds, South Carolina was plagued by a series of wars and warlike situations culminating, of course, in a full-fledged revolution and the struggle for independence from British rule. Upon reflection, it is difficult to imagine how anyone could have devised a better recipe for chaos, turmoil, and trouble.

The first of these embroglios was the Cherokee War (1760–1761), really little more than a local phase of the French and Indian or Seven Years War, as it was called on the other side of the Atlantic. This on-and-off struggle involved a series of campaigns to punish the Cherokee for attacks upon outlying settlements and creation of some thirty impromptu forts along the frontier. Among these were at least three on the west bank of the Congaree and another to the east on Wateree Creek. In May of 1761, 121 women and children sought safety at Godfrey Dreher's fort at "the Congarees." Also, in the midst of this affair, a training camp or garrison was established nearby where, according to Henry Laurens, men "died like Dogs." Their quarters and supplies were so bad, Laurens wrote in March 1763, that "they were more than once upon the point of mutinying & in prospect of disbanding for want of Provision."[2]

19

Eventually, after several years of negotiations, the Cherokee gave up territory below a line that conforms to the boundary between Anderson and Abbeville counties. At the same time, colonial authorities established a 225-square-mile reservation for the Catawba Indians near present-day Rock Hill. These moves of course opened still more of the back country to white settlement and ended the Indian threat to the Midlands for all time. But before this conflict ceased, it wiped out entire settlements, destroyed and impoverished scores of families, left orphans wandering in the wilderness, and, in the opinion of some historians, set the stage for the troubled times that followed. David Ramsay, writing in 1808, expressed this view most forcefully.

> The war was ended, but the consequences of it continued. It tainted the principles of many of the inhabitants, so as to endanger the peace and happiness of society. When settlements were broke up, industry was at an end. The prospects of reaping were so faint, that few had the resolution to sow. Those who took up their residence in forts had nothing to do. Idleness is the parent of every vice. When they sallied out they found much property left behind by others who had quitted their homes. To make use of such derelict articles did not appear to them in the odious colors of theft. Cattle were killed—horses were sold—household furniture, and plantation tools were taken into possession in violation of private rights. The wrong-doers lived easily at the expense of the absentees, and acquired such vicious habits that when the war was over they despised labor and became pests of society. To steal was easier than to work. The former was carried on extensively, and the latter rarely attempted. Among all kinds of theft none was so easy in execution, so difficult in detection, and at the same time so injurious in its consequences as horse-stealing. On the labors of that useful animal, the cultivators of the soil depended for raising the provisions necessary for their support. A horse when grazing is as easily caught by a thief, as by its owner; and will as readily carry the one as the other to a distance where he might be sold or exchanged, to the serious injury of an helpless family. Practices of this kind became common, and were carried on by system and in concert with associates living remote from each other. The industrious part of the community were oppressed, and the support of their families endangered.[3]

In essence, the aftermath of the Cherokee War and a sudden influx of newcomers created two societies in upland South Carolina. One, hard-working and eager to get ahead, yearned for stability and order. The other—perhaps, as Ramsay describes, devastated and corrupted by war-fare—was adept at squatting, poaching, sneak thievery, and getting by with little physical effort . . . individuals sometimes called "white" Indians. These folk were not full-blown outlaws and similar groups could be found in many regions. They were the unfortunate riffraff of the frontier, fugitives from various colonies, individuals who had served out their indentures, deserters from his majesty's forces, mulattoes, mixed bloods, runaway slaves, and so on. They were, in all, a battered class often lacking the fundamental ingredients of daily life, including a basic diet. In simplest terms, this was a division between those who existed largely by hunting and those who farmed. Hunters, men who paid no heed to the rights of private property, left animal carcasses lying about that attracted wolves, and drifted across the landscape at will, were a constant threat to stability and normal day-to-day life. What made the South Carolina situation of the 1760s so explosive were the great numbers involved, the development of coordinated outlaw activity, and the absence of local government.

Until the eve of the Revolutionary War, the only voice of authority in the back country was the justice of peace. Appointed by the governor, he usually "sat" on a Saturday at some central location such as the old fort at "the Congarees" or one of the stores that had appeared nearby. At that time, the militia mustered and paraded a bit, merchants hawked their wares, and flowing rum might produce revelry, laughter, fisticuffs, and sore heads. Militia companies, groups ranging from 50 to 125 men, were a potential source of authority; however, they usually were effective only in emergencies such as Indian attacks.

As for the justices, their powers were limited. They could issue warrants, administer oaths, take depositions, verify appraisal returns, issue certificates for the heads of wild animals so hunters could get their bounties, and take charge of stray stock. They also could settle civil cases involving sums up to £20, but had no voice in criminal matters. Constables carried out their orders.

But, as Ramsay emphasized, the governor, "with his scanty means of information," occasionally chose inept (or even dishonest) individuals as justices.

> The greatest villains had generally the most money, and often the most friends. Instead of exerting their authority to suppress horse-stealing and other crimes, some of these justices were sharers in the profits of this infamous business. Before such it was difficult to procure the commitment of criminals. If the proofs of their guilt were

too strong to be evaded, the expense of transporting them to Charleston was great; the chances of their escape many. When brought to trial, the non-attendance of witnesses from a distance of two hundred miles, and other circumstances were so improved by lawyers to whom the horse thieves were able and willing to give large fees, that prosecutions though for real crimes seldom terminated in conviction.[4]

Although writing nearly half a century later, Ramsay struck at the heart of the matter: the pressing need for local courts to dispense justice and establish order in the back country. Charleston was not unaware of the desire for courts and on several occasions before 1750 made half-hearted efforts to satisfy this demand. However, when lawyers refused to attend sessions held outside of the city and authorities in England axed such proposals, nothing happened. (Of course, there always were those eager to keep *all* judicial matters in Charleston because of the business created by such activity.) In 1754 a bill to establish courts in "the Congarees," Beaufort, and Georgetown died in the Assembly after one reading. Eleven years later a similar measure passed the House; however, the Council took no action.

In February of 1766 "the inhabitants about the Congaree's"—which was interpreted to mean those living in or near Ninety Six, the Saluda and Broad rivers, "& places adjacent"—sought relief from their plight.[5] Perhaps despairing of action on courts, these petitioners instead listed their complaints in terms a lowcountry man might appreciate. The land where they dwelled, they said, was not divided into parishes and the limits of counties were "uncertain and undetermined." They had no representative in the Assembly to relate how they suffered from the acts of "Neighboring Savages as well as from Fugitive White Men." Their produce had to get to market "wholly by Land Carriage, because there is no Navigation that can yet be made use of. . . . " They had no churches, no schools. The main thrust of this protest was, however, an "unEqualed and Grievous Taxation," for all land in the colony—upcountry and low—was taxed annually at forty shillings per acre. This injustice, the petitioners argued, discouraged settlement and attracted "Itinerants and Vagabond Strollers" who squatted in unoccupied territory and disrupted their daily lives. Taxation based upon true value would, it was claimed, bring great benefits to all concerned and revenues soon would exceed sums now being collected each year.

It is easy to view this document as a "taxation-without-representation" cry, but that is not quite true. These backwoods folk were interested, first and foremost, in lower, more equitable levies upon their property. Representation in the colonial assembly, churches, schools, parishes, even county boundaries and allusions to the rigors of frontier life were just side issues, arguments to buttress their plea for lower taxes. And one suspects action on that single item would have taken much of the steam out of their protest. However, that was not to be, and within a few months a crime wave that engulfed the back country gave new significance to what had been secondary concerns.

The activities of these brigands have their roots in conditions already described. But why this upsurge of robbery, murder, and mayhem erupted in the mid-1760s is not entirely clear. Perhaps the best explanation lies in sudden population growth and tantalizing opportunities present on any lightly governed frontier. Most of the "lower" element lacked the energy for an all-out crime career, yet sometimes provided recruits—as did decent, property-holding families. These outlaws, living in riverbank communities with their women, children, and old folks, developed ties to still other gangs, often accepted mulattoes and runaway slaves into their midst, and dealt in all sorts of nefarious pursuits from stealing horses and smuggling to daytime robbery at gunpoint. Significantly, although not Robin Hoods, they enjoyed the general approbation of the lower classes and (as Ramsay wrote) the tacit cooperation of some justices and constables as well.

Throughout much of 1766 and 1767 the back country was at the mercy of these rogues, who plundered almost at will. When a colonial official visiting in Camden tried to raise that community's militia late in 1766, no one answered the call to arms. By the summer of 1767, according to Charleston newspapers, poverty was becoming a preferred state in the upcountry. Any frontier family thought to have money soon was host to unwanted visitors. And at the peak of these outrages in June and July of that same year, an infamous gang swept though the Dutch Fork area and Saxe-Gotha burning and looting, torturing victims presumed to have items of value, raping wives and daughters, and making off with horses, furniture, and household goods. Residents of the headwaters of the Edisto (a region called "the Ridge") and the Camden community suffered a similar fate. In this instance, the relative isolation enjoyed by those living between the Congaree and Wateree—an inland peninsula with more attractive targets on its flanks—may have been a godsend.

Strangely, we have an on-the-spot account of daily life in the back country during this tumult, the journal of Charles Woodmason, a former Pee Dee merchant and planter, who in 1766 began a six-year stint as a roving Anglican minister based, for the most part, in Camden.[6] Since Reverend Woodmason viewed everything non-Anglican with a jaundiced eye, one must weigh his words with some care; nevertheless, some of this man's observations ring true. Throughout his travels, shocked by immorality, sluttishness, ignorance, and irreligion he saw on every hand, Woodmason did spirited battle with Baptists, Presbyterians, and other "sectarians." Technically, land west of the Wateree was not within his territory, but in the summer of 1768 he made this entry in his journal.

> Saturday September 3 / Rode down the Country on the West Side of the Wateree River into the Fork between that and the Congaree River—This is out of my Bounds—But their having no Minister, and their falling (therefrom) continually from the Church to Anabaptism, inclin'd me to it—The People received me gladly and very kindly. Had on Sunday 4—a Company of about 150—Most of them the Low Class—the principal Planters living on the Margin of the Rivers.
>
> Baptiz'd 1 Negroe Man—2 Negroe Children—and 9 White Infants and married 1 couple—The People thanked me in the most kind Manner for my Services—I had a very pleasant Riding but my Horse suffered Greatly.[7]

A few years later Woodmason moved to the "Congaree Distric," where he lived and preached for twelve months, but his journal does not cover that sojourn. What his writings describe in great detail is the riotous state of affairs of the late 1760s and the rise of the Regulators, America's first vigilante movement. Interestingly, this man of the cloth scorned this grass-roots protest against backwoods crime so long as it was led by Presbyterians; once prominent Anglicans joined in, he became its most ardent spokesman.

At the outset of these disturbances, Charleston's attention was riveted on the Stamp Act controversy, not what was happening in upland regions. Petitions and appeals were quickly filed away and forgotten, and in March of 1767 a new governor, eager to win favor, pardoned five of six outlaws convicted of robbing homes and stealing horses. A few months later, his excellency offered a £50 reward to those who apprehended evildoers and took them to Charleston. This was followed by a general order for all brigands to disperse and cease their unseemly way of life.

In the summer of 1767, perhaps encouraged by reward money, some frontier families began to strike back. At first they joined together merely to protect their property, but then they went on the offensive. Early in October, the governor informed the Council that numerous settlers living between the Santee [Congaree] and Wateree rivers had assembled and "in a Rioting Manner had gone up and down the Country Committing Riot and disturbances and that they had burnt the Houses of some Persons who were reputed to be Harbourers of Horse Theives [sic] and talk of Coming to Charlestown to make some Complaints."[8]

The Regulator movement had begun, and—as this report indicates—the Richland County area was in the thick of it. Not only had frontiersmen of this region taken justice into their own hands, they also had issued a threat to march on Charleston to air their grievances. Ironically, communities established to protect the lowcountry now loomed as a potential menace. The government answered with the only means at its disposal: another proclamation ordering all rioters to disperse and enjoining various officials to keep the peace. In succeeding weeks, the governor organized a new militia unit in the Saluda River area (which turned out to have at least one Regulator officer who had to be dismissed), a Charleston court summarily convicted both outlaws and Regulators of misdeeds, and governor, Council, and Assembly speculated about what course to follow. On 30 October 1767, the *South-Carolina & American General Gazette* reported that disturbances were continuing in the back settlements, although the bandits had "almost" been driven away. This editor then added, rather ominously, that—despite a general return to good order—the gentry were not "altogether satisfied."

A week later tangible evidence of this dissatisfaction arrived in Charleston in the form of Woodmason's well-known "Remonstrance," a detailed document that opens with this salvo: *"We are* Free-Men—*British Subjects—Not Born* Slaves!" This often audacious litany of frontier grievances, signed by four Wateree planters who claimed to speak for 4,000 settlers and backed by a threat to invade Charleston, if necessary, brought almost immediate results.[9] Within four days an Assembly committee reported favorably on proposals to set up a court system, enact vagrancy laws, and establish back-country garrisons to maintain order. The raising of two companies to man those posts in effect gave the Regulators temporary legitimacy, since many of the men and officers were part of that movement.

If the story ended at this point, all would be well, but it did not. The court bill passed by the Assembly in April 1768 was less than perfect and couched in terms that made rejection by London inevitable. Also, various justices continued to arrest Regulators and charge them with illegal acts. In June "a vast number" of Regulators gathered at "the Congarees" and drew up plans to continue their war on evil-doers in defiance of

Charleston courts. Writs and warrants emanating from the colonial capital, they said, were to be served only with *their* approval.

On 13 June 1768, the *South-Carolina Gazette* observed that it was "hardly probable" that back-country disorders would cease until that region had circuit courts. Each day, the editor continued, word reached Charleston of "new irregularities committed by the people called Regulators, who, seeming to despair of rooting out whole gangs of villains that remain among them any other way, still take upon themselves to punish such offenders as they can catch."

Early in August, 3,000 Regulators again met at "the Congarees," but this time moderation, not defiance, was the order of the day. Their goal, they claimed, was to establish parish bounds so they could vote in the next election. Following this meeting, which the *South-Carolina Gazette* termed "unjustifiable," the settlers themselves surveyed parish lines. Later that same month, the *South-Carolina & American General Gazette* (26 August 1768) had this interesting comment on developments in North Carolina where the Regulator movement began somewhat earlier and had far different goals: "They tell us from North Carolina, that the inhabitants of the western parts of North Carolina, are destroying the County Court Houses and Prisons. The Regulators in this Province are loud in demanding County Courts, that they may have justice at their Doors, without the Trouble of coming to, and continuing in, Charleston, at an enormous Expence, seeing Lawyers, &c." By contrast, the North Carolina movement was a "throw-the-rascals-out" campaign, while the Regulators of this colony wanted local courts and jails.

When a special election for Assembly seats was held in October, some backwoods landowners rode up to 150 miles to get to polling places in the lowcountry. But this effort accomplished little, for the governor soon dissolved the Assembly after it endorsed measures critical of the Townshend Acts. Then he compounded his problems in March of 1769 by dispatching one Joseph Coffell to arrest Regulators in the Saluda River area. Coffell, a man of ill repute, assembled a large body of men—some of them thugs once targets of Regulator wrath—who made arrests and also occasionally plundered as they went about the countryside. Mixed in with this unruly element, however, were individuals distressed by Regulator efforts to "regulate" all aspects of frontier life. In short, many who supported the campaign to curb banditry were less enthusiastic once "regulation" became a moral crusade in the winter of 1768–1769. Eventually, to avoid bloodshed between two opposing forces, the governor had to disavow Coffell's activities. In July 1769 the Assembly passed a circuit court act that finally became effective three years later. One of the new districts established by this measure was Camden, which included land lying between the Congaree and Wateree rivers.

So, the Regulators achieved their main goals and outright conflict between colonial authority (the lowcountry) and the back country was avoided. How had it happened? To begin with, the coastal region, fearful of slave uprisings, never had sufficient manpower to handle this inland revolt, and this hard fact was recognized at that time. Also, the elite of the lowcountry was sympathetic to some aspects of the movement, since outlaw gangs threatened property (slaves) and provided a haven for runaways. But attempts by Regulators to dictate morality and stamp out sin, not just suppress robbery and horse stealing, fueled a backlash that undermined support.

A two-hour whipping of a Noble Creek man with chains early in 1769, for example, just because he was "roguish and troublesome," led to the rise of what Richard Maxwell Brown calls the "Moderators."[10] And, although this group included in its ranks rascals eager to settle scores with Regulators, this opposition, coupled with widespread disenchantment with Regulator excesses and passage of a circuit court act, restored a semblance of order to the back country.

There is little doubt that this movement, essentially an attempt by rising, upwardly mobile landowners to create a stable milieu, found favor among some residents of the Richland County area. As noted, Regulators met on several occasions at "the Congarees," and Brown, on the basis of pardons issued in the early 1770s, was able to pinpoint the homes of at least 120 Regulator stalwarts. Among them was John Goodwyn, a transplanted Virginian, who lived on Mill Creek. However, Brown's research indicates the greatest centers of Regulator strength lay farther up the Broad River (Fairfield and Newberry counties) and in the Camden area. As to the total number of people actually involved, Brown believes there may have been 3,000 Regulators scattered throughout various frontier communities.

Of course, in a real sense this phenomenon reveals the coming of age of upland South Carolina. It now had people and was largely free of the Indian menace, but lacked both the structure and trappings of normal society—schools, churches, courts, effective local government, and day-to-day political machinery. All of these things would come to Richland County, much sooner than many thought in the early 1770s. Ahead, however, lay yet another time of strife and trouble: the Revolutionary War.

The broad outlines of that struggle are widely known—the outbreak of hostilities in New England, the agony of Valley Forge, a turning point at Saratoga, help from the French, and finally victory at Yorktown. And

South Carolinians are well aware of efforts by a Council of Safety to establish provisional government in 1775 and an unsuccessful attempt by the British to occupy Sullivan's Island in Charleston Harbor in May of 1776. However, the interplay of forces that ensued is less well understood. What began as a typical confrontation among those who sympathized with rebellion, those who did not, and still others who didn't give a damn ("a pox on both your houses") gradually disintegrated into a real *civil* war, splitting families and pitting brother against brother.[11] In addition, back-country life was complicated by scars left over from the Regulator uproar, as well as upcountry-lowcountry antipathy of long standing.

As for the correlation among Regulators, Moderators, rebels, and those loyal to the king, historians fail to agree—if, indeed, any ever existed. Nevertheless, certain facts are apparent. At the outset, loyalty was stronger in the upcountry than in coastal regions. Then, after a flurry of activity (1775–1776), war hardly touched South Carolina until 1780 when the British, misled by earlier events and exaggerated claims of back-country support, returned with plans to subdue and occupy this state. What followed was a vicious struggle that ended only with the departure of the British and their hard-core Loyalist allies in December of 1782.

Richland County's role in this drama is far from clear. Edwin Green, for one, concluded it was "impossible to give a detailed narrative of the part this section played in the Revolution," although he thought most residents favored independence.[12] Robert Goodwyn, Thomas Taylor, John Hopkins, and William Howell were among those representing this region at provisional legislative sessions (1775–1776), and Taylor and Goodwyn also served as colonels in local regiments in the years that followed. Other officers—all of them with Virginia roots—included Robert Lyell, Uriah Goodwyn, William Goodwyn, Joel McLemore, John Taylor, Hicks Chappell, David Hopkins, William Taylor, and Timothy Rives. In all, according to Green, about 100 area residents bore arms in behalf of the patriot cause.

William Henry Drayton, who toured the back country in the summer of 1775 to stir up support for the Council of Safety, got a favorable reception when he visited the east bank of the Congaree. Drayton conceded that some individuals attended a meeting held on 8 August with "mischievous purposes" in mind, but he was so successful in converting them to his point of view that many immediately formed volunteer companies. He was less pleased with the reaction of Germans living on the west bank of the river, a hot bed of Loyalism. Fearful their land grants might be annulled if they heeded Drayton's words and none too happy about a body of rangers stationed nearby, they resisted both cajolery and pressure. Even the threat that they would be unable to sell their produce in Charleston unless they embraced the rebel cause changed few minds.

A report by James Simpson in the collections of the South Carolina Historical Society underscores the loyalty of the German population of the Midlands. Writing to Sir Henry Clinton from Savannah on 20 August 1779, Simpson, who technically was South Carolina's attorney-general, predicted that "the German inhabitants of the Congarees, will Submit to the Strongest Party, but the most opulent amongst them, wish well to the English, and I am pretty confident, they will peremptorily refuse to act against them. . . . " Simpson, who thought 5,000 troops could bring South Carolina over to the king's side, then proceeded to enunciate his usual theme that British generals were too "soft," that they should take "an eye for an eye" approach and meet each patriot measure with stern action of their own.

Research by Robert S. Lambert indicates that the prime source of Loyalist strength in South Carolina was the newcomer, whether from the British Isles or Virginia, and the back country had more of them in 1775.[13] In addition, upland regions at that time had no real quarrel with London, while the mere mention of Charleston could stir old wounds. Lambert estimates that perhaps one-fifth of this state's free population could have been classified as Loyalist during the struggle that followed. But, he cautions, as a result of the ebb and flow of war these same individuals may have aided the patriot cause, too. Lambert sees two high points of Loyalist sentiment: at the outset of hostilities when initial choices were being made and again in 1780 when British troops invaded the state.

In the intervening years war was largely a faraway matter, something happening in the northern colonies, although residents of the Midlands certainly furnished both foodstuffs and manpower to aid those favoring independence. Of regional significance was the development of a small commercial center on the west bank of the Congaree at Friday's Ferry. This community in the lower part of Saxe-Gotha Township, long referred to vaguely as "the Congarees," had—by the outbreak of hostilities—become Granby. This name apparently honored Charles Manners, fourth Duke of Rutland and Marquis of Granby. A youthful advocate of colonial rights, Granby evidently won the admiration of Joseph Kershaw, an influential merchant, who in 1768 changed the name of Pine Tree Hill to Camden for the same reason, that is, to pay homage to Charles Pratt,

Lord Camden, for similar views. (An early reference to Granby dated 10 December 1774 can be found in Kershaw's account book.)

Kershaw, a power to be reckoned with, had several stores scattered along the frontier, as well as operations in Charleston, Camden, and Granby. However, at about this time he began to dispose of these far-flung holdings, and the first Wade Hampton (1754–1835), who would play a prominent role in Richland County history, acquired the Granby store. With the aid of various relatives, Hampton soon built up a brisk back-country trade based at that point with ties, of course, to Charleston. During the late 1770s, according to Ronald E. Bridwell, he was an active supplier of foodstuffs to rebel forces, helped recruit soldiers from time to time (an activity not incompatible with buying trips into the Piedmont), and also served as paymaster to troops commanded by Thomas Sumter.[14]

With the fall of Charleston on 12 May 1780, Hampton, like many well-known South Carolinians, assumed the war might be over and made his peace with the British. Indeed, most rank-and-file citizens followed this same course, that is, until Tory reprisals and British atrocities began to stir resentment. When the drift toward independence began, as noted earlier, one usually had the luxury of three choices: for, against, or neutral. But when Cornwallis, Tarleton, Sumter, Marion, and Greene squared off in mid-1780, those choices narrowed considerably. Now there was only one—that of the person holding a musket to your breast and soliciting your cooperation. Or, in the case of Hampton and some lowcountry gentry, economic considerations and belief that Parliament perhaps had learned a lesson loomed large.

With patriot voices momentarily silenced, the British easily overran the state and established bases of operation at numerous sites, including Granby, where Hampton's house and storage facilities became part of a fort and a collection point for grain. Also, a small post was set up just across the Congaree at the eastern end of Friday's Ferry as added protection for that installation, and it was here that the only wartime skirmish on Richland County soil would occur.

One turning point in this tale came only a few weeks after the fall of Charleston when Banastre Tarleton, a gifted, if cruel, campaigner, allegedly massacred rebel troops at the Waxhaws. This event, together with other outrages by Loyalist forces and efforts to make colonials bear arms, stirred anti-British feeling once more. Naturally enough, such moves were answered in kind as various individuals also settled old scores, always, of course, acting in the name of "patriotism." Andrew Jackson, who lived through these horrible times, once conceded that both sides were guilty of cruel acts, adding that, if the rebels were provoked into retaliating, they took full advantage of those opportunities.

As for organized warfare, the two-year campaign that followed was something of a draw, which meant defeat for the invader. Rebel forces were routed at Camden in August of 1780, but won at King's Mountain two months later . . . even though both sides actually were Americans: Tory vs. patriot. This setback forced Cornwallis to leave Charlotte and establish temporary headquarters at Winnsboro. In January of 1781 the rebels posted a spectacular victory at Cowpens, followed by yet another defeat near Camden in April of that year.

Meanwhile, as various contingents of organized troops and less disciplined partisans roamed about the state seeking support, supplies, plunder, and the enemy, they sometimes swept through the Richland County area. The roads they used include two that were made public thoroughfares in July of 1766—McCord's Ferry Road from the southeast corner of the county north along the west bank of the Wateree (now Route 601 and still known by the McCord name) and another highway parallel to it from Howell's Ferry near Mill Creek north into Fairfield County. The Mouzon Map of 1775 also shows a third road, really the old path to the Catawba Nation. This highway extended northward from the juncture of the Saluda and Broad to intersect with the Howell's Ferry Road and then curved to the northeast above the sand hills to join the McCord's Ferry Road on the banks of the Wateree in Kershaw County. However, Edwin Green notes that other roads, not public but passable, must have existed. General Nathanael Greene on one occasion marched from Winnsboro to Friday's Ferry, and troops also went directly from that ferry to McCord's, indicating that Bluff Road at that time could be traversed its entire length.

Soon after Cowpens, General Sumter laid siege to Fort Granby, still called "Camp Congaree" in some accounts. This move coincided with Wade Hampton's decision to sever his ties with the British, who were becoming increasingly wary of his true intentions. Bridwell believes the siege and Hampton's outward conversion were related. In short, Hampton, who had been furnishing foodstuffs to Fort Granby, knew supplies were low and told Sumter (an old friend with whom he may have maintained contact throughout 1780) that the post could be taken with relative ease; however, British reinforcements thwarted this scheme.

Two months later, Sumter returned to the Congaree with Hampton at his side. The first order of business, easily accomplished by newly organized state troops, was the taking of a block house on the east bank near

Friday's Ferry. The battle, during which that structure was burned and twenty-seven Tories killed, was a brief affair. Then, on 2 May Sumter once more laid siege to Fort Granby, defended by 340 men under the command of Major Andrew Maxwell. Inside, guarded by two twelve-pound guns, was a large assortment of plunder gathered from farms and plantations on both sides of the river. Four days later, Sumter departed for yet another enemy stronghold, Fort Motte, leaving Colonel Thomas Taylor and rebel militia to continue the siege. Taylor, whose Richland County lands had been confiscated and turned over to a Tory, had special reason to press the enemy hard, as did many of his men, since goods stolen from them were stacked inside Fort Granby.

On 16 May, however, Maxwell surrendered the fort to Colonel Henry Lee, who had been dispatched to the site by General Greene, under terms that so infuriated Sumter he threatened to resign his command. Lee, a Virginian with no ties to this area, allowed the defenders to take with them all of the private property they had collected without any inquiry whatsoever as to true ownership. And, as Lee described in his memoirs, Maxwell and 340 men (sixty regulars and the rest Loyalists) quickly departed with "baggage of every sort, two pieces of artillery, and two covered wagons."[15] The victors did, however, acquire public stores of ammunition, salt, and liquor, as well as numerous slaves lodged at the fort or living on Tory-held lands nearby, some of whom were handed over to rebel soldiers as payment for their services. With the departure of the enemy contingent, Taylor assumed command of Fort Granby.

In the months that followed, the British and their friends, unable to assert effective control of the countryside, gradually withdrew toward the coast. The last major confrontation in the state was at Eutaw Springs in September of 1781. Although not a clear-cut rebel victory, the British could not mount a major offensive after that engagement. With the convening of the state legislature in Jacksonborough early in 1782, civil government was re-established in South Carolina, even though the British did not evacuate Charleston until the close of that year.

As noted earlier, it is difficult to pinpoint with much accuracy the political sympathies of those living in what soon would become Richland County, and this British invasion further complicates any analysis of sentiment. County or district boundaries were yet to be established, and claims subsequently registered with the British government (even if related to this region) usually represented absentee landlords, not residents. Nevertheless, we know that three of the four men chosen to command Loyalist regiments raised in Camden District after the fall of

Charleston were associated with this area: Camden merchant Henry Rugeley, Winnsboro's John Phillips, and Virginia-born James Cary, a former Regulator. Of this trio, Cary, a justice of the peace in 1776, is the only one who may have lived briefly in Richland County. In any case, in 1780 Cornwallis appointed him not only colonel of a regiment but also "Conservator of the Peace" for the land lying between the Congaree and Wateree rivers.

In 1783, South Carolina authorities compiled a list of rebel soldiers who had gone over to the British and a summary of their confiscated property. According to this compilation, thirty-five men in Colonel Thomas Taylor's regiment, presumably residents of the Midlands, switched sides during the struggle.[16] Of that number, four are cited by Green as early Richland County landowners: Alexander Daley, William Leadenham, and James Bell, Senior and Junior. None of these thirty-five men had much property, the most affluent being John Thompson, who owned 400 acres of land, eleven cattle, three feather beds, three pewter dishes, four plated dishes, two pots, one table, six chairs, and four sheep, all of which were confiscated. William Fortune, perhaps the lone professional soldier in the group, was the only one who later presented a claim to London authorities.

Yet neither the departure of the British nor subsequent seizure of the property of those who supported them brought peace to the Midlands. At the end of July 1781, back at Friday's Ferry after campaigning with Sumter, Wade Hampton was shocked by what he saw. "Almost every person that remained in this settlement after the army marched," he informed Greene, "seems to have been combin'd in committing Robberies the most base & inhuman that ever disgraced mankind."[17] Hampton also told of "Horrid murders" that had taken place on the road from Granby to Ninety Six and Augusta. With the help of state troops and militia "who had spirit," he tried to restore order, yet remained deeply troubled. Plundering had become a way of life along the banks of the Congaree, and many of those accused of stealing property were men under his command (state troops). Greene, emphasizing that he had always dreaded "this evil more than any other," replied that he foresaw the day not far off when state forces and local militia would fall to wrangling among themselves. To prevent this turn of events, he set up strict rules governing the transport of property, especially horses, by both soldiers and civilians.

What Hampton, Greene, and the solid citizens of the Midlands were witnessing was a return to conditions that had given birth to the Regulators. Yet, although banditry continued to plague the Richland County area for several more years, the 1780s were not the 1760s. Despite the popular adage, history does *not* repeat itself. Circumstances may be similar, but never identical.

To begin with, the balance of power between Charleston and the rest of the state had shifted dramatically during these troubled times. In the fifth General Assembly (1783–1784), for example, the district between the Broad and Catawba rivers had ten representatives, as did three other regions—land "eastward" of the Wateree, New Acquisition, and Ninety Six. In theory, at least, these individuals (who included Richland's Thomas Taylor) could out-vote the thirty men who spoke for Charleston. Saxe-Gotha now had six representatives, among them Wade Hampton and his brother, Richard. But to add to Charleston's unease, its delegation in the lower house no longer spoke with one voice, for a new, less affluent element representing city artisans and mechanics now held some seats and frequently aired opposing views in a vigorous newspaper war. In addition, ultra conservatives could not look across the Atlantic for help; London's veto was no more.

In 1784 this new breed of upcountry legislator, men who often sat quietly and said little, was able to secure more equitable taxation (1 percent of the value of all land instead of a flat per-acre rate as before), thus finally achieving a goal sought by "the inhabitants about the Congaree's" two decades earlier. And as they gained confidence their demands increased, as did their victories. In 1785 the huge districts created in the late 1760s were divided into counties, yet another Regulator objective, and the following year—after much maneuvering—the General Assembly agreed to move the capital inland to a site near Friday's Ferry. In general, the argument for a new capital was much the same as that put forth for county courts: a centrally located facility more accessible to those it served. Meanwhile, various officials were actively trying to deal with petty and serious crime by erecting whipping posts, suppressing vagrancy, and handing down stiff sentences, including death. In a sense, then, the Regulators won their struggle, albeit nearly twenty years after it began.

To understand the mood of the back country in the mid-1780s it is necessary to consider two other factors: the continued influx of still more people and new interest in a crop long grown in lower Richland. Many of these settlers, as before, came from Virginia and North Carolina. Fleeing high taxes and searching for cheap land, they brought with them tobacco. In 1773, the colony of South Carolina had exported 536 hogsheads of tobacco; in 1785 nearly five times as many were shipped, and by the late

1780s that figure had swelled to 6,000 hogsheads. The legislature soon was establishing inspection stations to maintain quality, one appearing at Camden in 1783, others at Cheraw and Friday's Ferry in 1784, and still another at Winnsboro in 1785. People were excited by this new crop, some ex-Virginians even claiming the local product superior to that grown in the Old Dominion. Production of these broad green leaves and the task of getting them to market led to the construction of new roads and plans for canals. It also spread slavery and the plantation system, as well as hope, throughout upland South Carolina. For the first time in the memory of many, things were being built, not torn down, burned, or carried off.

All of these developments, in the opinion of Jerome Nadelhaft, led to what he calls "the awakening of the interior."[18] Political muscle at both state and local levels, meaningful efforts to suppress crime, expanding settlement, and an improving economy injected new spirit into what long had been a snarling, factious, frontier society. And nowhere was this spirit more vigorous and more apparent than on the banks of the Congaree, where soon would rise a new town, the seat of both county and state government.

Notes

1. Carl Bridenbaugh, *Myths and Realities: Societies of the Colonial South* (Baton Rouge, 1952), p. 128.
2. Philip M. Hamer, George C. Rogers, Jr., and David R. Chesnutt (editors), *The Papers of Henry Laurens* (12 vols.; Columbia, 1968–   ), III, p. 319.
3. David Ramsay, *The History of South Carolina* . . . (2 vols.; Charleston, 1809), I, pp. 210–11.
4. *Ibid.*, p. 212.
5. "House of Commons Journal," 27 February 1763.
6. See Richard J. Hooker (editor), *The Carolina Backcountry on the Eve of the Revolution: The Journal and Other Writings of Charles Woodmason, Anglican Itinerant* (Chapel Hill, 1953).
7. *Ibid.*, p. 60.
8. Quoted in Hooker, p. 171.
9. See Hooker (pp. 213–46) for the text of this "Remonstrance."
10. See Brown, *The South Carolina Regulators* (Cambridge, 1963).

11. In some instances, however, divisions were intentional, especially among the well-to-do. By having a family member in each camp, one might be able to salvage something, no matter which side prevailed.

12. See Green, *A History of Richland County*, pp. 83–109.

13. Lambert, *South Carolina Loyalists in the American Revolution* (Columbia, 1987), pp. 306–8.

14. Ronald E. Bridwell, "The South's Wealthiest Planter: Wade Hampton I of South Carolina, 1754–1835," Ph.D. diss., University of South Carolina 1980, pp. 100–107.

15. Henry Lee, *Memoirs of the War in the Southern Department of the United States* (New York, 1869), p. 352. In fact, under these liberal surrender terms, Lee even provided Maxwell with the two covered wagons he used, as well as an armed escort to British lines, and permitted all within the fort to keep their horses. This edition of Lee's *Memoirs*, edited by his famous son (Robert E. Lee), says nothing about Sumter's displeasure, stressing instead that Greene was "delighted with this happy event."

16. Robert W. Barnwell (editor), "Reports on Loyalist Exiles from South Carolina, 1783," *Proceedings*, South Carolina Historical Association (1937), pp. 44–5.

17. Hampton to Greene, quoted in Bridwell, pp. 167–70.

18. Jerome J. Nadelhaft, *The Disorders of War: The Revolution in South Carolina* (Orono, Me., 1981), pp. 125–42.

New County,
New Town

CHAPTER THREE

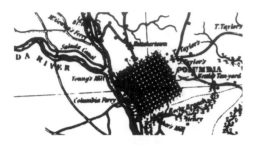

In March of 1783 the General Assembly set into motion the machinery that would create Richland County when seven men, including Thomas Taylor, were given the task of dividing up sprawling Camden District. The result, two years later, was the counties of Richland, Chester, Claremont [Sumter], Clarendon, Fairfield, Lancaster, and York. At the same time, all of the other districts formed in 1769 were split up in a similar fashion, although the general grouping by districts (the area served by a *district* court) continued to have some significance until the close of the 18th century. The original boundaries of Richland—named for fertile land found along the banks of the Congaree or a plantation owned by Taylor—were described in this manner: " . . . beginning at the corner of Clarendon county line, at Person's Island, thence up the Congaree to the mouth of Cedar creek, thence on a strait line to the mouth of Twenty-Five Mile creek, thence down the Wateree river to the beginning, and shall be called Richland county."[1]

Not everyone was pleased, and some landowners tried to change these borders in the decade or so that followed. In 1791 and again in 1792, the northeastern boundary was altered somewhat, transferring land to Kershaw County (established in 1791). Then in 1797, the Richland-Fairfield line was moved slightly northward, adding property to Richland.

To make these new counties of the 1780s a reality, the justices of peace in each one, acting as justices of a county court, were to erect a courthouse, jail, pillory, and stocks in the "most convenient" place. They also were to assess, levy, and collect taxes and hold elections for officers such as sheriff, coroner, and clerk of court. The General Assembly gave these officials jurisdiction over taverns, roads, and bridges and set up a detailed schedule of fees to be charged for various services.

During the next few years, some (but not all) of these goals were realized. In February of 1787, Joel McLemore became Richland County's
first sheriff and Philip Pearson, the first clerk of court. Four years later,
under a new apportionment scheme outlined by the Constitution of 1790,
the county for the first time had its own spokesmen in the House of Representatives: James Green Hunt and Hicks Chappell. Chappell replaced
Wade Hampton, who decided instead to become sheriff of Camden
District, a more prestigious post. At the same legislative session (1791),
Thomas Taylor represented Richland, Fairfield, and Chester counties in
the state Senate.

On the morning of 6 August 1792, Richland County citizens gathered
at the home of William Sanders Taylor on Mill Creek to select the site for
a courthouse. Their choice was Myer's Hill, the home of William Myer
and his son, Frederick, located about a dozen miles east of Friday's Ferry
and Granby, an elevation now known as Horrell Hill. Within two years,
according to Charleston's *City Gazette & Daily Advertiser* (10 October
1794) a courthouse had been built; however, it was soon abandoned in favor of a Columbia location.

This change probably was brought about by the desire of lawyers to
conduct business at the emerging state capital, as well as reorganization of
the district court system. From time to time in the 1790s, the General
Assembly grouped Richland, for general judicial purposes, with various
nearby counties, including Kershaw in 1798, only to break up that short-
lived union twelve months later and convert every county throughout the
state into a district. With this development, Richland County (called a
district until 1868) can be said to have begun its existence as an independent entity. At that time the old county courts were abolished, and administrative matters such as roads and care of the poor placed in the
hands of commissioners. Also, the act elevating Richland to district status
stipulated that its *district* court would be held in Columbia, thus, in effect, making that community the county seat.

In August of 1800, four commissioners appointed by the General Assembly contracted with Jesse Arthur to erect a jail in Columbia. This two-
story, brick structure, with foundation walls two feet thick, soon appeared
near the corner of Washington and Richardson [Main] streets, and the
following year a disagreement arose concerning the location of the courthouse relative to the jail. Some local residents, who eventually won out,
urged lawmakers to build the seat of local government opposite the jail,
while others wanted it several blocks to the south near the new state

house. In December of 1803, Richard Clarke, hired by the General Assembly to construct Richland County's second courthouse, was granted an eight-month extension, provided he used slate on the roof instead of shingles. When he agreed, members appropriated $1,050 to cover additional costs involved, and Clarke proceeded to finish the job. Edward Hooker, a young Connecticut-born tutor who arrived in Columbia in 1805, described the courthouse, which, like the jail, was a two-story, brick edifice, as "a much handsomer building" than the state capitol.[2]

Meanwhile, the Horrell Hill courthouse had found a new role. In December of 1801, the Minerva Society (incorporated the following year) asked the General Assembly for permission to use the empty structure as a grammar school. Their intent, they said, was to create an institution where "the poorer class of men may find it more convenient to bring forward their Children in the rudiments of Literature."[3] The Assembly acceded to this request, but some years later the society erected its own school building near Hopkins, giving birth to a small community known as Minervaville. According to Laura Jervey Hopkins, the original courthouse, abandoned once more, became a playground of sorts during the early decades of the 19th century.[4] Her ancestors, she relates, sometimes raced their ponies from plantation homes in lower Richland to summer retreats in the sand hills, with a rest stop at the courthouse where they would sit in the judge's chair and pretend to hold court.

As for the "new" courthouse, General Assembly records reveal it soon became a center of activity and controversy. In 1805, Sheriff Charles Williamson successfully sought reimbursement for a pillory he had built, a structure carefully described by blacksmith Benjamin Rawls, a Georgia native and later himself sheriff, who lived in York for about a decade before moving to Columbia in October of 1802.

> . . . it was made so as that a man could stand on a plank 7 or 8 feet from the ground, and [at] a right height for his neck [,] a plank fixed edgewise, with a semicircle cut in the upper edge *to fit half of his neck;* another plank like the first, was made to lift up, having a semicircle cut in the under edge to fit the *other half of his neck;* so that when he was fixed right, his head was on one side of the plank and his body on the other; but for his accommodation there also was a place for each arm, that fitted just close to the hand. They had a gent in it one day for an hour or two, but I did not see him in it; his name was

Robert Merit, he lived out in the Sand Hills, and merited the pillory for taking too much notice of some person's cow.[5]

That same year (1805), the courthouse grounds evidently were the site of Richland's first execution when a slave was put to death for plotting an insurrection. Lamb, owned by Benjamin Scott, confessed to the charge, even though no overt act ever was committed. Two years later, Scott, who agreed it was proper to make an example of Lamb for the public good, maintained that the public treasury should pay him for his loss. He sought $250, but got only $122.40.

During the next few years, local citizens filed numerous complaints concerning the courthouse, and the jury room still was unfinished when an earthquake rocked the structure on 15 December 1811. Benjamin Rawls writes that these tremors, the first shocks of the famed phenomenon centered in New Madrid, Missouri, damaged several brick buildings in the town and, since it coincided with a revival meeting then going on, prompted some to listen more intently to the words of the speakers. Three years later, legislators ruled it would not be necessary to tear down the courthouse; it could be repaired. But in 1816 they concluded that "the ruinous and insecure state of that Building" required that it be "prostrated and built anew," for "Breaches" extending from bottom to top endangered the lives of all who entered. They appropriated $8,000 for that purpose and subsequently paid builder Robert Yates another $3,500 for plastering, painting, and other finishing touches. Although the tremors of 1811 undoubtedly damaged the unfinished structure so much admired by the young tutor from New England, one suspects that faulty foundation work or low-grade mortar, which caused some concern as South Carolina College was taking shape, may have contributed to this disaster.

Thus, after decades of protests and appeals to both colonial and state officials, Richland County came into existence with relative ease, its birth pangs marred only by minor boundary disputes, legislative indecision concerning what sort of court system South Carolinians should have, an earthquake, and a twenty-year struggle to erect a satisfactory courthouse. Yet, although county government was indeed a prerequisite for the development and growth of the region between the Congaree and Wateree rivers, throughout the 19th century it did not exert great impact upon the day-to-day lives of most citizens. The county was a passive factor that gave stability and continuity to society. Its officers kept records, investigated crime and punished those found guilty, issued a variety of licenses, paid lip service to public education and the needs of the poor, and with indifferent success supervised the maintenance of roads and bridges.

Counties, first and foremost, served an organizational function. Nevertheless, in a milieu both agricultural and rural, a county could inspire intense loyalty and pride. Perhaps these emotional ties arose from association with family and friends, devotion to a local political luminary, militia duty, or even fear of the unfamiliar and affection for the known, but they were indeed real.

Creation of the community that became Richland's county seat, as well as South Carolina's new state capital, was quite another matter. The process was, strangely enough, both traditional and highly innovative . . . and, needless to add, extremely controversial. Transferring a functioning government to a more central spot was nothing new. Maryland did so in the 1690s, moving its capital from St. Mary's City to Annapolis, and all of the other thirteen colonies (except Massachusetts) would someday do the same thing, usually choosing an inland or westward location. Also, purchasing privately held land as the site for a new city or a new capital was well-established policy, as was the creation of a grid pattern of streets and avenues.

What was different was the unprecedented proposal to move a government, along with its records, clerks, and various functionaries, from a comfortable urban setting to fields and forests, a place devoid of organized communal life. Four years after South Carolinians decided in 1786 to take this bold step and abandon Charleston for the banks of the Congaree, federal leaders followed their example and established the city of Washington. And two years after that, North Carolinians voted to transform the county seat of Wake County, admittedly a virtual wilderness, into the city of Raleigh. In time, states such as Mississippi, Ohio, Indiana, and Missouri carved new capitals out of largely uninhabited territory, and in our own century several nations (among them, Australia, Pakistan, and Brazil) have done much the same thing.

The rationale for this unique decision of 1786, as well as the motives of those opposed to it, is easily understood. As the tumult of war subsided, the much more populous upcountry, flexing its muscle, began to pepper the General Assembly with suggestions for all sorts of reforms. These included county courts (which soon became a reality), recording of legislative votes, publication of measures enacted, a new constitution with a more equitable apportionment plan, colleges in Winnsboro and Ninety Six, and a bounty on the heads of outlaws. But a recurring theme among these appeals was a request, really a demand, that the seat of government be moved to a more "Centrical" place. And, although everyone was aware that *where* lawmakers met was a boon to tavern owners and shopkeepers and also made legislators subject to local pressures, these truths rarely were mentioned; instead, advocates of change talked only of the need for a more *central* location.

In February of 1786, the upcountry finally forced the General Assembly to confront this issue head-on, and for nearly four weeks members wrestled with the question of transferring state government inland. A committee appointed to select the most convenient place reported on 22 February that its choice was Camden and suggested that the next legislative session be held there; however, House members rejected this proposal. Opponents said Camden could not provide adequate accommodations, while others thought that community not "central" enough. Charleston spokesmen, on the other hand, argued that their city, despite geography, actually was *central* to trade, navigation, and commerce, adding that upcountry lawmakers, more accustomed to traveling great distances, experienced no real inconvenience when they came to the peninsula between the Ashley and Cooper rivers. Still others worried that an "itinerant" government might lose dignity, expose its records and treasure "to the mercy of a small number of banditti," or become little more than a wandering "band of Tartars." But a suggestion to amend the motion to read the *most proper* place instead of the "most convenient" was voted down in the House on 1 March.

Amid such maneuverings, Senator John Lewis Gervais of Ninety Six District introduced a bill on 4 March outlining a comprehensive plan whereby state government could be moved to a site near Friday's Ferry at no cost to taxpayers. His proposal, later much modified, was for the state to buy 140 acres of land on the plain and hill where James and Thomas Taylor lived, divide it into lots, and, when one-fourth of them were sold, use the proceeds to erect public buildings. As soon as those structures were complete, the government would move.

Five days later the Senate began to discuss this measure, and low-country members soon warmed to the attack. The site, they said, was not truly central, it was low and unwholesome, and "the people in that part of the country had hoisted the banner of defiance against the laws" and driven out judges.[6] When these thrusts failed to deter proponents, Arnoldus Vanderhorst (Charleston's intendant) proclaimed derisively that this capital would become a place where laws were "laughed at and despised" and sheriffs nothing but "harmless, inoffensive men." Under such conditions, he scoffed, there the desperate would seek asylum, and thus the new community should be called "Town of Refuge." "Col. Gervais said," according to published accounts of the proceedings, "he had no objection to its being a town of refuge, but not in an opprobrious way; he hoped that in this town we should find refuge under the wings of CO-LUMBIA, for that was the name which he wished it to be called."[7] This statement led to still more skirmishing, some advocating the name of a live hero (Washington) instead of a dead man (Columbus), who, it was noted, actually had nothing whatsoever to do with North America. But Columbia won out, 11–7.

On 11 March the House tackled what was now the "Columbia" problem, and in the days that followed the same arguments were aired once more: healthfulness, centrality, navigation on the Congaree, and so on. Thomas Taylor, members were told, was sickly until he moved to the hill where he now lived, "but soon after recovered, and had enjoyed pretty good health ever since." Thomas Sumter agreed Friday's Ferry was close to the center of South Carolina, but then directed attention to the nearby High Hills of Santee. Since he owned land there, he was, he conceded, reluctant to speak out; nevertheless, undue "delicacy or modesty might prove injurious to the public benefit." Friday's Ferry, in his opinion, was much less healthful and could boast only of barren soil and pine timber not fit for building. "To the westward and southwestward of it, the lands were mostly worn out, so that in many parts of it planters were not to be seen within ten miles of one another."[8] Compared to the Wateree, navigation on some stretches of the Congaree was "extremely bad."

Patrick Calhoun of Ninety Six District rose in rebuttal. The High Hills, he said, were as broken and barren as the land around Friday's Ferry; one had to go farther west to find good timber. Yet there was fertile soil along the Congaree, plenty of good streams flowed into it, and that region certainly was closer to the center of the state than the Santee hills. Some years earlier, Calhoun added, he had seen a saw mill near Friday's Ferry operating no less than *seven* saws at once!

Edward Rutledge vowed he recently had been at the site being praised and had "looked in vain for those numberless beauties and advantages to be dwelt on." But the House, perhaps tired of this bickering, refused to be swayed and voted 65–61 for a revised version of the Gervais Bill, which now called for a city two miles square with 60-foot-wide streets (thanks to a suggestion by Charleston's Dr. John Budd).

A few days later, Rutledge took the floor once more and persuaded House members to move "Columbia" to the confluence of the Congaree and Wateree. His most telling arguments were that the southeastern corner of Richland County was at the head of navigation, more so than Friday's Ferry, and that the new location would attract commerce from North Carolina. But the Senate held out for "Taylor's Hill," and on the final day of the session (22 March 1786) the two chambers approved a comprehensive act appointing commissioners to purchase land at that site "for the purpose of building a Town, and for removing the Seat of Government thereto."[9] Those named—Alexander Gillon, Richard Winn, Richard Hampton, Thomas Taylor, and Henry Pendleton—all owned land in the Midlands and thus had a personal stake in this venture. Missing from the group, however, was Wade Hampton, whose firm hand can be seen throughout these proceedings.

Hampton, along with Pendleton, was one of six representatives for Saxe-Gotha District in the 1786 session of the General Assembly. His brother, Richard, was senator for Saxe-Gotha; another brother, John, spoke for the "lower district" between the Broad and Saluda rivers in the House; and yet another, Henry, was a representative for the region between the Broad and Catawba. Thomas Taylor's brother, James, also represented the Broad-Catawba territory in 1786.

Until quite recently, Wade Hampton's interests lay on the *west* bank of the Congaree, not in Richland County. There he had a flourishing store, and it was the Granby-Saxe-Gotha area that he represented in the state legislature. But marriage in 1783 to a wealthy widow, Martha Epps Goodwyn Howell, made him master of considerable land on the *east* bank of the river. (The bride died in 1784.) In March of 1785, Richard and Wade Hampton purchased the rights to Friday's Ferry, and in April of 1786—one month after the General Assembly agreed to create the city of Columbia and on the *same* day that the commissioners purchased land for the new capital—the two brothers acquired about 1,000 acres on the Richland side of the river, property that included the eastern terminus of that important ferry. As Ronald Bridwell notes with some awe, Wade Hampton apparently owned no land until 1778. A decade later, at age thirty-two, he was a wealthy planter, master of several hundred slaves, and owner of numerous commercial enterprises as well.

Tutor Edward Hooker, who traveled with Hampton en route to Columbia in 1805, found him "a very singular man." According to Hooker, he talked much of energy and enterprise, as well he might with a reputed income by that date of $50,000 a year. "The leading traits of his character," wrote Hooker, "are boldness and originality of scheme, remarkable foresight in the judicious means for the accomplishment of this scheme, and undaunted perseverance in the application of those means."[10]

Nowhere is this boldness and foresight more apparent than in the "scheme" to make Columbia a reality. Long before others, Hampton sensed the impending move of state government inland and began to add to his initial holdings near Friday's Ferry. Then, he adroitly let Gervais lead the charge, while enlisting the aid of the Taylors, his brothers, and various other upcountry lawmakers who held similar views. Once South Carolina's leaders became reconciled to moving the seat of government and embraced the concept of centrality, Columbia's only serious rival was Camden. But that community's obvious spokesman, Joseph Kershaw, plagued by financial woes, was not a member of the General Assembly in 1786, and Thomas Sumter (one of ten representatives for the district east of the Wateree) became an outspoken advocate for his own property, a mistake not made by Wade Hampton and Thomas Taylor.

Late in April of 1786, following instructions of the General Assembly, the five commissioners purchased 2,471 acres of land near Friday's Ferry from ten property owners for £4,747, roughly eight dollars per acre.[11] They were:

Thomas Taylor	398 acres
Richard and Wade Hampton	381 acres
John Compty	362 acres
James Taylor	361 acres
Nathan Center	298 acres
Henry Patrick estate	222 acres
Stephen Curry	192 acres
John Henry Faust	172 acres
William Arthur estate	85 acres

Any of these men living within the confines of the new town could reserve 2 acres as a home site, land not subject to sale. Records at the South Carolina State Archives reveal they got half of the money due them in 1786 and the remainder in various payments during the next two decades. Although these individuals certainly suffered no loss, neither did they enjoy any great windfall; profit was realized instead by those who subsequently purchased desirable town lots or, like the Taylors and Hamptons, owned property on the borders of this new community that increased greatly in value. Even before these transactions were completed, the *Charleston Morning Post and Daily Advertiser* (1 May 1786) reported that embryonic Columbia was buzzing with activity: "A gentleman lately arrived from the neighborhood of Friday's Ferry informs that the new town called Columbia appears in a very forward way of being soon erected; saw mills are building on every stream within its vicinity, and such an opinion is entertained of the utility of this new undertaking that land thereabout has risen 150 per cent."

Meanwhile, the commissioners, who would govern Columbia for nearly two decades, went to the banks of the Congaree and divided the two square miles they had acquired into a grid of ten streets to the mile, making a total of 400 blocks, a few of which, it later developed, were under water. Eight acres were reserved for public buildings, and an effort was made—at least at the outset—to dictate the size and construction of new houses. According to this plan, the principal north-south street (Assembly) and the principal east-west street (Senate) intersected at the capitol grounds and divided the town into four equal parts. These two avenues and "boundary" streets (those on the borders of the community) were to be 150 feet wide; all others, 100 feet. Streets parallel to Assembly were named for Revolutionary worthies such as Sumter, Marion, Bull, and Pickens, while those parallel to Senate honored George Washington, his wife (Lady), various local citizens (Taylor, Greene, and Devine), and several well-known crops (wheat, rice, indigo, and tobacco). Some street names have been changed through the years, but the grid plan is virtually intact. And, although this basic scheme often is scorned by town planners as monotonous, Columbia's broad thoroughfares are the envy of scores of cities and a delight to tourists and travelers.

The first sale of half-acre lots was held a few months later in Charleston on 26 and 27 September and in Columbia on 10 November. Choice property along the principal streets, near the river, and in the center of town sold well, and the state received (in theory) nearly £12,000. The largest buyer, Richard Hampton, acquired sixty-four lots for £1,395, some of which he soon disposed of to other parties. The *Charleston Morning Post and Daily Advertiser* (24 November 1786) reported that, on average, lots had sold for upwards of £25, and many purchasers had contracted for houses "far superior" to what the law required. Waxing eloquent concerning the potential of Columbia, the editor praised streets 100–150 feet wide, especially Richardson [Main]. "The street will, no doubt, soon be built up with good houses and commodious stores, as the trade will mostly center there."

Yet there were problems. Thomas Burke, who bought fifty lots, refused to pay for them when he discovered some were in the Congaree River and promptly was sued by the commissioners. Also, the original survey turned out to be inaccurate, and others besides Burke, for various reasons, failed to honor commitments made so enthusiastically at auctions. These complications, together with the fact that buyers were making partial payments—so much down, the remainder over so many years—endangered the neat arrangement outlined by Gervais whereby income from sales would pay the costs of erecting public buildings.

The most important of these was, of course, the State House. In mid-November of 1787, Charleston's *City Gazette* announced that construction had commenced on a structure 130 by 60 feet, one story high, above a stone basement. During the next few months, work progressed very slowly, presumably under the direction of James Brown, a Camden builder. Brown may have been using plans drawn by Irish-born James Hoban, who later designed the White House in Washington. But Ronald Bridwell says only "circumstantial evidence" links Hoban to this building, and his name is not found in any records relating to it. Hoban, who emigrated to Philadelphia in 1785, was in Charleston by April of 1787 and lived there until 1792. However, it seems unlikely that the Columbia commissioners would have sought the help of such a recent arrival, a virtually unknown individual.

In any case, this unfolding saga took an unexpected turn in February of 1788 when the Charleston state house went up in flames. Some members wanted to rebuild the structure immediately; others thought this ridiculous since the government was about to set up housekeeping in Columbia. Amid this confusion, House members once more agreed to move to Camden (temporarily), but then changed their minds. Eventually they voted to rebuild their former meeting hall, which would become the Charleston County courthouse when state officials left . . . however, it could not, they ruled, be called the "state house." During these same weeks, distressed by the sagging sale of Columbia lots after an initial wave of buying enthusiasm, legislators agreed to loan the commissioners £3,500 to assist in the construction of public buildings. It is quite possible, of course, this was yet another lowcountry-upcountry deal: Charleston County got a new courthouse; Columbia, funds for construction.

By April of 1788, the basement offices of the new Columbia "capitol" were nearly finished and, according to Charleston's *City Gazette*, some fifty houses had appeared nearby. Early in October the State House was "raised," that is, the frame and roof of the main floor were erected, an occasion marked by patriotic toasts; and, in the evening, "a very numerous and polite assembly partook of a ball."

Six months later, in March of 1789, the General Assembly ruled that all records, except those pertaining to Charleston, Beaufort, and

Georgetown districts, should be shipped to Columbia, and the commissioners subsequently reported that chests measuring four feet by two feet by two feet were being constructed for that purpose. In May of that same year, they assured lawmakers that, despite frequent delays, the State House would be ready to receive them seven months hence and that adequate accommodations could be found in the immediate area. Columbia, they were told, had facilities for 217 people and 310 horses; Granby, for 109 individuals and 72 horses. In addition, Thomas Taylor's fine home was to become "government house," presumably meaning a residence for the governor, and they promised that a market would be built and stocked with foodstuffs.

Despite these assurances of basic shelter and food for both man and beast, the worst fears of lowcountry legislators undoubtedly were confirmed when they arrived in Columbia early in January of 1790. In contrast to the joys of urbane Charleston, the new seat of government was little more than a clearing in a pine barren wilderness. The only diversion (other than those found in taverns) was provided by a local jockey club, which had inaugurated a series of races in February of 1788. Among the organizers were Thomas Taylor and Richard Hampton, who obviously planned to duplicate what had become the culmination of Charleston's social season. Although these hopes were not realized, the lure of the track was so overpowering that some lawmakers tried unsuccessfully to ban horse racing within twenty miles of the State House during debates.

After only seventeen days, Columbia's first legislative meeting, the second session of the eighth General Assembly, came to a close. The brevity of these proceedings undoubtedly is proof of the keen distaste many harbored for their surroundings, as well as a general reluctance to embark upon a new course in a period of great change. During these months the federal constitution of 1787 was being implemented, testing new ground in the realm of nationhood, and South Carolinians were about to hold their own constitutional convention.

The main goals of this conclave were to tidy up a document some said had been written much too hastily in the midst of war and reapportion seats in the state legislature. Despite lowcountry objections, in March of 1789, General Assembly members agreed to convene a constitutional convention in Columbia in May of the following year. One would have thought the seat of government question resolved, but efforts by Thomas Taylor's son-in-law, James Green Hunt, to incorporate language into the new constitution fixing Columbia as the *permanent* state capital opened old wounds and led to angry words once more. An attempt by Charleston's

A Trip to Columbia

Come, *Citizens!* take up your parts,
　To *Columbia's* sweet Banks we'll repair;
Let's quit the gay scenes of the Town,
　Pregnant with suits and despair.

Near the centre of State we'll convene,
　Sagely devised by the *People;*
Adieu, to your pompous parade!
　Adieu, to your Balls and your Steeple!

Our roads may be sandy and ruff,
　Margin'd with fine lofy pine,
Directing our drover along,
　With herds of noble fat swine.

Our amusement, is *Business of State,*
　Centrically placed for our ease;
Without shrimps, or oysters in pies,
　So *delegates* fare as you please.

Your fair may out-dress us we own,
　An artless appearance we boast;
The feather which fills you with pride,
　Is not *the Columbian toast.*

This movement of Records may be
　American plodding or Dutch;
But the object well answers the end,
　And happy the state that has such.

Avaunt, then, you Nabobs of pomp;
　You fine-powder'd Bucks of the city;
With curl irons fixed in each pate,
　With Lasses sweet scented and pretty.

State Gazette of South-Carolina,
31 December 1789.[12]

C. C. Pinckney to table Hunt's proposal failed by only one vote (105–104), a reflection, no doubt, of the sentiments of men sleeping three in a bed and eating poor fare.

The delegates then proceeded to approve the motion by a vote of 109–105, but this was a hollow victory. To soothe bruised egos, a committee was appointed to compromise upcountry-lowcountry differences. The result, as embodied in the 1790 constitution, stipulated that the General Assembly would meet annually at Columbia ("which shall remain the seat of government, until otherwise determined by the concurrence of two-thirds of both branches of the whole representation"). The state, it was agreed, would maintain dual offices in Columbia and Charleston. A treasurer would reside in each city, and the secretary of state and surveyor-general (or their deputies) would operate in a similar manner. In addition, circuit judges were to meet first in Columbia to hear appeals from the upcountry and then proceed to Charleston "to transact all business of a similar nature." This arrangement, it might be noted, was not unique. Connecticut and Rhode Island had two capitals throughout much of the 19th century, and in our own day several states maintain extensive offices in cities located some distance from the communities where their legislatures meet.

The decade that followed was a "testing" time for South Carolinians both in external (state-federal) and internal relations, and this was especially true of those living on the banks of the Congaree. Columbia had won the right to be the seat of state government, but it was not yet a center of county affairs. For that matter, the relationship of counties to districts still remained unclear. Annual legislative sessions certainly boosted business each winter and added momentary zest to daily life, but the little community hardly could exist year-round on these infusions. The fundamental task facing the Taylors, Hamptons, and other families gambling on the region's future was nothing less than a restructuring of upcountry trading patterns. Produce and goods that had been traveling up and down the west side of the Congaree through Granby had to be redirected to the east side of the river, and farmers and storekeepers accustomed to dealing with outlets in Granby, Camden, and even Augusta and Charleston had to be lured to a new market place.

This was not an impossible goal, given certain geographical factors. The town was near the head of navigation on the Congaree; and, if the Broad and Saluda rivers could be cleared of obstructions, it might well serve as a convenient trading center for residents of the Midlands and Piedmont. But there were hurdles to overcome. The waters of South Carolina's rivers, although boats moved along them from time to time, were indeed capricious, often too high and too swift, in other seasons a mere trickle, and wagon traffic added much to the cost of goods. The Santee, until linked to Charleston by canal in 1800, was less than satisfactory, since produce shipped down the Congaree-Santee system faced a treacherous ocean voyage, and even that canal was of short-term benefit. In addition, Columbia merchants had to compete with their Charleston counterparts by providing services and goods at prices that made it advantageous for back-country folk to stop at the fall line rather than go all the way to the coast to transact business.

Ferries, roads, and bridges obviously would foster trade; and, beginning with the acquisition of Friday's Ferry in 1785, the brothers Hampton ushered in over a decade of improvements in regional transportation. These efforts, backed by various individuals, included re-chartering of at least half a dozen ferries (with connecting highways) and construction of several roads, among them, one from Friday's Ferry to the Augusta Ferry and others linking Columbia to points on the Saluda, Broad, and Bush rivers.

The Hamptons also tried to bridge the Congaree at Granby, and John Compty wanted to span the Broad just north of where it joined the Saluda; however, all of these attempts were thwarted by recurring freshets and floods. In fact, Wade Hampton erected no less than four toll bridges on the Congaree during the 1790s, only to see all of them washed away. His first bridge across the Savannah at Augusta suffered a similar fate; but, in time, he was able to rebuild that structure.[13]

The struggling little community of Columbia had internal problems as well. Since lots were not selling, in 1792 the General Assembly lowered the minimum price to be charged for land in certain areas and dispensed with all restrictions on the type of houses to be built on such property. Members also set aside 4 acres for the support of a free school and several years later donated two squares to the state's agricultural society. Then, in 1801 they handed over eight squares close by the State House to the trustees of South Carolina College, even though some of that land already had been sold.

As the town grew, the General Assembly realized that neither that body nor the commissioners (whose responsibilities had been reduced to peddling real estate) could provide day-to-day management. As a result, lawmakers approved the creation in 1797 of a commission of streets and markets to run the town; however, that group was reorganized two years later and given powers much like those of county road commissioners, that is, its members could compel residents to work on streets, issue tavern licenses, "fine and expel all keepers of gaming tables," and pass rules and regulations "they may deem proper and requisite for the promotion of the quiet and safety of the inhabitants of the town." Thus, until official incorporation in 1805, these men were Columbia's government.

The size of Columbia's population during these years is something of a mystery. It was, obviously, only a few hundred at most, but growing. The first federal census (1790) revealed that Richland County, which of course encompassed the little settlement on the Congaree, had 3,930 residents. This total included 1,306 white males (710 of them under the age of 16), 1,173 white females, 1,437 slaves, and 14 "other free persons." There were, in all, 480 households, 328 of which had no slaves. Only 4 men were masters of more than 40 slaves on plantations within the county: Thomas Taylor (160), Wade Hampton (86), John Goodwyn (55), and Benjamin Wade (46). By 1800, the county had 6,097 residents, 3,168 of them black.

Two revealing descriptions of early Columbia exist, one by no less an authority than President George Washington and the other by John Drayton, governor of this state at the time he published his remarkable *View of South-Carolina* in 1802. Washington, who toured the South in the spring of 1791, arrived in Columbia from Augusta on Sunday, 22 May, noting that the "whole road" along that route was "a pine barren of the worst sort, being hilly as well as poor." The following day he was feted at a public dinner at the State House and forty-eight hours later, early on the 25th, set out for Camden. "The Road from Columbia to Camden, excepting a mile or two at each place," he wrote in his diary, "goes over the most miserable pine barren I ever saw, being quite a white sand, & very hilly."

Delayed by a "foundered" horse, Washington spent Tuesday, 24 May, looking about South Carolina's newest community and thinking perhaps of the city he was striving to build on the Potomac. Here are his comments for that date.

> Columbia is laid out upon a large scale; but, in my opinion had better been placed on the River below the falls.—It is now an uncleared wood, with very few houses in it, and those all wooden ones—The State House (which is also of wood) is a large and commodious building, but unfinished—The Town is on dry, but cannot be called high ground, and though surrounded by Piney & Sandy land is, itself good—The State house is near two miles from the River, at the con-

fluence of the Broad River & Saluda.—From Granby the River is navigable for Craft which will, when the River is a little swelled, carry 3000 bushels of Grain—when at its usual height less, and always some.[14]

Drayton, said to have been the first governor to tour all of the up-country and a very active proponent of higher education, led the fight to create South Carolina College at Columbia in 1801. At the same time, perhaps inspired by Thomas Jefferson's well-known *Notes on Virginia*, he was busy completing an overview of the history, both natural and political, of his state. This unusual compendium contains, among other things, a botanical catalog, a list of native animals, birds, and fish, numerous statistics, agricultural and commercial data, and this description of the state's new capital.

Columbia is the seat of government of this state; and its situation is just below the confluence of Broad and Saluda rivers, on the eastern side of the Congaree river. It was so called by act of assembly in 1786; at which time measures were taken for the first settling of the town; and the departments of government met there in December, 1789; and continue to do so at stated periods. The town is laid off by a regular plan; its streets intersecting each other at right angles. The buildings are erected about three quarters of a mile from the Congaree, on a ridge of high land, near three hundred feet above the level of the river; from which a delightful prospect is presented. Here the state-house, situated on a beautiful eminence, is to be seen, at the distance of many miles, from various parts of the country. And soon, we hope, the *South-Carolina College* will rise an ornament to the town; respectable from its establishment*; but still more from the learning and friendship, which a national institution, like this, cannot fail to promote among the youth from all parts of this state; an object, particularly desirable to all true lovers of this country. Some successful attempts have been made, at Columbia, in raising grapes and making wine; a few casks of this grateful liquor have been there made by Mr. Benjamin Waring, whose flavor was agreeable, and not unlike Sicily wine. To this gentleman, also, the public is indebted for the erection of an oil mill in Columbia, by which, from a bushel of cotton seed, he extracts half a gallon of oil. And to Mr. Stephen Brown, also,

*By act of the legislature in 1801, funds were appropriated for establishing a college at Columbia, under the above name.

the public are obliged, for the establishment of a valuable rope-walk,
just without the skirts of the town; which is not only a great convenience to the interior of the state; but also much promotes the cultivation of hemp, as a new object of agriculture. Columbia consists of
about eighty or one hundred houses; and during the sittings of the
legislature, assumes a gay appearance. At other times a calmness and
quiet reigns, far different from the noise and bustle of a legislative
session; or to that of a large trading city. This tranquility is, however,
often roused into active business, by the arrival of loaded waggons
from the upper country; and were a suitable bridge thrown across the
Congaree, just below Granby, there is little doubt, but the trade of
this town would thereby experience a very happy increase.[15]

As Drayton makes clear, changes had occurred in Columbia during
the 1790s, including some pioneering attempts at wine-making and manufacturing. Yet the little community really had but two functions—government business from time to time and trade in agricultural products—
and these pursuits would occupy the attention of most residents for
decades to come. These same interests gave rise to a substantial number
of boarding houses, taverns, and hotels to serve the needs of visitors.
Timothy Rives was among the first to provide food and lodgings when he
opened his house during the 1792 legislative session for "the PRIVATE
accommodation of Gentlemen." His Richardson Street tavern near the
State House quickly became a popular meeting place in Columbia and, in
contrast to most, continued in existence for many years.

More typical were the operations of Samuel Green, a multi-purpose
individual who settled in Columbia in the early 1790s and gradually acquired land, slaves, and some local prominence. Born in Massachusetts
and educated in Rhode Island, Green was, by turns, merchant, druggist,
postmaster, tavern keeper, hotel owner, and land speculator. William John
Grayson, who entered South Carolina College in 1806, admired Green
(then also steward of the college) as "a general authority with his neighbors on all subjects ordinary and extraordinary," a man of simple speech
devoid of pomp. However, he described Green's hotel in this manner: "It
was a long, rough, wooden house with poor lodgings and worse fare."[16]

Samuel Green's papers, now at the South Caroliniana Library, consist largely of business accounts and letters to his brother in New York and
Massachusetts, prime supplier of items desired by Columbia customers.
For the most part, Green sought manufactured goods such as dry paint
(to be mixed with oil already on hand), books, glassware, medicine, all

sorts of carpenters' tools, bolts of cloth, thread, shoes (especially large sizes suitable for slaves), and foodstuffs.

In July of 1793, he wrote that stores were increasing "so fast in this place that the proportion of business each can do must be very inconsiderable." Perhaps, he mused, they should consider moving to Augusta. Two months later, however, Green was eager to stock up in time for the sitting of the legislature. His special needs were pocket registers, a barrel of gin, window glass, nails, and geographical dictionaries (for which there had been "great inquiry"). "Most of the People of this place are very fond of Politics," he stressed, "and are often at a loss to know when such and such Battles are fought, and I think we had best inform them if we can. . . ." At that time, he had on his shelves Bonnycastle's *Arithmetic*, *Pilgrims' Progress*, Enfield's *Prayers*, *Poems* by Robert Burns, and various self-help manuals. If possible, Green told his brother, he would like to secure copies of Dean's *System of Husbandry*, Paine's *Rights of Man*, Blackstone's *Analysis*, the writings of Baron von Steuben, and any medical pamphlets that might be available. Also, he noted in passing that Benjamin Waring, with whom he later cooperated in wine-making, had asked him to join in a tan-yard venture, which he eventually agreed to do.

Early in 1794, Green relayed several fashion notes. Ladies hats shipped south had sold well, although the brims should have been somewhat larger, but those made for men were much too high priced for the Columbia market. "Our ladies," he observed, "are all having their ears boared; whatever is fashionable in that way send me a few—some beads and necklaces if they are fashionable with you." In August of that same year, Green proposed opening a second store in Granby and perhaps buying a boat (or part of one) so as to lower shipping costs from Charleston. By that date he had become postmaster and reacted with these words when his brother suggested on 21 September 1794, that he move to Charleston: "I will comply notwithstanding that I would much prefer living in Columbia."

Throughout this correspondence Green tried to convey some understanding of problems he faced. Goods often sold well enough, but one had to extend credit. ("Capt. Taylor has many articles of me: I shall not be able to get any pay till some time in the Fall or Winter.") The medicines he received sometimes were inferior, and items frequently were damaged in transit. Nevertheless, his letters reveal that little Columbia, even in its formative years, exuded a certain pioneer charm. In July of 1793 he was "dubious" about the future of commercial operations on the banks of the Congaree and urged upon his brother the suggestion that they both move to the back country. Samuel Green complained of a climate "very unfavorable to a Northern constitution." A year later—now postmaster, involved in the tanning business, and associated with various other commercial enterprises—this New Englander had found a home.

Basic to this transformation was, of course, the excitement of forging a new town in the wilderness. In less than twelve months this discontented Yankee, who would remain in South Carolina for the remainder of his long life (he died in 1837), had discovered a land of opportunity in Columbia and Richland County. Many others, one might note, soon would follow in his footsteps.

Notes

1. Thomas Cooper and David J. McCord (editors), *The Statutes at Large of South Carolina* (10 vols.; Columbia, 1836–41), IV, p. 662.
2. Quoted in Green, p. 162.
3. Edwin Green Papers, South Caroliniana Library.
4. Laura Jervey Hopkins, *Lower Richland Planters: Hopkins, Adams, Weston, and Related Families of South Carolina* (Columbia, 1976), p. 13.
5. Benjamin Rawls, *Biblical Criticism and Reminiscences of Columbia* (Columbia, 1861), p. 32.
6. This is a reference to civil unrest that had occurred in Camden.
7. *Charleston Morning Post and Daily Advertiser*, 11 March 1786.
8. *Ibid.*, 15 March 1786. The traditional tale that Stateburg, created by Thomas Sumter, was considered as a site for the seat of state government apparently is apocryphal. That community never was mentioned in published accounts of these deliberations or in records of these debates.
9. See *Statutes at Large of South Carolina*, IV, pp. 751–52.
10. J. Franklin Jameson (editor), *Diary of Edward Hooker, 1805–1808* (Washington, 1897), p. 845.
11. Until the mid-1790s, South Carolina currency was expressed in pounds, not dollars. The Samuel Green Papers indicate that by that date a pound was worth about $2.50.
12. This anonymous poem, relatively upbeat, is a rebuttal to several composed by Philip Freneau (1752–1832). Freneau, a frequent visitor to Charleston, apparently was reflecting the views of his brother, Peter, then secretary of state. He portrays Columbia as a "sad, disheart'ning town," a place without "music, sermons, balls, or oyster-pies" where owls screech and bears break into stores. His final blast in the *Daily Advertiser* (5 February 1790) describes the trials of a beleaguered citizen:

Open the door, forsooth—the man is mad[.]
Lodging is not so easy to be had;
It is an article we do not trade in,
Nor shall my bed by all the world be laid in,
Our very garret is as full as can be,
Push off, I say, and try your luck at *Granby*!

13. Richard Hampton, who also erected a bridge over the Ashley River near Charleston, died in 1792, depriving the community of one of its most daring, if unfortunate boosters. His debts were so large that his administrators tried to void the purchase of town lots in Columbia, and two years later Samuel Green informed his brother that most local residents did not think Hampton's creditors ever would be paid what was due them.

14. Joseph A. Hoskins (compiler), *President Washington's Diaries, 1791–1799* (Summerfield, N.C., 1921), p. 37.

15. John Drayton, *A View of South-Carolina, as Respects Her Natural and Civil Concerns* (Charleston, 1802), pp. 211–12.

16. Richard J. Calhoun (editor), *Witness to Sorrow, the Antebellum Autobiography of William J. Grayson* (Columbia, 1990), p. 83. According to Grayson, a Beaufort native, the standard college meal at that time was bacon and "long" collards.

Colonel Taylor's Congaree Settlement

CHAPTER FOUR

One of this region's most prominent citizens for over half a century, Thomas Taylor was born in Amelia County, Virginia, in 1743. When he was about ten years of age, his father, John Taylor, moved to South Carolina and began to acquire land on the banks of the Congaree. This family's new home, gently rolling countryside near the fall line, interspersed with rivers and streams bordered by rich bottom land, was much like that they had left. The move south in the 1750s undoubtedly was prompted by the same factors that were pushing other Virginians, such as Thomas Jefferson's father, westward past the fall line into the Piedmont: pressures to find new soil for crops such as tobacco and wheat. The Taylors were, in fact, neither the first nor the last of their neighbors to settle in the South Carolina Midlands during these decades; and, by the outbreak of the Revolutionary War, a growing colony of ex-Virginians had appeared in the area now known as "lower" Richland.

At the time of his death in 1766, John Taylor owned property on both sides of the Congaree River, and his will, recorded in Saxe-Gotha, named Thomas, one of six children, as executor. The following year, this vigorous young man, 6'2" tall with reddish hair and hazel eyes, married diminutive (5'3") Ann Wyche of Brunswick County, Virginia. Their sixty-six-year union would produce twelve children and establish a dynasty long associated with Columbia and Richland County.

Beginning in 1775, Taylor threw himself headlong into the rush of events—local, state, and national—that took South Carolina from colony to partnership in a new republic. His patriotic service, beginning with a commission to receive the signatures of citizens willing to bear arms in defense of the province, led eventually to the rank of colonel under Thomas Sumter. In the early 1780s, he participated in at least six military engagements, was wounded and captured by the British, but managed to escape before reaching prison. Some of his lands and slaves were seized by the enemy, but his wife, living almost in the shadow of Fort Granby, somehow was able to keep her young family together and also plant and harvest crops. When the British and their Tory friends surrendered that outpost in May of 1781, Taylor took command.

Frequently a member of the legislature and various state-wide gatherings during the decades that followed, as a Richland County delegate he voted against ratification of the federal constitution in 1788. Six years later he was a serious contender for the office of governor (the favorite of the back country) and in the 1796 presidential election served as a Jefferson elector.

At the same time, Taylor was extremely active in local affairs, holding numerous posts and, perhaps more than any other individual, making certain that Richland County and the little town of Columbia functioned properly. He helped found both county and town, was trustee of a free school in Columbia (as well as South Carolina College), served as commissioner for roads, and supervised inspection of tobacco, clearing of rivers, establishment of a bank, and regulation of bread and flour. Taylor also conducted lotteries in behalf of "useful" manufactures and Columbia's First Presbyterian Church.

When George Washington toured the South in 1791, Taylor, together with Wade Hampton and other notables, conducted the chief executive from Augusta to Columbia, and many years later he welcomed Lafayette to the town he had laid out four decades earlier. As a veteran of an earlier fray, the colonel took great interest in the War of 1812 and reportedly wore a Revolutionary War plume in his hat whenever American arms scored a success. Even as he celebrated his eighty-seventh birthday, Thomas Taylor proved that the old fire still burned bright. In September of 1830, when Columbia's business and political leaders staged a states' rights meeting, he startled those present—including one of his sons, who was chairman—by speaking out forcefully in opposition to such ideas. The man who had fought to build a nation was not going to sit idly by and watch his progeny tear it asunder, so he spoke, anti-nullifiers said, "for the good of his country."

Taylor's will, written in August of 1832, mentioned the following property, some of which had been given to his children: eighteen squares and one lot in Columbia, hundreds of acres of land on both sides of the Congaree, as well as plantations and farms on Gill and Raiford creeks, and 248 slaves. An inventory following his death in November of 1833 recorded, however, only 115 slaves.

The often-told tale that Colonel Taylor acquired the site of Columbia in trade for an old mare, a long rifle, and a jug of whiskey clearly is untrue; and, since he was only one of a group of men who owned that land, it is rather unlikely that he ever said the legislature "ruined a damned fine plantation and created a damned poor town." Less flamboyant than Wade Hampton, a contemporary with whom he must have been compared on many occasions, Colonel Taylor certainly earned his position of community leadership . . . a community that he, more than anyone else, shaped and guided during its formative years.

When Taylor first saw central South Carolina, the region in and about the Congaree still was dominated by cattle, the last remnants of a "wild west" culture glimpsed by explorer Lawson a half century earlier. The will of pioneer Philip Raiford, dated 25 February 1747/8 and subsequently filed in Charleston, listed three basic commodities to be parceled out to his heirs: cattle, land, and slaves, with only passing reference to horses and household goods. John Taylor's will, written about two decades later, described beds, specific pieces of furniture, pigs, sows, dishes, plates, and a four-gallon pot, all to be divided among his six children. And in 1789, William Whitaker, Sr., left his heirs a riding chair, a "good" feather bed, a dining table, pewter, pots, knives and forks, a clothes press, hogs, and sheep. By that date, other residents were citing books, wheels, tools, crops such as indigo still to be harvested, notes due them, money on hand, and even funds to be set aside for education ("My beloved son, John, should have two years schooling"). All of these men were well-to-do citizens possessed of land, slaves, and livestock—which of course were mentioned—yet these seemingly routine lists reflect the transformation from rough frontier to settled community.

The easing of the Indian threat was a root cause of this change, but the type of settler coming to the Midlands also influenced these trends. Some, especially the Germans, clearly intended to stay. They built solid homes, cleared stumps from their fields, rotated crops and tended them with care, made good use of manure, planted vegetable gardens, and erected fences to protect their labors. The English, on the other hand, usually girded trees and let them die where they stood, planted around stumps for a time, limited their efforts to a few crops such as corn, wheat, indigo, and tobacco, and practiced crop rotation and manuring in a rather haphazard manner, if at all. As a group, they might be classified as "semi-permanent" settlers. They were here to exploit the land and move on if other opportunities beckoned. And then there were the "drifters," often Scotch-Irish. These folk, perhaps a combination of small farmer and hunter, frequently were content with a three-sided log hut open to the elements and eeking out a precarious existence.

Although Germans did not settle in Richland County in great numbers, their presence just across the Congaree in Saxe-Gotha could not help but affect life on the east bank of the river, and some of their superior agricultural techniques undoubtedly were copied from time to time. As for the English, predominantly ex-Virginians, some of them indeed did move on to Georgia, Mississippi, and still other frontiers. Yet a substantial number lingered along the Congaree and Wateree, beguiled by the good life produced by tobacco and cotton, as well as the opportunities a new seat of local and state government provided for careers in law, commerce, education, and all of the other pursuits associated with urban living.

The "drifters," of course, are difficult to trace. A few probably built a fourth wall on their log lean-to, added a chimney, cleared a patch of ground, planted a few fruit trees, and stayed put. Others drifted south or west, to town, or into the sand hills. With luck, they may even have acquired property, prospered, and risen far above the status of their forebears, because this was a fluid society.

Then there was a fourth group, the most numerous in Richland County by 1800, who could neither move nor drift, at least they were not supposed to. They were the slaves. Known simply as Harry, Cato, Tully, July, or Joney, they are now merely names in wills, inventories, and plantation records. In pre-cotton decades when few local households had much wealth, nearly all of these blacks were field hands, working at a variety of routine tasks such as planting, hoeing, and harvesting.

A newcomer, according to Meriwether, usually arrived in the Midlands during the winter months, thus able to gather crops at an old home and plant at a new one. Frequently the head of a household came alone in order to get title to land and build a rudimentary shelter, followed later by family members. Some brought little with them, perhaps not even a gun or a horse, but an *axe* was an absolute necessity. The well-to-do came with livestock, slaves, seed, guns, household utensils, furniture, farm implements such as hoes and plows, and quickly duplicated the life they had left behind.

In time, they might set up housekeeping in plantation cottages such as "Cabin Branch," built by John Hopkins (son of a pioneer planter bearing the same name) on land acquired in lower Richland in 1790. This structure, completed about ten years later, has a raised basement and exterior chimneys, a style of architecture found throughout Tidewater

Virginia. It subsequently was reproduced in the Piedmont and then spread southward along the Atlantic Seaboard. Most of these homes were constructed on the "double square" formula then in vogue, a house twice as long as it was high. Some cottages were only one room deep, others two, and in succeeding decades they often were expanded by adding more rooms or, as in the case of "Cabin Branch," another structure somewhat larger than the original.

Wary of rivers whose habits they did not know (for a sudden flood could wipe out a whole crop), a settler usually sought out streams and creeks such as those found in lower Richland. Smaller water courses had two other advantages: they could be crossed easily and provided fresh drinking water until wells were dug. Another consideration was a site not too close to other farms and plantations, but within ten miles of a neighbor.

Since South Carolina's meat exports declined in the 1750s, Meriwether concluded that these new back-country settlers lacked marketing skills and found it easier to sell hides than drive cattle to Charleston. Leather breeches, he noted, seem to have been very common at mid-century, although cows were kept for butter, some of which was sold in the lowcountry.

More importantly, perhaps, this new breed of South Carolinian was a farmer, not a stockman, and his goal was to grow crops. And what were those crops? By far the most common was corn. Virtually everyone, even the smallest farmer, grew some, for this universal staple could be planted in hills by hand and tended with a hoe, if at all. These hills usually were four or five feet apart with other crops such as peas, pumpkins, or squash placed in between. In September the ears of corn were gathered, put in corn houses to dry, and subsequently shelled by beating in cribs or flailing on a scaffold so kernels would fall on the ground where they could be gathered. Production varied, depending upon weather and growing conditions, but John Drayton wrote that thirty to fifty bushels might be harvested on an acre of ground in the "middle parts" of the state. Husks, stalks, and cobs frequently were saved and used as animal fodder and fuel.

According to Woodmason, the common folk of the back country of the 1760s ate two meals a day consisting of corn bread and pork in winter, corn bread and bacon in summer.[1] If they had beef (or perhaps venison) it was jerked and dried, but he indicated that he rarely saw meat in his travels. Meriwether noted that, while these pioneers certainly hunted deer from time to time, they apparently did not track them with dogs.

Faithful Fido had another and more important job to do: protect the homestead and warn of the approach of Indians or outlaws.

Strictly speaking, corn was not grown for export or trade, most of it being consumed right here in the Midlands. But there were two basic items that, at least at the outset, had to be obtained through trade. These were salt and iron. So, in time, wheat, flour, butter, cured meat, cheese, skins, furs, and other surplus goods made their way to the coast. On the return trip by pack-horse, wagon, or boat, merchants brought salt, iron and metal products, gun powder and shot, sugar, tea, and cloth.

Wheat, then, was the second major crop of the Midlands during early days of settlement. But, since it was heavy and difficult to transport, small mills that could turn out flour quickly appeared in Granby, Camden, and Ninety Six. Also, by 1748 ex-Virginian William Hay had erected a "gris mill" on Raiford Creek, which subsequently became known as Mill Creek. Drayton describes two methods of growing wheat. The first, which he called "a slovenly practice," was to sow wheat in a corn field after the corn had been gathered and simply plow the seed into the ground. With a minimum of effort a farmer could harvest perhaps twelve to fifteen bushels per acre. By plowing the soil before planting he could double his yield, but then, Drayton conceded, he faced the task of getting this relatively bulky product to market. As a result, many farmers were content to grow only enough wheat for their own use.

Some of these items such as corn, wheat, skins, and furs could be grown or procured by virtually any settler in the Midlands. Except for a hoe, gun, and perhaps a plow and scythe, no special tools were needed. If the year's work produced a surplus, then a small farmer might be able to get seed for still other crops such as peas, barley, or tobacco and equipment that would enable him to increase his output. Or, he might plant apple and peach trees that would give him cider and brandy, the principal local beverages, together with beer made from barley, a favorite drink on the west bank of the Congaree.

Yet this may be a much-too-optimistic scenario. Caught up in a cycle of unpredictable seasons and often inept agricultural practices, the average small farmer found it difficult to expand his horizons. Not being able to read and write in a society that was only 10 to 20 percent literate was no great handicap, but being a slave to established modes of behavior was.

Nevertheless, the settler who chose to begin life anew in the Midlands during the last half of the 18th century had certain advantages. Even if inherently conservative, he was living in an era of social and political change, which, in itself, encouraged innovation. Secondly, his was a most unusual frontier, for it was no cutting edge of civilization . . . at least not for long. Upon his arrival in Camden in the late 1760s, Reverend Woodmason was astonished by the size of the local population, much larger, he observed, than would be found in any comparable region of rural England at that time. And the back country of the Piedmont was filling up even more rapidly, creating trading patterns that quickly converted Indian paths into highways of commerce. Even before mid-century, for example, money from the Township Fund was used to transform the Cherokee Path along the west bank of the Congaree into a wagon road, and by 1775 Cheraw, Camden, Granby, and Augusta were linked, not only to Charleston, but to points in North Carolina, Virginia, and Pennsylvania.

Although these routes did not always pass through the region that became Richland County in 1785, traffic along the Congaree and Wateree made the Midlands a regional crossroads of sorts, and a growing population provided neighbors, customers, people with whom one could trade both goods and ideas. The result was a milieu quite different from that of the 17th century colonist pushing westward into the Virginia wilderness or the lonely sod farmer testing his will two centuries later on the Nebraska plains.

Into this land of corn, wheat, and small farms came three new crops that, during the last half of the 18th century, brought added wealth to those already well-to-do and provided the less fortunate of the Midlands with opportunities to improve their lot. They were, in chronological order, indigo, tobacco, and cotton.

By the late 1750s, the plant that produced the much-desired violet-blue dye was being grown extensively along the Congaree and Wateree, and for several decades it was second only to rice in the South Carolina economy. Planted in April and May, this native of India matured at different times during the summer months, resulting in several cuttings. Stems perhaps three feet long, together with leaves, then were steeped in a vat and allowed to ferment. The pulpy mass was subsequently dissolved, beaten, and drained several times before being dried, cut into squares, and placed in casks. It was a messy, smelly job, a task that attracted flies and mosquitoes and usually was assigned to blacks. Yet indigo possessed two great advantages. The output of an entire acre could be compressed into a cask weighing only eighty pounds that sold for upwards of £10 sterling. For the inland farmer, ease of transport and high return (thanks for many years to a bounty) were almost irresistible inducements to grow indigo.

By the 1770s, at least in the Richland County area, tobacco brought
south from Virginia was becoming another important crop. Cultivation
consisted of a few easily learned operations often performed by slaves under careful supervision. In the spring a seed bed perhaps 20 by 100 feet
was laid out and wood burned on it to destroy weeds and insects. Then
the tiny seeds were sown. As shoots appeared, they were transplanted
into hillocks three or four feet apart, preferably during rainy weather. In
succeeding weeks, worms and bugs were picked off, weeds pulled, dirt
heaped about the roots, and the plants "topped" so as to promote fuller
growth. Then, as the broad leaves began to ripen and turn brown, the
tobacco plant was cut and carried into a well-ventilated log curing house.

> The stalks, with the leaves adhering to them, are here hung up in
> pairs, on poles placed parallel to each other, along the building; leav-
> ing a sufficient space between them, that the plants may touch each
> other. They thus remain, to sweat and dry in the shade; and when
> sufficiently so, the leaves are stripped from the stalks; and are classed
> according to their respective goodness. They are then tied in small
> bundles, with one of the leaves, and remain thus in small heaps, until
> perfectly aired. After which, they are pressed into hogsheads, made
> of oak, containing 1200 to 1600 lbs. weight; and being duly inspected
> at the different tobacco houses appointed for that purpose, through-
> out the state, the tobacco is ready for export to foreign markets.[2]

The local inspection stations were those established at Friday's Ferry,
Winnsboro, and Camden in the 1780s. Once an official stamp was ap-
plied, the huge hogsheads were sent down river by boat or "rolled" to
Charleston, that is, hauled overland by horses.

Both of these crops, indigo and tobacco, presented the "little" farmer
with special problems. Preparing indigo for shipment was an exacting,
time-consuming process, and the man who grew only small quantities of
tobacco (say, less than a hogshead) had to sell his crop to a larger producer
or market it locally; for some tobacco was, of course, consumed here in
the Midlands.

Then in the 1790s along came cotton—or, to be more specific, along
came a method of cleaning cotton bolls quickly and effectively that
made the crop much more attractive. Cotton was grown in South Carolina as early as 1754 and received special attention during the Revolutionary War when, out of necessity, it was mixed with wool to produce
clothing. Unlike tobacco, cotton seed was planted in rows and later
thinned. However, once growth was under way, cultivation was somewhat

similar—weeding, hoeing earth around the roots, and perhaps planting other crops such as corn between rows. Blossoms appeared in early summer that gradually developed into pods, which, when ripe, burst into white bolls filled with seeds. "In small bags of oznaburgs, which are flung over the negroes shoulders for the purpose, the cotton is then picked from the pods; and is carried home to the cotton house. From whence, for one or two days thereafter, it is taken out and spread to dry on a platform, adjacent to the house, for that purpose; after which it is ready for ginning."[3]

As Governor Drayton was writing these words in 1802, the ginning process—separating seed from fiber—was experiencing great and important change. Until the 1790s, seeds were extracted by hand as folks sat around a fireplace in the evening or by foot gins, an almost equally tedious method. According to both Drayton and Lewis Du Pré, a Georgetown plantation owner, a worker could clean about twenty pounds a day with a foot gin, two small rollers turning against each other that were worked by a foot board or a treadle.[4]

Eli Whitney's famous invention, perfected in Georgia in 1793, revolutionized life in Richland County and throughout much of the South. A series of rollers with wire teeth that rotated against a hopper box (with brushes added to clean the teeth), this device could do the work of ten men if operated by hand, fifty if horse power was applied. Called a "sawtooth" gin, this mechanism actually was so simply constructed that almost any blacksmith could duplicate it, and several individuals soon claimed they had built something similar before 1793. Among them was a man named Holmes, who vowed he had developed a "saw tooth" on the Kincaid plantation in neighboring Fairfield County in the late 1780s. In any case, Wade Hampton generally is credited with first using water power to turn a "saw tooth" in 1799, the year that he introduced extensive cotton culture to Richland County by raising 600 bags of cotton on 600 acres, a crop valued at $90,000.

The full impact of this change to cotton is staggering. The cotton gin made it possible to grow short-staple or green seed, upland cotton for a profit, in the beginning, a very handsome one. It drove out indigo and tobacco, making South Carolina largely a one-crop, slave economy.[5] In 1790, for example, blacks constituted only one-fifth of the Piedmont population, but by 1830 the black-white population of that region was nearly equal. The same trend is apparent in Richland County. In 1790, only about one in three residents was black; in 1800, blacks outnumbered whites 3,168 to 2,929, and by 1830 the ratio was nearly 2:1, with 9,534 blacks to 5,238 whites.

But, like tobacco, cotton tended to exhaust the soil; and, in the absence of intelligent crop rotation and efforts to check erosion, this dependence on cotton initiated an exodus to new lands in Mississippi, Alabama, and Texas. This was especially true in the 1840s when the price of cotton plummeted; as a result, virtually every pioneer Richland family developed strong ties to those regions. Wade Hampton, for example, invested heavily (and very successfully) in Louisiana sugar plantations, and in the 1840s several members of the Hopkins family took up cotton lands on the Pearl River in Mississippi.

Until the little village of Columbia began to take shape, the cultural-social life of Thomas Taylor's Congaree community was pretty much what one would expect to find in any rural, largely frontier setting. There were virtually no churches or schools, although religious and educational pursuits were not entirely forgotten, both being carried on in some homes. Weddings, funerals, militia musters, and holidays such as the king's birthday were the focus of social occasions, a welcome opportunity to forget for a brief time the monotonous day-to-day routine. Presbyterians and Baptists often staged hymn "sings" in private dwellings, much to the distress of Anglican Charles Woodmason, who condemned these gatherings as excuses for debauchery, assignations, and the singing of blasphemous songs masquerading as hymns.[6] And, in time, court day was yet another occasion for revelry, a mix of business, legal activity, and social chatter.

As noted earlier, Reverend Woodmason, based in Camden, went to the fork of the Congaree and Wateree in September of 1767 to baptize, marry, and conduct services. Other men living in Orangeburg and Saxe-Gotha ventured into the Richland County area now and then for the same reasons. Although many residents were associated with no religious group, Baptists of various persuasions (English and German) and Presbyterians (Scotch-Irish) undoubtedly were the most frequently encountered of the well-known faiths. Yet Camden had a sprinkling of Quakers, Lutherans dominated the Dutch Fork area, and one sometimes met an Episcopalian. The extent of rancor and animosity among these groups, was, by today's standards, almost unbelievable. Woodmason's critics once released fifty-seven dogs in a meeting house where he was trying to conduct services, destroyed or mutilated notices he posted, and spread rumors that he had bedded down with a Baptist woman. Since all of the local magistrates were Presbyterians, Woodmason found it impossible to get any legal satisfaction, no matter how great the offense. "These Sects," he wrote in June of 1768, "are eternally jarring among themselves—The Presbyterians hate the Baptists far more than they do the Episcopalians, and so of the Rest—But (as in England) they will unite altogether—in a Body to distress or injure the Church establish'd."[7]

The special target of Woodmason's wrath, as well as that of Charleston officialdom, was the roving "New Light" or Separate Baptist minister. His emotional appeal also distressed Regulators of the same era, who claimed such religious fervor disrupted farm work. Woodmason once described these folk as "a Sett of Rhapsodists—Enthusiasts—Bigots—Pedantic, illiterate, impudent Hypocrites—Straining at Gnats, and swallowing Camels, and making Religion a Cloak for Covetuousness Detraction, Guile, Impostures and their particular Fabric of Things."[8]

Despite this blast, in 1766 one of these "Rhapsodists" established Richland's first congregation near Mill Creek. Reverend Philip Mulkey, who about 1760 founded a church on Fairforest Creek in what is now Union County, visited the banks of the Congaree four years later and, like Woodmason, baptized several converts. Then, on 30 November 1766, thirty-three individuals, with the assistance of Mulkey and Reverend Joseph Morphy, constituted themselves as an independent Baptist body and built a small meeting house on land given to them by William Howell. This structure, the first in this community, was located near William Hay's mill.[9]

In 1771, under the direction of Joseph Reese, this group became the Congaree Association—thus rejecting its "separatist" origins—and soon established branches throughout the region between the Congaree and Wateree rivers. However, political disagreements and war (Mulkey, for one, was a Tory) disrupted Baptist activity for nearly two decades, and there are no additional records of this congregation until 1790. Reverend Reese, still in charge at that date but very infirm, was adamantly opposed to joining Charleston's Baptist Association; however, following his death in 1795 those ties were forged. Nevertheless, the local church still was plagued by disagreements between pastor and flock and shortly after 1800 moved to a new site in southeastern Richland County about six miles above McCord's Ferry.

Reverend Woodmason wrote in the late 1760s of a "Congaree Chapel," but the location of this Anglican outpost is not known. A few years later he spent twelve months in the "Congaree Distric," then returned briefly to Camden, which, in his words, had been overrun by "Baptist Teachers." Thus it would appear that the little church on Mill Creek was Richland County's only house of worship prior to 1800.

The first religious group to attempt formal organization in Columbia was the Presbyterians. In March of 1794, Thomas Taylor and Benjamin

Waring solicited the services of Reverend David Dunlap, stressing that "it is greatly contrary to the interests of a young town to be growing up without the Sabbath day's observation." Dunlap was ordained and installed as minister at a ceremony held in the State House on 7 June 1795 and for several years preached in both Columbia and Granby. Gradually, however, as his salary dwindled, Dunlap become more and more involved with his duties as clerk of the state Senate and teacher at Columbia's academy established in 1795. Following his death in 1804 at the age of thirty-three, the Presbyterians were leaderless until 1810 when their congregation was reorganized.

Since Columbia had no churches, during much of this period itinerant preachers held forth in the State House, just as Dunlap had done, or in the new chapel at South Carolina College. According to the reminiscences of blacksmith Rawls, Lorenzo Dow, a primitive Methodist evangelist, spoke at the Male Academy in 1803. Dow, dressed plainly in shirt, homespun vest, and pants (no hat, shoes, or coat) "had no book, took no text, but commenced and preached" in a candle-lit room.[10] However, two years later, the Methodists erected their Washington Street church, the first in town, and within a decade the Presbyterians, Baptists, and Episcopalians had their churches, too.

Education in the Midlands to 1800, somewhat like religion, was scattered, spasmodic, and not very effective, often being carried on in private homes. This entry in Woodmason's journal (21 December 1766) describes what happened when he sought to enlighten the youth of Camden: "Found the School Room that was intended for me, turn'd by the Tavern Keeper into a Stable. Only 3 Boys offer'd, out of 2 or 300 that run wild here like Indians—But as their Parents are Irish Presbyterians, they rather chuse to let them run thus wild, than to have them instructed in the Principles of Religion by a Minister of the Church of England."[11]

Other clergymen tried to organize classes of instruction from time to time; but, in an era dominated by disorder and warfare, most young people probably ran "wild." Nevertheless, petitions to both colonial and state authorities reveal a general awareness that they should not. As early as 1792 a square in Columbia was set aside for the support of a free school, and in the summer of the following year a couple named O'Connor announced plans to open a private institution for young people. Mrs. O'Connor offered to teach young ladies spelling, arithmetic, English and French grammar, geography, and needlework, while her husband was prepared to "receive" young gentlemen interested in courses that stressed elocution, geography, history, and various mathematical skills.

The O'Connors, who unveiled these plans in Columbia's *South Carolina Gazette*, also proposed to conduct adult evening classes in French, promising an understanding of grammar within three months. Although there is no indication that the O'Connors ever taught anyone in South Carolina's new capital, two years later the legislature approved incorporation of an academy that turned out to be much like what the O'Connors had tried to establish, a private institution. Within thirty-six months a building was erected, and the first regular session began in January of 1798 with Abraham Blanding, a recent arrival from Connecticut, as principal. It was this school, Columbia Academy, that enlisted the services of Reverend Dunlap and also welcomed Lorenzo Dow.

And, as noted, shortly after 1800 a rural school appeared at Minervaville in lower Richland, the same one that, for a time, held classes in the original courthouse at Horrell Hill. Much more important, however, was the development and growth of South Carolina College. That institution would spawn numerous academies where young men could prepare themselves for admission and acquire rudimentary knowledge not readily available in their own communities, and it also would turn out teachers to man such classes.

The recreational activities of these young people, as well as those of their elders, might include horse racing, cock fighting, shooting matches, fishing, hunting, and various ball games. Among the latter were so-called "town ball" and "cat," precursors of baseball, and "fives," a form of handball. Minervaville and Columbia both had bowling alleys shortly after 1800, and in 1801 billiards were licensed at the county seat, the proceeds to be used to sink wells and buy a fire engine for the town. Gambling, dancing, and drinking were leisure pursuits, which, frowned upon by some, as always were enjoyed by others.[12]

Although entertainment of this sort often was monopolized by the well-to-do, almost anyone (including blacks) could revel in "mob" activity that attracted crowds of onlookers on court day or when militia units paraded about at Lykesland, Gaffney's Store near Gadsden, and in front of the State House in Columbia. Diarist Edward Hooker has given us this account of his first Richland County court day (18 November 1805).

> The present occasion enabled me to learn something of the appearance, character, and manners of the great mass of the country people in these parts. The contrast between them and the Columbians is very striking. They are indeed a rude, unpolished race. They are, both men and women, almost without exception, dressed in coarse

homespun cotton of a mixed color. There is nothing like fashion, taste or refinement about them. The women wore loose-gowns and petti-coats, and sun-bonnets of the same cloth. They were standing about in public places all day, gaping and staring at every body and every thing that was in any degree new to them. Some of the women had crying children in their arms. There are many girls of 18 or 20, who, with other women showed so little diffidence or sense of decency as to crowd up to the bar among the multitude, and even step up on the benches behind the lawyers to look over their shoulders. The street was full of hucksters' waggons and stalls as on public days in Connecticut. [13]

Interestingly enough, in little over a decade the demarcation line be-tween village and rural inhabitants had been drawn.

Culturally, socially, and economically, a turning point in the story of Colonel Taylor's Congaree settlement was creation of Richland County in 1785. No longer could residents rely upon communities such as Granby and Camden; instead, they had to set up their own market place. Even if the question of a state capital had not erupted, this new county would have developed some sort of crossroads for the transaction of local affairs. That Columbia happened to be the seat of state government as well merely hastened the process.

In the mid-1780s, Granby was a flourishing village located about three miles down river from where Columbia would appear. It was the "capital" of Lexington County with at least a dozen stores, and Columbia businessman Samuel Green urged his brother to open a branch facility there in 1794. Yet only eleven years later Edward Hooker wrote that the switch from tobacco to cotton had blighted the economic life of Granby. Once the center of an extensive tobacco inspection operation, business had declined sharply, and warehouses were shut and beginning to decay. A decade or so after that, the government of Lexington County moved to a more central location. Yet, even though its commercial importance was fading, Hooker thought Granby still a significant river port in 1805. Large, slow, unwieldy craft, propelled by poles and probably laden with huge bales of cotton, left frequently for Charleston, a trip that took at least a week. The return journey, he added, might require three times as long.

Camden, according to Drayton's *View of South-Carolina* (1802), was somewhat larger than Granby, having about two hundred homes. At the head of navigation on the Wateree, it had three "excellent" flour mills that promoted the growth of wheat in the Waxhaws and parts of North Carolina. Like Granby, it had become a seat of county government. Yet, although Camden may have been a focal point for Richland County families living among the Wateree, it could hardly attract the attention of those who saw the Congaree as their avenue to the coast.

Thus, in a very real sense, division of the sprawling districts of 1769 into counties forced each one to develop its own center of trade, business, and legal affairs. Some, such as the counties of Kershaw and Fairfield, were able to utilize functioning communities. Lexington tried to use Granby for a time before opting for centrality. Richland, on the other hand, flirted briefly with the same concept at Horrell Hill but then decided to merge local and state interests at a single site: Columbia. This decision led, as visitors observed, to a kind of "feast or famine" existence; for, during its formative years, Thomas Taylor's little village was a hubbub of activity when the legislature was in session and a very quiet place when it was not. Samuel Green, as we know, stocked up on liquor, books, and various other items he thought lawmakers would buy, and Edward Hooker, writing on 15 December 1805, revealed how very lively the town could be: "A riotous scene took place which made considerable disturbance. The Speaker of the H. of R. is said to have been the principal actor in it. He and several members of both houses together with some others went through the streets in high glee with a drum and fiddle; to *set the town to rights* as they term it. They went to the lodgings of a number of members, and in case of their failing to rise and admit them voluntarily, broke down the doors to their rooms."[14]

Pioneer merchants of the 1790s, in addition to Green, included William Purvis and Company. Purvis, a native of the north of England, ran a store in Charleston, while his brother, Burridge, operated the Columbia branch. Richard Bolan (formerly a merchant in Granby), Andrew Wallace, and Ainsley Hall also maintained local emporiums during that same decade or soon after. Immigrants Wallace and Hall both amassed huge fortunes, and the latter built two magnificent mansions that still survive: the Robert Mills House and the Hampton-Preston House. Although difficult to prove, it would appear that some of these men were carrying on the tradition of pre-Revolutionary War Scottish factors, bright young men with a head for figures, individuals eager to carve out commercial careers in a new land.

Benjamin Waring experimented briefly with a textile enterprise in Statesburg before moving to Columbia about 1791. Within a decade he had opened a tan yard (in partnership with Samuel Green), built a mill that was extracting oil from cotton seed, and was actively promoting vini-culture. At the time of his death in 1811, a Charleston newspaper praised this gentleman for his many contributions to the commercial life of Co-lumbia. Yet another industrial establishment was a rope walk erected by Stephen Brown in the late 1790s. Utilizing hemp raised in the Dutch Fork area, Brown was producing about eighty tons of "cordage, rope, and cables" each year and in 1799 provided rigging for the frigate *John Adams* constructed near Charleston.

In addition to merchants and businessmen, young Columbia at-tracted a handful of doctors and lawyers. Dr. Henry Tillinghast, one of the community's first residents, practiced here until his death in 1795. Samuel Green, sometimes identified as a "doctor" because he sold drugs in his general store, was an executor of Tillinghast's estate and subse-quently married his widow. Dr. Edward Foster, a Virginian who came to Columbia in 1801, practiced medicine in the community for thirty-five years. Prominent lawyers included Abraham Nott and John Hooker, both Connecticut natives. Hooker, Edward's older brother, first came to South Carolina as tutor to Wade Hampton's sons following graduation from Yale College in 1796. Thomas Henry Egan, born in Maryland and admitted to the Bar in Charleston in 1800, for many years was Hooker's partner. Rawls writes that Egan, who lived for some years with another man's wife, was known locally as the "Maryland stud." However, he adds (p. 30) that they finally got married "when the religious sentiment got in the ascendant." Revolutionary War veteran Robert Stark, a Virginia native, practiced law in Columbia from 1804 until his death in 1830.

The little town, sooner than most, got its own newspaper when the state printer declined to accompany the government inland from Charles-ton. According to official records, Robert Haswell, who died in 1791, pro-vided the General Assembly with 250 copies of a *Columbia Gazette*. None of them apparently exist today. The following year, Daniel Constable be-came publisher of the *South Carolina Gazette*, which lasted about six months. It was largely a collection of official proclamations, legislative proceedings, land sales, and tax notices. Then in January of 1794, the de-cision of William P. Young and Daniel Faust to revive the *Columbia Ga-zette* once more provided the little community with its own newspaper. Early issues contain several ads for "taylors" eager to make clothing for both men and women, and a surprising list of books available at the news-paper's office. In 1795, Young and Faust changed the name of their pub-lication to the *State Gazette*, reflecting their intent to become an official organ. A four-page weekly that usually appeared semi-weekly during

legislative sessions, this paper continued to publish under a variety of titles during the opening decades of the 19th century.[15]

As one would anticipate, men such as Stark, Egan, Young, and Faust
represented the educated minority. They were the core of local leadership and often held positions in town government. These individuals were
hardly typical; for, like patriarch Thomas Taylor, land baron Wade Hampton, and businessman Samuel Green, they were the pace-setters. Nor, for
that matter, was little Columbia representative of Richland County as the
community entered a new century. The town had become, as Edward
Hooker revealed, an outpost of urbanity.

All of this would have been a great surprise to Reverend Charles
Woodmason, who, only three decades earlier, had described the people
of the Midlands as "the lowest Pack of Wretches" he ever saw. They came
to religious services barefoot and almost indecently attired, refused to sit
still, and stirred about like a swarm of bees. He claimed that they rubbed
their hair with bear grease, slept together in a common room, dressed
"openly" without ceremony, and often flaunted their nakedness for all to
see. But in one particular, Woodmason, whose railings against sin and
whoring may have been influenced by the frustrations of impotency (he
had been kicked by a horse), was right on the mark. Nothing would
change, he vowed, until churches were built and "the Country reduc'd to
some Form." And that was what the flow of local events during the late
18th century was all about—"reducing" Colonel Taylor's Congaree settlement to "some Form." The form it took, of course, was that of a relatively
compact county whose seat of government also was the capital of the state
of South Carolina.

Notes

1. Hooker, *Carolina Backcountry*, p. 196.
2. Drayton, *A View of South-Carolina*, p. 136.
3. *Ibid.*, p. 131.
4. Lewis Du Pré, *Observations on the Culture of Cotton* (Georgetown, 1799), p. 17. Writing just as Whitney's invention was beginning to have impact, Du Pré was critical of most
   mechanical gins. He found them too imperfect or too complex and recommended that
   his readers continue using foot gins that "injure the staple less." However, Du Pré himself promised to introduce a better machine in the near future.

5. See Drayton, p. 168. His summary of Charleston exports (1790–1800) reflects a sharp decline in indigo, down from nearly 100,000 pounds in 1797 to only 3,400 pounds three years later, and the beginnings of a decline in tobacco as well. Meanwhile, cotton exports rose from about one million pounds in the mid-1790s to 6.5 million in 1800.

6. Hooker, *Carolina Backcountry*, pp. 97–98.

7. *Ibid.*, p. 43.

8. *Ibid.*, p. 42.

9. See Joe M. King, *A History of South Carolina Baptists* (Columbia, 1964), pp. 74–79, for a discussion of early religious activity in the Midlands, and Floyd Mulkey, "Rev. Philip Mulkey, Pioneer Baptist Preacher in Upper South Carolina," *Proceedings*, South Carolina Historical Association (1945), pp. 3–13.

10. Rawls, *Biblical Criticism*, p. 38. Rawls also tells of Main Street "scrub races," even on Sundays, and brags of helping clear the ground and measure for the foundations of the first building erected at the college.

11. Hooker, *Carolina Backcountry*, p. 11.

12. Benjamin Rawls, writing a half century later, says shop owners usually greeted customers with a drink . . . "the stores, in those days, set out liquor on the counter and any person drank free." See Rawls, p. 36.

13. Jameson, *Diary of Edward Hooker*, p. 862. In August of 1807, Hooker wrote that a local gentleman had informed him that, of the three hundred voters in Richland County, only about thirty or forty were "in tolerable circumstances (that is, with say, 100 acres of land and one negro to work on it)." Most, he added, were "very poor and very ignorant, generally lazy and often drunken."

14. *Ibid.*, p. 880.

15. Random copies of early Columbia newspapers are available at the South Caroliniana Library and on Readex Microprint at Thomas Cooper Library, University of South Carolina.

PART II

Image and Reality, 1800–1860

In these "Gone with the Wind" decades, South Carolina's Midlands could be all things to all people. Large, prosperous plantations with hundreds of slaves certainly did exist, and its growing urban center possessed much of what any American city of that era could offer—canal travel, railroad tracks, fire companies, telegraph wires, traveling stage shows, circuses, and numerous cultural and educational facilities, as well as an assortment of shops, dry goods emporiums, and saloons. Nearly every visitor was impressed by Columbia's fine homes and broad streets, its intellectual atmosphere, and the pervasive presence of blacks, some well dressed and well cared for, some not.

The region's economy, at least to the mid-1820s, was flourishing and healthy, even exhibiting boom-like conditions at times, but then, beset by expansion woes and competition from beyond the mountains, both businessman and planter had to wrestle for the next thirty years with a troubled present and an unpredictable future. It was under conditions such as these that the question of human bondage took on a new hue, especially when that institution became the target of national and even international criticism.

Amid this world of cotton fields and busy urban life were subsidiary realms about which we know all too little; for the sand hillers, less affluent white farmers, and blacks—both slave and free—have left comparatively few records. Now only names on census and tax rolls, they were born, cried, laughed, begat children, and died. If white, these folk often followed the dictates of some local squire and dreamed of emulating his way of life. If slave, they struggled to express human traits in a society that considered them property. And if black, whatever their legal status, they usually tried to be as free as possible despite state statutes, local ordinances, patrols, and custom. As a result, some were hunted down as runaways, others were whipped and put in chains, and still others simply disappeared.

Although these factors were evident in many communities throughout the antebellum South, Columbia and Richland County were, in several respects, somewhat unique. The largest inland city of the Carolinas, Columbia was an important commercial crossroads, and even in those years its day-to-day life spilled over into neighboring counties. Since it also was a center of government, its citizens, more than most perhaps, often were stirred by state and national issues—or, at least they were apt to hear considerable speech-making concerning nullification, slavery, abolition, and secession. South Carolina College was, in fact, a training ground for the flowery oratory so beloved during those decades and Columbia was the state's soap box.

Yet this city was South Carolina's *second* capital, a reality no one could forget for long. Nor could Charlestonians overlook the fact that Columbia's prominence and some of its commercial growth had come at their expense. Only one-fifth as large as Charleston in 1860, the "city of refuge" continued to exist in the shadow of what once had been the South's only metropolis, a bit unsure of itself and eager to please both upcountry and low.

Churches,
Commerce, Canals,
and Controversy

CHAPTER FIVE

The growth of Richland County during the first three decades of the 19th century was steady, but hardly spectacular. The total number of inhabitants rose from 6,097 in 1800 to 14,772 thirty years later, and in 1830 the town of Columbia had 3,310 residents. By that date, several nearby counties such as Fairfield, Orangeburg, Newberry, and Sumter were more thickly settled than Richland, while Kershaw (13,545) and especially Lexington (9,065) were not. Yet the new seat of state government was becoming more and more a crossroads of commerce and, at the very least, the "capital" of the Midlands.

In 1805, the community that Edward Hooker thought "a neat, handsome little town" and William John Grayson "a rambling, ill-built village" was officially incorporated by the state legislature as a town. The following year, in May of 1806, voters chose their first intendant, attorney John Taylor, son of Columbia's patriarch, and six wardens. These men, who replaced the commissioners of streets and markets, quickly assumed such responsibilities as keeping the peace, levying taxes, maintaining streets, issuing licenses, passing ordinances, and so on. (For a list of intendants from 1806 to 1855 when Columbia became a city see Appendix 1.)

It might be noted in passing that the birth of town government ended the activities of the original group of commissioners appointed to lay out and organize the new state capital. These gentlemen, it developed, did not deserve high marks as executives, salesmen, or bookkeepers. Upon investigation in 1808, the legislature uncovered a mass of confusion, incomplete records, and exorbitant fees. To bring order out of chaos, the General Assembly appointed a single individual, Benjamin Haile, as commissioner of Columbia lands, but three years later he was succeeded by James Sanders Guignard, who also was clerk of the Court of Common Pleas for Richland County. Guignard set to work trying to collect money due the state (efforts that included a suit against Wade Hampton), as well as paying debts owed by the former commissioners. He instituted periodic land sales with middling success and in 1818–1819, for example, was able to dispose of several squares at the minimum price of $134 per square.[1] Guignard also launched a scheme to erect a governor's mansion, but nothing came of these plans at that time.

Until the early 1820s, South Carolina rode the crest of good economic times and was, by some yardsticks, one of the wealthiest states in the young republic. Conflict raging in Europe increased demand for foodstuffs and cotton; and, although the brief War of 1812 caused some dislocation and inconvenience, the price of cotton nearly doubled between 1815 and 1818 before declining somewhat in succeeding years.[2] This general prosperity was, naturally enough, reflected in the day-to-day life of both Columbia and Richland County. The little college grew steadily stronger, new stores and businesses appeared, internal improvements abounded in the form of roads and canals, a few brave souls experimented with manufacturing establishments, and church spires changed the Columbia skyline forever. In the countryside, large homes and sprawling estates, especially in lower Richland, were clear proof of economic well-being for at least a lucky few.

Tentative manufacturing efforts included a mill owned by Thomas Taylor that turned out bagging for his cotton crop in 1809 and plans by several residents to build a full-fledged cotton mill; however, like Guignard's governor's mansion, nothing happened. Benjamin Waring's tanyard continued in operation, and in 1806 his son George began producing writing paper, newsprint, and wrapping paper. Young Waring claimed his mill was the first of its kind in the state, but the enterprise soon expired, even though he advertised in both Columbia and Charleston in an effort to secure rags for the paper-making process.

Yet another manufacturing establishment, unusual for an inland town, was Columbia's boat yard. Edward Hooker, who visited this facility in 1805, described two river boats then being built at the foot of Gervais Street. The larger one, 55' long and 9' 7'' wide, cost $500 and could carry up to 1,000 bushels of corn. However, because of shoals and rocks, such craft could be floated down to Granby only when the water was high.

An important local enterprise that would continue for many years was a factory established in 1806 by James Boatwright and Milton Glaze to turn out cotton saw gins. Within twelve months they completed three

Thomas Taylor (1743–1833).

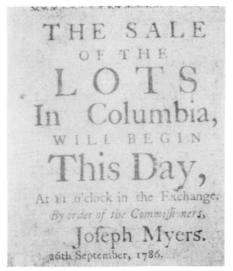

Advertisement in the *Charleston Morning Post*, 27 September 1786.

Old State House, *Frank Leslie's Illustrated Newspaper*, 17 August 1861.
By this date, Main Street had been closed and this structure moved to provide
a site for the present capitol. The famed Palmetto monument and
construction equipment can be seen to the right.

Keziah Goodwyn Hopkins Brevard (1803–1886).

Rutledge College ("South Building"), the first structure erected at South Carolina College.

This school was located at the corner of Washington and Marion streets, later the site of Columbia High School.

Thomas Cooper, president of
South Carolina College, 1820–1834.

The masthead of the *Palmetto-State Banner* (4 March 1851) hails railway development in the Midlands.

Sidney Park in the 1850s.

First Baptist Church, site of the Secession Convention in December 1860.

Flag of the Richland Volunteers during a review at Fort Moultrie, as shown in *Frank Leslie's Illustrated Newspaper* (23 February 1861).

Columbia in War Time. These drawings, which appeared in *Harper's Weekly* (20 February 1864), presumably are the work of a Union prisoner lodged in the Richland County Jail who subsequently was exchanged. The jail was located near the northwest corner of Main and Washington streets, the intersection referred to as a "public square."

REAR VIEW OF JAIL.

OFFICERS' QUARTERS

CITY HALL.

PUBLIC SQUARE.

OLD MAGGIE. (OFFICERS QUARTERS.)

Yankee troops cross the Saluda River with famed Saluda Factory burning in the background.

Looking north on Main Street after the fire. The ruins of the city hall and jail (to the north) are on the left; the county courthouse, to the right. Both drawings are from *Frank Leslie's Illustrated Newspaper* (8 April 1865).

Ruins of the old State House and walls of the present one, as shown in *Harper's Weekly* (1 April 1865).

such machines, and a short time later faced stiff competition from William Munson and James Young. Earlier, in 1801, Boatwright and Munson, as partners, had constructed the first gins built in Richland County.

Nicholas Herbemont, a Frenchman who intermittently instructed South Carolina College students in his native tongue, opened a cut nail factory in Columbia in 1813. It continued in operation for at least three years, but probably closed soon after trans-Atlantic trade revived following the War of 1812.

These examples reveal that manufacturing was not a significant factor in Columbia's early economy. Most of these enterprises employed only a handful of people, and what they produced often could be obtained with relative ease elsewhere. Only after the Civil War, thanks to rail lines and a much larger population, would Columbia begin to develop a true industrial base.

Of greater importance to some Richland County residents of this era was the growth of organized religion. South Carolina society, like that of most states during the last decades of the 18th century, verged on the hedonistic. Frontier life, wartime strains, the absence of basic education, and prevailing social mores were not kind to established faiths; however, in the early 1800s various groups began to exert moral influence in both town and country.

Columbia's Presbyterian congregation, reorganized in 1810, five years after the death of its original leader (David E. Dunlap), was formally incorporated in 1812. The following year the vestry sought help from the General Assembly concerning a site for a church. By an act passed in 1798, lawmakers had provided land for an interdenominational house of worship and a common burial ground in the square bounded by Bull, Marion, Lady, and Washington streets. But some individuals thought that location too close to the emerging residential area, others wanted their own church, and, as a result, no structure appeared. Eventually the legislature decided to sell the part of the square not used for graves, purchase another burial ground for the town, and divide any profit among the four congregations: Presbyterian, Methodist, Baptist, and Episcopal. However, each group still had a stake in the remaining part of the original site, and this dilemma was solved only when the Presbyterians decided to buy out the interests of all of the others concerned.

With the real estate issue resolved, the Presbyterians proceeded to build a structure that was completed in 1815 at a cost of $8,000, about $2,000 more than the original estimate. Money was raised both by subscription and state-authorized lottery. Thomas Taylor pledged $500, Wade Hampton, $400, and others gave smaller sums. A brick personage built in 1822 cost almost as much as the church. Some years later it was sold and transformed into a school run by Robert Edmonds.

Under the guidance of John Harper, who had been ordained by John Wesley in England in 1787, the Methodists formed a society in 1803 and within a year had erected a wooden meeting house at the corner of Washington and Marion streets on land donated by Harper himself. Bennet Kendrick, the first Methodist minister assigned to Columbia, died in 1807, two years after his arrival. Nevertheless, the church grew faster than any other congregation and by 1813 could count 147 whites and 170 blacks as members. Prominent among the Methodists were Andrew Wallace, a Scot who made a fortune as a local merchant; John and Robert Bryce and their sisters Mary and Jane, also from Scotland; Massachusetts-born Samuel Green, postmaster, merchant, and tavern keeper; and Ned Arthur, a black man who was licensed in the early 1820s to preach to members of his race.

Edward Hooker, who arrived in Columbia late in 1805, wrote in his diary that only the Methodists ("peculiarly engaged on the subject of religion") were holding Sunday meetings regularly and that "their noisy zeal" irritated some residents. However, he found that the order of service differed little from that of Congregational churches in Connecticut.

> The singing was much better than I expected it would be. The lines were read by the preacher [Mr. Kendrick] and sung by the audience alternately. Most and perhaps all of the singers sung the same part. If there was any bass, it was so small as to be overwhelmed by the burst of melodious sounds from the men, and women, in the gallery and below, promiscuously engaged in the same part. This was something new to me. It struck my fancy very much, and made a most agreeable impression. From the account which has been given me of Methodist meetings, I had expected to witness more indecorum and irregularity. Some groans were made; though I did not think they were very natural ones. The preaching did not entirely please me. A great deal of the sermon was certainly bordering on extravagance. I was glad to see the preacher warm, as every preacher should be: but I was sorry to see his warmth not in the least tempered by judgment. Whether repeating the text, quoting scripture, stating the heads of his discourse reasoning, or addressing the passions, it was all one uninterrupted current of affected pathos and monotonous roar. Even

between the different heads of discourse, he had no more stop or intermission of voice than between connected sentences—nor between different sentences had he hardly any thing more than common pauses. There was a closing prayer by another preacher (a Mr. Moore) which was excellent and well delivered. The audience appeared well dressed and respectable. I saw nothing like levity exhibited by any body present. The house was filled with people. All those who were in the gallery were blacks.[3]

Columbia's Baptist history began with the arrival of Jonathan Maxcy, the first president of South Carolina College. Maxcy, former head of Rhode Island College (now Brown University) and once pastor of a Baptist church in Providence, was preaching to students and townspeople in the college chapel soon after classes started in January of 1805. But Maxcy had to terminate his Sunday sermons six months later because of ill health and was succeeded by a student, William T. Brantley, who subsequently became rector of Richmond Academy in Augusta, Georgia. Nevertheless, Maxcy continued to play a prominent role in Baptist affairs.

William Bullein Johnson, who came to Columbia in 1809 from the lowcountry to study theology under Maxcy, quickly breathed new life into a struggling congregation. In the fall of that same year a Baptist church was formed, and the first person to be baptized was a very important convert, Ann Wyche Taylor, wife of Colonel Thomas Taylor, a staunch Presbyterian. Soon the Baptists were building "a commodious brick meeting-house 40 feet square" on the southeast corner of Sumter and Plain [Hampton] streets, a structure that was formally dedicated on 2 March 1811. Although not completed for some time, the Baptists could boast of the only brick church in town. However, in December of 1811, Johnson departed for Savannah, leaving the congregation in the hands of Maxcy and others, including Richard M. Todd and John Good.

For the next three or four decades, according the William Cox Allen's history of Columbia's First Baptist Church (1959), this group struggled against great odds. Until mid-century, pastors seemed to come and go with great frequency, often leaving the congregation leaderless for months, even years. Records are scanty and incomplete, yet one fact is apparent: black faithful far outnumbered white. In 1828, for example, the Columbia church had 171 members—26 white, 145 black; in 1837, 309 members—74 white, 235 black. Equally obvious was increased Sunday School activity, especially after 1830, and emphasis upon moral issues such as temperance and dancing. In 1836 it was agreed that no member would sell spirituous liquors, except as medicine, and the following year the devout pondered the problem of professors of religion who sent their children to dancing classes.

In contrast to the Baptists, Episcopalians established themselves in Columbia with relative ease. In the summer of 1812, Andrew Fowler, a minister engaged by the Society for the Advancement of Christianity in South Carolina, began to hold services in the State House. On August 8 of that same year, Trinity Church was founded by a large group of prominent citizens, among them, John G. and James S. Guignard, Edward Fisher, Benjamin R. Waring, Robert Stark, William Harper, Theodore Gaillard, William Branthwaite, William R. Davis, Samuel Percival, and William Marshall. Within a few months a church was being built, and on 14 December 1814, that structure was dedicated by Bishop Theodore Dehon. One of the most liberal contributors was Wade Hampton, who provided more than $2,000 and an organ. The Reverend Christian Hanckel became Trinity's first rector on 4 June 1815, also serving for a time as tutor and mathematics professor at South Carolina College. Hanckel, who resigned in 1818, subsequently accepted a call to a Charleston church.

From 1818 to 1834, the Episcopal story is much like that of the Baptists, a succession of pastors and sometimes none. Then in January of 1834, young Peter Shand, who gave up law to study for the ministry, took the helm, serving until his death on 1 November 1886. According to Reverend Shand's first annual report, in 1836 Trinity had forty-eight communicants and sixty-eight non-communicant members. A decade later, the cornerstone of the present cathedral was laid, a structure (without transcepts) that cost about $12,000.

Three other religious groups—Catholics, Jews, and Lutherans—had less impact upon the local scene during the opening decades of the 19th century. The first Catholics, Irish laborers employed in construction of the Columbia Canal, led to the erection in 1824 of a small sanctuary presided over by a Father Corkery, and two years later a $50,000 lottery (tickets $250 each, first prize $6,000) launched construction of a church. At that time, Corkery was replaced by Reverend Joseph Stokes, who ushered in a period of instability much like that experienced by Baptists and Episcopalians. In 1822, a Hebrew Benevolent Society appeared with the goal of establishing and maintaining a Jewish cemetery. That burial ground, located on Gadsden Street, was a gift of the De Leon family. The following year, a Female Auxiliary Jew Society was formed to assist those wishing to settle in the Midlands; however, it soon expired. A group of

Lutherans tried to organize a church in the late 1820s, but little came of these efforts until about 1840.

Yet by mid-century, Catholics, Lutherans, and Jews were on somewhat firmer footing. In 1848, Father J. J. O'Connell began a twenty-year career as leader of St. Peter's Parish that stressed the development of parochial education. Six years earlier, Reverend E. B. Hort had accepted a call to Ebenezer Lutheran Church, a post he held for nearly two decades. Although membership remained small (only twenty-nine in 1863, the year of Reverend Hort's death), the Lutherans were aided by the fact that their paster also was chaplain at the state hospital. And, according to the 1850 census, Copenhagen-born Philip S. Jacobs, age thirty-eight, was serving as this community's "Jewish minister." A decade later, however, he had become a bookkeeper for the weekly *South Carolinian*, having given up religious duties, at least temporarily, because of a salary dispute.

Apparently there were only a handful of rural churches during the early 19th century, most of them in lower Richland. The famous *Atlas* of Robert Mills, published in 1825, indicates that the region's original church, Congaree Baptist, continued to flourish about six miles from McCord's Ferry. Mills also recorded a church on Cedar Creek and a meeting house nearby, both in the Minervaville community. The Cedar Creek edifice may have been Beulah Baptist, an offshoot of Congaree Baptist organized in 1806.

William F. Medlin's *Richland County Landmarks* (1981) cites a few more early churches, chapels, and "preaching stations." These include a Baptist church on Colonel's Creek and a Methodist church on Mill Creek; however, Medlin's most interesting centers of religious activity are Logue's Methodist Church and Zion Episcopal Church. Logue's church and camp meeting ground, named for Presbyterian pastor John Logue, was located about four miles east of Horrell Hill and two miles north of the Sumter Highway. Logue, who was preaching in Camden during the Revolutionary War, built a meeting house at that site that subsequently was taken over by Methodists, perhaps their first church in Richland County. Although membership declined early in this century and services were discontinued in the 1920s, at least three Methodist congregations were spawned by this pioneer outpost in the same general area: Lebanon, McLeod's Chapel, and Antioch A. M. E. Zion. Eastover's Zion Episcopal Church began in 1820 as a chapel erected by William Clarkson for his slaves, an edifice soon used by whites as well. Some years later, construction of a parsonage a few miles to the north led in 1844 to creation of Zion Episcopal Church at the intersection of Garner's Ferry and

McCord's Ferry roads. During the following decade, another Episcopal church (St. John's) appeared in lower Richland, and by 1872 the two parishes frequently were being served by the same rector. Seven years after that, the Zion congregation moved to Eastover.

Missing from the local scene is much evidence of the evangelical revival that stirred many parts of the upcountry in the early 1800s. As this survey indicates, town residents built a few churches, and by the 1820s several more existed in rural areas. Hooker noted that Columbia's Methodists exhibited "noisy zeal" yet retained an order of service similar to that of other Protestants. The only camp meeting ground (a hallmark of the second Great Awakening) apparently enjoyed short life, and a pioneer chapel for blacks reveals the resolve of lower Richland planters to retain firm control over religious expression among their slaves.

It appears, then, that most families, whether dwelling in town or on a plantation, believed organized religion was an essential ingredient of civilized society. Nevertheless, they seem to have spurned evangelical gatherings and, judging from church records, frequently were not actually associated with any congregation. The truth is, during these formative decades, more worldly concerns dominated the thoughts of Richland County residents. Times were good, the price of cotton was high, the nation was expanding, and the future looked bright indeed. Writing in 1826, Robert Mills, statistician, architect, and canal promoter, noted that the pace of life in Columbia had quickened noticeably within the past five years.

> A considerable accession is yearly made, from the circumstance of the commercial, literary, and social advantages of the place. It has engrossed much of the trade which King-street, in Charleston, formerly enjoyed; the produce of the back country stopping here, to be transported by water to that city, instead of proceeding, as formerly, by land. Several of the King-street merchants have removed to, or established houses in Columbia; some also from the upper country and the northern states. Groceries and dry goods are now purchased in Columbia, on as reasonable terms as in Charleston.[4]

The population, Mills thought, was about 4,000; the number of houses, perhaps 500. Most of the business structures were three stories high, some of them built of brick. The town now had a board of health, no gaming tables, and, in his opinion, too few trees.[5] The wooden State House, to his eye, still looked temporary, although he had high praise for South Carolina College and three academies established for the training of young people. Mills had warm words, too, for the new state asylum (which he himself designed), the Columbia Canal (another of his handiworks), and the town water system.

This remarkable facility, the creation of Abraham Blanding, an associate of Mills in the promotion of canals, gave Columbia one of the nation's most advanced schemes for the distribution of water to homes, businesses, and public buildings. In 1819, the town fathers concluded a contract with Blanding that required him to have functioning pipes in the central part of the community within two years and complete the project in four. By December 1820, Blanding had purchased an English-made, twelve-horse-power steam engine that the *Columbia Telescope* thought was "more like the movement of a celestial system than a human invention." Located at the base of Taylor's Hill, it was capable of pumping water from a lower reservoir to a much larger one at the crest of that elevation (now known as Arsenal Hill), the highest point in town. From there, water was distributed underground by cast-iron and lead pipes. The entire system cost about $55,000, and until 1835—when Blanding sold out to the city—he was permitted to charge any rate he wished so long as his annual revenue did not exceed 14 percent of the original investment. Blanding, a shrewd businessman, was able to use excess steam power to run two mills grinding wheat and corn, and contiguous to his engine house were public baths that, in the words of Robert Mills, "prove a great luxury to the inhabitants, many of whom make use of them."

Columbia could boast in 1826 of a "respectable" town hall (which housed a produce market), a society for the encouragement of industry among the female poor, and a library for apprentices, as well as two circulating libraries and yet another at the college. There was also a Masonic lodge hall and a theater; however, the latter was not much used, for it was the opinion of Mills that "neither the population, nor habits of the place, are of a description to countenance such an establishment."

The market, according to this gentleman, was improving, but often was deficient in vegetables, meat, and fish . . . despite the presence of nearby rivers and streams and herds of livestock. Poultry, on average, cost $2 per dozen, geese $1, ducks 50 to 75 cents, turkeys $1.75 a pair. Beef cost from 6 to 10 cents a pound, mutton 12½ cents, pork 5 to 10 cents. Servants received wages from $6 to $10 per month, and rents, especially those charged for stores, tended to be rather high; however, one could board comfortably at from $4 to $6 a week in "the most respectable taverns" or with private families. Commercial enterprise, in the opinion of Mills, showed considerable promise.

The commerce of Columbia has been yearly increasing since its foundation. It is computed that not less than 30,000 bales of cotton are annually exported from this [place] to Charleston, equal to 10,000,000 of pounds, valued at 1,500,000 dollars. Two steam-boats have generally been employed to transport this cotton, besides a number of bay and canal boats; all of which return with full freight; the amount of which now is equal to 5000 tons. This will give an idea of the business transacted in this town.[6]

Mills was equally sanguine concerning a covered bridge being built across the Congaree at Columbia and a Broad River span two miles above the town recently authorized by state officials. The community, he emphasized, was rich in building materials such as timber, granite, and clay for brick, some of which were being used in the construction of the Congaree bridge. And by 1829 yet a third bridge was completed over the Saluda River, prompting the *Columbia Telescope* (14 August 1829) to boast that "you can now take your carriage and drive around Columbia, cross three beautiful rivers . . . and dash into town on the same side you set out from. . . . So much for Columbia and its enterprise."

In the 1820s, stage coaches connected Columbia with Charleston, Augusta, and Camden three times each week and once each week with Greenville. The only Richland County villages mentioned by Mills were Rice Creek Springs (fifteen miles northeast of Columbia), Lightwood Knot Springs (six miles north of town, called "Lighter Wood" by local residents), and Minervaville in lower Richland, each characterized by him as summer "retreats" or "watering places."

Edwin J. Scott, apprenticed to a Jewish merchant for six years in 1817, had a somewhat different view of the Columbia scene. Young Scott, who lived in nearby Sumter and Camden as a child, began working for Jacob Barrett when he was fourteen. Five years later, convinced that his situation was intolerable, he ran away and eventually settled in Lexington, although in 1839 he returned to the state capital as a bank teller. Scott's *Random Recollections*, published in 1884, form one of the most revealing portraits we have of early Columbia.

When he first arrived, a policeman cried the hours at street corners at night (there was no town clock), and a pump near the courthouse supplied water to most residents of the community. During his years with Barrett, Scott never saw a commercial salesman or a book agent, all writing was done with quill pens, and letters were simply folded sheets of paper since envelopes were not available. People traveled perched high on two-wheeled gigs or sulkies, not buggies, over roads that Scott characterized as "wretched." Right and left shoes, instead of the "straight" variety that fitted either foot, were just coming into vogue. ("Many people objected to them at first, because they could not be changed every day like the straight ones.") And forks—originally bearing only three prongs and called "split spoons"—were extremely rare.

By the 1820s, according to Scott, local merchants were doing a good business and kept large stocks on hand, especially in winter.

These they bought, mostly in Charleston, on a credit of six to nine months. To customers of good standing they sold on a year's credit, allowing accounts to run till New Year, when, if not paid sooner, they were expected to be settled by cash or note bearing interest at 7 per cent. All of the large dealers had their own boats, each manned by half a dozen stout hands, besides the captain or patroon. Light goods were hauled from Charleston by wagons, and sometimes, of a dry season, in the fall, when the river became too low for navigation, wagons were the sole reliance for transportation, and freights were enormously high, as much as four dollars on a sack of salt or a bale of cotton weighing a little over three hundred pounds. Salt sold at one dollar to one and a half per bushel, and for many years was hauled in bulk, an apartment in the hold of the boats and the back stores of the merchants being swept clean, in which it was poured loose and measured out to customers by the half bushel. Jamaica rum and Cognac brandy brought three to four dollars per gallon—the former being generally preferred as the more wholesome. Corn whiskey and New England rum (vile stuff made of West Indian molasses) retailed at one dollar per gallon. Very little fine wine was sold; sweet Malaga wine and mint cordial, retailing at one dollar per gallon, were very popular with women from the country, whom we always treated when they came in. Holland gin, with Stoughton's bitters, before breakfast, and shrub, composed of acid, sugar and spirits, made up the usual drinks of the people, who used stimulants freely, both in their homes and when friends met abroad. Up to 1820 no temperance societies existed. Merchants invariably watered their liquors before offering them for sale, the common ratio being a tub full to a hogshead, or in that proportion, and I have helped to carry many a one for that purpose.

Havana sugar, both white and yellow and "exceedingly dirty," arrived in 250-pound boxes; if loaf sugar, it came in hard conical packages wrapped in blue paper. Chewing tobacco was twisted into one-pound parcels, and the entire plant was sold for smoking, "the leaves cleaned, pressed and sweetened." Chalk pipes were popular, Cuban cigars less so because of high prices.

Male travelers, he notes, usually wore leggings to protect their pantaloons from mud and dust, and older women often had calico pockets suspended from waist bands. When indoors, these were replaced by scissors and pincushions hanging from chains about their necks. Madras handkerchiefs from the East Indies, "woven in bright colors and of good size," were worn by slave women as shawls and on their heads.

At Barrett's we kept dry goods, groceries, provisions, liquors (both at wholesale and retail), hardware, crockery, shoes, hats and saddles. Besides all of this, he sometimes bought a drove of hogs and made bacon for sale. He also speculated in negroes, horses, and real estate. Though hardly able to sign his name, and never looking into a book, he had unerring judgment as to the value of all sorts of property and a keen perception of the character and standing of his customers. One so shrewd, stingy and unscrupulous, situated as he was, could hardly fail, in such flush times, to become immensely wealthy, especially as he was aided by his brother Isaac in Charleston, who also was a keen business man, and, as his partner, bought goods and sold produce for him. Nothing that promised gain came amiss to him. At one time Isaac sent him a hundred Jersey wagons, costing with the harness, $25 each. These he sold in a few months at $75. Again, a cargo of government soldiers' condemned coats or jackets, bought at a great sacrifice, were readily taken by the planters for their negroes at an advance of one or two hundred per cent. over cost. A gang of some twenty negroes from Charleston he soon disposed of at very large profits, keeping for his own Armstead Booker, a good-looking, active carriage driver and barber, who attended to his horses and in the store, and Aunt Nancy, a first-rate cook, with her children.[7]

Barrett's was, of course, only one of several general stores in Columbia at that time, and Scott takes the reader on a leisurely tour of Main Street, describing various shops and their owners and relating what happened to them in succeeding decades. Two facts become evident as he strolls along the five-block business section north of the state capitol: the little town seems to have been blessed with an unusually large number of taverns, tailor shops, and drug stores, and many (like Barrett's) were multi-purpose emporiums offering a variety of goods and services.

In addition to grocery stores, law offices, and mechanics' shops, there were two book sellers and at least one milliner, butcher, and tin-smith. Whatever these folks were dealing in, most were being aided in some small way by construction going on at both South Carolina College and the new mental asylum, as well as this state's massive program of internal improvements.[8] The feeding and housing of workers, acquisition of materials being used, and transport of those materials to work sites in the area all added up to an outlay of public funds that could not help but affect the economic life of a community of only 3,000 souls.

Between 1817 and 1828, South Carolina spent nearly $1.9 million in an unprecedented effort to improve river navigation and roads, most of these dollars expended on waterways above the fall line. To put this sum in perspective, historian Daniel Walker Hollis has observed that the state appropriated almost as much for this program in a decade as it did for public schools from 1811 to 1860 ($2.1 million). Yet, in his opinion, backed by solid research, this adventure in transportation improvement was a "costly delusion."[9]

Much of this money was used to carve out eight canals on the Broad, Saluda, Wateree, and Congaree, all rivers of interest to Richland County residents; but, of course, the Columbia Canal on the Congaree was their special concern. Completed in February of 1824 at a cost of $206,000, it ran down the east bank of the river from the junction of the Broad and Saluda and soon was transporting over 30,000 bales of cotton a year past treacherous shoals and rocks. Three miles long, it had four locks that lowered south-bound craft some thirty-six feet.

This new facility was at the mercy of both dams and canals upriver on the Saluda and Broad, a system calculated to provide sufficient water for transport needs. However, the Columbia Canal often was inoperative, and during one such period in November of 1831 a writer to the *Columbia Free Press and Hive* suggested that the huge ditch be filled up and converted into a railroad. This gentleman, who signed himself "Rail Road," said that both the Saluda and Columbia canals with their thirteen locks, despite the thousands of dollars spent, should be "given up as a bad job." Yet cotton traffic on Columbia's canal reached a peak of 66,597 bales in 1833, but then declined sharply, and the waterway was closed for several years until a two-mile extension up the Broad River was opened in January of 1840.

Actually, despite such troubles, the Columbia Canal was perhaps the most successful of those built in the 1820s. Of eight canals, the six on the Saluda and Wateree were abandoned in 1838, the state refused to assume any responsibility for the Columbia Canal after 1840, and the Broad River's Lockhart Canal ceased operation in 1852. The basic problem, one already alluded to, was the capricious nature of this state's waterways, at times too much water and then too little. Hardly had the Columbia Canal reopened in 1840, for example, when it was ravaged by the worst "freshet" in nearly half a century, and the same story was repeated all too often on other rivers. As if "freshets" and dry spells were not enough, South Carolina's internal improvements program also was plagued by inept maintenance, the unrealistic, even outrageous promises of canal enthusiasts such as Abraham Blanding (of waterworks fame) and architect Robert Mills, and the tantalizing possibility of steam railway lines—all of which tended to undermine support of both lawmakers and the public at large.

Nevertheless, canal construction spawned a flurry of interest in steamboat traffic from the Midlands to Charleston. Between 1817 and 1824, merchants representing both Columbia and Charleston chartered no less than five companies in the vain hope of emulating the genius of Robert Fulton. Some individuals promised to reactivate warehouses at Granby, while others offered canal boat connections from that point to Columbia; however, seasonal conditions once more made service unpredictable and untrustworthy. Then, in the mid-1830s, cotton gin maker James Boatwright formed the Columbia Steam Boat Company with the intent of building a special shallow-draft vessel suitable for the waters of the Congaree. His boat, the *James Boatwright*, began service to Charleston in November 1835 and three months later made a record round trip in seven days and seven hours. On another occasion, the *James Boatwright* completed the down-river journey in only twenty-four hours' running time, that is, if one overlooks a six-hour delay en route. Despite such heroics, the steamboat, like the canal, and for many of the same reasons, did little to solve the transportation dilemma faced by Richland County residents.

Yet, even if the Columbia Canal failed to fulfill the dreams of its builders, it had great impact locally. In addition to the economic boost it gave the community during the 1820s and 1830s, the canal eventually became a source of water power for various mills employing hundreds. Also, during its heyday this waterway inspired John McLean to build a "street railway" from the cotton market on upper Main Street to warehouses on the canal. Chartered in 1831, McLean's horse-drawn line may well have been in operation some years earlier. Nevertheless, it was the steam version, not the horse variety, that seemed to be the wave of the future and thus the arch enemy of water transport that many thought both expensive and unreliable.

One of the many ironies of these decades is the fact that South Carolina launched its canal-building spree on the eve of a financial panic that gave birth to the first great crisis in American political life: the nullification controversy between the sovereign state of South Carolina and the United States government. Except for red-hot salvos hurled by college president Thomas Cooper—an aging but violent proponent of the doctrine that a state could nullify a federal law, that is, declare a statute enacted by Congress void and inoperative within its borders—few Richland County residents played prominent roles in the affair. This community was, however, the stage for dramatic debates, confrontations, conventions, and stormy legislative sessions as various factions jockeyed for position. By the time the smoke cleared in the mid-1830s, South Carolina, once relatively nationalistic in outlook, had become the acknowledged leader of sectional thought. [10]

The reasons for this change are complex. Until 1816, the federal government levied tariffs to gain revenue, which only incidentally protected young industries from foreign imports. But that year, northerners began to erect trade barriers to shield funds invested in factories during the previous decade. The financial crisis of 1819 increased demand in the Northeast for still more protection, and throughout the 1820s customs revenue mounted. As a result, the federal tariff, which averaged 25 percent of the value of imported goods in 1816, rose to about 33⅓ percent in 1824 and to 50 percent in 1828. This meant that the cost of foreign manufactured goods (bought primarily by southerners) soared; but, more important in southern eyes, since Europeans sold less in America, they bought less cotton. Thus the tariff, South Carolinians claimed, cut their income and raised their cost of living whenever they purchased imported items.

Had times been good in South Carolina in the late 1820s, reaction to higher tariff barriers might have been less intense. No other southern state, it should be noted, backed nullification officially; in fact, several of them condemned it. However, they did lend support to South Carolina's general assault on the tariff. But times were not good—or at least they did not appear to be as prosperous as they had been, although historian William Freehling emphasizes one has to weigh economic trends of those years with some care. The price of cotton grown in the Midlands certainly tumbled, from 30.8¢ a pound in 1818 to 12¢ in 1823 and continued low (about 9¢) from 1826 to 1832. Those growing sea island cotton and rice fared somewhat better; and, as a result of the 1819 panic, the cost of living for all South Carolinians declined about 70 percent during the 1820s.

However, many planters in Richland and neighboring upland counties faced special problems. Buoyed up by unrealistic prices in the years immediately after the War of 1812, they bought land and slaves too freely and contracted debts in inflated dollars that now had to be paid when their income had shrunk, the dollar was worth less, and new, more fertile lands beyond the mountains were sending more and more cotton to market. In 1801, for example, South Carolina produced 20 million pounds of cotton, half of the national crop. A decade later the planters of this state grew twice as much, still half of the nation's output; but, ten years after that, South Carolina's 50 million pounds was only 28 percent of the nation's cotton. One result, naturally enough, was the beginnings of an out-migration of both masters and slaves to new lands in Alabama, Mississippi, and Texas, an exodus that only increased the ill ease of those who remained behind.

Although yeoman farmers in sand hill and mountain regions probably were not much affected by these trends, having participated in neither the boom nor the bust, other groups in South Carolina were. These include white urban mechanics competing with black labor and Charleston retailers hurt by the decline in wagon trade as canal traffic to the upcountry increased. The Charleston business community was suffering from other blows as well; for the growth of inland towns such as Columbia had some negative impact, and internal improvements in other states (canals and roads) also diverted commerce elsewhere. As late as 1816, Charleston exports ranked second to those of New York, but soon declined, as did imports, down 50 percent in only five years, dropping from $2.4 million in 1823 to $1.2 million in 1828.[11]

Thus one root of nullification was a troubled economy, and the other may have been abolition. That movement was, in the 1820s, merely the plaything of a handful of northern visionaries, but lowcountry grandees—with remarkable prescience and leisure time to contemplate the ebb and flow of events—sensed the great danger it posed. Out of the economic woes of upland cotton planters (such as those living in the Midlands), a pervasive fear of federal interference with an institution basic to South Carolina's way of life, and the (for them) fortuitous Denmark Vesey Plot of 1822, these men fashioned their assault upon the much-hated tariff.

Freehling credits Vesey, an intelligent Charleston carpenter who purchased his freedom with lottery winnings, with bringing this state to a fever pitch. The result of this chilling episode was widespread distrust of all blacks and a deep-seated fear of both abolitionist propaganda and public debate concerning slavery. In the years that followed, many Charleston fires were blamed on slaves, and rumors of another plot packed the Georgetown jail in 1829. According to Freehling, Yankee peddlers who met with slaves at night and traded liquor for goods stolen from their masters were credited with spreading talk of freedom and fomenting almost any disturbance, real or imagined.

Reaction in Columbia to these trends was two-fold. In 1823, the community assumed responsibility for its own patrol, formerly a county-wide group of citizens detailed to ride about at night and make certain that slaves not on their masters' lands had permission to be wherever they were, and two years later a town guard was established. The latter body, the beginnings of a police force, consisted of a captain, two sergeants, and seven privates. In addition to maintaining the general peace, these men were given specific orders to disperse unlawful black assemblies and apprehend slaves at large without "tickets" from their masters. [12]

At the same time, the president of South Carolina College launched his campaign against rising tariff rates when he and two other local residents published a carefully worded protest in *Niles Weekly Register* on 13 December 1823. This "elaborate" essay on a bill before Congress, firm in tone, talked of "injustice, oppression, and ruin," but not of conflict or armed resistance. Then, the following year Cooper produced a wide-ranging account of the consolidation of American political parties since 1787. Declaring himself a staunch anti-Federalist and relying heavily upon defiance of federal law by Virginia and Kentucky in the late 1790s, Cooper cautioned that "the authority of constitutions over governments, and of the sovereignty of the people over constitutions, are truths which are at all times necessary to be kept in mind, and at no time perhaps more necessary than at the present."

Buried in this seventeen-page pamphlet were not-so-subtle references to the slave question and abolition. If Congress, Cooper asked, can pass an act to protect domestic and prohibit foreign manufactures, can it not then "legislate the Missouri question?" And, if John Quincy Adams became president and Arkansas sought admission to the Union, what would the "enemies of the South" do?

Although Cooper kept up his drum beat as the federal tariff continued to rise, many local residents were shocked when the English-born radical uttered these words at a meeting held in Columbia's town hall on 2 July 1827:

> I have said, that we shall 'ere long be compelled to calculate the value of this union; and to enquire of what use to us is this most unequal alliance? By which the south has always been the loser, and the north always the gainer? Is it worth our while to continue this union

of states, where the north demand to be our masters and we are required to be their tributaries? Who with the most insulting mockery call the yoke they put upon our neck the American system! The question, however, is fast approaching to the alternative, of submission or separation. Most anxiously would every man who hears me wish on fair and equal terms to avoid it. But, if the monopolists are bent upon forcing the decision upon us, with themselves be the responsibility.[13]

From this point on, largely at the urging of lowcountry fire-eaters who agreed wholeheartedly with these words, the nullification fury intensified and, in fact, moved to the national scene where it ensnared President Andrew Jackson and White House hopefuls such as John C. Calhoun, Henry Clay, and Daniel Webster. Meanwhile, back in South Carolina, after several rebuffs and the failure of various compromise schemes, in 1832 the Nullifiers won control of the General Assembly. In this bitter face-off, they carried predominantly black counties with ease. In Richland, for example, then 65 percent black, Nullifiers won three-fourths of the votes cast, although their margin state-wide was only 25,000 to 17,000. Yet J. P. Ochenkowski's careful analysis of returns indicates that loyalty to local squire—not concern for tariffs or abolition—may have decided the outcome, especially in rural precincts.[14]

In any case, once in the driver's seat, the Nullifiers organized a convention that met in Columbia in November of 1832 and passed an ordinance nullifying "certain acts of the Congress of the United States" relating to duties and imposts as of 1 February 1833. A short time later, state lawmakers passed a test oath requiring all officeholders to swear to uphold that ordinance, a move that incensed many Unionists; for, it should be remembered, this was not only a state-federal clash but an internal struggle that split families and ended friendships.

Amid military preparations in South Carolina and heated exchanges in Washington, those attending a public but unofficial meeting held in Charleston on 21 January voted to suspend the ordinance until after Congress adjourned, a bid—it would appear—for compromise. And at length a compromise of sorts was achieved. Congress agreed to reduce tariff rates over a period of ten years, and the Nullifiers regrouped in Columbia and rescinded their ordinance, at the same time nullifying President Jackson's "Force Bill" and declaring "victory." That bill, passed at the insistence of Jackson, gave him the right to (a) collect customs duties in South Carolina and (b) circumvent local courts in the event legal protests were lodged by Nullifiers.

The foregoing tale of nullification is largely the standard scenario, but younger scholars are beginning to question key elements of this story. Specifically, they believe South Carolina's pre-1820 nationalism has been exaggerated somewhat and that abolition had little to do with nullification. Instead, they emphasize this state's unique experience with civil strife in the 1780s and how the Revolutionary War shaped local views of federalism. For them, the root causes of the crisis that occurred a half century later were the tariff and hard times, not abolition, and they stress this is precisely what arch Nullifiers said throughout the controversy.[15]

There were, of course, so many political egos involved in this fracas that it is virtually impossible to say that anyone actually "won" this fight. When the chips were down, even some Nullifiers such as John C. Calhoun were, in the final analysis, Unionists at heart. Nevertheless, whether the focus of this drama was Washington, Charleston, or conventions and legislative debates held right here in Richland County, the impact of this tumultuous episode was great indeed. It was, in truth, a dividing line separating one era of local, state, and national life from another.

English traveler G. W. Featherstonhaugh, who visited Columbia in January 1835, just as the furor was subsiding, found it a "pleasantly situated" community with "airy" streets and "genteel-looking" houses that indicated "a respectable state of society."[16] Thomas Cooper, whom he had met previously, still was angry as he received his guest. "Almost bent double like a hook," Cooper rose from his chair, loudly denouncing Andrew Jackson and wielding a hearth broom as a sword, apparently eager to lash out at his adversary. The following day, Featherstonhaugh joined Cooper and several other friends at dinner, where he was struck by the total lack of caution whenever politics and religion were discussed. These gentlemen, he noted, seemed not to be talking to him but merely repeating opinions always expressed whenever they met.

> A stranger dropped in amongst them from the clouds would hardly have supposed himself among Americans, the language they used and the opinions they expressed were so diametrically opposed to the self-laudatory strain they too generally indulge in when speaking of their country or themselves. It was quite new to me to hear men of the better class express themselves openly against a republican government, and to listen to discussions of great ability, the object of which was to show that there never can be a good government if it is not administered by gentlemen.

Featherstonhaugh, not having shared much in the conversation, offered up James Madison as an example of a gentleman statesman, only to be told forcefully that "little Jamie" was "a false hypocritical dissembler," a favorite of the "Sovereign People," and one of the worst men in America. This, he quickly concluded, was because of the stand Madison had taken against nullification. "A short time after, something very extravagant having been said, I could not help asking in a good-natured way, if they called themselves Americans yet; the gentleman who had interrupted me before, said, 'If you ask *me* if I am an American, my answer is, No, sir, I am a South Carolinian.' If the children of these Nullifiers are brought up in the same opinions, which they are very likely to be, here are fine elements for future disunion."

Notes

1. To follow this tale a bit further, in 1849 the General Assembly made yet another effort to sell vacant lots. A. S. Johnston, chairman of this campaign, again found unclear records, squatters, and widespread confusion as to true ownership. Johnston reported in 1850 that still another survey had to be made, but he boasted of selling property worth $7,441 and marking lots with granite blocks. His plan to sell land in the southern and southeastern sections of Columbia stirred up a hornet's nest of opposition among those who viewed the woods of that region "as a barrier against the miasma of the river and swamps in that direction." Nevertheless, Johnston maintained that if the state attended to its rights in Columbia, it still might recover "an amount worth looking after." (See General Assembly records, South Carolina State Archives.)
2. In April of 1816, fourteen wagon loads of specie shipped to Columbia for safekeeping during the war with Great Britain were returned to vaults in Charleston (*Camden Gazette*, 18 April 1816)
3. Jameson, *Diary of Edward Hooker*, pp. 852–53.
4. Mills, *Statistics of South Carolina*, p. 699.
5. Billiards seem to have caused great concern in these years. In 1809 tables were heavily taxed ($500 for a license and a $2,000 fine for failure to obtain one), then in 1818 they were banned within fifteen miles of Columbia. This move brought a protest from Jesse De Bruhl, operator of a "house of entertainment" at Lightwood Knot Springs, and the law was relaxed in 1826 to permit billiards within five miles of town during summer months.
6. Mills, p. 708. As usual, Mills is overly optimistic since water traffic always was seasonal at best. According to his account, bay craft could carry 250 bales of cotton; canal boats, about half that number. Bay craft followed the Santee to the ocean, while canal boats went to Charleston via the Santee Canal.

7. Edwin J. Scott, *Random Recollections of a Long Life: 1806 to 1876* (Columbia, 1884), pp. 78–82.

8. Mills estimates that the original college buildings cost about $200,000, the South Carolina State Hospital (built between 1822 and 1827 to house 120 patients), somewhat "less than $100,000." See Wilton Hellams, "A History of South Carolina State Hospital, 1821–1900," Ph.D. diss., University of South Carolina, 1985.

9. See Daniel Walker Hollis, "Costly Delusion: Inland Navigation in the South Carolina Piedmont," *Proceedings*, South Carolina Historical Association (1968), pp. 29–43.

10. For a thorough analysis of this affair, see William F. Freehling, *Prelude to Civil War: the Nullification Controversy in South Carolina, 1816–1836* (New York and London, 1965).

11. For a provocative look at trans-Atlantic commerce, see W. M. Pine, "Atmospheric Determinants and the History of the Old South," *South Carolina Historical Magazine* (October 1989), pp. 313–21. Pine argues that a warming trend in the north Atlantic favored northern ports after the Revolution and hurt trade with Charleston.

12. There is substantial evidence, however, that rules restricting the activities of slaves were of little consequence except during times of crisis.

13. William F. Freehling (editor), *The Nullification Era: A Documentary Record* (New York, 1967), p. 25. Reprinted from *Niles Weekly Register*, 8 September 1827. Among those distressed by Cooper's words was Unionist John Taylor, reluctant chairman of the town hall assembly.

14. J. P. Ochenkowski, "The Origins of Nullification in South Carolina," *South Carolina Historical Magazine* (April, 1982), pp. 121–53.

15. See especially the research of Thomas S. Price, doctoral candidate at the University of Illinois-Chicago.

16. G. W. Featherstonhaugh, *Excursion Through the Slave States. . . .* (New York, 1844), pp. 155–58.

South Carolina College
—The Early Years

CHAPTER SIX

In the decades following the American Revolution, each of the thirteen former colonies wrestled with the problem of how best to create an educational system, whether to build from the bottom up or from the top down. This question, really a chicken-egg conundrum, is at the heart of the dilemma that to get able students one must have able teachers, who, at some point, were able students . . . and around it goes. For the most part, the Northeast relied upon sectarian colleges such as Harvard, Yale, and Princeton to provide advanced training in a variety of fields. Students attending those institutions came from a growing number of local academies, both public and private. Since educational facilities at all levels were less common in the South, state legislators—usually after rejecting proposals to build a network of grammar schools and academies as too expensive—created an institution to serve as the capstone of an educational pyramid that they hoped would somehow evolve. Georgia did so in 1785, North Carolina in 1789, South Carolina in 1801, and Virginia in 1819.

Of these four centers of higher learning, only that of South Carolina was called a "college" (certainly a more appropriate designation than university during a formative period), and only South Carolina College was located at the state capital. The choice of Columbia was no accident; for a prime goal of the patricians who guided the bill of incorporation through the General Assembly in less than a month was to unite upcountry and lowcountry. If the future leaders of the Palmetto State formed classroom friendships, they reasoned, then some of the animosities troubling South Carolina life might be ameliorated.

Other, less clearly enunciated motives also were at work. Although educational matters had concerned the General Assembly from time to time, no ground swell for a college was evident in 1801; however, the lowcountry was under increasing pressure to yield some of its political power to the more populous hinterland. Thus young Governor John Drayton, only thirty-three and the father of South Carolina College, saw this move as a concession that could benefit his lowcountry friends. Since the upcountry had the potential to become dominant in state affairs, Drayton and others who thought as he did decided to indoctrinate the elite of the backwoods in the ways of their tidewater world and thus forge a class of people that, they hoped, would adopt their culture and their views. And the scheme worked beautifully, aided, of course, by the cotton gin.

There was still another reason for choosing the little village of Columbia as the site for a college. Unlike other southern lawmakers, especially those in Georgia and North Carolina, South Carolina's leaders took a very personal interest in their handiwork and, naturally enough, wanted to monitor its growth and development. In antebellum decades they looked upon South Carolina College as a "department" of state government, lavished money upon it, and often attended academic functions in a body. What we now call commencement was, for many years, held in December while the General Assembly was in session, and members always had a special place in the line of march, as did townspeople. In addition, a new professor usually delivered his inaugural address, also in December, in the House of Representatives.

Of course, being little more than a stone's throw from the state capitol has disadvantages, too; for, if politicians interested in your welfare are giving you money, you may get involved in politics. Also, close association between government and college may explain why Columbia, unlike Chapel Hill, never developed into what one might call a "college" town. South Carolina College became an important factor in the cultural and economic life of Columbia and Richland County, true, but it was seen by local citizens as the handmaiden of state government or even as an integral part of it, not as a separate entity and thus deserving of special consideration.

To function, an institution of higher learning must have money, land, buildings, teachers, and students; and, within a relatively short time, only four years, South Carolina College had all of these basic ingredients.[1] The college was to receive, according to its charter, $50,000 outright and $6,000 annually. The trustees were to have their choice of unsold Columbia lots as the site for a campus, but this proviso created problems. They found it difficult to locate contiguous lots without owners, but eventually managed to gain possession of a 24-acre rectangle just east of the State House.

Although historian Daniel Walker Hollis faults the trustees for having little concept of future growth and the need for more land, the building program they initiated demands our respect today. The first structure completed was "South Building," subsequently renamed Rutledge College in the 1840s. Its central portion, containing a chapel and classrooms, was flanked by two dormitories. Three hundred feet away was a companion building, essentially a "mirror image," not finished until 1809. Known at first as "North Building" and later rechristened DeSaussure College, it also had a tall central section and two wings of dormitory rooms. Eating facilities soon appeared in the form of Steward's Hall (now the site of Harper College), followed by a president's house at the eastern end of the little campus and, in time, more quarters for students and faculty. The result, now beautifully restored, is a striking "horseshoe" of plain, utilitarian, but graceful buildings that complement each other, truly one of America's most charming academic settings and still the heart of the University of South Carolina.

While "old North" was taking shape, the trustees circulated a progress report that solicited the attention of prospective students and faculty members. Their words, copied from a Charleston paper, appeared in Boston's *Repertory* on 10 February 1804.

South Carolina College

With much pleasure we announce to our fellow citizens, that the buildings of this institution are in such forwardness, as to induce the Trustees at their last meeting to resolve, that they will proceed to the election of a President and a Professor on the 22d of April next. We believe no seminary of learning in the United States, possesses more liberal endowments than this. The salary of the President is settled at 2,500 dollars, besides a house for his residence; that of the Professors of natural philosophy, &c. 1,500 dollars each, and their board and lodging; and of each of the other Professors, 1000 dollars, and their board and lodging.

The buildings will consist of two ranges, each 250 feet in length. The philosophical apparatus will be equal, if not superiour, to any collection in America; and the library will open with near 5000 volumes of the most select books, in all branches of learning.—The whole of which, we are informed, is expected out from London in the spring of the present year. The situation of Columbia for such an establishment is certainly very eligible; the buildings are erected on an eminence that commands a most extensive prospect, and from its elevation, ensures free and salubrious circulation of air.

In addition to salubrious air, the trustees assured students that board would not be "above ninety dollars" and tuition and room a mere twenty dollars. Nothing was said, however, about such vital matters as admission requirements, courses to be offered, and rules of conduct, all of which were still being discussed. In April of 1804, as promised, the trustees chose Jonathan Maxcy as the new institution's first president. Maxcy, a young Baptist preacher from Rhode Island, had both experience and an impressive record. Elected president of his alma mater (Brown) when only twenty-four, he served at that post for a decade before moving to a similar position at Union College in Schenectady, New York. At this same meeting, the board named three professors; however, only one of them— Enoch Hanford, a recent Yale graduate living in Society Hill as a tutor— agreed to accept the call to Columbia. Thus the college's first term would open early in 1805 with a faculty of two: Maxcy and Hanford.

At the April meeting, the trustees also received a comprehensive report concerning rules and regulations that won formal approval eight months later. As Hollis emphasizes, this lengthy document was important because it shaped life at South Carolina College for the next sixty years. For the most part, the academic routine was organized along traditional lines with faculty empowered to carry out the will of the trustees. Borrowing heavily from New England models, the trustees established a hard core of classical studies with no electives and the usual four-tier system (freshman, sophomore, junior, and senior).

For admission to the freshman class, one had to be versed in both Latin and Greek, at least well enough to "render" into English such standard works as Caesar's *Commentaries*, Virgil's *Aeneid*, and passages from the Greek Testament by the Evangelist St. John. In addition, a candidate was expected "to give a grammatical analysis of the words [translated], and have a general knowledge of the English Grammar; write a good, legible hand, spell correctly, and be acquainted with Arithmetic as far as includes the Rule of Proportion."[2] First-year studies included Latin and Greek, plus a bit of arithmetic, English grammar, and elocution. In succeeding years, students were expected to explore higher levels of mathematics, French, and elements of philosophy, history, and public speaking, as well as still more Latin and Greek. Anyone seeking to enter at a level higher than freshman was to be examined in all of the courses his prospective classmates had completed, and seniors, in addition to a specific course of study (Millot's *Elements of General History,* Demosthenes, and Locke) were to review the junior year curriculum and "perform such exercises in the higher branches of the Mathematics as the Faculty may direct."

The weekday routine, as envisioned by the trustees, was equally rigid. Students were to rise at six for morning prayers in the chapel. Except for meals—breakfast at 8, dinner at 1, and supper at about 5:30 (preceded by more prayers)—the young men were expected to be studying in their rooms or reciting in lecture halls. Their only free time was from the end of supper to 9 in the evening, when they were to retire.

Several aspects of this organizational scheme have puzzled Hollis and others, as well they might. It is odd that the founding fathers borrowed so much from Puritan New England, including an especially strict code of conduct, and yet made no effort to promote theological study, even though Maxcy and three of the trustees were ministers. Also, it seems strange that South Carolina, then largely easy-going and materialistic, endorsed such a regimen for its future leaders.

Nevertheless, perhaps with some misgivings, nine students presented themselves for admission on 10 January 1805 and were duly enrolled. By the end of the first session in July their ranks had risen to twenty-nine and in January of 1806 stood at fifty-six. At the close of that same year the college staged its first public exhibition, an ambitious series of speeches, debates, and orations in English, Latin, and Greek. How much of these goings-on actually was understood by an audience of friends, parents, and townspeople is not known, but the *South-Carolina State Gazette* (6 December) thought the affair a "brilliant" display of "genius, learning, and eloquence."

A few weeks later, William John Grayson of Beaufort (destined to become a well-known writer and politician) arrived in Columbia to enroll as a sophomore in South Carolina College. Accompanied by a letter from his former teacher, a brother of President Maxcy, Grayson found the entrance examination much less formidable than he had feared. After this young man had recited an ode by Horace, Maxcy made a few comments about the beauty of the prose and the interview was over. Much more impressive, Grayson recalled in his autobiography, was his introduction to college life. The evening before he had been thrown into an uproar of "great jollity and good humor" as students filled a classroom with speeches, songs, and loud talk, much of it devoted to Tom Paine's *Rights of Man* and the ideas of the French Revolution.

Although Grayson came to admire President Maxcy, he found his fellow students less appealing. Released from the restraints of home, many of them had, in his opinion, no manners whatsoever. Greasy bones were tossed through the air at Steward's Hall and badly cooked food thrown under tables. Perhaps because of those dining hall melées, Grayson remembered fondly meals at the homes of Thomas Taylor and Wade Hampton, especially the latter since he was a more lavish host. He recalled in later years that his associates, some only fourteen years of age, quickly learned to smoke, chew, mix drinks, play billiards and cards, and ended up taking "degrees in arts and sciences about which his diploma is altogether silent."[3]

The conditions that so distressed Grayson led shortly after he arrived to a twelve-section ordinance on "misdemeanors and criminal offenses." Students faced disciplinary action and perhaps expulsion for blasphemy, dueling, fornication, forgery, card playing, profane language, associating with "bad" characters, getting drunk, and appearing "in indecent dress, or woman's apparel." They were forbidden to keep firearms or gunpowder, insult or strike an officer of the college, play any musical instrument during study hours or on Sundays, and (without specific permission) attend any "festival entertainment" in Columbia, visit a tavern, or bring liquor on campus, especially if it contributed to "the occasion of riotous conduct or tumult."

Some of these rules undoubtedly were promulgated to curb excesses that had already occurred, while others were designed to ward off disaster. Nevertheless, they point to a major problem that complicated the lives of Maxcy and his successors: discipline. In December of 1812, for example, the trustees were alarmed by a report that 504 panes of glass (a favorite target of student wrath) were broken or missing, fifty-three of them in the chapel. During the Maxcy years, despite rules, students frequented local taverns, stole turkeys and chickens from the backyards of Columbia homeowners, fought with boatmen along the Congaree, and used firearms pretty much as they pleased. Maxcy, no disciplinarian, tried to reason with his charges as "young gentlemen" and, as a result, nearly lost his job. Yet, after some tense encounters with both students and trustees, his sixteen-year rule closed on a relatively peaceful note.

Never robust, Maxcy died in 1820 at the age of fifty-two, much beloved and deservedly praised. To his credit, the first president proved to be a pragmatic administrator. Unable to secure professors in specific fields, he shaped the curriculum to fit the abilities of those he could attract to Columbia. The result was a drift away from classical studies to philosophy, science, chemistry, and a more utilitarian outlook. In the process, he established precedents that won for the college the respect of both lawmakers and the public at large. Maxcy is remembered today by a

Robert Mills monument that was erected in the center of the "horseshoe" by the Clariosophic Society. Egyptian Revival in style and topped by a golden globe, this obelisk clearly is a precursor of the famed Washington Monument. Long a focus of student activity and admired by generations of campus visitors, today only a handful of those who view it can read its Latin inscription.

Not all of Maxcy's pre-Civil War successors left much of an imprint upon college and community life, but several of them did. Thomas Cooper, whom we have already met as the arch-Nullifier, was, in the opinion of Hollis, "almost the complete antithesis" of Maxcy. A deist who loved controversy, this diminutive steam engine of a man did battle with Andrew Jackson, Presbyterians, and students (one of whom he hit with a cane after the young man hurled a chair at him). Despite a combative nature and efforts to raise academic standards and curb unruly activity, Cooper was popular with students, although his non-academic forays tended to harm the college in the eyes of the public. Enrollment, over a hundred during Maxcy's last decade, held up reasonably well until the early 1830s when it dropped to only fifty-two. In January of 1834, after fourteen years at the helm, Cooper relinquished the presidency and became a lecturer in chemistry, but student population continued to decline. At the close of that year, the trustees, noting that the faculty was not "acceptable" to the community at large, asked all members to resign, paving the way for wholesale restructuring of the teaching staff.

Cooper, who had a brilliant mind and seemingly could teach anything from political economy to chemistry and geology, certainly stimulated the intellectual life of South Carolina. Many eagerly embraced his views on nullification, while rejecting his religious tenets; for, as fundamentalist faith grew ever stronger, deism, materialism, and utilitarianism slid into disrepute. Controversial even in death, in 1839 Cooper was laid to rest in the Guignard plot near Trinity Episcopal Church, only a block or so from the college. A monument to his memory notes that it was erected not by all, but merely "a portion of his fellow citizens."

The task of reviving the college was put in the capable hands of Robert Woodward Barnwell of Beaufort. Only thirty-five, wealthy, and a Harvard graduate, he served admirably until overtaken by ill health in September of 1841. Young enough to recall student days at Cambridge (where he was said to have been an extremely accurate bread thrower), Barnwell appears to have had fewer disciplinary problems than his predecessors. However, he is remembered today for the fact that he literally rebuilt South Carolina College from the ground up—a six-foot brick wall (long talked about) soon surrounded most of the campus, old structures were renovated, more land was acquired, enrollment rose from 114 in 1836 to 169 five years later, and four new buildings appeared. These included two dormitories—Elliott and Pinckney, a double faculty residence subsequently called Lieber College, and a handsome library, the first separate building erected on an American campus to house books. Now the South Caroliniana Library, the large reading room is a replica of Bullfinch's Congressional Library in the United States Capitol. The exterior bears some evidence of the hand of Robert Mills and the structure often has been attributed to him, but apparently no proof of this assumption exists.

Although Barnwell lived to an advanced age and returned to the faculty after the Civil War, he was succeeded in 1842 by Robert Henry, a fifty-year-old professor who thought he should have been given the post years earlier instead of Cooper and Barnwell. After thirty-six months, however, largely because of declining enrollment, Henry handed over his responsibilities to William Campbell Preston and accepted a recently created chair in Greek literature.

The reputation of Virginia-born Preston, former U.S. senator, celebrated orator, and first alumnus (Class of 1812) to become president, attracted numerous students from Georgia, Alabama, and Mississippi and ushered in an era of growth and expansion. In 1849, enrollment reached 237, a total not equaled until 1905, leading to construction of two more dormitories, Harper and Legare. Since Preston was a familiar figure in the drawing rooms of Columbia and Richland County, his administration undoubtedly was looked upon with great favor; yet, plagued by ill health and internal bickering among faculty and students, his six-year stint was somewhat less successful than anticipated. A dispute between a chemistry professor and the junior class, for example, led to a riot in April of 1850 in which students burned their chemistry books. Preston, who left a vivid account of "confusion, uproar, and turbulence, beyond what I have ever seen," was unable to control the mob and eventually left the scene in disgust. A short time later most of the young men involved were suspended until end of term.

To replace Preston, the trustees turned to Presbyterian divine James H. Thornwell. An excellent teacher and a widely respected individual, Thornwell brought to the presidency both experience and a divided mind, for he seemed utterly incapable of choosing between pulpit and classroom. As Hollis points out, since joining the faculty in 1837, he was always resigning or threatening to do so and had made good those threats on at least four occasions. His election represented, of course, the triumph of fundamentalism and quieted much of the protest rising from religious quarters concerning college affairs. Although his tenure was brief, only three years, it was important. Thornwell replaced oral with written examinations, raised entrance requirements, reinforced classical studies, and publicly defended state-supported education at a time when new denominational colleges were gaining favor throughout the state. But in the end the pulpit triumphed. In November of 1854 he quit to accept a chair at Columbia Theological Seminary.[4]

Despite considerable success, the Thornwell years are often remembered largely because of the "Great Biscuit Rebellion" of 1852, so-called because of student-faculty confrontation over compulsory dining rules. As William John Grayson observed in 1807, bad food was a primary cause of student discontent, and various faculty members dealt with recurring protests with middling success. In 1842 the college instituted a bursary system with a bursar hired at a salary of fifteen hundred dollars a year to provide meals at three dollars per week per student. Attendance, however, was compulsory. This operation replaced the infamous "Steward's Hall," run by an unpaid individual whose income was realized by pinching pennies.

Although college authorities praised the bursary, students did not, and in the fall of 1852 over 100 of them joined together and demanded that the trustees abolish the compulsory requirement. The trustees, angered by this ultimatum, refused to do anything until the students disbanded. They proved equally firm, the governor declined to intervene, and many of the protestors packed up and left, reducing the student body from 199 in 1852 to 122 a year later. In a sense, the young men won, because in 1853 the college returned to a voluntary arrangement of earlier decades that permitted students to eat at licensed boarding houses.

Except for a near-fatal brawl, the administrations of Charles F. McCay (1856–1857) and Augustus Baldwin Longstreet (1857–1861) play virtually no role in local history, although it is of some significance that by those years only men from the Deep South could win trustee approval. McCay, veteran of a duel and a former mathematics professor at the University of Georgia, in effect permitted student discipline to get out of hand and his successor, once president of the University of Mississippi, restored it.

McCay had hardly arrived in Columbia early in 1856 when the long-standing feud between town police and students blazed out of control. On the evening of 17 February 1856, Edward Niles, an intoxicated junior from Camden, passed by the city guard house where he happened to see the town marshal, John Burdell. As a result of an old grudge, blows were exchanged and Niles was dragged into the guard house by Burdell's assistants. Meanwhile, Niles's excited companions rushed to the campus, spread word that their friend was being manhandled, and soon led a large and angry contingent to the center of town.

Two of the more aggressive students assaulted Burdell, said to have been a bully, even as President McCay struggled to restore order. As the uproar continued, the mayor summoned the militia and the students rushed back to the campus to arm themselves with guns from the cadet arsenal stored in the library. However, at that point Niles was released, paving the way for reconciliation.

By mutual agreement, McCay and Mayor E. J. Arthur decided to submit the matter to a panel of twelve citizens, but the next morning McCay was unable to gain student approval of this plan. The beleaguered president then turned to the faculty for help, but their discussion came to a quick end when the students armed themselves and rushed toward the guard house with McCay and all of the professors in hot pursuit. Hollis indicates that the same students who attacked Burdell the night before resumed their assault on the town marshal shortly after the meeting with McCay ended in confusion. The town bell was sounded once more, and within minutes 200 armed citizens and about half as many students, with rifles in their hands and fury in their eyes, faced each other.

When appeals for calm proved fruitless, someone had the good sense to summon Reverend Thornwell. Rushing to the scene, the former president urged the students to return to their rooms. He promised to investigate their grievances personally and told the students that, if they were right and a fight was indeed warranted, he himself would lead them into battle. Then, shouting "College! College!," Thornwell instead shrewdly led the agitated young men back to the campus. In the opinion of Hollis, "Probably no one else in the State could have done it."

In the aftermath of this affair, the governor, at the request of the trustees, seized the guns of the cadet corps and summarily disbanded a unit dating back to Lafayette's visit in 1825. Some of those who faced disciplinary action left school, while parents of others, alarmed by what had happened, summoned their sons home. But, to allow hot tempers to cool, classes were suspended for about three weeks.

The so-called "guard house rebellion" was by far the most serious of numerous town-gown confrontations, yet all of these disturbances from broken windows to burned books and hurled biscuits should be viewed in perspective. These outbursts at South Carolina College were not unique. Throughout the first half of the 19th century virtually every institution of higher learning in America experienced similar turmoil. Professors were attacked, shot, and on a few occasions killed, entire classes were expelled, and campus riots great and small occurred with amazing frequency. The reasons are many. Students, some well prepared and some not, ran headlong into professors who thought learning was serious business, for this was the age when colleges and universities became something more than mere finishing schools.

Also, many of these young men came from homes where cards, dancing, liquor, horse racing, and even cock fighting were standard fare only to be greeted by rules that banned almost any form of recreation. To add to the confusion, American society as a whole was in turmoil, and nowhere was this more apparent than in South Carolina. Beset by appeals from advocates of temperance, nullification, abolition, and fundamentalist beliefs (all heavily embued with "thou shalt not"), it is hardly surprising that college students of those years got drunk, smashed windows, ripped up fences, overturned privies, and raised general hell whenever given an opportunity to do so.

Nevertheless, such behavior should not obscure the educational achievements of South Carolina College during these decades. In addition to men such as Maxcy, Cooper, and Thornwell, all fine teachers, the faculty included, among others, internationally renowned Francis Lieber, the multi-talented Maximilian LaBorde, and scientists John and Joseph LeConte. During the antebellum period the college was a premier institution in the South and perhaps as good as any in the nation. Although young men went forth to become teachers, ministers, lawyers, physicians, and planters, South Carolina College was best known as a training school for orators. Competition between the Clariosophic and Euphradian societies, plus issues one could really sink teeth into—slavery, emancipation, annexation of Canada and Cuba, nullification, disunion, etc.—created the perfect milieu for hard-hitting, dramatic declamation. Yet not every verbal bout was so impersonal and somber. According to Hollis, in 1811 the Clariosophic Society debated whether highway robbery or seduction was the greater crime. Seduction of fair damsel lost by a single vote.

A key question is what impact the college had upon Columbia and Richland County. The answer depends upon what facet of local life one wishes to examine. To shopkeepers, contractors, carpenters, and masons, the college was customers and jobs. During its first half-century, South

Carolina College received nearly a million dollars in state funds that were used to build classrooms and dormitories and pay for salaries of a faculty that usually numbered a dozen or so. Added to this sum was money spent by students themselves, which by mid-century exceeded $50,000 a year.[5]

Sadly, in an age of widespread illiteracy, the college had a direct effect upon only a distinct minority of local households, largely those of the well-to-do. Also, whenever individuals it had trained departed for other regions—as so many did during these decades—both community and state suffered. Between 1805 and 1860, 305 Richland County residents were enrolled at South Carolina College and, of that number, 182 (60 percent) received degrees. Except in years when dormitory space was limited, college catalogs indicate that nearly all students, even those hailing from Columbia, lived on campus.

This pre-war Richland contingent included twenty-four Taylors and fifteen Adamses. In fact, out of twenty-one students in the junior class of 1833, four had the surname of Adams; however, the infamous "dish of trout" duel soon decimated their ranks. While dining, James G. Adams and A. Govan Roach, said to have been close friends, both grabbed a platter at the same moment and each refused to let go. The result was a meeting at Lightwood Knot Springs in which Adams was killed. College records state without further explanation that Roach and two other Adamses subsequently were "dismissed by request."[6]

The indirect impact of South Carolina College was more pervasive. Graduates became teachers in academies for both sexes, and the mere presence of an institution of higher learning stimulated the growth of preparatory schools, some of them, however, of brief duration. The most stable of these, Columbia Academy, established for local youth in the 1790s, by 1816 had given birth to a school for young ladies, Columbia Female Academy. After the Civil War, both schools became part of an emerging public school system.

Dr. Elias Marks, principal of the Female Academy for a decade, in 1828 established the South Carolina Female Collegiate Institute a mile or so north of town in Barhamville, a community named in memory of Jane Barham, the good doctor's first wife. Marks, who headed the school for over three decades, ran a tight ship. At first his charges were allowed only two trips to Columbia each term. They could attend, under close supervision, commencement at South Carolina College and festivities marking Washington's birthday. Each young lady was required to write her parent or guardian on the first day of each month. All incoming letters were open to inspection, and the school catalog cautioned that "letters of a trifling nature" were frowned upon since they interfered with more serious pursuits.

Despite such restrictions, this school—often called simply "Barhamville Academy"—was extremely successful. In the 1850s, for example, it usually had over 100 students, many of them from states other than South Carolina. In time the original rules were relaxed somewhat, and by mid-century, along with basic courses, embroidery, dancing, and music, a Barhamville girl could study bookkeeping.[7]

The story of Richland School, an academy for boys founded at Rice Creek Springs in 1828, is a less happy tale. A very ambitious undertaking, this institution was the brainchild of Rufus W. Bailey and H. L. Dana. A prospectus appearing in the *Columbia Telescope* (9 January 1829) outlined seven departments organized according to the "gymnasia" system: elementary, classical, belle lettres, scientific, commercial, agricultural, and military science and physical education. Students were to be divided into groups of twelve, each headed by a teacher who would be associated with the same unit at all times. They were to wear a uniform of blue coat with standing collar and brass buttons complemented by white pantaloons in summer and blue in winter. Tuition for older boys (those over ten years of age) was $272 annually; for younger students, $250.

In 1830, Richland School had eighty students from South Carolina, Georgia, Louisiana, and Pennsylvania, as well as two young men from Greece and Spain. Their ranks included some of the Palmetto State's proudest names, but within three years this institution had closed its doors.

Still other schools, some of them little more than tutorial classes in private homes, came and went in much the same fashion. In the fall of 1847, Columbia's *Daily Telegraph* listed no less than fourteen schools for young people within the town limits.[8] One of the most interesting of these was a no-frills academy for less affluent youth operated by the Odd Fellows from 1844 to 1879, sometimes called the "Palmetto Lodge School." At the outset, tuition was only twenty-five dollars per year.

By 1860, local youngsters could attend commercial classes taught by William B. Johnston and A. B. Brumby's Carolina High School, which had a staff of four, including a University of France graduate who taught French. During the preceding decade, Father J. J. O'Connell launched two parochial schools—St. Mary's Collegiate Institute for boys and the Academy of the Immaculate Conception for girls. In 1854, St. Mary's had over 100 students of various religious beliefs and the patronage of luminaries such as Wade Hampton III and William C. Preston, donor of an elocution medal. However, in the mid-1850s, this school, located at the northern end of Main Street, was attacked by Know-Nothing gangs who harassed students, stoned clergy, and even invaded classrooms. According to O'Connell, enrollment dwindled, and St. Mary's is not listed in the 1859 city directory. Although the girls school is cited, by that date it was an institution run by Ursuline nuns. In any case, the facilities of both schools were destroyed by flames that engulfed Columbia in February of 1865.

All of these academies, seminaries, and institutes mentioned thus far were private, yet public schools (such as they were) did exist. Legislation enacted by the General Assembly in 1811 created a board of commissioners to operate free schools in each county. The Richland group divided the region into seven districts: Columbia, Sand Hills, Kershaw, Garner's Mill, Crane Creek, Broad River, and Mill Creek. The state allocation for local pupils averaged about $1,000 a year until the early 1850s when it more than doubled.

Statistics published each year concerning the number of schools and students in the county are indeed impressive—for example, 29 schools and 450 students in 1831; 30 schools, 30 teachers, and 694 students in 1847.[9] But raw records at the State Archives paint a quite different picture. Since the state treasury paid so much per quarter for each student enrolled, commissioners throughout South Carolina inflated their annual totals by adding up four sets of returns. Thus a more accurate tally for Richland in 1831 might be seven schools and only 115 students.

In 1838 and again in 1842, Richland commissioner John Bryce pointed to these distortions, emphasizing that, except in towns, money spent on free schools was "money wasted." In the late 1840s, Robert W. Gibbes, another local commissioner, spoke out even more forcefully. He estimated that 850 area children needed free education. But the annual appropriation of $1.41 per child, in his opinion, was utterly inadequate: "Good schools cannot be established without the means to pay competent instructors."

Early in that same decade, Robert Henry, then acting president of South Carolina College, substantiated charges made by Bryce and Gibbes. In a special report to the General Assembly, Henry said, in his opinion, Richland's free schools lacked system and direction.[10] A teacher contracted to receive so many students at so much a head and agreed to provide proof of attendance. Regrettably, Henry observed, some pupils attended only a day or so, or at most a few weeks, because of pressures to work at home. Reflecting upon this dilemma, he made these recommendations to state lawmakers:

1. Free schools must remain "poor" schools, thus assuring that students would be from the same social class.
2. Instruction should be useful, incorporating elements of religious and moral truth, grammar, arithmetic, geography, and natural and civil history, and classes should be *identical* throughout the state.
3. Normal schools should be established to train teachers, and a board of control should oversee their classroom work.

Andrew Crawford, commissioner of Columbia's free schools, in 1852 petitioned lawmakers to consider a new approach to public education. With the cooperation of the town council, he had hired a competent male teacher who enrolled fifty-five students during the year. The experiment seemed to be a success, he added, but the community needed two more schools of the same size, one of them for girls, as well as more money. With increased funding, Crawford achieved at least one of his goals, and in 1860 Columbia had two free schools. Henry W. Powell was teaching boys in a building on Lincoln Street, and Mrs. M. S. Monteith was in charge of the Taylor Street school for girls.

J. F. Williams, author of *Old and New Columbia,* who was born in 1850, learned his ABCs at a free school in the northern part of the county that was coed. When he was six, his family moved to town and he became a Powell pupil. Williams indicates that his school, then on Washington Street, soon merged, at least temporarily, with the institution operated by the Odd Fellows on Lincoln Street.

Free classes obviously played a minor role on the local scene during the first half of the 19th century and their ties to South Carolina College were tenuous indeed. Yet alumnus Gibbes and community leaders such as Bryce and Crawford thought them worthy of attention even though few (if any) free school students ever got to the Columbia campus. Nevertheless, by the 1850s those favoring public education were beginning to question the generous annual appropriation to South Carolina College. Pendleton's Samuel M. Wilkes reminded members of the House of Representatives in December 1855 that *private* institutions should not receive state aid and moved that the college be given a final payment of $100,000 and no more. This motion, which also earmarked $800 for the education each year of two youths from Charleston's orphan house at South Carolina College, was rejected, 92–11. Four years later, a Richland grand jury revived Henry's plea for a normal school for teachers and suggested the selection of "able" boys to be sent to South Carolina College.

During these decades, three more institutions of higher learning appeared on the local scene, each of them quite different. In 1830, the Presbyterians moved their theological seminary from Lexington, Georgia, to Columbia where a handful of professors and students set up shop in the grand mansion Robert Mills had designed for merchant Ainsley Hall. The transfer of this ultra-conservative school to South Carolina's capital was inspired, no doubt, by grim resolve to counteract the religious views of one Thomas Cooper. On the eve of the Civil War, the Columbia Theological Seminary had five professors and fifty-six students.

In 1842, lawmakers established two military schools designed to train South Carolina youth—the Citadel in Charleston and Arsenal Academy in Columbia, both of which were to educate a certain number of free school graduates at state expense. Situated on the crest of one of the highest hills in Columbia, by 1860 Arsenal had five faculty members and about seventy students; however, this school was gutted by fire in February 1865 and never re-opened. The most tangible reminder of this ill-fated institution is, of course, its officers' quarters, now the home of South Carolina's governor.[11]

Columbia Female College, chartered in 1854, was part of a general proliferation of denominational schools during that decade. A Methodist institution, the college began classes five years later in a huge Italian-style complex—a four-story structure with a tower nearly 100 feet tall—located on the northern half of the square bounded by Pickens, Plain, Taylor, and Henderson streets. During the war years, since Columbia was thought to be a safe haven, enrollment swelled to over 300.

Thanks largely to the presence of South Carolina College, by 1860 education in its many forms had become a key element in the economic, social, and cultural life of Columbia and Richland County. Visitors from both the North and Europe were favorably impressed with the intellectual quality of the community, and as early as 1826 historian Jared Sparks paid the Palmetto State's little capital the supreme compliment.

In the spring of that year, Sparks toured the South searching for Revolutionary War records. After digging through musty files in Charleston and Milledgeville, Georgia, on 25 April he arrived in Columbia for a four-day visit. Here he met with Thomas Cooper, lawyer David J. McCord, William C. Preston, and various judges and professors. Following a congenial meal at the Preston home, Sparks wrote in his diary, "Since leaving Boston I have not found a more intelligent, literary, & hospitable society than in this place. The college doubtless has an influence on the literary air of the place."[12]

Sparks was right; it did. Perhaps John Drayton and his friends had done their job a bit too well; for, while raising up a backwoods elite to share their views, they had, in only a quarter of a century, created an intellectual outpost that posed a distinct threat to the regional dominance their lowcounty metropolis had so long enjoyed.

Notes

1. Much of the material in this chapter comes from the first volume of the sesquicentennial history of the University of South Carolina by Daniel Walker Hollis, published by the University of South Carolina Press in 1951. For the construction story, see John Morrill Bryan, *An Architectural History of the South Carolina College, 1801–1855* (Columbia, 1976).
2. Quoted in Maximilian LaBorde, *History of the South Carolina College* (Columbia, 1859), p. 30.
3. Calhoun, *Witness to Sorrow*, p. 80. See also, Robert Duncan Bass, "The Autobiography of William J. Grayson," Ph.D. diss., University of South Carolina, 1933.
4. By this date, students were attending three classes, Monday through Friday, at 7 A.M., 11 A.M., and 4 P.M. and a single class on Saturdays at 7 A.M.
5. Basic costs such as board, tuition, room, fuel, washing, servant hire, and lights rose from $181 in 1848 to $240.50 in 1860, while enrollment during those years averaged about 180, indicating an annual outlay of $35,000–$45,000 by students. This does not include, of course, money spent for clothing, travel, liquor, beer, and other recreational pursuits.
6. Although rumors of duels and near-duels surface from time to time during antebellum years, this custom does not seem to have been common in the Richland County area. The only other duel of note occurred "at the Fork" in November of 1854 following a disagreement at a Gadsden polling place. In this encounter, Dr. William D. Ray killed a Captain Gaffney. See Samuel Leland's diary for details. According to Leland, Gaffney was "a remarkably swayed back man" whose unusual form saved him during the first round of shots, but not in the second.
7. Marks retired in 1861 and leased the school to others. The buildings burned in 1869. See Hennig Cohen (editor), *A Barhamville Miscellany* (Columbia, 1956).
8. Academies in rural sections of the county were rare and led fragile lives. The Minervaville school expired soon after it moved to Horrell Hill, and Good Hope Academy— undoubtedly located near or on a plantation with a similar name—vacillated between private and public status during the 1820s and 1830s.

9. In 1840, the census taker recorded these totals:

	Academies	Students	Primary Schools	Students
Columbia	3	126	6	195
County	2	55	8	171

Forty-four academy students and eighty-two young people in primary grades were attending classes "at public charge."

10. *Reports on the Free School System, to the General Assembly of South Carolina* (Columbia, 1840), pp. 65–69.

11. The Arsenal was not popular with some local residents. In 1844, reacting to a petition that the school be abolished, a General Assembly committee vowed it was not "a public nuisance," but "a noble charity" worthy of state support. The lawmakers said these protests arose from "trivial causes" that had led to the suspension of several cadets.

12. John Hammond Moore (editor), "Jared Sparks Visits South Carolina," *South Carolina Historical Magazine* (July 1971), p. 158.

Slavery, Race, and Color

CHAPTER SEVEN

 Nothing has so shaped the South, and especially South Carolina, as the presence of blacks. As both slave and free, they have long been a key ingredient in almost every decision, be it political, economic, or social. For over a century and a half (1670–1820), Africans and their progeny were not a subject of great controversy. So long as Great Britain ruled, slavery was her policy, her problem. During the Revolutionary War, influenced by concepts such as freedom and the words of Thomas Jefferson ("All men are created equal . . ."), more and more Americans came to question the institution of slavery, and in the after-glow of independence residents of northern states began to emancipate their slaves. A few South Carolina masters endorsed such steps (at least in theory) and even supported the efforts of colonization societies to return to Africa those set free.

However, the cotton gin and the expansion of cotton culture wrote a quick end to such reflective thoughts. In 1790, only about one in three Richland County residents was black, but a black majority emerged ten years later that would last until the opening decades of the 20th century. In Columbia, blacks outnumbered whites in 1840 and again from 1870 to 1890. (See Table 1, "Local Population, 1790–1860.")

The most striking aspect of these columns of figures is the population loss of the 1850s, a time when the county suffered a sharp decline of nearly 2,000 (10 percent), largely because of worn-out soil and the lure of other regions such as Texas, Arkansas, and Florida. Yet Richland County was not unique. In the decade before the Civil War, four other South Carolina counties (Abbeville, Charleston, Kershaw, and Union) also lost population and nine more posted modest gains of less than a thousand. Thus half of the counties in this state had little or no population growth in the 1850s, while in the previous decade all of them were in the plus column, often with totals that increased by several thousand. One can only

Table 1. Local Population, 1790–1860[a]

| | Richland County | | | Columbia | | |
	Total	White	Black	Total	White	Black
1790	3,930	2,479	1,451	———	———	———
1800	6,097	2,929	3,168	———	———	———
1810	9,027	3,468	5,559	1,000[b]	———	———
1820	12,321	4,499	7,822	———	———	———
1830	14,772	5,238	9,534	3,310	1,807	1,503
1840	16,397	5,326	11,071	4,340	2,136	2,204
1850	20,243	6,764	13,479	6,060	3,184	2,876
1860	18,307	6,863	11,444	8,052	4,395	3,657

a. No returns are available for Columbia until 1830; also, the number of free blacks (included here with slave totals) is not always cited separately. In 1850, the county had 501 free blacks; in 1860, 439. In 1830, about 40 free blacks were living in Columbia. Their ranks rose to 149 in 1840; 196 in 1850, and 314 in 1860. However, since the 1860 census was compiled in a rather haphazard manner, it is possible some of these 314 free blacks actually were county residents.

b. Estimate, 1816.

conjecture as to how much these trends tended to exacerbate the frustrations of that era.

Since the county's black population dropped from 13,479 to 11,444, it is readily apparent that nearly all of this decline was caused by the sale of slaves or the migration of their owners. Some of the 2,000 blacks who left this region in the 1850s were taken by traders to new lands in Gulf Coast states. Although this traffic often was deplored, most southerners viewed it as a necessary evil, simply part of "the system." In 1902, Frederic Bancroft, author of *Slave-Trading in the Old South*, asked a group of Columbia blacks if they remembered slaves being sold here. "Did—dey sell 'em? Dey sol' 'em jess like yo' see 'em drive er hogs . . . 'er like dey sell chickens er tu'keys!'"

Nevertheless, Bancroft classified Columbia as a minor center of human commerce, believing instead that most sales in the Midlands were conducted privately. But a few men did gain notoriety as traders, notably Irish-born Charles Logan. On the eve of the Civil War, he and Alexander Forsythe each had small personal jails or "holding pens" where blacks were kept for a time, and a brick structure in the rear of Logan's home at the corner of Assembly and Senate streets long was pointed out as a "slave market," a somewhat incorrect designation. In addition to Logan and

Forsythe, both listed as "speculators" in the 1860 city directory, commission merchants such as L. T. Levin, A. R. Phillips, and D. P. McDonald & Company also dabbled in the slave trade.

After the war, Logan, once a shoemaker, advanced to horse trading and real estate, acquiring along the way a small fortune and reputation as a solid citizen, a pillar of the community. When he died in his eighty-ninth year, the *State* (30 November 1903) noted simply that his wealth was accumulated "through speculative deals of various sorts." Even this faint hint of tainted money was forgotten as soon as Logan's bequests became known. They included $60,000 to be divided among St. Peter's Catholic Church, Columbia Hospital, city schools (the major recipient), and municipal officials charged with preventing cruelty to animals. "Next to the care of children," the *State* proclaimed in editorial praise, "kindness to dumb animals is the mark of a kind heart."

As a result of this trade in slaves, migration, and relatively hard economic times, which probably had greatest impact, the number of local residents with over 100 slaves dropped from twenty-four in 1850 to fifteen a decade later. In 1850, various branches of the Adams family owned 1,125 blacks, while Benjamin F. and Sarah Taylor held about half as many, although some Taylor slaves lived and worked across the river in Lexington County. The plantation owner with the largest number within Richland County was Wade Hampton II, father of the Civil War general, who was master to 309. In 1860, three Adamses owned some 800 slaves, Frank Hampton, 260, the William Clarkson estate, 210, and Keziah Brevard, 209. Sarah Taylor, mistress of 224 Richland County blacks in 1850, reported only 123 a decade later.

The diary of Samuel Wells Leland, a young physician who was trying to build a practice in the Mill Creek community nine miles south of Columbia, describes what was happening in lower Richland. Leland, son of a professor at Columbia Theological Seminary, settled there in 1849 and remained for ten years, existing for the most part on "plantation business," ministering to slaves belonging to the Adams, Hopkins, and related families. His words, now at the South Caroliniana Library, touch upon numerous aspects of rural life, for Leland himself owned ten slaves and produced a bit of cotton, corn, and hay each year.

In August of 1852, a flood five feet higher than anyone could remember swept down the Congaree, ruining crops and smashing bridges. The next summer brought drought, and in the fall of 1854 crops again were disappointing. Leland complained that his 9 acres of cotton would yield only three light bales ("cotton is down very low"), the corn harvest was inadequate for his needs, and fodder was "trifling." On New Year's Day, 1855, he remarked that the preceding twelve months had been disheartening. Perhaps because of the Crimean War, he mused, provisions were expensive and cotton "a drug on the market." Planters had no money for doctors and his practice was so poor that (now a widower) he thought he might give up housekeeping, board with a neighbor, and hire out his blacks.

Although these plans were not carried out, Leland's diary nevertheless describes a community in deep trouble. He found the departure of William Creber and his family in December of 1853 especially disturbing. Creber, a fifty-year-old wagon maker born in England, did not leave the county, moving instead only a few miles away to the "Fork," the juncture of the Congaree and Wateree. Yet his shop had been a gathering place, a center of regional life, and Leland was certain that Mill Creek would miss him. "The neighborhood is breaking up fast," Leland observed. "James & John Hopkins, who owned large plantations in the neighborhood, have bought in Florida, and removed nearly their whole force there. The time is not far distant when I will be obliged to turn my attention to some thing else but the practice of medicine for support, if I should remain here."

And it was not only the well-to-do who were leaving. When Ruffin Jones and his family, "very poor, but very good, honest people," decided to try their luck in Alabama, Leland solicited funds to help them on their way. As Mrs. Matthew Howell and her children prepared to go to Florida in December of 1854, he remarked that only one member of that once prominent family was left in the community.

A few weeks later, Leland attended a sale day in Columbia at which four auctioneers were "crying" at once. Much property was sold, including two Mill Creek farms, but neither buyer intended to plant. One would grow timber and the other re-sell, so nothing, Leland noted, was added to the neighborhood. "Thus a whole section of the country is gradually breaking up. The people are dying or removing." However, the departure of Matthew Haley and his slaves for Texas was less distressing. "He was an Irishman, and a Roman Catholic—ergo—let him go." Several years later, Leland, now married to a Greenwood woman, sold his property and moved to Cass County, Georgia.

According to the 1850 census, these various families—Hopkins, Howell, Haley, and Leland—owned 133 slaves. Together with whites who also departed, including the Creber and Jones households, this translates into a loss of some 160 individuals and helps to explain the stark totals recorded in 1860. Yet as traumatic as these leave-takings were for members of both races, they had little effect upon black-white relations in this area. By mid-century the rules governing the master-slave world were pretty well agreed upon and firmly in place . . . even if not always honored to the letter.

Although these regulations remained formidable, pressures created by the American Revolution, emancipation societies, and the abolition crusade ameliorated some of the inhumane features of 18th century bondage. Under attack, many masters tried to improve the lot of their black workers, most of whom represented several generations of experience with the slave system.[1] Other factors also worked to promote accommodation by all concerned. These include *de facto* recognition by slave owners of family units and encouragement of religious life among blacks. The former made insurrection well nigh impossible since the wrath of whites would come down upon the loved ones of those who dared to mount rebellion. The latter preached individual morality and acceptance of one's present condition in return for salvation and a glorious hereafter.

It was easy enough for blacks to identify with the sufferings of the people of Israel, but more important was the fact that Christian faith provided a moral purpose for one's daily existence. In addition, the church offered an emotional and social outlet, relief from the tedium of hard labor, and—for a few talented orators—the path to leadership among their people.

Of course, not every master embraced paternalism nor every slave Jesus Christ, but these trends were real and strong during the first half of the 19th century. And all parties were motivated, it must be conceded, by self-interest. Simply put, contented, well-cared-for slaves could mean productive workers, good crops, more food, and perhaps better living conditions. Failure of a plantation might result in slaves being sold and families split asunder.

Both of these influences—religion, with its fundamentalist fervor, and paternalism—were evident in pre-Civil War Richland. As Edward Hooker observed in 1806, Columbia's earliest churches had sections reserved for blacks, usually in galleries, and they sometimes outnumbered whites. Records of the First Baptist Church indicate that the morality of *all* members, regardless of skin color, was serious business. Members of both races occasionally were cited for adulterous conduct, attending circuses, drinking to excess, or simply being "in disorder" or "unclean." (In 1816, a white brother arraigned for butchering cattle on the Sabbath in turn charged his accuser with selling dry goods to Negroes.) Ironically, at a time when slave marriage had no legal basis and might be ended on the auction block, blacks frequently were hailed before church elders for ignoring those bonds. Even before they entered the Baptist fold, church leaders usually "attended" to their "experiences" prior to baptism with great care, although thirty-four Hampton slaves seem to have been immersed in the Congaree with ease in August of 1821.

A typical entry in congregation minutes might be these words of July 1834: "Eliza and Grace belonging to Col. Cameron were suspended on account of a violent quarrel and intoxication. Elsy belonging to Mr. Bodie and Binah belonging to this person (the writer) are again censured for their old quarrel in which it is said that Binah struck Elsy. Daphney belonging to Mrs. Bull charged Paul with having attempted to lead her away to commit sin with her. On his positive denial and there being no other testimony, they were suspended from church privileges until further evidence can be developed."

At that time, Columbia's Baptist Church had 242 members, three-fourths of them black. Six years later this majority was greatly enhanced by a rapid-fire baptismal ceremony. According to church records, seventy-five more blacks went under the water, not in the Congaree, but in a special six-by-eight-foot pool built near the town spring. J. W. Clarke's watch indicated the entire proceedings took 17½ minutes, but a Mr. Jones vowed only 17 minutes elapsed.

Methodists were the other religious group most concerned with the welfare of local slaves, although Baptists always were more numerous in the black community. African-born Sancho Cooper, who died in April 1874 as he neared the century mark, long was "class leader" of his race at the Washington Street church. Once the body servant of Thomas Cooper, his strong Methodist ties made him a widely respected individual. Three other blacks—Colonel Taylor's Sancho, Merriman, who belonged to Jesse DeBruhl, and Peter, a Threewits slave—enjoyed similar privileges among Columbia's Baptists. Each of them was given the right during the 1830s "to exhort and instruct," in effect making them "assistant preachers." Their duties also included the investigation of charges concerning misdeeds among black members.

Columbia's Presbyterians, a much smaller group during the early decades of the 19th century, were reluctant to accept blacks unless those individuals belonged to white members. The case of Jack, a servant at South Carolina College lacking such ties, indicates what might happen. From April of 1820, when he first applied for membership, to July of 1821, Jack was held in limbo on probation, then on "extended' probation. At length, he was the subject of a special committee appointed to consider both his character and his "importunate" desire to become a Presbyterian. During these months, the faithful decreed that any black not associated with a "sister" church should be scrutinized with great care, only to be faced in 1827 with a black "transfer" from a Charleston congregation. The fate of neither Jack nor the ex-Charlestonian is known; however, it is most unlikely that either achieved full membership. Church records indicate that between 1819 and 1860 only thirty-four blacks enjoyed that high privilege.

Although this pattern of black participation soon was duplicated in rural meeting houses throughout the county, no one should have any illusions concerning who was running church affairs from day to day and dictating policy. Whites provided the financial support and were firmly in control of virtually all proceedings. Yet these religious bodies (especially the Baptists) created a strange, biracial world where spiritual equality, at least, was extended to slaves. Addressed as "brother" and "sister," they participated fully in all church activity, including communion, and were held to the same moral standards as their masters and mistresses.

The church also provided a forum for the resolution of disagreements. In the late 1830s, slaves Ben and Merriman, both loyal members of Columbia's Baptist congregation, got into a dispute concerning a crop they had grown jointly. After investigating the matter, a church committee awarded Merriman $21.25 (the total amount of his investment in the venture) and allowed Ben to keep the proceeds. And the church, not surprisingly, could become a center of controversy, too. When ministers advocated teaching slaves to read the Bible, masters often objected. In a series of letters that appeared in the *South-Carolina State Gazette* in the fall of 1822, H. W. DeSaussure cautioned that knowledge was power. For centuries, he emphasized, the precepts of Christianity had been taught solely by preaching and that practice must continue.

A decade later, in August of 1833, the appearance of a young, southern-born missionary at Columbia's Presbyterian Church stirred up a hornets' nest. John B. Phinney, a University of Georgia graduate who had been to Africa, apparently spoke several times concerning conditions in heathen lands. Some of his remarks about Liberia, comparing life there unfavorably with conditions in South Carolina, prompted some blacks to walk out in disgust. But the Columbia papers quickly labeled his address to Francis Goulding's black Sunday School class as a "colonization" talk. Within twenty-four hours an unofficial town meeting denounced Phinney and twenty-four hours after that convened once more and ordered the young man to leave town. Phinney and his Presbyterian friends tried to answer these charges, but tempers were too inflamed. His critics even waylaid the Augusta coach at the Gervais Street Bridge in an attempt to capture him; but, forewarned, Phinney escaped unharmed.

In the wake of this uproar, Thomas Goulding, a seminary professor, felt compelled to speak out in defense of his son's Sunday School. The class for blacks, he stated in a letter to the *Columbia Telescope* (10 September 1833), grew out of home instruction, was always *oral*, and was composed only of slaves who attended with the permission of their owners. No one, he stressed, was taught to read or write and discussion was limited to religious and moral subjects. Nevertheless, because of attitudes prevalent in Columbia, he said the class would be suspended.[2]

This incident usually has been interpreted as part of the emancipation-abolition controversy of those years, but that may not be the whole story. Instead, it was perhaps yet another skirmish in Thomas Cooper's anti-Presbyterian crusade. A few weeks before Phinney appeared on the scene, Columbia's *Southern Times and State Gazette* (thought to have been a mouthpiece for Cooper) attacked the Columbia Theological Seminary for actively soliciting funds in Boston to endow another professorship. The *Charleston Observer*, a Presbyterian weekly, countered on 10 August that, since northern religious bodies often sought money in the South, what was wrong with asking New England to assist in the training of southern ministers? Cooper thought otherwise, hence the attack upon Phinney.

Despite momentary shattering of the regional calm, emotional religious expression, with its many ramifications for both races, and white paternalism clearly became part of the social fabric during the opening decades of the 19th century. The latter is well documented by tales of faithful slaves who, even after the war, stuck by their masters and "stayed on the place." Although some of these stories probably are much embellished or even false, there were conscientious men and women who expended money, time, and energy in behalf of "their people."

In January of 1853, when the wife of one of his "boys" was to be sold by her master, Dr. Samuel Leland bought the woman. This was something he had vowed he would never do, but the outcry was so great that he yielded to his slave's pleas. Two years later, he bought yet another female slave, noting in his diary, "The object of the purchase is to free her, as much as the law will allow." Yet the following year, hard pressed for money, for the first time he sold one of his slaves for $900.

The brief diary of Keziah Goodwyn Hopkins Brevard, who owned property near Leland's Mill Creek home, reveals almost daily concern for her blacks. Mrs. Brevard, one of the county's wealthiest citizens and mistress of over 200 slaves, on the eve of the Civil War recorded her thoughts on black-white relations, religion, secession, and peace . . . observations that include these pertinent comments (1860–1861).

19 September—I wish to be kind to my negroes—but I receive little but impudence from Rosanna & Sylvia—it is a truth if I am compelled to speak harshly to them—after bearing every thing from them I get impudence. Oh my God give me fortitude to do what is right to these, then give me firmness to go no farther. At my death it is my solemn desire that Tama, Sylvia, Mack, Marie & Rosanna be sold. I cannot think of imposing such servants on any one of my heirs.

24 October—I wish every vessel that would go to Africa to bring slaves here would sink before they reached her soil. I would give up every ct. I own on earth if it would stop the slave trade.[3] My reason is this—we have a hard time with them & I feel for those who are to come after us. We never would have been unhappy with slaves if white people had been true to their white brethren & our negroes would now have been happy if all & every one had made the religion of Christ their North Star.

26 January—I have some good negroes & I wish them well. I pray God will place them in good places when I am taken from them—I have others who seem to dislike me & never care to look at me—such I hope may one day know they were well to do under my care. I don't wish them very bad luck. I only wish them to feel they are no better than other servants. . . . Negroes are strange creatures. I cannot tell whether they have any good feeling for their owners or not—sometimes I think they have—then I think there is nothing but deception in them. I am heartily tired of managing them—could I cast them off without scruples of conscience—I would do so as soon as we have peace—but I have thought all this over so seriously I cannot do it & feel that I have done right. They have been with us & our forefathers two generations back—have worked for us & contributed to our comforts & could I for a misdemeanor now & then cast them off without a rebuke from my Heavenly Father—while I believe I am an accountable being I cannot do it.

30 January—The truth is Sylvia *hates* a white face. I firmly believe this from the conduct of her whole life. Lord, if I judge wrong, forgive me.

3 February— . . . it has been my constant desire to make my negroes happy—& I am every now & then awakened to the fact that

they *hate* me—My God—My God—what are we to expect from slaves—when mine hate me as they do—it is nothing on earth but that I am *white* & own slaves—My Southern sisters & brothers who think their slaves would be on our side in a civil war will, I fear, find they have been artfully taken in. . . .

4 April—Our negroes are far more knowing than many will acknowledge. I had a little negro girl about the house to say to me the other day—'twas a sin for big ones like them to say sir to Mass Thomas & Mass Whitfield & little ones like them. . . . Now if black children have this talk what are we to expect from grown negroes? The same little girl has told me I did not know how negroes hated white folks & how they talked about me.

Writing to her sister in England on 12 August 1853, Matilda Lieber, wife of South Carolina College professor Francis Lieber, expressed a somewhat different view. In this instance, Matilda may have been basing her analysis largely upon experiences with hired servants. At that time, the Liebers apparently owned only two blacks, a forty-five-year-old female and a youth of sixteen. The general status of South Carolina slaves, in her opinion, had improved greatly during the last two decades, but improvement only sharpened dislike for their condition, "which the most informed amongst them fully understand and there are many who read, read the papers, and know all about the controversy in their behalf between the North and the South, that their condition of slavery is not sanctified by the whole union—yet I have no fear of them; they are so good natured—so grateful for any kindness shown them.[4]

But it was Keziah Brevard, a fifty-six-year-old widow who had to deal each day with scores of slaves, not just one or two, who gave voice to frustrations experienced by many of her Richland County neighbors in the 1850s. They did not like slavery nor did they like what it was doing to their society, but the matter seemed to defy solution. This was even more true once abolitionists and fire-eaters forced the slave into the political arena.

And how was slavery affecting the white population of Columbia and Richland County? For one thing, the proliferation of state laws and local ordinances during pre-war decades made every citizen a policeman and an informer, that is, if he or she actually obeyed these edicts. But, much like South Carolina College students and their rules, most local residents, be they white or black, simply ignored many of them.

The most important state statutes were a decision in 1820 to end emancipation, unless a slave was set free by an act passed by the General

Assembly itself,[5] and an 1834 law making it a crime to teach a slave to read or write.[6] Other statutes, such as those relating to patrol duty, slave passes or "tickets," the exclusion of blacks from certain occupations, and trafficking with slaves, were revised so frequently that it is obvious they were ineffective. The reasons why masters became so incensed when whites carried on commerce with their blacks were two-fold: (1) illicit buying and selling caused slaves to steal goods from the plantation, and (2) such trade often was conducted amid an air of camaraderie, especially if spirits were involved.

In the late 1850s, anti-trafficking fever soared to new heights with legislation that threatened anyone (except white females) with up to thirty-nine lashes if convicted of that crime. Subsequently, in even more ominous tones, lawmakers decreed that those guilty of circulating published or written material "calculated to disaffect any slave or slaves" were to be fined and imprisoned at the court's discretion. No penalty was spelled out, except a warning to free blacks that they might face corporal punishment.

At the local level, the first ordinance passed by Columbia authorities in 1806 stipulated that all blacks were to be home when the market bell rang at nine in the evening; but, for the most part, custom and state law regulated black life until 1851 when all town ordinances were re-written. The new rules included a comprehensive, fifteen-section litany concerning slaves and free persons of color. Some of these regulations applied only to slaves, others to all blacks. As one would expect, slaves once more were to be off the streets when the evening bell sounded and reside on their owner's property. They were not to become mechanics or pursue handicraft trades, be a clerk or sales person, purchase produce for re-sale, or keep a boarding house. All blacks were forbidden to gather in groups of five or more (except at funerals), unless a white person was present. Without the permission of town officials, they could not assemble for dancing or "merriment," and any such revelry had to cease by 1 A.M. Section 10 was perhaps the most interesting of these regulations.

> That any slave or free person of color who shall be found drunk, or shall otherwise misbehave, by acting in a noisy or boisterous manner, or by singing an indecent song or hallooing within the limits of said town, shall for each and every offence receive not exceeding one hundred lashes; and any slave or free person of color who shall smoke a segar in any street or in any open and public place in the town, or shall walk with a cane, club, or stick (except the lame, infirm, or

blind), shall for each and every offence receive not exceeding twenty lashes.

Throughout the remainder of the decade this network of rules was expanded and refined. In 1855, police were ordered to prevent blacks from assembling at military parades. The following year, both slaves and free blacks were forbidden to buy or sell cotton within the town limits without a permit, and any white person who bought cotton from them illegally might be fined twenty dollars. Police were told, if necessary, to search the homes and wagons of blacks in order to stamp out such traffic. Also, after 7 July 1856, no slave could be abroad after sundown without a pass for that date *and that date only.* (All militia members were supposed to ride patrol to be sure these and other measures were enforced.) A few months earlier, an all-inclusive ordinance stipulated that Columbia's blacks were not to play cards, shoot dice, gamble, or "otherwise offend against any law of this State." If convicted of such offenses, they might receive up to 100 lashes.

Life in the countryside was, of course, much simpler. It was the responsibility of each master to look after his slaves, and a patrol rode about from time to time to make sure slaves were where they were supposed to be. As a rule, patrols were most active in times of crisis; and, according to an essay by Belton O'Neall Townsend in the *Atlantic Monthly* (April 1877), members sometimes used their powers in vigilante fashion to exert social control over whites as well. Any upstart who threatened the plantation aristocracy might find his slaves whipped and mutilated, fences ruined, or crops damaged, all in an effort to hurt the property owner economically, a stern warning to mend his ways.

But much of the time patrol duty was a boring, onerous task that many whites tried to avoid. Some paid a small annual fee in lieu of participation; others simply failed to show up when called. In the summer of 1853, Dr. Samuel Leland stirred up a fuss when he refused to join a Mill Creek patrol on the Sabbath. Even when he did participate, Leland seems to have been eager to shield errant blacks from punishment, not apprehend them. The following March he noted in his diary that, while on patrol, he "saved a negro from a thrashing."

But the complexities of urban living, as ordinances of the 1850s reveal, presented countless dilemmas. No set of rules could control slaves who, after work, gathered in homes, churches, and grog shops where they often acquired new ideas and strange notions. There they were able to associate with free blacks (most of whom lived in cities) and white shopkeepers eager to sell them a variety of goods, including liquor.

The town was infinitely more exciting than the plantation, a greater variety of jobs was open to all blacks, and urban slaves usually were better treated. English lecturer J. S. Buckingham, who visited South Carolina in June of 1839, like most European visitors, thought rural slaves ill-clad, dirty, and miserable in appearance, while urban domestics presented a more pleasing picture. As he and his wife were approaching Columbia on the stage from Orangeburg, Mrs. Buckingham saw a gang of ragged blacks shuffling off to work at 4 A.M. and muttered "poor wretches." A fellow passenger immediately assured her that they were "among the happiest of human beings," and another berated English abolitionists for encouraging runaways. Fomenting a slave insurrection, they were told, was the British way of gaining revenge for the American Revolution . . . a view Buckingham said they heard on numerous occasions.[7]

And what occupations were open to urban blacks? According to the 1850 census, Columbia's free blacks were working as stable keepers, shoemakers, musicians, carpenters, tailors, cabinetmakers, and barbers. A decade later, a drayman, painter, gardener, teamster, huckster, railroad stewardess, cake maker, and numerous dressmakers, seamstresses, and washerwomen had been added to the list. Out in the county, virtually every free black household was somehow involved with farming, and most of them—there were only twenty-six in 1860—were clustered in a small enclave near Gadsden dominated by names such as Salmond, Jacobs, and Harris.

Under certain conditions, an ambitious Columbia slave could aspire to almost any occupation enjoyed by free blacks. Admittedly, he had to have a cooperative owner and some ability, but becoming a carpenter, musician, or barber was not an impossible goal. Slave Israel Smith, forty-eight years of age in 1860, was a successful carpenter with a free-born wife named Catharine. He had a shop of his own and for many years negotiated contracts. He acquired property in his wife's name and—except for paying his master twenty-five dollars a month—was virtually free. Smith, who could read and write, also was a musician in a local brass band.

Simon May's story was somewhat similar. An industrious slave carpenter and builder with a dressmaker wife (who was free), May took jobs on his own, hired workmen to help him, and also accumulated property in his wife's name. However, during the second year of the Civil War, his owner suddenly sold him, but his wife managed to gain his freedom by mortgaging their home.[8]

All of Columbia's barbers of the 1850s appear to have been black, and two of them are especially interesting. Alonzo Reese had a shop opposite the Congaree House on Main Street and, despite slave status, sometimes advertised his services in the *Daily Carolina Times*. It is unclear whether Alonzo or his master paid for this publicity. The other barber of note, an "almost white" free black, was the only member of his race listed in Columbia's 1859 city directory. Sam Glover, about fifty years of age and unmarried, also had a Main Street shop, but a year later he had disappeared, tarred, feathered, and run out of town because he allegedly became too familiar with a white woman.

Although no free black accumulated much wealth, in 1850 seven of them owned Columbia real estate worth $1,000 or more. Two of these individuals, carpenter Richard Holmes and stable keeper Jesse Rabb, also owned slaves. Holmes apparently was merely protecting a relative, perhaps his mother, a seventy-year-old female, but Rabb's two male slaves—ages thirty-two and fifty-five—obviously were laborers.

A decade later, only one free black, carpenter Green Guignard, was master of slaves. Guignard, the region's most prosperous black man, owned real estate valued at $5,000 and five slaves worth $4,000.[9] The two males and three females ranged in age from thirty-seven to fifty-two. Five other free blacks—two carpenters, a huckster, a musician, and a farmer—held real estate and personal property worth $3,500 to $8,000. The musician, Joe Randal, long a well-known figure throughout the Midlands, died two years later and named F. J. Moses of Sumter as executor of his estate. In retrospect, this was a revealing choice since the Moses family figured so prominently in South Carolina political life during Reconstruction; however, testimony before the Southern Claims Commission of the 1870s reveals that Columbia blacks knew who their friends were in the days of slavery, which men they could trust. When asked about the Union sympathies of John H. Heise, an ex-slave replied that he was "not one of that number."[10]

The most desirable vocations for blacks, whether slave or free, were in the building trades and music. One could earn a good living as a carpenter or mason, and the demand for musical entertainment—this community had no white musicians in these pre-war years—meant mobility. If a first-rate fiddler or banjo player, one's services were much in demand, and it was a simple matter to get passes to travel freely. And an adept young slave who was both bricklayer and musician is the key to one of the most intriguing sagas in local black-white history.

In 1820, James Wallace, a Jesuit priest born in Ireland in 1783, joined the South Carolina College faculty as a mathematics professor following brief stints at New York's Columbia College and Georgetown College in Washington D.C. Fourteen years later, when the faculty was restructured at the close of Thomas Cooper's administration, Wallace was not retained. No reasons were given, but perhaps it was because he was developing a black family, a phenomenon not unknown in many parts of the nation, North and South.

According to J. J. O'Connell's *Catholicity in the Carolinas and Georgia* (1879), Wallace "bore with fortitude the wintry blasts of a boisterous public life." Relieved of his obligations to the Society of Jesus, he moved to Lexington County and became something of a hermit. This one-time priest, in the words of O'Connell, "avoided all intercourse with the world and scarcely saw anyone but his confessor." A frugal man, he accumulated property that included three-and-one-half squares along the canal north of Gervais Street, valuable real estate indeed, and three houses located at the southwest corner of Gervais and Assembly streets. Columbia's slave census of 1850 lists James Wallace as the owner of four slaves—a female (forty-eight) and three young men (fifteen, twenty, and twenty-four)—who presumably lived in one of these structures. The following year, Wallace died and bequeathed his entire estate to the Catholic bishop in Charleston with instructions that it be used to found a male orphanage. This bequest, writes O'Connell, included slaves, "but the most valuable escaped to the Free States after his death."

Local newsman Julian A. Selby, author of *Memorabilia and Anecdotal Reminiscences of Columbia, South Carolina* (1905), reveals there is more to this tale, much more. By his will, Wallace granted freedom to his black family, but Catholic officials filed suit and got this provision annulled. At that juncture, Isaac Coleman, owner of facilities near the Catholic Church where circuses and other entertainments were held, became the "protector" of the Wallace boys. Coleman, an intelligent man who was reporter for the *Charleston Courier* during legislative sessions, also had fathered sons by a mulatto woman named Emma, but he sent them north to be educated where they, of course, remained. Under his guidance, these three young men acquired or perfected various skills, Andrew becoming a bricklayer, George, a barber, and James, a painter, and all of them became accomplished musicians as well. Then, in the mid-1850s (by this time Sarah, their mother, had died) Andrew obtained a four-day pass to play at an affair in Camden, but he failed to return. A decade later, Selby learned that he was living in Toronto, Canada. Shortly after An-

drew's departure, George and James disappeared . . . followed by Coleman himself.[11]

Needless to add, the world of slave and free, especially in an urban
setting, was becoming increasingly complex, and Selby's *Memorabilia* discloses yet another unexpected twist. When he was three, Selby and his
schoolteacher mother moved to Columbia from Charleston. In the boarding house where they lived, young Julian was much in demand; for, with
a white child by their side, the servants of that establishment could go
almost anywhere. Selby recalled that, as a result, he rarely missed any
momentous event, including the hanging of three negroes for the murder
of a Singleton overseer named McCaskill.

More important than the flight of the Wallace boys to the North and
young Julian Selby's presence at a triple execution was the changing nature of black-white relations during the middle decades of the 19th century. A cursory review of Columbia's ordinances and petitions to the state
legislature gives the impression that a legal network was getting ever
tighter. Some South Carolinians wanted to evict all free blacks from the
state or perhaps enslave them once more. Strange as it may seem, in the
late 1850s, at least three free blacks actually did institute legal proceedings to acquire masters. Just why is not known, but it would appear that
security of one sort or another was, in their eyes, more to be desired than
personal freedom.

Yet rules and regulations, as noted earlier, mean little if not enforced. Efforts to prevent Columbia's blacks from getting together (except
at funerals), "hallooing" in the streets, smoking "segars," and learning to
read and write indicate, not that the net was getting tighter, but that it
was full of holes that constantly had to be plugged. The state law against
circulation of material that might "disaffect" slaves was, in fact, tacit admission that some of them could read.

There also is evidence that a few Columbia slaves of the 1850s were
"passing" for free, perhaps with the connivance of their owners, if paid
enough. Israel Smith, who told federal officials in the 1870s that he had
been a slave until the end of the war, is listed as a free black in the 1860
census. Isaac Coleman's Emma is not among the town's free blacks in
1850, when she apparently was a resident, but is so listed ten years later.
Equally tantalizing are lists in Columbia's *Palmetto-State Banner* early in
1851 noting that among those who have mail waiting for them at the post
office are Alonso [sic] Reese and Emma Coleman. Since no other adults
in the immediate area had these same names (there was a white Emma
Coleman about one year old), it appears that a few privileged blacks, both

slave and free, were receiving mail, which helps to explain petitions to state legislators demanding that this practice cease.

This is no attempt to whitewash slavery, for it indeed was an evil, cruel system, and its horrors are well documented. J. F. Williams, author of *Old and New Columbia* (1929), lambastes one of the area's leading citizens, brickyard magnate John Kinsler, for the manner in which he treated his slaves . . . not that they were whipped or beaten, but because they were inadequately fed, housed, and clothed. As a result, writes Williams, they became a pest to the community, "the worst thieves in the country."

We are left, then, with a perplexing set of circumstances that raises many questions and provides few answers. The mobility of *all* segments of the population (even slaves), the dynamics of new religious faith, masters eager to make slaves happy, mistresses tormented by what servants thought of them, inter-racial relations day by day, free blacks, "virtually free" blacks, slaves "passing" for free—the picture becomes blurred and fuzzy for us today, and it must have been equally confusing for those who experienced this dilemma first-hand. The basic problem was that slaves were unlike any other form of property: regardless of rules and regulations, they exhibited and expressed *human* characteristics.

Thus at a time when neither slavery nor race could be defined satisfactorily, the criteria for social distinction became color. The local census taker recorded nearly all Negroes as black (B) in 1850, but ten years later many were classified as mulattoes (M). Subtle segregation was creeping into religious life, too. Sometime in the 1840s, Columbia's Presbyterians built a two-story lecture hall in the 1700 block of Sumter Street for Sunday School classes and prayer meetings. Whites used the top floor and blacks the bottom, reversing the normal, blacks-in-the-gallery routine. A Mr. Ladson, who was "catechizing" blacks in 1860 gave his name to Ladson Presbyterian Church that evolved there after the Civil War. In the 1850s, the Washington Street Methodists erected a similar building in the 1500 block of Sumter Street that, after 1865, became home to yet another black congregation, Bethel A. M. E. Church. Although both races used these halls, in the eyes of contemporaries they were "African" churches and are so designated on a map of the city drawn in 1860. Slavery, race, color. Unwittingly, Columbia, Richland County, and the rest of America were drifting toward segregation by the appearance of one's skin and into the age of Jim Crow.

Notes

1. The only exception would be 40,000 Africans legally imported between 1804 and 1807, many of whom remained in this state.
2. For details of this affair, see the *Columbia Telescope, South-Carolina State Gazette,* and the *Charleston Observer* (August-September 1833). At that time, the latter was publishing a series of articles with discussion questions entitled "Scripture Lessons for Coloured Persons."
3. Of course, any such traffic was illegal in 1860, although her half nephew, James Hopkins Adams (governor, 1854–1856), advocated re-opening that trade.
4. Lieber Papers, South Caroliniana Library. In September of 1859, two years after his parents moved to New York City, their son Oscar wrote to them from Columbia: "How negroes have risen in price! What with some carpentering that Henry has added to his accomplishments since you sold him, I am told he would fetch $1700." Francis Lieber often was accused of being an abolitionist at heart. Such sentiments—if they existed— obviously did not extend to Henry.
5. In 1823, a committee of the state Senate wanted to reward a Richland County slave for assisting in the capture of "outlaw Joe," a murderer. The group recommended that $700 be paid to a Mrs. Perrin, mistress of Royal, as soon as she set him free. Whether she ever did is not known.
6. As Matilda Lieber and others have indicated, this ban was not honored. James Stirling, who visited Columbia in 1857, said local slaves were holding evening classes at which, for $1 a month, they were teaching other slaves to read. See Stirling, *Letters from the Slave States* (London, 1857), pp. 295–96.
7. J. S. Buckingham, *The Slave States of America* (2 vols.; London, n.d.), II, pp. 6–8.
8. Data concerning Smith and May can be found in John Hammond Moore (editor), "South Carolina and the Southern Claims Commission, 1871–1880," pp. 237–41. Copies of this unpublished manuscript are available at the South Caroliniana Library and the South Carolina State Archives.
9. When Guignard died in 1865, he was mourned by the *Daily Phoenix* (22 October) as "a sober, respectful, and honest citizen."
10. Moore, "South Carolina and the Southern Claims Commission," p. 235.
11. Selby says that Andrew's fiancée, daughter of a prominent black carpenter named Lee, also fled to Canada. He describes Emma, the mother of Coleman's black progeny, and their daughter Maria as highly respected nurses. Maria married Charles Wilder, Columbia's postmaster from 1868 to 1885. Andrew and his family subsequently returned to Columbia where he became a successful bricklayer and contractor, dying in 1903, much beloved, at the age of seventy-seven. (See the *State*, 23 August 1903.) Isaac Coleman also returned after the war and served as a magistrate. According to the 1875–1876 city directory, Isaac H. Coleman, trial justice and coroner, was living at 72 West Plain Street; five years later, "Coleman Emma *c.*, wid of Isaac" was residing at 68 West Plain, the home of her daughter and son-in-law.

Columbia
at Mid-Century

CHAPTER EIGHT

Although older coastal cities such as Charleston, Savannah, and Wilmington were the Southeast's major urban centers during these decades, by 1850 Columbia had become a potent force in the region, thanks largely to its geograph-
ical position, the intellectual vitality of South Carolina College, and prominence as a state capital.[1] In that year, it had 6,060 inhabitants, a 40 percent increase over the 1840 figure (4,340) in contrast to only 8 percent growth for the state as a whole. Clearly, some country folk were moving to town, a trend that would accelerate in the future. In 1850 and again ten years later, Columbia (population 8,052 in 1860) was by far the largest in-land town in the Carolinas, its only rival being another seat of state gov-ernment (Raleigh), which at the outbreak of war was about half as large. However, South Carolina's capital had to share regional honors with several upland communities in Georgia. During the 1850s, Augusta (c. 12,000) was substantially larger than Columbia, while Macon was about the same size, and in that decade Atlanta and Columbus enjoyed booms that propelled them past both Macon and Columbia.

One cause of this sudden expansion was, of course, railroad trans-portation, an innovation that also was affecting life in the Midlands. Caught up in the mania of the 1830s, local businessmen tried unsuccess-fully to extend the tracks of the South Carolina Railroad's pioneer Charleston–Hamburg line to Columbia. However, in 1837, the Louis-ville, Cincinnati & Charleston Railroad acquired the right to build be-tween Branchville and Columbia, and in March of the following year a public celebration in front of the State House launched construction. Over a thousand people heard Robert Y. Hayne expound on the many benefits that the iron horse would bring and then watched as Hayne and railroad enthusiast Abraham Blanding each turned a symbolic shovel of dirt.

Although hard times frustrated the grand scheme to build all the way to the Ohio River, on 20 June 1842 the first passenger train from the coast pulled into Columbia's yet-to-be-completed depot at Gervais and Gadsden streets. Ten days later, this momentous event was marked by a huge barbecue attended by Charleston's Washington Light Infantry, the Richland Volunteer Rifles, various dignitaries from both communities, railroad officials, and some 5,000 citizens. Addressing this multitude, Columbia's intendant, William M. Myers, offered a toast that highlighted the theme of the day: "The metropolis and the capital: what man has magnificently joined together, surely God will protect against the ravages of time and the wars of the elements."

Robert W. Gibbes, editor of the *Carolina Planter*, wrote of more practical considerations. Now, for $7.25 one could be in Charleston in only twelve hours—breakfast at home, dinner in Charleston. In his opinion, rapid transportation soon would introduce shrimps, crabs, and other wonders of the deep to the upcountry, but the most immediate effects of new facilities that cost over $2.65 million were an increase in local property values and the development of business sites adjacent to tracks.

In the early 1850s, two more railroads—one to Charlotte and the other to Greenville—expanded Columbia's growing transportation network.[2] Both enjoyed strong local support, and the town fathers saw fit to invest $100,000 in the line to Charlotte and $60,000 in the one to Greenville. After some debate as to the site of a depot, the former began service in November 1852 from a station in the northeastern part of town at the intersection of Blanding and Barnwell streets. From that point, its tracks followed Laurens Street south, eventually turning to the southwest and merging with the South Carolina Railroad just below the town limits.

The Greenville connection   om the northwest, which joined the same railroad at its Gervais Street depot, began full operation a little over a year later in December 1853. Perhaps it should be noted that, during previous months, both railroads provided limited service to the "head of the line." In July of 1852, for example, travelers could ride twenty-two miles on the Greenville tracks and then connect with horse-drawn stages to Newberry, Laurens, and other communities in that region. And six months before that, similar connections were available at Winnsboro, that is, passenger service to that point and then a stage to Charlotte. Those arriving in Columbia by train could be transported to any part of town by an omnibus service operated by John Wells, fare twenty-five cents.

Little doubt exists that these rail lines, which linked Columbia with scores of towns other than Charleston, Greenville, and Charlotte, boosted the local economy in many ways, just as those that met at Atlanta helped that city grow. But, in time—especially after the Civil War— some Columbia residents began to question the wisdom of an investment that seemed to benefit the upcountry more than the Midlands. Boats and trains had lured to Columbia trade once centered in Charleston; and, in turn, Piedmont communities such as Greenville and Spartanburg discovered that, with rail lines, they could distribute goods once purchased in Columbia. As disturbing as these trends were, Columbians, like Charlestonians before them, really had no choice. Rejection of transportation facilities, even if their completion ultimately changed the nature of the local economy, was unthinkable.

Writing in the 1880s, bank cashier Edwin J. Scott recalled the relatively flush times of the 1840s and 1850s and alluded to the opposition of at least two leading citizens to railroad expansion. (Butcher Town and Cotton Town, which he mentions, were busy suburbs just north of town that specialized, obviously, in livestock and cotton.)

> The receipts of cotton, which reached a hundred and twenty thousand bales one year, and the live stock [sic] from Kentucky and Tennessee, made Columbia a lively place in the winter and employed all of the banking capital, amounting, after the opening of the Exchange Bank, to two and a half million. The present capital employed here in banking is less than one-tenth that amount. I have seen Main Street so crowded with wagons from the site of the present post-office to Butcher Town as to be almost impassable for carriages or gigs. Cotton Town was built up by the traffic in that staple with large grocery, provisions and storage establishments, which did a very extensive and profitable business till the completion of the up country railroads, contrary to our expectations, transferred this trade from Columbia to the towns and villages above. Thus our municipal and individual subscriptions to the stock in these roads, instead of benefiting Columbia, deprived her for a time of the main source of her prosperity and left her dependent upon the immediate neighborhood for support. This result was foretold by but two of our citizens—John A. Crawford and Stephen C. DeBruhl—who publicly opposed the subscriptions, and the latter afterwards boasted that they were the only sensible men in Columbia. But the spirit of progress was abroad in the land then and all opposition to its course proved useless.[3]

If Scott is correct, it would appear that Columbia was entering a period of economic stability, not rapid expansion, when war came. Railroads, much like canals, brought momentary benefits in the form of construction-related expenditures, and, temporarily at least, new markets. But the Midlands of those days lacked the network of little villages that dotted the upcountry, many of which soon were tied by railroad tracks to a chain of rival commercial centers stretching from Rock Hill to Anderson.

By 1854, two trains were leaving Columbia for Charleston each day at 7:15 A.M. and 4 P.M. Fare had dropped to four dollars, or only three cents a mile for intermediate travel. Blacks and whites usually rode separately, although Samuel Leland noted in his diary in September 1855 that a train he was on was so crowded that he "had to go into the Negro department." Travelers also could leave for Charlotte and Greenville early any weekday morning and for Edgefield in a two-horse coach on Tuesdays, Thursdays, and Saturdays. Within three years, service to Charlotte was increased to two trains a day, their arrival scheduled to connect with Charleston-bound traffic.

During this decade, the composition of Columbia's population changed little, the ranks of white and black growing apace, with whites slightly in the lead: 3,184 to 2,876 in 1850 and 4,395 to 3,657 in 1860. According to census rolls, free blacks increased from 196 to 314, although some of these individuals actually may have been rural residents. A comparison of 1860 returns with early city directories indicates that census taker Thomas P. Walker expended a minimum of energy that year. Instead of going from house to house in a systematic manner, Walker, for the most part, strolled through the business district recording storekeepers, clerks, black help, and perhaps an occasional lawyer and shopper wherever he encountered them. As a result, county folk occasionally were listed as city dwellers (and perhaps again in the county as well), a few Columbia residents also were cited twice, and a handful of names one would expect to find are missing entirely. These include, among others, free blacks Celia Mann and Bill Simons of Mann-Simons Cottage fame.

In 1850, free black households were nearly equally divided—sixty-eight in town and sixty-two in the country. Ten years later, according to Walker's returns, ninety-two such families lived in Columbia, while only twenty-six were in rural areas. As one would expect, the percentage of slave owners in both jurisdictions remained virtually unchanged, about half of all households reporting slaves. At mid-century, 360 of Columbia's 721 families owned blacks and nearly one hundred of them held ten or more. Artist William Scarborough, for example, owned fourteen; Episcopal clergyman Peter J. Shand, twenty; and Professor Maximilian LaBorde, twenty-nine. LaBorde had a large household (six sons and two

daughters aged two to twenty-three); however, most of his slaves undoubtedly were contracted to other masters, although a few probably
tended crops on his four-hundred-acre farm, seventy-three acres of which
were cultivated. And there still were thirteen small farms within the town
limits where slaves might work, as well as stores, businesses, and construction projects, and many of them easily could walk to nearby plantations each day. Thus it would appear that a substantial portion of
Columbia's slave population was "hired out" as agricultural, commercial,
or industrial labor.

Some, among them, Alonzo Reese, Simon May, and Israel Smith,
were "virtually free," existing much as they pleased so long as they
obeyed various ordinances and laws and paid their master or mistress a
small sum each month. Those who did not reside on their owner's property tended to live on the western or southern fringes of settlement, that
is, west of Assembly and south of the State House. The most impressive
mansions, the homes of the Hamptons, Prestons, and their friends, were
located in the northeastern quarter of the town.

Americans born outside of South Carolina were slightly more numerous in 1850 than immigrant stock, 474 to 366. Most had moved to Columbia from nearby states, were offspring of foreigners who tarried for a
time in northern ports, or were students at local institutions. North Carolina (85) led the list, followed by New York (80), Georgia (45), New Jersey
(40), Virginia (37), Pennsylvania (35), Alabama (31), and Connecticut (30).
A dozen other states, plus the District of Columbia, contributed a handful
of residents. Nevertheless, both groups—citizens from other states and
foreign-born—represented only a small portion of Columbia's total population at mid-century. Of the latter, Irish immigrants (168) were the most
numerous, followed by Germans (81) and English (73). Other foreign
homelands cited that year by census taker L. T. Levin were Scotland (19),
France (13), West Indies (4), Canada (2), and Denmark, Switzerland,
Sweden, Austria, Poland, and Spain, one each.

The small Irish community soon increased as the result of an influx
of stone cutters, masons, and sculptors hired to work on the new state
capitol building. According to the 1860 census, 107 of these skilled craftsmen were living in Columbia. Some brought families with them, while
others lodged in boarding houses. Ann Hislop had seven boarders in her
home at 234½ Richardson Street, and Cyrennius Loomis, who lived on
Pendleton Street between Sumter and Marion, had eleven.

These newcomers apparently were of little benefit to the town's tiny
Catholic enclave. Father O'Connell observed caustically in his history

that these workmen were only "nominally" of the faith and of no use whatsoever to his church. It is equally unlikely that these rough-and-tumble laborers had much to do with a local Hibernian Benevolent Society founded in March of 1851, an organization dominated by well-established businessmen. Some of the new Irish joined others who had created a small colony near the intersection of Greene and Gadsden streets, about three blocks southwest of the State House. Called "New Dublin," this little settlement was something of an outpost since the southern and western sections of the two-mile-square town were only partially occupied.

Richardson Street, often called "Main," and the only thoroughfare bearing numbers (from north to south, with odd numbers on the west side) was the heart of the business district. The blocks from Lady to Blanding, crammed with shops, were home to several hotels, a public market on the ground floor of the town hall, and the county's courthouse and jail.[4] By 1860, at least part of the city market had moved west to the center of Assembly Street, precursor of the famous "farmers' market" long associated with that area. Still farther west, the two railroad depots on Gervais or "Bridge" Street had begun to attract enterprises such as bars, boarding houses, and bordellos, though few of them found their way into early city directories. This region, at times called "Hell's Half Acre" or the "Holy Land," soon was the toughest section of the city.

And, after 1 April 1855, Columbia *was* a city, not a town, governed by a mayor and six aldermen, two from each of three wards. Three years later the community was divided into four wards, each represented by three aldermen.[5] However, except for substituting mayor and aldermen for intendant and wardens and increasing the authority to tax, the transition to city had little practical effect. In October of 1853, the principal town officers included a council clerk, a chief marshal and six assistants, the superintendent of the water works, a physician, overseer of streets, and keeper of the clock. To this group one might add the town's attorney, surveyor, and printer, as well as those responsible for public scales and the weighing of cotton. The council, which met on the first Monday of each month, was divided into committees that dealt with matters such as finance, public buildings, the alms house, free schools, and streets.

This arrangement changed little under the mayor-aldermen system, although expenditures increased substantially because of money spent to update the city's antiquated water system, in all, slightly over $100,000. This was, according to Mayor Allen J. Green, a necessary outlay that, to some degree, was balanced by funds invested in railroad stock. In his annual report of March 1860, Green boasted of numerous improvements made under his direction, including rock drains on many streets and a new town bell, which, he conceded, was "not, strictly speaking, all we could desire in tone." Major sources of revenue, in addition to real estate levies ($15,432.60), were taxes on merchandise sold in local stores and on slaves and horses, each of which brought in about $2,000 to $2,500. Water rents amounted to $5,252, while exemptions from street work for both whites and blacks earned the city $4,445. Patrol exemptions, on the other hand, produced much less, only $658.

Perhaps the most interesting part of Green's report card was his crime summary. Between March 1859 and March 1860, 650 slaves, 234 whites, and 40 free blacks were confined in the city guard house on Washington Street. The leading slave offenses were being out after hours (121) and having differences with owners who asked that they be locked up (182)—an indication that the frustrations experienced by Keziah Brevard were not unique. Gaming, running away, fighting, and insolence landed others behind bars, although only three slaves ran afoul of the smoking-in-the-street ordinance. Being drunk and disorderly were the principal crimes of whites (186) and free blacks (19).

In addition to marshals (called policemen after 1855, none of whom wore uniforms or badges), Columbia had several volunteer fire companies. At the beginning of the decade there were three such groups: the Independent Fire Engine Company, Monteith's Fire Engine Company, and the Hook and Ladder and Ax Company. Any free black or slave (with his master's permission) could join the engine brigades, but not the hook-ladder-ax crew. As such, he was exempt from street work and head tax (if slave), received five dollars a year, and shared in the liquor when a jug and cup were passed around during a conflagration. The names of these companies changed slightly during the 1850s—Monteith's becoming the Palmetto Fire Engine Company and the hook-and-ladder group, the Phoenix Hook and Ladder Company—and a city-sponsored contingent appeared with black firemen and white officers, the Vigilant Fire Company. Each had an engine house that served as social center and site for monthly meetings, and all (except the Vigilants) owned their engines.

Although a disastrous fire that destroyed twenty-nine stores and dwellings in April of 1842 stimulated reform efforts, it is unclear just how effective these men were in times of crisis. If only a few structures were involved, they apparently could contain the blaze. In the summer of 1858, an early morning fire engulfed a stable, house, and blacksmith shop on Sumter Street. According to the *Daily Southern Guardian* (31 July), visiting firemen from Charleston performed brilliantly, even though their engine had to be removed from a railway car. In addition, the *Guardian* had praise for the Independents and noted that "the colored company also did good service." The following year, the Palmetto unit acquired a Rhode-Island-built engine that could throw a stream of water horizontally over 200 feet.

Traditionally, fires and hangings were the best free shows in town, but during the 1850s and, as it turned out, for several decades to come, construction going on at the State House grounds provided stiff competition. On 15 December 1851, the cornerstone of a new capitol was laid, a move prompted by fears that the original structure was an unsafe depository for state records. Three years later the old building was moved slightly to the southwest so work could proceed, but shortly after that the recently laid foundation was discovered to be defective. Amid great consternation, the original architect was sacked and plans were revised by John R. Niernsee, a talented German immigrant living in Baltimore. At length, the new brickwork was torn down at considerable cost, and the building erected so as to face north-south, not east-west as originally projected. Also, in the process, Richardson Street (Main) was closed off to create more spacious grounds, thus destroying Russell's Garden, a favorite haunt of local citizens for many years and a horticultural facility that supplied plants and shrubbery for scores of homes.

Until war stymied these efforts, the task of transporting great blocks of granite from quarries near Granby to the construction site and then cutting them into slabs was an awesome spectacle. Iron tracks were laid from the river to the capitol over which teams of horses hauled the stone. Most of the quarry work was done by slaves, while white workmen cut and shaped the granite on the State House grounds. At the site itself there are hints of racial tension. Letters to the *Daily South Carolinian* in the summer of 1854, hot on the heels of ads seeking "white and colored carpenters," talk vaguely of unrest among local mechanics, even of mob action. This, of course, should be no surprise since white workmen always were wary of competition from slaves and free blacks. In any case, from the mid-1850s to the outbreak of war, 375 to 500 men, about 60 percent of them black, were at work on the new capitol. Put in perspective, this means that one out of every five or six adult males in the community depended, to some degree, upon this project for his bread and butter.

Other changes on the local scene included facilities on the northern limits of the city for the first state fair (1856), a few street lamps on the busiest streets, and a rather magnificent little park just north of the

Catholic Church between Assembly and Lincoln streets. The fair, out-growth of an "institute" first held in Charleston in 1849, was the result of the combined efforts of the South Carolina Agricultural Society, state authorities, and city officials. In time, despite a hiatus in the 1860s, it would become a premier event each autumn of political and social significance, as well as a meeting place for farmers, their wives, skilled craftsmen, and innumerable manufacturers of everything from ploughs and ox yokes to iron beds, stoves, and bricks.

In February 1851, the *Palmetto-State Banner* complained bitterly of Columbia's "ill-paved and unilluminated streets." Travelers getting off the Charleston train, the editor said, might well think they were alighting in Branchville by mistake. The problem was, in his opinion, that each shop-keeper thought only of his own welfare, not of that of the community as a whole. This was, he stressed, a form of "false" economy. Admittedly, maintenance of streets and roads was a never-ending battle throughout the 19th century, a struggle that nature usually won; however, creation of a local gas company and work on the new state capitol conspired to alle-viate Columbia's night-time gloom. Perhaps in response to editorial crit-icism, in August of 1851 the town council agreed to grade Richardson Street and add granite curbing. Members also voted to purchase street lights of post-and-iron-frame construction at a cost of $6.75 each, while specifying that lighting costs overall could not exceed $1,000 per annum. Within a few years, state officials decided to assume responsibility for il-luminating the enlarged capitol grounds, and the city was able to erect lamp posts throughout much of the business district, especially Richard-son and Sumter streets, and in front of most churches.

Sidney Park, carved out of hillsides near the city water supply and close by the house once occupied by John Taylor, has a tortured and ironic history. In the late 1840s, Virginia native Algernon Sidney Johnston, a warden of the town, launched a campaign to create a place of quiet beauty in and around the water works. Johnston, an editor and printer by trade, initiated the planting of shrubbery and flowers and the construction of roads and paths. In the words of Edwin Scott, what had been "a nuisance and eye-sore" was transformed into "a place of pleasant and healthful re-sort." Following Johnston's sudden death in September 1852, the town council named his creation "Sidney Park" and continued to lavish atten-tion upon it. Soon this four-block area was a favorite retreat of scores of citizens and the site of Fourth of July fireworks each year.

Decades later, in June 1899, the Seaboard Air Line Railroad an-nounced that it wanted the park for terminal facilities, hinting broadly that, if rebuffed, it would take its tracks and business elsewhere . . .

Swansea perhaps. In an age when railroad smoke equaled progress, the city complied, despite protests from a few citizens with respect for history and tradition. Nevertheless, Sidney Park, for several generations known as "Seaboard Park," was destined to reappear.

Directly or indirectly, in 1850 virtually all of Columbia's commercial and economic activity was related to cotton. That was the community's life blood. Rail lines that reached here in the early 1840s and then crept into the Piedmont a decade later were searching first and foremost for cotton bales, not passengers. Even the construction on the State House grounds and Algernon Sidney Johnston's pioneer "city beautiful" movement, in the final analysis, depended upon those fluffy white balls. Profits from cotton sales supported merchants, lawyers, doctors, bankers, and several small industrial establishments. If cotton was "sluggish" or "low," everyone suffered. Bills and taxes went unpaid, children were enrolled at less expensive schools or not at all, and gowns and frock coats began to show signs of wear. But when cotton was "high," Columbia took on the aura of an extravagant boom town.

The only challenge to the reign of cotton was a short-lived but vigorous trans-Appalachian livestock trade (cattle, horses, mules, and especially hogs) that created Butcher Town just north of the corporate limits. Until rail lines connected Columbia to Greenville, the state capital was the focus of numerous winter drives from Kentucky and Tennessee, and records of the South Carolina Railroad indicate that, beginning in the mid-1840s, a substantial number of animals were transported to the coast. But this commercial activity created problems, and in 1851 Columbia's town council passed an ordinance prohibiting passage of large herds of animals through the community. However, within two years Greenville became "head of the line," and with that mantle came the honor of dealing with hundreds of cows and pigs each fall and winter.

Basic to most of these local transactions in cotton and cattle were three banks established during the first half of the 19th century—a branch of the Bank of the State of South Carolina (1812), the Commercial Bank of Columbia (1831), and the Exchange Bank (1852). All existed under state charters that permitted them to issue paper currency in denominations from $5 to $100. Only the so-called Branch Bank was authorized to print smaller bills of one to four dollars and even invade what we now think of as coinage, notes of five, ten, twenty-five, fifty, and seventy-five cents.

Edwin Scott, who became cashier of the Commercial Bank in 1852, describes in his *Recollections* how business was conducted from day to day: "In the fall and winter months we assisted in moving the crops by advancing purchasers of cotton for their drafts, generally at thirty days' date, upon Charleston factors of good standing; whose acceptances were met at maturity from sales of the produce. When the winter was over we loaned freely to approved planters on six months' time, in anticipation of their crops. The law limited the rate of bank interest to one per cent. per annum, and we observed it strictly."

Scott also relates how his bank collected for Kentucky banks that advanced loans to drovers and tells of a unique, but highly profitable arrangement with Mississippi's Columbus Insurance Company. Since that state had abolished all banks following the panic of 1837, its citizens depended upon currency issued elsewhere—in this instance, Columbia, South Carolina. The insurance company, according to Scott, "borrowed our bills in large amounts and used them in advancing to the neighboring planters on their crops, taking drafts upon their factors in Mobile and New Orleans, which were forwarded to banks in those cities." In short, this was the same system used locally, but with one distinct advantage. The notes that Scott's Commercial Bank sent to Mississippi circulated at distant points for a long period of time, all the while earning interest, until at length forwarded to Columbia by collecting banks at a considerable discount.

As in all agricultural communities throughout the nation, Columbia's industrial production on the eve of the Civil War was limited to a handful of items, most of them necessities or associated with field and forest. An 1850 census survey, which included only industrial establishments turning out goods each year valued at $500 or more, listed twenty-two such operations within the town limits. Only three of them had, on average, more than ten employees—a sash and planing mill and two carriage manufacturers.

The carriage and wagon makers, Richard S. Pomeroy and John C. Thornton, had the most money invested and by far the most valuable output. Pomeroy told census-taker Levin that his twelve workmen, paid a total of $200 a month, built 150 vehicles worth $13,000 in the year ending June of 1850. Thornton's seventeen employees produced wagons, carts, and carriages valued at twice that figure, but he failed to disclose how many were constructed. Two mills turning out window sashes, blinds, and doors and William Preston's foundry were the only establishments powered by steam, all of the others relying for energy upon horse, water, or man. Four grist mills that ground corn appear to have been extremely profitable ventures. Jacob Geiger, for example, had only $1,000 invested in his water-powered mill; but, with the aid of a single helper paid twenty-five dollars a month, he claimed that he produced meal and flour worth $9,960 in 1859–1860. However, since grist mills traditionally ground grain and corn on shares for various farmers—that is, grinding so much and taking a percentage as payment—this sum may represent the value of Geiger's total output and thus be somewhat misleading.

Other establishments of special significance included James Boatwright's small factory turning out cotton gins and corn shellers and Patrick Flannigan's shoe shop, each of which had six workers. (The latter claimed he annually turned out 4,000 pairs of boots and shoes worth $6,500.) In 1850, Columbia also had two bakers, a confectioner, tinner, bookbinder, saddler, wood craftsman, saw mill owner, and blacksmith who were classified as "industrialists." Wood worker Joseph Long stated that, with the aid of an assistant, he had produced 170 washing machines worth $850 in the twelve months preceding the census. During the same period, James S. Anderson's saw mill turned out 350,000 feet of plank valued at $3,700, and Alexander Keenan—the only blacksmith to break into the "manufacturer" class—fashioned iron frames, horseshoes, and wagon parts worth $1,200.

Then, in 1852, James Boatwright joined William Glaze in an ambitious plan to produce weapons. According to the *States-Rights Republican* (24 May), the two men had invested $45,000 in an armory that already had orders from the state for 6,000 muskets, 2,000 rifles, 2,000 pistols, and 2,000 sabres at an estimated cost of $130,000. *DeBow's Review* (June 1853) had special praise for this "gun factory," which it said was going full tilt—"it is a fine building, of handsome proportions, and is situated on the top of a very high hill on the west side of town near the residence of Mrs. Taylor. The machinery is all of the most perfect description, the engine an admirable piece of work of Charleston manufacture—and all of the parts of the arms they make, rifles, muskets, pistols, and sabres, are made within the building in the most perfect manner." However, like other brave efforts, this factory had a brief existence, perhaps because of the death of Boatwright a few years later. By 1859, Glaze had abandoned guns and converted the operation into the Palmetto Iron Works, which produced steam engines, sugar mills, and iron railings.

This summary of industrial life in 1850 does not, of course, cite mechanics and workmen whose annual output was worth less than $500, nor does it include Columbia's newspapers, which, strictly speaking, were not industrial products. The town had two well-established daily newspapers in 1850—the *Daily South Carolinian* and the *Daily Telegraph*—each of which also issued tri-weekly editions. Within two years, the *Daily South*

Carolinian had acquired both the *Telegraph* and the weekly *Palmetto-State Banner*, which became the *Columbia Banner*, the *South Carolinian's* weekly edition. The *States-Right Republican*—a daily and tri-weekly established in July of 1850—ceased publication in the summer of 1852, soon after the first fury of secession excitement subsided.

In 1853, the *Daily Carolina Times* appeared to challenge the *South Carolinian*, and four years later a third newspaper entered the ring, the *Daily Southern Guardian*, bearing the masthead motto: "The South—Equality or Independence." And, in January 1859, yet another daily was launched, the *Carolina Bulletin*; however, finding the field too crowded, four months later it moved on to Charlotte, North Carolina. Of course, the real competition during these years was the Charleston press, which often hired special correspondents when the legislature was in session and frequently provided information not found in local papers.

Although nearly all of these Columbia newspapers tried to produce dailies, tri-weeklies, and weeklies, the four-page editions they turned out were long on advertising and short on news, much of it copied from other publications and often having no relevance to the local scene whatsoever.[6] Also, in an age when outspoken editors found themselves challenged to duels, most eschewed controversy. On 15 April 1851, for example, the *Palmetto-State Banner* printed an intriguing item about a brawl in a Richardson Street store involving two prominent citizens, Jesse E. Dent and R. P. Mayrant. The latter apparently attacked Dent (soon to be sheriff) with a pocket knife, whereupon Dent hit his assailant in the head with a hammer. The *Banner* promised more details the following week, but none were forthcoming.

One can discern perhaps three general themes in the day-to-day life of Columbia during these years: religion and temperance (so closely allied that they really constitute a single item), organization, and "southern-ness." These factors often were intertwined and frequently an outgrowth, quite frankly, of urban conditions that demanded some degree of regulation—or *organization*—to make such an existence tolerable. A drinking spree on a lower Richland plantation, whether in a slave cabin or up at the big house, disturbed relatively few people, but a similar gathering in town that might keep scores awake was quite another matter.

The growth of religious faith with its emphasis upon morality, Sunday school, and correct behavior for both races was perhaps the most striking change on the local scene during the first half of the 19th century. An essentially hedonistic, live-and-let-live attitude was supplanted in only two or three decades by what was ostensibly a strict and often intolerant moral code. In the 1820s, no celebration marking the Fourth of July or the birthday of George Washington was complete without free-flowing liquor and innumerable toasts. Thirty years later the Sons of Temperance (who really advocated abstinence) dominated such affairs and toasts were a thing of the past.

Garrulous Anne Royall, who visited Columbia for three days in 1830, had high praise for the community. It was, she wrote, a beautiful town not excelled by any other she had seen in her travels. Her quarters at the United States Hotel were "elegant," and the citizenry, "industrious, polite, and hospitable." But, she added, "I saw no ladies. I suspect they were at church, for notwithstanding this is the residence of the celebrated Dr. Cooper, the blue-skins here are as thick as yellow-jackets."[7]

German historian Friedrich, Baron von Raumer, who came to Columbia on the Charleston train on 10 May 1845, was stunned by a sermon he heard three days later. The preacher, probably a Presbyterian, was so certain of his facts that von Raumer concluded he was virtually an "assistant-ruler" in heaven. All angels, he was told, were students of church history, God instituted representative government (the *only* good government yet devised), every man bears the original sin of Adam, and each individual hates God and is impassive concerning his or her own conversion.[8]

During succeeding years, more and more of the "art" exhibitions seen in Columbia halls, collections of popular paintings and panoramic views, were Biblical in nature. A display in March of 1854 consisted of scenes from Bunyan's *Pilgrim's Progress*, and on 20 October of that same year (a Friday) stores were closed in observance of a locally proclaimed Thanksgiving Day, a religious holiday.

In time, this religiosity found its way into new local ordinances and attempts to enforce regulations already enacted. Blue laws concerning taverns, gambling, billiard tables, and houses of prostitution long had been on the books. How often they were invoked is quite another matter, but in June of 1856 a dozen shopkeepers faced twelve-dollar fines for being open on the Sabbath. Yet in a response quite typical, city authorities merely warned those found guilty to change their ways and not break the Sunday-closing law in the future.

There were those who did not embrace this new morality, at least not wholeheartedly. Their ranks included Irish laborers, college students, sand hillers, some merchants (especially purveyors of spirits), many blacks, and even a few women of secure social standing. Soon after a new German brewery opened on upper Richardson Street in May of 1860,

Oscar Lieber told his parents, with great glee, that Mrs. John Singleton and her daughters drove up in their carriage and purchased six bottles of beer. "I think that shows a most praiseworthy boldness, for I scarcely know another lady in Columbia who would have done the same." Then there were church-going Baptists, Methodists, and Presbyterians who paid only lip service to this reform wave, as well as militia members whose monthly musters often degenerated into drunken brawls and those seeking public office.

Samuel Leland, writing in his diary on 7 October 1854, told of just such a gathering near his Mill Creek home. A muster day crowd had anticipated that Colonel Hampton would provide a barbecue in preparation for an upcoming election, but only liquor appeared, no food. After part of the group had left, drinking began in earnest and Leland went home in disgust. "I suppose that Richland Dist., without any exception is the most thoroughly *corrupt* place in the United States. The inhabitants, for the most part," he observed, "sell their votes with such unblushing affrontery. The candidates do not even trust those they bribe, but only pay them after they are seen to vote by some responsible person."

Much earlier, such practices had given rise in Columbia to what was known as the "bull pen" system. Opposing factions literally corralled qualified voters in pens a few days before the close of a hotly contested campaign, plied them with food, liquor, and perhaps women, and then, at the appointed time, marched them off to the polls. Many of these individuals were sand hillers who came to town eager to pick up a few dollars, have some fun, and perhaps cast a ballot or two. "Old Joe Medlin, Charles Manning, some of the Goingses, and others," according to Edwin Scott, "made enough by the election [of 1840] to support their families for a year."[9]

Of course, this represents a form of organization, quite an effective one, and the same sort of coordination was increasingly apparent in almost every phase of local life, be it political, religious, social, or educational. By 1860, those interested in uniforms and martial music could choose among no less than eight local military units: the Volunteer Battalion, Richland Volunteer Rifles, Governor's Guards, Richland Guards, Emmet Guards, Columbia Artillery, Richland Light Dragoons, and South Carolina's 23rd Regiment. In addition to the Sons of Temperance and the Sons of Malta,[10] those so inclined could join any of seven Masonic lodges and three groups of Odd Fellows. There was also a Burns Club, a Sunday School Society, and a prestigious new private library, the Columbia Athenaeum.

The Athenaeum, largely the creation of onetime senator and college president William C. Preston (who donated his 1,600-volume library), opened in 1856 in the upper floors of a building located at the corner of Richardson and Washington streets. The intent was to create not only a library, but a place where city leaders could meet, talk, and listen to lectures. But members also opened their doors to the general public at times. In May 1857, for four nights one could view *two* spectacular exhibits at the Athenaeum: "Dr. Beale's Grand Illuminated Historic Voyage of Dr. Kane's Arctic Explorations," plus the siege, bombardment, and evacuation of Sevastapol. The charge was fifty cents for adults; twenty-five cents for children and servants.

At least two professional associations were formed in 1851—one by twenty typographers and the other by a group of teachers. The latter soon expired, but the typographers developed a potent organization determined to protect its rights. The motivation for this action apparently was a tendency of local publishers to hire temporary typesetters for "fat" work during legislative sessions, much to the distress of regular employees thus deprived of extra income.

Reverence for all things southern, a third discernible trend, expressed itself in ways well-known such as excessive praise of cotton culture and slave society, an abhorrence of abolition and crass Yankee ways, and threats to secede from the Union and go it alone. At times, this adulation went to extreme lengths. Robinson & Elrod's "Great Southern Circus," which brought its troupe of animals and performers to Columbia in November of 1851, assured the public that a musical chariot featured in the traditional street parade was drawn by twenty superb horses, all of them "raised in the South." (This assertion may have been designed to counteract frequent charges that traveling shows harbored individuals who encouraged slaves to run away or had links to the underground railroad and emancipation societies.)

As North-South animosities increased, few Columbia residents dared to discuss abolition openly or in a rational manner. In an undated letter written in the mid-1850s, William C. Preston told his friend Waddy Thompson that everyone actually disapproved of the proposal of Governor James Adams to re-open the slave trade; but, fearing their words would be misinterpreted, they kept silent. "In truth," he wrote, "we are under a reign of terror and the public mind exists in a panic." As hostilities loomed, at least two citizens were whipped, tarred, feathered, and run out of town because of alleged abolitionist sympathies. One was a stone cutter named Powell, the other a well-known businessman, Phineas

F. Frazee, who had purchased John Thornton's buggy business. Frazee, whose son died in Confederate gray, returned to Columbia after the war and for a time served as sheriff of Richland County.

In the spring of 1860, Edward G. Mason, a Yale undergraduate, visited Charleston and then Columbia, where he came face to face with a truly bizarre (and eye-catching) expression of "southern-ness." According to Mason, a Yankee, students at South Carolina College, as a patriotic gesture, had vowed to wear only fabrics made in this state. However, the supply of shoddy blue cloth woven locally for poor whites (probably at Saluda Mill in Lexington County) soon was exhausted.

> The only other dry goods actually manufactured in the State were some cheap and gaudy calicoes, intended for negro wear; and of these the crazy youngsters ordered whole suits of clothes. The effect was actually astounding. Here would go one youth, striped like a barber's pole, and glowing like a meteor in his fiery red and yellow garb; there, another, completely covered with bright green leaves upon an intensely blue background; yonder, two abreast, clad in patterns of gigantic vines and flowers; then, a whole company, arrayed from head to foot in the most startling colors, diversified with the most singular figures.[11]

Despite the strange ways this southern spirit had of manifesting itself—whippings, weird costumes, adulation of local culture, and denigration of virtually everything else—there was a positive side to this phenomenon as well. Divorced momentarily from politics and hyperbole, concern for the southern way of life could become constructive criticism coupled with suggestions for change.

Residents of fourteen states, including New Jersey and New York, competed for premiums at the first state fair held in Columbia in November of 1856. The principal speaker, Greenville's durable Benjamin F. Perry, chose the occasion to once more chastise South Carolina for its inordinate dependence upon one crop. Any agriculturalist, he said, should be able to grow enough food to feed his family and his livestock. South Carolina planters did neither and, as a result, the state was "positively poor" when compared with others. South Carolina's schools and colleges, he insisted, should be teaching the "mechanical arts" so as to foster manufacturing and industry. Then, in words Henry Grady would repeat three decades later, Perry uttered his plea for a "New South."

> When we sit down to eat, it is altogether probable that the table at which we are seated has been made in Europe or the Northern

States. The cloth which covers the table comes from abroad; the knives and forks, the cups and saucers, the plates and dishes, and every article of convenience on the table, is of foreign manufacture. When we ride out, either in our carriages or on horseback, we find again our dependence upon the North for the carriage, the harness, bridles, saddles, and blankets. If we are seated in our parlors, the same dependence stares us in the face, from the carpet to the window curtains. The very chairs we sit in, the bedstead on which we sleep, are from the North. If we look in a mirror, we see ourselves reflected by the mechanical skill and art of a Northern man. Shall this dependence continue? Can South Carolina bear up any longer under such a state of vassalage? Is it not time to divert a portion of our energy, industry, skill, capital and wealth, towards the achievement of real independence?[12]

For Perry, the answer was obvious. In his opinion, South Carolina's planters and farmers were little more than "overseers for the manufacturers and mechanics of the North! They plant the earth, and till it, and give to the Yankees its surplus products!" Perry even dared to compare his native state unfavorably with that fountainhead of abolition: Massachusetts. Nevertheless, he quickly balanced praise for the Bay State's industrial diversity with a stern defense of slavery. "Instead of assailing this Southern institution," he said, "the North ought to defend and protect it." Slave labor made cotton cheaper and provided that region with sugar, rice, tobacco, and wheat. These commodities gave employment to at least three million Yankee factory workers. The attack on slavery was, in his view, "a short-sighted policy, which seeks to check the political strength of the South. Its friends have never looked beyond the result. The religious fanaticism of the North has been enlisted in this crusade, until it has become formidable, and threatens to involve the whole country, North and South, in one common ruin!"[13] Thus kind words for slavery, a few jabs at the North, and an ode to "southern-ness" had to accompany any criticism of the local way of life, no matter how cautiously phrased.

But the fair was a new phenomenon, and those who heard Perry speak paid little heed to his plea for economic change. After all, this was but one of many events that dictated the ebb and flow of social life in the Palmetto State's capital at mid-century. Others, some of them already mentioned and much better established than the fair, included various political, educational, and religious gatherings, sale days at the courthouse, barbecues, fires, circuses, hangings, tournaments, militia musters, picture exhibitions, lectures, theatrical shows, meetings of fraternal orders, and, of course, holidays.

The most important holidays were patriotic in nature, Washington's Birthday and the Fourth of July, yet others such as Valentine's Day, May Day, Thanksgiving, and Christmas were beginning to gain some following. By the 1850s, valentines were being sold in local stores, schools were closed on May Day, and the Leland family, for one, had adopted the custom of having a holly Christmas tree, although some thought this smacked of "popery." Thanksgiving, as noted, still was a local affair celebrated late in October.

Any large indoor gathering usually was held at the college or in one of the auditoriums in the business district—American Hall, an annex to the American Hotel at Main (Richardson) and Blanding, Kinsler's Hall at Main and Taylor, often the site of lodge meetings, the Town Hall above the old public market on the west side of Main at Washington, and the Athenaeum in the upper floors of a building on the east side of the same intersection.

American Hall, for example, was host to General Tom Thumb, who in February 1851 appeared with the equipage given to him by Queen Victoria. Three years later, in January 1854, violinist Ole Bull and soprano Adelina Patti graced the same stage, and a short time after that a Washington's Birthday ball was held there. (On 11 May 1854, ex-President Fillmore, with little or no fanfare, spent the night at the American Hotel.) And in December of 1856, for two nights one could watch the antics of a troupe of "educated" dogs, monkeys, and goats brought to American Hall by Signor Donnetti and Colonel Wood. During these same years, a painting of De Soto discovering the Mississippi (later erected in the rotunda of the U.S. Capitol) was shown at the Town Hall, together with portraits of novelist Alexander Dumas and Algerian leader Abd-el-Kader, and in November of 1860 an opera company performed *Lucia de Lammermoor* and *La Traviata* at Kinsler's Hall. Another center for meetings, notably the Secession Convention in December 1860, was the First Baptist Church, a handsome structure erected in 1858. This building is the work of Columbia's first resident architect, George Edward Walker (1826–1863), who also designed the Lace House and the mansion that now is home to South Carolina's governors.

In the southern tradition, much entertaining was done at home. James Henry Hammond describes in his diary an all-male supper hosted by Professor Lieber in February 1841 that began at 8 and ended between 10 and 11. The fare consisted of turkey, duck, tongue, fish with truffles, and potatoes, followed by salad (an unusual winter treat), all washed down with sherry, hock, and wine. Dessert was a mulled claret with rum, "sweet and sickening stuff," according to Hammond. Suppers, he noted, cost less than dinners and were less formal.[14] This well-known figure, who soon would become governor, also recorded numerous evenings spent playing backgammon and smoking cigars and complained often of the vapid, inane conversation of some of Columbia's leading citizens, men who talked only of scandal.

Outdoor activities could take many forms such as hunting, fishing, horseback riding, cockfights, tournaments, ice skating on Fisher's Pond, a punch-up between youths living south of the State House and those who lived north of it, and similar free-for-alls among college students, "townies," and "powder monkeys" (Arsenal Academy cadets), as well as a Congaree cruise or a swim. Beginning in 1854, one also could clean up with hot and cold showers at the rear of the telegraph office between 6 A.M. and 10 P.M. each day, twenty-five cents per shower or a dozen for two dollars. And in December 1860, the Columbia Cricket Club was staging practice sessions at the college; however, it is not known whether any matches were played.

Each spring various military units held outings at nearby resorts such as Lightwood Knot Springs, but, except for the fair, the outdoor gathering that drew the biggest crowd was a horse race. Even before Columbia came into being, meets were being held here, and by mid-century this community was an important stop for various stables as they moved their horses south each year from Baltimore to New Orleans. These races, usually held in December and January, coincided with college commencement and sessions of the General Assembly. Although there were several tracks, the best known was that used by the Columbia Jockey Club (organized in 1828) located just east of town on land now owned by the Epworth Children's Home.

Sights that one could see about town were varied indeed—Charlie Logan, Mike Sharpe, and Alexander Forsythe with a fresh lot of slaves to be sold at the courthouse or an old man named Motley, a county resident, setting out with his hounds to track down a runaway. Sand hillers often appeared peddling blackberries, sassafras, mocking birds in cages (twenty-five cents), and small loads of firewood. Since hogs and other animals roamed pretty much at will, yard fences were common and trees not enclosed were boxed.

After April of 1851, matrons shopping downtown could partake of cakes, tarts, and French confections in an apartment "fitted up expressly for Ladies" at McKenzie's Ice Cream Saloon, 134 Main Street. And in the evening, unknown to them perhaps, their daughters might drive down "Lovers' Lane," a double row of trees stretching from Mill Creek to Bluff Road. According to Julian Selby, this extensive jaunt presumably was reserved for engaged couples. He notes in his *Reminiscences*, "The engaged young woman who did not enjoy one or more trips over this famous twelve-mile ride—down the Mill Creek Road to the Hampton private road, through his grounds to 'Millwood' and 'Woodlands,' then over the Bluff Road to Columbia again—would think she had been 'left out in the cold.' "

There are indications that Columbia was becoming something of a winter resort in the 1850s. Alexander Taggart McGill, a Pennsylvanian who taught at Columbia Theological Seminary during the 1852–1853 term, on 3 February told his wife (who remained in the North) that "quite a concourse of strangers . . . from Philadelphia, New York, Boston &c." was in town, attracted, he thought, by pine woods and sand hills that were said to promote good health. "One thing is nearly certain to my mind, that, if you come to Columbia, you will not be willing to leave it again. It is just the place for you," he wrote. "Its charming walks and gardens, delightful circles of female society, balmy climate, fattening foods, and ebony hands to dress it, will take such a hold of your local attachment that you will refuse to move, any more. Are you then prepared, to become permanently identified with the South in general, and South Carolina in particular?"[15]

There was, in the daily routine that so charmed McGill, a certain rhythm. From October to May of each year, Columbia bustled with activity. Wagons filled with cotton clogged the streets, lawmakers and stage shows came to town, South Carolina College and various schools held public exercises, business was brisk, and both races enjoyed parades and holiday celebrations. As the mercury soared in June, however, the humidity stifled much of this activity, and those able to do so fled to the sand hills and the mountains. Until the cool breezes of autumn ushered in another round of parties, sales, concerts, and lectures, only the traditional Fourth and fireworks at Sidney Park broke the steamy monotony.

But the fall of 1860 was different, and so were the winter months that followed. The air was charged with the high drama of political rhetoric and secession. Fifteen-year-old Louisa McCord, who lived near the college, remembered years later the bonfires, the energy of the moment, a time of "so much hope and so much courage."

Former mayor E. J. Arthur, age forty-six, the man who faced a mob of angry students four years earlier, saw things quite differently. In February, writing to Edwin De Leon, U.S. consul-general in Egypt, he blasted the new government as a bunch of blundering fools. In a letter now in the South Caroliniana Library, he told his boyhood friend that affairs were in "a most deplorable condition." The young Confederacy had no money, no soldiers, no ammunition, and yet its leaders were squabbling over the design of a flag! Whenever another state seceded, tar barrels were burned, "high-falutin' Buncombe speeches delivered," "bad whiskey drank and worse speeches made by brainless men," and flags presented to yet another militia unit by "fair" ladies. The people were brave, but their leaders seemed to be overwhelmed by "apathy & indifference." Nothing needed to be done, they said, because Yankees won't fight. The truth was, wrote Arthur, "we are wholly unprepared," soon would be "thrashed," and then have to "slink" back into the Union.

As spring came, Oscar Lieber, thirty years of age, could talk only of the beauty he saw about him on May Day—pretty girls in riding habits, roses in bloom, the college campus bright with new growth. "Nothing to remind one of war," he told his parents in New York City, "except the uniforms of soldiers, for there are now about 3,000 men from higher up the country stationed here, awaiting orders." Lieber, who would die fourteen months later in Virginia, promised to continue writing, even if his letters had to be sent through Havana.

Excitement, chaos, and beauty—Columbia undoubtedly presented many faces during those troubled times. And it is equally possible that all members of this trio, even teenage Louisa, realized they were witnessing momentous events: the passing of old ways and the dawn of a new era filled with both promise and danger.

Notes

1. This chapter is based in part upon research by Mary Fulton Green, "A Profile of Columbia in 1850," published in the *South Carolina Historical Magazine* (April 1969), pp. 104–21.
2. At about this time, Columbia's *Palmetto-State Banner* added to its masthead a triumphant engraving of a train wending its way past the State House.
3. Scott, *Random Recollections*, p. 149.
4. See Appendix 2 for businesses listed in the 1860 city directory.
5. See Appendix 1 for a list of intendants and mayors, 1805–1865. The principal purpose of wards, drawn in an east-west fashion, was to establish districts for fire companies and

elections. The first ward was the lower part of the city south of Gervais. The second extended from Gervais to Plain; the third, from Plain to Laurel; and the fourth, from Laurel to the northern limits.

6. Copies of most of these papers are available at the South Caroliniana Library. The most complete files for the decade are those of the *Daily South Carolinian*. In addition to titles already mentioned, a Know-Nothing weekly, the *New Era*, appeared briefly, 1855–1856. The only general-purpose magazine published in Columbia during these years was Steuart Adair Godman's short-lived *Illustrated Family Friend*, a weekly issued in 1851–1852.

7. Anne Royall, *Mrs. Royall's Southern Tour; or, Second Series of the Black Book* (3 vols.; Washington, 1830–31), II, pp. 62–63.

8. Frederick von Raumer, *America and the American People* (New York, 1846), pp. 422–26. Von Raumer also attended an evening of student speeches at the college, of which he approved—although between each oration a black band played the same tune over and over—and visited the plantations of Wade Hampton II. He found there well-fed blacks who had assigned tasks they usually could complete by 2 P.M., leaving them free to raise poultry, etc. The nature of slavery, he shrewdly concluded, depended solely upon the owner's character.

9. Scott, *Random Recollections*, p. 152.

10. The Sons of Malta, a strange, non-Masonic group, lasted only a few decades, dying out during the Civil War. Initiation included an outrageous cross-examination of candidates and a sometimes terrifying sojourn in a basket—often suspended from the ceiling while members partook of a sumptuous banquet below—or a shoot-the-chute affair from the top floor of a building to the basement.

11. Quoted from the *Atlantic Monthly* (February 1884) in Walter B. Edgar *et al*, *A Columbia Reader, 1786–1986* (Columbia, n. d.), p. 51.

12. *Address of the Hon. Benj. F. Perry. . . .* (Charleston, 1857), p. 12.

13. *Ibid.*, p. 30.

14. Carol Bleser (ed.), *Secret and Sacred: The Diaries of John Henry Hammond, a Southern Slaveholder* (New York, 1988), p. 26.

15. See Margaret DesChamps Moore, "A Northern Professor Winters in Columbia, 1852–1853," *South Carolina Historical Magazine* (October 1959), pp. 183–92. The family did not move south. McGill, who obviously was job hunting, returned to his position at Western Theological Seminary in Allegheny, Pennsylvania, and a year later joined the faculty of Princeton Theological Seminary, retiring in 1883.

Keziah Brevard's Richland County

CHAPTER NINE

 Large, expressive eyes, a hallmark of the Hopkins line, stare out from a portrait of this young lady painted when she was perhaps twenty years of age. Dark hair parted in the center and drawn back into ringlets frame a somber face; and, as it turned out, for Keziah Goodwyn Hopkins, life would be a serious affair indeed. Born in 1803, she was the daughter of Keziah Goodwyn and James Hopkins of "Oldfield" plantation, a property granted to John Hopkins of Hanover County, Virginia, in the mid-1700s and still owned by the Hopkins family. Her mother, widow of cousin Jesse Goodwyn, had three children by her first marriage, the most important on the local scene being Sarah, wife of Columbia merchant Ainsley Hall. By the second marriage there were five children—three boys who died in childhood, Keziah, and her younger sister, Caroline. In the 1820s, these two girls married brothers from North Carolina. Caroline's two sons died when young, and she herself failed to recover from the birth of the second child in 1828. Keziah had no children, and thus, when her father died in 1844, she became sole heir to his substantial holdings in lower Richland.

"Kizzie," as she was called within the family, probably was educated at nearby Minervaville Academy and at the well-known institution run by Dr. Marks in Columbia. She may have lived with the Ainsley Halls while attending classes there. If so, Keziah got a brief course in how quickly marital ties can become frayed. Her half-sister's marriage apparently was happy enough until she discovered a letter indicating that her husband was romantically involved with someone else. To Sarah's dismay, Hall not only admitted the relationship but defended the virtue of the "other" woman. It was, he said, entirely his fault. Sarah appealed to her stepfather, James Hopkins, who ruled out divorce since such a step would stain the family name. Only Hall's death in 1823 at a relatively young age—he was forty—resolved this impasse.

His widow completed the famous Mills-designed mansion then under construction, but in 1829 she sold the property to Columbia Theological Seminary. Sarah Hall subsequently built a home called "Bellewood," which was located out in the county near Garner's Ferry Road. There, according to family tradition, she became something of a recluse and more and more peculiar as years passed. When her health failed, she moved in with Keziah and died at her half-sister's home in April of 1867.

Keziah's story, although somewhat different, also encompassed grief and disappointment. In April of 1827, she married Alexander Joseph McLean Brevard, whose father owned considerable land in the Charlotte area. Brevard, who went by the name of Joseph, attended South Carolina College from 1818 to 1820, but did not graduate. By the mid-1820s, Keziah's sister, Caroline, had married Theodore Brevard, Joseph's brother, and the family also had close ties with Brevard cousins in Camden, so there were several routes by which any casual association spawned by college days or social gatherings could have blossomed into romance.

Joseph, two years older than Keziah, took his bride north to Charlotte where they set up housekeeping, and he served briefly in the legislature of that state. But the marriage soon was endangered by the groom's excessive drinking, and within a few years Keziah had had enough. One day she suddenly packed her things, ordered a carriage, and—like her half-sister before her—came home to father. Joseph followed on horseback; however, in contrast to the usual scenario, instead of pleading for his wife to return to their home, he decided to remain at "Oldfield." Just when these dramatic events occurred is not known, but recording of the elder Brevard's will in Columbia in October of 1831 indicates that his son, one of the executors, was living in Richland County at that time.

During the ensuing decade, Joseph was institutionalized on occasions, yet at length the young couple moved to her father's sand hills property that eventually became Keziah's principal residence. Now called "Alwehav," she referred to it as "Mt. Ed" or "Mt. Trouble," depending upon her mood, and once even considered calling an enlarged plantation house "Fountainebleau." This property, surrounded by huge magnolias, live oaks, and exotic trees and shrubs planted by James Hopkins, originally was a spacious cottage built about 1815. Following her father's death, Keziah moved that building several hundred yards to a new site and joined it to a handsome, two-story structure containing large rooms with thirteen-foot ceilings, a wide entrance hall, and porches typical of the period. At about the same time, Keziah purchased a substantial town house at the southwest corner of Bull and Blanding streets in Columbia; however, her diary reveals she soon tired of city life.

Joseph Brevard died in 1842, and his death was followed two years later by that of James Hopkins, Keziah's father. By his will, the forty-one-year-old widow inherited everything he owned, subject to two special provisions: if Keziah left no heirs "of her body," then all of the property, both land and slaves, was to go to blood relatives, and her actions and decisions were subject to approval of four trustees named by her father.

Any doubts James had concerning his daughter's managerial skills were ill founded. Her diary written on the eve of the Civil War, though brief, reveals a competent, no-nonsense mistress of several large plantations and over 200 slaves. According to census data, Keziah more than doubled the size of her holdings in the 1850s, while maintaining a creditable output of cotton, corn, wool, and sweet potatoes. No socialite, a woman who saw Columbia only as a place to transact business and buy plantation supplies, her idea of a good time was a relaxed family dinner such as she hosted on 27 July 1860. Ten relatives, both young and old, enjoyed a bountiful repast of ham, goose, mutton (roasted and boiled), cabbage, rice, beets, Irish potatoes, and tomatoes (cooked and uncooked). For dessert they had apple dumplings and "soft" peaches. To a lesser degree, she derived some pleasure from tea and conversation with neighbors. In November 1860, she wrote of a gathering at the home of ex-governor James Hopkins Adams at which she met Mrs. H., "a Charleston lady yet her manner is very natural."

Now nearly sixty years of age, Keziah liked to garden, preserve fruits and vegetables, take an accounting of all the foodstuffs on hand, and make wine by the gallon—some of which, to her distress, occasionally turned to vinegar. Frugal, but not parsimonious, she once referred to her family as "good, plain, unpretending people," and that characterization seems valid enough. Shortly after her father died, as noted earlier, Keziah enlarged her sand hills home, but she built no grand structure such as "Kensington" or "Magnolia."

Like any good farmer, the widow Brevard kept an eye on the weather and looked after the needs of those who worked her spacious fields under the direction of Abraham Rawlinson, a most capable overseer. When house boys Ned and Dick had to help harvest cotton, she expressed concern that they could not "stand the sun as the field hands do" and personally nursed little Harrison in his final illness, even bundling up the black youngster and taking him for rides in her carriage. Also, her diary indicates that she often loaned small sums to less fortunate neighbors.

Despite kind thoughts and good deeds, this lady's religious life defies easy analysis. Born into a world of relaxed morality, by mid-century Keziah invoked the mercy of God often and sought His guidance almost daily, yet her formal ties to religion were few. She rarely attended Sunday services, although frequently wrote that she wished she had done so. As a bride, she joined a Presbyterian congregation in North Carolina and over two decades later (7 April 1851) transferred her membership to the First Presbyterian Church in Columbia, noting that she was living in a settlement of Baptists "with whom she was not disposed to unite." At the same time, she mourned the passing of Beulah Church, a local Baptist institution long associated with the Adams family, and spoke scornfully of Adams cousins who had "gone clear over to the Episcopalians outwardly."

Keziah experienced turmoil common to this region in the 1860s, and at the close of the Civil War Sherman's men burned her birthplace, "Oldfield." (In the entrance hall of present-day "Oldfield" stands a handsome secretary with one drawer missing—taken, it is said, by one of Sherman's "bummers.") All of her slaves were, of course, set free, and whatever railroad stock she held became virtually worthless. Nevertheless, despite reduced income, this indomitable widow carried on amazingly well, maintaining one home in the sand hills and another in Columbia and occasionally riding forth in a grand carriage that always drew a crowd of onlookers. No longer able to collect rents herself, she hired a cousin, English Hopkins, to act as her business manager. According to tradition, Keziah Brevard never sold a slave or a tree, and an inventory following her death in 1886 indicates that at least the latter was essentially true, although she evidently had disposed of her city residence. James Hopkins left his daughter about 2,300 acres of land; she devised nearly three times as much to her heirs—6,710 acres.

Keziah's eighty-three years encompassed events both great and small, yet because of her many responsibilities and quiet nature, she often was more spectator then participant. Although not a recluse like her half-sister, her adult world was bounded by crops, weather, seasons, family matters, visits with neighbors, and the endless task of supervising slaves and lands. But one gala affair that she probably attended was the ball given in the basement of the State House on 12 March 1825 to honor Lafayette. We know that cousin Emma Hopkins, then only seventeen and a lifelong friend of Keziah, was among those greeting the aging hero of the American Revolution, and it seems likely that Keziah herself—having just turned twenty-two and not yet married—was present that evening. She also may have participated in gatherings in December of that same year

A Bride Visits Columbia

In June of 1827, on a honeymoon trip from Charleston to various points in North Carolina and Tennessee, Mrs. Henry W. Conner (Julia Margaret Courtenay) recorded these impressions in a diary now in the South Caroliniana Library.

Started early, passed through Granby, and but for its name would not have noticed it. Some dozen or twenty houses, looking as if they were deserted—not a sign of life or motion in the place, although it was formerly a place of business where all the boats landed. Tuesday, 12—proceeded on to Columbia. Crossed over a fine bridge which commands a beautiful view of the town which is handsomely situated on a hill of considerable eminence. Houses, many of them large and handsome—the public houses much more numerous and extensive than you would suppose from the size of the place. Indeed they are on a much larger scale than we have in C. Visited the water works which supply the town. The water is raised from the basin by means of a steam engine (which is so constructed as also to work a corn and wheat mill) to a reservoir which is on an eminence from whence it is conducted through iron pipes into the houses. From the cupola of Bridges Hotel we had a fine and extensive view of the town and its environs which is really beautiful, large gardens, and apparently great regard to neatness and taste in their buildings. Saw the Lunatic Asylum, a singularly constructed edifice, something of a semi-circular form and large enough to contain all of the lunatics in the United States. Passed the colleges which are nothing remarkable in their outward appearances. Went into the State House, a large wooden building in the upper part of which the Legislature sit during session. The lower part is occupied as a bank and Treasury.

The roads around the town are kept in excellent order, and in many places at a considerable expense. I returned much pleased with my ride and the general appearance of the place. Our time was too limited to admit of my seeing much of the inhabitants. We received considerable politeness and my impressions were altogether favorable.

honoring Bernard, Duke of Saxe-Weimar-Eisenach. The duke, shocked by the widespread custom of tobacco chewing (even when ladies were present), noted that a ball held at a Taylor plantation was marked by

> music of a singular kind; for the blacks, who had two days ago played very well at the governor's, were now drunk, and could not make their appearance. This was the reason that the whole music consisted of two violins and a tamborine. The tamborine was struck with terrible energy. The two others scraped the violin, in the truest significance of the word; one of them cried out the figures, imitating with his body all the motions of the dance. The whole of it amused me much; for the rest, I was astonished at the great plainness of the house. Besides the first room, there were three rooms open, which had white walls, and were without window-curtains.[1]

A decade later, English humanitarian and writer Harriet Martineau spent several days on a local plantation. The log houses where her stage stopped en route south from Richmond to Columbia were, she wrote, amazingly similar. Each had portraits of six U.S. presidents hanging on their walls (as well as a map with a greasy circle where too many fingers had pinpointed the site of that "inn") and served up the same meal: broiled venison, ham collops, eggs, an "infusion" called either tea or coffee, and "reeking corn bread."

By contrast, her Richland County visit was a pleasurable experience; and, although no friend of slavery, she conceded there was something in "the make-shift, irregular mode of plantation life" that was amusing once the cause was forgotten. She often awoke to find a group of black females staring at her and throughout the day was pestered by house servants wanting to know what time it was. After breakfast one morning, her hostess, having given orders to the staff, turned her attention to cutting out slave clothes. It was impossible, she said, to train blacks to do pattern work, and they wore out their garments so quickly. Asked about whippings, she replied that was the overseer's business, not hers; she never inquired into such matters. A few moments later this lady was called away to give medicine to a sick slave (they would take it, she emphasized, only if *she* administered the potion), returning just in time to greet morning callers.

After these visitors departed, everyone joined in a leisurely ride about the plantation in order to show the British guest the expansive fields, cotton gin, slave quarters, ice house, and even the overseer's bare dwelling with its fishing tackle, rifle, medicine chest, and shelf of books.

The group then returned to the "big house" for a brief rest before setting out for an early afternoon meal a few miles away in the sand hills. Their hosts, identified only as Mr. and Mrs. E., had a grand home in the city (Charleston?) but lived here in a simple cottage with broad piazzas. Mrs. E., mother of five children and expecting yet another, was delighted to be in the country. Disdainful of servants who taught their charges "improper" things and told them "falsehoods," she was greatly relieved that her brood now could romp and play without such supervision. Black nurses, in her opinion, were useless, and none of them knew how to wash a little boy's face. But, she concluded with a sigh, "Ladies must make the best of their lot, for they cannot help themselves."

The dinner was plentiful, including, of course, turkey, ham, and sweet potatoes; excellent claret, and large blocks of ice cream. A slave makes gentle war against the flies with an enormous bunch of pea-cocks' feathers; and the agitation of the air is pleasant while the ladies are engaged in eating so that they cannot use their own fans, which are hung on loops on the back of their chairs. The afternoon is spent in the piazza, where coffee is served. There the ladies sit, whisking their feather fans, jesting with the children, and talking over the last English poem or American novel, or complaining bitterly of the dreadful incendiary publications which Mr. E. heard from Mr. H., who had heard it from Mr. M., that Judge R. had said that somebody had seen circulated among the negroes by some vile agent of the hor-rid abolitionists of the North.

You go into tea, and find the table strewn with prints, and the pi-ano open, and Mrs. F. plays and sings. The gentlemen have done discussing the French war and the currency, and are praising the conduct of the Committee of Vigilance; frankly informing you, as a stranger, of the reasons for its formation, and the modes of its oper-ation in deterring abolitionists from coming into the neighborhood, in arresting them on any suspicion of tampering with the negroes, and in punishing them summarily if any facts are established against them. While you are endeavouring to learn the nature of the crime and its evidence, you are summoned. There is going to be a storm, and your party must get home, if possible, before it comes on. In such a case Mrs. E. will say nothing in opposition to your leaving her so early. She would not be the means of exposing you to the storm. You hasten away, and reach home during the first explosion of thunder.[2]

In years that followed, several other well-known individuals, in addition to personalities already mentioned, made their way to the land between the Congaree and Wateree rivers, among them, Phineas Taylor Barnum, William Cullen Bryant, Daniel Webster, and Solon Robinson. Circus impresario and showman P. T. Barnum arrived in Columbia in December 1836. Here he bought out a rival named Turner, reorganized his troupe, and went forth as "Barnum's Grand Scientific & Musical Theatre." Although the group disbanded a few months later in New Orleans and Barnum then launched his famous Manhattan museum, this marked his debut as a pioneer entertainer under his own name.

Poet and editor William Cullen Bryant tarried only briefly in Columbia ("a pretty town") in March of 1843, spending most of his time with friends in nearby Orangeburg and Barnwell counties. There he went on a raccoon hunt, watched with interest a corn-shucking and a slave dance, listened to black ballads and jokes, and ate, in his own words, "bushels of hominey [sic]." Bryant obviously enjoyed his three-week stay in South Carolina, but one aspect of rural life in this state puzzled him. No door, expect perhaps the principal one leading to the outside elements, ever was shut. The natives seemed to treat all others as mere ornamental appendages or "moveable" screens. In their view, Bryant concluded, a door was simply a ventilator to a room. Windows might be raised when it was hot, but doors always remained open. "On cold days you have a bright fire of pine-wood blazing before you, and a draught of cold air at your back. The reason given for this practice is," he wrote, "that fresh air is wholesome, and that close rooms occasion colds and consumption."[3]

Daniel Webster, who toured this region in May of 1847 to test the political waters, was wined, dined, and feted wherever he went . . . perhaps too much so. Quartered in the spacious Columbia home of William C. Preston, he sallied forth to inspect the cotton fields of "Millwood" and spend a day fishing in Richland County's rivers and streams. The "lordlike" Daniel also was hailed by South Carolina College students at an illuminated affair and guest of honor at a dinner given by the governor. But all did not go well. Webster, in the opinion of local residents, often appeared cold and rigid to the point of being discourteous. The reason, according to his biographers, was excessive southern hospitality. Not one to turn down food or drink and no longer a young man, the famous orator simple wore himself out in Charleston and Columbia and had to remain in bed for a time when he reached Augusta.

Agricultural reformer Solon Robinson, a frequent visitor to the South during the middle decades of the 19th century, came to South Carolina in April of 1849 and again in February of 1850. Both trips encompassed Columbia and Richland County and produced, among other things, an unusual handful of local recipes. (See p. 168.). The 1849 sojourn also embroiled Robinson, an avid writer on agricultural matters, in hot debate with Columbia's *South Carolinian*. His analysis of what it cost to grow a pound of cotton did not find favor here, and his words, together with those of editor William B. Johnston (who thought Robinson included items that were not true costs and thus painted an unfair picture), subsequently were summarized in *DeBow's Review* (November 1849).

Robinson's second swing took him to James Henry Hammond's Savannah River plantation, Charleston, and—once more—to South Carolina's capital city. Hammond, he observed, like most planters, allowed land not in cotton to "rest," that is, produce nothing but a crop of weeds. The former governor thought this highly beneficial, but Robinson was not convinced. In his opinion, clover or grass would have been preferable. Hammond, he wrote, planted cotton in rows four or five feet apart, with stalks every fifteen inches along those rows that produced perhaps thirty bolls or about 1,800 pounds to the acre. "He says he has seen 700 bolls and forms upon one stalk; and that it made 4 lbs. of cotton. It grew upon a dung heap. This is pretty conclusive proof that it would be profitable to grow the whole crop upon a dung hill.[4]

Hammond's corn yield was eight to ten bushels per acre, and Robinson indicated that was about average for "light" soil in upland regions of this state. His host reported that raising hogs actually was unprofitable because of "a most unconquerable love that negroes have for fresh pork."

A few weeks later, Robinson was back in Richland County, having traveled to Charleston and then to Columbia by way of the South Carolina Railroad. After leaving Branchville, he said one saw "only small patches of clearing and but two or three unimportant towns." But he found Columbia alive with hope and excitement in anticipation of the many benefits the new rail line to Greenville would bring. Once more Robinson dissented, distressed by the freight rates being levied here, much higher than those in the North. This was necessary, railroad officials claimed, because there were so few passengers. The rate on a plow that cost only $1.37½ in a New York store (to which sea charges of 12½¢ from there to Charleston were added) was 50¢, the same amount levied upon wheelbarrows, corn shellers, straw cutters, etc. This was wrong. In Robinson's view, basic agricultural implements such as plows should be carried by the railroads "almost" free.

At this time, it might be noted, another new rail connection was being constructed in the southeastern corner of the county. In 1848, the South Carolina Railroad built a branch line east from Kingville that

A Few More Trifles For The Ladies[5]

To Purify Tallow.—Mix 5 parts of beef tallow with 3 parts of mutton tallow, in a copper or iron kettle, with half a pint of water to each pound of grease. When melted, mix 8 ounces of brandy, 1 ounce of salt of tartar, 1 ounce of cream of tartar, 1 ounce of sal ammoniac, 2 ounces of pure and dry potash, with the tallow. Boil fifteen minutes, and set off to cool. When cold, take off the cake and bleach it in the air and dew for a few days and nights. It will then be hard and white. Candles, with a fine cotton-yarn wick (6 to a pound) will burn 14 hours.

Tomato Catchup.—First bake your tomatoes, then squeeze them through a sieve. Add to 6 quarts of juice an equal quantity of wine vinegar; boil slow until it begins to thicken; then add cloves, allspice, and pepper, ½ an ounce each, cinnamon ¼ of an ounce, and 2 nutmegs, all finely powdered. As it thickens, add four spoonfuls of salt, and when done, pour out in an earthen dish to cool. Bottle, cork, and seal, and it will keep years in a warm climate.

Potato Pudding.—Take ¾ of a pound of sugar, ¾ ditto of butter, and beat well together; add one pound of boiled potatoes (Irish or sweet) rubbed fine through a collander or mashed; six eggs, the whites and yolks beat separately, and a wineglassful of brandy and one of wine, a trifle of rose water, and cinnamon or nutmeg, as much as you like.

Rice Bread.—Take six tablespoonfuls of boiled rice, and one of butter; rub them together, and then pour in half a pint of milk; add two eggs, and six tablespoonfuls of wheat flour. Mix all well together and bake a little brown; and you will have a very good and wholesome kind of bread.

Solon

Columbia, S.C., April, 1849.

crossed the Wateree and then went north to Camden, a treacherous, thirty-eight-mile route largely over swamp land. Six years later, the Sumter County junction of Manchester, a key point on this road, was linked to Sumter, Darlington Junction [Florence], and the city of Wilmington in North Carolina. This facility obviously was not as important to most area residents as tracks leading into the Piedmont, yet it loomed large in the eyes of those living in the lower part of the county.

During these decades, young men from Richland County twice marched off to battle, although neither altercation had much immediate impact locally. On 11 February 1836, the Richland Volunteer Rifles boarded the steamer *James Boatwright* at Granby, arriving in Charleston three days later. There a man fell overboard and drowned, the only casualty the Volunteers suffered during their campaign to subdue Florida's Seminole Indians.

Then, in the fall of 1846, members of the same unit, together with the Governor's Guards and other local contingents, formed Company H of the famed Palmetto Regiment and set out for Mexico. Following a circuitous rail and water route via Atlanta and Mobile, they joined in the invasion of Vera Cruz and also participated in the assault upon Mexico City. On 27 July 1848, a huge Columbia parade honored these hardened veterans, followed by a grand reception and barbecue at South Carolina College. One lavish toast hailed their deeds as equal to "anything in the annals of Greece or Rome." Edgefield's Lieutenant Joseph Abney was more realistic as he saluted Company H: "In the war with Mexico the Richland Company did its duty."

Eight years later, the General Assembly bought for $5,000 the metal palmetto tree that honors their memory. Christopher Werner had constructed this unique monument, long a fixture on the grounds of the state capitol, for an insurance company that subsequently rejected his work. A more important result of the brief war with our neighbor to the south was acquisition of land that soon was attracting the attention of South Carolina planters unhappy with their worn-out soil.

Although it is difficult to recapture the mood of Richland County residents during the first half of the 19th century, petitions to the state legislature provide clues as to what was uppermost in their minds. Until 1800, the cry was "roads," followed by appeals for bridges, ferries, and schemes to clear rivers of various obstructions. Soon maintenance of existing transportation facilities was being stressed, and by 1815, beguiled by the promise of waterways and canals, local citizens were urging that some roads be discontinued. Fifteen years later, theft of wood, immorality, drinking, and illegal voting were objects of special attention, and fifteen years after that calls for more general support of public education frequently were voiced.

What this rough profile reveals is a community that, to the detriment of roads and canals, had become largely dependent upon railroads for transportation, and a people increasingly concerned with the nature of daily life. Theft of wood, an absurd crime before 1800, indicates the relative scarcity of the prime source of fuel, and interest in moral issues reflects the growing power of various ministers and their flocks. Also, charges of fraudulent balloting and appeals for classrooms were not unrelated. As democracy increased, the need for an educated electorate—at least one able to read and write—was becoming ever more apparent.

Yet some of these trends clashed head-on with the wishes of Richland's planter elite. Education, for example, was expensive and could increase taxes. Also it might well spread to blacks, and any center of activity in a rural landscape (even a schoolhouse) could attract a storekeeper who sold whiskey. On a visit to the site of old Minervaville in the summer of 1853, diarist Samuel Leland remarked that here once there had been "a considerable little village" with an academy and several large stores that were "the meeting place for all of the Planters & idlers for miles around." A lively setting famous for riotous brawls almost every evening, the ground now was planted in peanuts and potatoes, the would-be town ploughed under by members of the Hopkins family. Six years later, when the South Carolina Railroad sought to create a depot on Keziah Brevard's Mill Creek property, she said no. "I do not wish it myself," she wrote in her diary. "I had rather see Montgomery field converted to a gulph than to live to believe that one bad act . . . was ever committed on a spot of earth given for a depot near me." One cannot change man, Keziah added, but one can avoid aiding what will lead to wrongdoing.

The net result of attitudes such as these was the near-complete absence of village life outside of the city of Columbia. In 1851, for example, the county had only six post offices, all of them strung out along railroad lines. They were, in addition to Columbia itself, Gadsden and Hopkins Turnout in the lower part of the county, Littleton and Cedar Creek in the northwest corner close by the Broad River, and Level, located north of Columbia on the road to Ridgeway. At the same time, by way of comparison, Georgetown County had two post offices; Spartanburg County, thirty-eight.

There had been other post offices, but most, like Minervaville, soon disappeared. In the 1830s, postal facilities flourished for a time at Minervaville, Colonel's Creek, Rice Creek Springs, and Gaffney's Store, also called Piney Grove. Still earlier, post offices had appeared briefly at Miersville (Horrell Hill) in 1805 and at "the Fork" in 1816. Short-lived offices existed at Temperance (August–November 1841), Little River Depot (January–February 1851), Kingville (January–May 1855), and Tekoah (April 1857–January 1858). In 1852, a post office was established at Wateree, and in 1857 yet another began operation at Doko, a water stop north of Columbia on the Charlotte rail line. The latter probably replaced Level, which ceased to function in 1855.[6]

With community life severely restricted, it is obvious that industry would be virtually non-existent in a region dominated by agriculture. The 1840 census totals for Richland County, which include Columbia, list only a one-man pottery, three workmen turning out wagons and carriages, and seventy individuals employed at forty saw and grist mills. Strangely, no distilleries were reported at a time when Laurens County alone had sixty-four. Ten years later, there were thirty-six industrial establishments in rural Richland County. Again, most were saw and grist mills, four of them owned by women—Harriet English, Keziah Brevard, Mary McLaughlin, and Eleanor Percival.

All of these facilities used hand, horse, or water power and rarely employed more than one or two workers at wages of about ten dollars a month. Exceptions were the brickyard of John Davis (twelve employees) and the grist mill, saw mill, and cotton gin owned by Wade Hampton II. Hampton's establishment represented by far the most substantial investment ($11,000) and annually turned out products worth about $35,000.

Three years later, according to DeBow's Review (June 1853), Dr. Samuel Percival was operating a chair factory and tannery in the sand hills east of Columbia. (This apparently was an outgrowth of a saw and grist mill cited in the 1850 census.) Here he was providing employment for a few boys, offspring of the "wretchedly inert" inhabitants of that region, and a group of female slaves who caned chair seats. The writer conceded the business still was a small one but vowed it had great promise; however, editor DeBow never saw an industrial outlet south of the Mason-Dixon line, no matter how minuscule, that was not on the verge of doing marvelous things.

The area's best-known manufacturing center of those years lay across the river in Lexington County. The "Saludy" Company, so designated by the 1850 census taker, then had an annual output of cotton goods worth $100,000. Plagued by financial difficulties from its inception in the 1830s, in December of 1855 the Saluda Company was purchased by James G.

and Robert W. Gibbes and re-named the Columbia Cotton Mill. The new owners repaired a nearby dam, renovated idle machinery, and hired 200 white operatives to replace a slave labor force. Yet only during the war years, as demand for cloth soared, did this mill become truly profitable.

The census of 1860 discloses little concerning local industrial life. With typical zeal, Thomas Walker found only *four* manufacturing establishments in both city and county. His agricultural survey also may be defective but, in view of the overall population loss of the 1850s, probably was close to the mark.

In 1850, forty-five rural residents held real estate worth $10,000 or more, and of those farms and plantations only two contained less than a 1,000 acres. On the other hand, thirty farmers (about 6 percent) were existing on plots of 10 acres or less.[7] Most were sand hillers, not free blacks. The major difference between big and small farmers was that the latter planted little cotton, if any, and the poorest among them had few animals, perhaps not even a mule or horse. But virtually everyone grew corn, peas, beans, and sweet potatoes. About half of the sixty-two free black households in rural sections of the county carried on some form of independent agricultural activity, while the rest existed largely as hired labor. Rice production was widespread throughout lower Richland, although only two individuals (James H. Seay and Philip Schwarz) harvested more than 5,000 pounds in the year ending in June of 1850. James Gregg even grew 2,100 pounds within or close to Columbia's town limits.

On her two farms—2,600 acres valued at $22,500—Keziah Brevard had 6 horses, 20 mules, 90 cattle, 42 sheep, and 185 swine, livestock worth $2,160. In 1849–1850, she produced 7,073 bushels of corn, 525 bushels of oats, 45 pounds of wool, 700 bushels of peas and beans, 1,700 bushels of sweet potatoes, 200 pounds of butter, 43 tons of hay, and home manufactures with an estimated value of $180. She also ginned 190 bales of cotton and slaughtered animals worth $420. Keziah reported no rice, and apparently no one within the county grew tobacco.

This widow's operations actually were modest compared to those of some of her neighbors. Various members of the Adams family controlled 26,500 acres of land worth about $263,000. Wade Hampton II, perhaps the region's wealthiest citizen thanks to investments in Louisiana sugar and Mississippi plantations, owned 3,550 acres of county soil valued at $71,000. His fine collection of carefully bred livestock, one of the most impressive in the South, was worth nearly as much, $50,504. Several Hopkins cousins, although some of them soon would move to other states, held 8,600 acres of land worth about $100,000. Three other well-known names—Taylor, Clarkson, and Singleton—represented large concentrations of land, slaves, and power; however, the activities of these individuals often spilled over into neighboring counties. Substantial plantations also were owned by Caroline Weston, John D. Frost, James O'Hanlon, and Joseph A. Black.[8]

Moving down the scale, one comes to a small planter such as John Ledingham, a resident of the Hopkins-Adams neighborhood. Ledingham, age forty-five, lived with his wife Frances and seven children ranging in ages from one to sixteen on a 600-acre plantation worth $5,000. With the help of two teenage sons (Thomas and Joseph) and twenty-five slaves, in 1849–1850 Ledingham produced twenty-seven bales of cotton and substantial quantities of corn, oats, wool, peas, beans, and sweet potatoes. His young neighbor, Elihu Bates, owned a farm half as large valued at $1,500. The Bates household consisted of twenty-nine-year-old Elihu, his wife Elizabeth, and a baby daughter. Aided by two slaves, in that same year Elihu grew 900 bushels of corn, six tons of hay, and three bales of cotton. Both of these individuals also owned livestock appropriate to their needs, Ledingham reporting six horses, three mules, eighty-five cattle, twenty-six sheep, and thirty-five swine, while Bates had two horses, twelve cattle, and thirty swine.

Yet another Mill Creek resident, free black Robert Cline, owned 35 acres of land (21 of them cultivated) worth $100. Twenty-seven-year-old Cline, who had a wife and three small children, appears to have been a resolute worker. He owned two horses, twenty cattle, and thirty swine—animals valued at $316. In the census year, he produced 225 bushels of corn, 100 bushels of peas and beans, 100 pounds of butter, a ton of hay, home manufactures worth seventy-five dollars and, somewhat surprisingly, three bales of cotton.

At the bottom of the agricultural ladder were poor whites such as Philip Elkins and William Dow and free blacks William Pote and John Jacobs, each of whom managed to exist with their families on plots of less than 10 acres, perhaps by working part time as hired hands. Elkins (thirty-eight), with a wife and six children to support, owned a horse, two cows, and a pig. On his tiny, 3-acre farm he produced small quantities of corn, beans, sweet potatoes, butter, and honey. Dow, who was slightly older and father of five small children, lived on a 5-acre farm worth only $15. Owner of six cattle (no horse or mule), he somehow raised thirty bushels of corn in 1849–1850, as well as twenty bushels of peas and beans and forty bushels of sweet potatoes, and took to market fifty pounds of butter and twenty pounds of honey. In contrast to Dow, blacks Pote and

Jacobs, both in their thirties and responsible for smaller families, each owned horses and livestock, but produced much the same crops; however, Pote harvested several bushels of *Irish* potatoes, a vegetable not often grown on small Richland County farms at mid-century.

Some of the changes that occurred on the rural scene during the next ten years already have been alluded to—a sharp decrease in the slave population (c. 2,000) and the out-migration of numerous large landowners. As a result, the 1860 census returns reflect a general decline in many phases of local life. In that year, there were fewer animals on the farms of Richland County than in 1850, and those farms were producing less of practically everything. The number of horses and mules dropped from 2,991 to 2,129 during the decade, the cattle population fell from 11,575 to 8,521, and herds of sheep and swine were 40 percent smaller. Corn production was cut almost in half (433,998 to 233,401 bushels), the rice harvest nearly vanished (87,970 to 9,286 pounds), and even cotton declined from 11,365 to 9,946 bales. Hay production and the value of animals slaughtered rose slightly, and the number of rural residents owning real estate worth $10,000 or more edged upward from forty-five to fifty-nine.

The biggest change, however, was in the number of farms themselves, which in only ten years dropped from 543 to 203. Many that disappeared were small holdings, their owners having moved to town or to new lands beyond the mountains. In 1850, the county had sixty-nine farms of 20 acres or less compared with only three in 1860. On the eve of the war, about one-third of all local farms (seventy-four) contained 20 to 100 acres; another third (eighty-five), 100 to 500 acres. Sixteen had 500 to 1,000 acres; twenty-five, over 1,000 acres.

Keziah Brevard, through purchase, had increased her land holdings to 6,000 acres, her slave force was now somewhat larger (up from 180 to 209), and she had added rice (1,200 pounds) and honey ($175 worth) to her annual output of foodstuffs. But she reported none of the wine so carefully bottled; nor, like some of her neighbors, had she procured oxen to work her fields. John Ledingham seemed to be doing well, but smaller farmers such as Bates, Cline, and Elkins apparently had moved away . . . at least census taker Walker failed to find them.

Although no free black farmer living in Richland County during these years owned slaves or accumulated much money, by 1860 at least four of them had acquired real estate worth $1,000 or more. The leading members of this select group were Uriah Portee and Charles Frost, both of whom lived in the Gadsden area. Portee, whose name was recorded at times as "Pote" and "Porter," prospered greatly in the 1850s. At the beginning of the decade he had a horse, mule, and cow and was supporting his wife and six children on 25 acres of land said to be worth only fifty dollars. Ten years later, Uriah owned a 450-acre farm valued at $2,000 on which there were three horses, three mules, eighteen cattle, and fourteen swine. He took to market in 1860 the usual crop of corn, peas, beans, sweet potatoes, and butter, but no cotton. (After the war, this man would become a county commissioner and a prominent figure in lower Richland.)

In 1850, Charles Frost, age forty-four, was tilling 35 acres of land valued at seventy dollars. His family included his wife (Cecilia) and eight children. Despite the size of his property, Frost had a rather large number of animals—two horses, thirty cattle, ten sheep, and forty swine. Ten years later, although census records are a bit confusing, this industrious black man reportedly owned a 1,200-acre farm (one-fourth of it under cultivation) worth $8,000. He now had a mule, 3 horses, 77 cattle, 123 swine, and 10 sheep and produced that census year 300 bushels of corn, four bales of cotton, and 100 pounds of butter, as well as peas, beans, hay, and sweet potatoes.

Missing from this survey so far is any mention of the most numerous group in rural Richland County at mid-century: slaves. In 1850, those in bondage on farms and plantations scattered between the Congaree and Wateree outnumbered whites by nearly three to one—10,298 to 3,580. Yet today we know little about this great majority. Census records and estate inventories yield only lists of figures and first names. On rare occasions an especially troublesome house servant such as Keziah Brevard's Sylvia begins to assume vague form as one reads the pages of a diary or a collection of letters. Nevertheless, this picture nearly always is from the white perspective, not that of blacks.

But the slate is not completely blank, In 1879, Jacob Stroyer, then thirty-three years of age, published a slim volume entitled *Sketches of My Life in the South*, presumably the first part of his autobiography. However, part two never appeared, and in succeeding years this work was reprinted several times as simply *My Life in the South*. Stroyer, a minister of the African Methodist Episcopal Church in Salem, Massachusetts, was born in 1846 on the plantation of Matthew R. Singleton, the man who a few years later built "Kensington," a lavish, European-styled mansion now restored to its former glory by Union Camp Corporation. One of fifteen children and known as "Jake," Stroyer was no admirer of slavery; yet, although his words may be biased, some observations seem valid and he mentions individuals well known in the annals of this region. The tale he spins is a strange mixture of pride, casual recollection, and violence.

Even though this ex-slave sometimes portrayed Matthew Singleton in an unfavorable light, he still was proud to have been associated with a *large* operation—a master who owned 465 blacks quartered on several plantations, had a stable of race horses, traveled widely, and entertained in a grand manner. According to Jake, until old enough to work, he and his playmates spent the warm months at the Singleton's "summer seat" in the nearby sand hills. Cared for by women too old to pick cotton, they enjoyed a reasonably pleasant existence except for an endless diet of corn mush and clabber (sour milk). On Sundays, however, his parents would visit and bring him a feast of cow peas, rice, and bacon. (Jake's mother was a field hand; his father tended hogs.) Christmas, he recalled, was another pleasant time with presents, and there always was dancing, even by those who disapproved but dared not reveal their true feelings.

On Jake's plantation two families usually shared a cabin that had only one fireplace. Some of these little structures had partitions, others did not. Children stayed with their parents until they got married, boys sleeping in the part known as the kitchen, girls with their parents. If one entered a cabin and found two fires on the hearth, that meant there was bad blood between the families; one fire, it was a contented home.

As a small boy, Jake became interested in race horses and soon was riding them on practice gallops; however, beatings by cruel grooms for little or no reason quickly made his life miserable.[9] This practice, known as "overhauling," was rooted in the belief that a sound thrashing now and then kept a slave "in his place." According to Stroyer, both the Singletons and their neighbors, the Clarksons, subscribed to this view, and he tells of a dispute between Thomas Clarkson and his wife concerning "overhauling."

Isom, a house servant who once had belonged to Clarkson's father, disappeared following an "overhauling" by the younger Clarkson. In his opinion, the old man had too much religion and had made such a pet of Isom that it took "all of the salt in the country to cure him."

> "Well, Thomas," said Mrs. Clarkson, "I told you the other day, before you did it, that I didn't see any need for you whipping Isom, because I thought he was a good boy."
>
> "My dear, if South Carolina had many more such Presbyterians as you and Father Boston [his father], in a short time there would be no slaves in the state; then who would you have to work for you?"[10]

As it turned out, Isom had not run away but was merely hiding on his master's plantation. After several days, he was discovered eating a meal in the kitchen. Clarkson, who was acting as his own overseer, wanted to "overhaul" Isom once more, but his strong-willed wife interceded. Even though he had employed a slave hunter with dogs at considerable expense, Clarkson backed down amid his wife's cries that, if he had not whipped Isom in the first place, then none of this would have happened.[11]

What Stroyer's book reveals is tolerance for violence on some plantations that encouraged beatings and whippings, not only by masters, overseers, and slave drivers, but by rank-and-file members of the black community, the strong taking out their frustrations on the weak. Thus it should come as no surprise that the death of those condoning the blows was no occasion for grief.

According to this former slave, Matthew R. Singleton, who died suddenly in 1854 just as his dream house was nearing completion, never was a gentle master, but as his financial woes mounted—exacerbated by the failure of a Charleston factor for whom he had co-signed notes and the costs of "Kensington"—his mood became increasingly grim. When his remains were brought home from the Singleton's summer retreat in Flat Rock, North Carolina, the body was put on display. "After all the slaves who cared to do so had seen his face," Stroyer recalls, "they gathered in groups around mistress to comfort her; they shed false tears, saying, 'never mind, misses, massa gone home to heaven;' while some were saying this, others said, 'Thank God, massa gone home to hell.' "[12]

Following Singleton's death, his creditors took many of his possessions, including the race horses, and Jake, with the apparent approval of his mistress, tried to become a carpenter. The overseer objected, telling the widow Singleton that no slave ever should be permitted to choose his work. This disagreement led to a running confrontation and still more beatings. Then in 1863, this black youth was sent to Charleston to build coastal defenses. There he was wounded by a Union shell and shipped back to "Kensington." While recuperating, fighting ceased, and Jake the slave became Jacob Stroyer, a free man.

It was blacks such as Jake, obscure and unknown, who in the 1860s brought to a close the world Keziah Brevard had known for over half a century . . . not by any action on their part but by their mere presence. Throughout much of her diary, written just as the crisis of 1860–1861 was at its height, Keziah wrestled with the dilemmas presented by Abraham

Lincoln, abolition, and secession, as well as moral questions involved. She often invoked God's help in political matters but eventually concluded that, if the Almighty "set any one over us who is not worthy to rule this beautiful country," it was because the people deserved just such a leader. "I do hate a Northern Abolitionist," she wrote on 10 December 1860. "Lord forgive me—but who can love those whose highest ambition is to cut our throats?" A few weeks later she railed against abolitionists as "the selfish & envious sons of Satan."

Yet Keziah Brevard was wary of secession, fearful that any rebellion would "soon show distracting heads." Even the act of assembling a committee to prepare for the convention to be held in Columbia, she observed, fomented tension and discord. When the split finally came, she thought it much too hasty and, as months passed, bewailed the fact that only a handful of states had joined South Carolina. In her opinion, the movement was "doomed," and as late as 7 April 1861 she wrote these words: "I cannot believe the South did right to break up the Union. She ought to have been united. . . ."

Amid widespread fears of a slave insurrection ("we know not what moment we may be hacked to death in the most cruel manner"), this fifty-seven-year-old matron told herself that would not happen, adding that at times she actually felt "very safe." Nevertheless, when outbuildings on a nearby plantation went up in flames, she began to have second thoughts. Strangely, intermingled with war, peace, and talk of sudden death is an exultant tally of how many mice a new trap purchased in Columbia was catching each night.

Keziah Brevard's final entry, dated 15 April 1861, is indeed poignant.

> This is a very windy day—clouds brewing. One of my poor neighbors sat with me this morning. Two of her sons gone to Charleston in the Sixth Regiment . . . it left Friday or Thursday the 11th or 12th. The papers say a Mr. Edmund Ruffin fired the first gun on Ft. Sumpter [sic]. O Lord let the N. & S. now compromise & shed no more blood. This book is closed with the beginning of the War of 1861—I never believed I should live to see my Country severed & that by those who pretend to be the best people. My God save this country & do not let me live to see misery in this once favoured land. *Amen.*
>
> Col. Anderson of Ft. Sumpter surrendered on Saturday the 13th of April 1861. Now dark & it is raining hard—rain began to fall soon after sundown.

Notes

1. Bernard, Karl, Duke of Saxe-Weimar-Eisenach, *Travels Through North America During the Years 1825 and 1826* (2 vols.; Philadelphia, 1828), I, p. 212. Despite these rather critical remarks, the duke, like most European visitors, thought Columbia a pleasant community with elegant homes, lovely gardens, and broad streets.
2. Harriet Martineau, *Retrospect of Western Travel* (2 vols.; New York, 1838), I, p. 221.
3. William Cullen Bryant, *Letters of a Traveller* . . . (New York, 1869), p. 89. For another view of the Midlands during this same decade, see "Rambles in the Interior" in the *Charleston Courier*, 10 April 1845.
4. Herbert Anthony Kellar (editor), *Solon Robinson, Pioneer and Agriculturalist; Selected Writings* (2 vols.; Indianapolis, 1936), II, p. 347. The average yield in Richland County seems to have been about one bale (400 pounds) per acre.
5. *Ibid.*, pp. 214–15.
6. Eli Bowen, *The United States Post-Office Guide* (New York, 1851), pp. 129–32. See also, Harvey S. Teal and Robert J. Stets, *South Carolina Postal History and Illustrated Catalog of Postmarks, 1760–1860* (Lake Oswego, Ore., 1989). The origin of the word "Doko" is obscure. Doko, which soon became Blythewood (named for a girls' school), was located close to the Richland-Fairfield line. Contemporary maps show it in both counties; but, in any case, early in this century the region was annexed by Richland. Claude H. Neuffer in his *Names in South Carolina* (XII:44) says Doko presumably was an Indian word meaning "watering place," but he was not convinced that was true. A better explanation may lie in the fact that the Dokos were a pygmy tribe of southern Ethiopia, and one suspects that a short black man perhaps tended the water tower at that point . . . hence the word "Doko."
7. Actually, the number of farms this size was nearly twice as large (closer to 10 percent), but authorities in Washington, for various reasons, cut L. T. Levin's original list of Richland County farms from 623 to 543.
8. The man who captured the faces of many of these well-to-do people on canvas and in miniature was William Harrison Scarborough (1812–1871). A Tennessee native, Scarborough settled in Columbia in the 1840s and soon was a guest at numerous plantations, frequently staying several weeks as he painted portraits of various family members. See Helen Kohn Hennig, *William Harrison Scarborough: Portraitist and Miniaturist* (Columbia, 1937).
9. One of the first shocks of Stroyer's young life was the realization that neither his father or mother could protect him from such treatment.
10. Stroyer at this point interrupted the story to state that, as a rule, Presbyterians "made better masters than did other denominations among the slave holders in the South."
11. Jacob Stroyer, *My Life in The South* (Salem, Mass., 1885), pp. 66–67.
12. *Ibid.*, p. 31. Nor did Samuel Leland lament Singleton's passing, noting in his diary that the deceased was a victim of "his own extravagance" and that "the vast property accumulated by the Father [Colonel Richard Singleton] proved a curse rather than a blessing." When the colonel died in November 1852, Leland wrote these words: "Old Dick Singleton was killed today on the Camden Branch of the Rail Road. No comment." There may have been a bit of jealousy at work here. Leland and some of his neighbors were offended by the ostentatious display of the Singletons, as well as their refusal to allow preaching among their slaves.

PART III

War and Peace, 1860–1890

The three decades from Fort Sumter to Ben Tillman are among the most chaotic that this community has experienced. The war years and the Reconstruction era that followed have been described, dissected, debated, analyzed, praised, appraised, and re-appraised by diarists and politicians of those days, their children and grandchildren, and scores of historians, would-be historians, and laymen fascinated by tales to be uncovered and told. Whether we understand those times any better than those who lived through them is debatable, but no one can deny that the literature concerning the Civil War and its aftermath is indeed vast.

However, once affairs were "put right" by Wade Hampton and his Red Shirts in 1876, for many the story of life in city, county, state, and nation becomes a hazy Indian summer extending at least to World War I and perhaps all the way to the Great Depression and beyond. For example, D. D. Wallace's widely used "short" history of South Carolina devotes 550 pages to events before 1865 and 130 to those of the next eighty-five years. World War II, which lasted almost as long as the Civil War, rates ten lines.

Yet the final years of the 19th century were a time when much was happening. They brought to the Midlands the telephone and electricity, as well as improvements in education and rail travel, the beginnings of suburban life and mill culture, and organized leisure activity such as baseball. Perhaps general disinterest in such matters is rooted in the fact that many of these new forces tended to challenge cherished rural values and often were led by impersonal, outside (Yankee) forces. It seemed to be an age bereft of heroes. Flesh-and-blood men full of honor and courage who uttered stirring phrases and clashed on battlefields were supplanted by tight-lipped Wall Street tycoons and laboratory wizards in white coats busy with experiments only they could understand.

Nevertheless, the most far-reaching changes of the post-Civil War decades—innovations that affected every household in Columbia and Richland County—were essentially home-grown, not imported. These include the beginnings of a two-track, Jim Crow world, hundreds of small tenant holdings carved out of what once were sprawling plantations, and little crossroads settlements and rail depots that suddenly appeared throughout the countryside, much like new growth after a spring shower.

Although residents of the Midlands long would blame General Sherman for both real and perceived woes, Richland County's population doubled between 1860 and 1890, rising from 18,307 to 36,821, while Columbia registered a similar gain, 8,052 to 15,353. By the close of this era, although agriculture was in the doldrums, crop production and the value of farm buildings in this region equaled or exceeded totals recorded in 1860.

No one will deny that the economic, social, and cultural life of these thirty years was uneven. War and the upheaval of Reconstruction were tremendous blows. Then, caught between boom-like conditions in the Piedmont and lowcountry desolation, the Midlands steered an erratic course, searching for instant riches and alternately boasting of impending success and then bewailing its cruel fate when those dreams did not come true.

A business directory published in 1893 repeated this pattern. Columbia, we are told, had 20,000 inhabitants, "four hotels, two yarn manufacturies, two batting manufactures, two cotton oil mills and two fertilizer works, one ice factory, two bottling works, eight colleges (six white and two colored), a convent, good schools and churches and a branch of the Keeley Institute for the treatment and cure of intemperance." This organization, which was expanding to new quarters on Arsenal Hill and had just opened a branch in Aiken, was "saving thousands from an untimely death and a drunkard's grave, thus making glad the hearts of many wives and mothers throughout the land." Even as this directory was being written, an English syndicate with a capital stock of $20 million presumably was studying Columbia and Richland County with an eye to possible investment. Exultation, despair, dreams, and hope—all were part of the local scene during these tumultuous years.

The
War Years

CHAPTER TEN

Despite the prayers of Keziah Brevard and millions of other Americans, the "N. & S." did not compromise their differences in 1861. The result, an epic struggle that changed our national life, still exudes a strange charm that fascinates and beguiles present-day descendants of both winner and loser. They know the broad outlines of the story by heart, revel in its moments of high drama, and frequently delve deep into obscure incidents revealing heroism, valor, and intrigue, all in behalf of a just cause, either to save the nation established in 1776 or create yet another.

Except for the final fiery flourish of February 1865, Richland County's most exciting days occurred at the outset. Several local citizens played leading roles in these stirring events, and Columbia's new Baptist Church was the setting for a convention that opened on 17 December 1860 and quickly passed without dissent a resolution in favor of secession, 159–0. Maxcy Gregg was one of seven men chosen to draft the ordinance that was signed and proclaimed in Charleston a few days later, the convention having moved to the port city because of a small pox scare.[1] William F. DeSaussure helped compose an appeal for similar action by other southern states, John S. Preston went north to lobby Virginians, and ex-governor James Adams was one of a trio of commissioners who met in Washington with President Buchanan to discuss the crisis. (In addition to Gregg, DeSaussure, and Adams, William Hopkins and J. H. Kinsler also represented Richland County at the Secession Convention.)

This was a time of bonfires, speeches, rumors, waving flags, rosy predictions of future triumphs, parades, and marching feet . . . an exhilarating time when South Carolina's thirty-year dream of a nation free of Yankee interference and abolitionism seemed about to come true. Yet until the fall of Fort Sumter in April of 1861 it was unclear how large that new nation might be or whether, in fact, there actually would be a fight.

Columbia diarist Grace Elmore, like many southerners, clung to the belief that, if the border states joined in, the Confederacy would be so formidable that there would be no war. During these hectic weeks between secession in December and the first shots four months later, various local military units went to the defense of Charleston, among them, the Columbia Artillery, Richland Volunteer Rifles, and a re-constituted and somewhat controversial college cadet corps. The faculty, remembering what a similar group had done only four years earlier, viewed any revival with misgivings; and, in an effort to curb youthful spirits, the governor ordered the students to remain in Columbia, even though he knew they were determined to go to Charleston. To circumvent these restrictions, the cadets decided to disband, pay their own way to the coast, and then re-form once more. Using such tactics, these young men enjoyed several weeks of guard duty and drill on Sullivan's Island, cheered lustily as shells exploded over Fort Sumter, and then returned "in triumph" to Columbia and their classes.

Meanwhile, other military companies from the Piedmont began to gather at the fair grounds just north of town and still more were hastily formed by local men and boys. On 8 January the Columbia Grays, eighty-five strong, appeared, followed four weeks later by the Congaree Mounted Riflemen. On Saturday, 16 February, these two groups, together with the Richland Light Dragoons, Governor's Guards, and a veteran contingent of the Richland Rifles, paraded about the business district, much to the delight of onlookers. By the time Fort Sumter was in southern hands, two full regiments were encamped at the fair grounds, and Columbia ladies were discussing plans for "a temporary association for the relief of soldiers' wives and families, who need assistance."

The reaction of Richland County residents to impending hostilities obviously took many forms, some men rushing to don uniforms and their wives, daughters, and sisters eager to do their part. As we know, Keziah Brevard was wary of these trends, as was former mayor E. J. Arthur, although for quite different reasons. Keziah represented those who thought steps being taken were impetuous and not well thought-out, while Arthur spoke for individuals of one political persuasion who found it difficult suddenly to join forces with long-time adversaries. Then there were men like John Caldwell, soon to be ousted from his post as president of the South Carolina Railroad because of freely expressed coolness toward secession. Not pro-North, Caldwell, ever the pragmatist, simply thought the new Confederacy lacked sufficient resources to sustain itself. Columbia storekeeper Edward Pollard also got into hot water during these months. Already suspect because of Massachusetts birth, Pollard was so impolitic as to scoff at fears of a slave uprising when forced to do patrol duty. John Meighan, the Confederate captain in charge of the patrol, was so incensed that he attacked Pollard and broke his leg.[2]

Thus the attitude of local whites toward separate political status encompassed a wide range of views, although most of them clearly approved of what was transpiring in the winter of 1860–1861, enthusiastically so. What of blacks? (After all, if there ever was a "silent" majority, here was one!) It is difficult to believe that many of Richland County's 11,000 slaves wanted to remain in bondage, yet Pollard was right when he belittled fears of a revolt. The risk was much too great; and, if the Union prevailed, rebellion on top of rebellion was unnecessary.

Like nearly all of their brethren throughout the South, local blacks remained outwardly loyal and essentially passive, perhaps out of custom and habit, but also because they could do little else and, as is quite understandable, tended to prefer known perils to those unknown. In addition, wartime strains often made their daily life much more pleasant. Many plantations were operated by women not accustomed to directing the work of field hands, and hard-pressed city officials lacked the personnel to enforce various rules and regulations.

On 17 September 1863, the *Daily Southern Guardian* called upon Columbia's police to restore order and prevent "the confusion worse confounded, occasioned by loud talking, laughing and whistling of negroes upon public streets, both in the day and in the night." Taking a cue from this appeal, a week later a citizen complained in a letter to the editor of black youths who crowded about the intersection of Taylor and Main streets, filled up benches in front of the telegraph office, and sallied forth "into either street, and upon either pavement, cracking whips, throwing stones, and yelling at the top of their lungs." This rabble, he wrote, seemed to think they were free and that the streets belonged to them. A stranger, he added, might believe Columbia was occupied "exclusively" by a throng of noisy, ill-mannered blacks.

Seven months later, on 11 April 1864, the *Guardian*'s editor resumed the attack, emphasizing that Columbia's blacks lacked supervision and were not producing for the war effort as they should. Some were meeting wagons coming into the city, buying up goods, and re-selling them at handsome profits. Others were traveling into rural areas by train to secure produce. These folk, he thundered, were nothing but "blockade runners" in the "home department." They also received stolen goods, gambled, watched cockfights, and got into mischief. (He conceded that a few "low" white men were doing much the same thing.) "In cities and towns he [the black man] is comparatively under no control." These "drones" were using up food and clothing, which tended to increase prices for everyone else. The solution, this editor maintained, was to levy such heavy taxes on urban blacks that they would flee to the countryside where they would have to work.

William Beverly Nash, a Virginia-born slave then working as a waiter at a Columbia hotel, says local blacks kept up with the war's progress by reading the northern press. Nash, an intelligent individual who represented Richland County in the state Senate from 1868 to 1877, told a *New York Times* reporter (9 August 1867) that a highlight of meetings of the St. Cecilia Society—of which he was a member—were such reports. Nash conceded that on occasions these newspapers were buried to keep them out of rebel hands and boasted of reading a copy of *Uncle Tom's Cabin* owned by a hotel resident. He said he even had seen the celebrated "key" to that controversial novel and was "astonished" by its accurate portrayal of southern life.

What blacks were doing was, of course, but one aspect of life on the home front. The year 1861 was a time of temporary measures, short enlistments, and hopes for a short war as well. In May, various military companies returned from Charleston, re-grouped, and headed for Virginia. On 14 May, a third regiment of volunteers moved from the fair grounds to Lightwood Knot Springs where a "camp of instruction" would be maintained throughout much of the conflict. Soon excursion trains were taking visitors out to Killian's each afternoon, and late in June the first units of Hampton's Legion also set out for Virginia. In its original form, this organization—mustered in at Columbia on 12 June 1861—consisted of six infantry companies, four artillery companies, and one cavalry unit. Then one company each of infantry and artillery was added.[3] Student cadets at the college, eager to join these men, promised to return to classes after a summer of war, but faculty members rejected such a proposal.

News of victory at Manassas a few weeks later created considerable excitement at the telegraph office and stirred hopes of early peace. Nevertheless, war-related activities continued. Gadsden ladies met and collected $265 for the Soldiers' Relief Association, a call went out for nurses to care for the wounded in Virginia, and various committees attended to the needs of poor Columbia families whose breadwinners were at the front. On 29 August, despite the presence of 2,500 men, the *Tri-Weekly Southern Guardian* conceded that the camp at Lightwood Knot Springs really was not organized in a military fashion. Meanwhile, a huge crowd of women met to form the Columbia Ladies' Working Association, a group that would turn out clothing, knapsacks, and similar gear (for pay) for South Carolina's Quartermaster Department. A few weeks later, a more select gathering took initial steps leading to the organization of a hospital in fair grounds buildings vacated by men now at Killian's.

A unique development of these months was a "rest station" established in July by the Young Ladies' Hospital Association near the Charlotte Depot. The ostensible goal was to ease periods of delay soldiers experienced while waiting for trains, although it is quite possible that intermingled with patriotic zeal was a healthy dose of curiosity and a yearning for romance. Whatever the intent, older women quickly took charge and moved the facility to Columbia's older and busier depot on Gervais Street used by Charleston and Greenville trains. Although what became known as the Wayside Home or Wayside Hospital had limited objectives (i.e., provide food and drink for all men in uniform and aid the sick and injured in transit), this unusual establishment, the first in the Confederacy, soon was being duplicated throughout the South. In all, some 75,000 young men were assisted in some fashion at Gervais Street during the war. In time, yet another Wayside facility appeared at the Kingville rail junction in the southeastern corner of the county, and in October of 1862 a Ladies' Hospital was established at the Charlotte Depot, replacing the original "Soldiers' Rest."[4]

The arrival of 150 Yankee prisoners of war early in November of 1861 created almost as much excitement on the banks of the Congaree as news of Fort Sumter and Manassas . . . perhaps even more, for one now could see the foe first-hand. "The poor prisoners is all everyone can think of," Mrs. J. A. Moore scrawled in her account-book diary on 2 November. This lady virtually abandoned thirteen boarders in her haste to watch their arrival, noting that "everyone it seemed that was in Columbia and the surrounding county was present."[5]

To the editor of the *Southern Guardian*, these men, most of them from New York and Indiana units that had been fighting in northern Virginia, were a separate race. The "generous" southerner, he wrote on 4 November, knew *he* would not engage in aggressive warfare. But these individuals did so because of intense hatred for the South; and, as a result, the southerner gazes "with surprise, if not horror, for the first time upon a public enemy." Within a week, a reader was complaining that these POWs, "the lowest dregs of the meanest people on earth," were being treated as "unfortunate heroes." Permitted to lounge about the county jail, they chatted with those who passed by, flaunted their impudence and vulgarity, and occasionally even rendered lusty verses of "Hail Columbia!"

Soon this story took an unexpected turn. Early in the new year, according to a report in the *Charleston Daily Courier* (28 January), six prisoners, all loyal Masons, were guests at a local lodge meeting. Jacob Levin, chairman of a group outraged by such hospitality, called for action against those extending "the right hand of fellowship" to men bent upon "subjugating and enslaving us." Then, in mid-February the escape of thirteen prisoners led to a shake-up of the guard detail. Two years later, the *Tri-Weekly South Carolinian* demanded to know why a Yankee officer, under guard, was seen in the market place bartering with blacks, exchanging sugar for food . . . *how* could this happen? Prison officials apparently replied that, in the absence of a sutler, this seemed reasonable enough and, in turn, accused the editor of "sensationalism." This led to more charges by the *Tri-Weekly* (27 September), including a hint that the guards might be dealing in Yankee currency.

More Union prisoners were lodged in the Columbia area from time to time during the war, but until late in 1864 their numbers were small. Most soon were exchanged or moved elsewhere. Governor Milledge L. Bonham and local inhabitants fought Confederate efforts to establish a permanent prison here, fearing it would attract enemy raids and aware that POW food purchases would tend to raise prices. To some degree, this first outcry against Yankee prisoners may have been triggered by a federal assault upon Port Royal that occurred soon after these visitors arrived. Yet this exasperating pattern of exultation and disappointment was one area residents soon took in stride, for it would be repeated all too often during the next few years.

Despite such ups and downs, Columbia's first twelve months of war were marked by widespread euphoria, great enthusiasm for "the cause," and scores of schemes to deal in a temporary manner with the crisis at hand. Although men and boys marched off to fight and prisoners of war appeared in their midst, Richland County citizens, like most throughout both nations, North and South, still were grappling with the reality of their situation. They reasoned in a dream-like way that somehow volunteer efforts, a quick, all-out plunge, or an unexpected turn of fortune would bring peace; and, if Confederate, they often pinned their hopes upon European intervention.

But, as it turned out, volunteer zeal alone, however strong, could not bring victory. Attempts to land a knock-out punch (such as the Union drive on Richmond in the spring of 1862) fell short of their goals, Dame Fortune refused to play favorites, and England and France remained aloof. The result was a much more serious approach to the business of war during 1862 and 1863 that soon was reflected on the local scene. Specifically, these shifts in emphasis included more long-range planning, schemes to manufacture goods in short supply or find substitutes for them, and concern for home defense, all of which were accompanied by realization that inflation was increasing by leaps and bounds and that Columbia was fast becoming this state's number one refugee center. (On 9 December 1861, Amanda Sims wrote to a lowcountry friend urging her to come to Columbia: "You will find a haven of safety in this flower garden of the Sunny South.")[6] In an unusual departure, a crew of 500 blacks began digging the foundations of a direct rail route to Augusta, thus bypassing Branchville, but nothing much came of this venture.

In February of 1862, the State Executive Council, a controversial wartime body, designated the military camp at Lightwood Knot Springs an official reception center for troops and ordered Arsenal Academy cadets to serve, if necessary, as Columbia's police guard at night. A conscription law passed a few weeks later in Richmond, the first in American history, required all males between eighteen and forty-five to register for service, a measure that quickly led to the break-up of South Carolina College.[7] Despite the demise of male education, girls' schools flourished during the war years. Not only were Columbia's traditional classrooms crowded, new ones appeared in the nearby countryside, among them, Monticello Female Institute at Alston and Blythewood Female Academy near Doko.

Soon a state conscription office was established at Lightwood Knot Springs, and in October most of Columbia's volunteer agencies came under the control of the Central Association for the Relief of South Carolina Soldiers headed by Maximilian LaBorde. He and a small staff met each week to ascertain what was needed and, with the help of both state and private funds, dispatched foodstuffs and supplies to South Carolinians serving in various parts of the Confederacy. In 1864 alone, this group boxed and shipped materials worth over $1.1 million.

Long before this association began to function, the Fair Grounds Hospital had moved to the college, where it continued to expand despite faculty objections, and buildings at the fair grounds were converted into a medical laboratory. Under the direction of Joseph Le Conte and Dr. James Woodrow, workers turned out alcohol, nitrate of silver, chloroform, ether, and other vital supplies. Before peace came, Le Conte and his staff were producing up to 500 gallons of alcohol in a single day. At the same time, local officials struggled with the problem of retail liquor sales, and the city council considered closing all bars and saloons. In the spring of 1862, council members asked the governor to find out how cities such as Richmond and New Orleans were curbing price hikes without recourse to martial law, and in April of that same year the much-detested Executive Council established a passport system in Columbia and Charleston.[8] Without proper documents, one presumably could not travel extensively; however, these regulations obviously required the cooperation of railroad officials.

Although wartime Columbia hardly could be called a manufacturing center, various items of some importance were produced here. These included—in addition to military gear, liquor, and medical supplies—Confederate Treasury notes, gunpowder, swords and sabres, socks, hand cards used in the preparation of cotton for spinning, buttons, shoes, matches, and ink. Yet all of these enterprises were overshadowed by Lexington County's well-known Saluda Factory, re-named the Columbia Cotton Mill in the 1850s, where hundreds of workers turned out cloth for the Confederacy.

J. F. Williams notes in *Old and New Columbia* that "as the war went on everything became scarce and prices rose higher and higher. Various factories were started, but the stuff manufactured was for the use of the army." Scores began weaving their own cloth, giving rise, he says, to songs such as this:

> My homespun dress is plain, I know,
>   My hat is Palmetto, too,
> But it shows what Southern girls
>   For Southern rights will do.

Columbia, like many other communities throughout the Confederacy, was seized with a desire to produce niter needed for gunpowder. Animal carcasses, stable manure, and other decaying matter were dumped into pits north of the Asylum in an attempt to secure niter (saltpeter), but the results were disappointing. The fermenting process took longer than anticipated, and the major product, according to some residents, was merely "a terrible odor."

By September of 1863, about a dozen branches of the Confederate government were maintaining offices in various buildings scattered throughout Columbia's business district, and authorities at all levels were trying to halt soaring prices. Efforts to deal with increased demand and

dwindling supplies took many forms as refugees, war workers, and soldiers perhaps doubled Columbia's peacetime population of 8,000. Officials in Richmond proclaimed limits such as seventy-five cents for a
pound of bacon, four dollars for domestic wool jeans, seven dollars for a
pound of green tea, and thirty dollars for a bushel of imported salt . . .
ceiling prices that the market greeted with a shrug. Columbia's city council, searching for a better approach, passed ordinances prohibiting purchase of foodstuffs until 7 A.M. in summer months (8 A.M. during the
remainder of the year), as well as a ban on purchase for re-sale until items
had been displayed for at least two hours. The Columbia Mutual Supply
Association, formed on 14 November 1863, was yet another way, it was
thought, to solve this dilemma. A member who bought a $100 share of
stock could then buy up to that amount in goods each week at the association store. If an individual bought several shares or did not use up his
weekly allotment of $100, then those too poor to purchase shares could
acquire a quantity of goods at cost or close to it.[9]

There is little evidence that any of these stratagems had much impact. In November of 1863, Gustavus Augustus Follin, Jr., told his father
that he was getting ninety dollars a month as a clerk in the state adjutant
general's office and his expenses for the same period were $102 . . . "I
cannot live at this rate." A soldier visiting Columbia wrote to the *Daily
South Carolinian* (11 October 1863) to express shock at corn meal that
cost five dollars a bushel and bacon that sold for two dollars and fifty cents
to three dollars a pound! If true, this meant that bacon was selling in Columbia for four times the official price decreed by Richmond. During
these same weeks, Arsenal Academy teacher John B. Patrick tried to buy
a cow; but when he reached the owner's home, the animal already had
been sold for $225. "They sell at fabulous prices nowadays," he noted in
his diary. (Nine months later, Patrick was able to acquire a horse, harness,
and dray-wagon for $1,000.)

In an attempt to increase food stocks, in February of 1863 state authorities limited cotton planting to 1 acre per hand and, to prevent hoard-
ing and stimulate markets, in June of that year ordered farmers to deliver
one-tenth of their annual produce to collection sites within eight miles
of their homes. A group of city and county leaders met that same month
and established six committees of three men each to arrange for defense against enemy raids, and the names of both deserters (thirty dollars
reward) and women who had failed to complete soldiers' garments as
promised began to appear in the *Tri-Weekly South Carolinian*. This newspaper, like most throughout the South, now was only a single sheet. Its

rival, the *Daily Southern Guardian*, dealt with the paper shortage in a unique fashion, sometimes reducing the number of columns and also its name, appearing simply as the *Southern Guardian*.

A letter to the editor of that paper (28 September 1863) expressed concern that Yankee prisoners passing through Columbia were allowed to talk freely with blacks; more to the point, perhaps, they were exchanging greenbacks for Confederate notes: ten Union dollars for fifteen or more in southern currency. The latter would, of course, be useful if one escaped; and, asked the writer, should the police interfere with this practice? A few days later, James G. Gibbes held a gigantic auction near the South Carolina Railroad depot of items brought through the blockade by the steamers *Alice* and *Fannie*. In addition to dry goods, hats, shoes, leather, groceries, and medicine, Gibbes offered up 175 cases of Holland gin, 12 cases of sardines, 78 kegs of saltpeter, and 4 cans of Turkish opium.

What these bits and pieces reveal—rewards for deserters, blacks with relatively large sums of money in hand, taxes in kind, luxury goods auctioned off in a time of need—is the complexity of life in South Carolina's capital city during these years. There is little doubt that a few were finding the conflict to be a profitable venture, and scores of lowcountry refugees (as well as some local residents) were eager to buy whatever they had to offer. Also, Columbia's location made it an ideal site for conventions held within the Confederacy. During the war, bankers, railroad executives, teachers, and theologians from several states gathered here from time to time to ponder various matters. The most puzzling of these sessions was convened in the fall of 1861 by a group of Episcopal bishops who agonized for four days over what to call their church. Some were uneasy with the word "Protestant," and others did not like "Episcopal." But "Reformed Catholic" won little support, so eventually, as one could have predicted, that body became the "Protestant Episcopal Church of the Confederate States of America."

All of this activity made Columbia a lively, interesting city. Diarist Mary Chesnut wrote in May of 1862 that it was "the place of good living— pleasant people, pleasant dinners, pleasant drives. I feel," she added, "that I have put dinners in the wrong place. They are the climax of the good things here. This is the most hospitable place in the world, and the dinners are worthy of it."

In Washington, she explained, one had state dinners. In Montgomery there were few dinners. Charleston had all-male dinners; Richmond, balls; and Virginia, in general, lavish breakfasts.

Here in Columbia the family dinners are the speciality. You call or they pick you up and drive home with you. 'Oh, stay to dinner.' And you stay gladly. They send for your husband. And he comes willingly. Then comes, apparently, a perfect dinner. You do not see how it could be improved. And they have not had time to alter things or add for additional guests. They have everything of the best. Silver, glass, china, table linen—damask—&c. &c. And then the planters live 'within themselves,' as they call it. From the plantations come mutton, beef, poultry, cream, butter, eggs, fruits, and vegetables. It is easy to live here—with a cook who has been sent to the best eating houses in Charleston to be trained. Old Mr. Chesnut's Romeo was apprenticed at Jones's in town. I do not know where Mrs. Preston's got his degree, but he deserves a medal.[10]

Twenty-four months later, although the fortunes of war had shifted dramatically, Mrs. Chesnut probably still could have gotten a fine meal at any Columbia mansion. Insulated to some degree from the realities of both Gettysburg and Vicksburg, daily life on the Richland County home front steered an erratic course throughout much of 1864. The self-confidence of previous years was shaken, true; but, as if to defy the fates, volunteer efforts and contributions to the coffers of the Central Association mounted apace with lengthening lists of Confederate dead. During these months, Yankee POWs twice tried to tunnel out of the local jail, the "Bee" Store held huge sales of imported luxuries, a Confederate scout was hanged for killing a local madam and then his body dug up to be sure he was dead, civilian rail travel came to a halt, free small pox vaccinations were available to all who promised to turn in their scabs for army use, and Jefferson Davis visited town and made a strong appeal for all-out support, only to be followed within days by a call from Columbia's spokesman in the Confederate House of Representatives for a negotiated peace. Bands played twice each week in Sidney Park, concerts were held at the Athenaeum, and tournaments, barbecues, military "hops," and parties were so frequent that the *Daily South Carolinian* boasted in April of 1864 that Columbia was one of the "liveliest" spots in the Confederate States of America. It was, in short, a strange, topsy-turvy year.

Valentine B. Chamberlain, a Connecticut captain held in the jail from July 1863 until rescued by Union forces, escaped for ten days on one occasion but soon was behind bars once more. Copies of letters to his family reveal a tedious existence . . . "corn cakes in the morning and corn bread at night." However, a pet cat, a bit of whiskey at Christmas (sixty dollars a gallon), a little outdoor exercise each day, and ten volumes of Scott novels purchased for $225 helped pass the time. Meals, he assured relatives, were reasonably good, and one could hear music when a dance was held in a nearby hall and see "a fair form flit by the window." One such occasion may have been an "elegant hop and supper" held at the city hall on the evening of 5 May 1864 following a tournament at Hampton Race Course that starred twenty-five "knights" from Hampton's Legion.

Chamberlain was more fortunate than 1,400 fellow prisoners, who, late in 1864, were herded onto a 5-acre tract on the west bank of the Saluda River in nearby Lexington County. This site, known as "Camp Sorghum," was across from present-day Greystone Boulevard and slightly north of Riverbanks Zoo. It had no buildings, no tents, no latrines, no facilities whatsoever, and apparently Confederate authorities had no clear plans as to what would be done with these men. Rations consisted of corn meal and sorghum, hence the camp's name. Those held there could buy food at inflated prices, but few had utensils for cooking and eating. To survive, many dug holes in the ground for shelter or walked about at night in an attempt to keep warm. In November, guards permitted the prisoners to hold a mock election, promising to publish the results; however, Lincoln won by such a wide margin that no tally ever appeared. At least eight men died from disease and exposure and others escaped, although most soon were back in Confederate hands. Finally, in December the survivors were transferred across the river to the Asylum; and, as Sherman approached two months later, nearly all of these prisoners were hustled off to North Carolina. A few, however, got free and joined in the general assault upon South Carolina's capital city.[11]

Not far from where Captain Chamberlain languished for over eighteen months was the Columbia headquarters of the Importing & Exporting Company of South Carolina, usually referred to as the "Bee" Store because of owner William C. Bee, one of the Confederacy's most successful blockade busters. It was always a hubbub of activity whenever stocks were plentiful, and one young treasury clerk recalled that Bee's emporium sometimes was so crowded that any lady who fainted was laid out on a counter so she would not be trampled. When this store was about to close for a time, the *Daily South Carolinian* (10 March 1864) urged the management to set apart a day for blacks to shop as was being done in Charleston, and the following week the "Bee" Store was thrown open to them for two days.[12] This decision reveals that blacks, as a rule, were not shopping for themselves in Columbia stores, but by the spring of 1864 some had accumulated enough money to make them valued as customers. By this date, the "Bee" Store was accepting five-dollar bills at par; larger Confederate currency was being devalued by one-third.

Two other treasury workers had interesting comments upon the local scene during these months. Amanda Sims told Hattie Palmer on 22 June 1864 that occasionally there had been as many as 6,000 young men stationed in and around Columbia, and "we have had some romantic times, too." Concerning her work, she had these observations: "I sign my name 3,200 times a day and are occupied for six hours from 8 AM to 2 PM. It reminds me very much of school days. There are about two hundred ladies employed, each has her own desk, and I know Babel itself was not much more confusion."[13]

Bettie J. Clarke of Buchanan, Virginia, who came south when the treasury unit was transferred from Richmond, told of an immense hall filled with chattering women and tried to describe her surroundings to a friend back home. In the summer of 1864, Bettie was boarding at the Methodist Female College, "a very commodious & handsome" building, but would have to move when school opened. ". . . I must say I am somewhat disappointed in the South. I expected to tread on a flowery carpet, & breathe an atmosphere forever fragrant with the breath of the Magnolia & Cape Jessamine. While, instead my feet are parched on hot brick pavements, & my brain addled by this old South Carolina sun. . . ."

Yet she conceded the heat actually was no worse than Virginia, merely constant, and Columbia was a lovely town with gardens and trees on each side of its broad streets and often down the middle as well. "There is too much uniformity, about the place, & some of the people are stiff as ramrods— You know South Carolinians pride themselves on their hauteur of manner, these Columbians particularly. The refugees from Charleston, Beaufort, Sumpter [sic] are very different, so affable & charming." But this young lady quickly added that, in justice, she should note that many residents were exceedingly kind and frequently entertained treasury girls in their homes. In fact, she was going to the Prestons that very evening.[14]

One tale that certainly set tongues to wagging at the Treasury Department was the murder of Columbia's best-known madam in 1863 and the death of her assailant on the gallows in June of the following year. German-born Rosa La Grand, also known as "Dutch Rose," lived with six young women (ages sixteen to twenty-one) at the southwest corner of Gates and Lady streets. In the summer of 1863, a Virginia youth named Thaddeus Saunders, once a scout with Stonewall Jackson, came to town on leave, got drunk, and decided to steal Rosa's jewels. She objected; and, in an especially gruesome fashion, Saunders and an accomplice chloroformed and strangled the unfortunate Rosa. Game girl that she was, Rosa lingered long enough to identify Saunders and his friend. They were apprehended in Montgomery, Alabama, brought back, tried, and Saunders was sentenced to be hanged.

This should be the end of the story, but this young man was bent upon living. His first step was conversion to Catholicism, followed by ads in the *Daily South Carolinian* (25, 29 May 1864) soliciting signatures on a pardon petition to be submitted to the governor: "I now publicly state that, with the help of God and the interposition of the citizens in my behalf, I am willing to be placed in any position that may be allotted to me." In essence, if reprieved, Thaddeus Saunders would do all he could to beat the North, singlehandedly if necessary. This maneuver won him a two-week stay, but on 24 June Saunders was hanged in a field near the college. According to J. F. Williams, he was one cool customer, walking up the steps to the gallows unaided and pulling off his necktie, collar, and boots "just as unconcerned as if he were going to bed." John B. Patrick, who was not among the throng of onlookers, noted in his diary that it was indeed strange that "anyone should desire to see such a death."

Father J. J. O'Connell, a new-found friend, saw these events differently. Saunders, "as brave a man as ever lived," merely had gotten mixed up with the wrong crowd in "a disreputable house" operated by a notorious Jewess. O'Connell not only took the body of the deceased to his church for burial but published an ad in the *Daily South Carolinian* (25 June) signed by himself, Sheriff Dent, and others soliciting attendance by the general public at funeral services. Forty-eight hours later, those whom O'Connell characterized in his *Catholicity in the Carolinas and Georgia* as "arrogant, intolerant, and bigoted people" persuaded the governor to order an exhumation to be sure no popish chicanery was at work and that Saunders somehow still lived. With Wade Hampton in attendance, the grisly job was done, and it was established, beyond any doubt, that the man who killed Rosa was dead.

As bizarre as this tale is, it should not overshadow changes taking place in wartime Columbia. An island of security, war profiteers, and easy living, this crowded little city was developing an underworld that overwhelmed its minuscule police force. Especially troublesome was a growing number of unlicensed grog shops, the owners of which undoubtedly gained access to liquor being manufactured at the fair grounds.

In February of 1864 police salaries were raised somewhat, and the number of patrolmen increased to seventeen with plans to add eight more in the near future. Yet a year later, ten days before General Sherman arrived, few men had been hired, and at a city council session on 7 February 1865, twenty-two local residents, including well-known grocer John Heise, were fined $19.50 or more for illegal liquor sales. At this meeting, members again agreed to enlarge the force, voted to permit policemen to to continue dividing money received for whipping slaves and catching runaways, and once more chose John Burdell as captain. (Burdell, the man who perhaps instigated the notorious cadet riot of 1856, recently had offered a reward for one of his slaves, "dead or alive.")

By all odds, the visit of Jefferson Davis to Columbia on 4 October 1864 should have been a festive occasion, and perhaps it was. The chief executive, who stayed at the home of the Chesnuts on Plain Street, saluted a large crowd with praise for John C. Calhoun and the Palmetto State: "Her men are heroes, her women only less then angels." J. F. Williams, then a teenager, recalled schools were closed and he got a seat on a gate post and "heard him well." But, with enemy forces moving almost at will throughout the lower South, hopeful words and a call for renewed effort had little impact. During the winter of 1863–1864, most of the men in gray and butternut uniforms realized their cause was lost, and family letters at the South Caroliniana Library indicate that throughout 1864 rank and file citizens also were beginning to despair. By the end of that year, Columbia's gas works no longer functioned, and nearly everyone had grown accustomed to innumerable substitutes such as coffee made from parched seeds and soft soap from the country scooped up in buckets and pans. That Christmas season, young Williams went "in the street"—the 1860s equivalent of going downtown—and bought a pound of brown sugar for six dollars. With it his mother made a cake of corn meal and sorghum; and, according to her son, "It was first rate, too!"

All these sacrifices were both admirable and patriotic, but more and more frequently the question asked was why . . . what good would it do? Hardly had Davis left Columbia when Congressman W. W. Boyce, a Winnsboro lawyer-planter and this community's representative in the lower house of the Confederate Congress, made public a letter urging the president to call conventions in each state to discuss peace terms. The purpose of this proposal, which Boyce defended personally during a heated public meeting in Columbia's city hall on 18 October, was to divide the North. What the military had failed to do might be achieved, he argued, through diplomacy. Boyce advocated unity with northern Democrats to defeat Lincoln and thus put in the White House his rival, McClellan, a man more receptive to negotiation. Although this scheme went nowhere and Boyce was the target of much abuse, letters to local papers indicate he had his defenders. Interestingly, the congressman attracted much more attention than President Davis during these weeks, and nine months later some South Carolinians thought he should be appointed provisional governor of this state.

As far as Richland County residents were concerned, the opening months of 1865 were dominated by two memorable events—a gigantic bazaar at the old State House and the invasion of Yankee hordes led by General Sherman. The first, a breath-taking, three-day extravaganza, required almost as much organization and planning as the second. As early as November of 1864, Grace Elmore was soliciting contributions and making tobacco bags for this state-wide benefit for Confederate hospitals. Her mother remarked that their household was "bazaar" mad, and during the weeks that followed the madness continued to mount. (Early in December, Grace took part in a concert; and, while singing, she imagined she had the power "to decapitate Lincoln and enjoyed the thought greatly.") On 4 January 1865, she wrote in her diary that nearly every home in Columbia was in a state of frenzy concerning the upcoming bazaar.

> How strangely is the serious and the gay intermingled in our life, one moment gloomily considering the many chances of Yankee rule and the next looking with equally anxious earnestness after the pleasures and interests of the Bazaar. For with the Yankees almost at our doors, we still think of, work for and cheer our soldiers, sick and wounded in the hospitals. Money is scarce, so we will have a Fair to which the whole State is contributing. Each house has its corner to which tobacco bags, cloth babies, cushions, all odds and ends that can be raked or scraped from our needs, is consigned, there to rest until the great day when they will appear in the State House to tempt the fancy of every true Confederate. Since early November we've been ransacking the house for scraps, and bemoaning our extravagance in the first years of the war, in using up most of our material in foolishness for the soldiers. I remember cutting up two pretty dresses, and spending a lot of money on tassels, to make a lot of smoking caps for Captain Hoke's company. I presented them myself and was immensely pleased when the men whirled them around their heads and gave three cheers for 'the ladies.'

Now, she sighed, she wished she had those dresses to help sick, brave men really in need.

Meanwhile, with Sherman in Savannah and poised to march north into South Carolina, Mayor Thomas J. Goodwyn was trying valiantly to erect fortifications to protect this state's seat of government. On 30 December, pursuant to a city council resolution, he asked area residents to lend him slaves, wagons, carts, spades, and shovels. On 18 January, one day after the grand bazaar opened its doors, Goodwyn's request became a plea, coupled with frank admission that, to date, he had gotten neither help nor tools and public response actually was "mortifying."

But to the bazaar. On 17 January the old State House, with chairs removed and its walls draped and decorated, became a sea of color. Banners such as "Don't Give Up the Ship," "God Save Our State," and "Contribute to the Comfort of our Sick and Wounded Soldiers" floated over tables laden with food, toys, pictures, embroidered cushions, trinkets, and other odds and ends, some of them brought to town by railroads free of charge. The hall was open each afternoon and evening (admission one dollar), and the *Daily South Carolinian* reported 3,800 tickets were "taken up" the first day. The only discordant note, this paper said, was "a hundred or more rude boys" who, in packs of a dozen or so, dashed about tearing dresses and causing panic. *Real* coffee was drunk by the gallon, and all eyes were on a handsome wax doll from England that had the place of honor on the speaker's desk. In the words of Grace Elmore, "We were a gay crowd, every body left his bad spirits and anxiety at the door, and if Sherman was mentioned 'twas in a most casual way, nobody had time for blues, we jostled each other, laughed, quarreled, made fun and forgot for a time that the battle for home and fireside was soon to commence again."

Each Confederate state had a table named in its honor, and three of them offered restaurant fare. The Louisiana menu, startling in its complexity in either peace or war, must have attracted considerable attention: mock turtle soup, oyster soup, gumbo, roast turkey, boned turkey, daubed tongue, daubed beef, roast ham, partridge stuffed with artichokes, vol-au-vent of chicken, pork pie, chicken pie, oysters, chicken salad, giblet patties, mayonnaise, stuffed eggs à la Creole, French rolls, crackers, coffee, tea, six kinds of cake (black, jelly, sponge, pound, ginger, and ground-nut), doughnuts, trifle, jelly, blanc-mange, charlotte russe, custard, syllabub, and meringue. After three days, the remaining food and goodies were taken to the town hall, together with items that arrived late from various parts of the state, and the fun continued. Just how much money was made and how it was disbursed is not known. The *Daily South Carolinian* (20 January 1865) estimated each table took in $10,000–$20,000;[15] however, the records of Columbia's Wayside Hospital indicate it received only $24,936.50 from this three-day benefit.

The second great event, which also lasted about seventy-two hours, is, without doubt, the most controversial and closely analyzed period in Columbia's long history. It has been the subject of three exhaustive inquiries, a dozen or so books, and perhaps a hundred articles, most of which have tried without success to prove that General Sherman intentionally and according to prearranged plan burned one-third of the city on 17 February 1865. True, he was in command of South Carolina's state capital that terrible night, his armies having moved across the Saluda and Broad earlier that same day, and thus was responsible for maintaining order . . . amid war and *disorder*, it might be noted. And it is equally true that the great fire comported well with his avowed intent to destroy Confederate morale (a circumstance he never denied), but other factors must be considered. These include the defender, the invader, and the weather, and what each was doing in mid-February of 1865.

Like Mayor Goodwyn, South Carolina's new governor, Alexander Gordon Magrath, found it impossible to stir local interest in defense efforts or solicit support from other quarters. Lee on 23 January said he could not send help, although he soon dispatched Wade Hampton and 2,000 of Butler's cavalry to Columbia. When men of the 23rd South Carolina Militia were told to appear at the Richland County Courthouse on the 26th or face possible arrest, Colonel A. R. Taylor, the man who issued the order, received an anonymous death threat and a promise to burn down his house if he persisted in such a policy.[16]

During the next few weeks, Richland County residents existed in a perplexing state of confusion, doubt, and reassurance, uncertain whether Sherman was heading for Charleston, Augusta, or Columbia. On 10 February, Mrs. Emily Caroline Ellis, who arrived in the state capital from Orangeburg, noted in her diary, "Every thing seemed to be going on as usual in the city." That same day, Confederate authorities in Richmond, not state officials, ordered the evacuation of military supplies. On the 11th, the *Daily South Carolinian*, somewhat strangely, advocated a "scorched earth" policy—"let him [the enemy] find nothing on which to feed man or beast."[17] And the following day, the *Guardian*, amid a stirring call to arms, said Sherman's immediate goal was not Columbia and predicted a great victory was imminent . . . one that would prove "God is fighting on our side—although with vigor down—and that he has vouchsafed to South Carolina the proud privilege of closing, as she began, this war in triumph."[18] Forty-eight hours later, Mayor Goodwyn still was assuring citizens that their community would be defended, but few were listening as panic took over.

On the 15th and 16th, hundreds jammed the railway depots, hindering efforts to ship arms, medical supplies, and other vital materials to safety. Among those departing for Chester was General Beauregard and his staff, which left General Joseph ("Fighting Joe") Wheeler and, finally at 8 P.M. on the 16th, Wade Hampton—belatedly elevated to lieutenant general—with the task of defending South Carolina's proud capital city.[19] Before departing, Confederate soldiers, following a policy dictated by Richmond, moved hundreds of cotton bales into the streets for transport outside of town where they were to be destroyed so as to deny them to the enemy. Meanwhile, Wheeler's men, contrary to orders, burned the bridge across the Congaree and then proceeded to pillage and plunder Columbia's stores and shops. Motives undoubtedly were mixed—deny loot to the invader, as well as get even with merchants who had been charging what they thought were exorbitant prices. During this rampage, several of them had a hostile encounter with Hampton as he tried to interfere with their fun. When threatened, the general reportedly shrugged and attributed the altercation to liquor and high spirits.

On the evening of the 16th, Wade Hampton told Mayor Goodwyn that his forces would leave Columbia the next morning. The new lieutenant general also made two other fateful decisions. Unable to move cotton to fields outside of town, he ruled that it would *not* be burned because of the great danger any fire would present to Columbia itself; and, secondly, following consultation with Beauregard, he declined to destroy substantial supplies of liquor, both men taking the view that much of it was private property and thus not under military jurisdiction. By this time, Union forces had taken up positions on the west bank of the Congaree and occasionally were shelling the city, much to the distress of Charleston refugee Catherine Prioleau Ravenel. Still irked four decades later by such behavior, she wrote in *South Carolina Women in the Confederacy* (1907) that "No notice of such intention [to shell] was given to the authorities."

As word spread that Confederate forces were leaving, stragglers and the rabble of the town began to seize whatever Wheeler's men had not taken. Butler's cavalry, as it departed, burned the Charlotte terminal, and early on the morning of the 17th a huge explosion ignited by fire, ammunition, and looters rocked the other depot. In short, discipline evaporated and smoke and flames could be seen in various parts of the city. At about 10 A.M., Mayor Goodwyn, accompanied by three council members (John McKenzie, John Stork, and O. Z. Bates) met a Union colonel north of town and surrendered South Carolina's capital to him. As federal forces moved through Cotton Town, both blacks and whites greeted them with liquor in cups, bottles, and buckets. Sherman arrived a short time later as his men were establishing a semblance of order, yet it is obvious that widespread consumption of spirits and wine continued, and attempts to curb fires, often blazing in loose cotton, were spasmodic at best. According to regulations, the first Union brigade to enter Columbia served as provost guard, occupied important buildings, and established sentries. The rest of the men went into camp in the outskirts, and those without specific duties were free to roam wherever they wished. Meanwhile, still other units were dispatched to destroy rail lines and forage north and east of the city, notably in lower Richland where some plantation homes were burned and others were not.

During the afternoon, Sherman set up his headquarters, met with Mayor Goodwyn to assure him that the city was safe, and even called upon several old friends. The outlying mansions of Hampton and other prominent Confederates were torched, guards posted upon request at many homes, and Union officers tried to stem what seemed to be an endless flow of liquor. To sundown, the scene was somewhat chaotic, as was to be expected, but not especially alarming. Then, from 5 to 8 o'clock three major fires kept Columbia firemen busy. One was in cotton piled in the middle of Sumter Street between Washington and Lady, another was in the brothels near Gervais Street, and the third appears to have been in the center of town. The first two conflagrations were contained, but the last one, fanned by a high northwest wind, quickly spread to nearby buildings. The wind continued to blow until 2 A.M. as General Sherman himself, many of his men, and scores of Columbia citizens tried to subdue fires both great and small.

Both defender and invader actually battled three adversaries that night: fire, wind, and drunken, blue-clad soldiers who often impeded their efforts and on some occasions even set fires. Since Union troops had entered the city singing, "Hail Columbia, happy land, if I don't burn you, I'll be damned," such behavior must have been feared and anticipated. This was, after all, the capital of the state that started the war that had messed up their lives and caused them personal grief and pain. The *New York Herald*, for example, in an editorial of 16 February praised Sherman's forces and their "work of righteous retribution." "They know," this daily said, "they are shaking up the viper's nest in which this rebellion was hatched in shaking up, from top to bottom, the State of South Carolina. They feel they are instruments of divine justice, on a special mission, in the punishment of the thirty years' treason of South Carolina."

The most recent, in-depth analysis of what happened that horrible night is found in a book by Marion Brunson Lucas, *Sherman and the*

Burning of Columbia, published in 1976 by the Texas A & M University Press. Lucas, a South Carolinian by birth and recipient of a doctorate in history from the University of South Carolina, has pored through hundreds of documents, affidavits, and eyewitness accounts. He concludes that the Confederates erred in not keeping local citizens informed and in their policy concerning cotton, destruction of which by February of 1865 was pointless. Lucas faults both Confederate and Union leaders for not destroying liquor and especially the latter for not taking action sooner against drunken men, who, in effect, mounted a riot in the midst of a raging inferno. And then there was the wind, which, in his opinion, probably made the task of those fighting the fires well nigh hopeless.[20]

There is no doubt whatsoever that Union soldiers were to blame for what happened, some with intent, others by default in their drunken stupor.[21] Two Union diaries at the South Caroliniana Library contain pertinent observations. C. C. Platter, an Ohio infantry officer, wrote on 17 February 1865 of a day "long to be remembered." It was "a grand sight" as he and his men crossed the Broad River and came into town "with bands playing, Colors flying, &c. &c." to be welcomed by negroes "wild with delight." After admiring the new capitol ("a splendid edifice") and Columbia's impressive mansions, he and his men left the crowded streets and went into camp outside of town. From there, he watched the fire that night and then altered words written earlier that day: "Columbia is quite a nice city" was re-cast to read "Columbia *was* quite a nice city." The fire, this officer wrote, "does not reflect much credit on our army—a very disgraceful affair—but *whisky did it* and *not the* soldiers." On the 18th, Platter and his troops began tearing up railroad tracks leading to Charlotte. During the day, he noted, he saw an "innumerable number of darkies on their way to Columbia—all happy that the day of jubilee had come. This beats all the places for contraband I ever saw."

An Iowa enlisted man, Charles G. Ward, told much the same story.

17 . . . We then marched in to the city and Stacked arms in the Streets. Every man was soon to him self and whiskey and tobacco was the order of the Day. About 10 o'clock at night the city was Set on fire and all our Efforts to put it out amounted to nothing, for the Soldiers had cut the hoes [sic]. About midnight we were ordered from the city on account of the fire. Moved out one mile in to camp.

18 the 3 Brig is Doing as Drunken Duty in Town to Day as ours Did Yesterday. the 2n Brig relieved them but Done no better.

The results of the holocaust that overwhelmed Columbia were staggering, but (according to Lucas) not quite as devastating as later claimed.

Except for one structure, the Main Street business district was wiped out, and many homes between Main and Bull were destroyed. However, the college, residential areas west of Main, and most outlying blocks east of Bull remained intact. The new capitol, yet to be completed, was scorched and damaged somewhat, and the old State House, scene of the recent gala gathering, was burned to the ground. One of the most tragic losses was intentional destruction of the home of Dr. Robert W. Gibbes on the north side of Plain Street between Sumter and Marion. Distinguished citizen, antiquarian, naturalist, and collector of historic documents, Gibbes and his friends saved the house as flames rushed past only to have it subsequently destroyed by a drunken band of Yankee "bummers."

The initial reaction among local residents (and perhaps some Union visitors, too) was stunned disbelief, followed by efforts to help the homeless. Upon request, Sherman had 500 cattle put on the college green with which to feed the poor, and he also gave Mayor Goodwyn 100 rifles and ammunition and all of the salt left at the Charleston depot. During the weekend, the Yankees went about wrecking railroad tracks and other public facilities of military value not already destroyed and, on Monday the 21st, marched out of town toward Winnsboro and Cheraw. Among those leaving with them were many blacks and a small band of Union sympathizers that included Mrs. Jacob Feaster and her daughter, the celebrated Marie Boozer.[22] Before departing, these two women, renowned for their beauty, abandoned their carriage and appropriated a fancier vehicle owned by Grace Elmore's family.

As destructive as the Columbia fire was, it should be put in context. A blaze engulfed a large section of Savannah late in January following an explosion at an arms depot, 200 buildings went up in flames when the Confederates burned cotton as they withdrew from Charleston on 17 February, and during these weeks Hardeeville, Barnwell, Orangeburg, and many other South Carolina communities experienced flames, smoke, and terror. Perhaps it should be noted that the occupation of Charleston—at least as far as the northern press was concerned—overshadowed the blaze in Columbia, which got scant mention, if any.

At first, many South Carolinians accepted what had occurred on the banks of the Congaree as one of war's misfortunes. When informed by her husband that Sherman's men had burned Columbia, Mary Chesnut wrote that "we had every right to expect they would."[23] But within a week the alleged murder of Yankee foragers and threats by Hampton to retaliate if Sherman avenged those deaths led to bitter words between the two leaders. Soon each was claiming that the other had started the fire that rav-

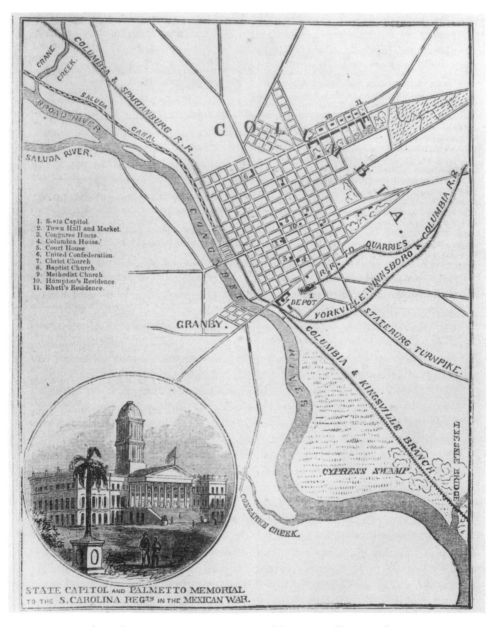

1. State Capitol.
2. Town Hall and Market.
3. Congaree House.
4. Columbia House.
5. Court House.
6. United Confederation.
7. Christ Church.
8. Baptist Church.
9. Methodist Church.
10. Hampton's Residence.
11. Rhett's Residence.

STATE CAPITOL AND PALMETTO MEMORIAL
TO THE S. CAROLINA REGᵗˢ IN THE MEXICAN WAR.

This rather strange map with an unusual "state capitol" appeared in
Harper's Weekly, 4 March 1865.

aged Columbia; and, a month later, when U.S. officers submitted their reports of action in the Columbia area, Sherman received abundant data to support his contentions.

Meanwhile, Hampton of course found scores of friends in his home town who embraced his views; and, since the city was not occupied or garrisoned by federal forces until late in May, residents were free to give vent to their grief, scorn, and hatred. On 7 March, Grace Elmore noted in her diary, "I get so confused over the accounts, they are so many and so much alike [,] nothing but robbery and insult." Also, there may have been a sense of guilt or collective embarrassment at work in the minds of some as they mounted their attack upon General Sherman, well aware they had done little to impede his progress. So, if he indeed did burn their city by some preconceived plan, they reasoned, then no amount of exertion on their part could have averted the disaster that ensued.

As this controversy was growing hotter, Columbia and Richland County struggled to resume a normal routine. By late March schools had reopened, shops and stores were doing business in temporary quarters, wagon lines were supplementing rail service, and city, state, and Confederate officials were trying to pick up the strands of day-to-day life.[24] The governor asked the legislature to meet in Greenville on 25 April to discuss the "invasion" and suggested transforming all military academies into "camps of instruction," a move that, in his words, would "conscribe" all young men ages fifteen to seventeen. In a proclamation issued early in April, Mayor Goodwyn bewailed the low state of morals, cutting down by some citizens of shade trees on public streets, and importation of liquor at a time when residents needed food instead. The city council decreed on 4 April that slaves without verified passes were not to be ferried across the Congaree and voted to sell $30,000 in Confederate bonds held by the city, "provided they bring par value, or nearly so."[25]

In succeeding weeks, merchants offered cabbage and beet plants for sale or in exchange for other produce, various authorities tried to collect all firearms (including those Sherman had given the mayor), and a group of citizens met to discuss how the patrol system might be revived. Then on 18 May a U.S. Army lieutenant and some fifteen soldiers rode into town with dispatches for Governor Magrath (who had fled to the Piedmont), and a week later yet another federal detachment appeared and quietly established the headquarters of a military government unit in a building on the south side of the college campus.

"The city is garrisoned, a Yankee wretch at every corner," Grace Elmore wrote on 27 May. "We hold our parasols between us and Yankee faces, but we can't escape a sight of their hateful blue legs and feet. Negroes are free." After nearly four-and-one-half years of ecstasy, turmoil, hope, frustration, and disappointment, for some South Carolinians the agony was over; for others it was just beginning.

Notes

1. Since Columbia's board of health reported four cases of the disease late in November, it seems strange that the Secession Convention even began its deliberations here. The board of health told the city council on 1 January 1861 that there had been thirteen deaths (nine blacks and four whites), and a few days later the college postponed the opening of classes until 15 January.
2. Moore, "Southern Claims Commission," pp. 238–39. Pollard, who also ridiculed the wearing of blue secession badges, submitted two postwar claims for goods burned by Union soldiers in February 1865. One was disallowed, but he eventually was able to collect $1,387 for flour, bacon, syrup, coffee, rice, and oats that allegedly went up in flames.
3. In the spring of 1862, just before the Seven Days Battle, the seven infantry companies (which continued to be known as Hampton's Legion) were attached to Hood's Texas Brigade, while cavalry and artillery personnel joined other commands. For the full story and the names of those involved, see the *State* (11 October 1908).
4. Grace Elmore, a frequent visitor to various hospitals, describes in her diary, now at the South Caroliniana Library, how Yank and Confederate were intermingled and admits that on one occasion she snubbed a Georgian and offered a delicacy to a Massachusetts man by mistake.
5. Mrs. J. A. Moore Diary, South Caroliniana Library.
6. Amanda Sims to Hattie Palmer, Palmer Papers, South Caroliniana Library.
7. In retrospect, conscription may have been a mistake. Those eager to fight volunteered, and conscription highlighted the inequities of a "rich man's war" and a "poor man's fight." A better approach to the manpower problem might have been more attention to the needs of servicemen's families, a prime cause of desertion as time passed. *Note:* Because of the manner in which Richland County residents entered the service—militia companies, short-term enlistments, cadet units, and conscription—it is impossible to determine with much accuracy how many actually were in uniform, 1860–1865.
8. According to J. B. Patrick's diary at the South Caroliniana Library, martial law began in Columbia late in March of 1862; however, enforcement seems to have been lax since it appears to have been re-imposed from time to time in succeeding years.
9. One drawback was the fact that one still had to have money in order to buy. During 1863, in an effort to forestall bread riots such as occurred in Richmond, a Corn Association tried to supply bread to Columbia's poor. In an unique gesture, on Christmas eve of 1863, butcher John Seegers offered free beef to any soldier's family that came to his shop. In 1864, according to one report, 1,152 individuals were on Richland County's relief rolls.

10. C. Vann Woodward (ed.), *Mary Chesnut's Civil War* (New Haven and London, 1981), pp. 346–47.

11. See Francis A. Lord, "Camp Sorghum," *Sandlapper* (August, 1975), pp. 29–33.

12. The day after the "Bee" Store said it would serve blacks, the *Daily South Carolinian* (16 March) carried an intriguing ad seeking someone to share costs of a trip through the blockade (authorities permitting) to purchase goods in New York City.

13. Palmer Papers, South Caroliniana Library.

14. Bettie J. Clarke to "Lizzie," 27 August 1864, South Caroliniana Library.

15. This issue also featured a poem, "The Doom of the Yankees on Carolina's Soil," that concluded with these words: "For Lee, in his anger, had drawn his bright sword, and struck down the foe in the name of the Lord." Nine days later, without comment, the *New York Herald* published an entire column from this Columbia daily that described the bazaar in great detail.

16. John G. Barrett, *Sherman's March Through the Carolinas* (Chapel Hill, 1956), p. 65. This order stated that all men ages sixteen to sixty not in service were to appear with four days' rations "prepared to go into camp."

17. Quoted in the *New York Herald*, 19 February 1865.

18. Quoted in the *New York Tribune*, 20 February 1865.

19. Hampton, naturally enough, was in a foul mood. Sent south with no men to command and technically outranked by Wheeler, a man half his age, he confided in a letter to a friend that he was considering applying for a transfer to the infantry.

20. A year earlier, in January of 1864, somewhat similar conditions (wind and cotton, but no liquor) resulted in "a most disastrous fire" when four warehouses, John Alexander's machinery shops, and several homes were destroyed in the vicinity of Lady, Wayne, and Lincoln streets. The loss was said to have been in excess of $3 million. Arson was suspected, but never proven.

21. In fact, payment of postwar damages to men such as storekeeper Edward Pollard for goods lost in the fire was *legal* admission by the U.S. government of its responsibility for what occurred in Columbia on the night of 17–18 February 1865. *Note:* The research of Lucas brings together virtually all of the published work concerning this affair. For a dissenting view, see Allan D. Charles, "The Burning of Columbia," *Southern Partisan* (Spring/Summer 1981), pp. 8–10.

22. According to J. F. Williams, "She [Marie] was a notorious character, and her mother was equally bad. They were both beautiful women, but that does not go far if it has not the character to back it up." Some of those fleeing Columbia (not the Feaster-Boozer group) died early in April when the steamer *General Lyon* burned off Cape Hatteras. Asked about Sherman in 1871, a local bootblack told a *New York Times* reporter (25 April), "Yes, sah, mighty glad to see him come, and more glad to see him leave!"

23. Woodward, *Mary Chesnut's Civil War*, p. 725. Mrs. Chesnut, who had fled to Lincolnton, N.C., called the Confederate retreat "disgraceful" and bemoaned the fact that Wade Hampton had not taken charge of South Carolina's military affairs six months earlier . . . "I believe he could have save us. Achilles sulking in his tent—at such a time!"

24. Sidney Andrews, who visited Columbia in September of 1865, reported that railroad tracks had been torn up for about thirty miles in all directions from the city. Some had been wrapped around trees, true, but many had simply disappeared. See Andrews, *The South Since the War . . .* (Boston, 1866), pp. 29–30.

25. *Columbia Phoenix*, 6 April 1865.

Adjusting to New Realities

CHAPTER ELEVEN

The years from 1865 to 1877, usually known as the "Reconstruction Era," are among the most controversial in America's past. Until quite recently they have been portrayed as a dark, dismal period when newly freed blacks ran roughshod over the wishes of their former masters in a carnival of corruption and misrule. One of the pioneers in efforts to reshape this story was Edgefield native Francis Butler Simkins, who in 1932 co-authored *South Carolina During Reconstruction* with Duke professor Robert H. Woody. They conceded that certain aspects of the traditional picture were true and that some of this state's officeholders of those years, nearly all of them at the highest levels white men, were downright scoundrels. However, the two scholars stressed that these same much-reviled leaders ushered in numerous overdue reforms, among them, universal public education, uniform assessment and taxation of property, a revitalized system of local government, and substantial change in an antiquated judiciary. They also wrote an official end to slavery and imprisonment for debt, enhanced property rights of women to some degree, authorized divorce, outlawed dueling, and established fundamental legal principles such as equality before the law and civil rights for all citizens.

What is most revealing, according to Simkins and Woody, is that—despite smoke, fire, and passionate rhetoric—Ben Tillman's constitution of 1895 retained virtually everything proclaimed by a convention of blacks, scalawags, and carpetbaggers in 1868. In the opinion of these historians, major differences between the two documents are found only in "suffrage provisions and in declaration of rights."[1]

For obvious reasons, Columbia was the focus of considerable attention throughout Reconstruction. Reporters, journalists, travelers, and tourists flocked to the banks of the Congaree to watch a legislature whose members included ex-slaves. At times, both state and national political issues intruded onto the local scene. Yet, through it all, Colonel Taylor's community was simply the stage for much of this drama and actually had a life of its own somewhat independent of momentous changes occurring on all sides.

Uppermost in the thoughts of most residents of Columbia and Richland County during these years were two concerns: making a living or, put another way, the economic life of the Midlands and, secondly, the role of thousands of new citizens in that economy. Given the realities of the day, the answers to such questions were self-evident. Columbia's well-being, as in antebellum years and for several decades to come, would be based upon agricultural produce and the distribution of goods and services related primarily to the needs of its rural hinterland. As for the region's blacks, even though they outnumbered whites two to one in the county as a whole and by about a thousand within the city of Columbia, it was apparent that, in time, a better-educated minority possessed of money, land, and experience would somehow prevail and establish the kind of economic and political order it preferred. Just how this might be accomplished was a task that native whites struggled with throughout this period.

In a general way, the rural economy of Richland County continued along lines laid down in the 1850s, that is, a decline in both herds of livestock and agricultural products. Although such might be anticipated amid war and its aftermath, census statistics indicate this was a long-term trend that Sherman and his "bummers" merely nudged along a bit. According to the 1870 survey, there were then about half as many animals on local farms as in 1860, and the production of all crops—except rice, which rose from 9,286 to 26,823 pounds—also declined by about 50 percent. The greatest change in the countryside, however, was an increase in the number of individual farms, which during the first years of peace rose from 203 to 1,138. More than half of these new holdings (639) contained 10 to 50 acres.

An important by-product of the breakup of large estates was the creation of village life in Acton, Eastover, Gadsden, Hopkins' Turnout, Kingville, and Clarkson's (or Wateree), all lower Richland rail depots that by the mid-1870s had post offices, as did Frost's Mill and Littleton on the Greenville line and Killian's and Doko on the way to Charlotte. Other less important stops included Simms, Woodward, and Wateree River on tracks leading to Sumter, Hampton's and Adams on the South Carolina Railroad, and Sharp's, located just north of Killian's.

Richland's overall population grew from 18,307 in 1860 to 23,025 ten years later, while the number of Columbia residents increased somewhat less than anticipated, 8,052 to 9,298. Yet, as limited as these gains were, they contrasted sharply with losses experienced by neighboring Midlands counties such as Fairfield, Kershaw, Lexington, Newberry, and Orangeburg as hundreds of freedmen departed for other regions. Only Sumter reported a small increase of about 1,500. During the 1870s, local population growth paralleled that of the previous decade, Richland County adding another 5,000 residents, the city of Columbia, 700, and in 1880 all nearby counties were in the plus column, too.

By that date, the number of Richland County farms had swelled to 2,246, and this upward spiral would continue throughout the rest of the century. Although livestock were increasing, because of changes taking place upon individual farms (greater need for horses and mules and less reliance upon cattle and especially sheep), farm animals never again would be as numerous as in 1850 or even in 1860. Corn production increased somewhat in the '70s, as did the rice harvest, but much more important was the output of cotton—10,958 bales in 1880, double the figure reported ten years before and nearly equaling the record crop of 1850.[2]

The industrial life of Columbia and Richland County during these postwar years was mostly pipe dreams and promises, not production and profits. Census takers counted sixty-nine manufacturing establishments in 1870 and eighty-one in 1880. These operations employed some 500 men, women, and children who earned $100,000 a year turning out goods worth five times that amount.

A promotional booklet published by Columbia's Board of Trade in 1871 pointed to four iron foundries, two saw and planing mills, a cotton seed oil company, a broom factory, and local railroad shops as a basis for claims that South Carolina's capital city was "the Future Manufacturing and Commercial Centre of the South." But, for the most part, the board (organized in September of 1867) was pinning its hopes on a Rhode Island millionaire who owned extensive cotton mills in New England and, it was thought, planned to build yet another alongside the Columbia Canal. However, William Sprague, who served his state as both governor and senator, proved to be something of a disappointment—some would say a disaster—and Columbia would have to wait until the 1890s to get the large manufacturing plant so earnestly desired.[3]

Lying not far beneath these cold agricultural-industrial statistics are two factors that must be considered: the effects of the Civil War and the repercussions of the political turmoil of these years. As devastating as Columbia's fire of February 1865 was, that holocaust gave birth to a mild construction boom during the first months of peace, and repair of railroad tracks in outlying areas also created jobs.

The *Daily Phoenix* (24 June 1865) reported that twenty-five Main Street merchants were back in business and published these prices current: pork, mutton, and beef, 10¢ a pound; coffee, 50–75¢ a pound; green tea, $2.50 a pound; draft ale, $2 a gallon; and peach brandy, $3.50 a gallon. Editor Julian Selby no longer was willing to accept produce in payment for his paper; he wanted cash. A few days later, as a result of the heavy loss of equipment in February, Columbia's three fire companies merged into a single unit. And on the Fourth of July, some 5,000 men, nearly all of them black, walked in pairs from Marion and Blanding streets to the college chapel where orators read the Declaration of Independence and urged everyone to get to work.

Following these remarks, a huge barbecue and picnic was held in nearby woods where one table was reserved for whites. According to the *Daily Phoenix*, the occasion was both festive and orderly, and in the evening the crowd enjoyed a fireworks display. Among those attending these festivities was "Marcel," who wrote in the *Nation* (27 July 1865) that he saw no U.S. Army personnel between Orangeburg and Columbia. He met men in gray returning home, he said, but encountered no special ill will. As one local lady remarked to him, "When they fought, they fought; and when they were done, they were done." Columbia was, he noted, "a sad sight."

A few weeks later, a U.S. Army band entertained citizens gathered in Sidney Park, and on 15 August a local group staged a "Soiree Musicale" at the Methodist Female College, the first such entertainment since the war ended. In the fall of 1865 the city council announced plans to build a new public market on Assembly Street and decreed that, in the future, only brick structures, not wood, would be erected on Main Street. In mid-January of 1866 the first train arrived from Charleston. A month later there was still a seven-mile gap on the Columbia and Greenville Railroad bridged by a stage line, but by April tracks to Charlotte were complete once more.

To stimulate interest in the latter undertaking, rail executives staged a contest between teams of whites and blacks, each crew starting from one end of the project and working toward the other. The result, officially at least, was a draw—sixteen miles of track laid in five weeks. In recognition of this "fine achievement," the company hosted whites at a barbe-

---

Headquarters Provisional Brigade
COLUMBIA, S.C., June 9. 1865.

To the Freedmen:
THE time has come for you all to do your best to show that you are fit to be free men in this great Republic. Observe sacredly the marriage tie. Learn to read and write. No one must leave his wife, children, or aged parents while he can assist them. Thieves and idlers and people strolling about the country will be punished. Be prudent, and quiet, and orderly. If you have trouble, report it to the military authorities. This year you cannot do much more than get a living for yourselves and families; those will get the best pay next year who work best now.

Let no one be either proud or ashamed of the form or color that God has given him. Be proud of the chance to do for yourselves and for each other.

A. S. HARTWELL
Brevet Brigadier General

[*Daily Phoenix*, 10 June 1865]

---

cue held at Lightwood Knot Springs, while blacks enjoyed a similar repast at Killian's Mill. At about the same time, through service was restored from Branchville to Augusta; however, in order to make some of these repairs, the South Carolina Railroad took up a spur track to Camden that was not replaced until May of 1867.

Even though Columbia's pre-war rail connections now were in place, this network had one obvious defect: no direct link to the west, all traffic having to be routed via Kingville and Branchville to Augusta. So, work started during the Civil War was resumed. In November of 1867 a 1,042-foot bridge was completed across the Congaree, and on 5 February 1868 Lexington residents greeted the first train from Columbia with barbecue and speech-making. Soon bales of cotton were flowing into the Columbia market from communities in Lexington, Edgefield, and other counties served by this new railroad. A year later, the *Daily Phoenix* was boasting of through service from Augusta to New York, a schedule that permitted a Columbia resident to depart on a north-bound train at 1:40 P.M., arriving in Richmond at 11:15 A.M. the following day and in Washington in time for supper.

This line soon merged with tracks leading to Charlotte, creating the Charlotte, Columbia, and Augusta. The venerable South Carolina Railroad, not pleased with these developments, at times used its engines to block traffic where the two railroads crossed and even removed track until disciplined by court orders. Meanwhile, the Wilmington and Manchester, frustrated by that same railroad's uncooperative attitude, decided to bypass Wateree Junction (Manchester) and construct a direct line from Sumter to Columbia that in 1870 gave birth to the Wilmington, Columbia, and Augusta.

This activity was transforming South Carolina's capital city into something of a rail hub, and in the fall of 1867 the South Carolina and Columbia-Greenville railroads, alarmed by the threat of competition, suddenly reduced freight rates. The Board of Trade, delighted with this news, credited the Piedmont Air Line linking Charlotte to points in Virginia with bestowing such benefits upon local businessmen. However, when the Air Line extended its tracks through Spartanburg and Greenville en route to Atlanta, smiles turned to frowns, for this move, more than any other, would thwart the growth of the Midlands in coming years. (On 26 April 1873, the *Columbia Daily Union* noted that, since the opening of the new railroad, Spartanburg merchants had slashed $1.50 from the price of a barrel of flour.) The populations of Greenville and Spartanburg increased three-fold in the 1870s, and by 1880 (only seven years after the Air Line was completed) Greenville, Spartanburg, and Anderson counties each could boast of over a hundred manufacturing establishments, compared with only eighty-one in Richland County. Twenty years later, the combined population of Greenville and Spartanburg exceeded that of Columbia; and, if suburban mill villages were added to this total, the difference was even greater.

But back to the 1860s and 1870s. Most textbooks divide these years into Presidential Reconstruction (1865–1867) and Congressional or Radical Reconstruction (1868–1877), but at the grass-roots level those terms had little meaning. If white, a Columbia resident of that period probably would have characterized the era as a time of momentary chaos followed by the horrors of black rule and, finally, the grand redemption of the Palmetto State under the leadership of Wade Hampton and his noble Red Shirt legions. Any black contemporary perhaps would have viewed the course of events differently. Yet it is quite possible that, while citing conflicting root causes, this pair might well have agreed that the onset of Reconstruction was a period of great apprehension and confusion.

The reasons are many, some of them a reflection of political turmoil on the national scene, but one of the most troublesome issues here in Richland County and throughout much of the South was a reluctance to grant ex-slaves the rights of citizenship. Whites clearly intended to retain the reins of government and exert all of the economic and social control they had long enjoyed. South Carolina's first post-war constitution, for example, restricted suffrage to whites, and forty pages of rules subsequently enacted, usually known as "Black Codes," decreed that for all practical purposes ex-slaves would be house servants and field hands. The practice of any other trade or occupation required an annual license. Such regulations, it was claimed, were necessary and actually were designed to "protect" blacks.

Freedmen, in the beginning at least, were more interested in land and education than in any of the niceties of citizenship. The dream of "forty acres and a mule" died hard, and Sidney Andrews, who visited Columbia in the fall of 1865, said blacks often asked, "When is de land goin' fur to be dewided?"[4] In his opinion, labor was demoralized and disorganized, yet he found a "certain air of easy dignity" in South Carolina's capital city not evident elsewhere, "not even in Charleston." This arose, he thought, from the fact that Columbia was the seat of government and home to a college. Women seemed less apt to snub Union soldiers than in Charleston, some of the middle class were now their wives, and a few elegant ladies sometimes even welcomed the attention of those in uniform.[5]

In an article published in the *Atlantic Monthly* (February 1866) Andrews, who had attended constitutional conventions held in Georgia and the Carolinas, said South Carolinians seemed to want a monarchy, not a republic. Since nine out of ten white men in this state had as little to do with public affairs as blacks, both races were, in a sense, virtually enslaved. Loyalty in North Carolina, he wrote, was a sham, while residents of its neighbor to the south existed amid an air of "cool arrogance" and made no pretense of loyalty but were passionately devoted to their *state*. Wade Hampton, Andrews observed, in November of 1865 had urged everyone to support President Andrew Johnson "so long as he manifests a disposition to restore all of our rights as a sovereign State." Most whites, he added, assumed that blacks would not work unless compelled to do so, thus the main issue of the day was a struggle between whites and blacks over compulsion, the former unable to comprehend that freedom might mean the same thing for both races.

Nevertheless, many local blacks—desperate for food and perhaps goaded by the U.S. Army—did agree to work contracts in 1865, and a document in the Heyward Family Papers is a good example of those arrangements. On 5 June of that year, 248 laborers on "Goodwill" Plantation, with a military representative standing by, promised to be obedient, industrious, and faithful and "to conduct themselves in such manner as to gain the goodwill of those to whom they must always look for protection." Their ex-master, in return, agreed to clothe, feed, and house these freedmen "as usual," allow "medical attendance," and protect the old and infirm until the contract expired on 1 January 1866. He had the right to punish those guilty of unlawful conduct, laziness, desertion, and insubordination. Any individual banished from the plantation no longer shared in the crop at the end of the year. All other workers were to get one-third of the agricultural produce once it was "gathered and housed." Then they could subdivide their portion of the crop according to a pre-arranged plan. Elderly and young, it should be noted, often signed up for less than a whole share. Of the 248 blacks who scrawled Xs on this document, twenty-two were not at "Goodwill" six months later, sixteen of them having run away and six having died.

Considering the many complaints at the end of 1865 concerning contracts violated by all parties involved, this seems to have been a rather successful venture. Yet on 18 July 1866, E. B. Heyward described in a letter to a friend his new scheme of "wage" labor. Neighbors, he said, thought he was crazy, while clinging to the notion that they somehow could get work done and not pay for it. "I knew it would cost something *as before*," he wrote. Soon, as blacks on nearby farms became disgusted with share agreements and quit, he had all the workers he needed. The great advantage was, Heyward stressed, "[I] only pay for what I get."

This young man also told of plans to break up his plantation into smaller farms to be rented, for in the present climate he was not willing to sell or buy since one often had to deal with strangers. There was plenty of law, he wrote sarcastically, but no justice. "Everything is new and I am afraid all our old men will be incapable of adapting themselves to the change." But being young, Heyward believed he could succeed. To date, he added, he had seen nothing in the "boastful" Yankees that compared with "the energy & noble patience of our Southern people."

What Heyward was struggling with was, of course, merely one step along the road to traditional share-cropping. This experimentation was made all the more difficult by several disastrous growing seasons. The 1865 crop, smaller than anticipated because of late planting and various disruptions, was followed in 1866 by a severe drought. In fact, the only good harvest between 1865 and 1870 came in 1868. Under such conditions, it is not surprising that members of both races considered migrating to other regions.

In December of 1865, Freedmen's Bureau officials in Columbia reported they were providing transportation to the coast for about 250 adults each week and issuing 4,500 rations to the needy every month. Yet bureau-sponsored schools were beginning to function, the first being a black institution established in a Baptist church basement by T. G. Wright with the aid of New York money. Six months later, in the midst of drought, conditions for some freedmen were becoming desperate. When employers were unable to furnish basic necessities, many abandoned their fields and sought out farmers such as Heyward. Crops suffered, workers sometimes were arrested, and the spiral of discontent increased. In October of 1866, a Freedmen's Bureau spokesman estimated that 10,304 individuals (perhaps half of all Richland County residents) were destitute. The center of greatest need was Hopkins' Turnout where hundreds of helpless freedmen and their families had gathered on what were known as "government" plantations. At the end of this tragic year, he credited the generosity of many ex-masters with saving scores of lives and pointed to the only bright spot in the bureau's program: nearly 2,000 pupils enrolled in thirty day schools and five night classes.[6]

Although the Freedmen's Bureau was much maligned—whites thought its schools much too political and blacks were certain agency personnel helped only their "pets"—it obviously performed yeoman service in a time of great need . . . and not just for blacks. An undated report in bureau records indicates that about 20 percent of those given rations by the Columbia office during the famine of 1866 were white, many of them elderly and crippled. Also, perhaps because Columbia was the state capital and a center of bureau activity, Richland fared especially well at its hands. In 1868, for example, local residents were given plantation supplies worth $12,596, while Fairfield County citizens got goods valued at only one-tenth that amount.[7] The bureau continued to function locally until 1872; but, after the first months of 1869, its work was almost exclusively in the field of education, not welfare.

In March of 1866, just as that troubled year was getting under way, Richland County officials told a grand jury that they were unable to perform their duties. The courthouse and jail were in ruins, there was no money for free schools, and, being "but little removed from paupers themselves," they had been forced to abandon the poor. "The public roads, in many parts of the District, are almost impassable, owing to the want of necessary funds to repair the bridges, and [to] the destruction of our old and cherished system of labor, [as well as] the ignorance of the Commissioners, for a long time, as to the mode of reaching the negro in his emancipated condition, and the uncertainty which still exists as to whether the 'wards of the nation' will obey their orders."[8]

Another product of emancipation and hard times was a marked increase in burglary and petty theft in and around Columbia. Some undoubtedly stole because of need, while others, especially ex-slaves accustomed to the general ownership of all goods and supplies by the master of their plantation and having long, in fact, been property themselves, failed to comprehend the true meaning of *personal* property. In mid-1866, as the drought worsened, reports of stolen items became commonplace in the columns of the *Daily Phoenix*. The local chapter of the Union League of America, a prominent black association, in July published a resolution condemning vagrancy and larceny among "our people." A short time later, residents of Columbia's Fourth Ward met and organized a "city guard" composed of all males sixteen to sixty; and, for a few months, this self-styled militia patrolled the streets with the permission of the U.S. Army.

As the year dragged to a close, the *New York Times* (28 October 1866) reported that Columbia presented a sorry sight. After a brief building spurt, construction had slowed to a snail's pace. Of about 250 structures destroyed by fire in February of 1865, 170 remained untouched and debris still littered Main Street. Business was dull. The college had only sixty-five students and the theological seminary, seven. Academies and other private schools languished, too, and the drought brought in its wake sickness and disease. In the opinion of this journalist, Richland County planters had only themselves to blame for some of their woes. Having lots of land at their disposal, they farmed in an indifferent manner, caring little how many acres were used to produce whatever they thought they needed. And, although this report did not mention failure to use fertilizer, many local farmers were only gradually becoming aware of its benefits.

But six months later change was in the air. After nearly two years of indecision, it was apparent that the federal government was not going to provide free land and mules for blacks and that freedmen, like other citizens, would have to look out for their own interests. This meant, of course, that rigid control of their lives by southern whites would not be permitted. More importantly, in March of 1867 the U.S. Congress, now firmly in Radical Republican hands, abolished South Carolina's state government, reinforced military rule, and set in motion the machinery for a new constitutional convention in which freedmen would participate. The *Daily Phoenix*, while deploring these decisions, conceded editorially there were benefits: property now would be secure and settlement of various vexing matters should bring tranquility to the region.

Two events on the local scene demonstrated how sweeping change might be. One was the appearance of black and white leaders on the same platform; the other, an imbroglio that led to the ouster of Columbia's mayor and five councilmen. In March, blacks held numerous meetings to celebrate the passage of civil rights legislation by Congress. The most interesting of these was a public gathering on the 18th near Nickerson's Hotel attended by William H. Talley, E. J. Arthur, James Gibbes, and Wade Hampton. Talley stressed that southern whites and freedmen must be united. "They are parts of the same society, inhabiting the same land, under the same sun, breathing the same atmosphere," he said. "And, if the lessons of history taught anything, they taught that, under such circumstances, the two races must prosper or perish together." And to prosper, Talley added forcefully, there must be peace.[9] Hampton, whose presence elicited national comment, also called for unity and urged freedmen to give their white friends an opportunity to help them. Ex-slave William Beverly Nash, a former waiter at a local hotel who was emerging as a respected and able voice in public affairs, called for enfranchisement without restrictions of all whites, a suggestion that he later admitted caused him some political embarrassment.

Five days later, writing to his friend James Conner in Charleston, Hampton cautioned, "We can control and direct the negroes if we act discreetly, and in my judgment the highest duty of every Southern man is to secure the good will and confidence of the negro. Our future depends on this."[10] Even if civil rights legislation was struck down by the Supreme Court, he was willing to let educated, tax-paying blacks vote. His goal, Hampton emphasized, was to save state government. If that meant black Congressmen might represent South Carolina in Washington, so be it. If necessary, he told Conner, he would send Nash to Charleston to confer with him. This man, he added, was "a power and I believe true."[11] Two weeks later, Hampton wrote Conner again, reiterating his belief that, although compromise might be required, he thought the black vote could be controlled.

The second development, which occurred largely behind the scenes away from public gaze, also involved Nash. According to Freedmen's Bureau records, sometime in June of 1867, Nash met with Mayor Theodore Stark in an effort to get two destitute blacks admitted to the city alms house. That institution, Nash maintained, was supported by tax dollars and yet served only whites. Stark wanted to know "why in the hell" didn't he go to the bureau? Freedmen were the government's "pet lambs." This meeting was followed by a general protest to the city council concerning still other public facilities not open to both races such as the orphan house and schools. The *New York Times* reported on 1 July that municipal authorities rejected these overtures, asserting that state-federal funds, not local, supported these institutions.

On 24 June, 19 July, and 2 August, a U.S. Army officer wrote Stark concerning the alms house; and, on 3 August the mayor finally responded, saying he was unaware that Columbia blacks lacked such facilities until so informed by federal officials. He promised everything would be done "to advance the status of the coloured people, both as to their education and the support of the poor" once civil government was restored; but, at the moment, the only buildings available had been built for whites and were fully occupied. The mayor tried to buttress his case by observing that out of 2,923 black males required to pay taxes only 118 had done so; however, this assertion, in the eyes of the bureau, merely proved that blacks were being taxed to support public facilities they could not use.

Although the U.S. Army command in Charleston agreed that Columbia's poor house must be open to all citizens, apparently nothing was done about this matter for several months. Then, on 19 June 1868, military authorities summarily removed Stark and five aldermen, installing Colonel Francis L. Guenther as mayor and naming six other individuals to the council, among them, three blacks: Joseph Taylor, Charles M. Wilder, and William Simons. No reason was given and it seems unlikely that the alms house issue alone was serious enough to warrant such action, yet this was a warning, if any was needed, that hostile, uncooperative behavior on the part of local officials no longer would be tolerated.[12]

Much had happened by the time the military sacked Stark and his associates. In January, 124 delegates (67 of them black) met in Charleston to write a new constitution. Richland residents were represented by four Republicans—Thomas J. Robertson (soon to become a U.S. senator) and three prominent blacks, Nash, Wilder, and Samuel B. Thompson.[13] Despite biased press coverage, in the opinion of Simkins and Woody, this body acted with dispatch and in fifty-three days produced a document that, among other innovations, transformed this state's old judicial districts into counties, established county boards of commissioners to oversee highways and the collection and disbursement of public funds, provided for the popular election of county officials, and divided counties into school districts and townships. The township system was scrapped two years later; however, the same geographical units were retained for tax purposes.

In mid-April of 1868, Richland voters approved the new constitution, 2,502 to 1,257, and subsequently chose W. Beverly Nash as state senator (a position he would hold until 1877) and four House members—Charles Wilder, Samuel Thompson, William Simons, and Aesop Goodson—all of them black. Six weeks later, a Radical slate captured all of the county offices. Then, in a special election held in November, restaurateur John McKenzie beat out iron monger John Alexander by thirty-two votes to become Columbia's mayor; but, in April of 1870, Alexander and his Radical allies swept to victory.

For a few weeks, the old council refused to give way, insisting its term did not end until 1872. At issue were two state statutes, one that had provided for special elections in all towns and cities in 1868 and another, passed in 1870, that extended Columbia's boundaries 954 feet north of Elmwood and east of Harden, thus increasing somewhat the black majority. Early in May, to the surprise of no one, the state Supreme Court ruled in favor of the Radicals.

Virtually all of this community's black political figures—whether holding state, county, or city offices—appear to have owned property. Some, such as Wilder, Nash, carpenter Israel Smith,[14] grocer Augustus Cooper, and farmer Uriah Portee, clearly were men of proven ability, even if they lacked the polish of the classroom. As a result, these freedmen gave the Reconstruction years of Columbia and Richland County a quiet quality not found in all parts of South Carolina. At times, blacks held a majority of seats on the city council, as well as most of the newly created and largely untested county offices, but key positions such as mayor, sheriff, and any post dealing with finance remained in white hands. In fact, Nash told a *New York Times* reporter in 1867 that local blacks "hooted" when "white strangers" proposed that they elect a black mayor. The Ku Klux Klan, significantly, was nowhere to be seen. The only evidence of any activity was a notice (which may have been a crude joke) that appeared in the *Daily Phoenix* on 24 July 1869 announcing that the "Cotton Town Rangers" and the "Knights of the Black Circle" would meet at midnight in "Skull Valley." In time, area residents even could treat the Klan in a light vein. One of the local baseball teams was known as the "Ku Klux" in the summer of 1871, and in that same year farmer James Carroll LaBorde recorded in his diary a bull named "Ku Klux," as well as cows called "Lost Cause" and "Dixie."

There are numerous reasons for this rather unique situation, and one should not discount the good will of lower Richland planters such as Wade Hampton and Keziah Brevard. The community's urban milieu with its nucleus of three or four hundred blacks accustomed to freedom contrasted sharply with a rural expanse such as Edgefield County. In 1860, with a population more than twice that of Richland, Edgefield, for example, had only 173 free blacks, and all but eleven of them lived on isolated farms, not in the tiny villages of Edgefield Court House and Hamburg. Even if not free, slaves such as Nash, through constant association with patrons of the hotel where he worked, managed to compensate for whatever drawbacks that status entailed. Added to this home-grown talent was a group of newcomers, teachers at Columbia's emerging black schools and colleges. Even rural neighborhoods were developing black leaders as separate congregations, most of them Baptist, appeared throughout the countryside. In November of 1865, three black Baptist ministers were ordained in lower Richland, men who soon established independent Shiloh (1866) and Beulah (1867), which three years later became "New Light Beulah Baptist Church." Within two decades, eighteen black Baptist churches were functioning in that section of the county.

Post-war business ties that paid little heed to race and politics also were an important element in this new society. Edwin W. Seibels, who in 1869 left an Edgefield County farm to found a real estate-insurance firm that eventually would develop into Seibels, Bruce and Company, was extremely active in local Democratic circles. Yet his business records of the early 1870s reveal he had an account with the Republican Printing Company and his customers included blacks such as Nash and R. B. Elliott and several white Radical stalwarts, among them, T. J. Robertson, S. L. Hoge, L. Cass Carpenter, and Timothy Hurley. In 1875, when it became clear that William Sprague would build no mill, Nash, Wilder, and some of Columbia's most prominent businessmen (L. D. Childs, John Alexander, John Agnew, and W. B. Stanley, to name a few) met at the office of Edwin Seibels to form the Congaree Manufacturing Company, which, as it turned out, like Sprague's "mill," also never produced anything.

These bits indicate that, although the seat of state government, this community put economics before politics in an age we have been led to believe thought of little else but torchlight parades and ballot boxes. Conservative Democrats were, naturally enough, alarmed by frauds being perpetrated at the state level, as were some Radical Republicans. But efforts to highlight what were said to be similar conditions in Columbia's city government often misfired. On 13 January 1872, for example, the *Daily Phoenix*, delighted with court action that stopped work on what it claimed was a scandal-ridden scheme to build a new city hall, complained editorially of a "city ring." Yet the following day, in the final installment of a Board of Trade series designed to lure business to Columbia, this same daily conceded that the municipal government, of which it obviously did not approve, was operating with an annual surplus of about $27,000.

Even though those out of power would charge three years later that Columbia's debt had increased by nearly fifty percent, they seemed unable to mount an effective challenge. In April of 1876, no less than four groups dubbed Republican, Regular Republican, Citizens', and People's fielded candidates in the biennial election. This in-fighting permitted Republican John Agnew to beat W. B. Stanley, the Citizens' nominee for mayor, by twenty-three votes. The new, twelve-member council (three men from each ward) was equally divided between Agnew and Stanley supporters, with whites outnumbering blacks by a seven-to-five margin. In fact, the lone success local Democrats could point to was the election of John T. Sloan to the state House of Representatives in 1874, the first white man so honored since 1868, and that victory had been achieved only with the cooperation of W. Beverly Nash.

Several truths are evident. Wade Hampton's secret plan to control black voters was not working, community life was not split into hostile factions unable to treat each other in a civil manner, and, as a result, no political group seemed able to develop a cohesive, disciplined organization. Blacks, despite some disenchantment with a tendency of white Republicans to monopolize top offices in city, county, and state governments, could not forget who had given them freedom and who had kept them in slavery. Democrats, on the other hand, battling demography and threats of federal intervention, vacillated between offering blacks the hand of friendship and using a whip.

As is often the case, this stalemate was broken by developments far from Richland's borders. These include a growing weariness in the North with the turmoil of Reconstruction and widespread concern over economic distress engendered by the Panic of 1873. Two years later, desperate for recovery and eager to revive southern markets, the federal government did nothing when Mississippi Democrats used whips, as well

Columbia in 1871

When a Pennsylvania man who was thinking of moving to the South inquired about local prospects, real estate dealer Edwin W. Seibels, founder of what is now the oldest business still operating within the city limits, the Seibels Bruce Group, was quick to reply. His answer, published in the *Daily Phoenix* (28 January 1871), provides an essentially accurate, if somewhat biased portrait of the heart of the Midlands at that time.

COLUMBIA, S.C.,
January 26, 1871.
A. L. H., Esq., Titusville, Pa.:

DEAR SIR: Yours of 21st inst., is to hand and in reply we beg leave to make the following statement: Columbia is situated on the east bank of the Congaree river, which is navigable for steamboats to Granby, two miles below. Boats seldom come up this far on account of the cheapness of the railroad transportation. First class freights from New York and Baltimore only cost merchants one dollar per 100 pounds. Lower classes at cheaper rates. The falls of the Congaree river, directly at the city, afford unlimited waterpower, which is now about to be utilized by Senator Sprague, of Rhode Island, who is now working at the canal, which will afford 15,000 horsepower for manufacturing purposes. This will be completed as rapidly as possible.

The population as per census of 1870, is above 10,000, and rapidly increasing; and bids fair to rival any city in the South in manufactures and population.

The health of Columbia is surpassed by no place in the world. A gentleman, a native of New Jersey, who is now present, has just made the remark that it is the "Garden of Eden" as regards health. He has been a resident for twenty-four years past. Of the large number of persons from the Northern States who have settled here since 1865, but one death has occurred.

In regard to society, there is none superior to it. Polite, refined, intelligent and sociable, ever ready to welcome any one of good character.

A good class of merchants, a liberal Board of Trade, an Agricultural and Mechanical Society, who hold a fair once a year—in November—which has always proved a success in promoting the industrial pursuits of the country.

Schools—we have located within the city limits the University of South Carolina, formerly the South Carolina College, which has a full corps of professors; a Female College, under the auspices of the Methodist Church, the exercises of which are suspended at present, but will be resumed after the 1st of September next; the Male Academy, under Professors Thompson and Davidson, besides a number of private schools, with the very best teachers, both male and female, with ample facilities for ordinary education at the public schools. The Ursuline Convent and Academy, at "Valle Crucis," about three miles from the city, is a place where young ladies can get a most polished education. This is a very popular school from the fact of its superiority of government.

As for real estate, knowing ones say it is bound to advance, and even now, some of the best financial men in this country are investing in unimproved property. Rents are high and pay landlords well. We can sell you property at any price, from a $50 unimproved lot to a $15,000 furnished residence; and, in truth, we know of no place that presents as many advantages to a business man and capitalist, as does Columbia, at the present time, and would advise you to run down to see us, and become convinced for yourself. Should you desire further information, we will cheerfully give it.

Very respectfully,

E. W. SEIBELS & CO.

as guns, to "redeem" their state. In 1876, Matthew C. Butler, Martin W. Gary, and their Red-Shirt faithful stormed out of Edgefield and convinced the rest of the state to do the same thing.

With Wade Hampton at the head of the Democratic ticket, they succeeded. Tales of freely given black support obviously are untrue, although Democrats, now unified, used every tactic imaginable to intimidate their adversaries. A *New York Times* reporter wrote in mid-October of that year that it was difficult to see how anyone could exist in Columbia unless he promised to vote for Wade Hampton. A shopkeeper who refused to do so had no customers and could not get a loan at the bank. Laborers and mechanics who clung to the Republican standard found themselves unemployed. Six decades later, mulatto Martha Richardson, a lifelong resident of Columbia, remembered these days as the most exciting she ever experienced. "You never seen so much talkin', fightin', and fussin' as dat. You know de Yankees was still here and they not 'fraid, and de Hampton folks was not 'fraid, so it was a case of knock down and drag out most of the time."[15]

Nevertheless, on election day these tactics did not work, perhaps, as the Edgefield crowd would contend, because they were not applied sternly enough as voters went to the polls. For whatever reason, Hampton lost Richland County to Daniel H. Chamberlain by some 1,400 votes, and Republicans sent an all-black delegation to the General Assembly . . . although two members (Senator Nash and Representative Charles S. Minort) subsequently resigned under fire and were replaced by whites. [16]

However, following resolution of the Hayes-Tilden, Hampton-Chamberlain controversies in the spring of 1877, ousting Republicans from city and county governments was a snap. (For details of this exciting story from the national perspective, see C. Vann Woodward's classic, *Reunion and Reaction*, first published in 1951.) By gerrymandering and pressures both subtle and not so subtle, which included jettisoning Hampton's campaign pledge to respect the rights of blacks, conservative Democrats gained complete control of local political life. The municipal election of 1 April 1878, which W. B. Stanley won, along with a slate of white aldermen, was hailed by the *Daily Register* as a "glorious" result, "a day of regeneration and redemption." This paper, successor to the *Daily Phoenix*, praised "sensible colored men" who voted for the winning ticket, described how eager Democrats flocked to the polls at an early hour, and told of cannon fire signaling victory. It all sounds thrilling and quite impressive until one realizes that there was only *one* slate to vote for, hence *no opposition!*

The dispirited Republicans fielded no candidates on that April Fool's Day, and six months later they made only a half-hearted attempt to mount a campaign at the county level. During the fall canvass, the *Daily Register* did not even dignify the contest, such as it was, by publishing the names of those seeking office. Of course, a reader would have known that Wade Hampton was campaigning for re-election as governor, but little more. Nevertheless, Acton precinct went Republican by fifty votes, the only region in Richland County to stray from the Democratic fold.

In the eyes of most city-county residents that election wrote an end to the Reconstruction era. Yet, despite this sudden reversal of fortune, blacks did not simply vanish from public life. Charles Wilder, Columbia's postmaster in the 1870s, continued to serve in that capacity into the 1880s, and in 1885 the assistant chief of police (Joseph A. Randell) was a black man. Blacks also were much in evidence when disaster struck, for two of Columbia's fire brigades continued to be manned by blacks—the Vigilants and the Enterprise Fire Company, both organized during Reconstruction.

Viewed from the local perspective, one of the most enduring by-products of this era was urban-rural disagreement over race relations. The Richland-Edgefield clash of the 1870s was merely symptomatic of attitudes that still would be apparent a century later. Men such as Edwin Seibels and Wade Hampton were quite willing to meet and do business with the Nashes, Wilders, and other able spokesmen for their race; But-ler, Gary, and their successors were not. But of even greater significance, what many voters of Columbia and Richland County thought had been settled in November of 1878 was, it turned out, not settled at all.

Notes

1. Francis B. Simkins and Robert H. Woody, *South Carolina During Reconstruction* (Chapel Hill, 1932), p. 562.
2. Despite this upsurge in cotton (or perhaps because of it), production of wheat, corn, and wool lagged far behind totals reported in 1850 and 1860.
3. See David Carlton, "The Columbia Canal and Reconstruction: A Case Study," an un-published paper at the South Caroliniana Library. Carlton concludes that Sprague was merely a speculator, who, unable to get full control of local water power and thus set rates, at length decided to pull out. Sprague purchased the rights to develop the old canal in 1869 for $200, did some excavating, also bought Columbia's water works, and then four years later—blaming Reconstruction politics—offered to sell everything back to the city for $300,000. However, the Panic of 1873 intervened; and, when the Sprague empire collapsed in 1878, Columbia was able to get back its water company on much more reasonable terms.
4. Andrews, *The South Since the War*, p. 97.
5. *Ibid.*, p. 35.
6. Methodist clergyman William Martin, who spearheaded church relief efforts in the Mid-lands, reported in March of 1867 that "actual famine" existed. His pension list for Rich-land County included the names of 428 heads of families, most of them widows, who represented 1,359 individuals, "nearly all of whom are persons incapable of supporting themselves." See *The Southern Famine Relief Fund of Philadelphia* (Philadelphia, 1867?), p. 19.
7. Louis J. Bellardo, Jr., "The Social and Economic History of Fairfield County, South Carolina, 1865–1871," Ph.D. diss., University of Kentucky, 1979, p. 58. According to a report in the *Nation* (15 August 1867), sand hillers seeking aid in Columbia sometimes addressed U.S. officials in a respectful manner as "the enemy," and bureau personnel often heard the North referred to as "those foreign states."

8. *Daily Phoenix*, 9 March 1866. By "our old and cherished system of labor," these officials meant the traditional duty of all able-bodied men to work on roads so many days each year, not slavery *per se.*

9. *Ibid.*, 19 March 1867. The following month, a similar meeting in Gadsden, addressed by three whites and three blacks, passed resolutions against "outside interference" and in favor of the selection of former masters as delegates to the upcoming constitutional convention, men who respected the wishes of freedmen and would speak in their behalf.

10. Hampton Family Papers, South Caroliniana Library.

11. It is not known whether Nash visited Conner, but an interview in the *New York Times* (9 August 1867) reveals that he soon was working for Hampton in a private capacity, transporting field hands to the general's Mississippi plantations, for example.

12. On 26 November 1871, the *Daily Phoenix* described a visit to the alms house, which then had twenty-seven inmates, including two black men, the rest being white women and children. A reporter found the facility in reasonably good condition, but he was distressed to learn that it was being run by a black "Uncle Sam."

13. The college's Euphradian Society was so infuriated by the actions of Robertson and Sumter's Franklin J. Moses, Jr., governor from 1872 to 1874, that members expelled both from its ranks.

14. Smith, who unsuccessfully sought compensation from the Southern Claims Commission for foodstuff taken by U.S. soldiers during the invasion of Columbia, had a unique story to tell. As a slave with a free-born wife, he paid his owner twenty-five dollars a month for the privilege of "hiring out his labor" and otherwise was virtually free. He maintained his own shop, negotiated contracts, and acquired land in his wife's name. In fact, the 1860 census lists Smith as a free black holding property worth $1,200. A decade later, he was worth ten times that figure. During the war, Smith aided escaped Union prisoners, but early in the conflict he made the mistake of voluntarily accompanying a local rifle company, first to Charleston and then to Richmond. He went as a musician, a paid member of a brass band; but, in the eyes of Southern Claims officials, these outings were inconsistent with true loyalty. Thus, even though they thought this carpenter "unusually intelligent," his claim was rejected.

15. WPA Records (D–4–18), South Caroliniana Library.

16. Accused of fraud, Nash resigned from the Senate on 15 October 1877 and made restitution for funds the Democrats said he had obtained illegally. Minort stepped down when indicted for bribery in connection with the election of U.S. Senator John Patterson. *Note:* In 1874, Chamberlain had carried Richland by a somewhat larger margin, 2,483.

The Enigmatic Eighties

CHAPTER TWELVE

The 1880s were an important period in the life of the Midlands, the state, and the nation. Seemingly bland, a time of calm between the turmoil of Reconstruction and the Populist upheaval of the "Gay 90s," these years were, in fact, a significant turning point in many facets of daily life. These include the rural-urban equation and white-black relations, as well as tensions arising from the "standardization" of our society. The 1880s were, to a large degree, a dividing line between an America dominated by disparate and widely scattered rural elements and a nation receptive to and often molded by urban innovation. Until that era, country life, in the main, was as appealing as that in town, perhaps more so. But the telephone, home mail delivery, electricity, streetcars, and graded public schools—all of which appeared in Columbia in the 1880s—quickly made an urban address infinitely more desirable.

This contrast was further heightened by a troubled farm economy. Between 1875 and 1885, the average price of cotton—Richland County's prime crop—declined from roughly twelve to six cents a pound, giving birth to frustrations that would propel Edgefield's Ben Tillman into the governor's mansion. Amid these trying times, the state's population increased by 15 percent, up from 995,577 in 1880 to 1,151,149 a decade later, and both Columbia and Richland County kept pace, the city registering a 50 percent gain (10,036 to 15,353), while county population overall rose from 28,573 to 36,821.

Under such depressed conditions, change in rural areas was not extensive, although by 1890 the value of Richland's farm land and buildings was slightly more than in 1860 (about $2 million), and corn production, which rose from 171,040 to 280,008 bushels during the 1880s, also exceeded that of 1860. The number of mules and swine continued to increase, as did individual farms (2,326 in 1890 compared to 2,246 a decade earlier). The most striking trend was added reliance on cotton despite dwindling prices—13,915 bales harvested in 1890, nearly 3,000 more than in 1880. To no one's surprise, the picture emerges of scores of tenants dependent upon cotton, corn, and hogs . . . and the production of each would rise in the 1890s, as would the number of farms.

Nevertheless, subtle as it might be, change was taking place. In 1880, Eastover was incorporated by the state legislature as a separate community, an area extending one-half mile in all directions from the railroad depot. This new entity, Richland County's second urban center, was to be governed by an intendant and four wardens. The following year, an amendment to Eastover's charter prohibited the issuance of liquor licenses within the corporate limits of the town. Of much greater concern than the sale of spirits was the appearance of new fences following passage of a controversial "stock law" in 1877. Adopted township by township in the early 1880s, this measure forced farmers to keep their animals on their own land. To those accustomed to fencing in crops and letting cattle and hogs run free—and especially to forage in forests long viewed as public domain—this was nothing more than another irksome burden forced upon the poor by the rich. Although local reaction was less violent than in some coastal counties, when a sand hills warehouse owned by pottery makers Landrum & Stock burned in February of 1882, the *Daily Register* blamed the "stock law." These folk, according to the editor, had fenced in their pastures as they began open cultivation of fields, moves resented by some of their neighbors. Two months later, city fathers decided to enforce the "stock law" in Columbia itself, and there are indications that fences played a major role in the autumn campaign of that year as disgruntled whites in the eastern half of the county listened intently to Greenback orators. This discontent, precursor of more to come, caused some apprehension in Democratic ranks, although the party won handily enough.[1] (For a list of prominent Richland County citizens of this era, see Appendix 3, a "Gazetteer" from the *Columbia City Directory* of 1879–1880.)

Meanwhile, the coming of age of a generation, both white and black in town and country, that knew nothing of the casual, good-natured banter and mutual respect sometimes present in the master-slave relationship gave rise to greater rigidity in racial attitudes. This ever-widening gulf, often encouraged by those seeking political office and augmented by rural distress, fostered the perfect milieu for a conscious re-writing of recent history and contributed directly in the decade that followed to the onset of separation of the races by law, not custom.

The "standardization" of American life in the 1880s took varied forms and presented local residents with a painful dilemma. These innovations often smacked of Yankee ways, yet *standard* time, a *standard* rail gauge, the beginnings of national advertising campaigns in behalf of *standard* (name) brands, and even graded public schools could by seen as an integral part of the much-desired industrialization of Columbia and its environs. Factories had made the North rich (and victorious, it might be added), and similar structures, some individuals argued, could solve the economic woes of this region.

Unlike events that transpired during the war and its aftermath, these changes frequently were gradual and undramatic and, as such, went virtually unnoticed or, on occasions, were viewed simply as steps long overdue, things that should have been done much earlier. Street signs and house numbers that appeared in the summer of 1887 in preparation for free mail delivery undoubtedly were seen in this light.[2] In addition, for over two decades (1870–1890) the eyes of the Midlands were riveted on the waters of the Congaree, not on mundane day-to-day happenings. Once the canal was completed, it was said, factories would rise majestically on its banks and provide jobs for hundreds, even thousands.

On 18 March 1881, Mrs. Fitz William McMaster, wife of a lawyer who was emerging as a prominent local figure, wrote to their twenty-year-old son, John, in Colorado concerning the latest campaign to make his home town an industrial center. "Do you know the Canal is booming! over $60,000 has been subscribed in the city in the last two days." As soon as $1 million was pledged, work would begin, and, in time, he would be able to find "a place as a factory boy" instead of roaming about the Rockies among people he didn't know who didn't care "one cent" for him. Perhaps, she wrote, he could become a spinner or a ward keeper. In any case, this mother, who obviously knew nothing about factory life, expressed the hope that something would turn up for Columbia so "all of her home-grown young men may find employment within her borders."

Lost in a dream world, local citizens from all walks of life, much like Mrs. McMaster, largely ignored the slow, but steady growth of a dozen or so small industries. Even businessmen succumbed to these attitudes, although, conscious of a vigorous economy in the Piedmont and stagnation in Charleston, in 1880 they revived their somnolent Board of Trade in an attempt to counter the threat posed by the mills of Greenville and Spartanburg.[3] This group's next annual report (September 1881) lashed out at deplorable highways and failure to make the Congaree navigable,

Happy Holidays, 1880

Columbia, December 26.—Business of all kinds was entirely suspended in Columbia yesterday, and Christmas was more generally and joyously celebrated than it has been since the war. Early in the morning a disagreeable, cold, drizzling rain set in and continued nearly all day, consequently an embargo was placed upon outdoor sports and exercises. But notwithstanding the chilling atmosphere, mud and slush, the streets were filled during the day and night with boisterous merry-makers, who indulged in all kinds of provoking pranks, such as carrying off gates, removing bridges, discharging giant crackers and blowing ear-piercing, sleep-destroying horns, all to the great annoyance of those who preferred quiet enjoyment around their hearthstones, burning the Yule log and telling Christmas tales. Most of the bar-rooms were closed, but unlimited quantities of liquor were drunk, and there was much drunkenness, disorder and street-fighting. As far as I can learn, there were not many casualties. A negro boy had an eye destroyed by a ball from a Roman candle, a white boy lost two fingers by the premature explosion of a package of giant crackers which he was carrying in a box, a colored man from the country was badly beaten and left insensible by a crowd of negro toughs, and a colored woman was run over by a dray and severely injured.

Charleston *News and Courier*,
27 December 1880.

which could be accomplished, members claimed, with the aid of federal funds. The roads of central Africa, they said scornfully, were as good as those of the Midlands, and a few weeks later the board offered a fifty-dollar prize for the best treatise on the construction and maintenance of public roads. Apparently there were few entries; for, six months later the contest deadline was extended and the long-standing appeal for the development of water power on the Congaree aired once more.

Throughout the 1880s, well into the 20th century for that matter, the potential of cheap river transportation continued to mesmerize local entrepreneurs. In 1887, another little steamer, the *John M. Cole,* made Granby its home port; however, as before and after, nothing much came of this experiment. To begin with, this ship's path to the sea was blocked by a low railroad bridge at Kingville, forcing the crew to transfer cargo to a second vessel at that point. And, as usual, the seasonal nature of the Congaree—waters too high and dangerous or too low and rock-strewn—thwarted schemes to make Columbia an inland seaport.

Nevertheless, some cotton did make its way down the Broad and Saluda to local markets from time to time, and the old Columbia Canal (as noted) was much in the news as a source of water power for industrial use. In February of 1882, the canal commissioners turned the property over to the directors of the state penitentiary, and within a few weeks work on the canal was resumed, largely with the aid of convict labor. According to plans widely hailed, the new managers proposed to transform the old waterway (four feet deep and fifteen feet wide) into a magnificent channel ten feet deep and 150 feet wide. When completed, the *News and Courier* boasted on 16 June 1883, the Columbia Canal would have a wider bottom than that of the mighty Suez!

Yet in an age dominated by rail travel, neither canals nor roads fared well. The basic reason was an inability to sustain interest in projects, which, if properly carried out, would cost a lot of money. Each spring Columbia's streets were packed with red clay and sand, and county road commissioners continued haphazard maintenance of Richland's highways with the reluctant assistance of residents who were required to work on them so many days each year. This forced labor, resented by freedmen who found the practice reminiscent of slavery, led to charges of favoritism, fines, and recrimination. The end result was that county roads, as well as city streets, generally were in deplorable condition and often impassable during wet weather. As for the canal, in the late 1880s it passed into city hands and, in time, fulfilled some of the rosy predictions of these decades.

Perhaps the most irritating problem of the 1880s was mud. In the summer when reservoirs were low, city dwellers complained of muddy drinking water; in the winter, of muddy streets. Crack trains could whisk one from Charleston to Columbia in three hours and forty minutes, and an individual could travel about the capital city in relative ease by buggy and streetcar, vehicles first drawn by mules and horses and then electrified. But it often was well nigh impossible to cross Main Street on foot![4]

On 15 February 1876, the *Daily Register* pleaded for a decent crossing on that thoroughfare . . . "anywhere in the business section of the city, so that citizens may not have to swim in the mud." Ten years later, in December of 1886, the *News and Courier* vowed that street still was "a disgrace . . . a miry bog!"

This same daily subsequently noted that mud was so thick in Columbia that streetcar drivers and their teams often strayed from the tracks. City employees tried scraping and sanding street crossings and even installed granite-block stepping stones at some intersections, but only the coming of the bicycle and the auto and the protests of their owners would bring true relief.

The streetcar, first proposed during Reconstruction, did not actually appear for another ten years. In February of 1876, twenty-four local citizens—among them, merchants William B. Stanley, W. C. Swaffield, Frank N. Ehrlich, John C. Dial, and John Agnew, broker William G. Childs, bankers Wilie Jones and John P. Southern, Attorney-General S. W. Melton, and two well-known blacks (State Senator William B. Nash and C. J. Carroll, commissioner for Richland County schools)—joined forces to form the Columbia Street Railway Company, capitalized at $100,000. Their charter outlined plans to commence construction within twelve months and to begin service within five years; however, the political turmoil of 1876–1877 ended any hope of launching such a project.

Five years later, the *Daily Register* (27 August 1881) asked, "What has become of the street cars which were to run in Columbia? Does the corporation still exist or will another have to be formed?" This query apparently was inspired by discussion then going on in the business community; for, early in 1882 another company bearing the same name appeared. This corporation, capitalized at only $25,000, received a thirty-year charter that also required full operation within five years.

The principal backers were three prominent businessmen—livery stable owner William D. Starling, Thomas D. Gillespie (manager of the local office of the Southern Express Company), and lawyer John R. Abney. Starling, who obviously had a special interest in the success of this enterprise, became manager of the railway when it began operation in 1886. Cars at that time served several key points: the cemetery, state fair grounds, and asylum on the northern edge of the city, the Main Street business district, and Columbia's two railroad depots. In other words, the streetcar line was a giant "T" formed by Elmwood and Main streets, together with two side tracks. At the base of the "T", cars turned in front of the capitol and went west on Gervais to the new Union Depot (opened in 1883) that accommodated all railroad passengers except those bound for Charlotte. Then, part way up the "T", another spur track went east along Laurel and Blanding streets to the Charlotte terminal. Colored signals designated the destination of each car.

Service began on 12 October 1886 (fare five cents) following the arrival of twenty mules from Kentucky and two cars from Troy, New York, which soon were joined by four more. During the first three days of operation, some 4,000 passengers experienced the thrill of being hauled along iron rails. In March of 1887, mules gave way to horses, which could pull the cars at a top speed of six miles per hour. This was, according to an 1876 ordinance, the accepted rate for those traveling on Main and Assembly streets; elsewhere it was one mile faster. The downhill run along Gervais Street, however, could be made without animal assistance; and, on at least one occasion, when brakes failed to work, passengers bound for Union Depot arrived somewhat sooner than expected . . . and undoubtedly exceeded the speed limit en route.

The end of horse-drawn travel was foreshadowed in December of 1890 with incorporation of the Columbia Electric Street and Suburban Railway and Electric Power Company. This new entity subsequently purchased the old street railway, which never was financially robust, and announced plans to expand service on both sides of the Congaree. Although no electric cars appeared until 3 May 1893, there is little question that the "trolley" played a major role in the development of suburban Columbia during the next two or three decades.[5]

Other forms of travel, notably by train and bicycle, also experienced fundamental change during the 1880s. On 1 February 1883 (as noted earlier), a new Union Depot opened on Gervais Street. This magnificent structure, built by the South Carolina Railroad at a cost of $18,000, also served passengers of the Columbia and Greenville and Wilmington, Columbia, and Augusta lines. It had spacious waiting rooms with eighteen-foot ceilings and frescoes by a Charleston artist. The ladies' area was painted lilac; the gentlemen's, buff. There were electric gongs to announce arriving trains, double-reflecting gas lights, sparkling chandeliers, telephone and telegraph connections, large washrooms, and a refreshment stand—everything any weary traveler could wish for.

Ten months later, in November of that same year, Columbia and the rest of the nation adjusted their clocks and watches to "standard" time. Until then, this community had *three* times—its own, Charleston time (four minutes faster), which was used by the South Carolina Railroad, and Washington time (sixteen minutes faster), that used by all other railroads.

At noon on 19 November 1883, the hands of local clocks were advanced twenty-four minutes so as to conform to the system adopted nation-wide. Three years after that, in June of 1886, all major railroads moved their rails to "standard" gauge, four feet, nine inches, that used by the Pennsylvania Railroad. In most cases, this meant an adjustment of only a few inches, perhaps three; nevertheless, this task was an awesome undertaking.

Shortly after the decade came to a close, in June of 1890 Columbia welcomed a new railroad line when the Columbia, Newberry, and Lau-rens ("Crooked, Noisy, and Late") began service between the state capital and Prosperity. Thus by 1891, the city directory could boast that Colum-bia was "a great rail centre" with direct ties to Charleston, Augusta, Greenville, Laurens, Spartanburg, Charlotte, Camden, and Wilmington. Its authors also told of a projected line from Washington to Florida via Columbia and Savannah that would become the most direct north-south line along the Atlantic Coast. At that time, three of Columbia's rail-roads—the Charlotte, Columbia, and Augusta; Columbia and Greenville; and Spartanburg, Union, and Columbia—were part of the sprawling Richmond and Danville system, which, after 1886, was ruled by a group of New York financiers. Subsequent expansion into Georgia and the panic of 1893 led to disaster, out of which emerged the Southern Railway of J. P. Morgan.

The real importance of the bicycle on the local scene, much like that of the streetcar, lies in the 1890s, but its roots go back to the late 1860s. The first of the velocipedes, as they were called, arrived in Columbia in 1869. In May of that year, Captain John Heise raffled off one of these contraptions at his confectionery store, and soon after that a short-lived velocipede "rink" offering free instruction was established in Janney's Hall. But these early "bone-shakers," little more than mere novelties, could achieve neither speed nor much of a following until transformed into the big wheel-small wheel "penny farthing," and by November of 1881 hardware merchant John Agnew was prepared to outfit any daring young man with just that sort of machine.

Seven months later there were enough excited cyclists to form a club, and in the fall of 1882 a handful of Columbia and Charlotte riders thrilled hundreds of onlookers at the state fair. The following year, much larger crowds, as many as six thousand fair-goers, watched thirty dare-devils from Charleston, Newberry, Greenville, and Columbia race around a special, twelve-foot-wide, oval track, six laps to the mile, as they competed for prizes such as a silver pitcher, a gold-headed cane, bicycle shoes, and a gold pen case. On this occasion, the Columbia Club appeared in canary-yellow silk shirts with a locally designed monogram.

Nevertheless, this exhibition, South Carolina's first inter-club meet, did not spark widespread interest. These pioneer bicycles still were too expensive, too dangerous; and, as local cyclists discovered a short time later when they tried unsuccessfully to ride to Winnsboro, country roads were not ready for this mode of travel. Also, on at least two occasions these two-wheel vehicles were tried and found wanting. In the summer of 1884, Columbia Club members who were riding near Trinity churchyard cornered a thief who had broken free from a constable. But, according to the *News and Courier* (8 August), "before his would-be captors could dismount from their iron steeds he leapt quickly over the fence and made good his escape." Then, races staged at the fair grounds in May of 1885 between a champion bicycle rider and a horse usually were won by the latter, much to the delight, it is assumed, of country excursionists who had crowded into town for the event.

Within a few years, however, English inventors produced a chain-driven model with equal-sized wheels much like the "bike" of today, as well as rubber tires, and the great craze of the 1890s was born. By the turn of the century, at least 3,000 area residents were commuting to work on bicycles, and many of them thought the problem of "short-distance" travel at last had been solved.

Roller skates, a less spectacular form of wheeled transport, enjoyed much greater popularity in the 1880s than the bicycle; in fact, local young people had been "skating" in various public auditoriums along Main Street since the late 1860s. This was, in effect, a winter sport provided by enterprising northerners who appeared each fall with several hundred skates, set up shop, and in the spring returned to whence they came, presumably to open a summer rink there. The Columbia Roller Skating Academy of the 1879–1880 season, for example, had quarters in Clark's Hall where during mornings and afternoons the only cost was rental of skates. In the evening, on the other hand, admission was charged, and in at least one year (1881) the season closed with a colorful costume carnival on wheels.

Other recreational pursuits of the decade included such traditional fare as tournaments with knights and ladies, barbecues staged by political parties and fraternal orders, cockfights, minstrel shows, shooting meets (often sponsored by the Schuetzen Verein organized by local Germans in July of 1874), dances and balls, church fairs and picnics, and, of course, traveling shows that appeared at the Opera House from time to time.

Buffalo Bill and his Wild West troupe were among those who graced that stage in 1881, and three years later—precursor of an attraction that still packs a wallop—Columbians enjoyed a full evening of Graeco-Roman wrestling, also at the Opera House.[6]

Yet, as in other realms of daily life, change was evident. On two nights in August of 1881, for a quarter (children, ten cents) one could enter the armory of the Richland Volunteers and listen to a wonderful machine developed by a Mr. Edison. According to the *Daily Register* (19 August), "It Talks, it Laughs, it Sings, it Cries, it Whistles, Plays Cornet, &c." Apparently local citizens approved of Edison's creation; for, by 1890 they were bragging that their city had more nickel-operated phonographs in its stores than could be found in all of Charleston!

However, if the number of phonographs increased during the 1880s, cockfights did not. Few approved of cocking mains held near the college from time to time, usually on holidays, but city fathers concluded that, until banned by state law, it was prudent policy to license the sport and thus retain marginal control. In 1887, the legislature finally acted, outlawing cockfights within three miles of any chartered institution. Thus Columbia's lone legal cockpit became history amid a final flurry of blood, feathers, and dollars—a three-day extravaganza pitting South Carolina birds against those from the Tar Heel State. Each side entered twenty-one cocks, with winners getting fifty dollars and the grand champion $500.

If there was a common thread in the new wave of recreation, it was an emphasis upon *organization*.[7] In contrast to earlier times, thanks largely to improved rail service, leisure activity often was provided by semi-professional groups such as baseball teams and firemen or centered upon school commencements in June and the annual state fair in November. Baseball, made popular by the U.S. Army during Reconstruction, gave birth in the 1880s to town teams, factory teams, college teams, midget teams, black teams, lean teams, fat teams, even teams representing various boarding houses. In November of 1884, a group of Yankee lovelies from the Northeast—the Blondes and Brunettes—swept into town and challenged the Mechanics. They wore, in the words of the *Daily Register* of 13 November, "fancy costumes after the pattern of suits, which gave free play to their limbs." Southern chivalry notwithstanding, the Mechanics won 12–10, but that evening the victors graciously "devoted themselves to their visitors, who lodged at the Hendrix House."

Although local teams seemed to appear and disappear with alarming regularity, one could count upon Columbia being represented each season by one or two relatively able white teams, a South Carolina College nine, and a group of eager black players. According to this account that appeared in the *News and Courier*, the latter, using community facilities, staged a fine show early in September of 1886: "The base ball park was the scene of a great contest between the Columbias, a local colored team, and the Congarees, a stalwart and very black team from lower Richland. The slugging was only surpassed by the muffing of the flies. There were spurts of good work, however, and the game, errors and all, proved very entertaining. The visitors started out handsomely, but the Columbias won by a score of 31 to 20, shutting out the enemy in the ninth inning by actually making a triple play."

During these years, devotees of this new sport also were developing keen interest in the progress of metropolitan teams, so much so that Al Meehan's Billiard Parlor in the Columbia Hotel was posting telegraphic reports inning by inning. As for football, it was virtually unknown. The game evidently enjoyed fleeting popularity among college students in the winter of 1884; the *News and Courier* reported on 2 February that a group of them, eager to arrange a "match" game, was unable to find any other "experts" in this state. However, in the early 1890s, pigskin and gridiron finally got a toehold in South Carolina. On 14 November 1891, Trinity (Duke) beat Furman 96–0 at the state fair grounds, and on Christmas Eve of 1892 Furman rolled over USC 44–0 in a game played at Charleston's Baseball Park, the first such contest ever seen in the "Holy City."

Yet, for every individual who crowded around a Columbia baseball diamond in the 1880s, ten applauded the exploits of local firemen, whether battling actual flames or going through competitive drills. At the outset of the decade, the city had five groups of volunteers—two black engine companies (Vigilant and Enterprise), two white engine companies (Independent and Palmetto), and a white hook and ladder unit (Phoenix). Membership in the white companies ranged from twenty to forty, while each of the black organizations had about seventy-five names on their rolls. These men, not baseball players, were the true athletes of the era, idolized by youngsters and their older sisters, and any inter-city tournament in which they participated was an excuse for parades, banquets, and balls.

Of course, each race organized its own outings, but this was one realm of daily life where the color line often was blurred. This is quite understandable since, if disaster struck, *all* firemen rushed to the scene and joined forces to fight the blaze. When blacks from Winnsboro and Greenville came to town for a parade and tournament in June of 1881, for example, the mayor was on hand to greet them, and so many whites attended a two-day fair staged for the benefit of the Enterprise Fire Engine Company in October of 1882 that blacks thanked them publicly for their support.

Nevertheless, as two incidents of those same years reveal, interracial cooperation was a fragile flower. In the fall of 1880, few black firemen participated in a parade marking the opening of the state fair. According to the *Daily Register* (13 November), only thirty-three Vigilants joined the line of march, and no one wearing an Enterprise uniform appeared. Why? In the opinion of this editor, rumors that this was "a political dodge" to trap and massacre blacks alarmed many who might otherwise have been present. And, although this gentleman railed against such "a mean and contemptible method" of exciting distrust and fear, it is obvious that the heat of the recent national election campaign had to cool before daily life in Columbia would be normal once more.

Then, in June of 1884, Mark Reynolds told his Stateburg sweetheart of a bizarre twist that occurred during a grand, three-day program of foot races and reel contests hosted by local white firemen. When hundreds crowded into the business district where bleachers had been erected for 1,500 spectators, Melvin Kinard, co-owner of Kinard & Wiley's haberdashery, decided to garner good will by throwing bits of clothing from the roof of his store. Reynolds, a struggling young lawyer, wrote that he largely ignored these festivities, but conceded he left his office from time to time to watch blacks scrambling for shirts, socks, and underwear. "Occasionally [roofing] slates would be thrown down—and several Negroes were cracked on the head. I was in hopes that I might get a case from some innocent bystander for damages caused by injuries sustained on this interesting occasion but was disappointed."[8]

Reynolds, who subsequently became a fixture in Sumter legal circles, earned a special niche in local annals when he became the first person in Columbia to master the typewriter. In February of 1885, his boss, Wade Hampton's son-in-law, Colonel John C. Haskell of the firm of Pope & Haskell, returned from the North with one of these machines, and young Reynolds quickly taught himself the requisite skills. His first letter to "Lizzie" (11 February) opened with these words: "Are you pleased to see your name in print?" Reynolds reported that the book he was using said it might take up to six weeks "to write twice as fast as with a pen" and told of offices Haskell had visited in Washington where scores of young ladies write "so fast that they looked as if they were playing pianos and yet could laugh and talk among themselves. . . . You will perceive," he added, "that I have not arrived at such a state of proficiency yet." Two

William Beverly Nash (c. 1822–1888).

Hampton in Triumph. This drawing of the new governor being hailed by enthusiastic supporters appeared in *Frank Leslie's Illustrated Newspaper* (13 January 1877).

The Pavilion at Shandon—a short-lived structure near Five Points that gave its name to "Pavillion Avenue." This drawing appeared in the *State* (29 May 1894).

C. H. Baldwin & Son, 1601 Main Street, purveyors of fine groceries in 1897.

The View from the State House, c. 1895. Looking west toward the railroad depot and "Duck Mill" and (bottom) southwest toward Olympia and Granby mills. Note the massive telephone poles and how close residential housing is to the capitol grounds.

Richland County Courthouse, the third such building, stood at the corner of Main and Washington streets until razed in 1935.

Fun at Camp Fornance. Local women and Spanish-American War soldiers enjoy a festive meal and a bicycle outing.

But bicycles were for all ages. These youngsters, properly chaperoned, were about to participate in a local bicycle parade held on 13 June 1896.

Main Street, c. 1905 (Security Federal Savings and Loan Association Collection).

Richard Carroll (1860–1929), Columbia's "Booker T. Washington," as portrayed on the front page of his *Christian Soldier* in May 1899.

Columbia's City Hall and Opera House, Main and Gervais streets. Opened 1 December 1900, this structure was the setting for Carroll's race conferences and many other famous gatherings. Replaced by the Wade Hampton Hotel four decades later, that landmark gave way in the 1980s to the AT&T Building. An arrow (lower right) points to one of the city's troublesome drains that for many years were crossed by small foot bridges.

years later, the colonel raised this young man's salary to fifty dollars a month, a princely sum that permitted him to ask "Lizzie" to become his bride.

Another wonder of the age, the telephone, arrived in Columbia somewhat earlier and enjoyed immediate acceptance. In January of 1880, a representative of the National Bell Telephone Company announced that, if he could secure twenty-five subscribers, service would be established here. This total was exceeded in less than a week, and by June telephones were being installed, largely in stores, business offices, and public institutions, at a cost of $46 a year. Nine months later, the *Daily Register* (which had a telephone) was able to publish a comprehensive listing. (See pp. 242–43.) By February of 1883, the number of subscribers had grown to ninety-one, enabling the company to initiate night service.

Electricity, perhaps because its proponents still were debating the merits of direct and alternating current, did not exert much influence locally during the 1880s. The city council discussed the advantages of electricity for street lighting as early as March of 1882, but then voted to expand gas illumination instead. When the State House turned on a primitive electrical system two years later, the *Daily Register* expressed keen disappointment, and state authorities subsequently reverted to gas. Finally, in December of 1887 the Congaree Gas and Electric Company appeared, backed by W. H. Gibbes, John P. Thomas, Jr., T. T. Moore, John T. Sloan, Jr., and B. L. Abney; and, in the fall of 1888, just in time for the state fair, arc lights were installed on West Gervais and Main streets.

Although two small generating plants were built in the early 1890s, one on Gates Street, the other on the canal, electricity for residential use was severely limited until after 1900. Meanwhile, in 1891 the various gas, electric, and street railway interests merged to form the Columbia Electric Street Railway, Light and Power Company. This utility, after absorbing various smaller rivals, in 1924 became the Broad River Power Company, which in March of 1937 assumed the now-familiar name of South Carolina Electric & Gas.[9]

The story of education in the 1880s, much like that of electricity, is something of a mixed bag. The greatest improvement was apparent in Columbia's graded school system and in the training of teachers. Once the city became a separate school district free of county control in 1880, community leaders, among them, Fitz William McMaster, who is generally considered the "father" of modern public education in Columbia, initiated a drive for a one-mill tax that would be used to lengthen the ninety-day school term and improve other aspects of the overall program.

Columbia Telephone Exchange

We were pleased to hear Mr. D. J. Carson, General Superintendent of the Southern Bell Telephone and Telegraph Company, who is on a tour of inspection to the different exchanges throughout the country, say that we have the best appointed and most complete exchange that he has yet visited. While the list of members here is still small, Manager Cathcart has arrangements made for the accommodation of many more, and the polite and efficient attendants, Messrs. Cantwell and Bateman, would be delighted to serve double the present number.

We publish the following classified list of present members of the Columbia Telephonic Exchange, all of whom will testify to the convenience and great benefits derived therefrom:

Attorneys at Law

McMaster, F W
Melton & Clark
Monteith, W S

Banks

Carolina National
Central National

Beer & Liquor Dealers

Habenicht, C C

Cotton Buyers

Blakely Bros
Crawford, Daniel, & Sons
Davis, W R
Dickson, E B
Griffin, B F
Haltiwanger, P H
O'Neale, Richard, Jr

Express Offices

Southern

Factories

Saluda Cotton

Fire Engine Company

Independent, John F Sutphen, Secretary

Family Grocers, Wholesale and Retail

Aughtry, T B, & Co
Griffin, B F
Haltiwanger, P H
Lorick & Lowrance
Laurey, C J
Martin, W T, Richardson street
Martin, W T, Taylor street
McKay, E B & D
Morris, J M, & Co
Rawls & Willhalf

Fertilizers

Laughlin, A C

Hardware

Dial, J C
Lorick & Lowrance

Hotels

Columbia

Insurance Agents

Keenan, R A
Swaffield, W C

Ice Dealers

Habenicht, C C

Livery Stables

Starling, W D

Machine Shops

Tozer, Richard

Merchant Tailors

Swaffield, W C

Millers

Gibson & Co

Newspapers, Daily

Register, Columbia
News & Courier, Charleston,
  branch office

Physicians

Talley, Dr A N

Public Institutions

State Capitol, Governor's Office
State Lunatic Asylum, Male
State Lunatic Asylum, Female
State Penitentiary
City Hall, Clerk's Office
Guard House

Residences

Coles, J S
Childs, W G

Residences Continued

Cathcart, W R
Clark, W A
Gillespie, T D
Hagood, Johnson, Governor
  South Carolina
Lipscomb, T J
Melton, S W
McMaster, F W
Talley, Dr A N

Railroad Offices

Agent South Carolina
Agent Greenville & Columbia
Agent Charlotte, Columbia &
  Augusta
Agent Wilmington, Columbia &
  Augusta
Charlotte, Columbia and Augusta,
  General Office

Restaurants

Heitsch, Henry
Pollock's, T M Pollock Proprietor

Telegraph Offices

Western Union

Wood & Coal Dealers

Gary & Tappan

Daily Register
18 March 1881

Efforts were rebuffed by voters in 1881 and 1882, largely because of reluctance to fund education for blacks, but finally succeeded in 1883. (On several occasions, the *Daily Register*, while ostensibly supporting this campaign, attacked black teachers who had the audacity to work actively in behalf of the Republican party.) In the meantime, the state inaugurated summer teacher-training institutes, with whites meeting in Greenville and blacks in Columbia, and local businessmen soon were keenly aware of benefits derived from these month-long sessions. When the editor of the *Daily Register* mislaid an address concerning the activities of the black South Carolina Teachers' Association in May of 1882, he apologized profusely on the day it was published and boasted of hospitality awaiting members of the group who planned to come to the state capital in July.

With the promise of new money, the school board began the task of restructuring Columbia's educational system. Howard School, built at the corner of Lincoln and Plain streets during Reconstruction, was considered suitable for black students, but the principal white structure near Sidney Park was much too small to handle an expanded program. As a result, city authorities decided to lease buildings owned by historic Columbia Academy, with the proviso that it always would be able to name two members of the board.[10] Aided by Tennessee-born David B. Johnson, appointed superintendent in June of 1883, school officials established a scheme whereby older white boys would attend classes at the former Male Academy on Laurel Street manned by four teachers, white girls and younger white boys would be taught by seven teachers in the old Female Academy on Washington Street, and all black children, as before, would be housed at Howard School, which had a staff of eight.

On 28 September 1883, classes began for 930 youngsters—550 white, 380 black—and within a month enrollment had increased to 1,120. The first eight grades of this ten-year program were free to all Columbia residents. Those living outside of the corporate limits had to pay one to three dollars a month, depending upon courses taken, and anyone enrolled in what were considered high school classes paid a monthly tuition fee of two dollars and fifty cents.

As would be expected, the curriculum consisted for the most part of basic skills that increased in difficulty from year to year. In grade one, for example, a student had to learn to count to 100 "forward, backwards, and by twos and threes, &c.," write, read, spell, and master the geographical features of "land and water, &c., in and around Columbia." In the third grade, a student graduated to world geography, in the fourth studied American and English money, in the sixth tackled South Carolina history, and in seventh moved on to that of the United States. Tobacco and eating or chewing were forbidden, as was the advertising or announcing of any public meeting or entertainment. Corporal punishment could be administered at the discretion of each principal. At the school for white females, a piano gave the signal for assembly, recess, and dismissal; at the boys' school, student movements were directed by drum beats.[11]

Nine months later, with piano chords and drum rolls ringing in their ears, Columbia's white students gave a rousing "finals exhibition" at the Opera House. The audience, said to have been the largest ever assembled there, had to pay an admission fee (twenty-five cents) that was earmarked for the library fund, and still scores were turned away. For over three hours, young people of all ages sang, recited, went through drills, and formed statuary scenes to the delight of relatives and adoring parents. At the conclusion, school officials announced that 1,494 students, 60 percent of those eligible, had been enrolled during the year, among them, 246 whites and 76 blacks who attended classes for the first time.

In addition to a graded system, another encouraging development on the local scene was Winthrop Training School, an outgrowth of the summer seminar for white teachers first held in Greenville. This institution, the personal creation of Superintendent Johnson (with the assistance of the president of the Peabody Fund, Robert C. Winthrop, hence the name), was launched in the chapel of Columbia Theological Seminary in November of 1886. The goal was to train teachers for schools throughout the state, and by the end of the decade more than fifty students were enrolled. Eventually, benefiting from the efforts of various prominent South Carolinians, especially Ben Tillman, this school achieved collegiate status and in the mid-1890s moved to Rock Hill.

Classes at two black schools—Benedict Institute founded in 1870 and Allen University, formerly Payne, which moved to Columbia from Cokesbury in 1880—were another bright spot. From the outset they inaugurated some of the truly innovative work being done in the field of education in this state. Benedict, founded by the American Baptist Home Mission Society and named for its first major benefactor, Mrs. B. A. Benedict of Pawtucket, Rhode Island, was really a multi-level private school that trained teachers, taught such industrial trades as shoemaking, painting, carpentry, printing, and dress-making, and provided college preparatory and college courses, both heavily embued with theology. Allen, a Methodist institution located just south of Benedict on the eastern edge of the city, carried on a similar program, plus an unusual law school that graduated its first class in 1884. This group included four young men, two of whom were clerks at the city post office. Allen also operated a primary school in the block bounded by Main, Richland, Sumter, and Laurel.

By contrast, old South Carolina College, Columbia Female College, the theological seminary, and various private academies were experiencing lean years. To some degree, this was a reflection of political ferment and hard times, as well as an enhanced public school system and interest in more practical studies that soon would be available at Winthrop and its male counterpart, Clemson College. Although the educational story of the previous decade will be explored more fully in the next chapter, it might be well to point out that, in the mid-1870s, South Carolina College—traditionally a white male enclave—had both black and female students for a time and then was closed for three years. The Methodist-sponsored women's college, converted into a hotel following the war, did not resume class work until 1873. And Columbia Theological Seminary, rocked by internal dispute, nearly folded and, in fact, was inoperative from 1880 to 1882.

In October of 1880, the oldest of these institutions opened it doors as the South Carolina College of Agriculture and Mechanics, a move that followed tacit agreement that this white school and Orangeburg's Claflin College (black) would share federal land-grant funds emanating from the Morrill Act of 1862. However, in the fall of 1882 "South Carolina College" reappeared, only to become a university in 1887 and then, in the early 1890s, a college once more. As Daniel Walker Hollis points out in his two-volume history of this institution, the red-hot rhetoric that surrounded the birth pangs of Clemson should not obscure the fact that some departments of the college/university/college actually were doing good work during the 1880s. Nevertheless, failure to develop an agricultural curriculum at a time when a majority of South Carolinians wanted one was a fatal mistake, especially in view of the Populist upheaval led by Ben Tillman and the bequest of Thomas Green Clemson providing land and money for just such a school. The end result was that, for better or worse, in ensuing decades this state would try to support *five* institutions of higher education instead of two, and the annual battle for funds often left scars that blighted growth and development at the proud old campus on Sumter Street.

The one event that each November melded together many of these diverse strands of everyday life—education, innovation, sports, even politics—and encompassed *all* levels of society was the state fair. Country folk came to town on excursion trains by the hundreds, even thousands, often accompanied by a small band of con artists, shysters, and pickpockets. There were shooting matches, sideshows, and horse racing, as well as standard exhibits of livestock, agricultural produce, farm machinery, and household goods. The eighteenth such event, which opened on Tuesday, 9 November 1886, featured a panorama of Gettysburg battlefield (also shown successfully in 1885) and many views of the earthquake that recently had devastated Charleston. There was a special WCTU booth and, as usual, restaurants and bazaars staffed by women representing local churches. Young ladies from Columbia Female College, carefully chaperoned by their president as they toured the grounds, undoubtedly admired prize-winning cakes, pies, jams, and jellies and marveled at needlework and china painting done by their contemporaries. There was, however, not much of a midway, most games of chance having been banned because of unpleasant incidents in 1885.

Following a custom inaugurated several years earlier, the Board of Trade operated an "intelligence office" that catered to the needs of visitors. Hotels were jammed, the Opera House booked shows calculated to please all ages, and gaily decorated commercial houses flaunted "sale" signs that offered enticing bargains. Among them were several "racket" stores (what a century later would be called "outlets") that more established merchants had tried without success to suppress.

This five-day extravaganza concluded with a lavish Saturday night ball given by the prestigious South Carolina Club and presided over by the governor and his wife. This event usually was held in the House of Representatives; but, since the State House was undergoing repairs, the aristocracy of the state gathered in Agricultural Hall, once the notorious Parker's Hall (or "Haul") of Reconstruction days. Music was by the Italian Band of Charlotte; the midnight dinner, a sumptuous spread complete with champagne; and, on Monday, the *News and Courier* regaled readers with columns that described in great detail "the magnificent toilet of the ladies." Miss Harriet English of Columbia, a reporter wrote, wore "a superb dress of old gold plush and exquisite light blue satin front, court train of plush, with revers of blue satin, neck V shaped, short sleeves; ornaments, natural flowers, diamonds, and turquoises." Her escort, as well as all other males who attended, were listed by name under a simple heading: "The Chivalry."

But while diamonds sparkled and elegant young couples danced the night away, Ben Tillman planned; for, he and his farmer friends, over 300 of them from all parts of South Carolina, also gathered in Columbia that week to map strategy for the upcoming meeting of the General Assembly. The truth is, the specter of a troubled rural scene hung heavy over these festivities, and the *News and Courier* conceded that crowds at the fair actually were smaller than in the previous year.

This picture of affluence amid hard times is a hallmark of the 1880s, as is Columbia's rather confused portrait of itself. The city certainly was growing and acquiring new jobs in both the public and private sectors. As Narcisco Gonzales of the *News and Courier* observed in January of 1883, it was experiencing "steady, comfortable progress." At that time, a hosiery mill and shoe factory were operating at the penitentiary, and by the close of the decade a small cotton factory had appeared near Union Depot, as well as a large compress and two cotton seed oil mills. The local trade in cotton more than doubled, up from 24,000 bales in 1882 to over 60,000 in 1888, and spending at various state facilities such as the asylum, penitentiary, and capitol increased somewhat during the same period.[12] Firemen's tournaments, conventions, excursions, and, of course, the fair also aided the economy.

But, caught up in the "New South" rhetoric of Atlanta's Henry Grady and others of that ilk, "steady, comfortable progress" was not what Columbia wanted. Instead, it was searching for something truly smashing, a real show-stopper that would wake up Charleston and make the Piedmont green with envy—a huge mill, a big canal, steamers that would provide direct access to world markets. Somewhat paradoxically, while dreaming industrial dreams, Columbia also yearned to become a quiet winter resort much like little Camden or Aiken. Yet, as this decade came to a close, South Carolina's capitol city had no public library, no hospital worthy of the name, and no first-class hotel.

If Columbia was confused about the future, the same cannot be said of its immediate past, for recent history was being rewritten with deliberate speed. Two examples perhaps will be sufficient to demonstrate what was happening. In 1880, ex-governor Robert K. Scott, then living in Ohio, got into trouble when he shot and killed a youth who, he claimed, was corrupting his son. Several Columbia citizens, including lawyer F. W. McMaster, who once had Scott as a client, wrote expressing sympathy and concern. Four years later, when McMaster launched a bid for a seat in Congress, A. B. Williams of the *Greenville News* unearthed his letter to Scott, updated it to 1884, and accused Democrat McMaster of consorting with Reconstruction Radicals. In reply, McMaster stated with much vehemence that, to the best of this knowledge, save for perhaps a servant, *no Republican ever had entered his house!*[13] However, this disclaimer did not save his candidacy; and, as the *News* had hoped, the nomination went to a Greenville man, not McMaster.

Three decades later, W. W. Ball, then editor of the *State*, dashed off a sketch of this community that appeared in *Columbia, South Carolina: Chronicles and Comments, 1786–1913*. In this Chamber of Commerce publication, he related how, "after the war," the area of the city was diminished by the General Assembly "in order that the danger of negro control in municipal affairs might be lessened." Ball's account, like much of Reconstruction lore, is only partly true. In 1870, Columbia's boundaries were extended 954 feet north of Upper Street (Elmwood) and a similar distance east of Harden. But blacks made no concerted effort to "control" municipal affairs, and eight years later the act permitting the 1870 extension was repealed. Instead, the southern boundary of the city was, for several years, Rice Street (cutting a three-block, east-west slice off Ward I, largely a black area); the northern, a line 417 feet, 4 inches, above Elmwood.

Both McMaster and Ball should have known better than to speak and write as they did, but their words reflect what may have been the most important trend of the 1880s: the increasing rift between the races. In its wake, blacks and anything or anyone associated with the Republican party had to be portrayed in the worst possible light.

Columbia soon got its "big" mill, even though river traffic and winter tourism never lived up to the charming pictures painted by local promoters. In time, an improving economy would ease rural-urban tensions, and some wonders of city living would spread to the countryside. But the racial split that began in this decade and was codified into statute in the 1890s cast a long shadow. Of course, this division of daily life into two streams was not initiated by Columbia and Richland County, or by the state of South Carolina, for that matter. The Jim Crow laws that evolved even can be viewed as part of an overall "standardizing" process, an effort to create uniform conditions throughout a state, a region, and perhaps a nation. Whatever the motivating force, their origin marks a dividing line in local life almost as potent as Fort Sumter and Appomattox.

Notes

1. When the Greenbackers met in Columbia in September of 1884, Narcisco Gonzales of the *News and Courier* termed their conclave "a convention of sneaks" and described the delegates as a band of seedy, slouching men spurting tobacco juice . . . "unshaven, unkempt, without collars, untouched by soap or shame."
2. Three years earlier, in July of 1884, the city council voted to convert east-west streets to "avenues" and change "meaningless" designations such as Greene, Lumber, and Laurel to names of South Carolina counties and towns. However, three months later, by a margin of 7–5, members reversed field and abandoned this scheme. Then, in November of 1892, this same body agreed that Winn Street would become Gregg and Medium, College. They also approved the official designation of Richardson Street as Main, a name long in common use anyway.

3. On 7 January 1883, in a rare outburst, the *Daily Register* called Charleston "the stumbling block of the State." Ever since the projected rail line to Cincinnati foundered, the *Register* said, that city's businessmen had done nothing to promote their community, waiting instead for commerce "to come to them."

4. It might be noted that, in much the same manner, in 1890 an Irmo resident could get to Columbia in seventeen minutes on the Columbia, Newberry, and Laurens line *provided* he could get to the station. Thus, in essence, the railroad solved the problem of long-distance travel, but short-distance travel (getting about a city such as Columbia or to a rural depot) often was impossible during inclement weather.

5. For an in-depth study of this subject, see David Charles McQuillan, "The Street Railway and the Growth of Columbia, South Carolina, 1882–1936" (Master's thesis, University of South Carolina, 1975). An extensive account of streetcar travel entitled "Behind the Mule," which appeared in the *Daily Register* (19 January 1887), is reproduced in this thesis as Appendix I (pp. 62–64).

6. This same structure was the setting for two unique forms of home-grown entertainment, competitive plume and broom drills. The plume drill of 1883 featured six rounds of precision marching on stage by local militia members. When only two performers remained, amid loud applause, a private received a red plume; a non-commissioned officer, a white one. That same year, on 29 January, fourteen young ladies dressed as Zouaves went through the manual of arms with brooms under the direction of Wilie Jones, commander of the Governor's Guards. This performance in behalf of the Baptist Parsonage Fund, watched intently by an audience of 700, was, according to the *News and Courier*, the "talk of Columbia" the next day. In this instance, Miss Kate Calvo was awarded a plume of an unspecified color.

7. Less organized recreational pursuits included nude bathing at the end of Gervais Street and sandlot baseball, both of which raised the ire of some citizens. Out in the northeastern part of the county, the Medlins and Jacobs carried on a lively feud, shooting at each other from time to time because of disagreements over road rights and similar presumed impositions. In February of 1882, four Medlins and several other sand hill residents were involved in a "sensational" free-for-all at McCreery's wagon yard. These country folk, camped for the night, got into a row that involved cards, liquor, clubs, knives, and guns. Several people (including onlookers) were injured before ten policemen finally subdued the participants and put them behind bars.

8. Reynolds Family Papers, South Caroliniana Library.

9. See Nell C. Pogue, *South Carolina Electric & Gas Company, 1846–1964* (Columbia, 1964).

10. This arrangement continued until 1972 when a new state law ended the right of private institutions to nominate public school officials.

11. See John P. Thomas, Jr., *Columbia Graded Schools: First Year, 1883–84* (Columbia, 1883).

12. In the 1880s, the number of asylum patients, some of whom paid at least part of their costs, rose from about 500 to 700. By 1891, doctors also were treating some 400 "out" patients. During this decade, the penitentiary population increased from 590 to 791, although up to 200 convicts usually were contracted out to private industry, railroads, and farmers. A small detail tended the State House grounds, while others were helping build Winthrop and Clemson. The decision to resume work on the capitol augmented the community labor force, as did additional clerks in various departments of state government, notably agriculture, which came into existence in the late 1870s.

Overall, the estimated cost of state government rose from $750,000 in 1879 to $1.1 million a decade later.

13. Ironically, family papers at the South Caroliniana Library reveal that in 1879 another Republican from Reconstruction days (R. B. Carpenter) wrote to McMaster from Leadville, Colorado, recalling "the many instructive and charming hours I have passed under your most hospitable roof in the society of your accomplished wife and daughter and yourself."

The World
of W. B. Nash

CHAPTER THIRTEEN

There he sits. A full-blooded black man, six feet high. He is a good-looking man, with pleasing manners. He was formerly a slave of W. C. Preston, and afterward a bootblack at one of our hotels. He is now a substantial citizen, and a prominent leader in the Senate and in the State. He handles them all. The lawyers and the white chivalry, as they call themselves, have learned to let him alone. They know more law and some things than he does; but he studies them all up, and then comes down on them with a good story or anecdote, and you better believe he carries the audience right along with him. All the laugh and all the ridicule is on his side. And when he undertakes a thing, he generally puts it through, I tell you. No, sir, there is now nobody who cares to attack Beverly Nash. They let him alone right smart.

This is how an unidentified black man described Nash as he and James S. Pike, a *New York Tribune* correspondent, watched South Carolina's lawmakers at work early in 1873. Nash was, Pike assured readers of his *Prostrate State* (published the following year), the leading figure in the local Republican party . . . "consulted more and appealed to more" in the upper house of the General Assembly than anyone else. "It is admitted by his white opposition colleagues that he has more native ability than half of the white men in the Senate."

This was, of course, the same individual that Wade Hampton had recognized as a "power" in March of 1867. Others have treated this ex-slave turned politician, land owner, and brickyard operator less kindly, accusing him of inconsistent policies, gross inefficiency, mismanagement of public funds, and billing the state for enough bricks "to build a Chinese wall around the whole of Columbia." The *Charleston Mercury* (14 February 1868) characterized Nash as "a genuine negro" who had sought notoriety in the political arena and was, in the opinion of that daily, "an unscrupulous, ambitious, [one-] fourth educated demagogue." True, this man's political career ended on a sour note in the fall of 1877, but the appraisals of Pike and Hampton seem more valid than the rantings of his detractors.

Nash, born in Virginia about 1822, was brought to South Carolina by the Preston family at the age of thirteen. In 1847, he married slave Dorcas Mitchell, by whom he had at least eight children, and at some point began working at a local hotel.[1] This job—variously described as porter, bootblack, and waiter—was the key to Nash's postwar career, for close association with legislators, travelers, and the public at large stimulated and developed his agile mind. In this atmosphere, he learned to read and write, although he conceded to a *New York Times* reporter in July of 1867 that he knew little grammar. At the time of that interview, Nash was operating a small stand near the city market on Assembly Street where he sold watermelons and ginger pop. However, even at this juncture his interest in politics was well developed and increasing.

Two years earlier, in September of 1865, W. B. Nash had organized Columbia's original Loyal (or Union) League, an innovative step that led to a seat in the first black convention ever held in this state. That body, which met in Charleston's Zion Church two months later, came together in reaction to the famous "Black Codes" promulgated by an all-white constitutional convention. In the months that followed, Nash's reputation continued to grow and soon he was being consulted by military authorities and sought out by northern journalists. The *New York Times* reporter, by the way, interviewed only two Columbia residents in the summer of 1867: Nash and the Governor James L. Orr.[2]

In response to this newsman's queries, Nash said he did not like military rule, but thought overall it had "a wholesome effect." White southerners, he noted, were "not conquered—not changed." Without the U.S. Army at hand, black rights would have been "a dead letter." Nash saw little hope for a moderate Republican party, scoffed at the idea of blacks holding key offices such as governor and mayor, and stoutly insisted that the black man was a good judge of character. He will know more of you in three days than you of him in three months, he told this reporter. "It has been his business all his life to find out the ways of the white man—to watch him, [discern] what he means." The state tax system, in Nash's view, was ridiculous. Instead of an annual sixty-cent levy on 100 acres of land, he advocated a much heavier tax that would force owners of large woodland tracts to sell their property, thus creating small farms.

As for tales that blacks stole and frequently were idle, Nash conceded they were true. Slaves had not thought taking their masters' goods was stealing and freedmen driven from plantations in 1865 and 1866, he countered, *had* to steal in order to live; but, in his opinion, black work habits were improving. They would improve still faster, he added, as wages replaced contracts. Personally, Nash favored "half" wages at the close of each month and the balance at year's end, a system he thought would teach freedmen to economize. When this reporter asked why he had not fled north before 1865, this emerging black leader replied that he couldn't. His mother was an invalid, and for seventeen years "I had to tote her in my arms, like a child." Nash said nothing about his wife and their growing brood as reasons for remaining in South Carolina.

Although William Beverly Nash does not appear to have played a key role in any of the public meetings he attended in the 1860s (the Charleston meeting of 1865, a national freedmen's conference held in Washington early in 1867, the constitutional convention of 1868, and subsequent sessions of the General Assembly), he did enunciate clear and *consistent* stands on vital issues. These include a plea for uniform taxation and the breakup of large property holdings by such means, opposition to federal confiscation of land and disfranchisement of prominent whites, and support for integrated public education at *all* levels.[3] In part, these views reflect personal experience. Certainly not one to advocate racial equality, Nash nonetheless knew how much he had learned through direct association with white people. And, unlike some of his contemporaries, he realized that the call of the black convention of 1865 for "even-handed justice" made little sense so long as many ex-rebels could not vote.

Shortly after the *New York Times* interview was published, General Sickles appointed Nash to his first official post, that of a Richland County magistrate. Then, in short order he was a delegate to the constitutional convention of 1868, also serving as vice-president of that body, and in the spring of the same year easily won a seat in the state Senate, a position he would hold until October of 1877. As he took the oath of office, Nash was one of ten black senators out of a total of thirty-one, while the House had a black majority, seventy-six to forty-eight. These ratios would not change much during the next eight years, although the ranks of white Republicans dwindled somewhat as those of black senators and Democratic representatives increased.[4]

Thus for a decade, ex-slave William Beverly Nash was the voice of Columbia and Richland County in the upper house of the General Assembly. According to Senate *Journals*, he offered only two bills during

the 1868–1869 session but in subsequent years, gaining confidence, became much more active, usually presenting fifteen to twenty measures
for consideration. These include a proposal to purchase land on Main
Street for a new post office and federal courthouse (now Columbia's city
hall),[5] incorporation of various business ventures in which he had a personal interest, creation of the Vigilant Fire Engine Company, and autho-
rization for a ferry across the Wateree, a bridge spanning the Broad River
(both in the Richland County area), and a street railway system for South
Carolina's capital city. Despite this diversity, his work as a legislator was
dominated by two major concerns: revision of existing statutes so as to
make more secure the rights of freedmen and the fostering of education
among young people, white and black. In March of 1876, for example, he
secured passage of a bill calculated to force all minors in Charleston and
Columbia to attend school. Any who failed to do so (or their parents)
might face a ten-dollar fine and/or fifteen days in jail. Nash also took special interest in plans to enlarge the Columbia Canal and quickly concluded that Sprague and his associates could not be trusted.

Throughout these years, leading figures in Columbia's white community found Senator Nash to be the sort of Republican with whom they
could do business, even as partners. He was articulate, relatively conservative where economic matters were concerned, sensible by nature, had
money to invest, could quote Shakespeare and tell a good yarn, and—
above all else—had political clout. At times, he joined Democratic stalwarts such as Hugh S. Thompson (governor, 1882–1886), John T. Sloan,
Jr. (lieutenant governor, 1902–1906), broker W. G. Childs, and insurance-
real estate man Edwin W. Seibels in ventures designed to promote manufacturing, street railways, and savings and loan associations. On his own,
in 1873 Nash established a brick yard with two black friends, Joseph Taylor and Henry Green. This facility, located at Laurel and Assembly
streets, was close by Nash's home at 23 West Laurel. He also dealt successfully in real estate and between 1868 and 1884 held title to 50 acres of
land in and around Columbia, property often purchased at sheriff's sales.
At the time of his death in 1888, Nash still owned five town lots and 26
acres on Wheeler Hill where he raised cotton and garden produce.

Two interesting twists in this man's unusual career include an outburst against mulattoes in January of 1873 and, in the following year, conservative endorsement of his slate of candidates for General Assembly
seats, among them, that of W. B. Nash. In the heat of a political clash, the
senator vowed that his ancestors had "trod the burning sands of Africa."
But why, he asked, should "mongrels" who were virtually white ally

themselves with blacks and prate of "our race"? Both incidents reveal splits within seemingly monolithic groups, for the truth is neither blacks nor conservative whites spoke with one voice during Reconstruction. Moreover, the decision of many of the latter to abjure politics paved the way for much of the success that freedmen enjoyed.

But there were those who chafed mightily under these conditions, notably ex-masters from rural areas such as Edgefield County. Each fall when they came to Columbia to attend the state fair—fast becoming an annual ritual of considerable socio-political significance—disgruntled Democrats saw enough evidence of urban decadence (i.e., racial mixing) to justify their worst fears. In November of 1873, William T. Gary, younger brother of Martin W. Gary, first president of the prestigious South Carolina Club, and later a judge in Georgia, led Edgefield's Palmetto Sabre Club through drill formations before a packed grandstand at the fair grounds. That group, he assured enthusiastic onlookers, was *not* political and had been organized solely for "the good of our people." Gary then delivered this "non-political" salvo: "Virtue, honor, and wisdom cannot be ruled by corruption, vice, and ignorance. We are not of those who despair. There is a just God, who presides over our destinies. Let us be mindful of our duties to our State. Let us organize with determined hearts to preserve our customs and civilization. Let us prove ourselves worthy sons of noble sires. Then, in the language of the motto inscribed on our flag, 'Resurgamus,' 'we will rise again.' "[6]

As these ringing phrases indicate, what really rankled was being out of power and the alleged "corruption, vice and ignorance" of those in power. As for white-black relations, Joel Williamson makes clear in his excellent study, *After Slavery: The Negro in South Carolina During Reconstruction, 1861–1877*, that the trend of those years actually was toward separation, not integration; and, at times, he cautions, blacks themselves encouraged such moves. By the close of the period, blacks had a legal right to use all facilities and accommodations open to the general public, but they rarely did so. As a rule, freedmen and their families bought cheaper, second-class tickets when traveling by train, sat in separate sections in theaters, stayed in black rooming houses, not hotels, and worshipped in their own churches. Convicts and asylum inmates were quietly separated by race, and—law notwithstanding—much the same thing happened in South Carolina's schools and colleges. When protest followed an all-white ball given by Governor Scott in January of 1869, he answered critics by holding an open house each Thursday evening, receptions attended only by black politicians.

The arenas in which the races mixed most freely were the State House and the market place, that is, elected officials dealt with each other in order to govern and men such as Nash and Seibels met to discuss common business interests. And there are occasional hints that some professions tried to ignore traditional racial barriers during Reconstruction. The *South Carolinian* (18 January 1873) announced that "A meeting of Tailors of the city, *white* and colored, is called at the shop of W. N. Roach, on Wednesday evening, at 7 o'clock." In addition, because Columbia was the state capital, a handful of blacks undoubtedly had more access to public facilities than anywhere else in South Carolina. But it is only when they flaunted their power that any outcry occurred. In December of 1868, Charles Minort and his wife nearly provoked a riot by taking front-row seats in a local theater,[7] and eight years later lawyer T. McCants Stewart was ejected from an Edwin Booth production of *Hamlet* because of a similar indiscretion. Perhaps the most interesting incident occurred in October of 1873 when the state's adjutant general and the senator from Georgetown ate and drank at the Exchange House but were denied use of the billiard hall, which, they were told, was a private club.

There was one other place where the races rubbed shoulders ever so briefly: the classroom. In an age when a term or a group of classes rarely lasted more than eight or ten weeks and each such session was considered to be a "school," the extent of black-white mixing is unclear. However, records submitted to the state superintendent of education for at least one period (1869–1870) reveal that about one-fifth of the "schools" in Columbia and Richland County had both black and white pupils. Among these were a large, three-teacher structure in Gadsden owned by blacks and a city school on Arsenal Hill, as well as classes at Spring Bluff, Jackson's Creek, and Bee Branch. These reports, now in the State Archives, fail to indicate how long this pattern of informal integration continued. Blacks attending Howard School at Lincoln and Plain streets, for many years the only public classrooms for their race within Columbia's city limits,[8] and whites enrolled at nearby private academies probably got reasonably sound training, and it is no surprise that these institutions became the nucleus of a municipal school system in 1883.

Until that time, education in both city and county was something of a makeshift affair with state, local, and private sources funding day-to-day operations. By 1875, the state superintendent had an annual budget of $426,462.99, yet he estimated that twice that amount would be needed to hold nine-month sessions throughout South Carolina. In 1874–1875, Columbia and Richland County spent $16,886.70 to educate 545 white and

1,683 black pupils in forty-three "schools." Slightly less than half of this sum came from state appropriations, the rest from poll taxes and local levies. But the community then had a school-age population of 1,637 white and 4,913 black youngsters, indicating that hundreds, even thousands, were growing up largely illiterate. Nevertheless, one must add a cautionary note. Free public education was a new idea, especially for blacks. It might even be termed "revolutionary"; and, in addition, officials at all levels were trying to build an educational network from the ground up in a time of discord, distrust, and deficits.

To some degree, any discussion of public education in the 1870s is misleading because private classes, sometimes with the support of public funds, continued to play a prominent role in urban life. A writer for *Scribner's Monthly* (June 1874) observed that "numerous private institutions of learning give the casual visitor [to Columbia] the impression that he is visiting a 'grove of Academe' rather than a perturbed and harassed capital." Although several of these schools, notably Howard, exhibited a mix of private and public support, there were at least six essentially private operations. These include the lower grades of Benedict Institute (founded for blacks in 1870), Mrs. Wigg's black classes, and a handful of white schools, some of which enjoyed the backing of the Peabody Fund.

Although there is no evidence of integration in local schools after the early 1870s, this was not the case at the University of South Carolina. In fact, the story of racial mixing on the campus of this state's premier institution of higher learning is well documented. In December of 1865, the old college became a university, and officials announced plans for more practical learning to be taught in eight schools. However, the U.S. Army continued to occupy several buildings, enrollment remained low (fifty or sixty students), and Reconstruction politics fostered an atmosphere of uncertainty and instability. Following approval of a new constitution stipulating that any center of learning receiving public funds must be open to all, regardless of race or color, Governor Orr suggested that the University of South Carolina enroll only whites and the Citadel (then closed) be opened to blacks.

Nothing came of this proposal, and until 1873 the Republican-dominated General Assembly did not interfere with life at the university and even gave it rather generous financial support. Then, in 1872 lawmakers decided to use Morrill land-grant money to create an agricultural and mechanical institute in connection with Claflin University, a new Methodist school for blacks being built in Orangeburg. In theory, this should have answered black demands for college-university training, but the Morrill dollars were squandered elsewhere. As a result, no state-sponsored school materialized until several years later, an institution that eventually became South Carolina State College.

At this juncture, those interested in aiding the struggling public school system decided to open a teacher-training facility at the university. That classrooms and dormitories stood empty and unused no one could deny. Nevertheless, those concerned with the university's welfare contended that a normal school for both sexes would have a degrading and demoralizing effect, but "the chapel and wings" (Rutledge) soon were selected as an appropriate site. Meanwhile, it became apparent that new trustees planned even more sweeping reforms, specifically the reshaping of the curriculum to meet the special requirements of blacks. Among these innovations would be a much-needed preparatory school. Despite the resignation of professors and departure of most white students, this program was put into operation, along with the opening of the normal school. The first black admitted to the university was Secretary of State Henry E. Hayne, a "nearly white" ex-senator from Marion County, who enrolled as a medical student early in October of 1873. Hayne was followed by others; and, as white undergraduates fled, the Radicals had to offer lucrative scholarships in an effort both to maintain a student body and save face.

By 1876, according to Daniel Walker Hollis, the university community was predominately black. At that time, twenty-seven males and fifty-one females (most of them about eighteen years of age and all of them presumably black) were enrolled in the normal school. That facility, operating independent of the university but with occasional lectures by newly recruited professors, granted certificates, not diplomas. As for the university students, Hollis writes that they were much like any others, with both "good and bad elements among them." Some, such as Joseph W. Morris (later president of Allen University) and William M. Dart (long associated with Columbia's public school system) went on to distinguished careers. An unexpected by-product of these years was this state's first intercollegiate athletic encounter. In August of 1875, black baseball teams representing USC and the Orangeburg school met on the local garrison diamond with the Columbia nine emerging victorious, 41–10.

The contested election of 1876 wrote a quick end to this experiment in bi-racial education. By cutting off funds, the Hampton government closed the Radical university, putting the proud old school in a state of limbo until the fall of 1880. Had the state provided a functioning black college as promised, it is quite possible that this episode, which left the

University of South Carolina weak and demoralized at a critical juncture, might never have occurred.[9]

Of course, not every development on the local scene related directly to race and politics. There were interesting new social organizations, prominent visitors, Confederate reunions, and the advent of labor-saving devices such as cook stoves and sewing machines. (For still more evidence of change, see "Minor Milestones," p. 262.) Grace Elmore, the Columbia lady who shielded her face from Yankee eyes with a parasol in May of 1865, tells in her diary of informing ex-slaves that she could not pay them and they were free to leave if they wished to do so. All of them promised to remain for a time, she says, but then simply disappeared.[10] On 25 June, she wrote, "I don't like to live among pots and kettles." This sentiment apparently was widespread, for one of the northern products soon in great demand was a heavy, cast-iron cook stove that replaced the open hearth and hanging pots long used by slaves. Stoves were followed by sewing machines, so many that by 1871 Columbia matrons could choose among makes costing as little as five dollars and a year later the "Sewing Machine Department" was the state fair's most popular attraction.

One of the most provocative social groups of the 1870s was the Grange. Largely a rural phenomenon and the first of several nationwide efforts to aid farmers and their families, by January of 1873 there were Granges in at least six local communities: Columbia, Cedar Creek, Jackson's Creek, Killian's, Grovewood, and "Upper Richland." Their avowed goals were an agricultural college, farmers' banks, a mutual insurance company, more favorable freight rates, and a state agricultural "bureau." Although the Grange soon declined in numbers and importance, members got their state department of agriculture in 1879, probably were instrumental in founding what is now Clemson University, and certainly paved the way for the more radical Alliance of the 1880s, Populism, and Ben Tillman.

In the winter of 1878, at a time when the University of South Carolina was locked shut and its future being debated, Thomas Green Clemson appealed to the *Daily Register* (1 February) for the creation near Columbia, with the aid of convict labor, of "a charitable institution" designed to encourage agricultural pursuits. What Calhoun's son-in-law envisioned—not quite a college, really—was an establishment of "practical benefit" to the state filled with trees, plants, nurseries, animals, birds, and so on, many of which would be for sale or exchange. However, no one paid heed, and not even an honorary degree awarded to Clemson by the university in May of 1886 deterred him from his dream of assisting South Carolina's hard-pressed farmers.

Although Richland County was host to numerous visitors during Reconstruction, none received a more heart-felt welcome than Robert E. Lee, frail of health, who stopped here en route to Florida late in March of 1870. Stores were closed for the occasion and, despite rain, hundreds flocked to the Charlotte depot where a grizzled veteran, tears in his eyes, yelled, "General, we were overpowered, not whipped!" Whereupon the throng took up the cry—"overpowered, not whipped!" Slightly over a year later, Jeff Davis received a more subdued reception. While in Columbia, the former president attended a concert and was serenaded by a band, but there were none of the tears and cheers that greeted Lee.[11]

Among those who may have seen Davis was a fourteen-year-old youth whose family had moved to Columbia from Augusta in the fall of 1870 when his father joined the faculty of the theological seminary. This young man, Thomas Woodrow Wilson, the twenty-eighth president of the United States, lived here for about three years—first at Pickens and Blanding streets and then at the corner of Plain and Henderson. During these months, Wilson attended private classes conducted by Charles H. Barnwell until he left in the fall of 1873 to begin his freshman year at Davidson College.

The following year, the family moved to Wilmington, North Carolina, where the Reverend Wilson became pastor of a wealthy Presbyterian church and young Thomas, unwilling to return to Davidson, prepared himself for classes at Princeton. Although Woodrow Wilson's Columbia sojourn was brief, it was here that he was admitted to church membership, developed a love of books, and spent, according to his own account, some of his happiest boyhood days. It is also quite possible that these months and years shaped racial attitudes he would espouse as this nation's chief executive.

In May of 1879, five years after the Wilsons moved to North Carolina, Columbia was host to thousands for the unveiling of the Confederate monument that stands on the State House grounds. For a decade, a ladies' group had been working and planning for this event. In 1871, they bought a site on Arsenal Hill overlooking Sidney Park and contracted with a Louisville firm staffed *only* by rebel veterans to construct the monument at a cost of $12,000. The foundation was to be made of Congaree granite, the marble portion imported from Carrara, Italy; and, surmounting it all, there would be a grand, seven-foot, three-inch figure of a Confederate soldier. Then it was discovered that a "substratum of quicksand below the soil" of Arsenal Hill rendered the proposed site unsuitable. For a time, the ladies considered erecting their monument in Elmwood Cemetery; but, still short of funds, they put it in storage instead. In 1878, a

Minor Milestones

1867

March Columbia greets Manhattan firemen who had planned to present a new hose to local fire fighters—"the hose of union upon the reel of friendship." However, that gift was lost at sea and had to be replaced several months later.

1868

Jan Burns Club holds 27th annual banquet at McKenzie's Saloon.
May Richland Fork Immigration Society formed to attract white settlers.
Dec General Assembly moves to university following disastrous fire at Gibbes Hall (Main and Taylor streets) in which two men were killed and three others seriously injured.

1869

May Confectioner John Heise installs soda fountain made of polished Tennessee marble.
Dec YMCA re-organized.

1870

Jan City warns forty tavern owners to renew licenses.
Sept John C. Seegers opens German-made, ice-making factory near Asylum, one of first in the nation. Using concentrated ammonia and various gases, this plant could turn out over 2,500 pounds of ice in five hours.

1871

March City council votes to rename streets in District of Columbia fashion (numbered avenues north and south and alphabetically designated streets east and west), but then abandons the idea.
Dec Theodore Pollock, Wheeler House proprietor, serves "something new" . . . much better than soda water, says the *Daily Phoenix* . . . ginger ale!

1872

March Gadsden blacks, led by Aesop Goodson, incorporate their American Union Literary Club.
Nov Woman's Suffrage Association meets at home of famed Rollin sisters to select delegates to national convention. These light-skinned ladies—Catherine de Medici, Charlotte Corday, and Louisa Muhlbach—conducted one of this community's most fashionable Republican salons during Reconstruction.
Dec New toll bridge—1,340 feet long and five feet higher than one burned in 1865—opens over Congaree at Gervais Street.

1873

March Senator T. J. Robertson presents city with English sparrows that are released in Sidney Park to attack insects, and B'nai B'rith holds second annual Purim Ball.
April *New York World* reporter says Columbia shows "more signs of life and progress" than any other southern community he has visited . . . "an

attractive resort" where northerners will be well received if they "behave themselves."

June Local ladies buy striped stockings in preparation for croquet season.

Oct Twelve members of Colored Bricklayers and Plasterers Union parade down Main Street.

1876

Jan Charleston lady opens dancing school at Richland Rifle Club—"the Glide Waltz a specialty."

Feb Army post band plays "Dixie" and "Yankee Doodle" at Richland Rifle Club Fair.

1878

March General Assembly ends public executions.

1879

Jan *Daily Register* issues plea for street railway. Columbia has, it says, two two-horse omnibuses, nine two-horse carriages, thirty-one single-horse hacks, an equal number of one-horse private wagons, and about thirty extra hacks during Fair Week—but NO street railway such as just began operating in Greenville!

March John C. Seegers announces he is bottling beer for family use, seventy-five cents per dozen bottles. Kegs also available.

1880

Oct Opera House begins six nights of lantern slides: "Tremaine's Grand Tour from New York to Jerusalem."

1882

April Five people killed and five more seriously wounded when steamer *Marion* explodes on Wateree.

1883

March Ellen Vogel, "noted courtesan," dies. This Louisiana native, also described as "a colored demi-monde," owned two houses on (east) Senate Street and much jewelry. Most of her $10,000 estate, according to the *Register*, went to "a prominent aged citizen," who turned out to be a former mayor.

1884

Feb Two Columbia citizens, one black, one white, fined ten dollars for not paying poll taxes.

1885

April Yeng Lee opens Chinese laundry. Seven years later, "Sam" Lee reportedly returned to China with $8,000 bank draft and much cash.

July Opera House engages thirty-one theatrical companies for coming season, and Columbia Lawn Tennis Club organized.

1889

April Construction of Columbia's first mill village, cottages for twenty-four families, begins near Congaree Cotton Mill.

more sympathetic General Assembly appropriated the amount needed to complete the work ($650) and also provided a new site. None of their contributions, the ladies boasted on the eve of the festivities, was tainted by intoxicating liquors.

From all accounts, the affair was a magnificent spectacle, certainly the most impressive seen in the Midlands since Wade Hampton became this state's chief executive in 1877. A Baltimore lady wrote a special poem for the occasion, two lines of which were:

Long may it stand, resist the storm, and proudly lift its head
In honor of their chivalry, our brave Confederate dead.

Ten thousand cheered the speakers—Governor William D. Simpson, John S. Preston, and others—who stood beneath a defiant banner bearing these words: "If I die now, I give my life cheerfully for the independence of South Carolina." And a few days later, Mrs. Fitz William McMaster penned these words to one of her seven sons.

I have not written to you for more than a week. We have been so crowded with company during the unveiling of the Monument and I have had so much to do entertaining that I have not had time to write. I wished so much that you could have been here to see the grand sight—The Military display was grander than ever seen before in Columbia, there were over *100* men under arms from Charleston alone. The street was just *ablaze* from Post Office to State house with brass buttons and muskets and epulettes [sic], and excursions being run from all parts of the state, hundreds of people came for the day and returned at night to their homes—I wish[e]d you could have been here, and enjoyed the sight—in its grandure clad with all the *glory* that attends the pomp and display of war!! *without* any of the memories, that *flocked* back, and made the hearts of those that were *active participants* of the *scene* commemorated, *sad*, and sorrowful— at times that day I found my self *in tears*, as the old days came back. . . .

But to return to the world of William Beverly Nash. As the political pot began to boil early in October of 1876, James Davis, a black Independent Republican from Hopkins who had served in the lower house of the General Assembly (1870–1872), rose at a meeting of the Richland Democratic Club to challenge what members were doing. He had not planned to speak, he said, and had come prepared to vote for their slate of candidates if it were "properly" drawn up.

. . . but as you have seen fit to frame a ticket discarding my race I must stand aloof. At the very first meeting held after the war to bring about good government I was in attendance. I as one am ready to concede that when we asked for unqualified suffrage it was a matter you could not readily grant. I have come to the conclusion that you have made up your minds that this is a white man's land and must forever remain so. If you come to my people and say to them we will give you what belongs to you[,] we will grasp your hand and help you drive out the carpetbagger. Colored men that are South Carolinians love South Carolina as well as you do. If this government is to continue the same as it has been in the past[,] I feel it that we will suffer. You have made money and have lands and if Hampton is elected can readily obtain any amount from the North, but what have we? Whilst I know that if the men you have nominated have their way, none of our rights would be endangered, yet what guarantee have I that their opinion will be regarded? You are fighting for the reins of government whilst my race is fighting to retain our liberties. I will agree with you that I and many like myself are not competent to run this government, but you must not draw a line and exclude all of my race. Give us representation and we will go together and reform the State together and we can then have good government. You may sift all that have come over to you and you will find that you will have to bull pen them to obtain their votes. I want good government: give us a fair showing and we are with you for reform and Victory![12]

This eloquence had no effect. Davis was answered by a Sumter black named Robinson who had toured the state with Wade Hampton, a man, he vowed, who could not tell a lie and would keep every promise made to blacks. A month later, the *Daily Register* (6 November), which fast was replacing the financially strapped *Phoenix* as Columbia's most popular newspaper, urged blacks to "get on the right side" and vote Democratic.[13] "If you want to educate your children," it warned, "vote for men who will honestly use the money raised for that purpose and not steal it . . . vote for your employers' prosperity, and thus secure your own . . . unite with us, and by your votes break down the color line." But, as we know, few black voters in this community were swayed by these words.

Early in the new year, as the Hayes-Tilden dispute mounted in intensity, Nash, a Republican elector, told a congressional committee that bank president L. D. Childs had offered him money to switch sides. The *Daily Register* ridiculed this charge, countering that the senator once had tried to bill the state twice for the same order of bricks. Soon, Charleston papers were publishing unsubstantiated reports of still more Republican chicanery, claiming that Nash and his cronies had used state funds to buy champagne by the case, gallons of whiskey, and boxes of cigars. "Brick" Nash (the *Register's* new name for the senator) quickly denied these allegations. Many people, he conceded, wanted him out of office; and, if he yielded to such assaults, he knew "Arsenal Hill would resound with peals of artillery."

Throughout the next few months, especially after Hampton gained firm control of state bureaucracy, these thrusts continued. Eventually, in October the Democrats at last struck pay dirt. Five years earlier, Nash had opposed a Radical Republican scheme to sell the state's interest in the Blue Ridge Railroad at a bargain price. At one point, he even turned down an offer of $25,000 to back a plan hatched largely by New York bankers; but, after it won legislative approval, he, like several others, accepted $5,000 in scrip. Why? Nash's weak reply, made under oath, was that he took the money because "I thought I might as well have it and invest it here as for them to carry it off out of the state."

Within a day or so of this confession, W. B. Nash resigned from the Senate, paid back the money, and never again had anything to do with politics. The *Register* (13 October 1877), delirious with joy, hailed the fall of this "ex-bootblack" who had "wielded a power as offensive to the decent citizens of Richland as his acts of legislation have been obnoxious to the civilized world." "This old negro man, who has had the audacity to walk the streets of Columbia as the representative of the people of Richland," the editor boasted, "has at last reached the end of his rope, and is now to be consigned to the oblivion which his misdeeds entitle him to. Nash was and is a fair specimen of the dregs which our revolution has brought to the surface."

During the next decade, Nash raised cotton and other crops on Wheeler Hill and collected rents from property he owned. In mid-January of 1888, on the day that Columbia voted to guarantee its canal bonds, Nash, still vitally interested in this seemingly endless project, went to the polls to lend his support. Soon after returning home he became ill and died a short time later.[14]

Although this man's sudden departure from the political arena fits the standard textbook tale, not all of the loose ends of Reconstruction were wrapped up quite so neatly. To begin with, there was the corruption issue, which presumably was at the heart of the Red Shirt campaign of 1876. Yet reform was nothing new and had been under way for some time at the insistence of many Republicans, notably Governor Chamberlain himself. As Joel Williamson has observed, once in power, Hampton and the Redeemers convicted *all* Republicans by innuendo and press reports of lavish spending but shied away from jury trials. Then, in the spring of 1879 the two parties concluded an out-of-court settlement of their differences: Democrats ceased criminal proceedings against Republicans in return for the latter dropping charges of alleged irregularities during the 1876 election.

No such "deal" is evident at the local level, although cries of Republican corruption were equally loud. Taking a cue from state officials, a commission was formed in 1877 to investigate Richland County affairs. As expected, the commissioners dutifully uncovered inept and corrupt practices and a debt of $31,507.09. However, according to press reports, that figure included accrued penalties, and the actual debt was a mere $4,437.04½. [15]

The situation in Columbia was more serious. Largely as the result of bonds issued in 1872 to pay for construction of a new city hall and opera house, the municipality was about $900,000 in the red. Appeals to the courts to invalidate these bonds, which critics claimed were sold illegally, and efforts to convince those holding them to accept a new, cheaper issue produced no results. In this instance, corruption charges became petty in the extreme when W. B. Lowrance alleged in December of 1878 that Mayor John Agnew, a Republican, had billed the city too much for six shovels that apparently cost eight dollars and ten cents. Lowrance boasted that he could have supplied the same implements for less. During succeeding months, the city debt continued to be a hot issue, often the subject of editorial comment and clearly one aspect of a relentless campaign to discredit Republicans. After 1880, having served its purpose, it faded from view.

The reason why alleged corruption at both state and local levels was largely swept under the rug and forgotten is obvious. Any close inquiry might have revealed conservative ties to some of the "horrors" of Reconstruction. Staunch Democrats, men one might classify as "closet" or "economic" scalawags, often advertised their products and services in the Republican press and joined Radicals in promoting numerous commercial enterprises. If in the legislature, they probably were tainted by some of the deals consummated there; and, as ordinary citizens, they may well have invested in the bonds used to build Columbia's controversial municipal building.

Charges of corruption could take still other forms, and those concerned with the moral health of the Midlands were quick to blame Republicans for perceived ills. In March of 1879, a Richland grand jury pointed an accusing finger at "a growing evil"—the expansion of Columbia's red light district toward the heart of the city. Jurors acknowledged that houses of ill fame always would exist, but those operating them, they said, should remain in the area "conceded" to them in the past, the neighborhood of Lady, Gates, Gervais, and Senate streets *west* of Richardson (Main). Municipal officials claimed they lacked the power to act, but jurors maintained that, if they could allow "a powder mill" to be built in the center of town, then they certainly could remove a "fornicarium." Jurors also complained of "idle people" on the streets and too many gambling saloons, which were, in their opinion, "the first step to ruin."

Four years later, after much debate, the city council passed an "ill fame" ordinance prohibiting females of "notoriously bad character" from riding horseback or walking the streets "dressed in a manner to offend modesty." However, efforts of temperance advocates to exploit the corruption issue fell flat. In December of 1884, when they finally got a referendum on liquor licenses in Columbia, wets breezed to victory, 940–170.

Other societal effects of emancipation and Reconstruction are so complex as to defy easy analysis. The same blacks who thought they might be massacred if they took part in a state fair parade in November of 1880 did so by the hundreds twelve months later. Whites often attended black concerts held in Columbia in the early 1880s; and, with the election of Democrat Grover Cleveland, the *Daily Register* (11 November 1884) predicted that a new spirit would sweep through the land.

> We expect to see race issues greatly relieved and the colored labor go to work with a will and purpose it has not done since 'freedom tuck in.'
> We confidently expect to see all race animosities fading away and each race meeting its own field of effort with an accord and mutual good will, which will be far better off for both races, as it cannot but fail to conduce to a greater production of the South.

But that was not to be. Six months later, an Episcopal conclave at Columbia's Trinity Church was split asunder when two black clerics took communion. "Many lay members subsequently showed a good deal of feeling about this," said the *Register*. Ironically, both men had impressive academic credentials, but education, of course, was not the issue. H. C. Bishop of Charleston was a graduate of New York's General Theological Seminary, and T. G. Harper of St. Luke's Church here in Columbia—a former British naval cadet—was an alumnus of London University and had studied at Leipzig. Then, in July of that same year (1885), Alderman Tilman Watson scandalized the community when he tried to publicly horsewhip George Shrewsberry (black) because of his attentions to a mulatto girl, Mamie Wiley. The mayor said the matter was "too disgusting" to talk about, although according to local newspapers most of the town did. Within a week, Watson resigned from the city council and withdrew from politics.

True, there was a new spirit abroad throughout the Midlands in the late 1880s, but it was far different from what the *Register* had predicted. In June of 1889, blacks met at the county courthouse to form their own state Alliance, a session followed in September by a conference of fifteen sub-Alliances representing communities such as Gadsden, Mill Creek, and Congaree. A few weeks later, executives of the Richmond & Danville Railroad announced plans to "experiment" with segregated cars on excursion trains to the state fair in Columbia. Blacks countered by organizing their own fair, the first of which was held early in 1890.

During these same weeks, Chapter CIX of this state's *General Statutes,* "Of Offenses Against Civil Rights," was repealed, although those favoring such action faced an uphill battle in the all-white Senate. This legislation was in response to an appeal by Governor J. P. Richardson, who, citing the recent "experiment," suggested that all common carriers should be relieved of restrictions found in Chapter CIX. Also, at Richardson's urging, a separate coach bill was introduced, but got bogged down in committee and was not enacted during the 1889–1890 session.[16]

Twelve months later, when a similar measure was being debated, Columbia blacks held an "indignation" meeting at a local church and elected a committee to confer with Richardson's successor, Benjamin Ryan Tillman. When the group appeared, Tillman's reception was indeed cool: "How long will you detain me?" However, according to the *News and Courier,* the one-eyed politico from Edgefield County then discussed their concerns for a brief time.

Two decades earlier, in March of 1867, William Beverly Nash sat in the gallery of the House of Representatives in Washington and watched intently as members passed the first Reconstruction Act over the veto of President Andrew Johnson. "I felt," he told a Columbia audience a short time later, "that the clock of civilization had been put forward a hundred years." We can only conjecture as to what he might have said had he been in the galleries of South Carolina's State House in December 1890 or among those meeting with Ben Tillman.

Notes

1. Census records indicate there may have been four more children. The best summaries of Nash's life are found in Bailey, Morgan, and Taylor, *Biographical Directory of the South Carolina Senate, 1776–1985* (3 vols.; Columbia, 1986), II, pp. 1,191–94, and Lawrence C. Bryant (ed.), *Negro Senators and Representatives in the South Carolina Legislature, 1868–1902* (Orangeburg, 1968), pp. 103–12.
2. For the full text of "Libra's" report, see the *New York Times* (9 August 1867). Interestingly, this gentleman devoted almost two columns to Nash and only one and one-third to Orr.
3. At the constitutional convention of 1868, for example, Nash spoke only ten times. His most impassioned speech was an unsuccessful attempt to prevent Governor Orr from addressing that body. He claimed that Orr had tried to make him a "fence-sitter" and, if allowed to speak, would only confuse those who heard him. Orr, he said, "tumbles so fast that it makes a man's head 'dizzy' to look at him." Nash much preferred ex-governor Perry, who everyone realized would "'cuse and abuse us," but one knew where he stood.
4. These men have been much maligned (often deservedly so), and it is generally conceded that some blacks in the lower house were incompetent and perhaps illiterate as well, but recent scholarship is beginning to shed new light upon their activities. See Thomas Holt, *Black Over White: Negro Political Leadership in South Carolina During Reconstruction* (Urbana, 1977) and Michael Edwin Thompson, "Blacks, Carpetbaggers, and Scalawags: A Study of the Membership of the South Carolina Legislature, 1868–1870" (Ph.D. diss, Washington State University, 1975).
5. See Florence Bacher Myers, "Columbia Court House and Post Office: the Building and its Architect, 1870–1874" (Master's thesis, University of South Carolina, 1977).
6. *Daily Phoenix*, 13 November 1873. Sabre and rifle clubs, actually extra-legal white militia units, would play a prominent role in the Red Shirt campaign of 1876. Technically, the state militia was open to both races during Reconstruction, but whites refused to join once blacks enrolled. The best-known local contingent was the Richland Rifle Club, also known as the "Governor's Guards," organized in July of 1874.
7. In 1873, Minort (then a Richland County representative) charged his wife with adultery and sued for divorce. The *Daily Phoenix* (19 October 1873) said this was perhaps the first separation suit ever heard in Columbia: "The revelations were such as it would be indelicate to reproduce in a newspaper."
8. Howard School, completed in October of 1867, soon had twelve teachers and seven hundred pupils. According to Freedmen's Bureau records, at that time those able to do so paid a monthly tuition fee of twenty cents.
9. When this institution celebrated its centennial in 1905, apparently no one who graduated or left school between 1873 and 1881 attended the ceremonies; and, according to rumor, a search in the 1950s for the oldest alumnus was quietly abandoned when the man to be honored turned out to be black.
10. As they discussed the future, "Phylis," whom her mistress described as half white and very intelligent, said she had no complaints about treatment she had received. Nevertheless, she said she would like to see what freedom was like and told of a friend who had bought her liberty: "It was a very sweet thing to be able to do as she chose, to sit and do nothing, to work if she desired, or to go out if she liked, and ask nobody's permission."

11. A decade later, ex-President Grant—if one believes the *Daily Register* (1 January 1880)—was hailed only by blacks when his train stopped briefly in Columbia.

12. "Richland Democratic Club Minutes and Scrapbook, 1876–1880," South Caroliniana Library. Pasted inside the volume is this campaign ditty:

> "Hampton, Hampton is my man;
> For Hampton live and die;
> I belong to the Hampton clan,
> And feed on Hampton pie."

13. Julian Selby's *Phoenix* (1865–1879) apparently fell victim to a labor dispute. In 1875, several of his printers started the *Register*, which lasted until 1898. Other Columbia papers of this era include two short-lived Republican dailies that eventually merged as the *Union-Herald*, the *Palmetto Yeoman* (1879–1885), and the *Daily Record* (1885–1893).

14. Upon the death of his widow in 1903, the *State* (15 June) praised Dorcas as an industrious, much-respected woman devoid of airs and recalled that her husband, adept at making money, "always had a smile and a good word for his old time white associates."

15. *Daily Register*, 26 October 1877. Two years later, this paper stated that Richland County's tax rate was 8¾ mills, which compared favorably with those of surrounding counties. That of Sumter was the same, Lexington's slightly less, and rates levied in Kershaw and Newberry were a bit higher.

16. Opposition to segregation by railroads themselves may explain why this legislation experienced difficulty. Many rail executives thought such arrangements expensive, impractical, and unnecessary.

PART IV

A Dynamic Half Century, 1890–1940

These decades open with a rush of industrial might and the long-overdue reforms of Benjamin Ryan Tillman and close with the dogs of war howling once more. In the years between, Columbia and Richland County experienced highs and lows common to similar communities of that era. These include expansion of the city outward and upward and two decades of general prosperity from the turn of the century to World War I. The other thirty years were somewhat less pleasant, especially in rural areas. Changes in travel—trolleys, autos, buses, hard-surface roads and streets, and even airplanes—are indeed striking, as is the appearance of huge cotton mills and Camp Jackson.

Some dreams obviously came true; others did not. As Columbia became something of a manufacturing center, any hope of attracting winter tourists and emulating Aiken and Camden evaporated. And schemes for becoming an inland seaport—the most resilient of dreams that may resurface even as we approach the year 2000—also were frustrated.

Centrality, the very reason for Columbia's birth, proved during these years less of a blessing than once thought. By the 1920s, the Chamber of Commerce was boasting that South Carolina's capital, in the absence of a metropolitan rival in the Midlands, was the hub of a trading area representing 500,000 potential customers. Actually, in 1930 Richland and contiguous counties (Lexington, Newberry, Fairfield, Kershaw, Sumter, and Calhoun) had only 283,808 residents, many of them black and most too poor to buy much of anything. Thanks to changes in transportation, centrality had taken on new meaning, and cities on the busiest rail lines such as Charlotte, Greenville, and Atlanta enjoyed special advantages.

On the other hand, a central location still could pay dividends. Whenever the national government set out to establish agencies and boards at the local level, as it did in World War I and again during

the Great Depression, Columbia was the obvious choice as headquarters of any group concerned with matters relating to the state of
South Carolina.

The word that best expresses the mood of Columbia during these decades is moderation. Having been burned (literally) by the extremism of
the 1860s and had a front row seat during Radical Reconstruction, residents tried, for the most part, to steer a middle path in what sometimes
was a bitter struggle. This political tug-of-war, as usual, pitted upcountry
against low, while each faction exacerbated rural-urban tensions in an
endless search for support, first among farmers and then mill workers.
Chief executives such as Tillman, Blease, Johnston, and even kindly old
John Richards, with his blue-law blitz, raised Columbia's collective blood
pressure. In December of 1894, F. W. McMaster wrote to one of his sons,
"We are glad that the populistic legislature has left—They looked like
strangers in a foreign land—They hid out in little boarding houses in the
back streets, &c." The rantings of Blease and Johnston's national guardsmen ringing the Calhoun Building undoubtedly moved other McMasters
to stronger language in decades that followed.

Although moderation failed to produce a Richland County governor,
it stymied Klan activity in the 1920s and created a racial climate that some
communities must have envied. This is not to suggest that Columbia was
a model of bi-racial harmony; but, Richland County apparently was free
from lynch-mob violence during this half century, frequent conferences
brought whites and blacks face to face with issues of the moment, and
leaders of both races were not strangers. Segregation was, of course, the
accepted mode of behavior, for this was the age of Jim Crow. Yet the black
community, enhanced by the presence of two institutions of higher learning that often had more students than their white counterparts, used
white athletic facilities and held meetings in the courthouse, YMCA, Hotel Jefferson, and Main Street theaters.

Some 2,500 people heard Booker T. Washington speak at the Columbia Theatre in 1907, an audience that included 300 whites in a special section. Another 2,000 individuals of both races were turned away. Racially
mixed audiences also greeted Billy Sunday in 1923; and, when "Uncle
Jaggers" died the following year, stores closed in tribute to an ex-slave
whose home for elderly blacks won wide respect. Three thousand attended his funeral, among them, the mayor, an official representative of
the governor, and ex-governor Richard Manning. Less attractive, however, are recurring charges of police brutality and community policies
concerning hospitals, libraries, and schools.

If moderation produced a relatively pleasant community, a good place to live and work, it had the disadvantage of inhibiting innovation. Except for the first decade of this century—a moment when Columbia was startling the South and the nation with big mills and skyscrapers—its leaders seem to take their cues from what was happening somewhere else. There were exceptions, of course, such as banker Edwin Robertson, the father of Camp Jackson, and Daniel Reed, the man who created what is now the nation's oldest community theater. Yet, having said that, Columbia of these decades really was both the South and much of the nation in microcosm: a community caught up in economic forces it did not comprehend and buffeted by autos, chain stores, and stock market gyrations over which it had no control.

Suburbs, Streetcars, and Skyscrapers

CHAPTER FOURTEEN

The decades from 1890 to 1920 were a time of sweeping change in urban America, and residents of Columbia experienced joys and frustrations common to all cities of that era, among them, growth, expansion, and rampant boosterism with its fantastic claims and rosy predictions of things to come. Population more than doubled and after 1900 grew increasingly white.

Statistics for all of Richland County are equally impressive (36,821 residents in 1890, 78,122 in 1920); and, although some rural acreage was annexed by Columbia during these decades, such losses were offset by acquisition in 1912 of much of Lexington County's Dutch Fork neighborhood and a strip of Fairfield in 1913 that included the town of Blythewood. At times, Richland also cast covetous eyes toward parts of Kershaw and New Brookland (which in 1938 changed its name to West Columbia)[1] and even dreamed fitfully of merging with all of Lexington County to create a new entity.

Columbia's willingness to spread across the Congaree was, as we shall see, part of a general desire to control suburban growth and increase both population and tax revenue. Outlying communities, on the other hand, usually joined forces with Richland in order to get better schools, better roads—and in the case of Dutch Fork—free access to markets. As early as 1890, the legislature gave area residents permission to buy bridges spanning the Broad and Congaree rivers from their owners or build new ones, but until 1912 no feasible plan emerged. Then, in December of that year, Lexington County authorities and officials representing Columbia Township agreed to purchase both structures for $90,000 and convert them into "free" bridges.

This news, as welcome as it was, did not shake the allegiance of those living in New Brookland, who in January of 1901 had rebuffed annexation by a margin of 35–9. That vote culminated a two-year campaign to make

276

Table 2. Columbia's Population, 1890–1920

Year	Population	White	Black
1890	15,353	6,563	8,790
1900	21,108	11,244	9,858
1910	26,319	14,772	11,546
1920	37,524	23,067	14,455

one county of two, a proposal that flew in the face of the contemporary trend to split up counties, not merge them. On 11 July 1899, beating the drum for a "greater" Columbia, the *State* published a three-column editorial detailing benefits that would flow from such a marriage. The two counties, it confidently observed, "lie in each other's arms, so to speak." And, since the name Richland actually was something of a misnomer for barren sand hills, to salve Lexington's pride, this daily suggested that the new creation might by christened "Congaree."

Outraged by such affrontery, the *Lexington Dispatch* exclaimed this could not be a serious proposition![2] The *State*'s Narcisco Gonzales, short of news and having cussed Ben Tillman from "A to izzard" so often that it was becoming monotonous, therefore had decided to chase this "preposterous" will-o-the-wisp. "Why it's undemocratic; it is in opposition to the Monroe Doctrine, why—er—er—er—perish the thought!" Merger, the *Dispatch* conceded, might reduce operating costs, but in the process Lexington would have to shoulder part of Columbia's awesome debt. As for calling any new county "Congaree," it noted sarcastically that "Gonzales" would be a more appropriate designation.

The *State* continued to trumpet the advantages of consolidation; but, in November of 1900 when Congaree Township, which included New Brookland, set in motion the machinery for a referendum on this matter, Gonzales poured cold water on any scheme for "petty scale" annexation. He wanted *all* of Lexington to join up with Richland, not just part of it. It was in this atmosphere that New Brookland rejected Richland and snuffed out any hope of creating a "super" county in the heart of South Carolina and simultaneously increasing the size and population of the city of Columbia.

New Brookland was only one of a dozen or so suburban enclaves that appeared just outside the borders of South Carolina's capital during the decades before World War I. The earliest were two functional centers just north of the city that included both business establishments and homes—Butcher Town and Cotton Town. As soon as rail lines reached the upcountry in the 1850s, stock drives to Columbia ceased and Butcher

Town vanished. But Cotton Town, a collection of merchants and warehouses on both sides of upper Main Street, grew in importance, especially in the late 19th century.

The first truly residential community outside of the city limits was Waverly to the east along the road to Camden (Taylor Street). Waverly, perhaps named for a Sir Walter Scott novel, was the property of wealthy Robert Latta, who died in 1861. Before his death, however, Latta began to divide his estate into blocks similar to those found in Columbia itself, and the Childs family, the post-war owners, continued this scheme, together with some random subdivision into lots. At about the same time, a similar neighborhood, Wheeler Hill, was taking shape to the south within the corporate limits. This little community was named for Dr. Ezra W. Wheeler, who came to Columbia from Ohio after the Civil War, built the Wheeler House in the center of the city (site of the Marriott Hotel), and presumably lived for a time on Wheeler Hill.

By the 1870s, house lots were being bought and sold in both areas, although neither was in any sense a "planned" subdivision marketed by real estate dealers. These communities had something else in common: a mix of black and white residents. Research directed by the University of South Carolina's Applied History Program indicates that, during the first two decades of this century, about two-thirds of the residents of Waverly were black.[3] In the same period, as the result of mill village construction, Wheeler Hill, once overwhelmingly black, exhibited similar characteristics. Two more clusters of late 19th century homes can be added to this list. They are Liberty or Quinine Hill, just east of Waverly, and Barhamville to the northeast, site of a famous school for girls. The latter, however, was transformed into Kendallville c. 1890 when a group of well-to-do blacks purchased land from Dr. F. D. Kendall and erected some sixty homes there.

As Kendallville was taking shape, three important forces began to change the nature of local suburban life: planned communities created by real estate developers, streetcar tracks, and villages for mill workers. The Columbia Land and Investment Company, chartered in February of 1889, was a pioneer in the field of residential housing, although those involved found the going rough until they teamed up with the city's new electric trolley system.[4] Assuming that the Congaree Bridge soon would become free, they purchased substantial acreage in Lexington Heights and at Horseshoe Lake near New Brookland, as well as 400 acres along the Congaree south of Gervais Street and some 600 acres southeast of Columbia. When plans to end bridge tolls were thwarted and work on the canal stalled, these men turned their attention to Shandon, the area that would become Columbia's first planned suburb.

Early in 1893 they were boasting that streets corresponding to those of Columbia already had been laid out in this yet-to-be-named community. One could buy an acre lot there for $300, half an acre for $160, and a quarter of an acre for $90, and the company was offering purchasers low-payment building loans. Despite such enticement, twelve months elapsed before the first sale was recorded, and only with the arrival of trolley cars in May of 1894 did the cash register begin to ring.

The street railway and the developers (led by Robert W. Shand) celebrated that occasion by opening a 50' by 75' pavilion on Devine Street near Harden, an edifice now remembered only by "Pavillion Avenue." This structure, it was said, soon would be joined by fountains, bath houses, and facilities for swimming, baseball, tennis, shooting, and bicycle riding. At the same time, as sales increased, prospective customers were cautioned that anyone who bought land in Shandon (named in honor of Shand's father, who for over half a century was rector of Columbia's Trinity Church) had to erect a residence costing at least $1,500 within six months.

The pavilion, which overlooked Rocky Branch and the Five Points area—then often under water—seems to have been something of a disappointment. Dreams of making it the centerpiece of a resort community that would lure northerners bound for Aiken or Augusta never materialized, nor did most of the vaunted facilities. Dances, concerts, and magic lantern shows were held there occasionally, and completion of a trolley "Belt Line" that enabled one to circle throughout the southeastern quarter of the city for only five cents made the pavilion a favorite stopping place . . . but for whites only. About a month after this structure opened, several blacks who tried to enter were turned away amid promises that the owners of the trolley system soon would build them a similar facility. A decade later, when Shandon was incorporated as a town, it could count only 112 residents; however, in time that community would spawn suburbs of its own and become one of the most sought-after addresses in Columbia.

During these turn-of-the-century years, the thrust of suburban growth was north and south of the city, not to the east. But, before moving to those areas, we should tarry for a moment in Waverly. In August of 1902, individuals claiming to speak for 1,500 inhabitants living along Columbia's eastern boundary secured permission to hold a referendum on incorporation of the town of Waverly. The leaders of this movement, who tried to elect an intendant and council prior to the incorporation vote, soon faced an injunction filed by a handful of disgruntled Shandon residents. Twelve months later, this injunction became permanent, and within days the Shandon group—joined by neighbors living in the tiny community of Epworth near the orphanage of the same name—filed for incorporation of what they boasted would be "the whitest town in the South." The main reason for their action, they said, was to secure the services of a town marshal empowered to act against careless hunters and blacks and others who grazed cattle in their streets. It is apparent that the move to incorporate *all* of the eastern suburbs as Waverly raised the ire of some residents, hence the injunction. Less clear are the actions of Robert W. Shand during these proceedings, for he was the attorney for those who sought unsuccessfully to create the town of Waverly.

If Shand was the father of Shandon, then insurance man Frederick H. Hyatt surely was the genius presiding over suburban growth beyond Columbia's northern frontier. By the mid-1890s, Cotton Town east of Main Street already had assumed the more elegant name of Bellevue Springs, and a trolley line was being rushed out to a new pleasure palace two miles further north that would honor Hyatt himself. In a jocular fashion, the *State* often referred to this residential expansion as "Ward 5," while conceding it was not yet part of the city of Columbia. When the Hyatt Park Casino opened early in July of 1897, this is how it was described by that same daily.

> The big building is situated near the centre of Hyatt Park, which has in the last month been transformed into a place of beauty. It is only a stone's throw from the park's electric railway station. It is built like an East Indian bungalow, and is surmounted by a steep and attractive roof. The main hall is fully 80 feet long and almost as wide. The floor is a beautiful one. Leading into the hall are large double doors, front and back. There are, besides, plenty of windows. The building is equipped with heating apparatus for cool weather. Across the front of the building will be a large and handsome sign painted by Hamiter [artist for the *State*], bearing the inscription, 'Hyatt Park Auditorium, 1897.'
>
> Broad stairways lead up from the ground to the piazzas in the front and back. The whole building is surrounded by piazzas 20 feet wide, from which an excellent view can be obtained of the city in the distance. The piazzas are supported by 40 brick pillars about ten feet or more high. Underneath the main floor are gentlemen and ladies' toi-

let and dressing rooms, which will be supplied from a tank which has been erected near by. There will be an ample supply of pure water from the springs in the park. Close by these rooms will be bowling alleys, shooting galleries and so on. The Hyatt park spring is but a few steps from the rear of this structure.

This obviously was a much more impressive structure than the little pavilion in Shandon, and it served the interests of Hyatt and his associates admirably for nearly two decades.[5] However, all of their well-laid plans were almost scuttled late in September of 1899 when blacks began buying up land near the casino for a burial ground. Springing into action, within seventy-two hours twenty-two white homeowners rushed through incorporation proceedings, held a referendum, gave their community a name, and elected town officials who promptly passed ordinance #1—a prohibition against black cemeteries in the new municipality of Eau Claire. The area so protected was "the circumference of a circle, having its center at a point in the Winnsboro road, one mile northwardly from two hundred yards above the forks of the Winnsboro and Broad River roads, and having a diameter of two miles."[6]

Four months later, the opening of the Richland Country Club (the first in this area) lured still more prospective residents to Eau Claire. Then, in 1904 the Ridgewood Club appeared. This newcomer, which soon absorbed its predecessor, does not appear to have begun life as a true "country" club. At the outset, presided over by insurance magnate John J. Seibels, its 170 members could boast of bowling alleys, pool tables, a reading room, and showers . . . to which, in time, golf links and an auto club were added. Creation in 1910 of an 85-acre amusement complex (Ridgewood Park) in the same general area enhanced the appeal of the northern suburbs for many, and the following year Ridgewood Club members abandoned plans to move to Shandon or Dent's Pond, voting instead to enlarge their facilities. And, when the club house burned in the fall of 1915, it was immediately rebuilt.

All of these attractions were, of course, for whites. Somewhat belatedly, in 1901 the trolley company fulfilled a promise made seven years earlier when it opened Lincoln Park, an auditorium for blacks located in the highlands north of the city. Said to have been similar to Hyatt Park Casino, on opening night (24 July) it was thronged by some 4,000 patrons, all of whom made the trip from town in special cars earmarked for their convenience. According to the *State*, this gala performance ushered in a series of events to be held Monday, Wednesday, and Friday evenings throughout the summer months; however, there is no evidence this schedule actually was maintained. An announcement three years later that the Shandon Pavilion would be re-named Douglas Park and handed over to blacks (as soon as the Ridgewood Club opened) indicates that Lincoln Park probably had a brief and checkered career.

Meanwhile, riding a wave of success, Frederick Hyatt somehow found time to run a dairy farm, lead South Carolina's "good roads" movement, and give advice to farmers, while still carrying on his real estate-insurance business. At an agricultural rally held at his casino in August of 1905, Hyatt spoke out strongly for proper use of fertilizer and diversified crop production, noting with pride that the federal government's first "diversification farm" in this state was on *his* land only a short distance away. The following week he addressed a similar audience in Union, adding road construction and white migration to his message. In Hyatt's opinion, a smattering of education was ruining an entire generation of young blacks, most of whom then refused to hoe and pick cotton and drifted into town where they did as little as possible. Their place, he said, would have to be taken by European immigrants.

During this same decade, Hyatt (together with J. T. Sloan) gave Columbia College 40 acres of land in the highlands, enabling that institution to move to the northern suburbs in 1905. Much of this activity, it developed, was in preparation for a gubernatorial bid. Five years later, this multi-purpose businessman campaigned in the Democratic primary as a Prohibitionist who believed in "economical administration, good roads, and 15¢ cotton." Despite this appealing platform, Hyatt was snowed under, coming in fourth in a field of five, unable to stir much interest even in his home territory.

By the time Hyatt was going down to defeat, Columbia's suburban growth was moving into high gear. In 1904, the state fair, having outgrown its facilities, moved south of the city, and G. A. Guignard transformed the old site into Elmwood Park. Three years later, the *State* reported there was widespread support among residents of North Columbia for annexation. This was a real-estate development several blocks north of Elmwood Avenue on the west side of Main Street, yet another operation headed up by Robert Shand. This property, once owned by the Newman family, encompassed Camp Fornance, a short-lived Spanish-American War installation.[7] At this juncture, however, only Elmwood Park, said to have had one hundred homes, agreed to merge with the city. Then in June of 1913, North Columbia, Waverly, South Waverly, and Shandon followed suit, although the vote in North Columbia was close, thirty-nine for annexation, thirty-two against. Bellevue Springs, by the way, became part of Columbia a few weeks earlier in March of that same year.

These incursions into county territory, the last major surge until the mid-1920s, took a large bite out of the southwest corner of Eau Claire's circular domain (Earlewood Park and portions of North Columbia) and stirred homeowners in the Columbia College neighborhood into action. The result was a rectangular town by the name of Arden stretching out east of Eau Claire. In essence, annexation added a block of land nearly one mile square, most of it west of Main Street, to the original city, together with much of the State Hospital property and an uneven strip four to eight blocks wide east of Harden.

Beyond these new frontiers, one encountered a bewildering assortment of little fiefdoms, some of them sprinkled with dwellings, some not. Beginning due north along the Congaree and sweeping in a clockwise fashion to the southeast, these settlements included Alta Vista, Park Place, North Highlands, and North Highland Farms (all south of the carefully tended expanse owned by the Ridgewood Club). North of the State Hospital grounds lay Colonial Heights, Bellevue Place, Monticello, Eau Claire Heights, East Ridgewood, East Ridgewood Heights, Spring Brook, and College View #1 and #3 (but not #2). Moving to the northeast, Kendall (or Kendallville) was located just outside of the city, with Booker T. Washington Heights about a quarter of a mile away along the Southern Railway tracks. And a mile or so further out were Columbia College, College Place, Arden Heights, and Graham Place.

Just east of Waverly and Shandon lay Haskell Heights, Pinehurst, Liberty Hill, Hampton Place, Fairview, Melrose Heights, and an unnamed subdivision at the corner of Devine and Sims owned by cotton broker M. C. Heath, the man who would bestow his name upon Heathwood. South Shandon and Shandon Annex (but not Shandon Terrace) still were in the county, as were South End and Rose Hill.

Within the city there were two more new subdivisions, neither of which bore much resemblance to nearby Wheeler Hill. The first, which appeared in 1909, was Cherry Tree Hill. It was located in blocks bounded by Pickens, College, Gregg, and Greene streets, a bit of land that once had been the college golf links. The other was Wales Garden, "a splendid residence section" in the southeast corner of the city laid out by a prestigious Boston landscape firm in 1913. This ambitious undertaking was the brainchild of several prominent businessmen, among them, Edwin

WALES Robertson, August Kohn, William D. Melton, and three members of the Gibbes family. Construction of this posh development figured briefly in a local political campaign when critics alleged that public funds were involved.

Columbia's suburbs to the south—and New Brookland to the west across the Congaree—were mill villages, row upon row of often identical homes for hundreds, even thousands, of workers. By 1896, the Richland Mill had built quarters for 400 employees on Wheeler Hill (within the city limits), and some 1,500 individuals who worked at the huge "Duck Mill," now the South Carolina State Museum, lived in New Brookland. As still other mills appeared, notably Olympia and Granby, more villages sprang up.

According to August Kohn's famous survey, *Cotton Mills of South Carolina* (1907), 3,500 workers were employed in six local mills with an annual payroll of $819,000. David L. Carlton estimates that Columbia's mill district had a population of 8,700 in 1903. About 4,200 of these folk, he writes, lived within the city and represented 20 percent of Columbia's total population and a third of all white residents.[8] As this historian notes, Narciso Gonzales and others took great pride in this growth and expansion, yet poverty clearly visible from the south portico of the State House gave rise to what soon was being called "the mill problem." When those whose daily existence was regulated by whistle blasts began to vote for the Tillmans (Ben and Jim) and then Colie Blease, apprehension turned to fear and was, of course, one reason for annexation north and east.[9]

Conditions prevalent in these mill communities inspired welfare work, educational reform, and other progressive and idealistic campaigns. Although reformers insisted each innovation was for the benefit of the "reformee," upon reflection it becomes apparent that these do-gooders often had the well-being of their own class, not that of mill people, uppermost in their minds. This was something that Blease, for one, shrewdly appreciated, hence his widespread appeal and political resilience.

What held all of these scattered neighborhoods together—and even created some of them—was Columbia's street railway system, the first in the state to use electric power in 1893. By the turn of the century, tracks north to Eau Claire and the "Belt Line" circling east via Taylor and Heidt streets to the Shandon-Five Points area and then along Harden and Gervais to the State House were added to the old horse-drawn network concentrated largely in the business district. In 1900, service expanded south to the mill villages and still deeper into Shandon along Devine Street,

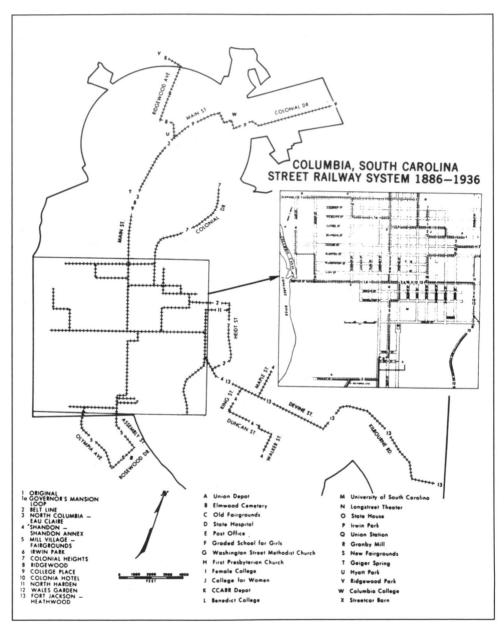

COLUMBIA, SOUTH CAROLINA
STREET RAILWAY SYSTEM 1886–1936

1 ORIGINAL	A Union Depot
1a GOVERNOR'S MANSION	B Elmwood Cemetery
LOOP	C Old Fairgrounds
2 BELT LINE	D State Hospital
3 NORTH COLUMBIA –	E Post Office
EAU CLAIRE	F Graded School for Girls
4 "SHANDON –	G Washington Street Methodist Church
SHANDON ANNEX	H First Presbyterian Church
5 MILL VILLAGE –	I Female College
FAIRGROUNDS	J College for Women
6 IRWIN PARK	K CCARR Depot
7 COLONIAL HEIGHTS	L Benedict College
8 RIDGEWOOD	
9 COLLEGE PLACE	M University of South Carolina
10 COLONIA HOTEL	N Longstreet Theater
11 NORTH HARDEN	O State House
12 WALES GARDEN	P Irwin Park
13 FORT JACKSON –	Q Union Station
HEATHWOOD	R Granby Mill
	S New Fairgrounds
	T Geiger Spring
	U Hyatt Park
	V Ridgewood Park
	W Columbia College
	X Streetcar Barn

FEET

Compiled by David Charles McQuillan, author of "The Street Railway and the Growth of Columbia, 1882–1936" (Master's Thesis, USC, 1975).

where, in time, a few shops would appear. Five years later, a spur was built past the penitentiary to a baseball field at Irwin Park near the city water works, and in succeeding years tracks reached Colonial Heights and College Park to the north. The last major lines to be built were those through Wales Garden in 1915 (a route still delineated by the median strip that divides Saluda Avenue) and to Camp Jackson via Kilbourne Road during World War I. By that date, Columbia's street railway was operating 100 cars over nearly twenty-five miles of track and in 1918 carried 11 million passengers.

From time to time there were rumors of still more expansion . . . trolley lines to Lexington, Camden, Sumter, Saluda, and perhaps even Augusta. The possibility of a Lexington connection was somewhat controversial since those tracks (to be operated by another company) would enter the city and might then compete with Columbia's urban system. In January of 1903, the city council, despite the *State*'s objections, voted 9–7 to grant just such a franchise; but, except for an Aiken-Augusta line, none of this proposed construction ever materialized.

In June of that same year, council members spoke out again, in this instance establishing Jim Crow seating on local trolleys. The *State* expressed regret that the "best" element of the black population was being forced to the rear, but whites, "by far the largest patrons," had to be protected, it said. The result was a brief black boycott, followed ten months later by a scheme for complete racial separation on "Belt Line" cars bound for the Shandon Pavilion (soon to become Douglas Park). According to this plan, cars moving clockwise around the loop would carry only blacks, while white cars would move counter-clockwise; however, there is no indication that this rigid arrangement ever was put into operation.

The purpose of trolleys was, of course, to move people about the city, to and from their homes (which might be located in new suburbs), downtown to work or shop, to school and college classes, or perhaps to zoos and other places of amusement built by or with the support of the street railway itself. Real estate developers, in cooperation with the trolley company, constantly stressed the wonders of suburban living. "Be a Bungaloafer" cried those promoting Colonial Heights.

> No boarding house mansion, no rented domain,
> Can equal my cottage or bungalow plain,
> For here I am monarch and owner of all
> And perfect content is my portion thereof.[10]

As Shandon Annex began to take shape in 1911, Walker, Ravenel & Company boasted of what it could offer those seeking a quiet paradise—

low prices, big lots, and electric lights, as well as telephone and trolley service. "Only $2,250.00 for that beautiful green bungalow at the end of the car line . . . very little cash needed, ½ acre of land."[11] But soon that green bungalow could be reached just as easily by an automobile that freed one from rigid trolley schedules, or the owner might be able to commute almost as conveniently by motor bus with its more flexible route systems. In any case, widespread use of the gasoline engine doomed the trolley to extinction. In July of 1920, for example, a public swimming facility opened at Boyden Arbor seven miles out Percival Road beyond Dent's Pond. Within three weeks, harbinger of things to come, T. B. Stack's motor truck was providing regular service out to that point at 6:30 and 7:20 each evening, with return trips at 8 and 9 P.M.

Facing competition similar to this, as well as private cars and "jitneys" (unlicensed taxis), in the early 1920s the Columbia Electric Street Railway, Light, and Power Company began to curtail service and remove tracks from some suburbs. These steps were an obvious effort to cut losses; for, unlike railroads, streetcar companies relied almost entirely upon passenger revenue, although it is apparent that "selective" bookkeeping procedures distorted the picture of income received from various operations of the local utility. Then, in the middle of the decade, its executives launched a concerted campaign to render trolley service unpalatable. They encouraged and even subsidized buses, saw to it that bus tickets cost less than those on trolleys, and even ran their streetcars directly *behind* buses whenever possible.

Finally, on 11 March 1927 trolley service ceased, and the following year the bus company went bankrupt, leaving the city of Columbia without any form of mass transportation. However, this state of affairs ignited a prolonged legal battle that in 1931 ended up before the United States Supreme Court. There, in a landmark decision, the justices ruled that a public utility must operate all franchises granted to it and that surrender of one monopoly invalidates all of those held by a company. As a result, seven streetcar lines began to function once more and continued to do so until 22 November 1936 when they were replaced by buses. So, tracks were paved over and cars sold for scrap or to other trolley companies, yet the imprint of the streetcar lines that created much of present-day Columbia is with us still. All one has to do is look closely, for telltale traces are evident to the discerning eye.

But the trolley was not the only form of transportation that altered life in the Midlands during these decades; the bicycle, auto, and train also exerted considerable impact. The first of these modes of travel, extremely popular in the 1890s, had socio-economic relevance far beyond mere

The Selling of Shandon, 1912.

MAP
OF PROPERTY BELONGING TO
THE COLUMBIA LAND & INVESTMENT CO
NEAR SOUTHEASTERN BOUNDARY LINE OF
COLUMBIA   SO.CAR
CORRECTED TO OCT 1st 1912

W B SMITH WHALEY & CO
ENGINEERS

numbers. In June of 1896, the *State* noted that sales were soaring, adding that dozens of "lady bicyclists" could be seen on Columbia's streets each day and musing about the political influence of "wheelmen" should they become a voting bloc. At that time, local enthusiasts could purchase new models for twenty-five to fifty dollars and used ones for ten to thirty-five dollars at a half-dozen shops, one of which styled itself as a "bicycle livery" equipped to lease vehicles as well as sell them. Competitive races, first staged in the 1880s, became ever more popular, and in December of 1899 blacks held a meet of their own at the fair grounds. As a new century began, an estimated three thousand area residents were commuting to work on bicycles.

This mania for wheeled travel quickly pitted riders against walkers, the former seeking better highways and gates that swung inward, the latter, lights and bells to warn of approaching speedsters. An attempt by city officials in September of 1900 to force bicyclists into the streets and slow their pace precipitated a huge outcry. Angry citizens charged that South Carolina's capital city had only one decent thoroughfare (Main Street), hence riders were forced to use sidewalks. They agreed with the *State* that a proposed five-mile-per-hour speed limit for cyclists was absurd. Any healthy businessman, they replied scornfully, could walk that fast!

Although the bicycle was seen less frequently in rural areas, it sparked interest in good roads among many segments of society—or, more precisely, it accentuated widespread demands for highway improvements already being voiced. For a century and a half, Richland County, like other American communities, called upon its able-bodied males to work so many days each year on roads near their homes. This form of forced labor was generally resented, neither worker nor supervisor knew much about road repair and construction, and the results were largely ineffectual. Railroads, for the most part, solved the problem of long-distance travel in any kind of weather, but getting to the depot over roads ravaged by rain often was impossible.

In the 1880s, South Carolina farmers began to complain of what they called the "mud tax," that is, the fact that poor roads not only isolated rural households, they cost their owners dearly in many other ways as well. In January of 1894, the General Assembly passed an extensive act designed to improve both county administration and highway maintenance. A county supervisor, elected for a two-year term, was given "general jurisdiction" over roads, bridges, paupers, bastard children, and all financial affairs. At the same time, several township boards were replaced by commissioners (three per township to be appointed by the governor upon the recommendation of the local legislative delegation). The supervisor and the chairmen of these commissions became the governing board of the county. If a supervisor wished to do so, he could institute a contract system for road work and receive a commutation tax from male citizens in lieu of annual labor. In addition, these statutes opened the door to the use of convicts to build and repair roads.

Thus the demands of bicyclists for better streets and roads reinforced the cries of farmers, who, nonetheless, probably had nothing but contempt for wheelmen. In September of 1895, a "road congress" convened in the Senate chamber of the state capitol, and two years later Richland County officials announced the first of many plans to construct macadam roads with free labor. According to this scheme, those within five miles of Columbia would be twenty feet wide, while others more distant and less used would be narrower. In 1911, apparently unable to grasp the vision of "through" highways, county authorities proposed thirty-foot roads within ten miles of the city and a twenty-six-foot width in other areas.

By that date, the bicycle mania had run its course, and the automobile was benefitting from the pioneering work of its two-wheel predecessor. Not only did the bicycle breathe life into the "good roads" movement (one might even say it initiated it), it created scores of mechanics in communities such as Columbia and tended to promote social change. All-day Sunday outings, bloomers or divided skirts for women, and the demise of the chaperon (older women rarely took up the sport) are some aspects of this new freedom. Most important of all perhaps, the bicycle changed attitudes toward personal travel that, in turn, encouraged acceptance of the automobile.

In June of 1900, hundreds of local residents, including schoolchildren let out for the occasion, saw their first horseless carriage, a Locomobile touring the country to promote Octagon soap. According to the *State* (5 June 1900), the vehicle was "manipulated by two young men who had no difficulty in doing so." Impressed by what they saw, banker Edwin Robertson and bicycle dealer John E. Richard, destined to become this state's first auto salesman, each bought a Locomobile. The following year, Richard sold cars to Gibbes Machinery Company's A. Mason Gibbes and Eddie Jacobs, both pioneer auto enthusiasts. In time, Richard represented still other manufacturers, and in 1909 the Gibbes Machinery Company (agent for Chalmers, Hudson, Selden, Hupmobile, and Peerless and today the state's oldest dealer) sold 387 vehicles. Meanwhile, on 11 December 1906, Richard's Locomobile exploded in the backyard of his home at 1524 Pickens Street with near-disastrous results. The blast, which seriously injured one of his sons, scattered debris over a wide area, deposited part of a seat on a nearby church steeple, and confirmed fears of many Columbia residents that autos were downright dangerous!

There were then some fifty vehicles registered with the city clerk, most of them owned by physicians and businessmen. According to an ordinance passed in February of that year, in addition to getting a registration number and paying a small fee, owners had to make a tag bearing their numerals (in letters at least three inches high) and display it on their machine. The speed limit was 8 to 12 miles per hour in various parts of the city, and one had to give a signal at each intersection and stop if any horse became agitated. In 1908, following the arrest of the mayor for speeding, the limit was raised to 14 mph. Four years earlier an attempt by municipal officials to make bicycles and autos stop for *all* animals was ridiculed by the *State* (5 February 1904): "To insist that bicyclists or automobilists dismount on approaching an ox or mule that wouldn't blink an eye or hasten a step in the presence of an earthquake is to insure the law being regarded by the public as absurd and consequently guaranteeing it an immediate state of desuetude." Although not enacted, this proposal indicates the close ties existing between bicycle and auto.

For much of that decade, however, the public regarded the auto with a blend of awe and skepticism. Auto shows, races, and hill-climbing contests attracted hundreds, but all too often those four-wheel wonders failed to perform as anticipated. Nearly every community had its "test" hill where prospective owners tried out new vehicles, and one of Columbia's favorites was Hampton Hill on Garner's Ferry Road. Then, in 1909, Clarence L. Rawl made it up the State House steps in a Maxwell; and, with this seal of approval, even the city itself began to buy "auto engines" for firemen, police and other departments. [12]

A turning point in this saga came in February of 1915 when Governor Richard Manning signed a bill creating a local commission to oversee expenditure of $1,250,000 on "more or less permanent highways of first-rate description" radiating from Columbia. These dollars, editors agreed, would make Richland one of the South's leading counties and double the area's rural white population within a decade. Subsequent efforts to exploit city-county differences on this bond issue were attacked by the *State* as "shameful." Someday, it said on 26 March 1915, Columbia's suburbs would extend to the county lines. Businessmen would commute to the city each day and be county residents except during working hours. Their children, this daily predicted, would attend neighborhood schools, and their wives would participate in community affairs far from Columbia's city limits. Thus—influenced by bicycles, autos, and both regional and national trends—Colonel Taylor's town and its hinterland were moving toward creation of a comprehensive system of roads, an undertaking so formidable that it soon would be primarily a matter of state-national concern, not local.[13]

The railroad story during the years from 1890 to 1920 was a tale of consolidation and, for a brief time, of efforts to promote highway construction since the automobile was seen at first as a "feeder" to rail systems, not as a competitor. In May of 1899, as sixty-five passenger trains were entering and leaving Columbia each day, business leaders stressed the need for a central terminal, and early in 1902 a handsome brick structure (now a popular eatery) appeared on lower Main Street. However, in the intervening months, another major operator—Seaboard Air Line—built tracks through Columbia en route to Tampa and, for various reasons, refused to use that depot. Instead, Seaboard executives insisted they had to have Sidney Park for their station and freight yard, and eventually they prevailed . . . only to decide they really didn't want that site after all! (This comic opera imbroglio will be discussed more fully in the next chapter.) Under pressure from municipal authorities, who quickly became disenchanted with Seaboard, the latter built the red-brick depot on Lincoln Street used for some years by Amtrak.

By the 1920s, eleven separate lines intersected in Columbia to form a busy transportation hub. These tracks were operated by three trunk carriers (Seaboard, Southern, and Atlantic Coast) and an intra-state line, the Columbia, Newberry, and Laurens. Over 200,000 freight cars were being loaded and unloaded here each year, and the Chamber of Commerce boasted that Columbia had *direct* connections to all of the state's county seats. Travelers leaving South Carolina's capital city, according to chamber literature, could reach any point in the state in three hours and thirty-three minutes! (In 1925, the chamber said the same feat could be accomplished by auto in four-and-one-half hours.)

There was another mode of transportation that fascinated local residents of these decades, much as it had their forebears—river traffic via the Congaree and Santee to the Atlantic Ocean. Beginning in the late 1880s, federal dollars were spent dredging those waters, and scores of editorials described how Columbia would someday be a "seaport." On 4 December 1893, for example, the *State* waxed eloquent in an essay entitled "Columbia to the Sea."

> Imagine lines of steamships from Charleston to New York, from Charleston to Philadelphia, from Charleston to Baltimore, from

Charleston to Boston. Imagine a line of steamers connected, therewith, running from Columbia to Charleston through the waters of the Congaree and Santee rivers and the ocean. Imagine a transfer in Charleston to the freights that come from Columbia. Imagine wharves in Columbia, loaded with cotton for trans-Atlantic ports and heavy freights from the North Atlantic ports. Imagine through bills of lading from Columbia to New York, Boston, Philadelphia, and Baltimore, and from Columbia to Liverpool and [Le] Harve. Imagine Columbia, already the railroad centre of the State, the entrepot for the trade of all upper South Carolina, having such rates of transportation to and from the seaboard as no all-rail route can furnish to any city in the State. Imagine all this, and you will have an idea of what Columbia will soon be—the great focus of freights for South Carolina.

The expenditure of a few thousand dollars by the United States government will bring all these imaginings to realization. A mile or two of cleared channel, and the thing's done!

According to this rosy scenario, upcountry businessmen then would face only a short rail haul to Columbia and "a cheap water haul to the whole world." In only a few months, the great dilemma that long had vexed much of this state would be resolved.

Nevertheless, years passed without much progress, but shortly after the turn of the century it seemed that some of these "imaginings" might yet be realized. In March of 1904, the *Highlander* made its first 212-mile trip upriver from Georgetown in thirty-five hours. This craft—136 feet long and 23 feet wide—had a draft when empty of less than two feet. It could carry the equivalent of six railroad cars and had two staterooms and thirty-seven berths; however, in June of that same year the *Highlander* caught fire and burned. Another boat soon appeared, and in 1905 freight from Baltimore and New York was being unloaded just south of Columbia's city limits. Passengers presumably could sail to and from the coast three times each week. Sometimes these flat-bottom craft (never more than one or two ever were in service in the same season) even crept up to the foot of Senate Street; and, in 1909, inspired by such feats, a local group formed a yacht club whose members cruised the Congaree for a year or so.

Despite disappointment and frustration, in October of 1913 the Columbia Railway and Navigation Company purchased two new boats, and the Chamber of Commerce—to the dismay of some members— continued to support such ventures. When compared with rail charges, it said, one could save twenty-seven dollars per carload on canned goods shipped from Baltimore.

Yet this campaign to transform the uncooperative waters of the Midlands into highways of commerce always exuded an air of unreality. The previous century had demonstrated the futility of such schemes on rivers alternatively too high and too swift and then virtually nonexistent. Even more disturbing, most proposals for water transport were tied to revival of the Columbia Canal. But after 1891 the upper half of that controversial ditch was churning out the hydro-electric power that turned the machinery in Columbia's new mills. Because of competition for water, ship traffic did not comport well with those operations. In addition, the local boat terminus clearly was seasonal in nature (depending upon the depth of the Congaree), and those promoting riparian commerce never developed warehouse facilities equal to those provided by railroads.

The basic reason for all of this nautical activity was, of course, freight rates. If the specter of competition could be conjured up, the *State* said in September of 1895, then rail costs would come down, as they had in Augusta. Only one boat trip a year up the Congaree, this daily bluntly admitted, might convince federal authorities to reduce rail charges being paid by local merchants. Thus this seemingly endless tale of the Columbia Canal (and there's more to come) was, at this juncture, a scheme to apply pressure on the railroads, not a sincere effort to develop functioning steamship service.

Late in 1910, Columbia schoolchildren again enjoyed a holiday, just as they had a decade earlier when an auto came to town. This time it was so they could watch as the first airplane to be seen in this state soared aloft. On 7 December, Eugene B. Ely, barn-storming under the auspices of Glenn Curtiss, made three flights at the fair grounds and also bested a Buick in a brief contest around an oval track. His "Belmont racer," which arrived by rail, had been assembled in only eight hours, and the *State* greeted the performance with a remarkable headline: "LIKE GREAT WHITE HERON MAN-MADE BIRD CUT AIR." The following day, Ely was joined by another aviator, J. A. D. McCurdy; however, this meet, sponsored by the local Chamber of Commerce, drew disappointing crowds of only a thousand or so and was not a financial success. Among the spectators was New York balloonist August Post, in town to speak at the university on aeronautics. One result of this hoopla, according to press reports, was a new ailment known as "aviation neck," a malady experienced by both young and old.

Ely, the first man to take off from and land on a warship, crashed to his death in Macon, Georgia, in October of 1911. Richland County residents would see more airplanes in the years that followed, especially during World War I. Commercial air travel still was far in the future, but in July of 1919 local spokesmen expressed hope that Columbia would be on an air route being projected by a Milwaukee company. In December of that year, Jesse B. Roddey, Columbia's Buick dealer, purchased a Curtiss biplane as the nucleus of his newly formed Columbia Aircraft Corporation. He had, he told reporters, already flown to Charlotte to purchase automobiles.

From horse-drawn trolley cars to airplanes in a little more than a quarter of a century is a giant leap; and, although Columbia was proud of its growing suburbs, huge mills, and healthy economy, every breast swelled a bit at the sight of the skyline rising majestically above the Main Street business district. In January of 1901, banker and utility magnate Edwin W. Robertson startled the community with news that he would erect a twelve-story skyscraper on the southeast corner of Main and Washington streets at a cost of $250,000. Construction of a new home for his National Loan & Exchange Bank, long known simply as the "Robertson Building" and now called the "Barringer Building," drew daily crowds in ensuing months, and in April of 1903 hundreds watched one Saturday evening as S. B. McMaster dropped a bicycle from the top of the state's tallest building to the street below. McMaster promised to repair the slightly damaged vehicle and give it to the first customer who made a twenty-five dollar purchase at his shop. The local baseball nine, then known as the "Gamecocks," soon became the "Skyscrapers," permitting university teams to assume that now familiar name . . . although by 1911 the "Skyscrapers" had become the "Columbia Comers."

In March of the following year, the city was swept up in a flurry of construction costing over $2.5 million. These projects included the Union Bank Building at Main and Gervais, the Palmetto National Bank (with its underground rathskeller and a year-round roof garden cafe, located just north of Robertson's handsome brick structure),[14] a shopping arcade alongside Columbia's first skyscraper, and large hotels at Main and Laurel (the Jefferson) and at Main and Wheat (the Gresham). The latter, close by Union Station, was the second significant structure to appear on lower Main Street below the State House. Plans by Robertson to erect another twelve-story tower, a twin to his National Loan & Exchange Bank Building, subsequently were abandoned, as was a scheme to add wings to South Carolina's capitol.

The arcade, still a charming creation, elicited special praise when it opened. "Looks just like New York," murmured one young lady, and a newspaper headline hailed the two-story edifice as the "handsomest building on [the] continent." This unprecedented wave of construction, together with other developments on the local scene, enabled the boosters to sum up this community's achievements in a spectacular list that appeared in the *State* on 26 August 1915.

Some Things Columbia Has

Nine hotels.

Ten colleges.

Eleven public schools.

Commission government.

Thirteen bank and trust companies.

Banking capital of $2,209,286.

Bank deposits of $10,729,790.30.

Banking resources of $14,930,951.32.

Bank clearings over a million a week.

Nine lines of railroad.

One hundred and forty-four regular trains daily.

Fourteen thousand eight hundred and eight miles of railroad, radiating from it.

Every great railroad system in the Southeast.

Boat line to coast with tri-weekly sailings.

Population of 56,992 (City Directory).

Population of half million within radius 50 miles.

Fifty-one churches—all denominations.

Six cotton mills—241,000 spindles—annual pay roll $998,000.

Largest cotton mill under one roof in world.

First mill in world ever operated by electricity.

Six fertilizer factories.

Three oil mills—60 other manufacturing plants.

Twenty-five miles street car track—57 cars.

Fifteen miles paved sidewalks.

Ninety miles streets.

Forty-one miles sewerage mains.

Fifty-one miles water mains.

Thirty-six miles gas mains—15 miles more being laid.

Annual rainfall 46.7 inches.

Six-story Y.M.C.A.; 83 rooms in dormitory; Woman's building.

Building average, one new building per day.

Three skyscrapers—10, 12, 15 stories, respectively.

Capital invested (manufactures) $12,252,648.

Twenty-five thousand horse-power electric plant—cheap power.

Two hospitals—another ordered.

Two hundred and sixty-five thousand dollar post-office ordered.

Five theatres.

But one thing that Columbia still lacked was a slogan, something any growing city of those decades had to have. Catchy phrases such as "the Lowell of the South" and "the Square Meal Town" no longer seemed appropriate, and in 1914 the Chamber of Commerce launched an essay contest among schoolchildren ("Why Columbia is a Good City to Live In") that it was hoped would produce the desired results. However, sentences such as "In Columbia Prosperity is a Habit" and "When You Boost Columbia You Boost Yourself" failed to enjoy widespread support and soon were forgotten.

The most important work of the chamber on the eve of World War I was, strangely, not in Columbia itself but out in the county. After experimenting with a series of one-shot extravaganzas such as air shows, harvest jubilees, corn expositions, and music festivals (all of which flopped), civic leaders turned their attention to rural matters. The chamber helped pay the salary of Richland County's first farm demonstration agent (J. M. Napier) and even dared to say that agriculture was more important than any steamship line on the Congaree. Columbia could exist without boats, real estate man Bruce Ravenel declared on one occasion, but it could not get along without food! It was a "ridiculous situation," he said, when local farmers failed to grow even one-tenth of the fruit and vegetables consumed in area households. Soon agricultural institutes were being held where speakers talked of new crops, lime, fertilizer, and crop rotation, and those attending a statewide Conference on the Common Good, held in Columbia in August of 1913, discussed the needs of farm families and their schools and churches.

Several factors caused this shift of emphasis. As the dreaded boll weevil moved northward, many individuals realized that the region's one-crop economy was in jeopardy. Twin dreams of becoming a seaport or a tourist mecca seemed stymied, and annual festivals (except for the state fair) were greeted with yawns. As a result, it was becoming apparent that the Columbia-Richland County area, still overwhelmingly agricultural, might well have to rely upon its own basic resources; and, in any eventuality, a vigorous, prosperous hinterland would be a distinct asset. Rediscovery of rural values also may be evidence of an incipient reaction to unrestricted industrial growth. As Columbia's parks were torn asunder and its landscape reshaped, some residents began to realize that railroad tracks and cotton mills, despite their obvious economic benefits, were a mixed blessing. Yet the only guidepost to development of an urban economy, a new phenomenon throughout much of the American South, was experience, which could be a severe, even cruel, taskmaster.

Notes

1. New Brookland, essentially a mill village at the western end of the Gervais Street Bridge, probably was named for yet another suburb separated from a larger commercial center by a river—Brooklyn, New York; in fact, state records sometimes referred to it as "Brooklyn." However, since a black settlement on the Wateree in eastern Richland already bore that name, this community became New Brookland, which was formally incorporated as a town in December of 1894.
2. See the *State*, 14 July 1899. This newspaper, launched in February of 1891 by the Gonzales brothers to counter the rise of Ben Tillman, soon became a major force in both the community and the state.
3. In 1903, the twelve-block area known as Waverly had ninety black and forty-two white households (the nature of two was unclear). During succeeding years, black preponderance increased, especially after 1920. By 1943, there was apparently only one white

household amid 195 black homes, with seven classified as "unknown." Technically, Waverly lay south of Taylor Street, but the name usually referred to a neighborhood dominated by Columbia's black colleges, Allen and Benedict. At the turn of the century, many residents were associated in some manner with those institutions and railroads that maintained facilities nearby. See a copy of "Historical and Architectural Survey of Waverly: Columbia's First Suburb," Dr. Michael C. Scardaville, coordinator, at the South Carolina Department of Archives and History.

4. The original incorporators were George W. Parker, William H. Lyles, Edgar C. Haynesworth, J. W. Willis, J. S. Muller, and W. A. Clark. By 1893, C. H. Manson was serving as president, and the board of directors included Dr. James Woodrow, merchant J. L. Mimnaugh, and Robert W. Shand, who would emerge as the most influential figure.

5. When this building was razed in 1915, the *State* (13 August) noted that Columbia's first moving pictures probably were shown there, adding that the casino had been closed for several years.

6. *Acts and Joint Resolutions of the General Assembly* . . . (Columbia, 1900), p. 585. In this instance, the name was spelled "Eau Clare." Eau Claire (clear water) was named for nearby Bellevue Springs, a source of mineral water that in the 1890s was bottled and sold by the owner, Louis Marsteller.

7. Tennessee and Rhode Island volunteers transferred here from Pennsylvania in November of 1898 so named their new home in honor of Captain James Fornance, who was killed during the battle of San Juan Hill in Cuba.

8. Carlton, *Mill and Town in South Carolina, 1880–1920* (Baton Rouge, 1982), p. 135.

9. According to Carlton (p. 166), in 1902, residents of Columbia's southernmost ward gave James Tillman, nephew of the senator and the man who shot and killed Narciso Gonzales, 71.4 percent of their votes in his unsuccessful bid to become governor. Blease, he adds, could count on about 85 percent of local mill-worker ballots.

10. *State*, 6 June 1909.

11. *Ibid.*, 9 April 1911.

12. On 10 November 1906, a black youth earned twenty cents by riding *down* the capitol steps on a bicycle.

13. A strange by-product of the auto age was the community of Pontiac (formerly Jacobs), so named by R. Beverley Herbert, Sr., and fellow land developers soon after a Pontiac dealer appeared in Columbia on the eve of World War I.

14. Tornado-force winds that swept through Columbia late in December of 1912 reportedly blew the Palmetto Building, then ten stories high, "out of plumb." Contractors said, however, that the framework could easily be repaired.

Mills, Parks,
and War Camps

CHAPTER FIFTEEN

Our Fountain of Fortune

Never did Ponce de Leon and his devoted followers, toiling through the chapparel and the dark swamps of Florida, listen more longingly for the murmur of crystal waters that would reveal to them the fountain of eternal youth, than have the people of Columbia, heartsick with hope deferred, listened and longed for the roar of Broad River's tawny flood through the locks of the great canal, for many years her chief industrial hope.

Here at last, awaiting but the pressure of the lever to bring into usefulness the finest developed water power in the United States, is Columbia's completed canal.

Surely those who against heavy odds achieved so much, are entitled to the meed of praise Scripturally accorded to him who caused two blades of grass to grow where but one grew before.

Among the various enterprises which will prove potent factors in the future growth and prosperity of Columbia, the Columbia Canal and Water Power stands [sic] paramount to all others.[1]

For once, the lavish prose of a local booster of the early 1890s was essentially true. That waterway, although not really "completed," would provide the electric power that turned spindles, created jobs, and changed the economic life of the Columbia-Richland County community. On 21 November 1891, after years of frustration and disappointment, hundreds crowded the banks of the enlarged canal north of the city to watch as water began to flow. Some arrived in carriages or on foot, but most came by special train (fare twenty-five cents). Shortly after noon, following remarks by Mayor F. W. McMaster, bells pealed, whistles shrieked, and cannon roared from atop

300

Arsenal Hill as the gates opened for the first time. Six hours later, water was six feet deep under the Gervais Street Bridge. At that moment, there were no large mills to be seen, but horsepower greater than that found in most manufacturing centers of the Northeast already had attracted the attention of wealthy industrialists.

However, before describing the massive structures they would build, it might be well to finish the tangled story of the canal itself. Its roots, of course, go back to the 1820s and attempts to construct a network of waterways throughout South Carolina. After the Civil War, state authorities contracted with various individuals eager to convert the canal to industrial use, among them, financier William Sprague and engineer David M. Thompson. When their efforts failed to produce results, the state decided in 1887 to hand the property over to the city of Columbia. Profiting from the experience of others, engineers hired by municipal officials built a dam about three miles upstream from Gervais Street and enlarged and extended the upper half of the old canal so as to take full advantage of waters flowing from the Broad River.

A few weeks after this waterway opened, it was conveyed to the Columbia Water Power Company, a utility headed by Aretas Blood, the New Hampshire textile magnate who subsequently would spearhead construction of the "Duck Mill." Then, as banker Edwin Robertson put together his street railway, light, and power conglomerate in 1905, the canal passed into his hands. Soon the state was urging him to complete the lower half of the canal (a responsibility incumbent upon those leasing the property), at the same time insisting that the city of Columbia remove water mains it had constructed across that waterway. In 1912, a General Assembly resolution gave Robertson permission to build a much larger dam near the confluence of the Broad and Saluda. This structure, projected to be forty-five feet high, presumably would add another ten feet to the water level in the canal and have locks for passage of boats and fishways. Once more, lawmakers reminded Robertson of his obligation to extend the canal south from Gervais Street to Granby.

But the proposed dam never appeared. Instead, Robertson gained control of a partially constructed hydro-electric plant at Parr Shoals twenty-five miles north of Columbia on the Broad River, and—utilizing rights held by the previous owners—built his dam there. This led in 1915 to a confrontation with U.S. Army engineers, who said they had not been consulted, and protests by those promoting shipping on the Congaree.[2] In 1917, disturbed by these developments, the General Assembly took steps to regain control of the Columbia Canal, alleging that Robertson had failed to fulfill the terms of his lease, i.e., finish building that water-way. During the next thirty-six months, Robertson and his associates, state officials, and various ship owners continued to wrangle. Utility executives offered, under certain conditions, to complete the canal and release water downstream upon request, but no agreement was forthcoming. In 1920, the state of South Carolina seized the canal, only to be told by the U.S. Supreme Court three years later that it had acted improperly. In the 1930s, the South Carolina Public Service Authority was ordered to complete the canal, but never did so. Thus after over a century of dreams, disappointment, and dissension, the Columbia Canal faded from public view, although schemes to make the Congaree navigable would surface again after World War II.

Yet, even though never completed to the state's satisfaction, little doubt exists that for several decades that short stretch of water along Richland County's western boundary was an extremely valuable asset. Actually, the explosion of mill construction that occurred in the 1890s was but one facet of local economic trends. Although agriculture was in the doldrums, during the previous decade new companies had appeared at an ever-increasing rate. In 1880, only twenty were incorporated in all of South Carolina; nine years later, eighty-two were formed, ten of them in Richland County. These included ventures in real estate, granite, furniture, cotton seed oil, banking, wine and vinegar, medicine, chemicals, and phosphates. According to the Charleston News and Courier (4 September 1888), the total trade of Columbia—retail, wholesale, manufacturing, and cotton—had quadrupled since 1880, rising from $2.5 to $9.7 million. This survey indicated that nearly 60,000 bales of cotton were handled locally in 1888, most of them going to mills in New England and Europe, an outward flow that soon would decrease.

The Congaree Manufacturing Company, the first cotton mill within the city limits, was located on Huger Street south of Gervais in a building that formerly housed a bentwood chair factory.[3] This small, steam-powered plant began production in September of 1888. Capitalized with the assistance of Philadelphia investors at $100,000, it was the brainchild of banker A. C. Haskell and two friends, George A. Shields and Frank N. Ehrlich. Some 8,000 spindles were tended by 125 workers who turned out fine yarn used by South Carolina and Georgia manufacturers producing gingham. These employees, supervised by L. A. H. Schwartz, resided in fourteen cottages located on an adjoining lot. However, this mill, like its bentwood predecessor, did not prosper and closed its doors within three years.

But the opening of the long-sought canal, which may well have coincided with the demise of the Congaree Company, cast Columbia's role as a manufacturing center in an entirely new light. By 1910, the city and its southern suburbs were home to seven mills employing 3,600 workers. Most were large operations that, in time, came under the control of northern interests. Two exceptions were the Palmetto Cotton Mill, organized in 1898, and the Glencoe Cotton Mill, which appeared a decade later.

The first, located one-half mile below Union Station, really was a step-child of the Congaree Company, since it began production with much of that defunct concern's machinery. The Palmetto's 280 looms, operated electrically, turned out fancy cotton weaves. In 1907, this mill employed 187 workers and had an annual payroll of $28,000. In the succeeding decade, however, the company experienced financial difficulty and eventually became a unit of Martel Mills that ceased operations in 1930. Ten years later, machinery was removed and the building became a warehouse for Dixie Home Stores. Yet the Palmetto Mill left its mark in textile history. With the aid of flexible machinery, it could, in the words of one contemporary observer, turn out almost anything—handkerchiefs, dress goods, shirtings, broadcloth, and so on. Palmetto was a pioneer in the production of rayon fibers and also developed pajama checks used in making BVDs (Best Value Drawers).

Glencoe, another small mill, was owned largely by the Guignard family, members of which supplied brick for much of the construction going on in the Columbia area during these decades. Heirs to rights to some of the electric power being generated by the Columbia Canal, in 1910 various relatives decided to open this facility in the block bounded by Huger, College, Williams, and Pendleton streets. There some 200 workers produced high-grade twine, warp, and rope for nearly a quarter of a century. Until the Depression of the 1930s, this was a profitable venture, but Glencoe finally closed its doors in March of 1939. The site subsequently was divided into lots and sold at public auction.

Of the remaining mills, two (Richland and Capital City) were relatively small, but the other three (Granby, Olympia, and Columbia) loomed large in the textile world because of construction techniques and innovation and experimentation they brought to that industry. All of these, except Columbia Mills, were the personal creation of a remarkable individual. However, before discussing the work of William Burroughs Smith Whaley, we should look first at that of a transplanted Maryland mill operator, Charles K. Oliver.

In the 1880s, Oliver, trained as a bookkeeper and manager, was able to revive the fortunes of Druid Mills, a debt-ridden producer of cotton duck cloth located near Baltimore, only to discover that a new owner wanted to reward him with a lower salary. Miffed, he cast about for other opportunities; and, after surveying the Columbia area with its horse-power potential, Oliver decided to seek out the same financiers who had helped him rejuvenate Druid Mills. Among them was New Hampshire industrialist Aretas Blood, head of Columbia's water power company and a man familiar with the local scene.

Oliver asked Blood and his associates to loan him a million dollars, $700,000 for capitalization of a proposed duck mill and $260,000 to cover the cost of the canal. Seventy-two hours later, Blood agreed to do so . . . adding that, since he was convinced the sum was an accurate estimate of costs involved, if Oliver had asked for less he would have said no. On 15 January 1893, the *State* announced that a group of northern investors would build a huge mill near the canal. By April of that same year, 300 workmen had begun erecting the massive structure that today houses the South Carolina State Museum. Except for maple flooring five inches thick from Illinois, all of the brick, lumber, granite, and concrete they used was obtained locally.

One innovation was a remarkable heating and cooling system designed to regulate the flow of air by means of fans, which was accompanied by humidity control devices and automatic sprinklers. But, for the most part, attention was riveted upon the General Electric motors that supplied the power to run the mill. As F. DeVere Smith observes, "For the first time in the world, electric motors operated successfully in the propulsion of an entire cotton mill. The most significant feature of the Columbia Mill development was the complete use of electric power throughout. It meant that mills need no longer be located on the banks of streams to utilize water power. It meant that power did not have to be transmitted throughout the mill by belts from a single power source. With independent motors, much smaller shaftings could be used."[4]

In April of 1894, electric current began to flow, and two months later small-scale manufacturing was under way. As production increased, the world's first, electric-powered cotton mill was hailed by New England textile experts in much the same words as those used by Smith. Here, they said, was *true* innovation. No longer would one have to maintain long lines of belting or operate an entire mill when only a small section or perhaps a floor actually was involved in production. Temperature and hu-

"Domestic Science" and Tennis at the Presbyterian College for Women, c. 1911. This school, which opened in the Hampton-Preston Mansion in 1890, merged with Greenville's Chicora College in 1914 and Queen's College (Charlotte) in 1930.

Edwin Wales Robertson (1863–1928).

Main Street, 21 March 1913. The Palmetto Building under construction (left) and just beyond it, Robertson's bank headquarters (the Barringer Building). In the distance is the State House, finally completed after over half a century.

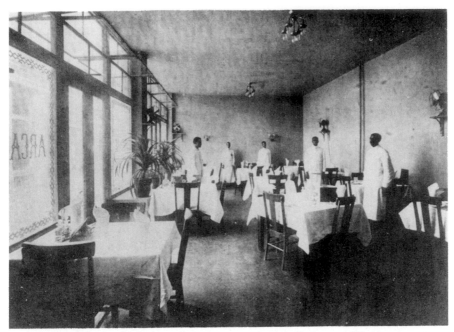

The Arcade Restaurant, 1912. A popular mid-town eating place in a well-known structure built by Robertson, it boasted of forty tables, eleven "polite and accommodating" waiters, and nine cooks and assistants.

A Camp Jackson Postcard, 1917. This facility also might be called a Robertson creation, for Columbia's banker-industrialist led the drive to establish this huge military base.

The Ridgewood Club, built in 1904 in the northern suburbs, became the Columbia Country Club in 1945 and two decades later moved to the Blythewood area.

The Tuesday Afternoon Club, wives of Columbia's black professional men, c. 1911. Front row (left to right), Ethelyn Thompson, Sarah Henderson, Shellie Gantt, Fannie Thompson; second row, Daisy Myers, Charlotte Seabrooks, Belle Vincent, Nell Simkins, Corrine Carroll Frederick; third row, Lydia Biggs, Maude Dillard, Jeanette Poinsette, Olive Shelton, Charlotte Garner, Belle Nix, Lottie Pinckney, Hattie Cornwell, Mittie Pugh.

The Jefferson Hotel, which opened 12 May 1913, long was a center of social, political, and economic life. Located at the northwest corner of Main and Laurel streets, it was replaced by Jefferson Square in 1970.

During the first season (1919), the cast of the Town Theatre, now the nation's oldest community theater, performed at several locations. The troupe subsequently moved to 1012 Sumter Street, where the present quarters were built in 1924.

Unloading 1911 Brush runabouts ($485, FOB Detroit) for the Gregory-Conder Mule Company, 1115 Hampton Street.

Purchased in Appalachicola in 1913, the *Ruth No. 2*—155 feet long—drew 18 inches light and 3½ feet loaded. It had a salon and eighteen staterooms and could carry up to 150 passengers. From 1913 to 1917 it was the flagship of what the *State* called the "Congaree Fleet" plying (sometimes) between Columbia and Georgetown.

Eastover Consolidated School, c. 1915.

All Dressed Up, 1920. Mary Waites Lumpkin (Mrs. Tom Pope) on College Street near where the USC College of Business Administration now stands. Today Capstone would loom in the background.

William Gonzales (1866–1937).

"Big Thursday" in the old wooden bowl at the fair grounds, October 1929. Although Clemson won (32–0), the Gamecocks had a relatively good season—six wins, two losses, and two scoreless ties.

midity control meant mills could be built practically anywhere in the nation, and electricity enabled one to locate them some distance from the source of power.

Workers, whose ranks had risen to 1,200 by 1907, lived across the Congaree in the village of New Brookland. (Originally, this community was christened "Aretasville" in honor of Blood, but that name soon was abandoned.) Like others living in Columbia's burgeoning mill district, they usually were on the job from 6 A.M. to 6 P.M., Monday through Friday, with an hour off for lunch, and worked only a half day on Saturday, 6 A.M. to 11:45 A.M. Average pay, which rose somewhat through these years, was about 75¢ a day in 1902 and $1.10 in 1907.

By 1896, the owners of the Columbia Mills had installed new and still better machinery and increased their supply of electric power. Annual consumption of cotton varied from 18,000 to 20,000 bales, the most used by any local factory. Looms that could weave high quality duck in widths from six to 124 inches turned out products such as sail cloth, as well as rope and twine, that were sold around the world.

According to Smith, the Columbia Mills enjoyed success from the outset, and in May of 1899 the board of directors proposed the addition of a wing that would nearly double floor space and increase consumption to 30,000 bales per annum. However, events in Baltimore, the center of cotton duck production, scuttled these plans. Instead of competing with rival manufacturers, the owners of Columbia Mills agreed to consolidate, on favorable terms, with thirteen other mills to form a trust controlling perhaps 80 percent of all duck produced in the United States. The monopoly thus created, the Mount Vernon-Woodberry Cotton Duck Company, would experience a decade and a half of corporate chaos before the local mill emerged as a separate entity once more. Nevertheless, throughout these mergers and reorganization schemes, the Columbia Mills usually showed a profit and was an important factor in the economy of the Midlands. One secret of this good fortune, in the view of some textile experts, was the optimum size of the operation alongside the Columbia Canal; for, not having expanded in 1899 as planned, this factory and its products were conducive to successful management.

While the Columbia Mills was subject to outside control from the beginning, the cotton empire of W. B. S. Whaley, son of a well-to-do Charleston couple, was based primarily in South Carolina. This fact, as we shall see, may explain some of the problems he faced. During his lifetime, Whaley would design and construct twenty-one cotton mills and numerous business establishments, as well as perfect several new types of engines. Following graduation from Cornell University in 1888 with a degree in mechanical engineering, he began working for a phosphate company in his hometown, but four years later Whaley came to Columbia and hung out his sign as a cotton mill engineer. Then in 1893, he joined forces with Gadsden E. Shand, a University of South Carolina graduate. By the turn of the century, the firm had a local staff consisting of a dozen engineers and draftsmen and a branch office in the heart of metropolitan Boston.

In the early 1890s, Whaley was hired to build mills in Union and Seneca, but only by providing personal leadership was he able to arrange financing for his first Columbia enterprise, the Richland Cotton Mill.[5] In October of 1895, production commenced in this four-story structure located below Union Station between Main and Assembly streets, a building now split up into student apartments. Whaley, who served as president, had a board of directors composed of well-known Columbia businessmen, among them, W. A. Clark, W. B. Lowrance, G. A. Shields, F. H. Hyatt, and R. W. Shand. For reasons not entirely clear, Whaley used steam, not electricity, to power this factory. This decision probably was prompted by realization that the Columbia Mills was using nearly all of the available hydro-electric power; and, with limited resources at his disposal, he was in no position to build his own generating plant. However, within months the Columbia Water Power Company would announce plans to construct a more substantial central facility.

Even before the Richland Mill opened, Whaley had turned his attention to a much larger development, the Granby Cotton Mills. Once more, he served as president, assisted by several of the business leaders associated with his first factory. This new facility, located south of the city limits near the remains of the old Columbia Canal of the 1820s, was designed to use electricity, not steam. It opened auspiciously on New Year's Day of 1897, even though much of the machinery was not in place and the supply of electric power was severely limited.

Within two years, Whaley unveiled plans to build an even bigger factory, the Olympia Cotton Mills, named for Admiral Dewey's flagship at the Battle of Manila Bay. Capitalized at $1.5 million, this grandiose project had virtually the same incorporators, officers, and directors as the Richland Cotton Mill. Olympia, even today an imposing mass of red brick, was built on a 104-acre lot adjacent to the Granby Mill. Power was supplied by its own electric plant, although for a time Whaley considered using that generated by the Columbia Canal. Construction of this large mill caused some concern in Augusta, then the South's leading textile center, when it was realized that Columbia soon would have more spindles than were operating there.

In August of 1899, just as Olympia's foundations were being laid, Whaley headed up a group of local investors who purchased the Columbia Electric Street Railway, Light, and Power Company for $257,500, the same amount that had been offered by a Baltimore syndicate. This gave Whaley access to a power house on the canal and, for a time, tied local transit and textile interests together.

Then, in 1900 the Capital City Mills, Whaley's fourth (and last) Columbia enterprise appeared near the forks of the Atlantic Coast and Southern tracks below the end of lower Main Street. A relatively small operation, this two-story factory used power generated at Olympia and often was singled out as "a gem" of mill design. In this instance, R. B. Jennings served as president, in association with Whaley, W. A. Clark, and B. F. Barnes.

Whaley's four mills had certain elements in common. They all were beautifully constructed, incorporated the most modern machinery and appliances, possessed facilities for the convenience of workers often not found elsewhere (including attractive villages), and turned out superior products. New England executives thought some of these outlays excessive, but their southern counterparts replied such sums might actually be sound investments. Good working and living conditions were needed to attract workers, greater initial expenditures could reduce long-term operating costs, and Columbia's unexcelled building materials at low prices made so-called extravagant fittings quite affordable. In addition, they added, the South often was profiting from the Yankee experience as it built new factories.

Sadly, Mr. Whaley's mills shared one other common feature: undercapitalization. Cash always was in short supply, perhaps a reflection of efforts to raise funds in the South and not in the North as Oliver had done. Granite, brick, wood, and labor were at hand, but machines were not . . . and they were expensive indeed. In June of 1901, as difficulties posed by limited working capital became obvious, the directors of the four mills began to exert financial control. Two years later, the Baltimore selling agents representing Whaley products refused to renew their contract, and early in November of 1903 a single board of directors was elected for all of the mills. Five of the nine men represented northern creditors; and, although Whaley was on the board, he resigned as president and was succeeded by Lewis W. Parker of Greenville.

Table 3. Cotton Manufacturing in Columbia, 1907

Mills	Capitalization	Spindles	Looms	Workers	Annual Payroll
Richland	$ 289,700	26,112	720	350	$ 84,000
Granby	706,300	57,000	1,542	536	135,000
Olympia	2,743,200	100,320	2,250	1,000	246,000
Capital City	293,600	15,000	300	150	36,000
Columbia	700,000	30,740	498	1,200	290,000
Palmetto	137,500	10,000	280	187	28,000
Total	$4,870,300	239,172	5,590	3,423	$819,000

SOURCE: August Kohn, *Cotton Mills of South Carolina*.

In essence, W. B. Smith Whaley, a man F. DeVere Smith describes as "a human dynamo," used his excellent credit to purchase machinery. He then sold the machinery to his mills in exchange for stock and pledged the stock as security for his debts; but, in time, these operations became over-extended. Facing bankruptcy, Whaley sold his spacious Gervais Street residence (now the Dunbar Funeral Home) and withdrew from his Columbia engineering firm, which subsequently became Shand and La-Faye. He then moved to Boston, where, except for one unsuccessful scheme to erect a huge cotton mill in Oklahoma, he devoted his time to building and improving internal combustion engines. Whaley died in New Rochelle, New York, on 17 April 1929, age sixty-three, of complications following an operation for appendicitis. He was buried on Long Island and specifically requested that no stone mark his grave. A man's work, Whaley said, should be his memorial, and his was the mills he had built.

Whaley's successor, Lewis Parker, an Abbeville native who also owned mills in the upcountry, struggled with the Whaley mills for over a decade. Between 1903 and 1914, Parker tried both refinancing and reorganization; but, in the end, he also failed, largely because of heavy borrowing and speculation in cotton futures. Late in 1915, negotiations began that led to the purchase of the Whaley Mills, now known as "the Hampton Group," by Pacific Mills of Massachusetts. The adjusted selling price was $3.2 million, which, by almost any yardstick, was a bargain. Efforts by several stockholders to challenge this sale in court were unsuccessful.

F. DeVere Smith notes in summary that the Whaley Mills represented "the culmination of many years of desire and effort on the part of the people of Columbia to utilize their water power for manufacturing purposes."[6] The cotton factories of the 1890s certainly fulfilled such dreams, but those managing the mills built by Whaley battled against great odds. As noted earlier, working capital never was truly adequate; and, according to Smith, from 1899 to 1915, cotton mill dividends in general declined about 5 to 10 percent before starting to climb once more as a result of market demands arising from World War I. However, these high-level management problems had little direct bearing upon mill communities springing up in New Brookland and along Columbia's southern boundary.

By 1903, nearly 9,000 new residents, mill workers and their families, had moved to this area, lured by the promise of jobs, steady pay, and a better life than they had known. Lola Derrick Byars, mother of author Alvin Byars, recalled vividly what happened in her household.

> My family came down from a farm in the Dutch Fork section of Richland and Lexington counties. We lived on a farm so poor it would grow nothing but rocks, my daddy cut cord wood on the side to buy food. He had heard about the mills opening in Columbia and one day he just decided to load up all our belongings and us onto the wagon and come to Columbia. He drove that old wagon onto the ferry at the Broad River and crossed. We went straight to the Granby Mill Village in 1898 and he went to the mill to get a job. I was 8 years old and worked at the Granby Mill until the Olympia Mill opened and then went to work there. We got one of those nice houses on Fifth Street. I was an experienced worker when I reached twelve years of age and could run eight sides. I had two new dresses and plenty of good food.[7]

It is impossible to know how many other families arrived in Columbia as the result of "snap" decisions, but most came for similar reasons. Also, it is apparent that their children, like eight-year-old Lola Derrick, often worked in the mills, although this practice began to decline after 1907 as a result of state legislation and campaigns waged by social reformers.

This was, of course, a predominantly *white* world that Lola and her family entered in 1898. Few blacks worked in the mills, except to clean up or handle cotton in warehouses, yet their ranks were so numerous at the Whaley Mills that Parker erected a school for black youngsters. In April of 1896, when several Greenville industrialists voiced fears that white labor was becoming scarce, the *State* pondered the question of black workers in cotton mills. By contrast, this daily saw no shortage. It stoutly maintained that mills were "schooling places," and the advantages offered should be reserved for whites. Blacks would create obvious social problems; and, since they could work for less, their presence might lower wages of whites. Besides, the *State* asserted confidently, blacks were healthier, happier, and more useful on plantations out in the country, far from towns and cities.

Despite such sentiments, in July of the following year plans to open a black cotton mill in Columbia were unveiled because, it was alleged, the supply of white labor was dwindling. The Elmwood Manufacturing Company, projected to have white management and black workers, was to be located in the old Congaree factory. However, this scheme eventually collapsed and that property became the home of the Palmetto Cotton Mill.

Although slaves tended machinery in the old Saluda Factory of the 1850s and blacks worked for many years in the penitentiary's hosiery mill (and at a short-lived branch of that operation located in Hopkins in the mid-1890s), both mill workers and their employers resisted efforts to introduce black labor. The reason, according to several contemporary observers, was because black people lacked the "temperament" such work required. This vague assertion never was explained; but, in an age saturated with Jim Crow thought, no explanation was necessary.

Thus the years from 1895 to 1905 were dominated, to a great extent, by factory construction and a sudden influx of several thousand workers, both of which added an entirely new dimension to local life. To "old" Columbia, mill people were an uncouth, rough, quick-to-fight lot, a bunch of lawless red-necks who spurned soap and schooling with equal fervor and tended to assert their independence by moving restlessly from one mill town to another. That this was an over-simplified and often false picture was of little consequence. For a generation or more, the gulf between settled middle class and mill-worker families was wide indeed . . . so wide that it led to a new form of city government in 1910. The commission plan—a mayor and four councilmen elected at large instead of three or four aldermen representing each ward—effectively diluted a mill vote favorable to men such as Jim Tillman and Colie Blease. Nevertheless, most Columbians exulted in a growing population, pointed with pride to "their" mills, and never missed an opportunity to boast of Olympia—"the largest cotton mill in the world under a single roof." Shortly before World War I, for example, the Chamber of Commerce proclaimed, "If the cotton goods manufactured in Columbia during 1913 were put together yard by yard, it would go around the world once and over 11 million yards would be left over!"

Despite such self-praise, leaders of the local establishment, who soon were talking openly of "the mill problem," harbored a deep fear of labor unrest. But this turned out to be a bugbear. Ironically, beginning in 1891 South Carolina's capital city established a tradition of huge Labor Day celebrations complete with parades, speeches, barbecues, baseball games, bicycle races, dances, and even church services, an annual salute to the dignity of work that might last two days. Store clerks, printers, and railroad men had their own unions, and—encouraged by the reformist conviction that *organization* could solve many of society's ills—others followed suit, including mill workers.[8] In the Labor Day parade of 1900, local members of the National Union of Textile Workers formed a double file over a block long. That same day, they helped form a state federation of labor that immediately issued a call for child labor legislation, a state bureau of labor with inspection powers, and reduced working hours.

Whaley, who already had fired operatives simply because of union affiliation, soon swung into action.[9] In March of 1901, the management of the Granby, Olympia, and Richland mills agreed to erect a public hall, library, and school for workers and their families, as well as contribute land for a church and $2,550 toward its construction. But this kindness failed to have the desired effect. So, in August, aware that union members would march in the upcoming Labor Day parade, Whaley issued orders that they work overtime on the two Saturdays *before* that celebration so as to make up hours that would be lost. Believing Labor Day a legitimate holiday, union members ignored threats of suspension if they did not comply; but, on Monday morning following the first "overtime" weekend, they were denied admittance to the mills.

This lock-out led to a union rally and angry words, but police dispatched to the area found the mill district quiet and peaceful. Unfortunately for the local union, which had few funds, in the passion of the moment its leaders began to accept new members. Whaley, in a bid for public support, pointed to the many services his mills provided for workers, noting (with some truth) that few other companies did as much. Management, he said, was "approachable" concerning the issue of the Labor Day parade, but unionism was quite another matter. According to the *State* (27 August), Whaley said bluntly that, as owners, he and his associates proposed to run their mills and would do all they could for those who worked for them: "We do not propose, however, to have any of this unionism business."

Local 211, still unwisely adding members to its rolls, tried desperately to avoid a strike; but, when management refused to talk to union leaders, on 28 August the order was given. Apparently over a thousand individuals heeded this call. The mills continued to run, however, with Whaley claiming three-fourths of his employees were on the job. The *State*, on the other hand, reported that by actual count no more than one-fourth were working. Infuriated by such statements, Whaley cut himself off from the press and scuttled efforts of editor Narcisco Gonzales to mediate this dispute. Meanwhile, within hours of the strike call, union faithful began receiving eviction notices.

On Labor Day, 2 September, all stores were closed as a huge parade wound its way through the streets of Columbia. Prominent in the line of march was Textile Local 211 led by two young ladies in white and some eighty children who worked in various mills. In their wake came several hundred defiant members. In speeches that followed, Mayor Fort Sumter Earle praised the union movement, while deploring strikes, and Governor Miles B. McSweeney, editor and publisher of the *Hampton County Guardian*, boasted of membership in the typographers' union.

In the weeks that followed, the strike simply fizzled out. The national union was unable to lend much assistance, so operatives had to shift for themselves. Some sought jobs elsewhere, especially Augusta, while others yielded to Whaley's demands, renounced the union, and went back to work. Without fanfare, what had been the largest textile local in the world disappeared. On Christmas Day, 1901, loyal workers presented Whaley with a gold watch, and the following September no group representing a textile union marched in the Labor Day parade.

W. B. Smith Whaley obviously won this fight, but it may have been a costly victory. In the process, he incurred the wrath of the press and irritated other mill owners with claims of "an iron-clad agreement" (immediately denied) that no one in the state would hire union workers. Also, forcing this issue at a time when his financial problems were mounting would appear to have been unwise. And, lastly, this confrontation embarked Whaley and his successors upon a fixed policy of out-bidding the unions for worker support.

Nevertheless, the results of that policy were impressive, at least until the Depression years of the 1930s. As president, Lewis Parker was an especially strong advocate of social and recreational facilities. Under his direction, streets were paved, swampy areas drained, windows screened, and sewerage systems installed. More school houses, as well as kindergartens (perhaps the first in the Columbia area), appeared. In 1909, the company built a large YMCA equipped with barber shop, showers, pool tables, bowling alleys, reading room, gymnasium, swimming pool, and theater. Under such conditions, athletics flourished, and basketball and baseball teams sponsored by Parker and Pacific Mills often met those representing local colleges and universities.

A parade and lectures on tuberculosis and flies were features of a YMCA fair held in September of 1912, and two years later, in August of 1914, 350 people attended an Olympia Village suffrage meeting where women appealed for male help in getting the vote and legislation establishing an eight-hour day and compulsory education.

By the 1920s, a community association was both initiating and organizing still more village activities. It would be incorrect to assume that all of these innovations were inspired by fear of unions, for this often was not the case. A worker shortage frequently prompted management to upgrade and improve facilities in the mill district; and, in any event, a healthy, contented labor force was a sound investment.

According to Alvin Byars, there were several brief strikes at the Whaley Mills (1905–1930), usually because of disciplinary action thought unfair or failure to promote qualified workers to better-paying jobs when vacancies occurred. What eventually led to unionization, in his opinion, was neither "outside agitation" nor any desire for added benefits. Instead, the problem was internal. Many workers were fed up with treatment meted out by overseers and other supervisory personnel, petty autocrats who came to view their part of the mill as a private preserve to be run by and for themselves and their cronies. The Wagner Act (1935) cleared the way for collective bargaining, and soon a few men were, in his words, "talking union" at meetings held in Olympia Cemetery, land not subject to the control of Pacific Mills. Finally, in July of 1938 the owners of all of Columbia's major mills agreed to sign union contracts.

Somewhat unexpectedly, Columbia's mill villages had direct impact upon the development of local parks, for Oliver, Whaley, Parker, and their successors set high standards at a time when municipal leaders seemed to be marching to a different drum. Almost from the beginning, New Brookland could boast of a park, school, and lyceum hall, and in 1906 Parker set aside a wooded, 5-acre area near the Olympia-Granby mills as a park and playground. Yet five years later, the Chamber of Commerce stressed the need for parks in Columbia itself: "It is regretted that in the whole of this city there is not a single public seat offered to our citizens or to our visitors where they can rest for a few minutes while walking over our city."[10]

This sad state of affairs had come about largely because of the destruction of Sidney Park in 1899. In June of that year, the Seaboard Air Line Railroad said it had to have that site for terminal facilities. Despite the objections of a few that the park was a well-established feature of municipal life, the city council—urged on by forty businessmen—concluded it was not. In short order, Seaboard paid the city $30,000 to lease the property for an indefinite period and immediately began clearing out trees, shrubbery, and walks that had been carefully tended for half a century at taxpayer expense. Two years later, in September of 1901, following an appeal by Edwin Robertson and two other area residents, a judge ruled this lease improper. Robertson, who was constructing a spectacular mansion atop Taylor's Hill, had been denied an injunction in 1899 when he tried to save the park, and the judge declared that he and his friends were entitled to damages. However, in the next breath, his honor agreed that, since Sidney Park no longer existed, the railroad could stay where it was.

But in July of 1902, Seaboard informed the city that it really did not want that site after all and wished to alter the terms of its lease. Instead of building a retaining wall along Assembly Street and replacing the home of a volunteer fire company that had been razed, railroad executives offered to pay the city to do both jobs. The city council not only rejected this proposal, its members also urged Seaboard to use Union Station that had opened in January of that year. Seaboard declined to do so, saying rights over tracks of rival companies would be too costly. Meanwhile, since the city was about to organize a paid fire department, the question of rebuilding the old firehouse became less relevant.

Late in 1902, Seaboard announced that it wanted to establish a passenger terminal on Lincoln Street near Gervais and tried once more to change the terms of its lease, only to be rebuffed again. Eventually, in March of 1903 a compromise was reached. Seaboard would pay the city $15,000 and build three things: what eventually became the Amtrak station, an additional track adjacent to it, and the Assembly Street wall. In return, the issue of the firehouse was dropped. Subsequently, when a railroad spokesman requested use of municipal grading equipment at the Lincoln Street site, the city said no.

A decade later, Seaboard decided to develop its railroad yard across the Congaree in Cayce and use the Sidney Park area for warehousing. Nevertheless, for the next seven decades that site would be known as "Seaboard Park," although it bore no resemblance to the bucolic loveliness it replaced.

During the years when Seaboard and the city were feuding, a concerted effort was launched to improve the physical surroundings of Columbia and its suburbs. In addition to what was happening in the mill villages and the loss of Sidney Park, this campaign also was fueled by the need to solve obvious urban problems and a national trend known as the "city beautiful" movement. This phenomenon, inspired by the "White City" created at the Chicago World's Fair of 1893, soon had cities such as St. Louis, Washington, and even little Columbia taking stock of their assets and liabilities.

In 1899, local authorities declared war on cellar doors and wooden awnings in the business district, as well as hordes of unregulated peanut stands. Two years later, the city erected two garbage dumps with incinerators and began work on an extensive sewerage system. Construction of that system, which took two years, required the help of some 300 laborers who laid nearly thirty miles of pipe.

Not surprisingly, it was banker-industrialist Edwin Robertson, who, in 1904, took the first concrete step toward solving the "park problem" when he bought a plot at the southwest corner of Laurel and Assembly streets (land adjacent to his home and once part of Sidney Park) and gave it to the city. He subsequently purchased property along Assembly Street from Laurel to Elmwood in 1909 that enabled municipal officials to create what was known for a decade or so as "Robertson Parkway."

By 1904, the year Robertson made his first gift to the city, a Civic Improvement League had been formed. And, on 29 November, F. Wellington Ruckstuhl, the sculptor who was shaping the equestrian statue of Wade Hampton that dominates the inner court of the state capitol complex, addressed this group. His advice, detailed indeed, was to take full advantage of Columbia's natural setting. In his opinion, manufacturing should be restricted to low-lying areas, with homes and stores occupying the plateau. Except for steeples, domes, and spires, no structure should be more than eighty feet high, and each block should strive for a uniform style of architecture. Ruckstuhl expressed regret that Columbia already had a skyscraper, but praised the fact that it was ornamented (finished) on all sides. And, since the Robertson Building existed, he suggested that another be erected on the opposite side of Main Street so as to create a "gateway" to the State House. Each, he added, might be topped with graceful bronze figures.

This gentleman's other recommendations included more parks, trees, and fountains, sand-clay streets (not macadam, "too hot and dusty"), stone curbs, street signs, "beautiful" lamp posts, and uniform garbage collection, with each homeowner having his own iron container.

Telegraph and telephone wires belonged underground, and Columbia should consider building a fine hotel that would attract winter visitors. Ruckstuhl concluded his remarks with this observation: "There was more art, and beauty, and elegance, and refinement in the South in days of yore than anywhere in the country. Why should it not be so again?"[11]

Both Ruckstuhl and Harlan P. Kelsey, a landscape architect who spoke to the same group a year later, praised this community's broad streets, although the latter emphasized overall planning and park land.[12] He deplored surface drainage in the business district and little foot bridges, often dilapidated, that spanned gutters along the edges of streets. In Kelsey's eyes, the Congaree River was Columbia's "most notable landscape feature," and most of the fourteen parks he proposed were somehow tied to that waterway and streams leading into it. The main thrust of his address, however, was to anticipate growth; and, in this instance, he strongly urged formation of a joint commission to facilitate city-state cooperation. Unlike Ruckstuhl, Kelsey thought Columbia's large blocks required alleys and expressed the view that a strict grid system of streets failed to take advantage of land contours.

Ruckstuhl's words led in 1906 to formation of a municipal Tree and Park Commission headed by Edwin G. Seibels, and Robertson, for one, took to heart this sculptor's vision of "dual" skyscrapers. But it was Kelsey who had the greatest impact, for his ideas would permeate any subsequent plan for suburban growth and development.

Two years later, the *State* welcomed the appearance of a temporary bandstand erected at municipal expense on Capitol Square, while calling once more for parks and playgrounds. In 1910, the Rembert Development Company, headed by R. W. Shand and R. C. Keenan, presented the city with 15 acres of land in McCreery's Bottom, the lower end of Rocky Branch, that soon assumed the much grander name of Maxcy Gregg Park. Upstream, closer to Five Points, that same waterway would give birth in 1912 to Valley Park, once the home of Shandon Pavilion.

In 1913, boys ages ten to eighteen were invited to join a City Beautiful Club as it launched a campaign to make Columbia "a spotless town," and a judge ordered municipal authorities to drain LaMotte's Bottom in the old Sidney Park neighborhood so as to alleviate malarial conditions. But the most important development of that year, as far as parks were concerned, was the emergence of Irwin Park, the creation of John Irwin, long chief engineer at the city water works.

Located on Laurel Street near the canal, this site quickly became a favorite rendezvous of local residents. One could take the trolley to the

Gervais Street Bridge and then walk up the canal past the penitentiary's forbidding walls to spacious lawns with curved cement benches and tables. Swans glided across the surface of several little lakes, and a small zoo (evicted from Hyatt Park when neighbors complained of noise) was home to monkeys, camels, ostriches, and other strange and wonderful creatures. A pergola was added in 1916, as well as a gun from the battleship *Maine*. Nevertheless, the president of Rotary International, who visited Columbia that year, chided his hosts for their inadequate park system, less than 1 acre per 1,000 residents, compared to 1 acre per hundred in cities of similar size. In the preceding year, the popularity of Irwin Park led to official segregation of that facility. Blacks were welcome only on Tuesdays and Thursdays, regulations that led, in turn, to a brief protest by those unable to use the park on weekends.

Despite the pleasure Irwin Park brought to many and the attention lavished upon it, during World War I it suffered the same fate as Sidney Park. When thousands of young men poured into Camp Jackson, municipal officials decided that the waterworks would have to be expanded. So, the park was torn up, the gun from the *Maine* dispatched to the State House lawn, and the zoo dismantled. But then peace came so suddenly that the projected expansion never took place. However, in 1919 R. C. Keenan gave the city a large block of land north of town at Smith's Branch, close to the Winnsboro Road and trolley lines, that became Earlewood Park. At about the same time, Hyatt Park, whose fortunes had waxed and waned, was transformed into Victory Park, and on 19 May its owners announced the opening of a new swimming pool. They had, they said, purchased no less than 800 bathing suits, and for only fifty dollars a family could swim for an entire season.

The story of parks in the Columbia area from the 1890s into the 1920s obviously is a tale of one step forward and two steps backward. But by the close of that era, Maxcy Gregg, Valley, and Earlewood parks clearly were established as municipal enterprises, as was Shandon Park on Wheat Street between King and Queen. Victory Park was the only "close in" commercial facility, although several rivals had appeared in more distant suburbs.[13] Public playgrounds were being maintained near a children's clinic adjacent to the Gervais Street Bridge, at Laurel and Pickens, near Howard School in the northwestern quarter of the city, and in Olympia Village.

While national trends stirring interest in parks and playgrounds often were subtle and felt only by a limited number of local residents, the patriotic outpourings of 1898 and 1917 were quite another matter. In May of 1898, following a call for volunteers to fight the Spanish, four small training camps filled with young men from all parts of the state appeared in the Columbia area—Camp Ellerbe (Hyatt Park), Camp Dewey (Geiger's Spring), Camp Fitzhugh Lee (Shandon), and Camp Prospect (Fair Grounds). Only a handful of these individuals ever saw the enemy, and by September some were being mustered out. However, when federal officials expressed interest in moving other troops from colder regions to winter quarters in the South, Columbia's mayor hurried to Washington. The result was a brigade headquarters known as Camp Fornance that housed contingents from Rhode Island and Tennessee. This installation honored a Pennsylvanian, Captain James Fornance, a West Point graduate killed in the Battle of San Juan Hill. The 2,500 men stationed there from November 1898 to February 1899 were transferred from Pennsylvania, and this fact undoubtedly explains how Fornance—a man who perhaps never saw the Midlands—bestowed his name upon one of Columbia's northern suburbs.

The presence of so many young men certainly added zest to the social season. Parades and concerts were held almost daily, and there were tournaments, dances, and sports events such as "roller-skate polo" at the Hyatt Park Casino.[14] Since the commanding officer declined to post guards around the camp, energetic blacks had a field day dispensing pies, fried chicken, and booze. Meanwhile, city officials, irked because Greenville had a *division* headquarters, sought to make Camp Fornance a permanent fixture. Although this campaign failed, the seed had been planted, and in succeeding years they would dream fitfully of greenbacks flowing into cash registers from a large military establishment located on the outskirts of their city. Civic leaders were able to draw some satisfaction from a federal decree in March of 1912 designating Columbia as a "point of war," the mobilization center for South Carolina should an emergency occur.

Three years later, as U.S. relations with Germany deteriorated, Edwin Robertson went to Washington and presented Columbia's case for a camp. In January of 1917, several army officers toured land east of the city; and, following that visit, Robertson and others, confident of success, began acquiring options on property in that area. At one remarkable meeting, the "Cantonment Committee" of the Chamber of Commerce collected pledges totaling over $50,000 in forty-five minutes, with Committee Chairman Robertson contributing $7,000. This banker-industrialist, subsequently honored as "father of Camp Jackson," was so certain of army approval that he already was purchasing material with which to expand his trolley system.

Even before war was declared early in April of 1917, rumors of a camp were rife, and on the 17th the *State* reported that Robertson had acquired rights to 1,000 acres of land lying between the Garner's Ferry and Old Camden roads. Then, about a month later, on 19 May, Major Douglas MacArthur, speaking in Washington, made it official: "Yes, Columbia has been selected as the site for one of our camps, but details concerning how many men will go there, just when they will be sent, and how long they will remain there must come from General [Leonard] Wood in Charleston."[15] In short order, the Hardaway Construction Company of Columbus, Georgia, agreed to build quarters for 30,000 men within ninety days, and in mid-June Major William Couper, the man who would direct this vast operation, arrived in Columbia. Couper's diary, a document resplendent with copies of official correspondence and pithy comment, tells a fascinating story.

Within a fortnight, 2,000 men were busy erecting the first 100 buildings; and, when Couper officially turned the camp over to the U.S. Army on 19 January 1918, he had spent $8,897,435.42. About half of that sum was paid to laborers working ten-hour days. In the process, they used 5,748 carloads of material (3,121 of them lumber) and handled 2,240 railroad cars filled with supplies. Shortly after Couper began, he was told to build a facility capable of handling 40,647 men and 12,247 animals. As fighting progressed, the camp expanded still more and, according to federal estimates, cost $12 million, a figure that includes another installation north of the city that was abandoned when peace came.[16] By that date, Camp Jackson consisted of 1,554 buildings on 2,237 acres, while the total federal reservation surrounding it covered 12,804 acres of sand hill land long thought virtually worthless. The first recruits, many of them from South Carolina, arrived on 1 September 1917, camp population peaked at 44,242 in July of the following year, and over 70,000 young men were demobilized there in 1919.

During his six months in Columbia, Couper had to do battle with plumbers who wanted more pay and shorter hours, workmen who used scarce roofing material as raincoats, rival construction firms that tried to lure labor away to other federal projects (his greatest headache), and conflicting views on salaries.[17] A local congressman badgered him to raise wages, while Frank Hampton urged him to pay less. In Hampton's view, field hands happy to get one dollar a day were receiving four dollars as carpenters simply because they could saw a board "without missing the line more than an inch or so." Couper also tangled with Hampton over rights of way and drainage of swamps near his property.

By mid-summer, he had over 10,000 names on his payroll. "The transformation of the streets of Columbia on Saturday night is a little short of marvelous," Couper wrote on 6 August. "The place now looks like a mining town compared with what it did six weeks ago." Late in October, the major noted with pride that Camp Jackson had the outward appearance of "a city that has always been there." A few days later, when the army staged its first review, Couper remarked that "the biggest impression on the spectators seemed to have been made by the Negro labor battalions—these troops carry picks and shovels on their shoulders instead of guns."

Camp Jackson, officially classified as a "Field Artillery Replacement Depot," also had an airfield, a balloon detachment, and an officers' training school. It was, of course, a wartime phenomenon with military significance, yet this camp's greatest impact was economic and social, various facets of which will be explored later. Suffice to say, sudden transformation of Columbia into "a mining town" brought great joy to the business community. As the *State* observed on 23 May 1919,

> The unvarnished truth is that Columbia, compared with most other Southern towns, was, until lately, poor in money. It had centrality of location, water power, railroad facilities, colleges and schools, and many other advantages, but it is not to be denied that the number of well-to-do businessmen was relatively small; hence the raising of a fund for any public enterprise could only be accomplished by severe straining. All that Camp Jackson has changed; scores of merchants and other businessmen now are on solid ground, whereas a little while ago those not cramped in their operations by lack of capital were few and far between.

Running through this tale of mills, parks, and war camps is a single, unifying theme: the decline of sectionalism and the rise of national feeling. Men who had nothing but disdain for Washington in the 1860s and 1870s were seeking its help to dredge the Congaree in the 1880s, and soon Yankee notions once more could attain a hearing on the banks of that same river. Patriotic ardor glowed bright in 1898 (much to the surprise of some northerners) and reached still greater heights two decades later. As World War I receded from view, factories were booming, cotton was selling for as much as forty cents a pound, and scores were proudly driving the first auto they ever owned. Unlike Ponce de Leon, perhaps the residents of Columbia and Richland County actually had found their "fountain of fortune."

Notes

1. *The City of Columbia and Richland County's Business Directory* (Charleston, 1893), pp. 78–79.
2. Ironically, in 1904 Robertson helped organize the Columbia and Georgetown Steamship Company. Other investors included August Kohn, Ambrose E. Gonzales, John L. Mimnaugh, John J. Seibels, Benjamin F. Taylor, and Lewis W. Parker.
3. See "The Economic Development of the Textile Industry in the Columbia, South Carolina, Area from 1790 to 1916" by Fenelon DeVere Smith (Ph.D. diss., University of Kentucky, 1952). Interestingly, in the late 1940s Smith served as superintendent of schools in the Olympia Mill district before joining the faculty of the University of South Carolina. Much of the material that follows comes from this dissertation.
4. *Ibid.*, pp. 78–79.
5. According to the *State* (21 February 1895), the brickwork on this structure was done by a black contractor, T. J. Bomar, an experienced individual who had built mills in several upcountry towns, among them, Pacolet and Union.
6. Smith, "Economic Development of the Textile Industry," p. 317. The Columbia Mills severed ties to a group of Boston financiers only a few months before some of them acquired the Whaley Mills.
7. Alvin W. Byars, *Olympia-Pacific: The Way It Was, 1895–1970* (West Columbia c. 1981), p. 29.
8. Although factory workers never made the list of "Trades and Unions" published in turn-of-the-century Columbia city directories, these groups did: railroad engineers, firemen, and conductors, carpenters and joiners, typographers, machinists, United Confederate Veterans, Sons of Confederate Veterans, United Daughters of the Confederacy, and the National Society of the Daughters of the American Revolution.
9. For details of this confrontation, see Melton Alonza McLaurin, *Paternalism and Protest: Southern Cotton Mill Workers and Organized Labor, 1875–1905* (Westport, Conn., 1971), pp. 169–74.
10. *State*, 25 April 1911. Of course, there were "pleasure resorts" such as Hyatt, Lincoln, and Ridgewood parks and the Shandon Pavilion, but these were commercial ventures; and, in addition, attractions of this sort seemed to blossom and fade from view rather quickly. *Note:* An earlier counterpart of Hyatt Park, the Schuetzenplatz, located near the intersection of Farrow Road and Colonial Drive, boasted of a shooting gallery, bowling alley, and restaurant. Although sponsored by German merchants, from about 1875 to the 1890s it was the site of picnics and social gatherings for many non-Germans as well.

11. F. Wellington Ruckstuhl, *The Value of Beauty to a City* (Columbia, 1905), p. 12. This was the Civic Improvement League's "Bulletin No. 1."

12. See Kelsey and Guild, *The Improvement of Columbia, S.C. Report to the Civic League* (Harrisburg, Pa., 1905).

13. William Couper, who visited Dent's Pond [Forest Lake] on 29 July 1917, describes that swimming resort as "quite a place. Entirely surrounded by woods, it lies at the foot of a dam, which impounds a considerable lake. The edge of the pond has been lined with a concrete wall and there are bath houses. A beautiful spot, especially on a hot day." Couper, whose unpublished diary is at the South Caroliniana Library, was in charge of the construction of Camp Jackson.

14. President William McKinley, several cabinet members, and General Joe Wheeler (who got the greatest applause) were serenaded by the Second Tennessee Band when they stopped briefly in Columbia on 19 December 1898.

15. *State*, 20 May 1917. "Columbia," this daily said proudly, "displaying the pluck that has ever characterized her efforts, has again scored a victory."

16. According to the *State* (2 December 1918), the North Columbia Cantonment was being build by 1,800 Puerto Ricans hired by the Hardaway Construction Company. Congress had appropriated $11 million for this project, which was about 25 percent completed when the war ended.

17. Mill executives, exasperated when workers quit to go to better-paying jobs at Camp Jackson, threatened to evict families from their homes, even if other members continued in their employ.

Boom, Bust, and a New Deal

CHAPTER SIXTEEN

The years leading up to the first World War were good times in Richland County. Population rose from 45,589 in 1900 to 78,122 in 1920. As the result of a black exodus to the North, especially during the war itself, three-fourths of this increase (24,110) was white, giving the county a slight majority of white residents for only the second time since census taking began in 1790. In 1920, the number of individual farms reached an all-time high of 3,889, two-thirds of them tenant operated. During the decades between 1900 and 1920, hog, horse, and mule population on those farms nearly doubled, as did the annual production of cotton, up from 14,213 to 26,690 bales. Most impressive, however, was the dramatic increase in the estimated value of farm land and farm buildings—$2.4 million in 1900, $5.1 million a decade later, and $18.4 million in 1920. Meanwhile, city population, augmented by annexation, rose during the same period from 21,108 to 37,524, and Columbia's new skyscrapers and cotton mills, obvious bastions of power, also reflected an aura of stability and well-being.

Against this background of general prosperity, war came in April of 1917, and its most powerful manifestation on the local scene was the huge training camp that appeared almost overnight just east of Columbia. Camp Jackson was one of several major installations in South Carolina that included Camp Sevier (Greenville), Camp Wadsworth (Spartanburg), and various naval facilities in the Charleston area. However, unlike Sevier and Wadsworth, from the outset Columbia's cantonment exuded an air of permanence—hundreds of wooden structures and printed records instead of tents and mimeographed materials. Camp Jackson soon had its own newspaper, theaters,[1] sports teams, and recreational facilities, as well as Emerson Flying Field (named for Lieutenant William Emerson, the first field artillery observer killed in action) and a base hospital that at the height of the influenza epidemic of 1918 was caring for 6,000 patients.

In December of 1917, however, just as this hospital was taking shape, 245 cases of spinal meningitis forced military authorities to make use of Columbia's Baptist Hospital. For a few weeks, a strict quarantine was in effect. Soldiers were restricted largely to their quarters, fed in the open air from side doors of their canteens, and cautioned to limit personal contact as much as possible. Posted placards spread this message: "If you wash before you eat, it will keep you well and make you neat." Early in 1918, the dread disease spread to Columbia. Schools, theaters, dance halls, pool rooms, and even churches were shut tight throughout much of February. Requests to import liquor for "medicinal purposes" from other states soared when as many as three hundred people a day sought the only means possible of obtaining what they hoped would ward off disease. (South Carolina had become legally "dry" on 1 January 1916.)

Early in the life of Camp Jackson, local citizens were stirred by government programs to "clean up" Columbia. Targets included not only meat markets, restaurants, and barber shops but also Gates Street (now Park), long this city's red light district. Such reforms were, in fact, the price communities paid for the privilege of hosting military and naval installations during World War I. Late in July of 1917 as the city council discussed outright suppression of prostitution, five hundred individuals—many of them businessmen—petitioned for mere "restrictions," arguing that campaigns to outlaw vice always failed. But the army remained firm, even threatening to abandon Camp Jackson, and the ordinance passed. So, on 27 July, according to the *State*, police told ninety-nine women living in "recognized" houses to cease their activities by 1 August.

A few weeks later, an article in *Survey* (18 August 1917) took a quick look at conditions in Columbia. Church women, it said, had offered to help any of 115 prostitutes living in twenty-one houses who wanted "to start life again." Two had accepted. Some presumably were leaving town, and others said they were planning to open boarding houses.[2] A *Survey* reporter met an elderly gentleman on Main Street who was much exercised by these developments: "I'm going to buy a pistol, sir. For twelve years I've lived in this town and never felt the need to protect my womenfolks. What do you suppose will happen when 40,000 virile, red-blooded young men come here to train for the army and find the segregated district wiped out? I know; and I'm going to buy that pistol, sir, and do it now!"

During these same weeks, a behind-the-scenes battle was raging over plans to send black soldiers to Camp Jackson. Senator Tillman, who happened to be in town, said such matters were up to the United States Army. After all, he added, you have your camp and may have to take "disagreeable things along with the good." Despite protests, blacks came, largely as labor battalions. In July of 1918, for example, there were 6,704 black enlisted men at the camp (compared to 35,562 white soldiers), and the following month their ranks reached a peak of 7,795.

As expected, the army got its way. In addition, the U.S. Public Health Service quickly enforced malaria control measures in the Columbia area and introduced standard practices for handling food, such as wrapped bread. Bakers, who no longer could get waxed paper, were told to use ordinary paper, although local authorities refused to lift a 1911 ban on ice cream cones, fearful small, unlicensed shops would use them. In time, no soldier could patronize any barber shop or restaurant not approved by federal officials.

Looking at the total war (1914–1918), one is struck by the economic crisis that engulfed South Carolina following the outbreak of hostilities. For a few months at least, this state found itself awash in cotton when normal sales channels were thrown into disarray. The temporary solution was a "buy-a-bale" campaign, the goal being for individuals to purchase cotton and keep it off the depressed market for a time. Winthrop students, circus performers, even stage actresses in Columbia for only a few days purchased bales, and in October of 1914 legislators met in emergency session and limited cotton production to one-third of all arable land. However, the market soon stabilized. Even before spring planting in 1915 the recently decreed limits were rescinded, and the great wartime boom was on.

At the outset, local matters such as the cotton crisis and a hot gubernatorial race overshadowed what was happening in Europe, although city and county residents always were partial to the Allied cause. Major events of the next few years included increased support for women's suffrage by both sexes at occasional rallies, precedent-breaking bond issues for roads and schools, and the demise of Ben Tillman's dispensary system with the advent of Prohibition.[3] Only about one-third of Richland County's qualified voters cast ballots in the liquor referendum of September 1915, but those who did voted "dry" by a 2–1 margin. Nevertheless, certain areas such as Spring Hill, Blythewood, and Ballentine went "wet," and the contest was close in Olympia, Eastover, and city wards one and five. Since dispensary profits long had supported education, this meant new revenue had to be found, hence the bond issues of that decade.

The actions of Mayor Lewis A. Griffith, a Blease partisan elected in 1914, caused concern among critics who the following year instigated a recall campaign. Griffith's pardoning policy and tendency to refund fines raised hackles, as did his presence at a ruckus in a Gates Street bordello. His honor claimed he was there making an inspection tour as head of the police committee, a position from which he was summarily removed by the city council. During an inquiry into this matter, a police officer was asked if he saw the mayor at the scene. When he answered in the affirmative, the next question was, what did he do? Answer: "I saluted and left."

Despite such confrontations, Griffith served out his four-year term, and in September of 1914 voters rejected by a 4–1 margin a proposal to abolish commission government. The big news of that year was creation of a regional Federal Farm Loan Bank headquarters in Columbia and growing uneasiness as area residents became aware of black flight to better-paying jobs in northern factories turning out goods for the European powers. A few weeks before America went to war, Mayor Griffith, convinced that someone was furnishing blacks with railroad tickets to Philadelphia, asked police to investigate and find out who was responsible for the departure of so many able-bodied workers.

On the eve of hostilities, four Reserve Officer Training Corps companies appeared at the University of South Carolina, and on 5 April 1917 the city staged a huge "Preparedness Day" parade headed up by Confederate veterans, Girls of the Sixties, and the UDC. They were followed by firemen, Boy Scouts, national guardsmen, school children, fraternal orders, business organizations, the Pacific Mills Band, Plumbers Union # 227, college students, women's clubs, and groups representing the Red Cross, YMCA, and post office employees. Despite rain, some fifteen thousand people participated in a patriotic outburst resplendent with choruses of "Dixie" and American and French flags. Three days before, across the Congaree, two hundred residents of Lexington County gathered at the courthouse to protest U.S. entry into World War I.

The immediate impact of war—other than the spirited campaign to secure a large army camp—was a rush to be part of the patriotic effort to save democracy. Black leaders assured Governor Manning that their people were eager to help, local women (led by Mrs. Julius H. Taylor of 18 Gibbes Street) initiated a program to grow vegetables in vacant lots, police promised to enforce vagrancy laws in order to secure labor, and early in June all males born between 1886 and 1896 registered for the draft.[4] By August, despite a rush to complete new apartment houses, accommodations were scarce, and a room registry had been established at 1211 Gervais Street. With the arrival of soldiers, military police appeared in

Columbia, and a Travelers' Aid office was organized to assist both service-men and their families. In October, the opening of the Columbia Cafeteria at 1607 Main Street, the city's first, was accompanied by ads explaining just what a "cafeteria" was.

The winter months (1917–1918) were dominated by shortages of all kinds, federally mandated prices for basic foodstuffs (rice, meat, sugar, grits, and eggs), a spinal meningitis scare, and the coldest weather in two decades. To conserve coal, many commercial establishments instituted "heatless" Mondays, and those in charge of Camp Jackson discovered they had to reinforce the floors of hastily constructed barracks because all of the occupants crowded to one section—the area near the stove. Military authorities commandeered 250 woolen shirts from local stores on the last day of 1917; and, when high winds wrecked telegraph lines, the *State* (13 January) published this tongue-in-cheek headline: "OUTSIDE WORLD CUT OFF FROM COLUMBIA."

On Washington's Birthday, 3,000 men from Camp Jackson's 81st Division marched down Main Street, the first of many such parades. With warmer weather, war bond rallies featuring celebrities such as Charlie Chaplin and William Jennings Bryan became commonplace. Meanwhile, on 31 March, as a wartime measure, local residents turned their clocks ahead one hour to Daylight Saving Time, an innovation said to have been used successfully in Europe to conserve energy. In June, war savings-stamp campaigns began in earnest, with whites soliciting whites and blacks soliciting blacks. On the 30th, thirty-five automobiles loaded with whites and twenty filled with blacks set out from the State House on what were called "Paul Revere Rides," on-the-spot appeals to boost stamp sales throughout Richland County. During that same month, as a patriotic gesture, Columbia College eliminated German language classes, and the city council passed a "disloyalty" ordinance. Anyone convicted of disloyalty and a breach of the peace could face a $100 fine or thirty days in jail. Also, soda fountains, unable to get sugar, milk, and ice, began to close, and restaurants served notice that customers faced "meatless" menus.

In August, citizens were asked to forgo Sunday driving to conserve fuel and to save peach stones, prune and date pits, and coconut shells needed in the manufacture of gas masks. The Fourth Liberty Loan parade held late in October was marred by tragedy. Airman Louis K. Godman, who was scattering appeals to buy bonds ("We are offering our lives! It's up to you to offer your money!"), crashed to his death in the backyard of an Assembly Street lot, although a companion escaped with minor bruises. A couple of weeks later, peace came with alarming suddenness, ending a massive effort that only in November of 1918 seemed about to shift into high gear. Within a dozen weeks or so, the population of Camp Jackson had dwindled to 15,000 and demobilization was under way.

This cursory view of the home front should not obscure truly important developments. These include expansion of agriculture to meet wartime needs, data gleaned from draftees concerning social conditions, and the relative prominence of women and blacks in the war effort. The cotton boom, of course, led to disaster in the decade that followed, but information about the health, intelligence, and educational levels of young Americans was valuable indeed. (The *State* was quick to point out in January of 1918 that the rate of feeble-mindedness among South Carolina draftees at Camp Jackson was only thirteen per thousand, compared to sixteen and one-half per thousand among those hailing from Tarheel land.) But epidemics of those years probably had greater impact than statistics as Americans came to realize that measles, spinal meningitis, and especially influenza had little respect for social and racial barriers.

Women of both races participated in Red Cross activities, organized social centers for servicemen, picked cotton, tended "victory" gardens, sold war bonds and savings stamps, and took on scores of tasks usually performed by men. The Equal Suffrage League sponsored a community cannery on Lady Street that for two years processed fruit and vegetables sold to Baptist Hospital, the university, and Camp Jackson. In 1918 alone, these women canned nearly 13,000 quarts of foodstuffs. Two years later, under the direction of Mrs. C. Y. Reamer (a lawyer), some of these same individuals formed a local unit of the League of Women Voters. Their initial program included how-to-vote classes at the university, as well as reporting "questionable" houses and whiskey dealers to the police.

Prominent blacks saw the war as an opportunity to improve the status of their race by playing an expanded role in local affairs, and whites, uncertain how long hostilities would last, welcomed their help. The story of black participation in the war effort will be explored more fully in a later chapter, but the patriotic fervor displayed by blacks and the frequency with which the governor, mayor, and military leaders addressed predominantly black meetings underscores what was happening. For example, "The Birth of a Nation" was shown in Columbia in 1915 and 1916 with little outcry concerning its stern racist message. Two years later, when that so-called photoplay was about to return, blacks objected, and the city council quietly voted, in effect, to ban the film lest it "stir up" racial feeling. And a few days before peace came, Western Union, noting it could find no white messengers, announced that black youths had been hired to deliver messages. The manager of the local office said an Allen University graduate was serving as captain of the group and that blacks fourteen to eighteen years of age already were working in a similar manner in Charleston, Atlanta, Savannah, and Jacksonville.

A roster of military and naval personnel published in 1929 indicates that nearly 3,400 Richland County young people donned uniforms during World War I—2,033 whites (including perhaps twenty army nurses and a handful of navy "yeomanettes") and 1,350 blacks. Of that number, sixty-two whites and forty black youths died while serving their country.

The world that veterans of that brief conflict returned to was somewhat different from the one they left. For the first time in history, according to the 1920 census, the United States was an urban nation; and, although this statistic by itself meant little, during the decade that followed national policies favored business and industry, not agriculture. It was an *urban* vision of America that dominated daily life, and newspapers, movies, radio, the auto, new highways, and consolidated schools all conspired to make country more like city. Yet, as the result of a sharp agricultural downturn in the wake of war, these factors had limited influence upon the local scene. To put it bluntly, except for foodstuffs and bare necessities, hundreds of families living in Richland and surrounding counties seldom could buy what Columbia merchants were trying to sell, nor could poorly paid mill workers of the city's southern and western suburbs. In 1930, for example, only one out of five Columbia households had a radio, and receiving sets obviously were found even less frequently in outlying communities such as Eastover and Blythewood. During that same year, half of the rented homes in this area cost occupants less than $15 a month. The number of Richland County farms dropped from 3,889 in 1920 to 2,787 in 1930, the value of their land and buildings from $18.4 to $7.9 million. Only 8,032 bales of cotton were produced in 1930, compared to 26,690 a decade earlier.

But it was not only rural distress that set the Midlands apart from the mainstream of the Roaring Twenties. Many of the great questions of the day, from the local perspective, were non-issues—things such as the Red Scare, Christian Fundamentalism, racism, the Ku Klux Klan, immigration quotas, and even Prohibition. Richland County had few (if any) card-carrying Communists, virtually no foreign-born residents (only 1.4 percent in 1930), and little need of Klan assistance in formulating racial attitudes. Religious life, perhaps neither as relaxed as Charleston nor as rigid as Greenville, was robust enough. According to a 1916 survey, 74 percent of Richland County residents over the age of ten were church members. Baptists led off with a total of 15,884 (12,479 of them black), followed by 9,301 Methodists (3,878 black), and far behind, each with less than 1,600 faithful, came Lutherans, Episcopalians, Presbyterians, and Catholics in that order. A decade later, Columbia alone had eighty-seven churches, fifty of them white, thirty-seven black.

As for Prohibition, having wrestled with Demon Rum for decades, residents of Columbia and Richland County probably were sick-unto-death of schemes to regulate drinking habits. Stills certainly existed in city, suburb, and swamp, and illicit whiskey often was transported throughout the Midlands over new and improved highways. Local newsmen became so jaded that they shortened Prohibition to "Prohi," and in 1928 county Democrats almost came to blows before finally endorsing a "dry" plank, 188-155.[5] Yet the previous year, during a stern lecture to Columbia's finest, Mayor L. B. Owens warned policemen to cease rude conduct and quit drinking while on duty. Since his honor won re-election several times and served until his death in 1941, this tolerant attitude evidently had wide support. Syndicated columnist Robert Quillen noted in his *Fountain Inn Tribune* (17 April 1930) that a Columbia bootlegger was arrested after he tried to advertise his services in the *Record*. A judge agreed to release him providing he left town . . . "we don't want your kind in Columbia." "The kind Columbia wants," quipped Quillen, "apparently is the kind that doesn't advertise." Then in February of 1931, Quillen told of sitting in a Columbia hotel lobby and watching as a maid struggled with a heavy hamper filled with "empties gleaned from the night's harvest of whoopee."

Most of these policies such as restrictions on immigration and booze were directed at the national level by business-minded men, Harding, Coolidge, and Hoover, all Republicans. As soon as the Democrats took over in the early 1930s and Franklin D. Roosevelt turned his attention to agricultural problems and recovery, any sense of alienation this region was experiencing quickly vanished.

Nevertheless, it would be wrong to conclude that the siren song of business growth was absent from the banks of the Congaree during the flapper age. The Chamber of Commerce never lost an opportunity to sing the praises of Columbia, and at a booster-night rally held early in 1921 six hundred individuals repeated a "good citizens' pledge." Each of those present, after promising to double their effort, enlarge their vision, and dream dreams, concluded this oath to progress with these words: "Thus today, on the threshold of a new era, while timorous peer doubtfully into the future, we take heart and, not content to wait for better times, proceed to make them."[6] To accent this theme, the *Record* added an ambitious slogan to its pages—"100,000 Columbians by 1930," and two hundred "Minute Men" were organized by the Chamber of Commerce to promote the city. It appears, however, that "promotion" in this instance meant hurrying vagrants out of town and forcing white prisoners to work on streets and roads instead of languishing behind bars.

Sadly, during the 1920s dreams were more common than solid accomplishments. Campaigns to establish a radio station and an airport made little headway until 1930, a war memorial auditorium that was supposed to cost $400,000 did not appear on the university campus until 1935 (and then in much reduced form), and another thirty-five years would pass before Columbia's population reached the 100,000 mark. As early as 1922, local boosters were seeking financial support for a radio station, and the *Record* began publishing a column of programs beamed from faraway points such as Pittsburgh (KDKA) and Newark (WJZ). Four years later, a 1,000-watt operation—WCU, "Wonderful Columbia Unlimited"—was scheduled to appear, but its place was usurped by WBBZ, a short-lived project staged by the Junior Chamber of Commerce on the roof of the Jefferson Hotel. At one point, the county secured $35,000 in state funds for this purpose, but the city council (reluctant to assume the expense of running a station) decided to use it instead for baseball facilities at Dreyfuss Field, thus replacing stands at the fair grounds that had burned.[7] Then, early in 1929, with the assistance of the *Record*, WBRW (another brief experiment) began Sunday afternoon broadcasts from a new Masonic Building erected in 1922. Finally, in 1930 WIS ("Wonderful Iodine State") appeared and became a permanent fixture on the Columbia scene. This strange name was a salute to a brief and somewhat embarrassing scheme to promote the iodine content of South Carolina soil, a slogan that also was featured on license plates for a year or so.

Except for a new post office completed in 1920 (now the home of South Carolina's Supreme Court) and the Calhoun Building (the first state office complex, erected in 1926), few structures of any consequence were built in Columbia during the decade. Chicora College began a $2-million campus in Shandon but, after putting up a few homes for professors and no classrooms, abandoned the project, moved to Charlotte, and merged with another Presbyterian school for young ladies, Queen's.

With a single important exception, to be discussed shortly, all of the major construction seen in the Midlands during the 1920s was somehow related to the automobile—paved streets, better highways, new bridges, and so on. The State Highway Department, established in 1917, would not be a key player in this story until after the tempestuous $65-million bond battle of 1929–1930. However, throughout the 1920s, this new arm of the state government was growing ever stronger, and counties often furnished department personnel with funds raised locally and asked them to build the desired facilities. In this fashion, highways such as U.S. 1 took shape as it crossed Richland County from Camden to the Congaree River, where a handsome new span appeared, as well as another over the Wateree on what is now Highway 76 en route to Sumter. The latter, which cost $210,000, was officially opened in July of 1923 at ceremonies held in both Eastover and Stateburg. Some 10,000 people heard speeches, ate barbecue, and then cheered as a chain was forged symbolizing inter-county unity and friendship. The Congaree structure, which cost nearly three times as much, welcomed traffic informally amid discord in November of 1927.

This bridge, a memorial to men of two counties who served in World War I, was quietly put in use without fanfare on Armistice Day. The problems were two in number—disagreement over who would (a) pave the Richland County approach and (b) pay for the electric lights on that span. The first issue apparently solved itself when a temporary surface proved satisfactory; however, only an act of the 1930 General Assembly dispelled the darkness. According to the *Record* (28 April 1929), the state had spent over $12,000 on an electrical system for the bridge but failed to provide for current, and for two-and-one-half years neither the highway department nor Richland County would assume that responsibility. Finally, on 23 April 1930 in an elaborate ceremony (too much so, really), bands played as the lights on the Congaree Bridge beamed for the first time and the structure also was bathed in floodlights.

Local businessmen, eager for customers, gave wholehearted support to fledgling, inter-city bus companies. In July of 1921, when service opened to the Saluda area, they crammed into fifty automobiles and escorted the first bus from Columbia to Lexington, Batesburg, and other communities along the way. Soon other lines were reaching out to Winnsboro, Bishopville, and Sumter, and by November of 1924 one could leave twice daily for Charlotte and Augusta from a terminal at 1519 Sumter Street. A year later, buses capable of carrying twenty-nine passengers appeared, and by 1926 twenty-five buses were arriving and departing from Columbia each day. Until November of that year, all patrons were white. When blacks applied for permission to establish a line of their own to Laurens, the highway department informed the applicants, much to their surprise, that buses were public carriers and, as such, open to both races.

The impact of autos and buses was especially pronounced in Columbia itself. During the opening years of the decade (1921–1923), the Chamber of Commerce staged "Palmafesta" (Palmetto State Festival), which was basically a spring auto show enlivened by a baby parade, coronation of a queen, concerts, and other attractions. And the seasonal stream of out-of-state cars along U.S. 1 to and from Florida (often called "foreign" vehicles by local businessmen) revived interest in the tourist dollar. This time, however, the goal was not to become a resort à la Aiken or Camden but merely to profit from this traffic. The Colonia Hotel opened in 1907 at Hampton and Pickens street as a winter haven for wealthy northerners, it might be noted, never prospered, while the commercially minded Jefferson, erected at 1801 Main Street in 1913 at a cost of $250,000, long was a center of business and social activity.

The first step in this campaign was organization of a motor club in the summer of 1922, followed by appeals for facilities that could win the endorsement of the American Automobile Association. In addition to garages and service stations, these included inexpensive (or free) accommodations, and for a time community leaders considered establishing a campground at Valley Park. Finally, in the summer of 1926 the Better Columbia Tourist Camp opened on the Camden road near the city limits. Its eight cottages could hold up to twenty-two people, and there also was a bath house, shoe shop, garage, filling station, and manager's residence; however, the success of this little village soon inspired others to cater to the needs of travelers. As the *Record* observed early in 1929, municipal camps were a necessity at the outset, but the future clearly belonged to their more opulent commercial rivals.

The twenties also brought non-curb filling stations (1920), numbered highways (1921), and Columbia's first traffic lights (1925), as well as one-hour, angle parking in the city's business district following a brief experiment with center-street parking (also in 1925). The following year, buses were permitted on Main Street for the first time, and the city council decided to shelve plans for an auditorium-civic center in favor of still more paved streets. At about the same time, Columbia got its first stop signs.

But increased use of autos and buses led to a dramatic transportation crisis. In March of 1927, the Broad River Power Company, which two years earlier had acquired the beleaguered street railway system, discontinued service. Nine months later, the city bus company, long subsidized by street railway interests, went bankrupt, leaving the community without public transit facilities. Within six weeks, municipal authorities were able to put together a makeshift operation, while at the same time launching a court battle that eventually restored trolley service from 1931 to 1936. Although few would dispute Broad River's claims that the trolley was a losing proposition, that company certainly did everything possible to hasten its demise. At the same time, the city never came to grips with the problem of jitneys (free-lance taxis) that were the bane of both trolleys and buses.

Yet, if this large utility lost friends during the transit dispute, it gained many more through close association with the vast construction project that produced Lake Murray.[8] This undertaking, by far the largest seen in the Midlands during the decade, cost $20 million and provided employment for some 3,500 men, who, in April of 1927, began clearing 65,000 acres of land northwest of Columbia. There, within three years, they erected a huge dam creating what was then one of the world's largest power reserves.

In the opinion of William E. Gonzales, editor of the *State*, the timing could not have been better. His correspondence reveals that he was deeply troubled by conditions in South Carolina during the opening months of 1927. Bank failures, in his view, had drained the spirit out of the Midlands, and the mental attitude of the region was "quite depressed," much worse than the financial picture actually warranted, he thought. On 3 June, writing to poet Archibald Rutledge, Gonzales remarked in passing that the power development on the Saluda River should dispel some of this malaise. It probably did; however, by the time electricity was being generated in the early 1930s, the Great Depression had set in and few could buy it.

The observations of Gonzales are supported by several disturbing trends such as large structures planned but not built and municipal funds shifted from one project to another, as well as numerous undertakings delayed, reduced in scale, or abandoned entirely. The near-frantic efforts of Columbia merchants to peddle their wares reveal that, for them, this was no carefree, high-stepping age. Thanks to the boll weevil and rural poverty, the twenties did not "roar" very loudly in the Midlands. County population increased less than 10,000 during the decade, only from 78,122 to 87,667, that of Columbia from 37,524 to 51,581, largely because city fathers annexed part of North Columbia in 1925 and assorted eastern and southeastern suburbs in 1926–1927. The latter included the Chicora College site near Harden and Wheat streets, Rose Hill, Hollywood, Capital Heights, Rosewood, Kilbourne Park, and Heathwood . . . in short, lands adjacent to Shandon, an area bounded roughly by Trenholm and Milford roads and Rosewood and Forest drives.[9]

Despite hard times, forces let loose by World War I such as health concerns and the new activism of women and blacks continued to be felt. The Ridgewood Tuberculosis Camp, organized in 1913 by Trinity Church women, by the close of 1921 had expanded to thirteen buildings with fifty-three beds, one-third of them for blacks. In that same year, Columbia Hospital became a county institution. This facility, organized by King's Daughters in 1892, had prospered since being taken over by twenty-six doctors in 1909, as had the Knowlton Infirmary, which became Baptist Hospital in 1914. In the 1920s, blacks were served by two small hospitals—Good Samaritan at 1508 Gregg Street and a sanatorium known by various names such as Waverly and Benedict.

More to the point, perhaps, was the beginning of public health units in Richland County in 1915 and in Columbia in 1921, as well as both local and state conferences. In July of 1921, for example, Blythewood mothers attended a "Better Baby" meeting, and six months later a week-long "Health Institute" was held in a Columbia theater. At a YWCA health contest held in April of 1922, Elizabeth Cowen was judged to have the city's most perfect foot, while Jessie Freeman took top honors for posture. As early as 1920, Columbia was staging an annual campaign to aid its Associated Charities (organized in 1900), YMCA, YWCA, Travelers' Aid, Door of Hope, Boy Scouts, and Red Cross. In March of 1925, a dozen such groups launched the city's first Community Chest drive.

The role of the county in hospitals and welfare activities demands a bit of explanation. The formal structure of Richland County government changed little during these decades, and outside of Columbia and its environs the region remained essentially rural. However, in 1890 the board of commissioners set up in 1868 lost power to the local delegation to the General Assembly when voters agreed to amend the state constitution. Thereafter, what had been an elective body was appointed by the governor. This change, in effect, gave the Richland County legislative delegation *de facto* control of community affairs, especially in the fields of finance and taxation. Thus, as matters of a communal nature arose— health, hospitals, schools, and libraries—there was a tendency to seek their assistance, hence county involvement became increasingly apparent in various aspects of daily life. In February of 1921, there even was talk of building a joint city-county administrative center.

By the early twenties, scores of local women were entering professions once closed to them. Columbia had a handful of female lawyers (Lester & Pierce being the state's first all-woman legal firm), a dental hygienist, osteopath, chiropractor, two interior decorators, and a photographer. The latter, Lelia Linder, a Lexington native, had begun studio work in Columbia in 1917. In 1922, women were delegates to the county Democratic convention for the first time, female golfers were testing their skills on the Ridgewood links, and in 1924 the old Civic Improvement League was transformed into the Woman's Club. Four years after that, Bessie Rogers Drake, wife of the Chicora College bursar and a Bennettsville native, was elected to Columbia's school board, the first woman to hold public office in the capital city.

Even before these pioneers began blazing new trails, numerous young ladies—often graduates of Columbia High School with a smattering of commercial training—were becoming secretaries in Main Street business offices. Christie Powers Zimmerman tells in *Receipts and Recollections* (1977) of her experiences on the eve of World War I with cotton broker M. C. Heath. She departed for work, she writes, with the admonitions of two elderly aunts ringing in her ears: "Be ladylike but not *aloof* [and] *never* step into an elevator crowded with men."

Although blacks lost leverage when peace came, in hard times they were valued as potential customers, and the *Record* was especially willing to publish news of their community. Baptist preacher I. E. Lowery, born a slave in Sumter County, contributed hundreds of articles and columns to that afternoon daily in the 1920s. Also, the rise of jazz was earning blacks a special status in the entertainment world. Ethel Waters, W. C. Handy, and Bessie Smith were among notables who performed in Columbia during these years. Interestingly, such shows at first played only to black audiences in the city's most prestigious *white* theaters, but soon white admirers took over the main floor, relegating blacks to balconies. More important than rhythm and blues and seating arrangements were functioning inter-racial committees, a hangover from the war years, and the fact that the term "race relations" had entered the local lexicon, supplanting what long had been known as "The Negro Problem."

Then came "Black Thursday" (24 October 1929), that memorable day when a turbulent stock market announced the beginning of a new age. But few area residents were listening. Only a handful had the wherewithal to dabble in stocks and bonds; and, of much greater importance, *that* was "Big Thursday" at the state fair, the annual clash between USC and Clemson, which the latter won, 21–14.

There were still other reasons why Columbia and Richland County tended to discount the bleak economic news that followed . . . at least for a year or so. To begin with, cotton mills and agriculture had been in trouble ever since the World War I bubble burst, so any business reversal had little immediate effect in those realms. In fact, the agricultural picture actually improved a bit in 1929, and farmers got more for their crops than they would at any time in the next ten years. In addition, South Carolina's capital had a diversified economy—a mix of assorted industries (none dominant), government offices, schools, colleges, and transportation facilities—that, for a time, got along reasonably well. Civic leadership, in the opinion of Paul S. Lofton, Jr., a scholar who has studied the city during the 1930s with great care, was strong and enjoyed the cooperation of able spokesmen in the black community.[10]

In 1930, Columbia was the center of a trading area with some 500,000 potential customers. It had 803 retail establishments, 280 of them food stores. There also were fifty-eight clothing and apparel outlets, fifty-seven restaurants and lunch rooms, fifty-five filling stations, thirty-eight pharmacies, twenty furniture stores, nineteen auto dealers, eleven shoe stores, nine cigar stands, five department stores (and an equal number of businesses marketing farm supplies), and one book store. One hundred and nineteen wholesale distributors, one-third of them dealing in food, were located in the city.

Work on Lake Murray was continuing to pump dollars into the economy, and Southern Railway passengers were welcomed by glaring electric signs: "COLUMBIA, THE POWER CITY." Two other notable construction projects were under way, but not without pitfalls, disappointments, and agonizing decisions. In 1928, voters approved a $300,000 bond issue to build a municipal auditorium and community center, but it quickly became apparent that sum was too small and the community center was scrapped. Those backing the auditorium then chose as a site what had been the boyhood home of Woodrow Wilson. Although the structure had fallen upon hard times, the American Legion and historically conscious citizens launched a successful campaign to save the building, and eventually the well-known Township Auditorium was erected on another nearby lot during 1929–1930.

The other undertaking, a pet project of Mayor Lawrence B. Owens that subsequently would bear his name, was a municipal airfield. In April of 1929, a site was selected three miles south of the city and preliminary work began, much of it done by the county chain gang. That summer, the Curtiss Flying Service agreed to build a hangar and runways, maintain the airport, and provide air taxis and a flying school. In September, Eastern Air Express made this emerging facility a regular stop on its New York-Miami run. Although Owens Field was dedicated with great fanfare in April of 1930 (an air show attended by 5,000 spectators), by that date the Post Office Department had abandoned plans for air mail service to Columbia, a principal reason for an outlay totaling $100,000.

Thanks to this construction—as well as the twelve-story Columbia Hotel at Gervais and Sumter streets, completed in February of 1931 at a cost of $822,000, and 122 single-family dwellings built in 1930—Columbia seemed to be swimming upstream against the national current.[11] According to the *Record* (19 August 1930), a survey conducted by a Manhattan-based institute indicated this city's mid-year business conditions were 11.6 percent better than in 1929, a surge exceeded by only two other communities throughout the nation, Davenport, Iowa, and Albany, New York. Yet statistics of this sort can be misleading. Month by month the number of families seeking help from various charities was increasing, and the ranks of transients being cared for by Travelers' Aid and the Salvation Army continued to grow.

Completion of the dam at Lake Murray and the "temporary" closing of two small cotton mills (Glencoe and Palmetto, the latter, it turned out, never re-opened), as well as ill-advised boasting of a healthy economy, added to local woes. By year's end it was quite apparent that the Great Depression had arrived. The annual Community Chest drive, as was customary, fell short of its $80,000 goal, raising only $56,000; however, that was $8,000 more than had been collected in 1929. The next year (1931), Chest officials sought professional help; and, although times were worse, they surprised everyone by achieving their target of $78,000 with relative ease.

In August of 1930, the city council refused to set up a municipal employment agency. Mayor Owens agreed the number of jobless might be increasing but declared there was no crisis. Ninety days later, prodded by state and national leaders, he reversed field, and shortly before Thanksgiving a temporary city-county office opened at 1106 Lady Street. Within two weeks, almost a thousand applicants had registered, most of them middle-aged men with families who had been unemployed for several months. Slightly less than half were black.

Despite a thwarted Community Chest campaign and a flip-flop on helping the jobless, when Christmas rolled around in 1930 Columbia did itself proud. Clothing, food, and toys were collected and distributed as never before by groups such as the American Legion, Knights of Columbus, Lions, Rotarians, Civitans, and Kiwanis. Even the Ku Klux Klan in robes and headgear handed out fifty baskets of food on Christmas Eve. During that joyous season, the *State*'s W. E. Gonzales initiated a project that lasted far beyond the 1930s. At his suggestion, Mayor Owens created a municipal woodyard where the destitute could get fuel. Sponsored by the *State* and run by the Salvation Army, it soon became a center where transients could demonstrate willingness to earn a room and meal and the unemployed could seek work. In succeeding years, the "Woodyard Fund" was augmented by financial contributions, all properly acknowledged in the pages of the *State*, as well as wood given by farmers clearing land and cut by those on relief.

Although times were hard in 1930, boosterism and politics still were key ingredients of local life. When it appeared in May that the census being compiled would show Columbia with slightly less than 50,000 inhabitants, the Chamber of Commerce, aided by the press, mounted a drive to find 500 more people. Two months later the official count stood at 50,201. But this triumph turned sour when it became known that, according to state statutes relating to cities over 50,000, the salaries of the mayor ($2,500) and each councilman ($2,000) automatically doubled, adding $10,500 to the annual budget. Citizen outcry increased even more sharply in November when a new councilman resigned because of ill health; and, instead of consulting voters, his associates chose a successor. "No Latin American country would submit to such subversions of fundamental principles without a bloody revolution," thundered the *Record* (25 November). Several heated public meetings ensued, and some critics advocated changing to the city-manager plan, which the *State* favored. However, within a few weeks the furor subsided; nevertheless, the salary issue would resurface from time to time, especially in election campaigns.

During the next two years, Columbia and Richland County, like the rest of the nation, sank deeper into economic stagnation. Yet there were bright spots, especially in 1931. These include the highly successful Community Chest campaign of that year and especially word from Washington in April that a 300-bed veterans' hospital costing $1.3 million would be built just east of the city close by Camp Jackson. Heartened by this news, the Chamber of Commerce launched a "Columbia Forward Movement" to stimulate business by advertising and promoting the city. The idea was for citizens to pledge the chamber budget for the next three years so as to enhance plans for conventions, new business, and various educational-cultural activities. Buoyed by enthusiasm over the soon-to-be-constructed hospital and a brief surge of economic confidence arising from a war-debt moratorium, this campaign achieved its goal of $156,900 in two weeks. This was an astonishing feat; but, as both chamber and Community Chest officials realized, a pledge was not money in the bank, merely a promise to *give* money at some future date.[12]

Encouraging developments of this sort were rare indeed as budgets grew tighter and workers were laid off in all parts of the community. In

January of 1932, for example, municipal paychecks were cut 10 percent. During the next two years, as tax revenues dwindled, many city employees received scrip, not money, as did the University of South Carolina staff in 1932. However, A. C. Flora, superintendent of Columbia's schools, somehow managed to meet all payrolls throughout this trying decade. Under these conditions, charitable organizations did whatever they could, churches tried to help members (despite ever-smaller collections), and families often looked after the needs of relatives. Yet in mid-1932, a *Record* reporter discovered a hundred people living at the city dump where they hunted for food scraps and slept in boxes and abandoned autos. A few months later, an estimated 12,000 Columbia residents were looking for work.

Bleak as this picture is, it was made worse by a drifting population of dispossessed sharecroppers, farmers who had lost their land, unemployed textile workers, assorted homeless individuals, and a surprising number of well-educated professional men. Early in 1932, up to 100 individuals were being cared for each night at the county jail and YMCA. There was, of course, no easy solution to this problem, and none would be found until national recovery programs began to work their magic. Columbia was a major rail center on a vital north-south highway. These factors, plus occasional boasts of a healthy economy, tended to attract those honestly seeking work and those who were not. At times, police simply hauled men to the city limits and told them to keep moving; on other occasions, they were lodged in temporary quarters at Camp Jackson. In 1935, Mayor Owens remarked that he once worried about such people, "but they don't worry about themselves, so I stopped worrying about them." And a councilman expressed his view quite forcefully: "I am 100 percent opposed to transients—they ought to stay at home."

Until the spring of 1932, all relief was local. Then Congress supplied the Red Cross with flour and cloth to be given to America's needy, and the Hoover administration set up the Reconstruction Finance Corporation (RFC) to make loans to states and cities. Local officials embraced these federal programs with great reluctance, but by year's end city-county residents were benefiting from RFC funds. In February of 1933, 23½ percent of Columbia's adult population had registered for work with the Richland County Relief Council; in rural areas, the figure was 44 percent. During the first four months of operation, the council paid 8,000 individuals $144,959 to work on 253 community projects financed by the RFC, which means each person (on average) got eighteen dollars. That is not much, but it was a beginning, and soon, under Roosevelt, the concept of work relief was winning more and more converts.

FDR's New Deal with its alphabet soup of agencies, boards, and commissions is a complex tale that takes one far from the realm of local matters; for, throughout much of the 1930s, the economic life of Columbia and Richland County was shaped on the banks of the Potomac, not the Congaree. This vast program spent $58.7 million in South Carolina between March of 1933 and June of 1939. Of that total, $38.1 million went for public works, and about half ($31.1 million) was in the form of repayable loans.

The most popular of these undertakings was the Civilian Conservation Corps (CCC), which shortly after Roosevelt took office put 285 young men from Richland County in forestry camps where they studied various skills and built parks, fire towers, and roads. Others followed in their footsteps, and one CCC unit, Camp Pontiac, was established in July of 1935 twelve miles northeast of Columbia. Out of the CCC experiment came the beginnings of South Carolina's state park system.

The best-known arm of the New Deal was, however, the Works Progress Administration (WPA). It seemed to be everywhere doing everything and anything that might stimulate the economy. An outgrowth in 1935 of the spectacular but trouble-plagued National Recovery Administration (NRA), the work of the WPA often was largely paint and fix up, but on a huge scale. WPA employees improved existing roads, streets, and playgrounds, repaired and renovated public buildings, prepared school lunches, copied historical documents, interviewed aged ex-slaves, painted murals, improved sewerage and water systems, and even taught individuals to sew, read, and write. In May of 1936, several Columbia women wrote to President Roosevelt to thank him for WPA-sponsored classes they were attending. Money received enabled them to feed and clothe their children, they said, adding they also had learned how "to sign our checks for the first time." WPA spending in Columbia and Richland County was modest at first, but by 1940 that agency was employing 2,781 local residents, and most of the $1.3 million allocated to this region that year went directly to them in the form of wages.

If the WPA was the most pervasive of the New Deal programs, the Public Works Administration (PWA) could point to the most spectacular results. Formed late in 1933, its goal was not mere renovation and improvement but new construction. A university stadium was erected at the fair grounds with RFC money in 1934, but the PWA subsequently provided funds for a water reservoir serving the southeastern part of Columbia, sheds for the Assembly Street market, three housing projects (University Terrace, Gonzales Gardens, and Allen-Benedict Court), a new courthouse for Richland County, and several university buildings.

These included four dormitories for men, one for women, McKissick Library at the head of the Horseshoe (now McKissick Museum), and a truncated War Memorial auditorium.

During these years, the erection of a new federal building transformed the old one at 1737 Main Street, through an exchange of land, into Columbia's city hall. The former seat of municipal affairs at Gervais and Main streets subsequently was razed and replaced by the Wade Hampton Hotel. Another project involving federal property was the five-story headquarters of the Farm Credit Administration built at Hampton and Marion streets in 1935. Other construction of note—buildings not tied directly to New Deal programs—included Dreher High School and Carver Junior High (backed by a $500,000 bond issue in 1937), Tapp's Department Store, a Greyhound bus terminal (now a bank), and Providence Hospital on Forest Drive, operated by Catholic Sisters of Charity.

To some degree, change wrought by the New Deal was merely a facelift, and much of the construction lacked the grandeur of W. B. S. Whaley's mills and the skyscrapers that appeared along Main Street in the years before World War I. With two exceptions (some would call them minor, others major), Columbia's New Deal experiences differed little from those of cities stretching from Portland, Maine, to Portland, Oregon. But those differences would have ramifications both political and economic. First, Washington's insistence upon a color-blind wage structure raised hackles throughout the South. In 1934, for example, when whites, with the support of a Richland County legislator, barred blacks from a Winnsboro Road project, federal authorities simply cancelled the job. Second, in the New Deal era, Columbia's central location and status as seat of state government made it the natural headquarters for scores of programs and projects. This trend, to the dismay of Charleston, Greenville, and other rivals, would be accentuated by World War II and events following in its wake.

Turning from city to countryside, during the 1930s both Columbia and Richland County registered modest population gains, but the 1940 census revealed a bleak rural picture. The number of individual farms, after rising slightly in mid-decade, dropped to 2,428, equally divided between white and black operators.[13] One-fourth of these units contained 10 to 29 acres, and twenty-two were plantation-sized spreads of 1,000 acres or more. One-fourth also were free of mortgages. Less than half (1,069) reported autos, and only 187 had trucks. One out of five Richland County farmhouses had electricity, and about the same number were located on hard-surface roads. Telephones (170) and tractors (120) were extremely rare. Corn, cow peas, cotton, and sweet potatoes were the most popular crops; and, despite a drive for diversification, only one farmer in six was producing peaches and peanuts.

Writing to a friend on 15 January 1934, W. E. Gonzales, reflecting upon the nation's woes, compared the United States to an auto stuck in the mud. The driver's back wheels represented American business, and Roosevelt's recovery program was feeding gravel, pine boughs, and wood into the mud in hopes of building a firm foundation . . . "something on which they [the wheels] can catch and hold." If there's quicksand, Gonzales cautioned, there's going to be trouble. But as material built up, "the wheels can take a firm grip, he will pull out and go merrily forward on his way." The driver, warned Gonzales, cannot know the results in advance and can use only whatever is at hand that promises results. Yet, because of the fear of quicksand, neither can he stand idly by. He has to do something.

This analogy, one Gonzales's friend in the White House certainly would have appreciated, was indeed appropriate. But the best evidence a half century later indicates the mud may have contained quicksand; for, despite the millions spent, it probably was World War II and not the New Deal that sent the auto "merrily forward." On the other hand, the recovery effort kept the rear wheels from sinking deeper. The boom of World War I enabled this gentleman to buy a car, the bust got him in the mud, and then Roosevelt got him out . . . or did he?

Notes

1. Although military authorities would have built some theaters, these facilities were larger than first proposed following failure of Columbia to permit Sunday movies. In October of 1917, the city council—supported by clergymen, the *State*, and WCTU—rebuffed such an appeal. A short time later, the army unveiled plans for a 3,000-seat auditorium.
2. Army brass, alarmed by conditions they had seen on the Mexican border, tried to suppress vice within five miles of all military installations. In October of 1918, Camp Jackson's commander, angry because as many as 3,000 of his men sometimes were ill with venereal disease, met with the city council to voice displeasure. In his opinion, the local government was singularly uncooperative. Those ousted from the old "segregated" district now were back in town, he said, often living in hotels and "acting in a suspicious manner."

3. The dispensary, a state-operated liquor monopoly instituted in the 1890s and often a hot political issue, gradually evolved into a county-option plan. By 1915, only fifteen counties, among them, Richland and Lexington, had dispensaries.

4. Not everyone was swept away by patriotic ardor. Before war was declared, Civil War veteran W. M. Reedy of Clio cautioned his sons not to volunteer: "It's a hard life, in fact, it's a dog's life." Six months later, while reading the *State*, he discovered that not one but *two* of his boys were in uniform at Camp Jackson. Furious, Dr. Reedy wrote demanding an immediate explanation (Reedy-Beacham Papers).

5. Police stopped two cars at the Lexington end of the Congaree River Bridge in October of 1922 and seized 400 quarts of whiskey. Eight months later, they uncovered a twenty-five-gallon tank of booze in the wall of a Gervais Street cafe.

6. *State*, 21 January 1921. In the mid-twenties, Mimnaugh's Department Store was selling aluminum auto signs: "Columbia—The City Unlimited."

7. The decision to build at Dreyfuss Field, once known as Fisher's Mill Pond Bottom, was preceded by heated debate when Mayor Owens tried to erect a stadium in Maxcy Gregg Park instead. Only after the state Supreme Court ruled against him in January of 1927 did Owens turn reluctantly to the South Assembly Street site now used by the Columbia Mets. *Note:* This field was named for Barney Dreyfuss, head of the Pittsburgh Pirates, the club then guiding the fortunes of the Columbia Comers.

8. New York industrialist William Barstow, the man behind Lake Murray, purchased the utility interests of Edwin Robertson in 1925. At that time, he wisely concluded an agreement with the state concerning the irksome Columbia Canal. In return for relieving him of any obligation to complete that waterway, Barstow agreed to supply the state with a specified amount of free electricity—some of which later lit up the Congaree Street Bridge.

9. At this time, the city tried once more to annex Eau Claire, but the vote subsequently was ruled invalid. Also, in 1928 the Richland County delegation split over renaming the "old" road to Camden. Senator James H. Hammond, who prevailed, wanted to call it Forest Drive, while House members favored "road," maintaining that "drive" meant only a short distance and was an improper designation for a major artery.

10. Paul Stroman Lofton, Jr., "A Social and Economic History of Columbia, South Carolina, During the Great Depression, 1929–1940," Ph.D. diss., University of Texas, 1977, p. vi. *Note:* Much of the material that follows comes from this research.

11. Work was supposed to begin in May of 1930 on yet another large hotel, a new version of the old Jerome at Main and Lady streets, but that structure never appeared.

12. The business community mounted still another campaign in 1931. Stung by words Sinclair Lewis wrote in 1920, merchants tried to change the name of Main Street to "State Street." They formed committees, held meetings, wrote letters, and took polls; but, in the end, nothing happened.

13. According to census returns, there were 2,787 farms in 1930 and 3,200 in 1935, reflecting an obvious population shift in the depths of the Depression. During the 1930s, the number of tenant holdings declined slightly (1,536 to 1,212), and the value of land and buildings also dropped ($7.9 to $6.9 million), as did the number of mules and horses, down from 3,642 to 2,890. Herds of cattle increased somewhat, but corn and cotton production remained virtually unchanged.

William E. Gonzales's Columbia

CHAPTER SEVENTEEN

The youngest of three brothers who guided the fortunes of the *State* for nearly half a century, William Elliott Gonzales (1866–1937) was the son of a foot-loose, impecunious Cuban revolutionary, Ambrosio José Gonzales, and Harriett Rutledge Elliott, daughter of lowcountry grandee William Elliott. In fourteen years, this unlikely pair produced six children. William, originally christened "Benigno," was fifth in line and the first born after the Civil War. His father, a veteran of that conflict, was a man who changed jobs and abodes with alarming frequency, and in January 1869 the family departed for Cuba where Gonzales achieved fleeting stability as a teacher. However, ten months later his wife fell victim to yellow fever, and within two years widower Gonzales deposited his brood with a collection of equally impecunious Elliott aunts and uncles living at "Oak Lawn" in Colleton County. He then drifted on to New York, Baltimore, and other points.

Although Gonzales reappeared from time to time and made some effort to be helpful, relations with his in-laws and progeny quickly deteriorated. By the late 1870s, his eldest son (Ambrose) refused to see him, and the Elliotts were delighted when Gonzales once more departed for Cuba. Then, in 1882, $10,000 inherited from an elderly aunt produced a distinct warming trend, especially when this new wealth paid back taxes on "Oak Lawn" and erected a more suitable dwelling for the Elliot-Gonzales household. Even Ambrose was willing to accept a $2,000 loan in order to educate his youngest sister, Harriett. But William, a student at the Citadel, declined to see his father and spurned financial assistance.

As Lewis Jones relates in *Stormy Petrel: N. G. Gonzales and His State* (1973), during the 1870s all of these youngsters received training in educational fundamentals from their aunts; and, as remarkable as it may seem, these ladies somehow managed to send the two oldest boys to struggling Virginia preparatory schools for a year or so. They then became telegraph operators on rail lines in the southernmost part of the state, jobs that eventually led to careers in journalism.

By the early 1880s, N. G. (Narcisco Gener), a reporter for the Charleston *News and Courier*, was able to send William to King's Mountain Military Academy in Yorkville and the Citadel. Although William liked cadet life, he was embarrassed by a tendency to stutter; and, with Narcisco's permission, left that Charleston institution in the spring of his freshman year. A short time later, he joined the *News and Courier's* Columbia bureau as a five-dollar-a-week assistant to his brother. The following year (1885), Ambrose, who had been working in New York City, became associated with the business department of the same daily, spending much of his time traveling about the state writing descriptive articles calculated to boost circulation. Unwittingly, perhaps, the foundations were being laid for a rival newspaper a few years hence.

In February of 1887, William took as his bride a striking Columbia belle, Sara Shiver, daughter of a well-to-do businessman. Although the Elliott aunts were not enthusiastic, the wedding was all one could ask for: twenty-six attendants, a vast throng at Columbia's First Presbyterian Church that included Governor John P. Richardson and the Richland Volunteers in full splendor, and a brilliant reception at the Shiver home on Arsenal Hill.[1] Within six months, William vainly sought a raise, noting it was difficult to live in a "respectable manner" in Columbia on twelve dollars and fifty cents a week. Soon after this appeal, those operating the *News and Courier*, in a cost-cutting move, decided to dispense with his services entirely. However, this young man soon was named private secretary to Governor Richardson.

Late in the following year (1889), Ambrose quit the paper to become secretary of the State Board of Agriculture. The year after that, Benjamin Ryan Tillman—the principal target of the soon-to-be-born *State*—swept to victory, stirring Narcisco, Ambrose, and their friends to mount a holy war against this agricultural reformer. But William, having gone to North Carolina to promote a resort near Asheville, was not party to these exciting proceedings, a fact he always regretted. Within two years, however, the real-estate scheme soured, and William (then "W. Elliott Gonzales") was back in South Carolina working for the *State*.

In the beginning, it was touch and go. Money was tight, the three brothers were pitted against well-entrenched rivals such as the *Columbia Register* and the *News and Courier*, and only dogged determination (especially that of Ambrose) kept the *State* alive. He was, in fact, "the balance wheel" of this trio—a good-natured, public-spirited compromiser, and a man often too generous with money. Forced to play the father role at a young age, contemporaries thought him the real power during the *State's* formative years. Yet, as time revealed, Ambrose did not really have a head for business, which may explain why he insisted on keeping the paper going when others, even Narcisco, thought it doomed.

By contrast, Narcisco Gener Gonzales, perhaps because he had weak eyes and was short-sighted, was a reserved, dignified appearing introvert. An aggressive editor, he often demonstrated the same "bad-tempered" demeanor that brother Ambrose commented upon when they were young. Writing in *Stormy Petrel*, Lewis Jones details a long list of scrapes and clashes in which Narcisco was involved. The cause, he notes, usually was right, but "his language rarely was restrained."

William, in the opinion of Jones, had "the most pleasing personality," although until Narcisco's death he clearly was a junior partner. An avid wheelman, William suffered a bad spill during a five-mile bicycle race at the fair grounds in June of 1894, which, according to the *State*, would force him "to lay up for some time." Two years later, this feature writer-reporter produced an amazing, eleven-part series on "The New Columbia" (3 June–13 July 1896), a penetrating analysis of the growth and development of South Carolina's capital city since 1880.[2]

Each of the brothers participated in the Cuban conflict of the late 1890s, and Narcisco told of his experiences in the columns of the *State* (8 September–7 December 1898), reports published in 1922 as *In Darkest Cuba*. Soon after the turn of the century, he once more was caught up in what Jones calls "Tillmania," but this time his adversary was Lieutenant Governor James Tillman, nephew of the senator, who also was a veteran of the Spanish-American War and at times a rival journalist. Their differences went back to the early '90s and included various personal disagreements, among them, a near duel. When Tillman decided to run for governor in 1902, the fight was on; although, in the opinion of Jones, Narcisco's thrusts lacked the humor displayed a decade earlier when he did battle with the well-known uncle. Despite bitter words—often four or more columns a day and not unlike what other newspapers were saying— Jim Tillman ran relatively well locally in the second primary, losing to Duncan Clinch Heyward 963–691 in Columbia and 1,529–1,077 in the county as a whole.[3]

Tillman stated in a circular letter that he blamed N. G. Gonzales for his defeat, but did nothing more until about 1:45 on the afternoon of 15 January 1903 when he walked up to Gonzales near the corner of Main and

Gervais and shot him at close range in the presence of several witnesses. Gonzales, who was unarmed, died four days later, and his assailant subsequently was acquitted ("self-defense") in a sensational trial held in Lexington County, not Richland.[4]

With the death of Narcisco, the task of running the *State* fell first to Ambrose and then William. In 1912, the latter labored hard for Woodrow Wilson, served as a Democratic elector, and was rewarded with the post of minister to Cuba. Six years later, he became ambassador to Peru (the first South Carolinian to achieve such rank), resigning, according to custom, when President Harding took office in 1921. William's return to Columbia also was prompted by the declining health of his elder brother. He first served as editor and then, upon the death of Ambrose in 1926, became publisher and president of the State Company.

William's tenure as head of what had become South Carolina's leading daily was a difficult eleven years. The boll weevil, agricultural distress, and the Great Depression all added up to trouble. Also, in the late 1920s, the *State's* afternoon rival, the *Columbia Record*, came under aggressive leadership that was determined to increase that paper's share of the local market. This confrontation was complicated by the fact that International Paper and Power, new owners of the *Record*, were the very people supplying newsprint to the *State*. Throughout these years, William, who died in October of 1937 during State Fair Week, struggled with various proposals to join the two dailies together; however, this did not occur until 1945 when the *State* purchased the *Record* for $550,000.

In the midst of these trials, William Gonzales had one well-deserved moment of triumph. In the summer of 1930, publisher William LaVarre, architect for a brief time of the *Record's* new activism, offered a gold watch to be awarded to Columbia's "most useful citizen." It took a five-member committee only fourteen minutes to select his arch rival as the recipient of this honor. LaVarre, not pleased, was absent from any ceremony that ensued and told the group by telegram that it would have taken him "much longer" to reach the same decision.

Unlike LaVarre, William Elliott Gonzales looked upon his newspaper as "a Columbia institution," not as a private enterprise, yet frequently chided local merchants for not using the pages of the *State* to lure potential customers living in outlying areas. He was fully as public spirited as Ambrose, but had more business sense, and clearly possessed little of the rashness of Narcisco. Friend of men such as Woodrow Wilson, Bernard Baruch, and Franklin D. Roosevelt, his seventy-one years encompassed exciting events in both South Carolina and the nation . . . as well as cer-

emonies marking the centennial of the first legislative session held in Columbia (1891) and this city's sesquicentennial in 1936.

Reflecting upon the half century from 1890 to 1940, it is apparent
that certain developments on the local scene have much more significance
than others. At the top of the list one would have to put the cotton mills
and mill villages of the 1890s and Camp Jackson, followed closely by the
appearance of more and more improved streets and highways. At the bottom would be ill-fated schemes to link Columbia to the sea and efforts to
transform the city into a winter resort for well-to-do Yankees. Also, a succession of music festivals, corn expositions, harvest jubilees, and Palma-
festas—none of which lasted more than a few years—served only to prove
that residents of the Midlands would support only one truly large annual
blow-out: the South Carolina State Fair. Somewhere in between lie still
other aspects of day-to-day existence such as various levels of education,
religious and cultural life, commercial activity, and efforts to promote Columbia as the hub of a far-flung trading empire. In such pursuits, Richland County and its city could point to growth and improvement, but
seldom were the results spectacular or unlike those experienced by similar communities during the same decades.

Cotton mills fulfilled a dream decades old, provided hundreds of
jobs, increased Columbia's suburban population, comported well with local labor practices, and represented a long-range investment of a few million. Camp Jackson was something quite different. It was a short-term
outlay several times as large that made mincemeat of the prevailing wage
scale and, together with the upheaval of war, shook Columbia's social fabric for the first time in forty years.

Although this installation, which often had a temporary population
greater than Columbia itself, existed in a formal manner only from September 1917 to September 1921, it was a force for substantial change.
Even after the last soldier left, it continued to exert influence as a summer camp for national guardsmen, a federal forest preserve, storage facilities for a growing State Highway Department, an experimental farm,
and target of various schemes for industrial development. Nineteen years
later, as war loomed on the horizon, it was transformed into Fort Jackson
and achieved the permanence long sought by Columbia's business
community.

Of course, all of these changes were chronicled by the Columbia
press. The best known of these newspapers were dailies such as the *Columbia Register* that folded in the late 1890s after nearly a quarter of a
century, the *State*, and the *Daily Record*, which was established by

George R. Koester in 1897 and became the *Columbia Record* in 1913. In the 1920s, under the skillful guidance of Charlton Wright, a Savannah native, this afternoon daily was a lively, innovative, highly interesting sheet that attacked lynching, aggressively promoted the arts, and told readers about any axe murder that occurred anywhere in America. Weeklies of note included N. J. Frederick's black *Palmetto Leader* (established in 1925), politician Walter Duncan's *South Carolina Gazette* (published in Columbia 1925–1930 before moving to Aiken), and the arch-conservative *Carolina Free Press* produced by Klansman Ben Adams throughout the 1930s.

During these fifty years, education prospered at all levels in a relative sense. That is, it improved markedly, but that improvement often was less than claimed, rarely reached desired goals, and failed to keep pace with national trends. Times, for the most part, were hard; money scarce. Those skeptical of public education's benefits were reluctant to spend tax dollars on schools, especially black schools. This attitude, by no means limited to the Midlands or to the South, for that matter, obviously was pervasive and rooted in self-interest.

In 1890, Richland County and the city of Columbia (a separate district with its own superintendent) were maintaining sixty-seven schools at a cost of $22,735. A half century later, city and county were spending over a million dollars to operate 92 schools. Table 4 shows how districts, schools, pupils, and budgets increased.

Several cautionary notes are necessary, however. The number of pupils represents actual enrollment, not daily attendance. In 1920, the names of 17,135 students were on the books, but average attendance was only 12,256. Twenty years later, the city-county area had 29,337 young people ages six to twenty, but only 21,090 were enrolled in school. There

Table 4. City–County Schools, 1890–1940

Year	Districts	Schools	Pupils	White	Black	Expenditures
1890	9	67	6,029	1,844	4,185	$ 22,735
1900	13	88	7,685	2,847	4,838	43,504
1910	16	104	10,894	4,584	6,310	139,125
1920	30	121	17,135	8,067	9,068	358,628
1930	36	120	19,665	10,057	9,608	852,833
1940	36	92	21,090	11,618	9,472	1,033,707

SOURCE: *Annual Reports, State Superintendent of Education.*

were other disparities, most of them known all too well. In 1920, the city term was 180 days, compared with ninety days in the county. By 1940, terms were about equal (170 days), except in fifty-six rural elementary schools for blacks, where sessions were shorter. Annual expenditures per student enrolled and salaries of instructors varied greatly. In 1930, $71.72 was being spent on each white pupil, $13.69 on each black student. That same year, teachers' salaries ranged from $1,787 for white males to $517 for black females. In 1945, by court order, this white-black salary difference was replaced by a system based upon merit and service.

Through the years, the rural educational structure became more like that of the city. In 1896, the county school commissioner was replaced by a superintendent and a board of education that gradually expanded to include one member from each township outside of Columbia. This board, in turn, implemented a graded system with high schools. By 1915, in addition to Columbia High School (eleven teachers and 281 students), there were "high schools" in Eastover, Heathwood, Hyatt Park, and Lykesland. But these institutions had only two or three teachers and a limited curriculum. That year the county superintendent boasted of a summer school for teachers held at the university, rallies in behalf of education, and a school fair held at Lykesland. Innovations included domestic science clubs, a mill-village textile school, and the addition of a health officer. Children in need of treatment could be cared for, the superintendent added, at a public clinic in Columbia.

Meanwhile, a drive was under way to consolidate white schools. In 1911, for example, a dozen, one-room operations with 104 students were transformed into a single school at Eastover with five teachers. These students were transported in five free hacks and furnished with free pencils, pens, and books. Music classes were available at no extra cost.[5] Fifteen years later, according to the *State* (26 June 1926), Frost was home to Richland County's only rural, one-teacher school for white children. At that time, outside of Columbia there were forty white and seventy-three black schools. Forty-eight of the latter had but one teacher.

The fifth annual report of the county board of education, which included city statistics, highlights some of the dilemmas faced in 1918–1919. Domestic science was being taught in seven schools, agriculture in five, and there were eight adult schools.[6] Among these evening classes, all held in the city, were three at the mills and one each at the penitentiary, YMCA, and Booker T. Washington School. The latter, erected for black elementary students in 1916, had become a high school in 1918. Despite progress, the superintendent called for uniform, nine-month sessions in all schools, stronger compulsory attendance laws, and teachers both better trained and better paid. Yet he conceded that so long as financial support varied from district to district within Richland County, so would schools.[7]

In these same months, his Columbia counterpart, E. S. Dreher, the man who succeeded Winthrop's D. B. Johnson as head of city schools in 1895, was in hot water. During his administration, several new buildings had appeared in response to an appeal for more classrooms. In the fall of 1902, for example, both white and black students were turned away, and some grades instituted double shifts. Among these new structures were Taylor (1906), McMaster (1911), Logan (1913), Blossom Street (1916), and Columbia High and Booker T. Washington (both in 1916). By annexation, the city had acquired schools in Shandon and Waverly. Much of this construction came after Dreher had complained in an annual report that the people of Columbia, as a whole, were interested only in material things, not intellectual pursuits. City-owned horses, he vowed, were housed better than this community's school children, adding that "a course of lectures on the care and protection of school children would be beneficial in many ways."[8]

But for some parents, bricks and mortar were not enough; and, in September of 1917, led by physician Joseph J. Watson, they demanded, in effect, that Dreher step down. At a monthly board meeting, Watson made two highly unusual offers: $1,000 to underwrite an investigation of city schools and $500 a year for five years to be added to the salary of Dreher's successor, if ———— was named to that post. The latter offer was rejected and Watson's choice not revealed; however, the board accepted funds for an inquiry. According to the Record (20 September), Watson exclaimed during the meeting, "Inefficiency! Inefficiency! That is the keynote of the whole matter!" One cause of discontent was the small number of students completing their education at Columbia High School. In 1917, only twenty received diplomas. That same year, communities such as Anderson, Florence, Greenwood, and Orangeburg all had more graduates. But it was Sumter, with thirty-four, that especially incensed Watson and his friends.

In the spring of 1918, federal educators submitted a survey of Columbia schools that Dreher immediately denounced as impractical and unfair. He subsequently was elected to another term as superintendent, but chose instead to resign and was succeeded by W. H. Hand. Hand, who had held joint positions as state high school inspector and professor

of secondary education at the University of South Carolina, would operate Columbia's schools until his death in August of 1928. During that decade, he instituted cafeterias, standard testing, dental clinics, classes for
retarded students, and a longer school day so as to provide study periods.

Hand's special passion, however, was practical courses of a vocational
nature and a twelve-year program, something Columbia would not have
until 1944. With a pen fully as sarcastic as that of Dreher, as high school
inspector he attacked the weak offerings of South Carolina's colleges.
Some of them, he said, would not be first-class secondary schools in other
states. Yet, by accepting students in preparatory departments they retarded both themselves and development of four-year high schools.[9]
Upon his death, Hand was succeeded by A. C. Flora, who administered
the city school system until his retirement in June of 1951. As noted earlier, Flora's management skills were especially effective during the Great
Depression, when, by careful counting of dollars and cents, he met all
payrolls. In 1930, Flora elevated C. A. Johnson, Booker T. Washington's
principal since 1918, to the newly created post of supervisor of black
schools and seven years later won approval of a $500,000 bond issue that
built Dreher High School for whites in the Shandon neighborhood and
Carver Junior High School for blacks on Elmwood Avenue.

Except at the kindergarten level, private education was hit hard by
the rise of public classrooms. Parochial schools such as Ursuline Academy
(and then High School) continued to educate Catholic girls, while
younger children attended St. Peter's. By the 1930s, there was a small
Hellenic school for Greek Orthodox youngsters, and throughout these
decades black children often attended mission schools operated by the
Episcopal and Presbyterian churches. Also, both Allen and Benedict conducted elementary and high school classes during much of the period.
Schools that went by a variety of names—Verner's, Davis High School,
and University High School (one existed c. 1910 and another by the same
name appeared in 1932)—prepared students for entrance to the University of South Carolina. But the most unique institution was Annie
Bonham's Bon Air School, which, for over three decades (1898–1931)
stressed, along with the three Rs, exercise and fresh air. All classes not
held outdoors convened in a room open to the elements on three sides,
where, if it got too cold, students sat bundled in woolen bags.[10]

Despite praise lavished on city schools, both public and private,
their country cousins undoubtedly had greater impact. A Richland
County school, especially if consolidated, became *the* social-cultural center for scores of families. Not only the setting for Christmas pageants and

end-of-the-year recitations, it also was a place to hold all sorts of meetings, dances, and other non-religious functions. In fact, scores of little school houses, both black and white, became a prime focus of local life and, since they touched virtually every household, were, in a sense, rivals of both church and Sunday School.

At the turn of the century, for example, Horrell Hill School also was home to Camp # 59, Woodmen of the World, and the Horrell Hill Literary Society. The latter, founded in 1896, met monthly, except during summer, to hear lectures, musical numbers, and recitations, discuss matters such as the legal status of women, compulsory school attendance, and coeducation, and listen to lively debates. Among issues considered were: reading of fiction should be condemned, the cow is more valuable than the horse, city life is happier than country life, the southern farmer is to blame for his failures, old maids and bachelors are a nuisance to society, and the Ford car is a greater benefit than the "aeroplane." When tornadoes hit the Horrell Hill-Lykesland area in April of 1924, killing twenty-three people, four of them at the school, the society helped rebuild that structure.

Columbia's colleges experienced weather almost as rough, especially during the decades before World War I. This city was, John Andrew Rice writes in his engaging *I Came Out of the Eighteenth Century* (1942), both a seat of learning in the 1890s and this state's "principal matrimonial agency." And those dual functions may be even more important today. Rice, whose father in 1894 became president of Columbia Female College (soon to drop "Female" from its name), recalls that the railroad depot was the main entrance to town. There were no window screens, much spitting, and consequently spittoons were everywhere. "I was born into a spitting world. Everyone except ladies and aspirants to that title, spat." Rice, then a youngster, says he went to school during the week but learned much more each Saturday when everyone came to town for market day.

Despite disastrous fires in 1895 and again in 1909, under the leadership of the elder Rice, this venerable Methodist institution dropped its finishing-school image and became a true college. Its Presbyterian rival, the College for Women, established in 1890 in the Hampton-Preston mansion, was less fortunate.[11] In 1915, it merged with Greenville's Chicora College, and the enlarged school bought property in Shandon and began to build a new home. However, hard times forced Chicora to move to Charlotte in 1930 where it merged with Queen's. Two other schools also left town: Winthrop, which moved to Rock Hill in the 1890s, and the Columbia Theological Seminary, which took up residence in Decatur, Georgia, in 1927.

On the other hand, Lutheran Theological Southern Seminary moved to Eau Claire from Mount Pleasant in 1911, and Columbia Bible Institute began classes at 1627 College Street in September of 1921. It soon was granting degrees and in 1927 moved to the Colonia Hotel, the same structure that had been the temporary home of Columbia College following the 1909 fire.

In the early 1930s, both Allen and Benedict phased out their preparatory departments, and by 1940 each had about 400 college-level students, small divinity schools, and thriving summer sessions. There also were cooperative programs sponsored by the two institutions, as well as evening classes.

A cursory review of the second volume of Daniel Hollis's history of the University of South Carolina, even a mere scanning of the table of contents, discloses the rocky road this community's premier institution traveled from 1890 to 1920. Ben Tillman first reduced the proud old school to a struggling liberal arts college, dispatching its technical department and equipment, in the words of F. W. McMaster, "to an obscure part of the state to foster an institution that exists in name only." Then having lavished attention and money upon Clemson and Winthrop, the governor became concerned that his administration would be held accountable if the university actually collapsed and reversed policy. He even pushed coeducation upon a reluctant faculty; and, beginning in 1895, a few young ladies enrolled in special courses. Three years later, Mattie Jean Adams of Lexington became the first female graduate.

In 1905, the college, with only 300 students enrolled, staged a stately centennial and the following year once more was officially designated as a "university." In the decade that followed, the departments of education, law, and engineering grew stronger, and by the mid-twenties the student body had swelled to 1,419 . . . larger than Clemson (1,032), but smaller than Winthrop (1,742). Of much greater importance, the state appropriation for 1926 was $528,903, the first time since the founding of the latter that the university had received more than its Rock Hill rival.

Hollis credits two presidents of this era—Samuel Chiles Mitchell (1909–1913) and William Davis Melton (1922–1926)—with doing much to improve academic life. Mitchell, a Mississippi-born history professor, became an educational evangelist, speaking everywhere and to anyone who would listen in behalf of the University of South Carolina. Although this true Progressive resigned after a bout with Governor Cole Blease, he left the old school much stronger than he found it. A decade later, Columbia lawyer Melton brought a vigorous, business-like approach to the presidency. His tenure was cut short by death, but he was able to stimulate public support and, in the opinion of Hollis and others, laid the groundwork for a modern institution capable of serving the interests of the entire state.

The 1930s would not seem to be a time for expansion; but, thanks to New Deal largess, the university was able to make numerous overdue repairs and build several dormitories, an indoor pool, a stadium, and a new library (WPA project # 4450). In 1940, ten divisions were offering twenty degrees, six of them at the graduate (master's) level. Enrollment during the previous decade had crept upward to 2,051. More important than mere numbers was the nature of the student body. Many of these young people had part-time jobs and represented a wide spectrum of society. No longer could the University of South Carolina be considered an elitist institution, what Tillman once characterized, not as a center of learning, but as one of "foppery and snobbery."

Local sports activity was, to some degree, tied to the fortunes of the university. This was especially true of football, which, after a shaky start in the 1890s, gave birth to "Big Thursday" at the state fair, the Carolina-Clemson classic. The university won the first contest by a score of 12–6, but the series did not become an annual event until 1909. A Barnwell youngster who saw the 1902 game recalled there was no passing, no quarters, just two halves of rough-and-tumble, bone-crushing football. Carolina prevailed, again by 12–6, which led to a near riot and no more meetings for seven years. In the decade that followed, Clemson usually emerged victorious, so often that Carolina alumni packed their team with "ringers" in 1915 and again in 1920 in a vain attempt to achieve victory.[12] Then, beginning in 1931, the Gamecocks won three straight. Interestingly, the 1932 game was the only time there were vacant seats, and the next contest was the last one played in the old wooden bowl that soon was replaced by a real stadium. But that encounter ushered in the "Great Drought," a seven-year famine that finally ended with a Carolina victory (18–14) in 1941.

Despite infrequent wins over an arch rival, in 1928 the Gamecocks beat the University of Chicago 6–0. Bands, fire trucks, sirens, and his honor the mayor greeted players upon their return from the Windy City, and 5,000 hailed the victors during a Main Street parade. In May of 1912, a similar outpouring, though somewhat less boisterous, honored a university student who placed first in a southern oratorial contest.

Basketball, called "sissy" ball in the university's 1909 yearbook, had few followers until after World War I, largely because of a lack of playing facilities. However, a community center built by Pacific Mills in 1909 gave workers and their families recreational advantages not found in other neighborhoods. Soon it was turning out top-flight men's squads, and in 1922 the "Pacific Terrifics" won the southern textile tournament held in Greenville. Five years later, the team beat Newberry, Wofford, Presbyterian, and Clemson and walloped a visiting New Jersey outfit, 105–31. Meanwhile, a program was started for mill girls; and, aided by gymnasiums built by Dreher and Hand, other local youngsters began to take up the sport. In the spring of 1929, Columbia High boys won third place in a national tourney held in Chicago.

At the university level, basketball existed largely in the shadow of the gridiron, its sole virtue being that the Carolina squad sometimes beat Clemson. In 1928, the *Garnet & Black* summarized the activities of the "Indoor Gamecocks" in six pages of sparse photographs devoid of scores. That year the football team had seven lovely coed sponsors; the basketball quintet, three. A decade later, the situation had changed little; in fact, track and boxing seemed to enjoy equal, if not more respect.

Boxing and wrestling, of course, had appeal far beyond a campus setting. Matches frequently were part of vaudeville programs through the years, although, because of racial overtones, movies of the Jeffries-Johnson fight were banned in Columbia in 1910. A decade later, at least two local arenas, one of them on Wheeler Hill, were providing evening fun for fight fans, with whites meeting whites, blacks, blacks before segregated audiences. In September of 1927, the *Record* broadcast a blow-by-blow account of a Dempsey-Tunney encounter for 5,000 delighted listeners. Blocks near the intersection of Sumter and Lady were cordoned off, and vendors dispensed peanuts, soft drinks, and other goodies to the crowd.

Even before Lake Murray appeared, hundreds, even thousands, participated in water sports each year. The *Record* (27 May 1928) greeted another season with claims of Columbia's advantages as "an inland watering place," pointing to Lakeview, Adams Pond, Twin Lakes, Moore's Pond, Bower's Branch, Boyden Arbor, Forest Lake, Caughman's Pond, and so on as solid proof. This did not, of course, preclude all-day beach outings by excursion train to the Isle of Palms (leave 3:40 A.M., arrive Charleston 8:15) and Tybee (leave 12:35 A.M., arrive Savannah 7 A.M.).

The bicycle races of the 1890s faded with the advent of the auto, and old-style tournaments with knights and ladies also lost favor, at least in urban areas.

Robert Moorman, writing in Columbia's sesquicentennial history, credits Columbia Theological Seminary with pioneering tennis play in the 1890s. Four decades later, country clubs, the university, and various municipal parks had courts, and Ridgewood and Forest Lake (which opened in 1925) also had facilities for golf. Interest in the sport of kings was sparked by some two hundred horses that the Buxton brothers trained each year at the fair grounds. In 1936, Bold Venture, a product of these stables, won both the Kentucky Derby and the Preakness. Less well-known sports included bull fighting (two Laurens bulls were supposed to meet at the 1892 state fair, but the SPCA intervened), fox hunts staged at Camp Jackson in the late 1920s, soap box derbies of the 1930s, and miniature golf played at a Five Points course during the same era.[13]

But the premier pastime throughout this half century, hands down, was baseball. Football probably made inroads during the 1930s, thanks to temporary eclipse of Columbia's professional franchise and a new stadium for gridiron fans. Nevertheless, only baseball touched the lives of all segments of the community—young, old, rich, poor, black, white—and aroused passions that closed stores whenever the local team began a new season. By the early years of this century, the *State's* sports column, dominated by baseball, was a standard daily feature, and for several years Brooklyn's National League club tarried here to play the university nine during its spring tour.

Both major newspapers staged elaborate re-enactments of World Series drama, first with the aid of telegraph and then radio. Sometimes action was merely described or diagrammed on blackboards; on other occasions, real men raced around real bases in a vacant lot. For several months in the summer of 1922, the *Record* even experimented with a "sports" extra that moved baseball news to page one. By the 1920s, the Comers, long associated with the South Atlantic (Sally) League, were part of the Pittsburgh farm system. However, in January of 1931, citing poor attendance over several seasons, the Pirates severed these ties. Except for a brief period in 1934, the city was without professional baseball until 1936 when a Florida businessman organized the Senators, a team loosely linked to Boston's National League club. A year later, a local group gained control and forged ties to the Cincinnati Reds, who, in turn, created the Columbia Reds. This team would provide local fans with quality baseball for the next two decades.

Despite the demise of the Comers, baseball fever was intense in the summer of 1931. The local American Legion junior team swept the southeastern and eastern series and then went on to the national finals. There, after fourteen innings, they lost (1–0) to a South Chicago nine. Upon their return, like the Gamecock eleven of 1928, they were feted as conquering heroes. The star, sixteen-year-old pitcher Kirby Higbe, went on to a career in the majors, and his teammates also won state championships in 1932 and 1934. In his memoirs, *The High Hard One* (1947), Higbe tells how he developed a strong right arm as a youth by throwing rocks and of his experience with street and "pick-up" ball games. On a Saturday, he and his friends would play a penitentiary team at noon (the "Caged Tigers") and a mill team at three. If, in their travels about town, they crossed through the "bottoms" where blacks lived, then rock fights with various gangs often erupted.

Another prime focus of social life, in addition to education and sports, was the church. This was especially true in the black community. For the most part, the religious world moved along in a normal manner, the usual struggle against the forces of evil, Demon Rum, back-sliders, and sin. On at least three occasions, however, church matters were in the forefront of local concerns. The first two occurred in 1893 and involved a telephone operator and allegedly light-fingered trustees of a black congregation.

Sally Means, the poor-but-honest switchboard girl, was forced to work for four hours on the Sabbath, whereupon Columbia's Second Presbyterian Church tried to oust her from its ranks. Sally, who according to the *State* merely read her Bible that day, fought back. The church's action subsequently was approved at a stormy session of the Charleston Presbytery, and Sally's defenders then appealed to a national conclave. There they won, Presbyterian worthies ruling that this young lady could not be summarily dismissed and must receive a proper letter of withdrawal, if one was requested. During these same months, a brief but much louder ruckus ripped through the black Sidney Park Methodist Church. The pastor accused two trustees of misappropriating funds, and they struck back with demands he resign. After an all-night session (12 March) peppered with calls for stringing up the trustees, a thousand angry members finally resolved this dispute without recourse to violence.

By contrast, the third event, a gigantic Billy Sunday crusade held in Columbia (25 February–8 April 1923) affected not only white Presbyterians and black Methodists, but people of many faiths, some of whom lived a hundred miles or more from South Carolina's capital city. A huge tabernacle known as the "Pine Temple" appeared at Main, College, and Greene streets, university students operated an auto parking lot, and an 800-voice choir sometimes was heard by as many as 6,000 in a single afternoon. Special trains and buses brought the curious to town, and Billy held services earmarked for all segments of society, among them, newsboys, children, mill workers, railroad men, women, policemen, college students, Shriners, Masons, and convicts.

Blacks often took part in these proceedings, seated in special sections, and local papers faithfully printed Billy's sermons in full for those unable to attend. Practicing the vigorous Christianity that he preached, on 27 March, Sunday (once a professional baseball player) umpired a game between Erskine and the university, which the latter won, 10–7. As the final week of this sawdust spectacular got under way, he was holding two services each weekday and four on Sundays. On 8 April, scores of devoted fans "ushered" the great evangelist to the depot, some of them hauling his silent Packard through crowded streets by ropes. The following evening, a segregated audience gathered at the "Pine Temple" to hear a black chorus and pledges (including one by Mayor W. A. Coleman) that work done "to cement better feelings between the races" would continue.

Essentially non-religious clubs, associations, societies, and organizations proliferated during these decades and embraced virtually every phase of local life. The roster of Columbia's secret, benevolent, and patriotic groups nearly doubled between 1920 and 1940, rising from about thirty-eight to seventy. Under certain conditions, one could join everything from professional unions for book binders and loom fixers to exclusive clubs whose principal function was to introduce debutantes each winter. Those so inclined could dress up in white sheets, white-tie-and-tails, fezzes, and knightly regalia, initiate community projects to help young people and destitute neighbors, or lay aside funds for a proper burial, a goal especially popular among black benevolent orders. Study clubs for women (New Century was the first, organized in 1901) provided an opportunity to review current literature, chat, and drink tea. Their husbands might listen to original papers delivered before the Kosmos Club, a town-gown group established in 1925, or gather informally weekday mornings at Gittman's Book Store (1125 Main Street) to discuss authors, politics, gossip, scandal, and whatever else came to mind.

Perhaps the range of possibilities can be illustrated by considering just three groups—the Oyster Club, Columbia Cotillion, and Ku Klux Klan. The first of these, originally composed of Mexican War veterans, had the simplest of goals: to meet and eat oysters in the spirit of good fellowship. In November of 1930, this organization began its eighty-second season in the basement of a Main Street clothing store. The only ingredients needed were a barrel of oysters, a barrel of beer, and stimulating conversation. (According to the *Record*, "near" beer was served that year, not the real thing.) A cook first roasted the oysters on the top of a stove and then turned them over to members, who completed the preparation in whatever manner they wished over their own gas jets. Shells were tossed on the floor, and whenever someone supplied another barrel of oysters (and beer), the club called another meeting.

The Columbia Cotillion, formed in 1890 by thirty socially elite young men one year after the rival Columbia Assembly appeared, presumably had antecedents in a group by the same name organized in 1873. Through the years, it staged three or four balls each season, first in various Main Street halls and then at the Hotel Jefferson. In 1913, distressed by current fads, the executive committee ruled that, since "an evening of terpsichorean pleasure may be gained without indulgence in the new dance steps, only the waltz and two-step may be engaged in." It is not known when this ban was lifted, but from 1911 to 1915 the equally prestigious South Carolina Club outlawed the one-step, hesitation, and fox trot. Unlike similar groups, the Cotillion did not embark upon the business of introducing debutantes until 1947.

The Ku Klux Klan, a reconstituted Reconstruction relic ready to save America from blacks, immigrants, and Catholics, first appeared publicly in April of 1921 when a lecture on the merits of the KKK was given in Craven Hall. Six months later, a flaming cross and effigies representing non-South Carolina critics were found on Millwood Hill, together with signs warning blacks to quit loafing and get to work. In 1924, Klan members of the General Assembly apparently decided to rid the university's board of trustees of Catholics, Republicans, and Jews; but, for the most part, this secret body does not seem to have become truly active locally until it was declining as a national force. In June of 1925, some 600 robed figures marched through the business section en route to a meeting at the fair grounds. The *State* found the silence "almost oppressive" and marveled at men with electric crosses on motorcycles. This paper, puzzled as to why anyone would march robed and hooded in 97° heat, noted pickets were in evidence. A few days later, the local Wade Hampton Klan staged Thomas Dixon's *The Awakening* at the Town Theatre. During the third act, six candidates actually were initiated into the order.

In the spring of 1926, mayoral candidate L. B. Owens was accused of Klan ties, something he neither confirmed nor denied, and that summer the state organization staged another, slightly larger parade. Then, the following year the Columbia contingent, re-cast as the Richland Educational Society, set up headquarters in an old firehouse at 916½ Main Street (tel. 3534). But, when Klan notables came to dedicate these facilities in October of 1927, there was no parade and any ceremony that took place was private. A few months later, House Speaker John K. Hamblin of Union was host at a barbecue luncheon held at the firehouse for members of the General Assembly.[14]

Within two years, the society disappeared and was replaced by a weekly newspaper, the *Carolina Free Press*. This publication, the brain child of Ben E. Adams (a Richland member of the lower house of the General Assembly, 1935–1938), was produced next door at 918 Main Street, but had the same telephone number as the old Richland Educational Society, *i.e.*, the Ku Klux Klan. However, as the New Deal began to flex its muscle, the strident message of the *Free Press* was heard by an ever-smaller audience.

Columbia's experience with "high" culture (art, music, literature, and theater) during the years from 1890 to 1940 was, with one exception, not especially noteworthy. In theory, the presence of several institutions of higher learning should have stimulated interest in such fields. Georgia O'Keeffe, who taught art at Columbia College for a semester in 1915, later said those months were important since it was here that she decided to "start anew" and experiment with charcoal black and white. In the 1920s, Edna Reed Whaley, who held classes in her studio, served as art critic for the *Record* and often published news of the art world in Sunday editions of that paper.

Much earlier, in 1899, an art league was formed that gave birth to a study group in 1913 and an art association in 1916. In years that followed, members staged exhibits in a downtown arcade, at various schools and hotels, and each year at the state fair. In January of 1927 they sponsored an "art week" and subsequently launched a drive for a museum home; however, that goal would not be realized until after World War II.

The music story is somewhat more upbeat. Efforts in the early years of this century to establish a festival similar to one being held so successfully in Spartanburg had spasmodic success, thanks, for example, to the presence of Victor Herbert in 1911. Fifteen years later, "Grand Opera Week" lasted for two or three seasons, and there were occasional concerts by visiting symphony orchestras. Finally, in 1929 the Shandon Choral Society, formed to promote the Community Chest drive of that year, ushered in a new era.

During the 1930s, members appeared with Washington's National Symphony in Township Auditorium and shared the stage with guest performers such as Grace Moore, Nelson Eddy, and Lily Pons. These triumphs led to formation of Columbia's own Southern Symphony in February of 1940. Within two months, this group, together with the choral society, gave twenty-two concerts in a dozen South Carolina communities. On 6 April 1940, the closing performance of that year's music festival (the first two acts of *Aida*) was carried by eighty affiliated NBC stations, an event evoking much local pride.

Literary output of these decades varied, but the most memorable books and articles were rooted in black culture—the Gullah stories of Ambrose Gonzales, works such as *Congaree Sketches* and *Nigger to Nigger* by E. C. L. Adams (tales based upon his experiences in lower Richland), and Julia Peterkin's novels. The latter, a resident of Calhoun County, was encouraged to write by Henry Bellamann, head of the music department at Chicora College for eighteen years. Bellamann, who subsequently produced several novels, including *King's Row*, won a $100 prize in a short-story contest sponsored by the *State* in 1921, beating out future luminaries such as Peterkin, Louis B. Wright, and J. McBride Dabbs. He served as editor of the *Record's* "Literary Byways" in the mid-'20s, even after departing for New York and a job with the Juilliard Foundation, and subsequently wrote for the *State* in the same capacity. It should be noted, perhaps, that both local dailies, especially the *Record* under the direction of Charlton Wright, did much to foster interest in books, literature, and writing.

An entirely different voice both startled and amused local readers at the turn of the century, that of J. Gordon Coogler (1865–1901), an incurable romantic who ran a tiny print shop, rode a bicycle about town, and wrote verse on order. His tortured rhyme scheme ("fewer/literature") has titillated thousands, including H. L. Mencken, and a recent revival of interest in the "Bard of Doko" has led to formation of a Coogler Society and even a Coogler Festival. Indeed, J. Gordon may have the last laugh (something he rarely did). His little verses actually sold well during his brief lifetime, and his fame increases while others are forgotten. Especially poignant are these words from his final poem: "Stand back; let me hang my harp on the tree; you are weary of the music it brings. . . ."

An incongruous aspect of the literary scene is scant support given the local library. In 1896, several ladies formed an association that moved its books from one downtown office building to another for over three decades. What had been the Union for Practical Progress became, in turn,

Minor Milestones

1891

May   Columbia marks centennial of first legislative session held here.

1894

Aug   Magic lantern show at Shandon Pavilion lampoons Tillman as bar tender.

1895

Feb   Allen University burns.

1897

May   Students and state militia clash at university when latter disrupt baseball game.

1899

March   City hall burns. Many say good riddance . . . "conceived in sin and brought forth in inequity." Replaced by structure that served as seat of municipal government until late 1930s.
July   Shoe store owner John Oliver leaves $6,000 bequest to aid poor.

1901

July   Carrie Nation arrives. Constables raid forty "blind tigers."

1902

April   Wade Hampton dies, age eighty-four.

1903

July   J. L. Tapp (formerly T. A. McCreery & Bro.) installs "moving stairway."

1904

Jan   City's five liquor dispensaries and three beer outlets report annual profit of $41,603.

1905

Jan   Salvation Army unit established here.
Nov   Hampton statue unveiled.

1907

April   Over 150 city hacks pass in review at annual inspection.
July   Boll weevil reported in lower Richland.

1909

Feb   County organizes rural police patrols.
Nov   President Taft here.
Dec   Woman's Exchange opens in downtown Columbia.

1911

June   Governor Woodrow Wilson of New Jersey speaks to state press association.
Oct   Film of Columbia shown at state fair.
Nov   Ninety-five Richland County residents pay state income taxes. Only three report five-figure incomes: J. L. Mimnaugh and Edwin W. Robertson (both $12,500) and Mrs. T. J. Taylor ($10,000).

1913

July   New county jail to be built at Hampton and Lincoln streets.
Nov   Secretaries want Saturday afternoons off.

1914

Feb   No "dead" (parked) autos to be left on Main Street from 8 A.M. to 6 P.M.
April   Dr. Jane Bruce Guignard heads local Suffragettes.

1915

April   Columbia Theatre to be altered for movies.

1917

Dec   War contractors seek black laborers at $2.25 a day.

1918
Dec Flu toll—whites 144, blacks 202, Camp Jackson 354.

1920
March Piggly Wiggly opens self-service store at 1229 Main Street.
Nov Business section expands to Sumter Street.

1922
Feb Trolley strike.
May University marshal shoots professor and then kills self.

1923
May Three marathon dancers each win $150 at Victory Park. Mayor, council, and hundreds watch as ninety-nine-hour ordeal ends.
Nov Jefferson Davis Highway marker unveiled in 1600 block of Taylor Street.

1924
April Marion Paul of Hyatt Park wins city marbles crown and goes on to capture state title.

1925
Jan Paul Whiteman's orchestra plays "Rhapsody in Blue" in concert. *State* praises jazz numbers, especially those featuring banjo.
July Departing Chamber of Commerce secretary advises city to build more schools, annex suburbs, and not show high school to visitors so long as approached over dirt roads.

1927
Aug Paul Redfern, local air pioneer, crashes in jungle while trying to fly to Rio.
Dec Columbia Theatre to feature vaudeville on Mondays and Tuesdays, movies the rest of the week, except for traveling shows.

1928
Nov Edwin Robertson, age sixty-five, dies of heart attack in New York City.

1929
July Room cooler (air conditioner) installed at Dunbar Funeral Home.
Sept First piano to cross the Atlantic by air (in *Graf Zeppelin*) purchased by music teacher Lelia Jo Caughman.

1930
Oct Belk's department store opens.

1931
Dec Trolley fare drops to seven cents.

1933
April Eighty cases of legal beer arrive at Hotel Jefferson.
Aug NRA codes implemented.
Dec Fifteen-year-old Hubbard Harris, Jr., murdered following bungled kidnapping.

1935
May Twenty-four "package" stores open here under new state liquor law.
Oct Governor Johnston declares war on state highway department.

1937
July Palmetto Theater opens at 1400 Main Street.
Aug Mrs. Inez Hutto of Pulaski Street, widowed mother of seven, receives state's first Social Security check.

1938
Feb Under state pressure, city police launch "clean up" campaign.
Dec FDR visits Columbia.

1940
April 1,200 parking meters installed after court battle with local merchants.
Aug Reactivated Camp Jackson becomes *Fort* Jackson.

the Columbia Library Association and then the Timrod Library. In 1924, the city assumed control, transforming Timrod into the Columbia Public Library. Five years later, this new entity found a permanent home in the Woodrow mansion at the corner of Sumter and Washington streets (once the site of a publishing company), yet it still was overshadowed by libraries in much smaller communities throughout the state. However, in the early 1930s, aided by the Rosenwald Fund and state appropriations, this institution greatly increased its holdings, which was just as well since people read a lot in the dark Depression days. Circulation doubled in 1930, compared to 1929, and nearly tripled by the end of 1932. Two years later, county responsibility resulted in a final name change, creating the Richland County Public Library. [15]

The star in Columbia's cultural crown was its Town Theatre, established in 1919 and now the nation's oldest community playhouse. That summer, Sgt. Daniel Reed, then stationed at Camp Jackson, organized the Columbia Stage Society, which the following year became the Town Theatre. Reed, who served twice as artistic director (1919–1927, 1936–1938), deserves much of the credit for this triumph. In ensuing years, Martha Graham danced, Julia Peterkin acted, Carl Sandburg read poetry, and Edgar Lee Masters listened to selections from his *Spoon River Anthology*. An organization that began with only 400 members had nearly twice as many two years later. In 1924, a $12,000 campaign put the group on a firmer footing and also sparked construction of a permanent home on Sumter Street near the university.

Why community theater did so well, so much better than related fields, is something of a puzzle. True, Columbia always has been a good "theater" town, eager to welcome circuses, vaudeville performers, Sara Bernhardt, Lillian Russell, and any other star who came this way. The answer probably lies in Reed's tenure, his ability to get the backing of Columbia's "movers and shakers," and, perhaps most important of all, quality productions that audiences found highly entertaining.

Near the close of this era, in March of 1936 Columbia's 150th birthday party brought together many diverse threads of community life. There were pageants, balls, parades, concerts, an inter-squad football game, a Town Theatre production of *The Pirates of Penzance*, and a commemorative legislative session with members looking anything but comfortable in wigs, knee britches, and frock coats. The most solid by-products were, however, Helen Kohn Hennig's fine history, *Columbia, Capital City of South Carolina, 1786–1936*, fifty-two historical markers, Sesquicentennial Park just east of the city, and the university's arboretum.

The community had come a long way since the dark nadir of 1890, a time when "country boys" ruled the State House and ran roughshod over the great Wade Hampton, the university, and everything else held sacred. Yet success has its price. Tillman, Blease, and others saw in the rise of Columbia the sinister machinations of a "ring" composed of business and professional leaders, men bent upon grabbing every political plum and every appointive office. Thus the upcountry-lowcountry clash took on a rural-urban dimension; and, since the *State* was considered the voice of this alleged conspiracy, William Gonzales himself became a key member.

There are ironies in this tale. Those said to be running the "Columbia Ring" probably were country born and undoubtedly were striving to improve life in their community no less than the bankers, real estate dealers, insurance salesmen, and farmers who met for coffee each morning in Barnwell, Bishopville, and Belton. In addition, Columbia, despite a few skyscrapers, still was firmly rooted in red clay, cotton, and corn. Until World War II, each major highway leading into town had a watering trough for mules and horses. Strangely, the charge of "ring," true or not, was something of a compliment, for it revealed begrudging recognition of a center of power that clearly did not exist until after 1900.

Notes

1. They would have three children: Alida (Mrs. Richard K. McMaster), Consuelo, who died young, and Robert, a handsome University of South Carolina graduate, who succumbed to pneumonia in 1916 while serving on the Mexican border. Note: The full story of the Gonzales family—especially the life of the general and his relations with his children—may be altered by the ongoing research of Cuban-born Antonio de la Cova.
2. Although typical of material often found in book form, these well-illustrated chapters apparently never were reproduced.
3. Heyward, a close friend of the Gonzales brothers, was born at "Goodwill" Plantation in eastern Richland County in 1864, although his family soon moved to Colleton County where he rose to prominence as a rice grower. During the campaign, both Ambrose and William advised their brother to temper his attacks upon Tillman.
4. Sadly, fatal encounters between prominent white businessmen, one of whom often was unarmed, were relatively common in South Carolina during these turn-of-the-century decades. Although this affair was not unique, it probably was the most sensational of such shootings because of well-known figures involved—a lieutenant governor, crusading editor, senator, and so on.
5. *State*, 31 July 1911.

6. City schools instituted manual training classes in 1908.
7. At that time, some districts levied special taxes in behalf of education, others did not. In 1924, with passage of the "6–0–1" law, the General Assembly tried to alleviate some of these inequities. This legislation fixed minimum standards and salary schedules, imposed a new, four-mill county tax, and pledged the state would provide supplemental funds to run schools for six months if a county or district operated them the seventh month.
8. In October of 1914, at Dreher's suggestion, Columbia High students signed a petition seeking a restoration of peace that was forwarded to the "monarchs of Europe." Apparently no reply ever was received.
9. In his 1914 report, for example, Hand noted that sixteen of this state's twenty colleges had such departments. He also was contemptuous of catalogs that talked of beauty, climate, and pure water but said nothing about libraries, laboratories, or educational standards.
10. See the *State*, 31 July 1912.
11. According to Rice, the presence of these colleges caused many a conversation to open with this query: "Are you a Presbyterian or Female girl?" Another common question was, "Are you a South Carolina boy?"
12. Despite a lackluster record, the university launched a football coaching school in the summer of 1921.
13. The Camp Jackson fox hunts led to formation of the Pine Tree Hunt Club in 1938. Five Points, destined to become Columbia's first suburban shopping complex, began to take shape about 1915 when Rocky Branch was sent underground through large culverts and Columbia streets continued eastward into Shandon.
14. During these same months, Hamblin's predecessor, Edgar Brown of Barnwell, spoke on "citizenship" at an Aiken Klan rally and served as counsel for residents of that community said to have been involved in the notorious Lowman lynching.
15. Lucy Hampton Bostick, who became head of the library in 1929, would guide its fortunes for nearly four decades.

Blacks: Outside Looking In

CHAPTER EIGHTEEN

During these decades, any Richland County black interested in the well-being of his race was taken for a ride on an emotional roller coaster. One rebuff after another dominated the turn of the century years as legal segregation à la Jim Crow became a fact of life on trolleys and railroads and in city parks. Other low points occurred in the aftermath of World War I and during the onset of the Great Depression. In the early 1920s, black morale suffered, not because of actual events in the Midlands, but fears that mob violence and Klan activity might spread to the banks of the Congaree.[1] Then, when economic life came to a halt in the 1930s, blacks were the first fired and last hired. On the other hand, 1917–1918 represented a brief moment when whites joined hands with blacks "to make the world safe for democracy," and Columbia's dailies even used "Mrs." when referring to black women aiding that effort. Two decades later, as New Deal programs began to take root and another war loomed, the future brightened once more. Through good times and bad, it should be emphasized, the flame of inter-racial harmony flickered but never went out, nurtured largely by Columbia clergymen.

Blacks reacted to these twists and turns in various ways. Most, caught up in day-to-day affairs, greeted each development with a shrug and went about the business of making a living. Others, attracted by high pay and the promise of a better life, fled north to Philadelphia, New York, Cleveland, and Detroit, especially during World War I. Although it is impossible to know how many departed permanently, census returns indicate that Richland County's white population increased five-fold between 1890 and 1940 (11,933 to 62,484), while the number of black residents merely doubled (24,885 to 48,359). During these same years, Columbia's black population rose from 8,790 to 22,195, but the white sector grew twice as fast, 6,563 to 40,201. By the early 1930s, tangible evidence of this

369

exodus, the local *Palmetto Leader* was publishing a weekly column of social bits from Brooklyn, New York.

A few Columbia blacks staged brief boycotts against Jim Crow, and a handful of ministers and educators redoubled their efforts to make sense out of what was happening. At first, these individuals tried to work within the confines of segregation and even use it to their advantage, seeking, for example, all-black military units in wartime (including officers) and black wards or hospitals staffed by black nurses and doctors. When requests of this sort were ignored, these leaders, often associated with Allen and Benedict, began to mount a cautious challenge to the system itself.

The years from 1890 to 1905 were unusually difficult. Blacks already had begun organizing their own state fair in the late 1880s, although they continued to participate in various ways in the annual white gathering. In 1892, a black man was felled "senseless" by "a brawny-armed countryman" when he peeked out of a canvas at the wrong moment in the "knock-the-negro-in-the-head" booth.[2] A month later, a Georgia black went eight rounds with a local white heavyweight at Clark's Hall, a match won by the home town boy. According to the *State* (22 December), the crowd was "a miscellaneous mass of humanity as far as color and social standing was concerned, and they witnessed one of the prettiest and hardest-fought glove contests ever seen in this city."

Of much greater importance, on the same day this fight took place, a dispute at the scene of a fire in the business district led to the demise of black fire companies. Just as a conflagration at the Lorick & Lowrance store was being brought under control, city police arrested J. L. Simonds, president of the Vigilants, and another black fireman when they refused to obey orders to leave. Angered by this action, both black companies voted to disband. Editorially, the *State* expressed regret but noted it might well be time to reorganize and establish a paid fire department. (When this was done a decade later, experienced black drivers were asked to join the force.)

Early in 1893, fifty members of Columbia's Lincoln Memorial Association—the group that for many years sponsored Emancipation Day celebrations—issued a straight-from-the-shoulder manifesto pointing to obvious racial shortcomings.[3] Blacks, they said, were divided, lacked foresight, and, for the most part, were failures in finance and business. Their ranks contained many teachers and laborers, but few clerks, salesmen, and merchants. Since community strength was centered in the church, they urged blacks use religious leadership to improve their lot. The *State* immediately endorsed these sentiments, conceding it spoke from a selfish viewpoint since spending by blacks would help everyone. "So long as the masses of the negro race remain non-accumulative, whether from idleness, or thriftlessness, or incapacity for profitable grades of labor, the South will suffer."

However, when these same blacks, stirred by talk of a constitutional convention, began to hold political caucuses, the *State* became alarmed. In March of 1894, 300 blacks met to discuss registration procedures for an upcoming municipal election, the first such gathering in years. Those present insisted they had no interest in holding office, but merely wanted a voice in local affairs. A year later, at a courthouse rally they talked openly of protecting their "rights," and in July of 1895 seventy-five blacks from all parts of South Carolina met in the Senate chamber to compose an appeal to federal authorities to block Ben Tillman's plans to disfranchise blacks. In the opinion of the *State*, this was the wrong approach; instead, it said, these men should endorse "restricted suffrage and honest elections," the goal of most whites.

Debate on a new constitution began a few weeks later, and Tillman, of course, got his way. Then, in 1898 the General Assembly finally passed a Jim Crow railroad bill, and in 1903 similar action at the local level separated blacks and whites on Columbia's streetcars. Perhaps it should be noted that South Carolina's capital city enacted few racial ordinances, relying for the most part upon custom and state statute.

Meanwhile, on Labor Day of 1900 the black Capital City Guards, while playing host to the Savannah Light Infantry, decided to hold a parade. As these men were marching down Main Street, a carriage filled with whites knocked several of them down, and a few moments later yet another buggy driven by whites broke into a drill formation in front of the State House. Some soldiers left ranks and tried to pursue the second group. Although it is impossible to know the circumstances involved, Governor McSweeney, who witnessed the fracas near the capitol, immediately disbanded the Guards. The *State* (6 September) called this unfair, stressing the men clearly had provocation to react as they did.

So, by the turn of the century, there were two state fairs each autumn, black firemen had quit in disgust, a new state constitution was disfranchising thousands of black voters, railway travel was "Jim Crow'ed," and Columbia's last black militia company had been sacked. Soon local streetcars would be segregated, and in 1904, for the first time, the city directory introduced a "colored" section.

Yet there were bright spots. In June of 1893, the old city "pest" house in the southern suburbs opened as the Good Physician Hospital for blacks. Strangely, this structure, operated by the Episcopal Church, had been renovated through the efforts of contractor Tilman Watson, the one-time alderman who only a few years earlier had been wielding a horsewhip. Although financial problems closed this facility three years later, in 1896 it cared for 100 ward patients, and some 200 individuals sought help at its dispensary.[4] But the seed had been planted, and other struggling little clinics would appear, although health care for blacks would be a source of much complaint in decades to come, especially after the city approved a $300,000 bond issue for hospital expansion in the 1920s but did virtually nothing for blacks.

In 1901, Matilda A. Evans, Aiken native and graduate of Oberlin and Pennsylvania's Woman's Medical College, founded Taylor Lane Hospital, a twenty-five-bed facility that also trained nurses. As the community's only female physician, Dr. Evans built up a practice among white women that, in effect, subsidized black charity patients. She also handled black railroad workers injured on the job and ran a truck garden and poultry farm that supplied food for her hospital. When Taylor Lane burned in 1914, it was succeeded by the Good Samaritan Hospital (1508 Gregg Street), developed by Dr. W. S. Rhodes and his wife, Lillian. At the same time, blacks launched a campaign to build a larger institution; however, this effort was frustrated by World War I and disagreement within the black community and did not achieve its goal until 1952.

The individual who did much to keep hope alive during these dark years was an unusual man who came to be known as Columbia's "Booker T. Washington." Richard Carroll, born a slave in Barnwell County in 1860 to a part-Indian mother and a white father he never knew, became an orphan at an early age. Carroll attended local schools and then worked his way through Benedict and Shaw University. By the mid-1890s, this energetic young man was traveling throughout South Carolina as an evangelist and Sunday School worker for the Home Mission Board of the Southern Baptist Convention. In June of 1895, on the eve of constitutional debate concerning the fate of blacks, he stopped at the Trenton home of Ben Tillman to interview the former governor (soon to be senator).[5] He came away convinced Tillman harbored little ill feeling toward blacks but feared political foes might use them against him. Thus, in Carroll's words, the situation was not unlike that of Lincoln and abolition. If disfranchisement would protect his administration and his program, Tillman would use it.

Three years later, speaking as a United States Army chaplain, Carroll told readers of the *State* (27 December 1898) that, as soon as he was a civilian once more, he planned to settle in Columbia and work for racial justice. Black meetings in the North dealing with problems in the South only created acrimony and confusion. What was needed, he stressed, was an appeal to the better class of both races. Whites should work to create sentiment for fair play, and blacks should elevate and reform the worst elements of their race so as to ease tensions. Here, for all practical purposes, was the core of Carroll's program for the next quarter-century. Yet he pointedly warned against social equality, "the fly in the ointment."

In April of 1899, Carroll, with the help of northern philanthropists, bought 90 acres of land near Epworth Orphanage and began a campaign to raise $25,000 to support a home for young people and elderly preachers. At the same time, he announced plans to hold religious conferences bringing together members of both races and, in words anyone could understand, issued this appeal to whites:

> We do not ask you to put us in your homes, but to help us get homes. We do not ask to get into your church pews, but help us build churches. We do not ask to get into your school houses, but want you to help us build schools. We do not want intermarriage in your race, but want you to help us produce women of our race. (They are all colors, and we are satisfied.) We do not ask you to let us run the government, but ask you to see that the government gives us justice. We do not ask you to give us '40 acres and a mule,' but a chance to buy and time to pay. . . . Fear not the Ethiopian, but take hold of his outstretched hand and help.[6]

Six months later, both blacks and whites participated in ceremonies dedicating Carroll's South Carolina Industrial Home for Negro Children, a facility that had grown to encompass 316 acres, three cottages containing twenty-two young people, and a livestock herd that included a bull contributed by Ben Tillman.[7]

For the next two decades, despite bouts with ill health, Carroll was in the forefront of virtually every local gathering dealing with racial matters and, in fact, did much to shape attitudes shared by both races. In April of 1905, he launched his lyceum career with afternoon and evening lectures at the Opera House in which he dispensed advice peppered with common sense and told of a visit with President Theodore Roosevelt. On the platform, Carroll was flanked by the mayor, governor, bankers, educators, leaders from all parts of the community. Blacks listened from the balcony, although Carroll—who would become even more popular with whites than with his own people—conceded he preferred to appear before the races separately. Soon after his oratorical career began in earnest, the reasons became obvious; for, he tended to speak bluntly concerning black shortcomings when addressing whites, so much so that some black ministers called him "the white man's pimp." Also, Baptist preachers were incensed when Carroll charged publicly (although he gave no names) that some of them were stealing from their congregations.

In the fall of 1905, Reverend Carroll launched a semi-monthly publication, the *Southern Ploughman,* and personally confronted Thomas Dixon when his play, *The Clansman,* came to Columbia on 14 October. Carroll, who had met Dixon at Baptist gatherings, was the lone black seated on the main floor. As the first act unfolded, he became uneasy; and, when Dixon got up and walked outside, Carroll followed and told the preacher turned demagogue that his drama was an outrage. Dixon replied he was being hasty and should see the entire play. Once he had, Carroll vowed Tillman's anti-black outbursts were "the voice of an angel" compared to the monstrosity created by Dixon.[8]

During the next two years, speaking in the North and Midwest, Columbia's premier orator told whites, you have the power, intelligence, and money. Since you will rule, he said, be just, pay better wages, provide better housing, treat blacks fairly, and help educate them. Blacks, whom Carroll characterized as followers by nature, not leaders, were cautioned to give good service, be honest, and obey the law. Whites, he advised, prefer black workers and, if they are dependable, will pay top wages. Race conflict, in his opinion, hurt blacks, not whites: "The negro must be made to see his condition and be aroused."

As a result of these travels, Carroll became convinced blacks should remain in the South. Since southerners were accustomed to their presence and their labor, he thought it offered greater opportunities than the rest of the nation. However, whenever mob violence erupted, he said blacks should move to another part of the region. In contrast to those who were troubled when states such as South Carolina offered land to foreign immigrants on liberal terms (something never done for blacks), Carroll endorsed immigration. In his view, it would foster another issue and thus divert attention from "the Negro Problem." Also, he believed competition from foreign labor might well stir blacks to greater activity.

In December of 1906, Andrew Carnegie gave Carroll $5,000 that enabled him to enlarge his school and move it to Irmo. On Emancipation Day, 1907, he was the principal speaker in Charleston, where he even charmed the *News and Courier.* During succeeding weeks, Carroll opened a black employment bureau at 1013 Washington Street. (There was no charge for this service; all one had to do was call 1180 to secure a cook, maid, or yard man.) And, he somehow found time to breathe new life into the black state fair.[9]

But the big event of these months was Carroll's first major race conference, which opened at the Opera House on 23 January 1907. Over a thousand delegates poured into Columbia, and both white and black were turned away when Booker T. Washington spoke. His speech, covered at great length by local reporters, included bits of pointed humor. A man, he said, once was told that, for a fee, he could attend a show displaying a sight no one else had seen or would see in the future. When the curtain parted, on the stage was a group of blacks *pulling together* on a rope. As for the race problem, Washington discussed various solutions and then, step by step, rejected most of them. Amalgamation, he warned, was not feasible since, by law, a white man had to be 100 percent white, and anyone with only 1 percent black blood was black . . . which, he added, demonstrated the power of black blood!

Similar sessions were held each January or February for at least a dozen years. These meetings—long on hymns, speech-making, and platitudes and always attended by fifty or sixty prominent whites such as the governor, mayor, and leading clergymen—help to explain the racial calm existing throughout Richland County during the opening decades of this century. These gatherings may not always have produced substantive results; but, as Richard Carroll had hoped, the "movers and shakers" of both races were meeting face to face and discussing common concerns.

However, at times even Reverend Carroll, an optimist with absolute faith in Progress and Social Darwinism, became discouraged. Following the 1916 conference, which, he claimed, was the biggest ever, Carroll unburdened his soul in a revealing letter to the *State* (14 February).[10] Over 1,600 delegates were present, among them, leading laymen of all denominations and preachers "who made from 50 to 75 bales of cotton last year." Yet financial support, as always, came from outsiders, not Columbia. When he took the black state fair to Batesburg in 1909, whites in that community contributed more in one year than Columbia had in eight; and, to add insult, the city council was ignoring the campaign to build a black hospital, even though a non-resident had given $5,000.

> Columbia has done nothing for the negro colleges in its midst. Allen University and Benedict College. It has the poorest public school building for negroes for any city of its size in the South. Something is wrong. Some other cities in the South have negro physicians to practice among the poor negroes, negro policemen, parks for

negroes. And I state here that I have not been a grafter. I do not drink whiskey or sport. I have caused to be spent in Columbia and around it $75,000, and I do not own a home. I have no bank account. If I die tomorrow I would not have enough money to buy a coffin. So I have not been begging for myself, but for others.

Carroll said he did not like to praise himself or parade his condition before the public, but vowed he had been a good citizen for two decades. He would, he declared, call no more conferences in any city that did not cover expenses involved and was abandoning all hope of erecting a black hospital. This mood may have had roots, as Carroll claimed, in poor community support or in ill health and realization that his pragmatic, nonpolitical approach was no longer working. Blacks who migrated north were telling friends and relatives of a different way of life, local black illiteracy was decreasing much faster than that of whites, and war with Germany soon would bring profound change to Richland County itself.

Before moving on to events of 1917–1918, it might be well to discuss a few developments *not* shaped by Reverend Richard Carroll. In the summer of 1910, Columbia's black merchants formed a business league that would assume greater significance in post-war decades.[11] Then, in June of 1912 blacks began plans to cooperate with Associated Charities, a forerunner of the Community Chest. Within six months, a full-time employee was added to the staff, a black woman whose work was subsidized by contributions (fifty dollars a month) from black citizens interested in welfare activities. In October of 1913, for example, this social worker handled forty-five cases, visited eighty-six families, and conducted fourteen office interviews. For the most part, she busied herself with requests for transportation, fuel, and food, but she also boasted of a crippled beggar who, with her help, had found work making quilts.[12]

In that same year, 100 white housewives of Columbia, distressed by a "servant problem" that was developing as blacks flowed northward, formed a Home Keepers' Association. On 25 March, members urged blacks to attend a special meeting at Ladson Presbyterian Church called for the purpose of discussing mutual concerns. In the fall of 1914, when the outbreak of war in Europe caused an economic crisis in the Midlands, these same ladies opened a free employment bureau, and Associated Charities set up a soup kitchen that fed hungry whites in the morning, blacks in the afternoon. During these weeks, in an unrelated matter, the *State* mounted an all-out drive for passage of a compulsory school attendance law. Opponents, who feared it would help blacks, were told that keeping the black man ignorant hurt the white man, too. A white farmer unable to employ blacks then had to compete with them, this daily said, and any attempt to draw the color line in industrial progress was both "folly" and "insanity." This campaign bore fruit in February of 1915 with enactment of the desired legislation, although a local option proviso weakened its effect.

On the eve of war two years later, blacks gathered at a local church, with Richard Carroll presiding, to whip up patriotic fervor. Not everyone cooperated. One local minister (Ralph M. Myers of Elmwood Avenue's Second Nazareth Church) expressed his views quite forcefully: "The white folks have the Winchesters, and you haven't even a little pop-gun. They'll not ask you whether you want to enlist. They'll just take you out and shoot you if you don't." To stifle protest and restore order, Dr. Matilda Evans jumped to her feet and launched a stirring chorus of "My Country 'Tis of Thee." Carroll then urged those present to grow potatoes and onions, quit baseball and sports, and enlist in the army. "We've had jim crow [railroad] cars, jim crow street cars, jim crow cemeteries, churches, and schools. Now let us have a jim crow regiment, surgeons, and hospital staff."

That same day (5 April), a huge preparedness parade, composed only of white units, marched through Columbia's streets, and forty-eight hours later Governor Richard Manning met with a black delegation headed by Carroll. Manning thanked the group for its interest in black officers, but said he had no plans to enlarge the national guard. Instead, he suggested blacks aid the war effort by remaining on farms and lashed out at those fleeing to factory jobs in the North. The following day, Manning offered a fifty-dollar reward for the arrest and conviction of labor agents whose false claims, in his opinion, were disloyal acts and actually harmed blacks. A short time later, however, the governor abandoned his knee-jerk reaction, named a committee (headed by Richard Carroll, of course) to coordinate war work of blacks with David Coker's State Council of Defense, and began to talk more openly of black patriotism.

In succeeding months, as the population of Camp Jackson soared, black churches opened reading rooms for servicemen, and the Phillis Wheatley Club (begun a decade earlier by teacher Celia D. Saxon for black working girls) developed a small recreation center at 1001 Washington Street. When Carroll's annual race conference opened in mid-March of 1918—a bit later than usual—delegates were entertained by the camp's black infantry band, and Manning was on hand to beat the drum for still greater exertion in behalf of God and country. After describing the death of his "mammie," he spoke out strongly against lynching, sin, and pool-hall loafers. To this litany, he added a stern admonition that war-time cooperation never could lead to social equality: "[It] will not be tolerated by the southern whites and wouldn't be good for the negroes."[13] In response Professor R. J. Crockett, a Carroll ally, assured Manning of all-out support and then launched into one of the strangest boasts of national valor ever heard in the Midlands.

> And let this assure you, sir, that any governor that stands for the principles and new standards you have proclaimed here today may count on Epharim [sic], Esau, Joshua, and Ham, and the offspring of the old black mammies you so reverently speak of. And take it from me and the negroes in khaki, we are with you. . . .
>
> We have not come up here today as in times past seeking 'rights,' but duties. We lay on the altar for this world's war our lives and property. And if a German u-boat sticks its ugly nose into a ship at Charleston the negroes of Camp Jackson will paint the waters of that harbor red with patriotic blood; and if a Prussian airship shall drop a death-dealing missile on the grave of our beloved Wade Hampton, the negroes of South Carolina will line the capitol square with the skulls of their heroic soldiers. . . .
>
> Your words about your black mammie's death stir me. And we will get rid of our foes—liquor and immorality of which you so feelingly speak. Yes, it is up to us to avoid what causes strife and lynching. We will do so:
>
> > And moving on from high to higher,
> > Become on fortune's crowning slope,
> > The pillar of a nation's hope,
> > The center of the world's desire!

Soon, local blacks were planting war gardens and promoting sale of bonds and stamps with even more gusto. According to press accounts, they purchased war bonds valued at $45,000 during the second national campaign and by mid-1918 had invested almost as much in stamps. Three months later, in yet another drive, they subscribed to bonds worth $50,000, and on 1 August nearly 200 individuals from all over South Carolina (including blacks) met at Chicora College to discuss health problems such as typhoid, tuberculosis, and malaria. At the conclusion of this two-day conference, blacks presented a resolution expressing their sincere appreciation for an opportunity to cooperate in the war effort, "feeling that we are part of this great commonwealth." In addition to promises of aid and assistance, they also thanked the Council of Defense and the State Board of Health for inviting them, as well as for "the luncheon served at the college." On the day war ended, a black hostess camp with quarters for visitors and a cafeteria opened at Camp Jackson. And on 12 November, a parade to the State House, band music, and remarks by the mayor helped dedicate yet another facility for black servicemen, the Red Circle Club at 1129 Washington Street.

Throughout 1919, conferences and meetings of one sort or another (all with racial overtones) were held almost monthly in Columbia. Motives were mixed—to welcome the boys home and make sure they did nothing "foolish" once they got here, press for reform or press against it, or take steps to avoid bloodshed such as was erupting in other parts of the nation. An Emancipation Day orator at Benedict College, after praising America's doughboys and racial goodwill engendered by war, lashed out at mob violence, inadequate schools, "horrible" railway cars, and denial of "a sacred heritage," the right to vote. At the annual race conference, Richard Carroll enunciated his usual conciliatory theme ("we can't win by making demands"), but another speaker called for *equal* education and *equal* justice: "We want the rights any other American citizen has." A month later, when Columbia turned out to welcome a black regiment back from France—forty-two white officers and 1,450 enlisted men who had trained at Camp Jackson—these appeals became more specific. Various speakers, with Governor Robert Cooper on the platform, called for a chance to vote and participate in government and the right to serve on juries and have their neighborhoods patrolled by black policemen.[14]

Columbia residents tackled some of these questions at a meeting held in July of 1919 at Sidney Park Methodist Church. In a frank exchange, thirty prominent whites and many more blacks discussed how religious leaders and city officials could improve community relations. A judge defended the police (a favorite target of the audience), while conceding they sometimes made mistakes. Yet patrolmen often had to deal with blacks "on dope," he added, and "some of the overseas men have come back with foolish notions in their heads." Several, this judge declared, had been caught with "obscene" pictures. A short time later, the pastor of Bethel AME Church, fearful an "ignorant" black might light the fuse that would start a riot, told his congregation to honor Jim Crow seating on streetcars, destroy pictures brought back from France, and take every precaution to avoid trouble. You stay on your side of the fence, he said, and whites will do the same. Meanwhile, leading clergymen met at the YMCA and drew up a resolution extolling wartime cooperation and condemning violence.

During that same "hot" summer of 1919, several prominent business-men formed the South Carolina Constructive League. Its goals, de-scribed in the James Heyward Gibbes Papers, were many and diverse: good government, law and order, better schools, just and fair taxation, hospitals and medical clinics for all, paved highways, cotton marketing fa-cilities, and programs designed to attract settlers, encourage military training, and foster respect for manual labor. The principal aim, however, was "the just treatment of the negro and the cultivation of harmony be-tween the races but at the same time the inculcation of the principle that our State shall be dominated by its white citizens." In addition to Gibbes, Irvine Belser, Wyndam Manning, and Dixie Carwile also helped chair-man R. Beverley Herbert launch this well-meaning but short-lived orga-nization for white males only.

Since Richland County came through the immediate post-war period unscathed, efforts such as these—spearheaded by both white and black—apparently paid off. Nevertheless, the racial question obviously was becoming more political and black leadership was changing. Carroll, laid low by a series of strokes, became bed-ridden in the mid-1920s. When he died shortly before his seventieth birthday in October of 1929, the annual black fair halted briefly in his honor, the *State's* lead editorial saluted him as a man of clear vision ("His were the ways of peace and constant endeavor . . . these are the ways that succeed"), and a delega-tion of white Spanish-American war veterans played Taps over his grave. W. E. B. DuBois marked Carroll's passing with these words in *Crisis* (February 1930): "He was the type Negro conservative who is welcome to Southern white people, but at the same time, he was not without ideals for his race and was a hard worker."

Carroll's place was taken by several individuals. One was I. E. Low-ery, born a slave in Sumter County in 1850 and a frequent contributor to the *Record*. His columns and articles, which began before World War I, form a running commentary on regional life, especially things Methodist, until the *Palmetto Leader* appeared in January of 1925. That weekly, which existed for three decades, was the creation of N. J. Frederick, an Orangeburg native educated at Claflin and the University of Wisconsin (A.B., 1901). Onetime principal of Howard School and director of sum-mer institutes for teachers, in 1913 Frederick was admitted to the South Carolina Bar. Although lawyer Frederick was involved in legal matters (notably Aiken's notorious Lowman lynching) and numerous business ventures, the *Leader* became the voice of black Columbia—and a strong one—until his death in September of 1938.

Isaac Samuel Leevy (1877–1968), a protégé of Richard Carroll, was a fixture on the Columbia scene for six decades. Beginning as a merchant tailor, Leevy soon was selling furniture and operating a barber-beauty shop, garage, farm, and funeral home. He helped found the Red Circle Club during World War I and Victory Savings Bank and was active in affairs of the National Association for the Advancement of Colored People (NAACP) and Republican party, even running for Congress in 1916, 1946, and 1954.

Frederick and Leevy were joined by various ministers, Benedict and Allen faculty members, and several women, among them, Dr. Matilda Evans, Matilda Griffin, and Modjeska Montieth Simkins. In addition to creating local health centers, in 1916 Dr. Evans organized a Negro Health Association that embarked upon a program of preventive medicine that, she stressed, could benefit both races throughout the state. A decade later, she built a recreational pond and dance hall on the outskirts of the city (Lindenwood Park) and in the early 1930s opened a free child-maternal clinic with the financial backing of both city and state authorities. However, this facility closed soon after her sudden death in 1935. Distressed when the state American Legion adopted an all-white policy, Matilda Griffin, whose sons Samuel and Clifton were killed in France, used their insurance benefits ($7,000) to build a two-story brick building at 2029 Taylor Street. This structure—commercial offices on the first floor and a meeting hall for black veterans and other groups on the second—was dedicated on Armistice Day, 1926. Among those on hand were the governor, mayor, and representatives of the Salvation Army. (Sixty-four years later, in the fall of 1990, this structure was razed to make way for new development.) Modjeska Simkins, a former teacher, spearheaded state-wide efforts to stem tuberculosis in the 1930s and, inspired by the work of Dr. Evans, spread her net to encompass the whole spectrum of health problems confronting blacks. After 1940, she would become well-known as an outspoken fighter for civil rights.[15]

In the mid-1920s, some of these individuals formed a local NAACP chapter that in January of 1927 launched a membership drive fashioned after the bond and stamp campaigns of 1918, complete with battalions of workers, battalion captains, and definite operational goals. In that same month, another group, the Negro Business League, met with city councilmen in an effort to secure for blacks a share of both skilled and unskilled jobs on permanent civic projects such as streets and sidewalks.

The league, which included both male and female entrepreneurs, embraced many NAACP ideals and often heard speeches from Chamber of Commerce representatives urging them to be good citizens and boost Columbia.

The principal goals of this emerging black leadership were a political role for their race, a real hospital, a public library, and better schools. They enjoyed some successes such as a branch library that opened at the Phillis Wheatley YWCA (1429 Park Street) in July of 1930, and the New Deal, of course, built new classrooms. Yet the 1920s and 1930s were, for the most part, an economic wasteland that inhibited innovation for all residents of the Midlands, regardless of color.

At times, divisions within the black community also hampered progress. Efforts of the Duke and Rosenwald funds to provide health facilities were stifled by bickering among black physicians. In 1934, Columbia Hospital, despite loud black protest, opened a segregated wing where, it turned out, black doctors could practice only on private cases, not charity, which were reserved for white interns (although the hospital did set up a training school for black nurses). Since indigents constituted 90 percent of black patients, black doctors, angered by such rules, restricted their activities to Good Samaritan and Waverly hospitals. In 1939, a long-standing feud between these black facilities finally ended, but by that date foundation funds were severely limited.

Action in the political arena was equally confusing. Blacks interested in such matters continued to support Republican candidates, although in August of 1926 Democrats discovered, somewhat to their surprise, a fully qualified black party member in a rural Richland County precinct.[16] When forty blacks registered to vote as Democrats in March of 1932, the *Record* said these individuals "unknowingly" had signed up for the Columbia municipal election. The *Palmetto Leader* countered they knew what they were doing. Although this move, instigated by the NAACP, was thwarted by court action, in 1939 an Allen University professor was summoned for duty on a county jury. Yet local blacks were wary when Franklin D. Roosevelt appeared on the national scene. The *Leader* noted in July of 1932 that he was "an adopted son of Georgia, and that in itself bodes nothing but ill for the darker brother." Despite FDR's popularity, in 1940—since they were barred from Democratic primaries—members of Columbia's black establishment still were in the Republican fold.

Until the mid-1930s, the local NAACP was not especially vocal, but a drive backing anti-lynching legislation before Congress led in 1938 to increased activism and formation of the Columbia Civic Welfare League.

This group, headed by forty-five prominent blacks, turned its attention to improving playgrounds and housing, reducing black crime, and curbing police brutality. When a new bus terminal opened in 1939 without a lunch counter for blacks, the league yelled foul. In November of that same year, members staged a city-wide rally condemning police brutality and issued a call for black policemen. The following summer, aided by white lawyer R. Beverley Herbert, the league confronted the city council with specific charges against several members of the force. The council merely warned police to be "more judicious," but even that was something of a triumph.[17]

Despite such outcries, there were a handful of encouraging signs. When Governor John G. Richards launched his iodine blitz in January of 1930, he took a cue from his World War I predecessor and named a black committee on natural resources, as well as a white one, of course. That same year, blacks organized their own division within the Community Chest. And, despite almost universal separation of the races, in at least two realms of everyday life the line was somewhat blurred, much as it had been in the 1890s at fires and prize fights. One of these was the market place; the other, the theater. In each instance, blacks had something whites wanted: their money, and the music and song they could provide.

Two factors tended to enhance blacks as customers. As many of them departed for northern cities, Columbia's black-operated businesses suffered a relative decline between 1900 and 1930, down from about 10 to 5 percent of all such establishments, and economic realities of the post-war years put any potential customer, regardless of color, in the driver's seat. In November of 1927, Tapp's took the plunge and began advertising in the *Palmetto Leader*. Two years later, when Belk's supplanted Mimnaugh's, it initiated a series of full-page ads, and soon these department stores and other merchants as well were bidding for black dollars, especially during the Yuletide season and whenever crowds came to town for a convention or fair. In time, they were joined by Penney's, Eckerd Drug, Colonial Life Insurance, R. L. Bryan, Kimbrell's, Adluh Flour, and J. Drake Edens's food stores. On occasions, even the Chamber of Commerce and the city itself welcomed black visitors. In 1940, the *Leader* was quick to praise a sandwich and drink facility that Silver's Five and Dime opened to everyone, "regardless of race or creed," and more editorial flattery was forthcoming when a remodeled Belk's provided rest rooms for blacks and added a dozen or so blacks to its staff.

These innovations were no challenge to Jim Crow, even though white clerks were waiting on black customers, but the world of entertainment

presented unique problems. It fostered an easy-going, relaxed atmosphere where itinerant black performers, whites (perhaps minstrels in
black-face), and individuals with varying opinions of Jim Crow mingled
freely. As a rule, those watching were segregated—whites on the orchestra floor, blacks in the balcony . . . or often in a so-called gallery up near
the ceiling.[18] But rules could be bent. Richard Carroll, we know, got an
orchestra seat at a Thomas Dixon play in 1905, and it seems possible that
other prominent blacks and their families were accorded similar privileges from time to time. Carroll's race conferences and especially jazz re-
vues of the 1920s also altered seating patterns. In the first instance, a
section or group of seats in some church or meeting hall was reserved for
whites; in the second, local theaters often gave blacks the entire house on
the first night, while restricting them to balconies on the second.

With the opening of Township Auditorium yet another wrinkle developed. When well-known black orchestras played there, blacks paid
eighty-four cents to dance; whites watched from seats in a spectators' gallery for forty-four cents. And it was just such an arrangement as this that
won Columbia fleeting fame in 1937. University students who crammed
into a small gallery at the Big Apple Club on Gates Street (a building that
once was a synagogue and now has been moved a short distance and carefully restored) duplicated steps they saw blacks performing. In short order, the "Big Apple" made its way to other cities and swept the nation up
in a short-lived craze.

But back to the theater for a moment. During the inter-war years,
Columbia was host to many jazz greats, among them, Ethel Waters,
W. C. Handy, Bessie Smith, Louis Armstrong, Ella Fitzgerald, Count
Basie, Fats Waller, Jimmie Lunceford, and Cab Calloway. Yet on stage
one is faced with the perplexing fact that in January of 1924 the Columbia
Theatre could present a black pageant with a cast of 200 (with seats for
whites) that portrayed cotton fields and slavery and talked of freedom and
loyalty, and no one objected. But five years later, when the Town Theatre
tried to produce *Potee's Gal*, a play based upon stories of E. C. L. Adams,
hardly a radical spirit, white protest was so great that the performance
was cancelled.

Special note should be taken, perhaps, of the appearance of black
tenor Roland Hayes at the Columbia Theatre in February of 1931. Half of
all seats were reserved for blacks, not the normal orchestra-balcony division, and Hayes subsequently was honored at a public reception and ball
at Township Auditorium. All of his party, except the star, stayed at the
Hotel Jefferson. Also, in the late 1930s, several "white" theaters along
Main Street inaugurated black only, Saturday night shows (beginning at

11 P.M. or later) that featured ten-dollar "Screeno" prizes. One by-product of special seating arrangements, shows only for blacks, and sections reserved for white spectators was the fact that members of both races had to read the fine print in any entertainment ad with care.

Black Columbia of the 1930s, much like its white counterpart, presents puzzling contrasts. Blacks lived largely in three areas, although residential segregation by law or ordinance did not exist. To the northeast, there was Waverly with two colleges, two small hospitals, and homes of the black establishment. Across town to the northwest, another group of black dwellings stretched from Seaboard Park to the waterworks, and to the south an arc of shanties (some soon to be replaced by New Deal housing) extended from Senate Street easterly below the university. Within this milieu, there was a black medical society, baseball teams, churches, schools, and an ever-changing mass of social organizations—Young Madams, Le Cercle Entre Nous, the Brawley Book Club, Radio Social Club (male), a veterans' group, Boy Scout troops, and a New Century Club, obviously named for a prestigious white group. On the outskirts of town one could find tourist camps such as Cabin in the Cotton near Ridgewood that offered lodgings, dancing, sandwiches, drinks, and plate lunches and the Taylor Tavern at Camp Fornance where patrons also could swim. In the summer of 1940, blacks took special pride in the selection of Miss Sepia America at the New York World's Fair—Helen Elizabeth Lewis, an Allen University sophomore.

W. E. B. DuBois, who visited Allen in February of 1929, remarked that his audience was "unusually intelligent and attentive," although he said a female quartet somehow managed to rip "every shred of melody" out of "Steal Away." DuBois wrote that he traveled throughout much of the South via pullman car by undisclosed arrangements, and files of the *Palmetto Leader* indicate some local blacks, either alone or in groups, often did the same.[19]

Seven years later, in November of 1936, William Gonzales replied to an inquiry from Walter White, executive secretary of the NAACP, concerning the condition of blacks in South Carolina. Gonzales boasted that his *State* was the first southern daily to actively oppose lynching. Blacks, he said, certainly deserved better justice and better living conditions, yet he insisted that, in his lifetime, improvement had occurred in Columbia. Gonzales was right, although Modjeska Simkins and friends could point to many areas where change was needed.

It is a giant step from being beaned by a baseball to serving on a jury, but that in essence is what had happened in five decades. And, as a result, it is apparent that the title of this chapter ("outside looking in") is somewhat inappropriate. According to the precepts of segregation, this was true. Nevertheless, as these years reveal, rules were not always adhered to, and blacks, strictly speaking, were not "outside" of life in the Midlands at all. As maids, laborers, and sharecroppers, they were very much on the *inside*, an integral part of the day-to-day world and witness to whatever was transpiring.

There are, of course, obvious parallels to earlier times. Jim Crow, the bastard offspring of slavery, ran into some of the same dilemmas his father faced. Both were schemes endorsed by part of a nation (and perhaps only a numerical minority of that section), and both were flawed by inherent exceptions and legal contradictions. Also, in a sense, both were brought down by war, one in 1865, the other eight decades later in 1945.

Notes

1. The only lynching in the immediate vicinity apparently occurred near Chapin in August of 1921 when a disgruntled black sharecropper shot and mortally wounded a respected white farmer. The cause was a festering dispute over division of cotton seed. Although police from three counties were involved in this affair, the lynching took place in Lexington and immediately was deplored publicly by area residents. At the same time, Richland authorities were searching Blythewood swamps for a black man who allegedly killed a popular Columbia policeman. He was not apprehended; and, as the investigation dragged on, it was far from clear that a black was to blame.
2. *State*, 17 November 1892.
3. *Ibid.*, 21 February 1893.
4. *Ibid.*, 24 December 1897.
5. *Ibid.*, 3 July 1895. Carroll, who was not asked to join Tillman on the porch, claimed he endorsed the Edgefield reformer in 1890, despite threats on his life by fellow blacks. Actually, the two men respected each other. The senator subsequently assisted Carroll's industrial home for young people and once remarked that Reverend Carroll "always has borne a good reputation and has a good deal of sense."
6. *Ibid.*, 18 April 1899.
7. During these same months, Carroll was the moving force behind an act passed in February of 1900 creating a juvenile reformatory for boys less than sixteen years of age. This legislation established a segregated facility in nearby Lexington County.
8. *State*, 17 October 1905. The *State* and other South Carolina newspapers also were critical of Dixon's work. See John H. Moore, "South Carolina's Reaction to the Photoplay, 'The Birth of a Nation,' " *Proceedings*, South Carolina Historical Association (1963), pp 30–40.
9. In 1909, under Carroll's direction, the fair was held in Batesburg, not Columbia. Local whites took considerable interest in these proceedings, which, like anything Carroll

touched, had a strong religious flavor. On the final evening, twenty-one white gentlemen of that community, stressing their great faith in his work, presented an astonished Carroll with a horse and buggy.

10. Carroll was on excellent terms with the Gonzales family, who helped pay for the education of his children, and he had no difficulty publishing articles and letters in the *State*.

11. In 1900, ninety-six black commercial establishments were scattered throughout the business district. By 1920, the number had risen to 220 centered upon the 1100 block of Washington Street adjacent to Main and the farmers' market. For the most part, these were groceries and personal service operations. See Paul Frederick Seman, "Structural and Spacial Distribution of Black Owned Businesses in Columbia, South Carolina, 1900 to 1976," Master's thesis, University of South Carolina, 1977.

12. *State,* 27 November 1913.

13. *Ibid.,* 14 March 1918.

14. At this juncture, municipal authorities were being roasted at mass meetings by angry white citizens for inefficiency and corrupt practices. Illegal liquor, too many soldiers, and too few police, plus various wartime strains, probably account for this outcry. Nevertheless, it is true that mayor and council were trying to recover $20,000 taken by a former assistant treasurer who left town in April of 1918.

15. See Edward H. Beardsley's *A History of Neglect* . . . (Knoxville, 1987) for a discussion of the careers of Evans and Simkins and regional health policies.

16. *Columbia Record,* 10 August 1926. Two years later, according to the *Palmetto Leader* (10 November 1928), Hoover carried Columbia's Seventh Ward by ten votes.

17. Paul Lofton, "The Columbia Black Community in the 1930s," *Proceedings,* South Carolina Historical Association (1984), p. 88.

18. When the Allen-Benedict choirs performed at the Town Theatre in February of 1930 at a benefit to raise funds for books in black county schools, the *Palmetto Leader* remarked, "Negroes were compelled to climb to the topmost gallery of the theater to hear their own people sing."

19. In these years, the Atlanta train station maintained a "secret" list of prominent blacks entitled to purchase pullman tickets when heading north, a privilege accorded others who (with the permission of those concerned) used their names to purchase tickets. It seems likely that a similar arrangement existed here in Columbia.

PART V

The Decline of Sectionalism, 1940–1990

Factors that have made the Midlands, South Carolina, and the South part of a homogenized America during the last half century are so obvious that they hardly need to be mentioned. World War II, industrial growth, franchise foods, television, interstate highways, and the demise of "white only" signs all have done their bit to make one nation of what often seemed to be a collection of semi-autonomous sections. Today, few doubt that the South is any longer far removed from the mainstream of U.S. life. Yet this theme can be stressed too much; for, hand in hand with uniformity comes a natural urge to preserve regional uniqueness. Also, climate, the innate composition of society, even voices one hears on the street tend to frustrate the best-laid plans of Madison Avenue. A blind man dropped into Columbia's business district soon will realize he is not in Portland, Pocatello, or Providence.

In nearby suburbs such as Shandon, Eau Claire, Cayce, and West Columbia, regional differences are more subtle. But any visitor from New Jersey will be struck by a population composed overwhelmingly of Anglo-Saxon and native-born and by proud Protestant citadels with their towering churches, offices, schools, halls, and even gymnasiums. He would look in vain for the flashing neon sign of a friendly corner tavern and might have difficulty finding Italian, Greek, and Jewish delicacies. Farther out, newer housing developments—Harbison, Grayland Forest, Quail Hollow, and Spring Valley—with their meandering streets and self-conscious architectural mix (except for magnolias and dogwood) could be found almost anywhere in the lower forty-eight.

Rounding out the urban picture are a handful of foreigners and a substantial number of blacks. Neither group is, in itself, unique, although the banks of the Congaree certainly are home to fewer immigrants and more dark-skinned residents than one sees in many American communities. In the 1980s, with upwards of half a million people living in the two-county area centered upon Columbia, slightly more than 2 percent of them were foreign-born and perhaps 25 percent black, with Richland County having a lion's share of both. According to the 1980 census, only 1.4 percent of Lexington residents were born outside of the United States, compared to 2.7 percent in Richland. At the same time, 13,654 blacks were living on the west bank of the Congaree and 103,955 on the east. Statistics such as these certainly reflect great change during the past century, although one should remember that in other times, say the early 1800s, the percentage of both foreign-born and black would have been much greater. (For population totals, 1790–1990, see Appendix 5.)

There is, through movement of peoples and pressure of national trends, a cloak of conformity being woven that conceals regional identity. Yet each of us is enough of an individualist, regardless of birthplace, to crave a dash of diversity and even swim against the current at times. Unlike most Americans, Midlands residents can drink countless glasses of iced tea during any season of the year, eat grits for breakfast day in and day out, and feast on barbecue and fried chicken several times a week without complaining. Whether white or black, they probably will have some familiarity with their forebears and brag of ties to a small-town, rural way of life a few generations back. And they will be conscious of their Midlands heritage, caught as they are between upcountry and low.

Columbia was, of course, born of compromise and has spent much of its life balancing views of contending forces—rural and urban, farm and factory, Piedmont and coastal. This conciliatory stance, a view some would label "pragmatic," was of paramount importance during the integration crisis of these decades and may serve equally well in years to come.

Over half a century ago, the WPA guide to this state characterized a typical South Carolinian as having "fire in his head, comfort in his middle, and a little lead in his feet." Concern for comfort remains as strong as ever in the Midlands, but to achieve that ease, fire and lead have been transformed . . . the former tempered by several wars and profound social change and the latter by desire to realize more fully the American dream. That dream, it might be noted, was closed to many residents of the Midlands in 1940, both white and black. In the 1990s it is not, and this, without doubt, is the most far-reaching development of these decades.

Battles
Big and Small

CHAPTER NINETEEN

During the decades from 1940 to 1970, residents of Columbia and Richland County were caught up in a series of campaigns, some of them with national and even international implications. These include World War II, a "police action" in Korea, and the Vietnam quagmire, as well as efforts to improve the quality of local life—better schools, wider streets and paved roads to handle more and more automobiles, and yet other facilities demanded by a burgeoning population, such as hospitals, parks, and basic urban services. And the key word is *urban,* for the local landscape was fast becoming less rural (2,428 farms in 1940, 799 in 1964, and only 530 in 1969) and increasingly part of a general residential-commercial sprawl that paid little attention to traditional boundaries.[1]

In these same years, Richland's population grew from 104,843 to 233,868, while that of Columbia rose from 62,396 to 113,542. Moreover, at mid-century, census officials, who considered Richland to be 77.6 percent urban, were dealing with a metropolitan complex encompassing towns and cities on both sides of the Congaree. Twenty years later, that domain was home to 322,880 people, one-fourth of whom lived in Lexington County communities such as Cayce, West Columbia, and Irmo, part of which was in Richland. This collection of 84,180 households was 26.6 percent black, although the ratio was slightly higher in Richland County alone (32 percent). About 14 percent of the families in this metropolitan enclave were existing below the poverty level; on the other hand, 375 households had annual incomes in excess of $50,000. Over 115,000 individuals were gainfully employed, largely as professionals, managers, industrial laborers, sales personnel, and service workers. But only 457 of them were classified as farmers or farm managers. Despite change, those dwelling along the banks of Congaree continued to be overwhelmingly of native American stock. In 1970, 3,381 foreign-born were living here, nearly a thousand Germans, followed by Asians, Mexicans, and former citizens of the United Kingdom in that order.

Turning to Richland County, by 1970 about one-third of its 233,868 inhabitants were enrolled in school and college classes, and another third (78,458) were employed in non-government jobs. Government workers—local, state, and federal—totaled 21,312, equally divided between male and female employees. Only 766 laborers were tilling Richland County soil. In summary, population totals for the region look like this:

Table 5. Regional Population, 1940–1970

	1940	1950	1960	1970
Richland County	104,843	142,565	200,102	233,868
Columbia	62,396	86,914	97,433	113,542
Lexington County	35,994	44,279	60,726	89,012
Columbia SMA	———a	186,844	260,828	322,880

a The Census Bureau did not begin systematic grouping of counties with trading centers of 50,000 or more as "Standard Metropolitan Areas" until 1950, later changed to "Standard Metropolitan Statistical Areas" (SMSAs). This table does not reflect Fort Jackson's World War II population of 40,000–50,000.

The source of this growth is no mystery. The Columbia area entered World War II with a relatively diversified economy—a healthy mix of agriculture, wholesale and retail trade, and professional services, supplemented to a lesser degree by jobs in construction, textiles, and government. In succeeding years, farming almost faded from view and government at all levels kept adding employees as it expanded into new fields. The wild card on the local scene was Fort Jackson. A hubbub of activity in the early 1940s and the source of considerable wartime profit and some consternation, "the fort" seemed about to close in 1949, then greatly increased its personnel (up from 2,239 in 1950 to 19,862 in 1960) and

---

"We don't have any cotton farming around here any more because of the labor problem. Why should anyone want to work the fields when they can go to Columbia or Sumter and get a job paying more money? All of the farmers around here are planting grain crops—soy beans, wheat, barley and oats—so they can harvest by mechanical means."

Mayor Earl T. Campbell of Eastover,
Columbia Record, 1 May 1960.

by 1965, for the first time, was constructing truly permanent buildings.[2] So, in essence, development and retention of that military base was yet another battle Columbia residents waged during these decades.

In October of 1939, after nearly two decades of limited activity as a state facility, Camp Jackson began to receive National Guardsmen on an extended basis, not just for summer training. Ten months later, federal authorities resumed control and christened the installation "Fort Jackson," emphasizing it would be a *permanent* post. Within a year, 21,000 men were in residence and construction totaling $17 million was under way. (President Franklin D. Roosevelt, who made the first of several visits in March of 1941, pronounced the base "simply great.") Meanwhile, late in 1940 it became an induction center for draftees, and thousands more— soldiers, civilian workers, wives, and sweethearts (real, potential, and alleged)—poured into the Midlands. Rents soared, restaurants and beer joints boomed, and, for all practical purposes, the Great Depression became a distant memory.[3]

As a result, the final year of peace was a hectic ordeal for many as defense-related activities strained local resources almost to the breaking point. Fort Jackson expanded to accommodate over 30,000 men and revealed plans to handle as many as 43,000, making it one of the largest bases in the nation. New facilities appeared in Lexington County (soon identified as "Columbia Army Air Force Base"), as well as at Congaree and Sumter. In September, the army launched maneuvers of staggering proportions when 400,000 men participated in a "Red and Blue" clash directed by officers stationed at Forts Jackson and Bragg. Bulletins from "the front," a battleground covering portions of two states and centered in the Darlington-Bennettsville area, even overshadowed news of real war in faraway Russia. And there were casualties as some thirty-five men died, largely in traffic accidents.

Although these maneuvers had little direct impact upon Richland County, local authorities were locked in a hard-fought battle of their own with illegal liquor, beer joints, and "transient women." In January of 1941, Fort Jackson spokesmen conceded that a monthly payroll of $2 million was attracting unsavory elements. According to the *Record* (9 January), some 150 females were in "registered" houses and whiskey was easy to get. One outlet in the county even had curb service. All patrons had to do was "toot" to get mixed drinks.

In ensuing weeks, Mayor L. B. Owens and the U.S. Army went on the offensive. Both wanted enhanced recreational facilities for servicemen and more police to curb crime; however, differences concerning how to achieve such goals quickly emerged. The military, for example, vowed Sunday movies were "almost imperative." The Chamber of Commerce agreed; ministers did not. Nevertheless, by mid-year the army got what it wanted. Councilman Fred D. Marshall, head of the police committee, was not pleased when the mayor invaded his domain nor with his honor's outspoken assault upon vice, although Owens tended to blame the public at large, not men in blue. In any case, with the cooperation of the sheriffs of Richland and Lexington counties, Mayor Owens ordered all prostitutes out of the Columbia area by noon of 21 March 1941. Within hours, he proclaimed that most of them had left. But fifteen months later, Governor R. M. Jefferies was seeking the old CCC camp in Pontiac as a detention home for Columbia's scarlet women, brazen white females who either defied the mayor's command or chose to return, and anti-vice drives were a recurring theme throughout the war years. In 1942, 507 women were arraigned on prostitution charges, compared with only sixty-one in the previous year, and in March of 1943, on average, police were arresting three women per day.

Strange as it may seem, even recreational centers for servicemen stirred controversy. Early in 1941, the Masons opened an enlisted men's club in an old bus terminal at Main and Laurel streets, Owens suggested GI parties be held at Township Auditorium, and military authorities began building a facility for a thousand blacks stationed at Fort Jackson. In August, a black USO opened at 1125½ Washington Street, and plans were unveiled for a huge white USO on Arsenal Hill. The site selected, land at Laurel and Assembly that Edwin Robertson had given to the city for a park, aroused the ire of insurance magnate Edwin G. Seibels, who had purchased Robertson's spectacular white mansion located nearby. Seibels launched a court battle to thwart federal take-over of municipal property but, after Pearl Harbor, threw in the sponge, sold his home, and moved elsewhere.

During these months of pseudo-peace, rents and traffic both increased about thirty percent. Use of city buses nearly doubled (up from 5 million passengers in 1940 to over 8 million a year later), and municipal officials proudly announced in June of 1941 that 400 parking meters erected along Main Street fourteen months earlier (despite strong merchant protest) had paid for themselves. Henceforth, they anticipated a weekly harvest of six hundred dollars in nickels and pennies. City workmen also installed more powerful street lights; and, although efforts were made to limit pleasure driving, in late summer filling stations began running out of gas.

By October of 1941, there were 1,836 Richland County men in uniform. Of that number, 472 were draftees, the rest enlistees or men called to duty as members of the National Guard. Their departure, as well as expansion of Fort Jackson and widespread patriotic fervor, stimulated arrangements to collect aluminum, entertain GIs, sell defense bonds, and stage "limited" blackout drills. Women began to hoard silk stockings, farmers expressed concern over a labor shortage, and the KKK rallied at the Hotel Jefferson and endorsed aid to Britain.

Except for preparation for war, and with 7 December the real thing, the biggest event of 1941 on the local scene may have been the opening early in September of a drive-in movie theater at the intersection of Fort Jackson Boulevard and Garner's Ferry Road. Capable of handling 300 autos and featuring the state's largest screen, it quickly became a favorite rendezvous of both soldiers and civilians. This was, of course, a precursor of future trends, recreational outlets far from Main Street catering to patrons on wheels. Two years later, with gas severely rationed, management rose to the challenge and provided lawn chairs for those who came on foot, by bus, or on bicycles.

Like most Americans, residents of the Midlands were stunned by the attack on Pearl Harbor. To prevent sabotage, troops soon were guarding the city power plant, major bridges, and local textile factories. The *Record* hurriedly produced a Sunday evening "extra" bearing a woefully inaccurate, flag-waving headline: "U. S. WINS FIRST CLASH." Mayor Owens, recovering from a bout with pneumonia at his son's home, sent a wire to the White House assuring President Roosevelt of Columbia's all-out support and placed the city's civilian defense force on a war footing. Forty-eight hours later, Owens succumbed to a heart attack, ending his fifteen-year reign, the longest in municipal history. He was succeeded by one of his severest critics, Fred D. Marshall, promoter of parks and playgrounds, who, in the spring of 1942, beat out Frank Owens (son of the deceased mayor) for a four-year term.

The elder Owens, a Louisiana native with family roots in Stateburg, was a doctor with a host of friends. According to the *Record* (10 December), he once introduced Huey Long to a Columbia audience by praising FDR and had as his goal for this city "a convention a day." "If red tape stood in his way, he cut through it. If it required that he run the risk of what appeared to be impolitic, he accepted the risk and still, often to the surprise of his friends, was all the stronger politically for it. He was," the *Record* concluded, "a builder of Columbia." (In the same issue, this afternoon daily provided advice on what to do in case of an air raid.)

In the closing weeks of 1941, Fort Jackson shelved plans to release draftees over thirty-six years of age, scores of young men flocked to local recruiting stations, and the USS *Columbia*, a 10,000-ton cruiser, slid down the ways in Camden, New Jersey, christened in proper fashion by sixteen-year-old Jean Adams Paschal. The struggle that ensued is reminiscent of both the Civil War and World War I. Shorter than the first and much longer than the second, from the American point of view it was an overseas affair and, despite slogans, speeches, and the pledge of Mayor Owens, never developed into a truly all-out effort. Of course, there were patriotic rallies, shortages, rationing, and millions of men and women in uniform, but what set World War II apart was an emphasis on planning and organization and concern for postwar America. To some degree, those directing affairs profited from experience learned in 1917–1918 and the 1930s.

To aid the war effort, volunteers conducted salvage drives to collect rubber, tin cans, and rags. Streetcar rails were dug up, and even J. R. Roddey's 1909 Buick racer joined the scrap heap. In July of 1943, Township Auditorium became the focal point of a "Share Your Clothes with Russia" campaign that amassed 80,000 pounds of shoes, sweaters, and socks for our brave wartime friends. Rationed items included tires, sugar, gas, meat, coffee, shoes, and canned goods. Fresh fruit and vegetables never required ration stamps, and in mid-1943 a community cannery appeared at 1112 College Street. There one could process garden produce for two cents a can or have it done by others for five cents, assuming willing hands could be found.

Before fighting ceased, 30,552 Richland County men registered with three local draft boards. Of that number, 21,447 had physical examinations, which 7,494 (35 percent) failed to pass. The most frequent cause was educational deficiency (1,525), followed by neurological problems (924). In all, 8,654 young men were inducted into various branches of the armed services, and 5,047 enlisted (a figure that included women), making a total of 13,701.[4] A five-volume compilation of South Carolinians in uniform indicates that at least 167 Richland County residents were among the dead and missing, 1941–1946.

Even if not quite as pervasive as the Civil War, this conflict, in some manner or other, touched virtually every home in the Midlands. Mrs. B. D. Derrick of 3601 Phillips Street, Eau Claire, had six sons in the service, eighty-seven-year-old Adaline Weed of rural Route 2 could boast of seventeen grandsons who were fighting for their country, and nineteen Little Mountain residents bearing the name of Shealy answered the call to arms. The Derricks, Shealys, and all of their neighbors got a crash course in basic geography as they tried to figure out where "their boys" were and, at the same time, keep track of fast-moving events. However, the headlines of the *State* and *Record*—bold, glaring, and *always* upbeat—often were misleading. As the Allies piled success upon success and American forces seemingly routed the foe at every turn, a few readers must have wondered why the war was not over. One event of particular interest was the daring air raid on Tokyo in April of 1942, especially when it became known that General James Doolittle and his bomber crews had trained for this exploit at the Columbia Army Air Force Base.

Two minor ripples on the home front were increasing prominence of women in the work force and the demise, for the duration, of Sally League baseball and sporting events such as the Carolina Cup. In December of 1942, female tellers appeared at Citizens and Southern Bank. Shortly after that, the city police department hired its first woman clerk, seventeen-year-old Margie McLendon, and two other women began pumping gas at a station located at Gervais and Harden streets. In time, still more were repairing cash registers, working on farms, and invading other fields once dominated by men. Inter-city baseball was replaced by a league composed of players from the community at large, including Fort Jackson and various mills, and with the help of naval trainees the university's sports program limped along as best it could. The state fairs (white and black) were held as usual each fall, as was Columbia's music festival. An appropriate and practical form of wartime recreation, victory gardens, in all shapes and sizes, flourished in various parts of city and county, although Eau Claire councilmen suggested no one tend potatoes, peas, and cabbages on the Sabbath.

But the most unique aspect of wartime Columbia was a head-over-heels love affair with the GI. In July of 1943, perhaps the crest of this emotional binge, those in uniform could select from a bewildering assortment of attractions that continued almost around the clock. Five USO clubs (two of them for blacks), an extremely active city recreation department, church groups, mill village community centers, and various fraternal orders vied with each other for the attention of off-duty servicemen. (The Elks patio at Hampton and Henderson streets, complete with outdoor dance floor, fireplaces, and picnic facilities, could accommodate a thousand or more.) A simple listing of bingo games, dances, block parties, athletic contests, movies, and song fests for a seven-day period covered a column and a half of fine print in the Sunday edition of the *State*. One also could roller skate, finger paint, or play bridge, whist, checkers, and ping-pong. And there were special meetings for wives of servicemen ("prenatal and infant care"), voice recording sessions ("say hello to mum and dad"), and discussion groups ("the peace that will follow the war"), as well as classes in art, foreign languages, music appreciation, sewing, and handicrafts.

At that time, the city was entertaining 100,000 service personnel each month, most of whom visited the main USO, a $300,000 structure that opened at Laurel and Assembly streets in the spring of 1942. On holiday weekends or pay day, as many as 25,000 young men might overwhelm movie theaters, restaurants, parks, and sidewalks, although by late 1944 their numbers were beginning to decline somewhat.[5]

The city recreation department, with two-thirds of its annual $80,000 budget supplied by federal funds, was especially active. Dance coordinator Isabel Whaley Sloan, daughter of mill builder W. B. S. Whaley and the lady who taught three generations of Columbians their ballroom manners, mounted an ambitious weekly schedule of events at all of the local bases, many of them formal. Young ladies who wished to attend merely called the recreation center in advance (4-1228 or 4-3241); however, they had to be transported in buses provided for that purpose, not by private conveyance. On one occasion, Mrs. Sloan hosted an extravaganza for 1,600 soldiers and as many girls at Township Auditorium, but her most memorable affair was a Christmas ball at Fort Jackson. The hundred or so youngsters who were attending the dance, packed and ready to spend the holidays with their families, learned shortly before the music started that they were heading overseas instead. "My, they were a sad-faced bunch of boys," she recalls. "Tears were everywhere. Those dances were supposed to end at 11, but I bribed the orchestra into playing two more hours. Then I accompanied each young lady to her door and, if necessary, told her parents what had happened. By the time I got home myself, my husband had the police searching for me!"[6]

Perhaps it should be noted that Columbia's civilian population was not forgotten entirely in this rush to entertain servicemen. Each week some events were earmarked for children and teenagers, and on Friday evenings the auditorium in the largest USO became a non-military canteen for jitterbugging youngsters.

Why Columbia greeted the GI so warmly is an intriguing question. Traditional southern hospitality is a partial explanation, and from its inception this community has loved uniforms, parades, and military pomp. Also, these dances, parties, and games were fun. They helped relieve boredom and, momentarily at least, banished concern over empty gas tanks, ration quotas, and loved ones far from home; for, prominent in the minds of many, was the hope that someone somewhere would do the same thing for "our boys."

The Midlands aided the war effort in still other ways. Factories and mills ran full tilt, and farmers did whatever they could, despite troublesome shortages of materials and labor. To some degree, the latter was relieved by boys too young for military service, women, and German POWs lodged in compounds at Fort Jackson and the Columbia Army Air Force Base. Air raid wardens held their drills, and Red Cross classes in first aid, surgical dressings, and home nursing abounded, sometimes as many as thirty-three in a single week. Bob Hope, Jane Wyman, John Payne, and Sergeant Alvin York came to town to sell war bonds (Hope also found time for a round of golf at Ridgewood Country Club), and visitors to Fort Jackson, in addition to FDR, included Winston Churchill, Jack Dempsey, Betty Grable, General George C. Marshall, and Joe Louis.

Among the fort's best-known residents was infantry officer Winthrop Rockefeller, grandson of famed "John D." In 1942, to mark the Yuletide season, Winthrop's mother and her Hudson River knitting circle presented all of the men in Company H, 305th Infantry, with hand-made sweaters. Another young man who attracted attention was a North Carolinian, the grandson of one of Barnum's Siamese twins.

With the successful invasion of Europe in mid-1944, any sense of crisis or emergency evaporated. Draftees no longer were arriving at Fort Jackson for training, blackout rules had been suspended, and few were interested in being air raid wardens or collecting rags and cans. That summer, the *State* and *Record* urged area residents to save fuel, money, and time by spending their vacations at home. In August, Mrs. Ruth Shaw McGarity (2228 Devine) won a fifty-dollar prize for a letter describing sights to be seen without leaving the city. During that same month, a Valley Park gathering was swept by rumors that Germany had surrendered. A short time later, a full-page ad in the *State* warned it was everyone's patriotic duty to aid local farmers: "Pick Cotton—Join the Cotton Picking Brigade."

After nearly three years of exciting headlines, war had to share the stage with regional concerns such as political campaigns, schemes for a "little TVA" on the Broad and Congaree rivers, and a proposal to move the university to the suburbs, perhaps out by the Veterans Hospital, although Kershaw County officials quickly offered a site near Camden. In March of 1945, Louis D. Drake became the first ex-serviceman to use a GI loan to purchase a Columbia home (2744 Burney Drive). Also in

March, because of deteriorating runways at Owens Field, commercial aircraft began using the Columbia Army Air Force Base in Lexington County.

However, the subject most frequently discussed in the spring of 1945 (other than the war itself) was a sensational murder that would garner headlines for many months. Virginian Samuel Epes—handsome, wealthy, associated with the U.S. Army's Medical Administrative Corps at Fort Jackson, but not a doctor—claimed he panicked when his young wife apparently died after taking pills he had secured for her at the base hospital. Lieutenant Epes first reported her missing, but after a week or so led police to the spot where he had buried her body. The trial that ensued involved legal and political figures well-known throughout South Carolina and was followed by several appeals for clemency, including one held before Governor Ransome Williams in a jam-packed House chamber in December of 1946. Epes eventually served thirteen years in prison and was released in December of 1959.

Meanwhile, in May of 1945 fighting ceased in Europe, a welcome event but not a cause for great celebration in the Midlands. The end of the war in the Far East on 14 August was, however, quite another matter. By 7 P.M., Main Street was bedlam—a sea of cars, soldiers, sailors, shouting civilians, and the noise of sirens, cow bells, firecrackers, auto horns, the university's chapel bell, and youths beating on tubs. Broken windows, petty theft, and inebriated revelers kept police busy throughout the night. Federal and state employees were given a forty-eight-hour holiday, and some stores also closed their doors.

With peace, Columbia residents, like all Americans, faced a myriad of problems. Streets, highways, schools, and public services had gotten a boost of sorts from the New Deal, but wartime maintenance and repair varied from inadequate to nonexistent. The private sector was equally chaotic as servicemen and defense workers scrambled for jobs, homes, and autos. In addition, the overriding fear from 1600 Pennsylvania Avenue to Bluff Road was an economic disaster such as followed World War I, and decisions made at every level of society during the first years of peace should be viewed in that light.

As war was ending, taking a cue from the 1930s, local leaders tried to spark interest in two huge projects: navigation of the Congaree and an educational-medical complex centered on the Veterans Hospital. The dream of "Port Cayce" foundered in succeeding decades when it mushroomed into schemes for hydroelectric dams and flood control. Federal authorities and South Carolina Electric and Gas were less than enthusiastic, and timber interests, whose lands would be under water, were adamantly opposed. Proposals to move the university—the trustees gave approval, but students and most alumni did not—never got much of a hearing once it became clear that the Medical College had no intention of leaving Charleston.

By the late 1940s, despite occasional outcries concerning escalating living costs, no "Great Depression" had appeared on the horizon, and it became apparent that regional investment in homes, apartments, and office buildings, as well as the day-to-day spending power of a growing population, was fostering a stable, postwar economy. The value of city building permits, slightly over $5 million in 1947, exceeded $10 million only three years later. Thus recession fears were supplanted by concern for traffic, downtown parking, schools, the future of Fort Jackson, and the changing nature of race relations.

Perhaps the scope of these dilemmas can be demonstrated with a few figures. Between 1945 and 1950, the number of motor vehicles registered in Richland County nearly doubled, rising from 25,679 to 49,650, and across the river Lexington experienced a similar increase, 8,969 to 17,406.[7] In 1941, Columbia had only twenty-four traffic lights; ten years later, 101. At mid-century, only half of the streets within the city limits were paved, and many of those that were needed re-surfacing. A few important thoroughfares had been widened and more soon would be, but mid-town traffic was beginning to frighten merchants, who became convinced that autos bumper to bumper was the community's number one problem.[8]

On the other hand, teachers, students, and parents might well disagree. Enrollment in Richland County schools rose from 21,090 in 1940 to 39,385 in 1960. Much of this growth was in Columbia itself, which in the 1950s added 1,200 new pupils each year and, on average, forty-seven classrooms. By 1965, total county enrollment was 46,893 (about 40 percent black), and the region had seventy-five schools (fifty-two of them elementary), all with more than four teachers and grouped in only three districts.

Fort Jackson, scheduled to close in 1950, was granted a reprieve by the Korean War and in 1954 issued checks worth $51 million to 30,000 servicemen and civilian employees. Various aspects of race relations, a matter that impinged upon the economy, schools, and even life at "the fort," will be discussed in the next chapter.

None of these special interests—traffic, schools, Fort Jackson, or race—existed in a vacuum. They often were related and therefore tended to stimulate limited inter-government cooperation. In the fall of 1946, Mayor Frank C. Owens, who beat out Lester Bates in the Democratic primary and then faced a Republican challenger (the first in seventy-five years), convinced county officials to share the cost of extending city water and sewer lines to suburban industrial sites.[9] These same gentlemen even could discuss forming a joint health department, but fashioning a three-way commission to administer a regional airport, formerly the Columbia Army Air Force Base in Lexington County, led to angry words. Finally, in September of 1947 a twenty-five-year lease was negotiated that seemed to satisfy the city and both of the counties involved. However, two years later a crisis arose when the Richland delegation to the General Assembly failed to supply its share of funds, and the city, on its own, arranged a new fifty-year lease. In return for one dollar a year and half the profits, Lexington County granted the city sole authority over what was immediately re-named the "Columbia Metropolitan Airport." Nevertheless, when a "jet port" was built in the mid-1960s, yet another leasing arrangement had to be hammered out.

During the late 1940s, there was bickering within Columbia's five-member city council as well, prompted, it would appear, by dissension in the police and fire departments. Simply put, some council members worked harder than others on municipal matters and often enjoyed greater clout because of governmental units they theoretically supervised. This system, which intermingled legislative and administrative responsibilities in a questionable manner, obviously was outmoded, and these debates led in June of 1948 to suggestions that the city hire a manager. Fourteen months later, voters gave approval (1,222–650), although this move failed to end wrangling among mayor, police chief, and county sheriffs concerning gambling and illegal liquor. In May of 1950, J. Macfie Anderson succeeded Owens as mayor, amid promises that each city department would control its own affairs with the "least interference possible" from council, and in August, Thomas P. Maxwell became Columbia's first city manager.

The federal census of that same year had a marked effect upon life in South Carolina's capital. It revealed that 8,541 homes, about 27 percent of all residential dwellings, were substandard. Of that number, one-third lacked running water and half had no inside toilet or bathtub. Soon an Urban Rehabilitation Commission was at work trying to relieve such conditions and, despite opposition from real estate interests, by 1954 the city had enacted minimum housing standards and renovated or demolished nearly 2,000 substandard units.

This campaign, which developed a general slogan, "Fight Blight," was city-wide in scope but concentrated upon about ten blocks in largely black neighborhoods. By the mid-1950s, property owners had spent $2 million fixing up property, and new buildings valued at nearly twice as much appeared on land that was cleared. Meanwhile, the city housing authority, under the direction of John A. Chase, Jr., continued the New Deal policy of erecting low-cost structures for those displaced. During the next two decades, eleven developments covering nearly 160 acres were built, the largest being Saxon Homes near Benedict College. Yet not everyone was happy. Some residents resisted plans to alter neighborhood life, especially when churches were involved, and black tenants often viewed this "war on blight" as little more than a white plot to move them elsewhere and mask their true plight. Admittedly, a major beneficiary was the university, for slum clearance paved the way for expansion south of the traditional campus all the way to Rosewood Drive and west beyond Assembly Street toward the river.

If the 1950 census triggered urban renewal, the 1960 head count had a quite different impact. In the mid-1950s, after nearly thirty years of bickering, Columbia absorbed Eau Claire's circular domain. This move added 14,000 people to the city and presumably pushed population over the 100,000 mark.[10] However, the Chamber of Commerce, wanting to make certain that figure would be surpassed in 1960, launched an annexation drive. The cheerleader was insurance man Lester Bates, who became mayor in June of 1958 following a primary run-off decided by only fourteen votes. Within hours of taking office, Bates was laying plans to build a new auditorium that soon was transformed into dreams of a huge, multi-purpose civic center. Six months later, his wish list had expanded to industrial sites, parking garages, a new post office, a Federal Reserve bank, a larger airport, a coliseum, and an orderly annexation program appropriate for a metropolis, which, he predicted, would have a population of 200,000 in 1975.

For whatever reasons—fear of higher taxes and "outside" control or racial concerns—this attempt to annex county land backfired. Between November 1959 and May 1960, six suburban neighborhoods became towns, at least on paper: Arcadia Lakes, Ardincaple, Bendale, Boyden Arbor, Independents, and Ravenwood. And across the river, Cayce and West Columbia held merger talks and even staged an election, but at length decided to continue their separate ways.

These newcomers joined four other incorporated communities within Richland County (Columbia, Eastover, Forest Acres, and Forest

Lake). Columbia and Eastover had roots in the 19th century, but the "forests" are more recent creations. Forest Acres, wedged in between Columbia and Fort Jackson, was born in 1935 to take advantage of a WPA program designed to deliver city water to rural homes. It contains part of historic Quinine Hill near the intersection of Forest Drive and Beltline Boulevard, land once owned by Hamptons and Taylors. During World War II, shops and stores appeared to serve GIs, and in the 1960s Forest Acres began to annex land that included the "paper" town of Ravenwood.

Forest Acres had no police force until 1962 and no property taxes until 1968. But by the mid-1980s, it could boast of an annual budget of $1.7 million and 6,000 residents.[11] Forest Lake, once Dent's Pond, was formed in 1951, also to get water, but by 1980 had disappeared. In fact, the census of that year indicates that, of the seven little towns established in the 1950s and 1960s, only Arcadia Lakes was recognized as a functioning community. However, during the 1970s two more organized communities appeared—Blythewood to the north (population ninety-two) and Irmo, a growing little town that straddled the Lexington-Richland line. Blythewood, first incorporated in 1879 and in Fairfield County until 1913, reenacted its incorporation in 1974. In 1980, about two-thirds of Irmo's 3,957 citizens lived in Richland County.

The upshot is, area population grew by a healthy 40 percent in the 1950s, rising from 186,844 to 260,828, but Columbia could find only 97,433 people within its borders in 1960, thus narrowly missing the 100,000 mark. Despite disappointment, South Carolina's capital must have been doing some things right, for it won "All-American City" status in 1951 and 1964 and came close in other years as well. This honor, then bestowed annually upon a dozen or so communities by the National Municipal League, was achieved in the first instance largely because of a successful citizen effort to implement city-manager government. Thirteen years later, peaceful integration brought national recognition once more.

Expansion fever flared again in the fall of 1968 when Columbia, with Pentagon approval, annexed Fort Jackson. This move increased the municipal domain from 20 to 100 square miles and, according to the *Record* (12 September), boosted population to 123,000. Yet, because of white flight to the suburbs, the official count in 1970 was 113,542, somewhat less than anticipated but well over the goal set a decade earlier.

Motives for annexation hardly need to be explained. Columbia, supplier of urban services (water, sewage lines, garbage disposal, fire protection, and so on), wanted to monitor growth in areas served, neighborhoods that someday might seek to join the city. Secondly, tax revenue from suburban homes and businesses, some of the latter refugees from Main Street, could offset losses caused by relocations. This same exodus, a fact of American life of the postwar era, stirred efforts to make "downtown" more attractive, as well as proposals to improve urban services, combine certain city-county functions, and perhaps even merge local governments into a single entity.

Schemes for upgrading the traditional business district took many forms. In the wake of World War II, the solution seemed to be wider streets, another bridge across the Congaree, a parking garage, and better bus service. But the growth of Five Points (especially the appearance of a huge, all-purpose grocery store in July of 1949 and "Sears Town" five years later, Sears having vacated a Main Street address) called this approach into question. Also, in May of 1954, Columbia's first "shopping center" opened on Rosewood Drive, followed twelve months later by Cayce's Parkland Plaza and in 1961 by Richland Mall, then the state's largest merchandise mart and the first in this area to incorporate a big department store.

In the late 1950s, led by the editorial staff of the *Record,* merchants began to promote the "Midlands" concept, the theory that Columbia was the natural market place for a band of counties stretching across the center of the state. And this "shopping capital of South Carolina," they said, had not only its well-known "downtown" but a dozen other shopping areas close by, thus making a virtue of suburban growth and change. In time, petunias and palmetto trees graced several blocks of Main Street, but proposals to create a pedestrian mall were rebuffed. If a female shopper, one even could attend free movies as guest of the Downtown Council of Columbia, a group that in 1960 was publishing full-page ads extolling the joys of "a pleasant stroll from 7,000 parking places" to local stores.

But the truth was, "strolls" along Main Street were not always pleasant, especially in the "combat zone." Men stationed at Fort Jackson in postwar decades still marvel at the transformation that has occurred, as do residents who recall almost nightly fistfights and brawls. In April of 1961, after long ignoring several Main Street spots dominated by bar girls, loud music, and cheap booze at fancy prices, city leaders and the press went on the attack. Their initial target was a group of night clubs in the 1800–1900 blocks such as the Town Pump, Stardust Lounge, Friendly Spot, and Pink Elephant, followed by several beer halls down by the capitol. In time, with the help of state officials who licensed these establishments and grand jury presentments deploring such "nuisances," both areas were cleaned up.

Meanwhile, in the late 1950s, a J. C. Penney store opened at 1423 Main Street, Tapp's expanded and built its own parking lot, and Belk's absorbed what had been Efird's. Also, at least three large motels appeared in the downtown area, and by 1965 still more new buildings were changing the Columbia skyline. Among these structures was a large post office at Seaboard (Sidney) Park, a state office building at Senate and Bull streets, and various high-rise apartments and university dormitories.[12] The following year, the city opened a parking garage at Assembly and Taylor streets served by a free shuttle that had carried patrons at the New York World's Fair. For three years, shoppers could park and then board this open-air contraption that wound slowly through the business district. But in June 1969, despite minor protests, the "Carolina Queen" made its last run. Twelve months later, Dutch Square—then the largest enclosed shopping center in the Carolinas—opened at the intersection of two interstates on land that only a short time before had been pasture. Downtown was putting up a good fight, but each group of suburban stores, always bigger and grander than its immediate predecessor and with ever more free parking, was providing stiff competition.

Efforts to improve urban services included all sorts of measures ranging from kicking hundreds of hogs off the city dump and replacing it with a landfill to banning chicken-raising within the corporate limits and pit privies where sewer lines were available. Yet state rather than local action often had more impact. Creation in 1946 of a Greater Columbia District for water lines, sewerage, and drainage, together with subdistricts, all under the control of a commission, established a pattern frequently duplicated. Soon other commissions for both Columbia and Richland County, with General Assembly approval, were borrowing money and supervising airports, rural recreation, historic preservation, ambulance service, music festivals, animal control, and streetlight systems. Of special significance was the fact that these bodies sometimes operated without regard for town, city, or county boundaries.

In February 1951, Columbia established a municipal planning commission, thus joining two words heard more and more frequently throughout these years. A decade later, at federal urging, urbanized areas of Lexington and Richland counties formed a joint planning commission to deal with highway development. And in April of 1969, Governor Robert McNair divided the state into ten planning districts, thus giving birth to the Central Midlands Regional Planning Council. This organization, covering four counties (Fairfield, Lexington, Newberry, and Richland)

and representing thirty-four units of local administration, has gained steadily in stature since its inception.

If commissions were an end-around maneuver to foster cooperation, to some extent so was planning. From the end of World War II into the 1970s, it seems that every man, woman, and child living in or near Columbia must have been asked to aid some group intent upon shaping this region's future. Not only average citizens but experts such as Wilbur Smith and Associates, Atlanta's Hammer, Greene, and Siler, and city planner Costantinos A. Doxiadis dreamed, probed, reflected, held meetings, and issued charts, diagrams, and recommendations. In general, they said enhance approaches to the river ("Congaree Vista"), coordinate overall planning, develop core areas for commerce, industry, government, education, and residential housing, get rid of railroad crossings, and establish a single administrative structure for city-county government so as to end duplication and promote efficiency.

But this last point, merging traditional governments, was too radical a departure for those accustomed to waging turf wars to contemplate. In addition, such a union never could win the whole-hearted approval of the Richland County delegation to the General Assembly. These lawmakers, the real power in local affairs, controlled appropriations for communities within the county, including Columbia, and were able to appoint or influence the appointment of numerous officials. In fact, as late as 1969, Richland's four senators and ten representatives somehow formed themselves into *eighteen* standing committees ready to deal with every aspect of daily life from agriculture to townships. Strangely, a state government that lamented the excesses of central authority in Washington sang a different tune in Columbia.

Nevertheless, proposals for city-county union or adaptation to meet changing needs were almost as common during these decades as suggestions for Columbia's future and schemes to convert the Congaree into a great waterway. At one point, civic leaders even considered turning Columbia into a *county*, a step that at least would provide the community with its own delegation to the state legislature. The most comprehensive of these merger proposals was, however, a full-page plan for a governmental body run by a fifteen-member council, published in the *State* on 1 September 1963.

Despite an apparent stalemate (the League of Women Voters already had thrown in the towel on this issue), change was in the air. In 1949, Charleston County took the first tentative step toward home rule when it won the right to elect a council, a move that foreshadowed the possibility of some form of managerial administration. Then in 1964, Columbia and Richland County got permission to enter into agreements designed to eliminate duplicating services, a legislative act notable for its vagueness. At the same time, Richland's seven commissioners, one from each township and long the nominal governing body of the county, were transformed, amid some outcry, into road commissioners. These officials were replaced by a five-member board of administrators elected at large, a group that in 1969 became a county council like that of Charleston County. Meanwhile, in 1966 the city and county agreed to coordinate tax procedures, an obvious example of official cooperation. Although efforts to build a city-county administrative center were frustrated, by 1970 the annual United Fund drive and Greater Columbia Chamber of Commerce, as well as an ambulance commission and various planning organizations, were operating with little regard for municipal and county boundaries.

If this era closed with promise of greater home rule and enhanced regional cooperation, it also was witness to one of the most disruptive episodes in the history of the Midlands. The precipitating factor was public disagreement over America's involvement in Vietnam. A small protest when General William Westmoreland, a Spartanburg native, received an honorary degree at the university in 1967 and ripples from the conviction of Captain Howard Levy that same year for refusing to train Green Berets at Fort Jackson were portents of things to come.[13]

In January of 1968, those trying to coordinate GI protest against the war opened the UFO Coffee House at 1732 Main Street, one of a chain of similar meeting places located near large military bases that served soft drinks, coffee, and antiwar and conventional literature. In the summer of that year, author Norman Mailer appeared and addressed 200 patrons. Some of them undoubtedly were SLED agents and federal informers, for the establishment already was distressed by what it thought was a nest of drug dealers, hippies, profanity, and radical political thought. Late the following year, after months of open harassment, the UFO was shut down, and five people who operated it charged with maintaining a public nuisance. Four of them—one fled and declined to return—subsequently were found guilty and sentenced to six years in jail. The UFO Corporation also was fined $10,000.

This verdict was so outrageous (compare it with what happened to those running bars in the "combat zone") that local authorities sought out lawyers representing the four and arranged a tacit, out-of-court settlement. In return for not appealing the verdict, which they readily conceded never could be sustained, county and city officials were willing to forget the whole affair. After all, the UFO was closed; they had achieved their goal. So, the verdict was set aside because of "errors" in the trial, and those convicted were permitted to leave the state.

During these same months, nineteen-year-old Brett Bursey, a USC student and instigator of numerous antiwar incidents such as burning a Confederate flag and selling Viet Cong flags on campus, attacked a local Selective Service office and poured paint over records. His companion in crime, supposedly his best friend, was, it turned out during the trial that ensued, a SLED informer. Eventually, Bursey served nearly two years behind bars, the only individual involved in the local protest movement of the 1970s who actually was tried, convicted, and locked up.

Smoldering yet insignificant antiwar sentiment would have amounted to little except for two developments on the national scene and two more on the banks of the Congaree. President Nixon's decision to invade Cambodia, after hinting for months that peace was just around the corner, and the Kent State tragedy were greeted with widespread horror and dismay. Here in Columbia, police began patrolling the university's student union (Russell House) to guard against action by what they said was a "UFO in Exile" movement, and Fifth Solicitor John Foard, citing transcripts of the UFO trial, launched a witch hunt to oust professors at both the University of South Carolina and Columbia College, who, in his opinion, harbored radical, even Communist ideas.

Forty-eight hours after Kent State, angered by Foard's attack, police in *their* student union, and developments at home and abroad, University of South Carolina students—despite an appeal from Governor McNair—began a two-day strike. On 8 May, forty-one of them were arrested when they refused to leave Russell House, the first of many who would feel the strong arm of the law. Soon police were joined by the National Guard. Interestingly, although all of these men were armed, no account of the disorder that ensued mentions gunfire. Columbia, in short, was *not* going to be Orangeburg.

On the 12th, the board of trustees suspended thirty-one students, whereupon their friends stormed the administration building where those gentlemen were meeting. This action, naturally enough, increased tension and led to a strict 9 P.M. to 6 A.M. curfew that lasted for four days. All gatherings of over six people were banned, and the campus was restricted to faculty, students, and, of course, lawmen. Despite such measures, over 100 individuals were arrested during the night of 12–13 May.

Tear gas drenched the campus, young people were clubbed (but never shot), and head wounds were acknowledged even by those booking alleged offenders. Some of those apprehended undoubtedly taunted police and defied the curfew, and both police and guardsmen were quick to respond, perhaps too much so. To add to the confusion, activist Jane Fonda, in Columbia to drum up antiwar support among GIs, spoke to 2,000 at Maxcy Gregg Park on the 14th. Her message, somewhat strangely, was a sermon on non-violence. Don't break windows, she advised, get political.

With the end of the curfew, faculty members began meeting with students to ease their anxieties, but Solicitor Foard, ever vigilant, chose that moment to attack university president Thomas Jones, alleging his handling of recent events was "weak." However, students, faculty, and Columbia newspapers quickly came to the president's defense. In July, despite a personal, two-hour appeal to the trustees, Foard was unable to unseat Jones.

Meanwhile, in June the university held graduation ceremonies as usual, something many institutions were unable to do that year, and thirty-six individuals, most of them students, were formally indicted for their activities in early May. On 18 June the trustees met once more and expelled a dozen young people. However, upon advice of counsel, all were eventually re-admitted; for the trustees soon became aware of the fact that the Bill of Rights and Constitution actually did have force within the ivory tower. They no longer could be accuser, judge, and jury.

What were the results of this bizarre episode? It clearly reshaped the trustee-student relationship, brought the issues of Vietnam and civil disobedience down to the local level (if ever so briefly), altered somewhat the normal reserve existing between student and professor, and obviously changed the manner in which USC students viewed authority. When police and guardsmen first arrived on campus in force, according to most accounts, they were jeered by 400 and cheered by 2,000. Following tear gas, beatings, and constant identification checks, especially the cards of good-looking coeds and long-haired males, that ratio was reversed. Those in uniform may not have won friends, but they certainly influenced people. The most chilling effect was damage done to the careers of those who stood up for what they thought were their legal rights. Some students clearly suffered because of their political views, and several professors at Columbia College and the university were sent packing as a result of association with the UFO Coffee House and various forms of protest. Interestingly, in the years since 1970, some of those representing authority at that time have conceded to former adversaries that they (the establishment) were wrong and the protesters were right.

As intriguing as this outburst may have been, it actually was a brief affair and had little impact beyond the center of Columbia. There were, however, three other developments of these decades, each quite different in nature, that were felt in nearly every household in city and county. These were the rise of air conditioning, the growth of television, and the ongoing struggle by blacks for their civil rights.

Air conditioning was nothing new; in fact, a few southern mills were being cooled by huge machines before World War I. During the 1930s, air conditioning spread to movie theaters, railroad cars, hotels, restaurants, and department stores. In July of 1950, Trailways proudly displayed a dozen air-conditioned buses at its local terminal. Then, in the spring of 1952, Columbia newspapers for the first time began to advertise home air conditioners, magic boxes that could transform any steamy room into a cool paradise. Early models, still quite bulky, sold for $229.95, but the price soon declined. Two years later, one could buy an air-conditioned home on Brentwood Drive, and by the close of the decade many public places in Columbia and Richland County, including churches and schools, were air cooled. In 1960, only 12 percent of South Carolina's homes were air conditioned, but ten years later the figure was 40 percent and in 1980 had risen to 68 percent.

Television, a contemporary of home air conditioning, was virtually unknown until the early 1950s. According to the *Record* (9 June 1949), Columbia then had only two receiving sets. One was owned by radio repairman Melvin Levkoff, who claimed he could get an Atlanta station, except when an old-time car went by his shop. By September of 1950, local papers were publishing the weekly schedule of a Charlotte station, and Columbia's stores were advertising sets for sale. In June of 1952, many of them mounted a concerted drive to sell air conditioners and TVs so families could watch the political conventions of that year in solid comfort, and this appeal apparently got results.

By the spring of 1953, Columbia had four radio stations (WIS, WCOS, WNOK, and WMSC, the first two also producing FM broadcasts), and the race was on for television transmission. The winner was WCOS, Channel 25, which began operating on 1 May, the state's first TV station. (That same day, the Wade Hampton Hotel announced that 100 sets had been placed in its "larger" rooms.) In September of that year, WNOK, Channel 67, joined in, yet many were waiting for a huge WIS tower that had been under construction for several months. On 6 November, Columbia's premier radio station made a spectacular television debut: full coverage of the UNC–USC football game. Although South Carolina's capital city could boast of three TV stations, a year later program schedules still were somewhat abbreviated, usually lasting only from mid-afternoon to 11:15 P.M. Nevertheless, television had arrived, and in September of 1955 WIS began experimenting with color transmission.

The full impact of these innovations upon daily life is almost incalculable. They altered the very rhythm of family routine. Entertainment, sports, and news were right there in the living room, and the living room was *cool* during summer months. Now to another vitally important development of these mid-century decades: the battle for civil rights.

Notes

1. The agricultural census of 1969 counted only thirty-seven tenant farms in Richland County, sixteen of them operated by blacks. Three decades earlier, on the eve of World War II, the county was home to 1,212 tenant farmers, but by 1950 their ranks had dropped to 647.
2. According to *The Economy of Metropolitan Columbia, South Carolina*, compiled in 1965 by Hammer, Greene, Siler Associates of Atlanta for the Richland-Lexington Counties Joint Planning Commission, in 1964 government employment accounted for 20,200 jobs (20.6 percent of the civilian sector), compared to only 3,900 in agriculture (4 percent). That same year, 20,500 service men and women were stationed in the Columbia area.
3. The 1940 city directory listed only seven emporiums where beer could be consumed legally, five of them on Main Street. Two years later, nineteen were cited, five of them for black patrons. During the same period, according to telephone books, the number of restaurants, grills, and luncheonettes grew from fifty-six to well over a hundred. In addition, there were many more yellow-page ads for both restaurants and taxis. The 1940 book had only three small ads for eating places, two for taxis. Twenty-four months later, the ratio was twenty-two to ten, with those serving "colored" clearly identified. The 1942 edition also had this warning splashed across its cover: "STOP! THINK! Is the call you're about to make really necessary? If not, please don't make it. Help keep Lines and Central Offices Clear for War Business." A year later, according to the *State* (11 May), this community had thirty-three liquor stores; however, supply was so tight that all were closed on Wednesdays. Otherwise, business hours were 10 A.M. to 7 P.M.
4. For additional details, see Holmes B. Springs, *Selective Service in South Carolina, 1940–1947* (Columbia, 1948). The *Record* (18 July 1941) noted that the first area residents sum-

moned for physicals were Walter Paul Baldwin, 909 Sumter Street; James Rivers Roberson, 4718 James Street; and Sam Bernard Dowdy, Eastover. Each held 196, the number picked in a national lottery.

5. In June of 1945, the Laurel Street USO awarded a $100 war bond to Bronx PFC Irvin Simels, the two-millionth man to visit that popular facility, said to have been the nation's largest such operation.

6. Interview, Isabel Whaley Sloan, 20 March 1989.

7. In succeeding years, these totals would continue to mount. By 1970, Richland was home to 112,994 motor vehicles of all sorts (94,304 of them automobiles), while Lexington reported 53,424 (41,317 of them cars).

8. In September 1950, a new Farmers' Market opened near the university stadium, thus clearing Assembly Street of stalls and booths long associated with that area. This move may have been hastened by a serious gas explosion in November 1946. Five individuals were killed when a machine used to cure bananas blew up. On the debit side, wider streets and more highways (especially interstates) have produced a proliferation of billboards that has won Columbia unfavorable publicity in some national publications.

9. In March of 1946, the General Assembly established a Greater Columbia District with four subdistricts, all under the control of the Richland County commissioners, to supervise sewerage, water lines, drainage, and similar matters in heavily populated neighborhoods.

10. In December of 1949, the city annexed about nine square miles to the north and east, an arc stretching from Edgewood to Devereaux Road and home to about 12,000 people, the largest addition of territory since 1927.

11. *State*, 15 August 1985, 24 November 1989.

12. In March of that year, seven workmen were killed when a retaining wall at Seaboard Park gave way and engulfed them in 3,000 tons of red dirt and clay.

13. See these materials at the South Caroliniana Library: Doris B. Giles, "The Antiwar Movement in Columbia, South Carolina, 1965–1972," and interviews Ms. Giles recorded with student activist Brett Bursey and ACLU lawyer Laughlin McDonald, a Winnsboro native.

Reviving
Reconstruction

CHAPTER TWENTY

As the half-century heyday of Jim Crow recedes down the hallways of history, the more he becomes an aberration that defies easy explanation. Federal statutes enacted in the wake of the Civil War remained intact (1890–1940), and state laws and local ordinances concocted in his behalf often were enforced in a capricious manner. This was especially true in urban areas that were more receptive to change than rural communities bound by custom and tradition. Also, two world wars and the Great Depression had impact in all parts of the nation, not just the South. Put another way, an enemy without and hard times within tended to sap Jim Crow's strength. South Carolinians less than forty years of age probably cannot remember the vestiges of legal segregation—"colored" and "white" signs, to the back of the bus, and so on. If teenagers, even the ferment of the 1960s is, for them, prehistory.

Throughout the past century, the race question often thrust Columbia into a difficult role. Being the state capital, it was seen as a symbol of regional values. This usually meant views held by rural legislators, who were, in effect, local residents part of each year. At the same time, this city was a crossroads of commerce and home to several institutions of higher learning, as well as a large military base. Thus travelers, students, and soldiers composed a constantly shifting mass not tied to the Midlands that might march to a different drum . . . or even spurn or have little interest in prevailing attitudes toward race and skin color.

In addition, even when Jim Crow was riding high, a minuscule few struggled to make meaningful the phrases found in both the Declaration of Independence and the Constitution. Most were educated blacks, often ministers and associated with Allen and Benedict. Ironically, in 1941 two of their goals were the same as those enunciated in 1919: the right to vote and black policemen in Columbia's black neighborhoods. But times had

414

changed, too. As the result of a U.S. Supreme Court decision, in February of 1941, South Carolina's black teachers asked for pay equal to that of their white counterparts and, for good measure, an eight-month term, one accredited black high school in each county, and bus transportation where needed.

Several weeks later, following a mass meeting, a black delegation presented the Columbia city council with three major grievances: wage discrimination, difficulty getting old-age pensions, and harassment of black businesses by white military police from Fort Jackson. In April, white CCC youths and black GIs clashed at "the fort" when both groups, disregarding specific orders, went swimming in the same pond. A black got dunked, rocks were thrown, fists flew, and all black soldiers in Columbia (but not white servicemen) were ordered back to base. Meanwhile, the army lifted all restrictions on black enlistments, and the U.S. Supreme Court ended segregation on inter-state trains.[1] Shortly before Pearl Harbor, the city contributed $1,500 to a black USO, a sum that contrasts with $25,000 given to a white facility.

War created unprecedented opportunities for blacks. They became air raid wardens and nurses' aides, participated in bond and salvage drives, served on Richland County's rationing board from a separate office at Benedict College, formed a black division of the Community Chest (the first such group in years), held "March of Dimes" balls, and mounted a $100,000 drive to build a joint Good Samaritan-Waverly Hospital. This campaign for medical facilities faced many obstacles and did not achieve its goal until 1952; however, in March of 1943 the Columbia Hospital unveiled a 165-bed black wing with black nurses and white supervisors that cost over $700,000. Army officer training schools were opened to black candidates in mid-1942, and the following year black Women's Army Auxiliary Corps personnel (WAACs) arrived at Fort Jackson. Hundreds from Columbia's black communities entertained GIs at various USO clubs, old Howard School, and Allen and Benedict. A black baseball team, the Columbia White Sox, enjoyed several good seasons at Allen Park, and in December of 1943 the *State* was featuring a column of black social news. Blacks also were reading John McCray's *Lighthouse and Informer*, a lively, aggressive weekly closely associated with the NAACP that moved to Columbia from Charleston in 1941.[2]

Yet there were disturbing incidents, too. Columbia police, waging a "work or fight" campaign, hassled blacks unable to prove they were employed or in the service. On one occasion, to their embarrassment, they jailed the rector of St. Luke's Church by mistake. Some of this "hassling" occurred in "Congo Square," the 1000 block of Washington Street, an area presumably off-limits to men from Fort Jackson. According to editor McCray, black GIs usually congregated along Gervais Street in the Waverly section, which they dubbed "Burma Road."

In the summer of 1942, reacting to rumors of Axis activity in Georgia, Governor R. M. Jefferies asked police and merchants in various communities, including Columbia, to report on sales of guns and ammunition and organization of "Eleanor Clubs." (The latter, named for Eleanor Roosevelt, allegedly were being formed by black cooks in an effort to improve working conditions and wages.) Sheriffs, constables, and pawn brokers could find nothing, a Fort Mill official replying that no one seemed to know anything about "Ellers" clubs.

But the following summer, gun play did lead to tragedy when two white men, who had been drinking, shot and killed a black teenager near Ridgewood Country Club. This seems to have been little more than a random, unprovoked shooting inspired by too much liquor. Both men subsequently were sentenced to two-and-one-half years in prison. Then in October of 1944, two black military policemen were wounded by gunfire while patrolling in a black neighborhood. Their assailants evidently were disgruntled blacks.

On another level, issues such as equal pay for teachers, graduate education for blacks, and the right to vote simmered and bubbled. At length, arbitration talks with teachers broke down, and early in 1945 blacks filed suit. In May of that year, a federal judge ruled that Columbia's black teachers should receive pay equal to that of whites with similar experience. In succeeding years, however, this victory was clouded by a concerted effort to strip blacks of official certification, the state alleging they had cheated on examinations. Scattered requests by blacks for graduate training led in 1945 to a $25,000 appropriation for such classes at South Carolina State College and arrangements for tuition payments to out-of-state institutions. Two years later, South Carolina State opened a law school for blacks.

But the heart of the matter was the ballot box. In the spring of 1942, with the backing of twenty-one prominent whites (including D. W. Robinson, Jr., and R. Beverley Herbert), a group of Columbia blacks tried to vote in the municipal Democratic primary. The view expressed by these white leaders was that it was time to enfranchise blacks proven to be "good citizens." At length, a handful were allowed to enroll; but, in order to vote, they had to prove they had been loyal party members since 1876, thus eliminating anyone less than eighty-seven years of age. Governor

Olin Johnston further muddied the waters in the summer of 1943 during a speech at Fort Jackson to state defense forces. "If any outsiders come into our state and agitate social equality among races," he said, "I shall deem it my duty to call upon you men to help expel them. . . . God didn't see fit to mix them [the races], and I am tired of people agitating social equality of races in our state."[3] Blacks countered no one had done so. All they were seeking, they maintained, was *equal* opportunity, *equal* teacher pay, and the right to participate in state government.

Late in February of 1944, the state House of Representatives, taking a cue from Johnston, passed a fiery resolution condemning "amalgamation of the races on the basis of equality." The sponsor, John Long of Union, once secretary to Cole Blease, vowed acts of northern agitators were treasonable and played into the hands of our Fascist enemies. The *State* deplored Long's invective, and the *Record* advised the House to keep "its mouth shut and do something to eliminate the inequities which will be seized upon by the agitators to prove their case." As for blacks, they again denied that racial amalgamation was their goal, noting whatever had occurred to date was largely the fault of whites, and questioned who actually was playing into Nazi hands.

In mid-April, South Carolina's lawmakers met in special session in response to a Texas court decision and turned the Democratic party primary into a private function, stripping the process of all ties to state government.[4] A month later, John McCray, Osceola McKaine, and Reverend James M. Hinton, an effective NAACP leader, created South Carolina's Progressive Democratic party. This group, almost exclusively black, would send representatives to national party conclaves in 1944, 1948, and 1956; and, although not officially seated, its members paved the way for other southern delegations who were admitted in the 1960s. Also, in 1944 this new party began organizing grass-roots Lincoln Emancipation clubs throughout the state.

As war was ending in Europe, the city council turned down yet another appeal for black policemen, and in May of 1946 the CIO voted to meet in a union hall after the Wade Hampton Hotel refused to admit black delegates. The following year, however, blacks were seated at a local Episcopal convention, a black drive-in theater opened in Colonial Heights (said to have been the first in the South), and various courts ruled that South Carolina blacks *could* vote in primary elections.

Less than a hundred cast ballots in the city canvass in April of 1948, but many more voted in the state primary in August. During intervening weeks, Columbia attorney R. Beverley Herbert addressed the University of South Carolina's graduating class concerning race and the ballot. In his opinion, the dictates of the courts had to be obeyed. If we continue to swindle blacks, he said, we only debase ourselves. "Are we, then, to resort to deception and duplicity? Are we to endeavor to circumvent the decisions of our own courts? Are we to rear a generation of white tricksters and set an example of dishonesty to eight hundred thousand colored people and expect our state to prosper in the way of right thinking and right living? Such a course," he predicted, "can end only in strife and discord leading to disaster."[5]

During that same year, Herbert published a pamphlet entitled *What We Can Do About the Race Problem*. In it he continued to expound his strange brand of conservative liberalism. All Americans should recognize the nature of the South's dilemma, he wrote, and blacks should be encouraged to migrate to other parts of the nation so as to ease tensions. Both segregation on public conveyances and outside interference should cease, and until blacks become accustomed to voting they should not be urged to do so. This struggle to be even-handed was admirable, but the message probably appealed to few readers.

Meanwhile, another black delegation presented the Columbia city council with facts and figures concerning allocation of recreation dollars. Blacks constituted 40 percent of the population, and 40 percent of them owned taxable property. Yet they got only 1 percent of the money spent on twenty white parks and playgrounds and two "ill-equipped" areas allocated to blacks. City officials did not dispute these statistics, but countered they were "trying" to correct such inequities. Then, fresh from voting for the first time, yet another group revived the age-old plea for black policemen. They noted black MPs walked Columbia's streets during the war; and, in their opinion, black policemen would reduce tensions, curb juvenile delinquency, and foster civic pride. After a month of deliberation, the council agreed to accede to this request.

In the early 1950s, blacks finally got their policemen, as well as eight firemen at a new engine house on Harden Street, a large recreational center at Seegers (Drew) Park, and a representative on the city planning commission, Dr. R. W. Nance. On the eve of the opening of a new $300,000 county library in October of 1952, library officials, in answer to a NAACP query, denied that privileges of the facility were withheld from blacks.[6] A short time later, the U.S. Supreme Court banned segregation on all trains, and in December those attending a racial conference at Allen called for an end to segregation everywhere. In less than a decade the race issue at the local level was being transformed from a question of equal facilities to one of integration.

During these same years, segregation ended in the armed forces, and soon Fort Jackson was a large island of integrated life on Columbia's eastern boundary. This led to confusion as black GIs sometimes refused to go to the rear of city buses. In November of 1953, forty-eight black soldiers and their white officer (who allegedly interfered with the arresting official) were arraigned for just such an offense. It appears that these men, in sequence, took turns sitting next to the lone white female passenger.

Of greater significance, however, was what was happening in sports. The Columbia Reds, a Cincinnati farm team, revived Sally League action in the spring of 1946 with the help of young Ted Kluszewski. "Klu" led the league in batting that year and helped lure over 177,000 fans to Capital City Park, a new season's record. Seven years later, both Savannah and Jacksonville came to town with blacks on their rosters. On 22 April 1953, Jacksonville beat Columbia 7–5 with the aid of a homer, double, and single by second baseman Henry Aaron. Attendance soared, and the Reds announced more seats would be provided for blacks. In December of that year, hundreds turned out to welcome Booker T. Washington graduate J. C. Caroline, a University of Illinois sophomore, who had won All-American honors as the nation's leading rusher. A bi-racial committee headed by Judge John C. DuPre organized a motorcade and Township Auditorium reception for Caroline, who subsequently played for the Chicago Bears. When the man of the hour missed connections in Knoxville, the committee even chartered a plane to bring the football star to festivities where he was hailed by city officials, the Chamber of Commerce, Merchants Association, Junior Chamber of Commerce, and a host of friends.

A few months later, the Reds signed Cuban-born Chico Terry, a black short stop, who on 13 April 1954 hammered out a triple and single. This was the reaction of one white fan as Chico and the Reds beat Charlotte 6–1: "It don't make no difference what color he is, so long as he can hit that ball!" Soon Terry was joined by two more blacks, pitcher John Jackson and eighteen-year-old Frank Robinson. The latter, a California high school star, then playing third base for the Reds, got four home runs in his first two games.

But the focal point of the race question was the classroom, not the baseball diamond. In November of 1950, the NAACP initiated a Clarendon County court suit designed to challenge segregated schools throughout South Carolina. The state, in turn, asked for time to equalize its system of public education, while launching a massive building program and assuming control of all school buses. The General Assembly, under

the leadership of Governor James F. Byrnes, also embraced "massive resistance" and enacted whatever legal barriers members could devise to
protect segregated education.[7] In October of 1952, Columbia's League of
Women Voters searched in vain for a debate speaker who would defend
an amendment ending the state's obligation to operate free public
schools, yet it soon was approved by a 2–1 margin statewide and by a vote
of 13,532 to 3,792 in Richland County. Six months later, a proposed hospital bond issue went down to defeat, largely because of opposition from
local blacks, since it offered them nothing, and the *Record* (12 June 1953)
published an unusual editorial: "Must Face Possibility of Segregation's
End." Failure of the justices in Washington to rule on separate schools
during the spring term indicated, according to the *Record*, that segregation might be eliminated "root, branch, and limb." But even if it was, this
daily cautioned its readers to use common sense, for the state still would
need the same number of classrooms to educate its young people.

The turning point in this tale is, of course, the Supreme Court decision of May 1954 ending "separate but equal" schools, and one of the
cases involved (*Briggs v. Elliot*) related to Clarendon County. For the next
eight or ten years, as far as Columbia and Richland County were concerned, this drama was played out in various courtrooms, followed by a
similar period of grudging, but increasing and almost totally peaceful integration of local schools.

South Carolina's initial reaction to what nine men in Washington had
said was relatively moderate. After all, this state had supported reform in
the past such as Ben Tillman's version of Populism in the 1890s, Wilson's
New Freedom, and Roosevelt's New Deal. Even before the court spoke,
Columbia's Lutheran Theological Southern Seminary announced it was
ready to train blacks for the ministry, and in the fall of 1954 Catholic
schools in several South Carolina communities were integrated. But leading political figures, especially George Bell Timmerman, Jr., who succeeded Byrnes as governor in January 1955, were becoming increasingly
intransigent as they silenced anyone advocating accommodation.

Early in 1956, the state association of White Citizens' Councils held
a huge rally at Township Auditorium. (A small block of seats was reserved
for blacks, but none appeared.) Featured speakers included Olin
Johnston, Strom Thurmond, Sol Blatt, and Mississippi's James O. East-
land. Even if actual editorial endorsement was withheld, their words enjoyed the obvious approval of the *State* and *Record*. Soon, White Citizens'
groups appeared throughout rural Richland, although a Klan organization
based in Georgia was unable to secure a local charter. Meanwhile, Tim-

merman and others weighed the possibility of denying state jobs to NAACP members (such a law was enacted but then repealed under threat of adverse court opinion), and unknown gangs for a second time shot at Dentsville's Sinbeth Motel, a facility owned by the family of Modjeska Simkins, an outspoken integrationist.

With the public school question tied up in court, the battleground became instead a series of bus seating skirmishes and attacks by the governor upon Allen and Benedict for allegedly employing "un-American" professors. In June of 1954, Sarah Mae Flemming, a black domestic then living in Eastover, was arrested for refusing to move to the rear of a city bus, and four months later another maid, Sadie Brevard, faced similar charges. Sadie, who at first refused to accompany an arresting officer, was quoted as saying, "You try to run us over. You want us to work for you, but you can't get along with us." The judge, who suspended sentence because Sadie was employed by prominent families, advised recourse to the Golden Rule: "I think the spirit of cooperation would accomplish a great deal in such matters."[8]

Sarah Mae Flemming, on the other hand, almost achieved the fame reserved for Montgomery's Rosa Parks. As the result of an NAACP-sponsored suit against South Carolina Electric and Gas (she claimed a bus driver hit her), a federal circuit judge outlawed segregation on city buses, a decision endorsed by the U.S. Supreme Court in April of 1956. Whereupon the state Public Service Commission said no, South Carolina law was supreme, a view Union's John Long tried unsuccessfully to enact into statute a few months later. (John Hart, also from Union, proposed a "chivalry" bill stipulating no male could sit next to a female on a public conveyance without the latter's permission, but it died in committee, too.) In May of 1957, Sarah Flemming went before a local judge for the third time suing only for damages and lost.

That fall, Allen University presented segregationists with a unique challenge when Hungarian freedom fighter Andre Toth, age twenty-four, enrolled as a student. Within days, the state Department of Education withdrew certification of Allen's teacher graduates, loudly proclaiming that the cause of this action was not Toth but three Allen professors who harbored "subversive" tendencies. Early in 1958, the same charges were leveled against a trio of Benedict professors amid calls in the General Assembly for a full-scale probe of both institutions. By June, however, the fire had gone out of this campaign. Several factors account for this change. To begin with, the six professors left, as did Toth after completing two full terms. More importantly, in January of 1958, several Allen and Benedict students applied for admission to the University of South Carolina. Although unsuccessful, according to new state laws, if only one had made it, that institution would have been closed. Thus the threat was posed: blacks, with federal help, had the potential to shut down any state-supported school, college, or university in South Carolina.

Three other events of the 1957–1958 school year should be noted in passing, two within the state, the other several hundred miles away beyond the Mississippi River. The first was the appearance of a little pamphlet (eighty-nine pages, fifty cents) entitled *South Carolinians Speak: A Moderate Approach to Race Relations.* Twelve contributors, including R. Beverley Herbert and several ministers, called for calm, reason, and "integration by evolution not revolution." Actually, their words might have gone unnoticed except for strident attacks by segregationists long before the booklet was released and a bomb thrown into the home of a Gaffney woman who wrote one of the essays. Then on 5 October, the North Carolina State band, with two black members, traveled to Clemson for a football game. When word spread that they had dined with white students in the campus cafeteria, Lake City residents, over 200 miles to the east, began circulating a protest petition to be forwarded to the governor in Columbia.

The third development, far more important, was the Little Rock crisis in September of 1957. The use of federal troops to enforce integration enraged South Carolina's political leaders. Olin Johnston vowed he would fight if a similar situation arose here, but L. Marion Gressette, chairman of the legislative committee charged with maintaining the status quo, assured the senator it could not. By state law, he emphasized, any institution ordered to integrate would automatically be closed. To demonstrate his personal displeasure with Washington's policies, Governor Timmerman resigned from the U.S. Naval Reserve.

Strangely, at the moment an Arkansas high school was torn by racial strife, Columbia High School students were helping rehabilitate the home of an elderly black woman, Patsy S. Ceasar. As part of the city's urban renewal program, this structure at 1113 House Street had been partially torn down to comply with building codes and left in an unfinished state. Students learned of the owner's plight and, in connection with Youth Government Day, decided to make her problem their project. After working in shifts on Saturdays and holidays for two months, some 900 young people were able to complete the job late in November.

So, as the 1950s came to a close, a segregated way of life still was relatively secure in the Midlands, although protective barriers were beginning to fall in nearby states. Virginia's "massive resistance" crumbled early in 1959, and in the fall of that year a handful of North Carolina school systems bowed to token integration. Thirty-six months later, Clemson admitted Harvey Gantt, and in September of 1963 three black students enrolled at the University of South Carolina, among them, Henri Montieth, niece of Modjeska Simkins. The following autumn, thirty-one black youngsters entered local schools that previously were white.

These changes did not occur without some anguish and protest, and the full story of behind-the-scenes maneuvering to forestall violence is yet to be written. Nevertheless, it is obvious that Little Rock exerted great impact, as did turmoil in other communities such as Oxford, Mississippi, and Birmingham, Alabama. Businessmen, eager to sustain and expand South Carolina's economic growth, were especially wary. They knew no new industrial plants appeared in Arkansas's capital city during the four years following troop action there, and this point was driven home at Hampton's traditional watermelon festival in the summer of 1961 by no less a figure than Piedmont industrialist Charles Daniel. This economic argument was, in fact, the opening salvo in a campaign to keep Clemson from closing its doors. In short order, politicians such as alumnus Edgar Brown fell into line, and by year's end others were beginning to abandon diehard stands. Governor Ernest Hollings, who in April of 1959 told a Congressional committee that proposed civil rights legislation was unnecessary, would "hurt everyone," and promote discord, now said it was time to be "flexible." Allendale's Robert McNair, candidate for lieutenant governor, observed that various localities throughout the state might wish to solve problems posed by integration in different ways.

Hollings also was being pushed by other factors such as marches and lunch counter sit-ins in the Columbia area in the spring of 1960 and again in 1961. And there were similar protests in Rock Hill, Denmark, Orangeburg, Florence, and Charleston as well. The Columbia incidents were essentially non-violent, except for a minor stabbing by a white man at a lunch counter early in March of 1961. At the same time, 187 young people who marched to the State House were jailed, the only such action here. (Two years later, their convictions were set aside by the U.S. Supreme Court.) In April, blacks were barred from a Democratic party dinner held at the Wade Hampton Hotel, a decision that drew fire from the White House; and, three months later, when twenty blacks were turned away from Richland's Sesquicentennial Park, a court suit began to push for integrated state parks.

These spasmodic disturbances, even if not especially disruptive, concerned community leaders of both races. On 6 April 1962, in an effort to head off what was becoming an annual ritual, Reverend James Hinton, the presidents of Allen and Benedict, and other prominent blacks contacted Mayor Lester Bates. How, they asked, could concessions be arranged without recourse to demonstrations and similar forms of public pressure? A short time later, several department store executives, a prominent Columbia banker, and the editors of the *State* and *Record* went to Atlanta and Augusta to see how limited desegregation was working in those communities. By early summer, according to a letter written by a Woolworth district manager, gradual, voluntary integration had the approval of Columbia's Chamber of Commerce, its city council, and local ministers.[9]

On 21 August, the lunch counters of eight downtown chain stores quietly served blacks for the first time. (Those backing this move had planned to act on 15 June, but political primaries delayed this momentous step for two months.) The Associated Press and out-of-town dailies told readers what had happened, but Columbia papers did not. On the 28th, two white male USC students picketed one of the stores, and four days later the *State* carried a two-column ad, "Is the Curtain Drawn on Our News?" Sponsored by "Deeply Concerned Columbians" and signed by John Adger Manning, it claimed what had been done "should be undone—without secrecy." Other small protest ads followed, and Republicans charged that Mayor Bates had orchestrated this opening wedge of integration, something he vehemently denied. In weeks that followed, the black community, by prior agreement, began to supply Main Street merchants with a steady flow of cooperative black customers.

Actually, this transition came at a most opportune time, for public attention soon was diverted elsewhere. At the end of August, Bates unveiled plans to build a civic center complex at the fair grounds that would serve the university, the State Fair, and citizens of Columbia, the Midlands, and the state at large. The Committee for Conservative Government, headed by A. Mason Gibbes, quickly attacked the project as too expensive ($8.9 million), asserting that (a) the city had more pressing matters that needed attention and (b) it had no business providing facilities for college students and fair patrons. But the real issue was race. As the controversy heated up, some voters feared the center's theater, coliseum, and exhibit halls would be integrated; others feared they would not be. When pressed for an answer, proponents—including the *State, Record,* and Chamber of Commerce—clouded the debate by replying that the proposed facilities would be "operated like others in this state." This answer proved too vague, and on 7 November voters rejected the center, 12,231 to 11,487.[10]

Even as this battle raged, Richland residents also had to consider the riot at the University of Mississippi in response to federally induced integration. With Clemson facing orders to admit a black student, what happened in Oxford had special significance. Segregationists wanted Governor Hollings to join southern protest; but instead, converted to realism by recent events, he sent the head of SLED to Mississippi to learn how to prevent trouble. Ironically, for several years SLED did all it could to protect segregation, then turned around and used its powers to dismantle it with as much dignity and grace as possible. This new mood was aided by frequent editorials in the *State* and *Record* preaching moderation . . . violence must not blacken our proud heritage . . . South Carolina must act responsibly in this time of crisis. And when Gantt appeared at Clemson early in 1963, all went smooth as clockwork. The *Record's* headline on the following day (26 January) had a note of pride, even triumph: "First in Secession—Last in Desegregation."[11]

Returning to the banks of the Congaree, integration of lunch counters bought Columbia several months of racial peace. But as trouble flared in North Carolina and Alabama in the spring of 1963 (protest in those years seemed to come with warm breezes and longer days), community leaders once more became concerned. These fears led to formation of a group of essentially informal committees by Mayor Bates, although he at first denied that any bi-racial body existed. Early in June, the city council met with black leaders; and, when pressed by reporters, Bates conceded similar sessions had been held in the past. A few weeks later, following an outburst of violence in Birmingham, he summoned eighty-seven white businessmen to what proved to be a stormy meeting. Eventually, however, the pragmatists, using stark economic arguments, convinced those less enthusiastic to begin desegregation of various aspects of community life. That hurdle overcome, Bates named a public committee (twenty-five whites and the same number of blacks, who at first met separately) and a smaller group that worked in secrecy.[12]

These two bodies were the newest members of a collection of local organizations concerned with racial matters. The oldest of these was the South Carolina Council on Human Relations, founded in 1919 under a different name, that worked behind the scenes through churches, Benedict, Allen, and the university. Then there was the city council, Chamber of Commerce, and the NAACP. The latter often was too radical for the Chamber of Commerce, especially its board of directors, but even farther to the left was the Richland County Citizens Committee, formed in 1944 and chartered in 1956. Modjeska Simkins, one of its more vocal members, was a gadfly quick to call attention to any and all forms of discrimination.[13] Even though critical of the policies of Lester Bates, she actually helped him on numerous occasions; for, Columbia businessmen, fearing her committee might launch a boycott, opted for ideas proposed by the mayor that they otherwise would have rejected. On the far right, there were White Citizens' Councils, L. Maurice Bessinger's National Association for the Preservation of White People, as well as his South Carolina Independent party, and spasmodic Klan activity in communities such as West Columbia and Irmo.

By the fall of 1963, as the University of South Carolina was enrolling three black students, many vestiges of segregation were vanishing from the Columbia scene. Public facilities such as restaurants, hotels, and theaters were integrated, "white only" signs had disappeared, blacks were members of several municipal boards and commissions, and the city had adopted a non-discriminatory hiring policy. According to the *State* (13 September), of 527 municipal employees, 215 (41 percent) were black. Their ranks included many low-level workers, but also nine firemen and eight policemen. At that time, the county sheriff also had two blacks on his staff.

Perhaps the most innovative measure devised by Bates was the creation of a guidance center to coach blacks eager to apply for visible, responsible jobs formerly held by whites. In time, this organization evolved into the Greater Columbia Community Relations Council, and five years later claimed it had found meaningful employment for 1,200 applicants.

Whether this overall program was for real may always be debated. Some blacks, including Modjeska Simkins, thought it nothing more than high-powered public relations. Her citizens' committee in 1969 characterized Columbia as "a machine-ridden city" that was poorly governed in secrecy. The mayor's "hand-picked" Community Relations Council was "a distinct farce" and the police force a bunch of "political hacks" and "antiquated military men." These blasts were delivered in a letter to *Look* magazine as the city was trying (unsuccessfully, it turned out) for an unprecedented third All-America award at the close of the decade.

But five years earlier in 1964, what Bates and others had done won All-America status and nationwide recognition. A seven-page article in *Newsweek* (3 May 1965) heaped praise upon Columbia as a city that had "liberated itself from the plague of doctrinal apartheid." Profiles of area residents highlighted the experiences of aristocrats, businessmen, "good ol' boys," blacks, and mill hands. Perhaps the most interesting remarks were those of a middle-aged textile worker. He could recall, he said, when anyone who worked in a cotton mill faced scorn from Main Street merchants. Once they realized you were from Olympia or Granby, "they wouldn't much care if they sold you anything or not." Now the black man, in his opinion, was starting the same climb up the ladder that he and his friends had made.

That climb continued throughout the 1960s, but there were tense moments. In April of 1965, 500 blacks marched from Allen University to the State House to protest legislative foot-dragging on anti-poverty programs. A white youth who joined in was attacked by two white men. Three years later, the "Orangeburg Massacre" ignited an emotional outburst, as did the assassination of Martin Luther King, Jr. Thirty fires on the evening of 8 April 1968 (seventy-two hours after King's death) convinced the mayor to impose a night-time curfew that lasted for a week. During that period, scores were arrested but no major damage occurred.

Meanwhile, integration of Columbia and Richland County classrooms proceeded apace, with blacks at first moving by written application to formerly white schools. About 1,250 had exercised this right of "choice" by the fall of 1966, and a dozen teachers also had crossed traditional racial lines. During the next three years, local, state, and federal officials wrangled over what path to follow. In September of 1968, 3,100 black youngsters were in integrated schools, although Washington was threatening to cut off federal funds unless "zone" or "neighborhood" plans replaced "choice."[14] Finally, in the summer of 1970 it became clear that unrestricted racial mixing was inevitable. That September, city and county schools opened peacefully. By that date, Booker T. Washington High School, traditionally black, was 60 percent white. Several weeks later, a minor fracas erupted at A. C. Flora, which may have been sparked by aides to a gubernatorial candidate; but, for the most part, police were rarely seen. These changes sent some students to private classrooms in both city and county; however, in February of 1970, Governor McNair's two youngest children were enrolled in an integrated public school.

Another battleground, although the fray was muted by comparison, was the state park system. In this instance, authorities faced a legal tangle, since much of the land involved might revert to former owners if not operated as parks. Hunting Island Beach near Beaufort presented a special problem. The conveyance relating to that park said nothing about race, merely stipulating that the facility was to be open to the public at all times. In addition, if the question was segregation and no parks or integration and parks, South Carolinians clearly preferred the latter by a wide margin, a fact underscored at hearings held throughout the state in summer and early fall of 1963. This may indicate a shift in opinion after a decade of controversy, willingness to make a decision when presented with definite choices, or more grass-roots tolerance of integration than politicians cared to admit. (Segregation was a fine hobby horse to ride at election time, especially since it diverted attention from other matters.)

Here in Columbia, twenty spoke for integration, three against. In Greenville, the margin was 20–5, in York, 26–1, and in coastal communities such as Georgetown and Myrtle Beach hardly anyone supported segregation. A retired textile worker, who emphasized he spoke for ten children, forty grandchildren, and a dozen great-grandchildren, expressed this view in Greenville: "My grandfather would turn in his grave if he could hear me . . . but we adults have too many deep-rooted prejudices. The kids have more at stake; let them have a voice, and I'll bet the parks remain open."[15] Integration of state parks began on a limited basis in the spring of 1964 (no swimming, no sleeping in cabins), but then localities were permitted to do as they wished and those bans quickly vanished.

By the late 1960s, other things were happening in the public arena that would have raised eyebrows (and fists) only a few years before. In 1965, the white South Carolina Education Association voted to drop racial requirements, thus opening the door to black teachers. The following year, students meeting in a mock legislative session approved integrated college athletics, a stand applauded by the *Columbia Record*. In December of 1968, six black high school players were named to the metropolitan area's all-star football teams (with a black coach on offense), and pictures of black debutantes who were making their bow at Township Auditorium appeared in the *Record*.

Yet another noteworthy milestone was selection of Lower Richland's Ernie Jackson as the region's outstanding athlete of the 1967–1968 school year. This football-track star was headed for Duke on a scholarship and certainly deserved the honor; but, in all of the accolades appearing in the press, race never was mentioned. Also, by this date Columbia's newspapers no longer were identifying local semi-pro baseball players by color. In 1969, both houses of the General Assembly had black pages for the first time, and the next year three blacks were elected to the state House of Representatives. Two of them, Leevy Johnson and James Felder, were from Columbia. And in June of 1970, black and white youngsters were swimming together at Drew Park.

Getting the vote, integrating many aspects of local life, including classrooms and swimming pools, and sitting in the state legislature—all of these things occurred in slightly more than two decades and with a minimum of fuss and fury. To understand *why* this was happening, one has to look far beyond the waters of the Congaree and Wateree. World War II altered attitudes toward race and skin color both at home and abroad, and that conflict transformed the United States, for the first time, into a global power. Cast in a new role in a changing world, America's leaders had no choice but to jettison Jim Crow.

To understand *why* change occurred so peacefully here in the Midlands, one does not have to roam quite so far afield. For one thing, South Carolina's leaders certainly delayed the inevitable as long as they possibly could; but, in this instance, procrastination paid huge dividends. It provided conservative diehards with an opportunity to try their hand at stemming the tide, thus they rarely were able to charge in succeeding years that their views were ignored. In addition, Little Rock, Birmingham, Oxford, and even civil strife in North Carolina increased the ranks of those advocating accommodation, for those tragic events affected local thought in at least two ways. First, turmoil and bloodshed created firm resolve that similar outbursts of violence would not stain this state's honor; and, second, they reinforced an innate sense of pride, the feeling that South Carolina possesses a regional superiority perhaps shared only with Virginia.

Then there is the rise of a two-party system and the industrial health of the Midlands to be considered. The former gave some individuals an outlet for expressing frustrations engendered by change, and the latter muted its effects. As Columbia area whites left traditional jobs for better-paying positions with new plants built by Argus cameras, Dictaphone, Elgin National Watch, Westinghouse Air Brakes, and Allied Chemical, blacks moved in to replace them . . . part of that climb up the ladder for both races, in fact.

That South Carolina's capital city was willing to yield on what some thought were truly fundamental issues should not come as a great surprise. Columbia was conceived in compromise and has spent much of its lifetime balancing the views of upcountry and low, rural and urban, agriculture and industry, old and new, and so on. But in the final analysis, credit must go to those individuals who made peaceful change possible. Richard Carroll, dead for nearly half a century, brought black and white together at a time when meaningful contact was rare indeed. Various

Allen and Benedict professors, R. Beverley Herbert, and D. W. Robinson, Jr., continued those associations; and, when crisis came, Mayor Bates, Reverend Hinton, and editors, merchants, and bank presidents used them to great advantage.

At the outset of this integration/segregation crisis, politicians stressed the confrontation between state rights and federal power ("outside interference"), but by the early 1960s the debate had become largely a state or local matter. Columbia was determined not to be Little Rock or Birmingham and, if possible, avoid the strikes and boycotts of Charleston and the bus burnings of the Piedmont. With the help of able leadership and restraint on the part of marching students, as well as White Citizens' Councils and black activists, it somehow succeeded in doing so.

Notes

1. In March of 1942, an irate army major protested to Governor R. M. Jefferies that he was unable to secure a pullman berth at Orangeburg, while six blacks got sleeping accommodations on an Atlantic Coast Line train. In reply, Jefferies said integrated train travel was a fact, adding that the race problem was "becoming more and more serious in this state."
2. This publication was created by merger of the *Charleston Lighthouse* and the *People's Informer* of Sumter. By 1944, under the able direction of McCray and Osceola McKaine, an ex-patriate driven out of Belgium by Hitler, the *Lighthouse and Informer* had 14,000 readers. It ceased publication in July 1954, shortly after McCray quit to become South Carolina correspondent for the *Baltimore Afro-American*. Unfortunately, few copies exist, although McCray's personal papers are at the South Caroliniana Library.
3. *State*, 17 July 1943.
4. While this brief session was in progress, Dillon attorney Joe P. Lane wrote these words to Johnston: "It's inevitable that the negro is going to vote in South Carolina in a short time anyhow. You can not put the uniform on a negro and then always deny him the ballot. Suppose we run them out of the lower part of South Carolina, then who's going to do the work and produce the annual wealth? Not us whites. We are not going to do much hard work." Johnston Papers, "Special Session," Box 4, South Carolina Department of Archives and History.
5. For the full text of this speech, see the *Southern Christian Advocate* (17 June 1948), p. 5. At that time, Herbert's views were endorsed by many leading newspapers, including the Charleston *News and Courier*. A decade later, according to the *Record* (23 May 1958), 58,122 South Carolina blacks had registered to vote. In Richland, the figure was 6,645 (17 percent of all registered voters); in Lexington 213 (1.4 percent).

6. This evidently meant blacks could borrow any book through their branch library, for eight years later in April of 1960 the main library was the scene of protest and a brief sit-in. Also, the fact that the new library opened without ceremony may indicate some nervousness on the part of various officials.
7. The role of Byrnes in the school segregation fight is somewhat puzzling. As John G. Sproat writes in *New Perspectives on Race and Slavery in America* (Lexington, 1986), this elder statesman was an internationalist who must have known that attitudes toward race and color were changing throughout the world. In addition, as a Washington bureaucrat and politician, he had done much to expand federal power. Thus, in Sproat's opinion, his "massive resistance" stand probably was influenced by failure to gain the vice-presidency in 1944 and disagreement with the policies of Harry Truman, the man who did.
8. *Columbia Record*, 6 October 1954.
9. F. P. Evans, head of Woolworth's Atlanta office, to Edward O. Herron, district manager for Eckerd's, Charlotte, 13 August 1962. This correspondence was prompted by fears of Evans that Tapp's and Eckerd's Columbia outlets wanted to fight integration. Woolworth's, he assured Herron, had desegregated 165 stores to date with few problems and little effect on sales. This course, in his opinion, created fewer problems.
10. The city approved the complex by 420 votes, while the county rejected it by a margin of 1,164. The following year, the same forces clashed again, and the center lost even more decisively, 14,273 to 8,179. After that defeat, the project was abandoned.
11. On 15 January, the day before a final order concerning Gantt was issued, Spartanburg attorney Donald Russell succeeded Hollings as governor. During his inaugural, the former USC president invited everyone to a paper-plate barbecue picnic at the governor's mansion. Over 11,000 people, including a hundred blacks, accepted.
12. For details of these arrangements, see a four-part series by Thomas M. Walker in the *Columbia Record*, 21–24 January 1964, and Paul S. Lofton, Jr., "Calm and Expediency: Desegregation in Columbia, South Carolina," in Elizabeth Jacoway and David R. Colburn, *Southern Businesssmen and Desegregation* (Baton Rouge, 1982), pp. 70–81.
13. During these years, in the *State* and *Record* newsrooms, she was referred to simply as "that Simkins woman."
14. Heyward McDonald, caught up in this controversy as a member of the District One School Board, recalls making a forceful speech in which he vowed onetime opposition to integration but firm support for desegregation, now that it was the law of the land. Political leader Tom Elliott subsequently told McDonald he never thought a man could alienate everyone by uttering a simple sentence, but *he* certainly had managed to do just that!
15. *State*, 20 July 1963. L. P. Hollis, former superintendent of a Greenville school district, strongly backed integrated parks and attacked the Gressette Committee for spending unknown sums of tax money and doing "untold damage to this state." See "Desegregation, 1955–1956," State Parks Division, South Carolina Department of Archives and History. As early as 1956, Edisto Beach was the scene of confrontation. When a park there was closed to keep out blacks, white tourist trade declined, so much so that local businessmen appealed to politicians such as Edgar Brown to solve the problem.

The Urban Vision
of Lester Bates

CHAPTER TWENTY-ONE

 An "unflagging optimist," a born salesman unwilling to take "no" for an answer, a purveyor of "down-home" humor, a superb after-dinner speaker with clearly defined goals for himself and for his community—such a man was Lester Bates, who, together with those following in his footsteps, notably Kirkman Finlay, Jr., did much to shape present-day Columbia. "Everything is salesmanship from salt to salvation," he once remarked. "While most of the worthwhile things in life are free," he added, "there are those who must tell the story with confidence and conviction." And this Bates did for over half a century, whether selling burial insurance to blacks, greeting convention delegates ("It's a *financial* pleasure to have you with us"), welcoming patrons to his Laurel Hill supper club, or promoting South Carolina's capital city.

Early in 1971, having voluntarily relinquished the post of mayor after a dozen years, Bates still was in fine form. At a breakfast held in his honor, he told a huge audience that Columbia had "more know-how, drive, talent, resources, and imagination than any city of comparable size in the country, but," he cautioned, "these must be harnessed." Also, in passing, the ex-mayor told his friends that "being thought of as a 'has been' doesn't appeal to me at all!"

The Bates saga is, above all else, a rags-to-riches, Horatio Alger tale. Born in Berkeley County's Hell Hole Swamp in 1905, eighth of fifteen children, Bates had little formal education and, except for a freak accident, might have lived out his days in an isolated region widely known for bootleg corn liquor. At the age of twelve, Bates got a job as water boy with a logging crew that paid three dollars a week. Soon after beginning this twelve-hour-day routine, one of his legs was seriously injured by logging machinery and he was shipped off to a Charleston hospital for treatment.

New Deal Housing of the 1930s—Allen-Benedict Court.

The Assembly Street Curb Market, c. 1930.

In the 1950s, palmettos appeared on Main Street and also lent their name to the "Palmetto Trials." Bottom, Mrs. J. Macfie Anderson, wife of Columbia's mayor, honors a 1952 winner. Trainer Max Hirsch (right) long was associated with this spring-time social-sporting event.

Protest on Main Street, c. 1960.

Modjeska Monteith Simkins, veteran human rights activist, was the subject of a special South Carolina ETV documentary in February 1990.

Lester Bates (1905–1988).

The skyline he helped to create, as seen from Arsenal Hill (Herb Hartsook).

Model of Richland County's new library under construction at Assembly and Hampton streets (Brian Dressler).

A Day at the Zoo. Ride a turtle and watch elephants and their trainers. Since its inception in 1974, Riverbanks Zoo has been host to thousands of visitors (Emily Short, Riverbanks Zoo).

Sidney Park restored (Robbie Robertson).

There he saw a new world, one he never imagined existed, and overheard a casual remark that changed his life. An older relative, nodding to where Bates lay in bed, commented to a doctor that a poor kid like that never would amount to much. Stung by these words, Bates vowed to prove him wrong, an attitude that gave birth to one of his favorite dictums: "To improve your circumstances, you must improve yourself."

After several weeks in Charleston, which he grew to love, Bates returned to his swamp home, but within two years he was back in the "Holy City" attending night classes sponsored by the Salvation Army and working at a variety of jobs. Then, at age seventeen, he became agent for an Atlanta insurance company, and his spectacular performance soon attracted the attention of superiors. Special training followed, as well as managerial responsibilities and marriage in 1927 to Julia Burk, a local girl he met at a dance. Four years later, they moved to Columbia where Bates continued to break sales records as head of the regional office of the Atlantic Coast Life Insurance Company.

In February of 1936, with little money and much hope, Bates struck out on his own and, assisted by a single employee, launched Capital Life & Health Insurance Company in a one-room office over a store located at 1111½ Taylor Street. Promoted with jokes, short speeches by the founder, gospel songs, and renditions by a well-known WIS group called the "Hired Hands," this new institution took root and prospered. (As Bates quipped, "Anyone can get you a speaker, but where can you get one with a quartet?") Within eight years, Capital Life expanded to the gracious old Robertson-Seibels mansion on Laurel Hill and in 1949 moved to a new structure nearby. In the early 1950s, the company was transacting business worth $5 million each year and had 400 employees, some of whom received salary equal to their service pay while in uniform during World War II.

And it was during the war years that Lester Bates began his political career as a member of the city council, serving from 1944 to 1952, when he declined to seek a third term. Although plans to become mayor were frustrated until 1958 and two gubernatorial bids also sputtered (1950 and 1954), Bates was much in demand as a speaker. He was, in fact, the man who successfully presented Columbia's case for All-America status in 1951 and again in 1964.

In September of 1953, Bates embarked on a third career when he opened a restaurant on Laurel Hill near his company headquarters. The ostensible goal was lunch facilities for employees, who already enjoyed unprecedented health and hospitalization benefits, but the "supper club" soon became a prime night-time rendezvous. "It was always crowded," one local resident recalls, "and there we heard Patti Page, Julius La Rosa, Andy Griffith, Mel Torme, and lots of other big names." Just why Lester Bates branched out into the entertainment world is unclear, but about this time he sold Capital Life (under circumstances with political over-tones), quit the city council, and began laying plans for a second bid for this state's highest office. Admittedly, Bates always was keenly interested in music in its many forms and, as a promoter of Columbia, sincerely be-lieved that a growing, cosmopolitan center deserved top-flight talent.

Bates won the Democratic nomination for mayor in 1958 by fourteen votes, a triumph, he boasted, that earned him the sobriquet of "Land-slide Lester," and the supper club faded from view as his attention turned to municipal affairs. Despite many successes during a twelve-year reign, the local power structure warmed up to Bates rather slowly. There were at least three reasons: humble origins, flamboyant showmanship to the tune of country ballads, and rumored rapport with the black community. The latter, an obvious asset in the turbulent 1960s, was an outgrowth of day-to-day business contacts, as well as recognition of the fact that blacks soon might be casting ballots in substantial numbers.

On 24 July 1945, editor and political activist John McCray asked Bates why the city council had spurned a request for black policemen. A week later Bates replied, reminding McCray of his past record and active friendship for blacks: "When called upon, I have responded, without hes-itation, with my time and my means to any worthy request made upon me in the interest of the welfare and happiness of the colored citizens of Co-lumbia and the State." He was, he noted, deeply disturbed by charges of police brutality and other matters "affecting not only your party, but the question of properly promoting the best interests of all colored citizens, and by the help of the Lord, I expect to act and vote as I think will best promote the interests of all of our citizens, white and colored, and pre-serve harmony between the races." Yet five years later, Bates stood "Four-Square for Segregation" in a vain attempt to become governor, and McCray—schooled in the Byzantine world of racial politics—undoubtedly understood why.

As mayor, although his greatest feat was peaceful transformation to integrated schools, lunch counters, and public facilities, Lester Bates cut several miles of ceremonial ribbons, made countless speeches, told hun-dreds of jokes, and welcomed scores of visitors. Some of his dreams for Columbia were realized, others were not. But basic to all of his programs and policies was planning for the future, while trying to make the right choices along the way so as to create a milieu in which government and private enterprise could function harmoniously. It was easy enough, he often said, to expand a city such as Columbia. "But quantity in itself is no virtue," he told a Kiwanis luncheon in February of 1968. "It's quality that makes a city a worthwhile place in which to live." And quality required hard work each day, he warned. Left to its own devices, South Carolina's capital city would simply "sprawl" and foster new problems, new headaches and eyesores.

As Bates stressed in an article published in 1971,[1] the Doxiadis Plan and a foundation established in 1970 to implement its recommendations would go far toward making his "vision" come true. Although no longer mayor, he continued to speak out for better housing, a Main Street pedestrian mall, a beltway around Columbia and a transportation hub for all buses and taxis, greater use of the river front, a civic center near the new USC Coliseum, and coordination of city-county government and municipal relations with the university. When asked where the money for such innovations could be found, Bates quoted Doxiadis, who, when queried, replied that in coming decades millions would be invested in Columbia. "The real question," Doxiadis emphasized, "is not where the money is coming from, but will that investment be controlled in such a way as to implement the Plan."

Bates apparently hoped to run for governor a third time after leaving office, but chronic health problems prevented him from doing so. Nevertheless, until laid low by a stroke in 1980, he continued to be a familiar figure in downtown Columbia. Although he lost personal control of a second life insurance company (New South) when it experienced financial problems in the early 1970s, in the middle of that decade he still was following a strict regimen: up before dawn, coffee with his wife at their home of many years (2408 Marion Street), breakfast at the Elite Café with friends, to People's Barber Shop for a shave, and then to his office, often being the first to arrive. After an early afternoon nap, the former mayor (who occasionally talked of seeking his old job just one more time) went back to his favorite barber for a steam facial.

When he died in 1988 at the age of eighty-two, survived by his wife and two children, Lester Bates had been an invalid for nearly a decade and to many was a relic of a bygone era. Yet the *Columbia Record* remembered how much he accomplished as mayor (urban renewal, numerous new buildings, and plans for the future), while not forgetting his controversial stands and several goals not achieved. Others recalled his many charitable acts and sincere devotion to Park Street Baptist Church, which he attended twice each Sunday so long as he could, although Bates characterized himself as only "a nominal Christian."

But it was left to Columbia's blacks to pay special tribute to his memory. To them, he was a man who got things done—playground equipment for their children, black policemen to patrol the streets of their neighborhoods—a man who called a married black woman "Mrs." and "somehow knew just the right thing to say or do." When invited to their meetings, he came and *stayed*, no matter how long they lasted. Others remembered Bates assuring them he would be strong, firm, and, above all else, fair. A mayor had to weigh conflicting pressures, he declared, and make the decision that is best for all concerned. Modjeska Simkins, frequently one of his severest critics in the 1960s, summed up the political career of Lester Bates in one simple sentence: "He did more for progress in Columbia than any other mayor before or since."

As we all know, the years when Bates was active on the local scene, 1945 to 1970, was a complex age indeed. Civil rights agitation, the rise of suburbs and shopping centers, school integration, Vietnam, and the pervasive influence of television and air conditioning all are part of the story. And so is the growth and diversity of that era and the two decades that followed.

In 1945, the city telephone book, only a quarter of an inch thick, had fifty-six pages of residential and business listings and about twice as many yellow pages. Twenty-five years later, the Columbia directory was four times as large and included Eastover and Lexington.[2] By 1970, "tea rooms" and "soda fountains" had disappeared, along with the word "colored," from 400 pages of display ads and commercial listings. Twenty years after that, a volume two inches thick would talk of "acupuncture," "yogurt," and "video games" (all new terms) and provide customers with still another 400 yellow pages, phone numbers in Chapin and Little Mountain South, and thirteen-and-one-half pages of government offices—local, state, and federal.

Census returns are yet another yardstick by which change can be measured. In 1960, 70.7 percent of all Richland County residents were native South Carolinians (in Lexington County, the figure was 86.7 percent). Twenty years later, these totals had declined to 66.3 percent in Richland, 70.4 percent in Lexington. Also, residents of the Columbia metropolitan area were a restless lot. Over half of them (59 percent in Columbia itself) moved to a new address between 1975 and 1980. And, although the region's foreign-born population was minuscule, only 2.7 percent in 1980, census rolls contain some surprises. In 1950, almost as an afterthought, Richland reported, in addition to 161,151 whites and 103,955 blacks, eleven American Indians, ten Chinese, and two Japanese. Three decades later, the county's ethnic population included 4,446 individuals of Spanish origin, 740 Koreans, 395 American Indians, 336 Chinese, 275 Asian Indians, 239 Filipinos, 238 Vietnamese, 229 Japanese, 82 Hawaiians, and a handful of Guamanians, Eskimos, and Samoans. Across the river in Lexington, the same nationalities were represented to a lesser degree, although that region could boast of twenty-eight Eskimos, while Richland had only fourteen.

Three segments of the local economy account for much of this diversity and growth: various levels of government, education, and wholesale-retail trade. In short, whether one weighs figures for city, county, or the entire urban sector—except for agriculture, which has almost disappeared[3]—regional income depends upon some of the same factors that gave birth to Columbia over two centuries ago. The number of local, state, and federal employees living in Richland County rose from 8,700 in the 1950s to 36,700 in the 1980s. (For the urbanized, two-county area, the total, which would include nearly all of those involved with education but not individuals in uniform, was 51,000.) In general terms, in 1980, 35 percent of Richland's 116,637 workers were government employees. Another 20 percent were associated with the distribution of goods, that is, wholesale-retail commercial activity, and 15 percent were providing services needed by various sectors of the economy. The latter included everything from waste and garbage disposal to telephones, computers, paper, and office space.[4]

As the metropolitan population grew in the 1980s, up from about 410,000 to 470,000, the ranks of those engaged in distribution and services continued to expand, while the number of government employees and those working in manufacturing experienced relative decline. In 1988, for example, only one Richland County manufacturer (Westinghouse, with nearly 1,200 workers) ranked among the state's largest industrial operations. Overall, some 20,000 individuals living in the Richland-Lexington area were turning out manufactured goods in the 1980s; however, only 3,800 of them were in textiles, an industry that once loomed large on the local scene. On the other hand, "high-tech" employment was booming. Between 1970 and 1980, the number of Richland County citizens in such fields grew from 5,890 to 14,250, while the ranks of their employers rose from 672 to 1,735. Lexington County experienced similar, although less spectacular growth, its "high-tech" work force rising from 3,829 to 7,140.

"The fort," an important but sometimes frustrating factor in the economic picture, finally began to put down roots and build permanent structures in the 1960s. During that same decade, it also merged with the city of Columbia, a union that cemented long-standing ties. By that era, military personnel were participating in blood drives and annual United Funds, attending University of South Carolina classes taught on the base itself, and often choosing to settle in the Midlands when their duty tours came to a close. Those who did frequently contributed to the ethnic diversity and cultural enrichment of this area.

In 1988, that bustling training facility was home to nearly 15,000 servicemen and women and employed 3,856 civilian workers. Their combined annual payroll was $281.6 million, while another $142.1 million was allocated for construction, supplies, and services. Much of this total ($423.7 million) was spent in the Midlands. During that same year, McEntire Air National Guard Base near Eastover, a much smaller operation, had a budget of $18.9 million.[5]

But even as government payrolls grew longer, more stores appeared in larger and more opulent shopping malls, tall office buildings changed the Columbia skyline, and Fort Jackson assumed an air of permanence, it was education in its many forms that dominated the public mind. The reasons are obvious. Classroom activity touched thousands of households, new schools often were the focal point of daily life in new suburbs (together with the neighborhood mall), and these sprawling, air-conditioned structures served many functions. There children learned, played, fought, and formed friendships, while their parents attended meetings, political rallies, and cultural and sports events . . . and perhaps voted on election day. In addition, the integration fury of the 1960s thrust the school forward as a matter of special concern and gave rise to "white flight." However, by the mid-1970s that phenomenon had lost some of its force. At the end of the decade, Richland County had seventy-one public schools with 40,663 pupils, while Lexington was operating forty-five public schools with 32,550 students. Another 4,292 Richland youngsters were attending eighteen private academies, nearly all of them church affiliated. Lexington had only ten such institutions with an enrollment of 975.

Changes wrought by integration and population shifts of these decades were far-reaching and often painful. This was especially true for graduates of old Columbia High School, who, in the early 1980s,

mounted an unsuccessful battle to save their Washington Street structure. Other well-known high schools that vanished included University
(1966), Olympia (1971), and Booker T. Washington (1974). The passing of
Olympia marked the demise of a remarkable mill-village institution that
fostered community pride and produced more than its share of fine
athletes.[6] And this was a fact that many who faced the "Red Devils" could
attest to. As one local resident recalled, "Whenever we played them we
got beat twice—once on the field and again afterwards!"

New classrooms appeared at public high schools such as A. C. Flora,
Richland Northeast, Spring Valley, and Lower Richland, as well as at a
handful of private institutions, among them, Heathwood Hall, Cardinal
Newman, and Hammond Academy. Heathwood, which opened in 1951 in
a famous mansion that gave its name to a Columbia neighborhood, began
as a modest kindergarten-grammar school but soon added higher grades
and moved to a new campus south of the city. Cardinal Newman, successor to famed Ursuline Academy, began classes in the spring of 1961, and
Hammond opened its doors in the fall of 1966, following the closing of
University High School three months earlier.

Contemporary developments in higher education were almost as unprecedented as what was happening in grades one through twelve. The
most spectacular growth occurred at the university, although Columbia
Bible College moved to a suburban site during these years, Midlands
Technical College made its debut, and Columbia College bounced back
from a disastrous fire. Aided by urban renewal programs, the University
of South Carolina expanded in virtually every direction, including up. In
the decades following World War II, student population increased over
ten-fold, from 2,220 to 26,000. By 1990, there were seventeen academic
units on or near the Columbia campus, including a medical school established in conjunction with the Veterans Hospital in 1977, and eight
branches in other parts of the state attended by another 13,000 students.

In addition to traditional courses, the university now was offering a
full range of evening, extension, and correspondence classes and was
home to a variety of institutes and research centers. Through able leadership, it was prepared, perhaps for the first time in its long history, to
serve the needs of *all* South Carolinians, including those, it might be
noted, behind bars. As one alumnus commented, "When I graduated in
1950, USC was a college where southern-educated teachers lectured to
southern students, most of them, quite frankly, South Carolinians. When
I returned twenty years later, everything had changed. It was a *real* university. And it was not just the new buildings, you could sense a much

more cosmopolitan atmosphere. For example, look at Five Points! That wasn't part of USC in 1950, but in 1970 it sure was."

A cursory review of college bulletins indicates these observations are indeed valid. In 1950, USC had 263 teaching faculty. Of that number, 109 (about 40 percent) were alumni, and another seventy-three had attended southern institutions. Two decades later, the Arts and Sciences division alone had a staff of 363, 100 more than the entire faculty of 1950. Only fifty-three were USC graduates, and many held degrees from prestigious American and foreign universities. Also, during the 1970s, black enrollment increased from 279 to 3,070, and in the fall of 1979 the student body included 356 foreign nationals and residents of every state except Montana.

Some credit for this growth must go to Texas-born Thomas F. Jones, an affable Purdue University engineering dean, who became president of the University of South Carolina in 1962. During the next twelve years, he battled to raise faculty salaries and add established scholars to the staff, while at the same time overseeing construction projects valued at $68 million. His overall goal, he often said, was "to create a vital environment in which things were happening." Similar efforts continued under James B. Holderman, a youthful educator formerly associated with the Lilly Foundation, who guided USC fortunes from 1977 to 1990.

To advance his dream of a national role for the university, Holderman crafted an enlightened public relations program, launched unprecedented fund-raising campaigns, brought scores of celebrated and distinguished figures to Columbia (including stage, screen, and TV stars, U.S. presidents, and Pope John Paul II), and coordinated academic and regional life in a manner that delighted the business community. The papal visit in the fall of 1987 prompted banker Robert V. Royall to hail Holderman as "the most attractive economic tool we have today." A stellar byproduct of this town-gown camaraderie was the Koger Center for the Arts, which opened in January of 1989. Next door was the Carolina Coliseum, a huge structure where basketball games, auto shows, religious revivals, circuses, and graduation ceremonies had been held for two decades. Although not called a "civic center," these two buildings went far toward fulfilling the frustrated hopes of Lester Bates.

Other institutions could point to various achievements during these same decades. Midlands Technical College began life in 1963 as the Richland Technical Education Center; then, following a name change and merger with several similar schools, it grew into what, by the late 1980s, was this state's fifth largest educational complex. In addition to two busy campuses in the Columbia area, one on each side of the Congaree, there were continuing education centers at Fort Jackson, Harbison, and Winnsboro. An outstanding example of regional cooperation, Midlands offered practical training in a wide range of one- and two-year programs, everything from court reporting and dental hygiene to commercial graphics and diesel mechanics.

Columbia College, which flirted with coeducation in the late 1940s and even fielded an impromptu football eleven and awarded degrees to a few males, eventually decided to stick to its traditional role as a Methodist-oriented institution for women. Benedict, more so than Allen, which was plagued by internal disputes, benefitted greatly from federal largess of the Kennedy-Johnson years and foundation grants. New dorms and classrooms were built, as well as an impressive library, and by the late 1980s that predominantly black institution had about 1,500 students, slightly more than were enrolled at Columbia College.

For nearly forty years, Columbia Bible College, largely the personal creation of Robert C. McQuilkin, was housed in the old Colonia Hotel and nearby structures. In 1953, the school purchased a 300-acre site north of the city, and at the close of that decade faculty and students, many of them destined to become missionaries in foreign lands, moved to a new campus near Interstate 20. This relocation paid unexpected dividends, for it stirred efforts of historically minded Columbians to save from destruction a building that had served for some years as that school's library and male dormitory.

The fate of this gracious brick edifice, built for merchant prince Ainsley Hall in 1823 according to plans drawn by architect Robert Mills, hung in the balance for some months. By November of 1961, however, the Historic Columbia Foundation, headed by Jennie Clarkson Dreher, had inaugurated a campaign that, in turn, led to formation of a city-county historical commission. Soon, individuals, banks, businesses, and government agencies pitched in, and this remarkable display of community purpose succeeded in saving what became known as the Robert Mills House. By January of 1967, that mansion, set in an entire city block, was restored, and during the next five years, period furniture, outbuildings, and gardens appeared. According to *Be It Remembered*, a massive report issued in 1974, this undertaking cost slightly more than $800,000.

This triumph inspired other restoration efforts such as the nearby Hampton-Preston House and homes associated with Woodrow Wilson, Maxcy Gregg, Mary Boykin Chesnut, and noted free black Celia Mann. In the early 1970s, the university began refurbishing its "Horseshoe";

and, in succeeding years, the state created "Governor's Green," a 9-acre complex encompassing the Lace House, Boylston House, and the traditional residence of South Carolina's first family.

Heightened historic interest also played some role in the development of several area museums, among them, facilities at Lexington, Cayce, and Fort Jackson, the university's McKissick Museum, and especially the new State Museum located in the former "duck" mill on Gervais Street. In 1973, South Carolina officials launched plans for the latter and even selected a site; however, the decision of the owners of the famed Columbia Mill to cease operations paved the way for acquisition of that impressive structure in December of 1981. Seven years and some $15 million later, the museum opened to widespread acclaim.

The roots of concern for the past are easy to identify. Urban renewal of the 1950s and destruction of several landmarks to make way for downtown office buildings sparked scattered resentment, and historical awareness also was fueled by commemorative events marking anniversaries of the Civil War, founding of colonial South Carolina, and the American Revolution. In addition, cities such as Savannah were demonstrating that preservation made good business sense, and one never should discount the desire to keep pace with that rival citadel of bygone culture: Charleston.

Yet this was not simply preoccupation with or glorification of the past, for cheek-to-jowl with every scheme to preserve remnants of the 1800s were plans for Columbia after the year 2000. Interestingly, the vision Lester Bates presented to the All-America city committee in 1951 concentrated upon citizen participation and the effectiveness of city manager government. Thirteen years later, he still was emphasizing citizen power but had expanded his story to encompass race relations, urban renewal, *and* historic preservation. In addition, Bates spoke glowingly of plans for a new post office and a new community hospital. The latter, by the time it opened in 1972, cost $24.5 million and had been re-christened Richland Memorial Hospital.

Missing from his 1964 presentation, somewhat strangely, is any reference to the zoo, as well as true appreciation for growth and expansion of the University of South Carolina. The idea of a zoo, at first seen as a facility for children, not their parents, goes back to the 1930s. A decade later, the Chamber of Commerce revived the proposal, secured options on a site near the Veterans Hospital, and in 1961 hired a zoo planner. By the mid-1960s, a fund drive was under way, and in April of 1974 a full-fledged zoo opened on the banks of the Saluda, not east of the city as first envisioned. Originally supported by Columbia and Richland and Lexington counties, what became Riverbanks Zoo experienced management and financial problems during the first year or so and nearly was taken over by the state. However, in time, as the result of hard work and a Lexington County referendum that demonstrated citizen support, Riverbanks expanded and evolved into what is now this state's top publicly supported attraction. In the year ending in June of 1990, for example, it was host to 930,000 visitors, many of them out-of-state tourists.

In 1969, during a final (and unsuccessful) pitch for national recognition, Bates did cite plans for a zoo and the university's coliseum, which made its bow in November of the previous year when USC eked out a 51–49 basketball win over Auburn. Perhaps his honor hesitated to say much about Riverbanks until it became a reality, although he seemed willing enough to talk of other proposed projects, some of which really were not municipal undertakings. But failure of the mayor and his associates to make more of changes going on at the university is both puzzling and perhaps revealing. On one level, it is possible the full impact of what was happening on and around the old campus was not yet comprehended; or, memories of a battle with a church and forced relocation of 250 families and thirty-five businesses to make way for the coliseum and a new law center may have been painfully fresh.[7] Also, university acquisition of Wheeler Hill, with the cooperation of the city, was being questioned by black activists.

But it was not only the University of South Carolina that was gobbling up real estate, so was state government, so much so that by the 1980s, according to Mayor Kirk Finlay, 43 percent of all land within the city was not subject to taxation. The first major construction of this era for state administrative purposes was the Rutledge Building at Senate and Bull streets, completed in 1965. Then, a few years later, as a bicentennial project, the state began building an impressive quadrangle of offices and underground parking facilities south of the capitol. This finally put to rest a 1945 proposal to complete the State House "tower" according to original plans and another scheme in 1958 to add a dome and flanking wings similar to those of the national capitol in Washington.

At least four other mid-town buildings of these years demand attention, two because of sheer size and two more because of unique qualities. The Bankers Trust tower (now NCNB) and the AT&T Building, which replaced, respectively, the Columbia and Wade Hampton hotels, are simply big, functional blocks of steel, concrete, and glass with banks of elevators and hundreds of office cubicles. Cornell Arms, on the other

Minor Milestones

1941

Feb Lotte Lehman and Southern Symphony perform at Township.
May KKK meets at Hotel Jefferson and endorses aid to Britain.
June NAACP holds second annual state conference at Sidney Park CME Church. Edwin Seibels honored as inventor of vertical filing system.
Dec Woman's Club opens headquarters at Maxcy Gregg Park.

1942

Jan Municipal workers get 10 percent raise.
May Gas rationing: three gallons per week.
July A. C. Flora elected head of National Education Association.

1943

Jan USC launches three-semester schedule. Olin Johnston rides to inaugural in surrey.
May Restaurants begin meatless days.

1944

Feb Farmers urged to plant kudzu.
Aug Colonel D. W. Seigler (ninety-seven), last local Civil War veteran, dies at Confederate Home.

1945

Sept Syphilis blood-test campaign: "Bring Them Back to a Healthier Columbia."
Nov 2,244 students inundate USC.

1946

Feb Dreyfuss Field becomes Capital City Park. USC students picket State House seeking expanded facilities.
Dec Male "coed" football: Coker 34, Columbia College 7.

1947

Jan New airport terminal burns. Paul Robeson at Allen University. Baptist Hospital expands.
April Pine Tree Hunt (founded in 1938) holds sixth annual trials.
July James F. White, 3012 Kirkwood Avenue, wins Soapbox Derby.

1949

Jan South Carolina National Bank opens drive-in window in Five Points.
March William J. ("Uncle Billy") Cayce, age eighty-four, founder of Cayce, dies.
April Marian Anderson, who first appeared at Bethel AME Church in 1927, sings to a packed Township, with races segregated at every level: arena, dress circle, and balcony.
May Movie star Esther Williams opens Maxcy Gregg Pool.
June Richland County Court grants first divorce under new laws.

1950

Feb Billy Graham concludes crusade before 40,000 at stadium.
March Oral Roberts preaches to thousands in thirteen-day tent revival.

1951

June Columbia is being served daily by twenty-five passenger trains, eighty-six inter-city buses, and sixteen planes.
June Herb Brown, Jr., wins national junior tennis crown.
Sept Miniature train, "Carolina Special," begins operation at Valley Park.
Dec Voting machines arrive.

1952

Aug Columbia Reds win league pennant, first ever.

1953

July　Blossom Street bridge opens.
Dec　Door of Hope closes after fifty-five years. City bans livery stables.

1954

Jan　YMCA marks 100th birthday.
Oct　Police find 3,600-gallon still in Gill Creek Swamp one-and-one-half miles from VA Hospital.

1955

June　"Big Apple" to become Bethel Bible Institute.
Nov　Harden Street extension aproved. Columbia Polo Team organized.

1957

May　JFK gets honorary degree at USC.
Aug　Data processing center opens on Millwood Avenue.
Nov　Construction of Elmwood Avenue bridge begins.

1959

Aug　A. C. Flora High School opens. Representative Ryan Shealy water-skis to Charleston to demonstrate potential of Congaree.
Oct　Clemson wins last "Big Thursday" contest, 27–0.

1960

Aug　First annual jazz festival held at Legion Lake (Heise's Pond). I-26 opens to Pomaria.

1961

Nov　USC outlines building plans costing $13.3 million.

1962

March　Confederate flag appears over State House.
June　Spring Valley Country Club to open. Columbia Country Club (Ridgewood) planning to move to Blythewood area.

Oct　Passenger train service to Charleston ceases.

1963

April　Malcolm X attacks integration as "trick" in West Columbia speech originally scheduled for Township.

1964

April　Desree Jenkins (4228 Monticello Road) crowned "Mrs. America."
June　Doris Giles, senior employee at Columbia Pacific Mills, retires after fifty-nine years. Charles Bolden, Jr., C. A. Johnson salutatorian, to attend Naval Academy.

1965

Aug　Jet service begins at enlarged municipal airport.
Nov　Congressional hearings reveal Heritage Garment Works (522 Howard Street) makes and sells KKK robes.

1966

June　Assembly Street post office opens.
Nov　Local voters back liquor reform, but proposal defeated state-wide.

1967

March　Work begins on USC Coliseum.

1968

May　Singer James Brown awarded key to the city.
June　"Liberty Tree" historical drama opens at Sesquicentennial Park.

1969

Jan　Benedict senior William Gray becomes Senate's first black page.
Oct　Last Palmetto Fair held.

1970

April　Chamber of Commerce scraps controversial postal meter slogan: "General Sherman visited here . . . why don't you?"

Sept USC offers non-credit computer courses.

1971

Oct Without fanfare or comment, integrated State Fair opens.

1972

May *Osceola*, alternative weekly, begins publication.

1973

Aug Good Samaritan-Waverly Hospital closes.

1974

March Five hundred "streak" at USC. Plans for Harbison unveiled.

1976

June WLTR-FM, educational radio station, begins broadcasting.
Oct Congaree Swamp National Monument wins congressional approval . . . $35.5 million allocated for purchase of 15,200 acres of land in lower Richland.

1977

Feb Elvis in sell-out concert at coliseum.
July Work begins on Thurmond federal building.
Aug Parks & Recreation softball league has over 200 teams.

1978

Nov In "blue-law" dispute, Richland sheriff closes Sunday crafts show at fair grounds.

1979

Dec City buys 27,250 garbage carts ("Herbie-Curbies") for $1.1 million.

1980

Sept Home milk delivery ends.

1982

July Work begins on Riverfront Park.

1983

March First St. Patrick's Day fete at Five Points.
July Union Camp to restore "Kensington."
Nov Blythewood holds "Coogler Festival."

1984

June Ban of *Chocolate War* by School District Two creates outcry, soon rescinded.
July Reagan attends Caribbean Conference at USC.
Sept Union Camp opens $550-million pulp and paper plant near Eastover.

1985

Feb In less than twenty-four hours, USC fans buy ninety stadium parking places at $7,500 per space.
May Sunday retail sales become legal. Robert Marvin presents his "Vista Plan" to civic leaders.

1986

March Columbia celebrates 200th birthday.
Oct Knight-Ridder, Inc. buys State-Record Company.

1987

Sept Pope John Paul II visits Columbia.

1989

Feb Benedict College honors Annie Greene Nelson, well-known black novelist, at exhibit and reception.
Sept Seibels-Bruce marks 120th year.

1990

Sept Greenville native Charles P. Austin becomes first black to head city police department.
Dec After much controversy, Sidney Park opens to rave reviews.

hand, is a residential complex, which, when completed in November of 1949, was the tallest such structure (210 feet, eighteen stories with 119 apartments) between Richmond and Miami. Named for owner Cornell G. Fuller, president of the Bank of Barnwell and head of a trucking firm, it also was the tallest building that the Federal Housing Administration ever had financed. Not surprisingly, the demise of a third hotel, the Jefferson, now site of Jefferson Square, led to appeals for new facilities, and during his administration Mayor Finlay put together a $60-million package known as the Palmetto Center, which includes a distinctive office tower, parking garage, and the Columbia Marriott (302 rooms) that opened in the fall of 1983.

Also, both as councilman and mayor, Finlay pushed hard for implementation of the "Seaboard Park Plan," an ambitious scheme to rejuvenate a fifty-block area encompassing Arsenal Hill, Sidney Park, and the "Congaree Vista," a region stretching westward from the traditional business district to the river. Virtually everyone agrees that Columbia is indeed fortunate to possess such a large in-town area ripe for development, yet there are major hurdles to be overcome. Two of them, however, already have been surmounted. With a judicious mix of federal money and local funds, Finlay was able to relocate the railroad tracks that so irritated Constantinos Doxiadis, and state officials have agreed to move the penitentiary (Central Correctional Institution) to Lee County.[8]

Turning to other matters of regional concern, in April of 1968, the U.S. Supreme Court expanded its "one man, one vote" decision to encompass local government, a move that had impact akin to that of the 1954 segregation ruling. By the mid-1960s, the General Assembly already was grappling with reapportionment proposals that eventually granted Richland four senators and ten representatives. Thus federal action and increasing urbanization set the stage for fundamental change in local government, together with simultaneous revival of still other suggestions for reform. Among the latter was talk once more of a city-county merger, sparked in part by secret sessions of Richland's new, five-member council and controversial surveys of various county departments.

In the spring of 1972, Richland legislators agreed to seek General Assembly approval of greater council authority over local affairs, as well as referendums on both merger and a new courthouse. That fall, the courthouse squeaked by, 25,213–24,260, but merger apparently lost, 23,503–20,785. One has to say "apparently" because, as it turned out, 4,200 voters in two precincts (Greenview and Dentsville) either failed to receive merger ballots or, if they did, their ballots were not counted.[9]

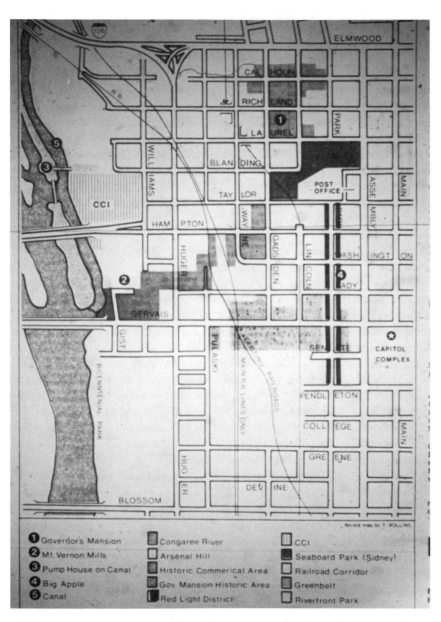

The Congaree Vista Takes Shape, 1981. This map appeared in the *Columbia Record* (30 July 1981) in a five-part series on urban development authored by Katherine King.

Early in 1973, reacting to criticism, county council members pledged to hold, with certain qualifications, open sessions. (It might be noted that city officials during the Bates administration and after often faced similar charges, namely, that important matters were decided in private and public meetings were *pro forma*.) And on 1 June 1973, the council hired Robert G. Mauney as "county executive." The following year, members voted 4–1 to place merger on the ballot once more, but local legislators axed this proposal, presumably because a "home rule" amendment, already ratified, was to become effective in June of 1975. Soon after that date, voters in both Richland and Lexington counties approved a council-administrator form of government and also enlarged their councils. In Richland, membership rose to eleven; in Lexington to nine. Meanwhile, in an unrelated matter, Columbia and Richland County agreed to an exchange of downtown property that cleared the way for construction of an $11-million courthouse that is now known as a "judicial center."

Few doubt that "home rule" is an important departure in South Carolina public life. Yet in a three-volume analysis of the state constitution, James Lowell Underwood points out that (a) municipalities already possessed some of the advantages promised by "home rule," (b) a mass of special commissions, districts, and boards formed before 1975 remain in place, and (c) through appointive powers and other rights embedded in the constitution itself, county delegations often continue to play a major role, especially in fiscal matters, highway decisions, and school affairs.[10]

However, some individuals active in Richland County politics see matters a bit differently. To varying degrees, James Leventis, Heyward McDonald, and Timothy Rogers believe home rule and single-member districts (to be discussed shortly) ushered in substantial change. In fact, Rogers sees a circular development. The demise of the delegation's grip on local government was succeeded by single-member districts in the House in 1974 and in the Senate a decade later, which, strangely, pushed both representatives and senators back into the local arena once more. Nevertheless, a definite shift in emphasis has taken place. Two decades ago, the delegation wielded veto power; now its members are being forced into an advocacy role by local constituents lobbying for pet projects.

Richland's county council has had, according to most accounts, a rather tempestuous childhood. Personality clashes and political infighting as a two-party system takes root are part of the story, and rapid turnover of administrators in the early 1980s would indicate reservations on the part of some elected officials concerning the merits of managerial government. The city council, on the other hand, has struggled to find a formula for federally mandated representation. Two proposals for limited single-member districts were defeated at the polls before a 4–2–1 plan finally won approval in December of 1981. (Four members chosen by districts, two others and the mayor elected at large.) Thirteen months later, in January of 1983, federal authorities rebuffed an attempt to reduce the size of the county council, which continued to be elected at large until 1988 when single-member districts were instituted for all eleven seats.

The cultural-social story of these decades is far more complex than any struggle over "home rule" and "one man, one vote." Its overriding themes are the pervasive influence of television and suburban life, the rise of big-time sports at USC, and the multiple interests of a growing and increasingly diverse population. Looking at just one aspect of popular culture (movies and facilities for large audiences), in 1950 this community had eight motion picture houses capable of handling 6,800 patrons, five drive-in theaters, and two major auditoriums—Township seating 3,500 and the university fieldhouse, 3,000. As always, all sorts of gatherings were being held in churches, lodge halls, and schools. During the next two decades, the number of movie theaters increased slightly, and in 1970 five of them still were downtown. The massive Carolina Coliseum, seating 13,000, had just opened and, although primarily a basketball arena, could accommodate drama, concerts, circuses, trade shows, and so on.

Twenty years later, the Koger Center for the Arts, costing $15 million and seating 2,300 people, appeared nearby. But there no longer were any drive-ins, only one Main Street theater (the Nickelodeon), and nearly all of this community's eleven movie outlets were multiple screens tucked away in shopping malls. Reliable old Township, home to everything from wrestling matches to opera and political bombast, had been joined by smaller auditoriums at various schools and colleges, which, in turn, staged plays and musical events of their own. The Columbia City Ballet, for example, made its debut at Dreher High School in April of 1962.

In short, the scope of cultural activity expanded to the suburbs, and "the tube" exerted direct impact upon the nature and location of movie theaters and even dictated how thousands spent their leisure hours. Similar factors wielded considerable influence upon the content of Columbia's daily newspapers. The afternoon *Record*, which long featured pretty girls and any murder committed anywhere in North America, in the early 1960s began to pay attention to suburban life, especially after the annexation fiasco of those years. In 1962, it launched a "metro" section and each Friday published considerable television and entertainment news. By October of 1974, this coverage had grown into "Weekend," and in the fall of 1981 "Neighbors" appeared, an ambitious attempt by both dailies to reflect life in six "zones" of metropolitan Richland and Lexington countries.

Although TV and suburban sprawl played a role in this evolving story, so did the challenge of various weeklies. Paramount among these was *Osceola*, a spin-off from Clemson's *Tiger* that, from 1972 to 1977, set high standards for local journalism. Yet television coverage, at least for the *Record*, may have been a fatal will-o-the-wisp; for, in a pattern repeated throughout the nation, subscribers of afternoon dailies were choosing to watch the evening news, not read it. And in April of 1988, after ninety-one years, the *Columbia Record* published its final edition.

Local residents also were watching sports, match-ups that sometimes featured the USC Gamecocks. Just when those directing university fortunes decided to go big-time is not known, but trends of the 1950s and 1960s reveal that bowl-hungry trustees were calling the shots. The seating capacity of the stadium grew from 27,676 to 42,338; and, in December of 1969, as part of a $112-million construction program, USC disclosed plans to add another 30,000 seats. Other lavish facilities for both players and fans appeared, as well as football coach Paul Dietzel and basketball wizard Frank McGuire, and the 1971 yearbook opened with . . . football! By the 1970s, under the guidance of Yankee star Bobby Richardson and June Raines, the USC baseball team also was contending for national honors, and in these years a dozen players went on to the majors. A decade later, in 1988, fifteen former Gamecocks were playing with minor league teams as well.

This sudden emphasis led to faculty criticism and a recurring crisis throughout the Holderman years. The president, in a largely successful bid for control of both the athletic program and its bank account, sought to restructure lines of authority. The result was a series of contract disputes that cost the university $1.1 million, reflecting little glory upon those concerned. And the socio-economic impact of tailgate hoopla was felt throughout the community each autumn, even if one did not park in a space costing five figures, revel in an ornate clubhouse, and sip drinks in a railway caboose equipped with basic facilities (not to mention luxuries) that some Columbia homes still lack. Basketball and baseball crowds were, of course, much smaller, although USC baseball benefitted to some degree from the absence of semi-pro teams.

In 1952, the Columbia Reds won their first Sally League pennant and duplicated that feat three years later, only to depart for Savannah. The next season, local fans were unable to convince players to return the pennant (they claimed it had been won in Columbia and should remain here) and had to fashion their own. The Reds were succeeded for two years by the Gems ("Columbia the *gem* of the ocean"), a Kansas City franchise. Then, in 1960, the Reds came back for a couple of seasons. During the next two decades, the years when the Gamecocks were becoming a collegiate powerhouse, local fans had no city team to root for—that is, until the Columbia Mets made their debut in April of 1983.[11] The Mets lost the opener to Greenwood but went on to win the league title and draw 111,209 fans during their initial season.

Baseball, basketball, football, and similar sports were played during these years at other colleges and schools throughout the region, and Township continued to feature wrestling and boxing cards. In 1951, Fort Jackson staged a service bowl game, but the score (Jackson 7, Carswell AFB 32) snuffed out plans for an annual event. The Palmetto Trials, a single day of horse racing held at the fair grounds each March, at times was a social rival of the Camden Cup. Launched in 1952 by veteran trainer Max Hirsch and sponsored by the Junior League, these meets ceased in 1968, largely because earlier openings at New York tracks were luring trainers and horses to the north.

Meanwhile, in 1961 USC fielded its first soccer team, and the Columbia Polo Club (organized six years earlier) in the 1970s spawned the Wildewood and Rainbow Farms clubs. Another local sport, however, was smothered by suburban housing. Soon after World War II, the Columbia Speedway opened in Cayce, and it was there that auto daredevil Richard Petty scored some of his first triumphs. But in the late 1960s, neighbors began to complain of noise; and, in 1972, as their numbers increased, they demanded and got a 10:30 P.M. curfew. Under such pressures, the track eventually closed and in 1983 moved to a more bucolic setting near Gaston.

By contrast, as noted earlier, suburban growth tended to strengthen art, music, and theater. More people with varied backgrounds translated into more participants and patrons, as well as larger audiences. For the most part, although not always, cultural activity had academic ties. One stellar event was the opening of the Columbia Museum of Art in the Taylor mansion on Senate Street in March of 1950. Thus after decades of hanging paintings in schools, department stores, libraries, the USO, and even abandoned police stations, the local art association, led by Walter

Bedford Moore, Jr., had a home of its own. In 1941, this group had mounted an ill-timed drive to acquire the Hampton-Preston House, but in the decade that followed, their appeals were aided by paintings and art objects donated by Edwin Seibels and a European adventure with unforeseen consequences.

In the spring of 1948, Columbia joined in a campaign to help French communities still suffering from the effects of war. This city's special concern was Berck, a resort town of 12,000 on the Atlantic Coast south of Boulogne. By October, gifts worth $75,000 had been collected, and Mayor Frank C. Owens and his wife decided to go to Europe and present this donated food and clothing to the citizens of Berck. Owens, as he later admitted, was deeply impressed by museums he saw in towns much smaller than Columbia and returned a convert. In the first ninety days of operation, this new facility had over 10,000 visitors and, under the guidance of John Kraft, director from 1950 to 1977, added an art school, theater group, and valuable works from the Kress Collection. It also developed a planetarium and science museum and often was the setting for Sunday afternoon recitals.

The Columbia Music Festival Association, an organization founded in the early 1930s as a state-wide arts council and directed throughout the 1940s by James Y. Perry and his wife, had general oversight of musical affairs throughout these decades. As such, it promoted an annual artist series and coordinated the work of groups such as the Lyric Opera, City Ballet, Choral Society, Palmetto Opera, and the Youth Opera. In its initial season, the Columbia Philharmonic (successor to the Southern Symphony and South Carolina Philharmonic) was under Festival auspices, but in 1964 it became an independent organization.

As usual, the theatrical world was especially robust, thanks to pioneer work of the Town Theatre. The somewhat more experimental Workshop Theatre, born in the mid-1960s, soon was producing five shows each season. Among them were two smash hits, *Cabaret* in 1975 and *Oliver* in 1981. By the late 1980s, one also could cheer the hero and hiss the villain at the Koger Center, USC, and Columbia College, Act One in West Columbia, Village Square Theatre in Lexington, Chapin's Community Theatre, and Trustus and Upstage Children's theaters in Columbia.

For those interested in writing and books, the most encouraging signs were vigor displayed by the university's English Department and the growth of libraries. Until the 1950s, when USC began to expand by leaps and bounds, an important center of intellectual thought was James T. Gittman's bookstore in the 1200 block of Main Street. Gittman, a

Virginia native, came to Columbia shortly before World War I and soon established himself as an authority on rare books.[12] An amateur pugilist, he also coached the university's first boxing team, but more important were his morning coffee sessions during which writers and would-be writers traded ideas. Among those attending from time to time were Henry Bellamann, Julia Peterkin, Havilah Babcock, Chapman Milling, Frank Wardlaw, and photographer Carl Julien. It was Wardlaw, managing editor of the USC Press (established in 1944), who, over coffee at Gittman's, teamed Milling with Julien to produce *Beneath So Kind a Sky*, a book that has gone through eight editions. By the 1960s, the literary focus had shifted to the university scene, enlivened by visiting scholars, lecture series, and individuals such as Ben Greer, Pat Conroy, Columbia's own "southern fried" William Price Fox, and poet-novelist James Dickey of *Deliverance* fame, who joined the USC faculty in 1968.

In the fall of 1952, the Richland County Library moved into a $300,000 home at Sumter and Washington streets and, in time, set in motion an active program to provide branch facilities for suburbs and outlying communities. New libraries also appeared at virtually every center of higher learning in the region. Especially impressive was the Thomas Cooper Library, an Edward Stone structure built at USC in the early 1970s, much of it below ground in what librarian Ken Toombs liked to boast was "the biggest hole ever dug in this state." To round out the picture, under the leadership of Estellene Walker, an invigorated state library system, with new headquarters on Senate Street, took shape, and bookstores proliferated to keep pace with these trends. In 1950, the metropolitan area had five bookshops; in 1990, there were ten times as many. A handful were specializing in religious material, metaphysical publications, and adult books, while others catered to regional interests and educational needs.

Some innovations of these decades such as adult bookstores, historic preservation, polo ponies, and $15,000 parking spaces certainly were not part of the original vision of Lester Bates. His ideal world was largely a Chamber of Commerce dream of controlled growth, civic pride, a dynamic downtown, and economic well-being for all. At the same time that Bates offered up the Doxiadis Plan to achieve these goals, USC president Tom Jones was juggling burgeoning enrollments and state appropriations so as (in his words) to provide "a vital environment in which things were happening." Two decades later, it would appear that both men—*and their associates*—succeeded far better than they realized, and the Columbia area is richer for their efforts.

Notes

1. See Lester L. Bates, Sr., and Joe C. Norman, "Columbia 2000," *South Carolina Urban & Regional Review* (June, 1971), pp. 3–6. In February of 1971, while addressing a leadership conference, Bates expanded his "wish list" to include new liquor laws, revision of the state constitution so as to remove "the noose from the necks of cities," relocation of the penitentiary, and an interstate highway to Charlotte. According to Dennis Daye, speech writer for Mayor Bates, his boss had an uncanny memory. Given the draft of an address, he read it slowly, carefully, and, on the spot, memorized every word. Thereafter, Daye recalls, efforts to alter the original text usually were futile.
2. In 1970, Lexington listings covered only ten pages; in 1990, forty-three pages.
3. According to the 1980 census, only about 2,000 individuals were employed in agriculture in Richland and Lexington counties. In 1987, Lexington had 702 farms; Richland, 326. Three years later, Richland's last dairy farmer, Hopkins resident Sam McGregor, gave up and sold his herd.
4. In 1980, midtown Columbia had 1.5 million square feet of office space, which by 1990 had increased to 4 million; however, regional totals reflect an even greater gain, rising from 2.8 to 8.6 million square feet during the decade.
5. This field came into being in 1943 as part of the Columbia Army Air Force Base. By 1948, the National Guard had taken over, and in November of 1961, this facility was renamed in honor of Brigadier General Barney B. McEntire, the first commander of this state's Air National Guard, who lost his life in a Pennsylvania plane crash in May of that year.
6. See Alvin Byars, *Olympia-Pacific* . . . , pp. 153–473.
7. From 1965 to 1970, members of the Greene Street Methodist Church waged a spirited and eventually successful campaign to remain within an area marked for urban renewal by municipal and federal authorities. At one point, university trustees voted to raze the church, but then recanted and deleted church property from their plans.
8. In September of 1977, the Capital City Development Foundation organized in 1970 to promote the Doxiadis Plan, disbanded. A spokesman for the group admitted efforts to create a transportation hub had been thwarted by the uncooperative stance of bus companies and conceded that no "Vista" could take shape so long as CCI remained where it was. However, as noted, a decade later relocation of that sprawling facility was under way.
9. In this election, aided by the Nixon landslide, Republicans did well, gaining a 3–2 margin on the county council and a 5–2 advantage on the District One School Board.
10. See James Lowell Underwood, *The Constitution of South Carolina* (3 vols.; Columbia, 1986, 1989, 1992), II, pp. 245–249.
11. That same year, USC joined the Metro Conference in basketball and spring sports, having quit the ACC in 1971 in a dispute over academic qualifications for athletes. In September of 1990, the Gamecocks became affiliated with the Southeastern Conference.
12. Gittman, who died in October of 1951 at the age of seventy-eight, worked for the Pullman Company when young in order to see the country. He subsequently became a representative for Scribners and owner of a chain of bookshops in the Carolinas. Eventually, however, he sold all of them except the Columbia outlet and proceeded to make it an institution of considerable regional importance.

The Heart
of the
Midlands at 250

CHAPTER TWENTY-TWO

In February of 1957, Henry Cauthen, Carlton Truax, and fellow staff members at the *Columbia Record* launched a year-long campaign to promote the Midlands. Despite such efforts, much like "the Congarees" of the early 18th century, this inland empire remains an elusive concept. In their eyes, it was a sixteen-county expanse centered upon Columbia that extended from the Savannah River shores of Edgefield, Aiken, Barnwell, and Allendale to the eastern frontiers of Lancaster, Kershaw, Sumter, and Clarendon. Three decades later, geographers Charles F. Kovacik and John J. Winberry defined the Midlands as a modest, east-west band of four counties: Aiken, Lexington, Richland, and Kershaw.[1] Meanwhile, formation of the Central Midlands Regional Planning Council in July of 1969 focused attention upon a slightly different grouping, communities located in Lexington, Richland, Newberry, and Fairfield counties. Nevertheless, little doubt exists that the heart of the Midlands is the Columbia metropolitan area—South Carolina's capital city and its suburbs in two counties, Richland and Lexington.

In 1980, this region had a population of 410,088, a figure that is expected to rise to 530,100 by the year 2000. In an attempt to sketch a rough profile of the rapidly changing Columbia scene, the summary that follows has been assembled from the pages of the *South Carolina Statistical Abstract* for 1990, a compilation of local, state, and federal data. It may contain a few surprises; and, since different agencies express similar findings differently, slight distortion can occur.

As most residents already know, the two counties are about the same size; and, from the onset of European exploration and settlement, their destinies have been closely linked. Garrisons and trading posts appeared on the west bank of the Congaree from time to time in the early 1700s, facilities that obviously served the entire region. Then in the 1730s, German-Swiss immigrants carved out the first farms of the Midlands in what was known as Saxe-Gotha, several years before pioneers from North Carolina and Virginia began moving into lower Richland. Through-out succeeding decades, at least since 1800 when districts (counties) achieved definite form, Richland has been more densely populated and home to far more blacks and fewer little towns and villages than its neighbor.

Agriculture, long the primary occupation, now is dwindling in importance on both sides of the river. Yet, even in decline, vestiges of by-gone days still remain—expansive plantations in lower Richland, small, self-sufficient farms in Lexington, a region that in some ways actually resembles Piedmont more than Midlands. On the eve of the Civil War, for example, only two Lexington residents owned more than 100 slaves, compared to fifteen in Richland, and Lexington always has had more whites than blacks within its borders. Lexington experienced especially rough days in the late 1860s when its population dropped 17 percent, down from 15,579 to 12,988. During the Depression decade of the 1930s, the number of residents again declined somewhat and in 1940 stood at 35,994, about one-third that of Richland (104,843). A half-century later, following several wars and decades of unprecedented social and economic change, here are some of the factors shaping day-to-day life in the heart of the Midlands.

Table 6. The Columbia Metropolitan Area in the 1980s

	Richland	Lexington
Population (1980)	269,735	140,353
White[a]	161,130	125,463
Black	104,050	13,856
Other	4,555	1,034
Estimated (1988)	285,900	170,600
Per square mile	375.4	241.3
Projected (2000)	323,200	206,900
Total area (square miles)	771.38	757.23
Land	761.58	707.00
Water	9.80	50.23

a. Although overall totals remain the same, white-black population originally was reported somewhat differently: Richland 161,561 white, 103,955 black; Lexington 125,503 white, 13,654 black.

Table 6 (*continued*)

Total acres	487,411	452,480
Woodland	320,106	246,892
Percentage of total area	65.7	54.6
Roads (miles)	2,565.83	2,488.19
Interstate	52.19	51.94
State primary	286.83	237.26
State secondary	1,267.96	1,190.49
County paved	228.03	190.00
County unpaved	346.93	777.00
Municipal maintenance	383.89	41.50
Motor vehicles registered (1988)	190,693	137,150
Accidents	12,253	5,494
Injured	4,531	2,163
Deaths	53	48
Mortality rate[b]	27.7	35.8
Economic loss (millions)	$ 57	$ 34
Local governments[c]	15	27
Municipalities	5	15
School districts	2	5
Special districts	7	6
With tax power	3	5
Total registered voters (1988)	125,015	71,083
Votes cast	89,660	56,212
Percentage voting	71.7	79.1
Public schools (1988)	63	47
Enrollment	38,130	33,987
Operating cost per pupil	$ 3,667	$ 3,240
High school drop-outs	484	256
Drop-out rate	3.8%	2.2%
Private schools	18	7
Enrollment	3,249	748
Farms (1987)	326	702
Average size (acres)	190	116
Average value (land and buildings)	$223,117	$145,989
Farming operator's main occupation	40.5%	38.5%
Average age of operator	55	53
County land in farms	12.7%	18.0%
Cattle	7,300	15,300
Hogs and pigs	3,000	2,900
Work force (1980)	1,051	1,178

b. Deaths per 100,000 registered vehicles.
c. Includes county governments.

Table 6 (*continued*)

Housing units (1980)	91,868	52,650
Households	85,461	47,617
Owner occupied	51,734	36,398
Renter occupied	33,727	11,219
Persons per household	2.8	2.9
Families	61,013	38,367
Persons per family	3.3	3.3
Marriages (1988)	2,825	1,587
Divorces (1988)	1,187	884
Total personal income (1987, millions)[d]	$ 3,747	$ 2,443
Per capita personal income[e]	$13,270	$14,455
Estimated per capita income (1987)	$10,914	$11,681
Highest (by community)	$19,771	$13,349
Community	Arcadia Lakes	Irmo
Lowest (by community)	$ 6,407	$ 7,155
Community	Eastover	Swansea
Employed age 16 and over by industry (1980)		
Farming, forestry & fisheries	1,481	1,487
Construction	6,992	5,907
Manufacturing	15,247	13,948
Transportation	2,811	2,845
Communications & public utilities	4,467	3,250
Wholesale trade	4,730	3,711
Retail trade	18,002	9,693
Finance, insurance & real estate	10,294	5,666
Business & repair services	4,055	2,575
Entertainment & recreational services	5,116	2,384
Health services	12,816	3,912
Educational services	13,440	5,201
Other professionals	6,456	2,946
Public administration	10,730	4,848
Employed age 16 and over by class of worker (1980)		
Private wage & salary	74,326	49,815
Federal government	7,168	2,229
State government	21,204	7,979
Local government	8,380	4,085

d. Personal income, in contrast to estimated per-capita income, includes income (monetary and non-monetary) derived from *all* sources, as well as that received by non-profit institutions, private trust funds, and private health and welfare funds, which, for personal income purposes, are classified as "persons" by the federal Bureau of Economic Analysis.

e. In 1987, the top county in South Carolina was Beaufort ($14,601), followed by Lexington, Greenville, York, and Richland.

Table 6 (*continued*)

Self-employed	5,251	3,992
Unpaid family workers	308	273
Businesses, workers & annual payrolls (1987)		
Contract construction	582	532
Employees	9,993	4,289
Payroll (millions)	$ 194	$ 66
Manufacturing	252	203
Employees	17,935	9,271
Payroll (millions)	$ 403	$ 204
Over 1,000 employees	Westinghouse	Allied Fibers
Number of employees	1,188	1,332
Transportation & public utilities	213	128
Employees	8,191	2,468
Payroll (millions)	$ 277	$ 55
Wholesale trade	632	275
Employees	8,971	2,820
Payroll (millions)	$ 199	$ 58
Retail trade	1,931	884
Employees	26,410	9,920
Payroll (millions)	$ 262	$ 96
Finance, insurance & real estate	889	191
Employees	17,469	1,295
Payroll (millions)	$ 336	$ 27
Services	2,824	1,023
Employees	35,370	8,438
Payroll (millions)	$ 544	$ 108
Civilian labor force (1988)	141,250	94,190
Employed	136,210	91,790
Unemployed	5,040	2,400
Percentage unemployed	3.6	2.5
Gross sales (1988, thousands)	$ 5,403,825	$1,931,405
Banks and offices (1988)	10 / 74	7 / 37
Deposits (thousands)	$ 2,170,477	$ 623,961
County finances (1987, thousands)		
General revenue	$ 183,785	$ 78,806
General expenditures	153,727	74,806
Debt outstanding	86,656	57,375
State tax allocations to counties:		
1987	$ 9,972,427	$5,240,349
1988	10,553,829	5,640,040
1989	11,125,570	5,884,915

These columns, in the aggregate, deal with place, people, their institutions, and how they make a living. Missing is any sense of cultural-social activity and recognition of those bonds that bind diverse groups together, as well as strains that pit county against county, city against county, and even one small community against another a short distance away. In light of recent annexation squabbles and go-it-alone policies sometimes advocated by citizens of Columbia and Richland and Lexington counties, it would be folly to deny the existence of such forces, which are, after all, quite normal. Loyalty to hearth, school, and neighborhood is an admirable quality. Yet such sentiments can be divisive, and one cannot ignore the fact that race often is a root cause of these divisions.

At the same time, the power of regionalism is indeed real. The idea of the Midlands, the work of a four-county planning council, and a federally ordained metropolitan area all mitigate against an every-man-for-himself approach. In addition, interstate highways and sprawling suburbs, both of which have limited respect for political boundaries, go far toward making a solid quilt out of many pieces. As many observers have noted, seen from a plane the Columbia area looks like a single entity. It is only on the ground or when one studies a map that scores of jealous little fiefdoms assume reality. Nevertheless, as urban, suburban, and even rural Midlanders begin to face similar problems, the potential for cooperation increases. Political union may always be an anathema to some area residents. Yet the clear blue sky remained intact in 1966 when Columbia and Richland County agreed to institute joint taxing procedures, and there are those willing to bet that additional functional relationships are possible, even desirable and potentially beneficial.

In March of 1990, leaders from various local governments, the University of South Carolina, Greater Columbia Chamber of Commerce, and Central Midlands Regional Planning Council held a two-day "summit" to ponder the present situation and chart a course for the future. Discussion centered upon growth, drugs, solid waste management, and education. But basic to all suggestions for change was an emphasis upon *regionalism* and recognition of the fact that the quality of daily life depends upon greater *regional* cooperation. Common themes among those discussing growth were calls for a park system to enhance use of the area's rivers and lakes, new measures to protect the environment, a true public transit system, consolidation of public utilities, and economic cooperation across political borders.

Recognizing that efforts to merge city and county had gone nowhere and annexation usually stirred up a fuss, these individuals advocated a three-pronged plan: tax-base sharing, more thoughtful analysis of current problems by the media, and a stronger Central Midlands Regional Planning Council. Tax-base sharing, simply put, means sharing both the cost of attracting new business to the Midlands and the revenue it brings. The press, in the view of some participants, excels in highlighting problems but is short on solutions. An ill-informed public, they stressed, is not well equipped to make decisions. Restructuring the regional council, giving it "teeth," would require new state statutes, yet many of those attending this "summit" believe that is the way to go. In their view, membership should be mandatory, not voluntary, and the council should be given limited legal authority to deal with inter-jurisdictional squabbles.

The decision to concentrate attention upon growth, drugs, solid waste, and education was no accident, for a pre-conference survey revealed widespread concern for these matters and gnawing fear that elected officials were not cooperating as they should to meet these challenges. And although, like most such meetings, this one was long on talk and dreams, it soon produced results. Six months later, Lexington County began replacing its catch-all "green boxes" with trash compactors and separate receptacles for "recyclable" materials, and in October the four-county area received $1.6 million in public and private funds to beef up its "Fighting Back" campaign designed to curb drug abuse. The preliminary survey, taken early in 1990, also disclosed that Midlands residents rated their schools "fair" and their roads "adequate." Most individuals queried were merely "satisfied" with the pace of growth and the tenor of daily life, not "very satisfied," and expressed belief that problems such as drugs (the number one bugaboo) could best be handled through regional cooperation. But, when asked to evaluate their local governments, they gave them only a middling grade of "C."

This response from 333 area residents can be contrasted with a nationally based study of some 300 American cities conducted at about the same time. In the summer of 1990, *Money Magazine* rated Columbia the sixty-eighth best place to live in the United States. This survey by 252 readers was based upon the quality of air and water, crime statistics, and the number of hospitals and doctors. A year earlier, the Columbia area was 242nd out of 300 communities. Quite a leap in only twelve months!

During the 1980s, various individuals also gave voice to their personal impressions of South Carolina's capital city and its suburbs. To poet-novelist James Dickey it was "an easy-going place, with some fine old homes, good local theater, and the most imaginative small zoo" he had ever seen. Dickey also stressed "the meridional aspect" of this urban complex: a unique balance between Appalachia and the Atlantic.[2] Another well-known Southern writer, John Egerton, thought it "a pretty city" that moved without any sense of urgency and usually did things piecemeal, partly, he surmised, because of a fragmented governmental structure, splintered as it was by the special interests of a large city, two counties, and a clutch of towns and villages.[3]

Washington Post travel writer John Sharkey found the region rife with serendipity, pleasant surprises in a leisurely, uncrowded setting where tourist attractions were staffed by individuals always ready to chat.[4] Sharkey liked the outdoor murals and broad avenues that "seemed more suited to a city much larger" and all but eliminated traffic jams. "Turn your head briefly," he wrote, "and you will miss what passes for the evening rush hour." His Midlands, which encompassed Edgefield, Camden, and even Greenwood, was a place where "landscape and history come together for the curious traveler." And, curious traveler that he was, Sharkey's special joy was "an unexpected cache" of newsreel films at USC's McKissick Museum.

As Dickey, Egerton, and Sharkey emphasize, this is a multifaceted community that defies easy classification and possesses a large dose of what one might call the "double N" factor: it is neither this nor that. Almost from the beginning it was home to a college, but clearly is not a college town. It built cotton mills and acquired a huge military base, yet never became either a mill town or a "soldier" town, except perhaps in wartime. Scores of entrepreneurs have dreamed of the Congaree's potential, but Columbia failed to become a river port. Ironically, today, thanks to Lexington's Lake Murray, it is, if anything, a "lake" city. It welcomes tourists and, as Sharkey discovered, has something to offer them, but their dollars are not a prime source of revenue.

"It's a wonderful city. . . . It's still a big small town—it's small enough that you are always running into someone you know, but not so small that you know everyone."

Georgia-born Clay Burnette, noted
Columbia basket maker, *Southern Accents*
(November 1990), p. 64.

Thomas Taylor's community of 100,000 or so obviously is not a bustling metropolis; neither is it a sleepy little county seat. The *Greater*

Columbia Visitors Guide, the pages of the *State* almost any day (and especially on Fridays and Sundays), and those of *Point,* the independent newsweekly that may become the *Osceola* of the 1990s, quickly dispel any ill-founded notion that nothing is going on. Yet the pace of this "easy-going place" can be fast or slow, depending on whether one is attending a USC football game with 75,000 rabid fans, elbowing through crowds as Five Points pays tribute to Ireland's patron saint, hoisting a beer at Jaco's Corner, or eating a breakfast of eggs, grits, and bacon at the Capitol Restaurant on Main Street.[5] And a general reluctance to be pigeon-holed is, in the opinion of newsman Robert Pierce, this city's greatest asset. Although some may see weakness in diversity, to him this "amorphous blend" makes South Carolina's capital "Everyman's city."[6] If nothing else, thanks to this many-splendored mix, Columbia, not its satellites with their shopping malls and housing developments, defines the region that is the heart of the Midlands.

Turning to Richland County, anyone who roams through its swamps, fields, streams, and sand hills will be struck by the constantly changing landscape. South of the Sumter highway lies a broad domain, flat as a table top and dotted largely with one-story homes and rare clusters of tall oaks hiding proud old mansions that somehow eluded Sherman's torch. This expanse, reminiscent of scenery found in much of the coastal plain that arcs southward through Georgia, Alabama, and Mississippi, ends, of course, in the awesome silence of Congaree Swamp . . . and it is the only part of the county where trees flaunt delicate swags of Spanish moss. Yet this miniature "Deep South," once cotton fields, also is home to a trio of massive 20th century wonders: Westinghouse, Union Camp, and the Wateree Station of South Carolina Electric and Gas.

North of the road to Sumter lie Fort Jackson, much of the city of Columbia, and what at first glance seem to be endless suburbs. But drive out Monticello Road to the northwest along the Broad River; and, shortly after passing Columbia Bible College, four lanes become two and one is surrounded by pine trees and dense undergrowth. That corner of the county, from the river to the Winnsboro Road (Route 321), remains a quiet, forested enclave with an occasional church and few homes and farms. The same cannot be said for the west bank of the Broad along I-26 or Richland's northeastern quadrant, land bounded by the highway to Rock Hill (Route 21) and Fort Jackson's northern frontier. There, lured by accessibility promised by two interstates (20 and 77), real estate moguls have sliced the sand hills and the first ripples of the Piedmont into "mini" farms and housing lots. This is a region where, unlike the dogwood and honeysuckle, signs bearing the words "For Sale—Residential Sites" bloom year-round.

In some parts of the county, with a bit of imagination, it is possible to watch Colonel Thomas Taylor lead a band of patriots in pursuit of the British foe and see Keziah Brevard's huge carriage rumble along a dirt road as she sets forth to visit a neighbor. But Columbia has changed so much that it is difficult to envision W. B. Nash or even William Gonzales slipping easily into the urban scene. If Taylor were to look out over the city from what is now Arsenal Hill, Sidney Park would lie at his feet. In the distance, the Palmetto Center certainly would catch his eye, as would the AT&T tower and other Main (Richardson) Street structures that all but blot out the capitol dome. Yet the low lands to the southwest, wrapped in blue haze, would look much as they did two centuries ago. If the colonel ever voiced doubts concerning transformation of one of his plantations into a town, which seems highly unlikely, this panorama of present-day Columbia should put such thoughts to rest. "It was," he might conclude, "a damned good swap after all!"

Notes

1. Kovacik and Winberry, *South Carolina*, pp. 212–13.
2. James Dickey, "Why I Live Where I Live," *Esquire* (April 1981), pp. 63–64.
3. John Egerton, "Columbia, S.C. A Southern Center Where There Still May Be Time," *Osceola* (7 November 1972), pp. 10–11. Reprinted from *City* (Summer 1972), pp. 52–56.
4. John Sharkey, "Columbia, the Gem of the Midlands—South Carolina, That Is," *Washington Post* (2 April 1989), pp. E 1–2.
5. The Capitol Restaurant (1210 Main) and Jaco's at Rosewood Drive and Bluff Road, also known as the Spit & Argue Club, apparently trace their origins to the years immediately before World War I. The runner-up as veteran purveyor of food and drink is the Seaboard Diner, which began life as the Seaboard Cafe in the early 1920s.
6. Robert A. Pierce, "Columbia's Strength Lies in Her Diversity," *State* (24 February 1985), p. B 2.

Intendants and Mayors, 1806–1865

Intendants

John Taylor	1806	William F. DeSaussure	1826–1827
Abraham Nott	1807	E. H. Maxcy	1828–1829
Claiborne Clifton	1807	William C. Preston	1830
John Hooker	1808	William C. Clifton	1831
Daniel Faust	1808	E. H. Maxcy	1832
Simon Taylor	1809	M. H. DeLeon	1833–1835
Robert Stark	1810	John Bryce	1836–1838
Simon Taylor	1811	Robert W. Gibbes	1839–1840
Daniel Faust	1812–1814	Benjamin T. Elmore	1841
William E. Hayne	1815	R. H. Goodwyn	1841
James Gregg	1816	William M. Myers	1842–1844
Daniel Morgan	1817	William B. Stanley	1845–1846
James T. Goodwyn	1818–1821	Joel Stevenson	1846
David J. McCord	1822	Edward Sill	1847–1849
James T. Goodwyn	1823	Henry Lyons	1850
David J. McCord	1824	A. H. Gladden	1851–1852
James T. Goodwyn	1825	William Maybin	1853–1854

Mayors

Edward J. Arthur	1855–1857
James D. Tradewell	1857–1859
Allen J. Green	1859–1861
John H. Boatwright	1861–1863
Thomas J. Goodwyn	1863–1865

Terms usually began in April of each year. Mayors, like intendants, at first were elected for twelve months; but, after Arthur and Tradewell won re-election, the council initiated a system of two-year terms.

Columbia Business Directory, 1860

BUSINESS DIRECTORY

AUCTIONEERS AND COMMISSION MERCHANTS

Jennings J. H...88 Richardson
Levin L. T..210   do
McDonald D. P. & Co 198   do
Phillips A. R...................Taylor bet Richardson and Assembly
Wood Wm. S...........Washington bet Richardson and Assembly

BAKERS

Dial Wm. H......................Taylor bet Richardson and Sumter
Gardner Samuel...104 Richardson
Mann Solomon...231   do
Simmons H 246   do
Stadtler George...207   do

BLACKSMITHS, WHEELWRIGHTS, & c.

Kennedy A. W.......................................Upper cor Sumter
Gruber John ....Sumter cor Upper
Monckton & Wright ....Laurel bet Richardson and Assembly
McAndrew William...........Washington bet Assembly and Gates
Mason G. T...Gervais cor Pulaski
Young R. E......................Assembly bet Washington and Lady

BOARDING HOUSES

Creight Miss N ....117½ Richardson
Gibenrath Mrs. Elizabeth ....54 Richardson
Hislop Mrs. A. E ....234½ Richardson
Hunt E ....76 Richardson
Loomis Cyrennius...............Pendleton bet Sumter and Marion

From *The Columbia Directory*, published by Julian A. Selby and printed in Columbia on the power press of R. W. Gibbes.

McCully John ....34 Richardson
McMahon Mrs. Mary...........s s Senate bet Sumter and Marion
Shiver Wm ....n w cor Taylor and Marion
Speck Mrs. D. C..89 Richardson
Stratton Mrs. M. W.................n w cor Gervais and Assembly
Wells James H ....240 Richardson

BOOK-BINDERIES

Carolinian Bindery.......Washington bet Richardson and Sumter
Stokes E. R ....rear 177 Richardson

BOOK-SELLERS

Glass Peter B ....175 Richardson
Townsend & North......................................162   do

BOOT AND SHOE DEALERS

Bruns & Eilhardt ....105 Richardson
Ehrlich M 91   do
Flanigan Thomas...174   do
Flanigan P. H. 148   do
Oliver & Bro..197   do
Thompson G. M. & Co 190   do
Young W. H..173   do

BUILDERS

Beck Robert...............s s Laurel bet Richardson and Assembly
Johnson Robert W.............Henderson bet Laurel and Richland
Troy James ....n e cor Taylor and Henderson
Waring Clarke..........................s w cor Lady and Henderson

CARRIAGE MANUFACTURERS

Brennen & Carroll.................s e cor Washington and Sumter
Frazee P. F.........n s Washington bet Richardson and Assembly
Greenfield W. K ....Gervais opp Charleston Railroad Depot

CHINA, GLASS AND EARTHENWARE

Nichols Henry C...133 Richardson
Stanley William B 180   do

CLOTHIERS

Abrahams, Harris & Co................................119 Richardson
Anderson R. C. & Co 157   do

Blume Lewis..124   do
Bull Thomas 242   do
Drieson Julius...87½   do
Fullings E. & Co 141   do
Himan & Rich..250   do
Jacobs M..236   do
Johnson G. M 138   do
Kaufman Henry 83   do
Kaul L..113   do
Lilienthal Moses 212   do
Peixotto D. C..213 Richardson
Roth H 191   do
Swaffield R ....3 Granite Range
Townley, Farley & Co...............................206 Exchange Row

CONFECTIONERY AND FANCY GOODS

Heise John H...152 Richardson
Kirsten C. H..95   do
LeFort Victor L...204   do
Mann Solomon...231   do
McKenzie A...136   do
Simmons H 246   do

COOPERS

Hennies William ....19 Richardson
Norman Charles ....64½   do

COPPERSMITH

Perpignon F...72 Richardson

DENTISTS

Dargan K. S ....266 Richardson
Reynolds & Reynolds 140   do
Gregg D. P..............................s e cor Richardson and Plain
Sigesmond S. B. ....3½ Granite Range
Smith George...163 Richardson

DRESS TRIMMINGS

Poppe Mrs. A. H.......w s Richardson bet Plain and Washington

DRUGGISTS

Fisher & Heinitsh ....100 Richardson
Griffin W. B 171   do

McGregor Peter G...92   do
Miot C. H. 196   do
Purse W. W 55   do
Sill Edward 123   do

DRY GOODS

Bedell Charles A...165 Richardson
Clarke & Goodwin 121   do
Dye J. C 220   do
Elias L 229   do
Falls & Kinard...169 Richardson
Goodwin A. G.............................1 Granite Range   do
Gracey John I. & Co.......................................118   do
Green J. C.................................2 Granite Range   do
Lopez Samuel..77   do
Sims & Baldwin.........................5 Granite Range   do
Walker J. C..177   do

EXPRESS COMPANY

Adams'..117 Richardson

FRUIT DEALERS

Allworden G. V..188 Richardson
Beard H. & S 226   do
Bahlmann John 99   do
Brill C..237   do
Hertwig F...75   do
Huffman H 62   do
Sessford W. K...94   do

FURNITURE WAREROOMS

Bower George S ....214 Richardson
Berry Milo H...135   do
Squier A. C 172   do

GILDER

Brown Joseph...112 Richardson

GROCERS

Bates O. Z..199 Richardson
Baldwin C. H..52   do

Beard John 37   do
Bollinger William...145   do
Brown Matthew ....n s Gervais bet Gadsden and Wayne
Bryce Robert...87 Richardson
Cantwell P 252   do
Dye J. C..220   do
Feaster J. N..194   do
Ferguson Mrs. Sarah 241   do
Forbes John G. 48   do
Franck H. C...232   do
Friday James K 223   do
Hinrichson H 110   do
Hope Edward...80   do
Lyons J. C..245   do
Lyles William ....64 Richardson
McGuinnis Michael..................s w cor Gervais and Assembly
McGuinnis William...20   do
McMahon J. S ....178 Richardson
Maguire Robert...234   do
Milling J. & Co 163   do
Mordecai I. D. 128   do
Moore Mrs. M 250   do
Muller & Senn...249   do
Nunamaker G. B 11   do
Seegers J. C..101   do
Smith E. C. & Bro...219   do
Smith Peter B 97   do
Stenhouse E...68   do
Thompson G. D ....cor Richardson and Medium

GUNSMITHS

Kraft P. W ....184 Richardson
Reckling H 79   do

HARDWARE, CUTLERY, &c.

Allen & Dial..192 Richardson
Baldwin C. H..52   do
Fisher & Agnew & Co 168   do

HATS AND CAPS

Fuller P. W...238 Richardson
Remsen C. P 187   do

HOTELS

Assembly House......................Plain bet Assembly and Gates
City......................................s w cor Richardson and Laurel
Congaree................................n w cor Richardson and Lady
United States............................s e cor Richardson and Lady

ICE DEALERS

Gage A. & Co..........Washington bet Richardson and Assembly

IRON FOUNDERS AND MACHINISTS

Alexander John & Co........................n e cor Lady and Wayne
Glaze William.............................n e cor Laurel and Lincoln

LAGER BEER BREWERS

Bauman J. & Co..101 Richardson
Grieshaber & Wolf.........................29, 31 and 33   do

LAWYERS

Arthur E. J..2 Law Range
Bachman & Waties..1   do
Bauskett John...8   do
Black J. A..196½ Richardson
Black S. R..196½ Richardson
DeSaussure W. F..3 Law Range
Gregg & Adams...7   do
Green John S..........s s Washington bet Richardson and Sumter
McMaster F. W..5 Law Range
Wallace William......s s Washington bet Richardson and Sumter
Pearson John H..rear Court House
Talley Wm. H...4 Law Range
Tradewell & DeSaussure.................................6   do

LIVERY STABLES

Green & Bailey...............w s Sumter bet Blanding and Laurel
Hitchcock W., Lady bet Richardson and Sumter, and cor Lady
   and Assembly
Reardon G. W......s s Washington bet Richardson and Assembly

MARBLE WORKERS

Boyne and Sprowl.....................s e cor Richardson and Laurel
Duane T....................w s Richardson bet Laurel and Richland

MILLINERS

Cooper Mrs. M. S......................................124 Richardson
Kenneth Mrs. M. E...................................164   do
Smith Mrs. S. A 156   do

MUSIC STORES

Gardner Samuel.......................................196 Richardson
Newman Joseph..151   do
Rawls John G 142   do

PAINTER—PORTRAIT

Scarborough W. H ....Marion bet Pendleton and Senate

PAINTER—SIGN AND ORNAMENTAL

Newton G. G.......s s Washington bet Assembly and Richardson

PAINTERS—HOUSE

Brown James ....58 Richardson
King Charles ....w s Barnwell bet Senate and Gervais
Hines Joseph A ....n e cor Sumter and Lumber

PAINTS, OILS, &c.

Allen & Dial ....192 Richardson
Brown James...58   do
Fisher & Agnew & Co 168   do
Baldwin C. H...52   do

PAPER HANGERS, &c.

Barnes A. J. & Co ....49 and 137 Richardson
Brown James...58   do
Engelke Frederick.......................................86   do

PHOTOGRAPHERS, AMBROTYPES, &c.

Wearn & Hix ....170 Richardson
Zealy J. T..2 Granite Range

PHYSICIANS

Boatwright John H ....e s Sumter bet Plain and Washington
Fair & Huot ....8 Fair's Row
Freeman William C.........e s Sumter bet Plain and Washington

Gaston J. McF. ....n s Plain bet Richardson and Sumter
Gibbes Robert W. & Son ....Plain bet Sumter and Marion
Goodwyn T. J ....Gervais bet Richardson and Sumter
Kennedy A. W ....Laurel bet Richardson and Assembly
King Barrington S....................................173½ Richardson
Logan C ....Room No. 1, 78 Richardson
Lynch John.......................w s Assembly bet Taylor and Plain
Nott Junius..208 Richardson
Powell & Templeton ....s s Plain bet Richardson and Sumter
Talley A. N..................s s Washington bet Marion and Sumter
Taylor B. W ....e s Sumter bet Lady and Washington
Trezevant D. H. & Son....................n w cor Plain and Marion
Watkins B. F......................n w cor Richardson and Pendleton

PLATER—GOLD AND SILVER

Kraft H. F...184 Richardson

SADDLE AND HARNESS MAKERS

Hawley Levi ....201 Richardson
Hopson & Sutphen.....................................147   do
Hoagland C 1   do
Brady B. H..71   do

SASH, BLIND AND DOOR MANUFACTURERS

Beck Charles.................s s Laurel bet Richardson and Sumter
Killian & Wing ....Pickens bet Washington and Plain

SALOONS

Berry Thomas W...111 Richardson
Claffey James...235   do
Grieshaber & Wolf........................29, 31 and 33   do
Hunt A. M..............................s e cor Lady and Richardson
Mordecai I. D ....128 Richardson
Mundle Samuel D....................s w cor Laurel and Richardson
McKenna Charles ....239 Richardson
Shodair Louis..195   do
Stork & Hussung 205   do
Stork John..193   do
Turner Bernard 243   do
Seegers J. C...101   do
Vogel Theodore ....225 Richardson
West William H. ....under Congaree House

SCHOOLS

Brumby & Davidson.............w s Barnwell bet Taylor and Plain
Stuart Barnwell S ....n w cor Laurel and Henderson
Reynolds Misses Jane A. & Sophia M.........n w cor Washington
and Marion
Johnston W. B ....n e cor Washington and Bull
Ursuline Academy..................s e cor Richardson and Blanding
Zimmerman Dr. & Mrs ....e s Pickens opp Washington
Evans J. E. B ....n s Taylor bet Sumter and Marion
Sosnowski Mrs. C.....................s s Taylor bet Bull and Marion
Reddoch Mrs. R....................n s Taylor bet Marion and Bull
Selby Mrs. M. A. C ....w s Gates bet Washington and Plain
Walker C. Bruce........................s w cor Pickens and Gervais
Crowe J. W.......................s s Sumter bet Blanding and Taylor
Powell Henry W. (Public)..............w s Lincoln bet Washington
and Plain
Monteith Mrs. M. S. (Public)..............n s Taylor bet Assembly
and Gates

SEGAR STORES

Beard H. & S ....226 Richardson
Feaster T. D 185   do
Feininger Adolph...211   do
Volger C 203   do

TAILORS

Eisenmann J. F. & Co...................................150 Richardson
Johnson G. M 138   do
Miles Aaron...74½   do
Walker W. W..186   do

TIN AND SHEET IRON WARE AND STOVES

Due John S ....107 Richardson
Palmer A 222   do
Pearse Samuel..108   do
Walter Wm. T...115   do
Smith James W ....Plain bet Richardson and Assembly

UPHOLSTERERS

Barnes A. J. & Co ....49 and 137 Richardson
Engelke F. W...86   do

WATCHES AND JEWELRY

Gazetteer of Richland County, 1879–1880

GAZETTEER
of
RICHLAND COUNTY, S.C.

An Alphabetical List of the Villages in the County, giving
their Location, and the names of the Business
Men in each, and the Principal
Farmers in the County.

Acton
(30 miles s e of Columbia)

Ariel Rev W H, pastor
  Methodist Church
Clarkson Alex G, merchant
  and planter
Clarkson John H, farmer
Garner Gilbert, farmer
Garner S G, merchant
  and farmer
Green A J, atty at law

Joyner Belton, farmer
Rives W Hampton, merchant
Singleton C K, planter
Singleton Richard, postmaster
  and merchant
Stiles Rev C A, pastor
  Baptist Church
Tillinghast Rev J H, rector
  Zion Church

Eastover
(On W C & A R R, 27 miles s e of Columbia)

Clark M R, physician
Cloud D L, farmer
Cross H W D, farmer

Dowdy W H, farmer
Gayden John, farmer
Green Allen J, atty at law

From *Columbia City Directory, 1879–1880*, printed in Charleston for Charles Emerson
& Co.

Henry S G, farmer
House Jesse, farmer
Joyner Mrs M C,
  telegraph operator
Joyner P Hamilton,
  postmaster, Express
  and R R agt
Keith W W, physician
McLaughlin John, farmer
McLaughlin W B, farmer
Morris Tobias, merchant
Oakman W, merchant
Rhame L F, farmer
Scott T K, farmer

Shoolbred Mrs. Fannie,
  farmer
Shoolbred James, merchant
Sloan W S, farmer
Taylor J H, school teacher
Taylor J T, farmer
Taylor Simon, physician
Taylor W S, farmer
Tillinghast Rev J H, pastor
  Episcopal Church
Van Bokkelen A H, merchant
Walker H W, merchant
Weston Wm, farmer
Wright F P, farmer

Gadsden
(On S C R R, 21 miles s e of Columbia)

Adams H W, farmer
Adams J I, farmer
Adams W, farmer
Dwight J S, postmaster
Garick John, farmer
Garick J P, farmer and
  merchant
Huguenin A, farmer
Huguenin J G,
  notary public
James J B, farmer

Kaminer G A & Bro,
  merchants
Leman E P, farmer
McKenzie S W, farmer
  and physician
Oakman & Williams,
  merchants
Scott T A, farmer
Weston W W, farmer
Williams G K, farmer
Williams J G, farmer

Grovewood (Postoffice)
(On W C & A R R, 12 miles s e of Columbia)

Hopkins Turnout
(On S C R R, 12 miles s of Columbia)

Adams J R, farmer
Bush G B, farmer
Chappell F M, farmer
Chappell P G, farmer
Hopkins E, farmer
Myers J A, farmer
Pagett J N, farmer
Pagett J R, farmer
Pagett R A, farmer

Patterson A, farmer
Reese A H, farmer
Smith C T, farmer
Smith Edward, physician
Spigner R W, farmer
Suydam Dr C H, farmer
Sykes J H, trial justice and farmer
Sykes J G Jr, farmer
Sykes Z T, farmer

Kingville
(On S C R R, 25 miles s e Columbia)

Adams Warren, farmer
Bradford W R, R R trestle
master
Carroll John C, farmer
Carter Joel, farmer
Drafts Geo M, merchant
Douglas C M, trial justice
Fouts W T, R R section master
Green T C, R R agt
Joyner N C, farmer
Joyner Ruffin, farmer
Lenoir W Eugene, postmaster
Seay J Robt, farmer
Touchberry J E, farmer
Trumblo James, R R supervisor

Wateree (Postoffice)
(On W C & A R R, 32 miles s e of Columbia)

Mayors, 1865–1990

James G. Gibbes	May 1865–April 1866
Theodore Stark	April 1866–July 1868
Francis L. Guenther	July–August 1868
Cyrus H. Baldwin	August–November 1868
John McKenzie	1868–1870
John Alexander	1870–1878
William B. Stanley	1878–1880
Richard O'Neale, Jr.	1880–1882
John T. Rhett	1882–1890
Fitz William McMaster	1890–1892
Walter C. Fisher	1892–1894
William M. Sloan	1894–1898
Thomas J. Lipscomb	1898–1900
Fort Sumter Earle	1900–1904
Thomas H. Gibbes	1904–1908
William S. Reamer	1908–1910
Wade Hampton Gibbes	1910–1914
Lewie A. Griffith	1914–1918
R. Johnson Blalock	1918–1922
William A. Coleman	1922–1926
Lawrence B. Owens	1926–1941
Fred D. Marshall	1941–1946
Frank C. Owens	1946–1950
J. Macfie Anderson	1950–1954
J. Clarence Dreher	1954–1958
Lester L. Bates	1958–1970
John T. Campbell	1970–1978
Kirkman Finlay, Jr.	1978–1986
T. Patton Adams	1986–1990
Bob Coble	1990–

Guenther and Baldwin were appointed by military authorities in 1868. With inauguration of commission government in 1910, mayors began serving four-year terms. Also, until 1950 the mayor was chosen by the council, not the voters.

Population, 1790–1990

| | Richland County | | | Columbia | | |
Year	Total	White	Black	Total	White	Black
1790	3,390	2,479	1,451	——	——	——
1800	6,097	2,929	3,168	——	——	——
1810	9,027	3,468	5,559	1,000[a]	——	——
1820	12,321	4,499	7,822	——	——	——
1830	14,772	5,238	9,534	3,310	1,807	1,503
1840	16,397	5,326	11,071	4,340	2,136	2,204
1850	20,243	6,764	13,479	6,060	3,184	2,876
1860	18,307	6,863	11,444	8,052	4,395	3,657
1870	23,025[b]	7,842	15,177	9,298	4,002	5,295
1880	28,573	9,185	19,388	10,036	4,338	5,698
1890	36,821	11,933	24,885	15,353	6,563	8,790
1900	45,589	17,513	28,070	21,108	11,244	9,858
1910	55,143	25,609	29,533	26,319	14,772	11,546
1920	78,122	41,623	36,499	37,524	23,067	14,455
1930	87,667	49,520	38,127	51,581	32,062	19,519
1940	104,843	62,484	48,359	62,396	40,201	22,195
1950	142,565	92,071	50,494	86,914	55,671	31,243
1960	200,102	134,930	64,845	97,433	67,789	29,488
1970	233,868	159,092	73,437	113,542	78,677	33,998
1980	269,735	161,561	103,955	101,208	58,798	40,762
1990	285,720	160,063	119,394	98,052	52,625	42,837

a. Estimate, 1816.
b. After 1870, totals may include races other than Caucasian and Negro.

Sources for Columbia–Richland County History

This story is based largely upon materials found in the South Caroliniana Library and the South Carolina Department of Archives and History and relies heavily upon newspapers and census data, both published and unpublished. The bibliography that follows has two goals: indicate what books, articles, papers, and individuals were consulted in the telling of this tale and point the way to resources and collections that others interested in a similar adventure may find useful.

Books and Articles

Abbott, Martin. *The Freedmen's Bureau in South Carolina, 1865–1872.* Chapel Hill, 1967.

Acts of the Legislature of South Carolina, Relating to the Town of Columbia. Columbia, 1851?

Adallis, D. *History of the Columbia, S.C., Greek-American Colony, 1884–1934.* Columbia, 1934? Brief account.

Adams, Lark Emerson, and Rosa Stoney Lumpkin, eds. *Journals of the House of Representatives, 1785–1786.* Columbia, 1979. A volume in the State Records Series, 1776–1794.

Address of the Hon. Benj. F. Perry, Before the South Carolina Institute, at Their Third Annual Fair, November 1856. Charleston, 1857.

Allen, W. F. ["Marcel"]. "A Trip to South Carolina." *Nation* (27 July 1865): 106–107.

————. "State of Things in South Carolina." *Nation* (10 August 1865): 172–73.

Allen, William Cox. *A History of the First Baptist Church, Columbia, South Carolina.* Columbia, 1959.

Andrews, Sidney. *The South Since the War. . . .* Boston, 1866.

————. "Three Months Among the Reconstructionists." *Atlantic Monthly* (February 1866): 237–45.

Annual Report of the Mayor of Columbia. Columbia, 1860.

Applied History Program, University of South Carolina. *Cultural Resource Survey of Goodwill Plantation, Richland County, South Carolina.* Columbia, 1985?

Project coordinated by Michael C. Scardaville; Katherine Hurt Richardson, editor.

Arsenault, Raymond. "The End of the Long Hot Summer: The Air Conditioner and Southern Culture." *Journal of Southern History* (November 1984): 597–628.

Art Work of Columbia, S.C. Chicago, 1905. Nine folios of turn-of-the-century photographs. Text by August Kohn.

Bailey, N. Louise, Mary L. Morgan, and Carolyn R. Taylor, eds. *Biographical Directory of the South Carolina Senate, 1776–1985.* 3 vols. Columbia, 1986.

Baker, Steven G. *The Historic Catawba Peoples: Exploratory Perspectives in Ethnohistory and Archaeology.* Columbia, 1975.

Bancroft, Frederic. *Slave-Trading in the Old South.* Baltimore, 1931.

Barnum, Phineas Taylor. *Struggles and Triumphs.* . . . Buffalo, 1889.

Barnwell, Robert W., Jr. "Reports on Loyalist Exiles from South Carolina, 1783." *Proceedings*, South Carolina Historical Association (1937): 43–46.

Barrett, John G. *Sherman's March Through the Carolinas.* Chapel Hill, 1956.

Base Hospital, Camp Jackson. *As You Were, 1917–1918.* St. Augustine, 1919.

Bateman, John A. *A Columbia Scrapbook, 1701–1842.* Columbia, 1915.

Bates, Lester L., Sr., and Joe C. Norman. "Columbia 2000." *South Carolina Urban & Regional Review* (June 1971): 3–6.

Be It Remembered. Columbia, 1974. Describes creation of Robert Mills Historic House and Park.

Beardsley, Edward H. *A History of Neglect: Health Care for Blacks and Mill Workers in the Twentieth-Century South.* Knoxville, 1987.

Bernard, Karl, Duke of Saxe-Weimar-Eisenach. *Travels Through North America During the Years 1825 and 1826.* 2 vols. Philadelphia, 1828.

Bleser, Carol, ed. *Secret and Sacred: The Diaries of James Henry Hammond, a Southern Slaveholder.* New York, 1988.

Boles, John. *Black Southerners, 1619–1869.* Lexington, 1983.

Bowen, Eli. *The United States Post-Office Guide.* New York, 1851.

Brevard, Keziah Goodwyn Hopkins. *The Diary of Keziah Goodwyn Hopkins Brevard (1860–1861).* Columbia, c. 1974. Brief, but important record of plantation life in lower Richland.

Bridenbaugh, Carl. *Myths and Realities: Societies of the Colonial South.* Baton Rouge, 1952.

Brown, Richard Harwell. *The South Carolina Regulators.* Cambridge, Mass., 1963.

Bryan, John Morrill. *An Architectural History of the South Carolina College, 1801–1855.* Columbia, 1976.

Bryant, Lawrence C., ed. *Negro Senators and Representatives in the South Carolina Legislature, 1868–1902.* Orangeburg, 1968.

Bryant, William Cullen. *Letters of a Traveller.* . . . New York, 1869.

Buckingham, J. S. *The Slave States of America.* 2 vols. London, n. d.

Byars, Alvin W. *Lintheads.* Cayce, 1983.

————— . *Olympia-Pacific: The Way It Was, 1895–1970.* West Columbia, c. 1981.

Calhoun, Richard J., ed. *Witness to Sorrow, the Antebellum Autobiography of William John Grayson.* Columbia, 1990. See also, Samuel Gaillard Stoney's earlier edition of this same work in the *South Carolina Historical Magazine* (July 1947–April 1950).

Carlton, David L. *Mill and Town in South Carolina, 1880–1920.* Baton Rouge and London, 1982.

Cauthen, Charles E., ed. *Family Letters of the Three Wade Hamptons, 1782–1901.* Columbia, 1953.

————— . *Journals of the South Carolina Executive Councils of 1861 and 1862.* Columbia, 1956.

Central Midlands Regional Planning Council. *An Analysis of the Columbia, S. C., Urbanized Fringe Area.* Columbia, 1973.

————— . *The Central City Development Plan: A Progress Report on the First Five Years.* Columbia, 1974.

————— . *Central Midlands Regional Planning Council—First Six Years, 1969–1975.* Columbia, c. 1976. These publications are merely representative of ongoing reports and studies relative to Columbia, Richland County, and the Midlands produced by this body, which maintains a small library at its headquarters.

Charles, Allan D. "The Burning of Columbia." *Southern Partisan* (Spring/Summer 1981): 8–10.

Childs, Arney R. *Planters and Business Men: The Guignard Family of South Carolina, 1795–1930.* Columbia, 1957.

Citizens Committee for the Metropolitan Area. *Citizen's Design for Progress, Columbia, South Carolina.* Columbia, 1965.

Clark, W. A. *The History of Banking Institutions Organized in South Carolina Prior to 1860. . . .* Columbia, 1922.

Cohen, Hennig, ed. *A Barhamville Miscellany.* Columbia, 1956.

Columbia Art Association, 1915–1975, Columbia Museum of Art, 1950–1975: A History. Columbia, 1975.

Columbia Board of Trade. *Columbia, S. C., The Future Manufacturing and Commercial Centre of the South.* Columbia, 1871.

Columbia Chamber of Commerce. *Columbia, South Carolina: Chronicles and Comments, 1786–1913.* Columbia, 1913.

————— . *Columbia—Unlimited.* Columbia, 1925.

Columbia City Directories. Columbia [and other cities], 1859 +.

Columbia Graded Schools. *Annual Reports.* Columbia, 1883–1928.

Cooper, Thomas, and David J. McCord, eds. *The Statutes at Large of South Carolina.* 10 vols. Columbia, 1836–41.

Coulter, E. Merton. *The Confederate States of America, 1861–1865.* Baton Rouge, 1950.

Cousins, Ralph E., *et al. South Carolinians Speak: A Moderate Approach to Race Relations.* Dillon, S.C., 1957.

Crewdson, Robert L. "The End in the Carolinas: Burning Columbia." *Civil War Times Illustrated* (October 1981): 10–19.

Davidson, Chalmers Gaston. *The Last Foray—The South Carolina Planters of the 1860s: A Sociological Study*. Columbia, 1971.

Derrick, Samuel M. *Centennial History of the South Carolina Railroad*. Columbia, 1930.

DeSaussure, H. W. *A Series of Numbers Addressed to the Public*. . . . Columbia, 1822. Letters to the *South-Carolina State Gazette* concerning Vesey Plot and slavery.

Dickey, James. "Why I Live Where I Live." *Esquire* (April 1981): 63–64.

Directory of Social Organizations of Columbia, South Carolina. Columbia, 1918. Apparently the first of several similar publications.

Doxiadis Associates, *et al*. *Central City, Columbia, S.C., Master Plan*. n. p., 1969. An exhaustive study that has shaped attitudes toward development throughout the late 20th century.

Draine, Tony, and John Skinner, compilers. *Richland District, South Carolina: Land Records, 1785–1865*. Columbia, 1986.

Drayton, John. *Memoirs of the American Revolution*. . . . Charleston, 1821.

———. *A View of South-Carolina, as Respects Her Natural and Civil Concerns*. Charleston, 1802.

Dunlap, Benjamin. *Columbia: Memories of a City*. Columbia, 1986.

Du Pré, Lewis. *Observations on the Culture of Cotton*. Georgetown, 1799.

Economic Development Commission of Greater Columbia, Richland and Lexington Counties. *Greater Columbia Data Book*. Columbia, c. 1976.

Edgar, Walter B., N. Louise Bailey, *et al*, eds. *Biographical Directory of the South Carolina House of Representatives, 1692–1815*. 3 vols. Columbia, 1977–84.

Edgar, Walter B., and Deborah K. Woolly. *Columbia: Portrait of a City*. Norfolk, 1986.

Edgar, Walter B., *et al*. *A Columbia Reader, 1786–1986*. Columbia, n. d. Fine collection of firsthand impressions of city.

Edgar, Walter B., and J. Cantey Heath, Jr. *A Training Guide for Kensington*. Eastover, c. 1985.

Edwards, Ann D., *et al*. *The Governor's Mansion of the Palmetto State*. Columbia, 1978.

Egerton, John. "Columbia, S. C. A Southern Center Where There Still May Be Time." *Osceola* (7 November 1972): 10–11. Reprinted from *City* (Summer 1972): 52–56.

English, Elizabeth D., and B. M. Clark. *Richland County: Economic and Social*. Columbia, 1923.

Fant, Christie Zimmerman. *The State House of South Carolina: An Illustrated Historical Guide*. Columbia, 1970.

Featherstonhaugh, G. W. *Excursion Through the Slave States*. . . . New York, 1844.

Foote, Shelby. *The Civil War: A Narrative*. 3 vols. New York, 1958–74.

Ford, Lacy K. "Self-Sufficiency, Cotton, and Economic Development of the South Carolina Upcountry, 1800–1860." *Journal of Economic History* (June 1985): 261–67.

Fox, William Price. *Southern Fried Plus Six*. Philadelphia, 1968.

Freehling, William F., ed. *The Nullification Era: A Documentary Record*. New York, 1967.

Freehling, William F. *Prelude to Civil War: The Nullification Controversy in South Carolina, 1816–1836*. New York and London, 1965.

Furman, Richard. *Exposition on the Views of the Baptists Relative to the Coloured Population of the United States*. Charleston, 1823.

Graydon, Nell S. *Tales of Columbia*. Columbia, 1964. Well-told vignettes of the local scene.

Green, Edwin L. *A History of Richland County*. Columbia, 1932. First part (1732–1805) of a projected two-volume study. Green's research notes are available at the South Caroliniana Library. This book was re-issued in 1974.

Green, Mary Fulton. "A Profile of Columbia in 1850." *South Carolina Historical Magazine* (April 1969): 104–21.

Hamer, Philip M., George C. Rogers, Jr., and David R. Chesnutt, eds. *The Papers of Henry Laurens*. 12 vols. Columbia, 1968–.

Hammer and Company, Associates. *The Columbia Area: Development Potentials*. Atlanta, 1959.

Hammer, Greene, Siler Associates. *The Economy of Metropolitan Columbia, South Carolina*. Atlanta, 1965.

Hennig, Helen Kohn, ed. *Columbia: Capital City of South Carolina, 1786–1936*. Columbia, 1936. Brings together considerable regional information in pertinent essays. Reprinted in 1966 with a mid-century supplement.

Hennig, Helen Kohn. *William Harrison Scarborough: Portraitist and Miniaturist*. Columbia, 1937.

Herbert, R. Beverley. *What We Can Do About The Race Problem*. Columbia, 1948.

Higbe, Kirby. *The High Hard One*. New York, 1967. Unusually frank account of a career in baseball.

Higginson, T. W. "Some War Scenes Revisited." *Atlantic Monthly* (July 1878): 1–9.

Hill, James D. "The Burning of Columbia Reconsidered." *South Atlantic Quarterly* (July 1926): 269–82.

Holcomb, Brent H., ed. *Record of Deaths in Columbia, South Carolina, and Elsewhere as Recorded by John Glass, 1859–1877*. Columbia, c. 1986.

Hollis, Daniel Walker. "Costly Delusion: Inland Navigation in the South Carolina Piedmont." *Proceedings*, South Carolina Historical Association (1968): 29–43. Perceptive analysis of the canal mania.

———. *University of South Carolina*. 2 vols. Columbia, 1951, 1956. Comprehensive history of college and university, 1801–1956.

Holt, Thomas. *Black Over White: Negro Political Leadership in South Carolina During Reconstruction*. Urbanna, 1977.

Hooker, Richard J., ed. *The Carolina Backcountry on the Eve of the Revolution: The Journal and Other Writings of Charles Woodmason, Anglican Itinerant*. Chapel Hill, 1953. Incisive, if biased account of life in the Midlands.

Hopkins, Laura Jervey. *Lower Richland Planters: Hopkins, Adams, Weston, and Related Families of South Carolina*. Columbia, 1976.

Hoskins, Joseph A., compiler. *President Washington's Diaries, 1791–1799*. Summerfield, N.C., 1921.

Ivers, Larry E. *Colonial Forts of South Carolina, 1670–1775*. Columbia, 1970.

Jameson, J. Franklin, ed. *Diary of Edward Hooker, 1805–1808*. Washington, 1897. Unusual account of life in early Columbia.

Jarrell, Hampton M. *Wade Hampton and the Road Not Taken*. Columbia, 1949.

Jones, Lewis Pinckney. *South Carolina: A Synoptic History for Laymen*. Lexington, 1978.

———. *Stormy Petrel: N. G. Gonzales and His State*. Columbia, 1973. Perceptive study of an important editor.

Kellar, Herbert Anthony, ed. *Solon Robinson, Pioneer and Agriculturalist; Selected Writings*. 2 vols. Indianapolis, 1936.

Kelsey & Guild. *The Improvement of Columbia, S. C. Report to the Civic League*. Harrisburg, Pa., 1905.

King, Edward. *The Great South*. . . . Hartford, 1875.

King, Joe M. *A History of South Carolina Baptists*. Columbia, 1964.

Klein, Rachel N. *Unification of a Slave State: The Rise of the Planter Class in the South Carolina Backcountry, 1760–1808*. Chapel Hill and London, 1990.

Kohn, August. *The Cotton Mills of South Carolina*. Columbia, 1907.

Kovacik, Charles F., and John J. Winberry. *South Carolina: A Geography*. Boulder, Colo., 1987.

LaBorde, Maximilian. *History of the South Carolina College*. Columbia, 1859.

Lambert, Robert. *South Carolina Loyalists in the American Revolution*. Columbia, 1987.

Larsen, Christian L., and Robert H. Stoudemire. *Columbia City Government*. Columbia, 1948.

Latimer, S. L., Jr. *The Story of the "State," 1891–1969, and the Gonzales Brothers*. Columbia, 1970.

Lee, Henry. *Memoirs of the War in the Southern Department of the United States*. New York, 1869.

Lefler, Hugh Talmage, ed. *A New Voyage to Carolina by John Lawson*. Chapel Hill, 1967. Important account of life in the Midlands before European settlement.

Lofton, Paul Stroman, Jr. "Calm and Exemplary: Desegregation in Columbia, South Carolina." Jacoby and Colburn, ed., *Southern Businessmen and Desegregation* (Baton Rouge 1982): 70–81.

———. "The Columbia Black Community in the 1930s." *Proceedings*, South Carolina Historical Association (1984): 86–95.

Lord, Francis A. "Camp Sorghum." *Sandlapper* (August 1975): 29–33.

Lucas, Marion Brunson. *Sherman and the Burning of Columbia.* College Station, Texas, and London, 1976. Brings together virtually all of the research on this controversial subject.

Lumpkin, Henry. *From Savannah to Yorktown: The American Revolution in the South.* Columbia, 1981.

Mackay, Alexander. *The Western World.* . . . 2 vols. Philadelphia, 1849.

McDowell, William L., ed. *Colonial Records of South Carolina: Documents Relating to Indian Affairs, 1754–1765.* 2 vols. Columbia, 1958, 1970.

McLaurin, Melton Alonzo. *Paternalism and Protest: Southern Cotton Mill Workers and Organized Labor, 1875–1905.* Westport, Conn., 1971.

McMaster, Fitz Hugh. *History of the First Presbyterian Church and Its Churchyard, Columbia, S. C.* Columbia, n. d.

Malone, Dumas. *The Public Life of Thomas Cooper, 1783–1839.* Columbia, 1961. Reprint of a 1926 edition.

Martineau, Harriet. *Retrospect of Western Travel.* 2 vols. New York, 1838.

Massey, Mary Elizabeth. *Refugee Life in the Confederacy.* Baton Rouge, 1964.

Mathews, R. Arthur. *Towers Pointing Upward.* Columbia? 1973. History of Columbia Bible College.

Maxey, Russell. *The Columbia High School Story: In Memoriam, 1915–1975.* Columbia, 1984.

————. *South Carolina's Historic Columbia: Yesterday and Today in Photographs.* Columbia, 1980.

Medlin, William F. *Richland County Landmarks: Volume 1, Lower Richland.* Hopkins, S.C., 1981.

Meriwether, Robert L. *The Expansion of South Carolina, 1729–1765.* Kingsport, Tenn., 1940. In-depth study of regional life in the mid-1700s.

Meyer, Jack. *William Glaze and the Palmetto Armory.* Columbia, 1982.

Milling, Chapman J. *Red Carolinians.* Chapel Hill, 1940.

Mills, Robert. *Statistics of South Carolina.* . . . Charleston, 1826.

Montgomery, John A. *Columbia, South Carolina: History of a City.* Woodland Hills, California, 1979. Intriguing illustrated survey with bibliography and index.

Moore, John Hammond. "South Carolina's Reaction to the Photoplay 'Birth of a Nation.' " *Proceedings*, South Carolina Historical Association (1963): 30–40. Reprinted in Lander and Ackerman, *Perspectives in South Carolina History: The First 300 Years* (Columbia, 1973): 337–47.

Moore, John Hammond, ed. "Jared Sparks Visits South Carolina." *South Carolina Historical Magazine* (July 1971): 150–60.

Moore, Margaret DesChamps. "A Northern Professor Winters in Columbia, 1852–1853." *South Carolina Historical Magazine* (October 1959): 183–92.

Mulkey, Floyd. "Rev. Philip Mulkey, Pioneer Baptist Preacher in Upper South Carolina." *Proceedings*, South Carolina Historical Association (1945): 3–13.

Myers, H. Melville, Jr., compiler. *The Stay-Law, and All the Amendments. The Tax Law of 1866. An Ordinance of the Convention. Freedman's Code. New Constitution of the State of South Carolina.* Charleston, 1866.

Nadelhaft, Jerome J. *The Disorders of War: The Revolution in South Carolina.* Orono, Maine, 1981.

Newby, I. A. *Black South Carolinians: A History of Blacks in South Carolina from 1895 to 1968.* Columbia, 1973.

Nicholson, William A. *The Burning of Columbia.* Columbia, 1895.

Ochenkowski, J. P. "The Origins of Nullification in South Carolina." *South Carolina Historical Magazine* (April 1982): 121–53.

O'Connell, J. J. *Catholicity in the Carolinas and Georgia: Leaves of Its History.* New York, 1879.

Official Roster of South Carolina Servicemen and Servicewomen in World War II. 5 vols. Columbia, 1967.

Official Roster of South Carolina Soldiers, Sailors, and Marines in the World War, 1917–18. 2 vols. Columbia, c. 1932.

Ordinances of the Town of Columbia. . . . Columbia, 1823, 1851. Various editions of city ordinances are available, 1858 +. Most of these compendiums include state statutes relating to Columbia.

Osburn, George C. *Woodrow Wilson: The Early Years.* Baton Rouge, 1968.

Padgette, Minier, *et al. History of Columbia Hospital, 1947–1966.* Columbia, 1967.

Pancake, John S. *This Destructive War: The British Campaign in the Carolinas, 1780–1782.* University, Ala., 1985.

Parkinson, B. L. *A History of the Administration of the City Public Schools of Columbia, S. C.* Columbia, 1925.

Pierce, Robert A. "Columbia's Strength Lies in Her Diversity." *State* (24 February 1985): B 2.

Pike, James S. *The Prostrate State: South Carolina Under Negro Government.* New York, 1874.

Pine, W. M. "Atmospheric Determinants and the History of the Old South." *South Carolina Historical Magazine* (October 1989): 313–21.

Pogue, Nell C. *South Carolina Electric and Gas Company, 1846–1964.* Columbia, 1964.

Pope-Hennessy, Una, ed. *The Aristocratic Journey.* . . . New York and London, 1931.

Proceedings of the Colored People's Convention of the State of South Carolina Held in Zion Church, Charleston, November 1865. Charleston, 1865.

Proceedings of the Constitutional Convention of South Carolina, January 14–March 17, 1868. Charleston, 1868.

Quint, Howard H. *Profile in Black and White: A Frank Portrait of South Carolina.* Washington, 1958.

Ramsay, David. *The History of South-Carolina, from Its First Settlement in the Year 1670, to the Year 1808.* 2 vols. Charleston, 1809.

Raumer, Frederick von. *America and the American People.* New York, 1846.

Rawls, Benjamin. *Biblical Criticism and Reminiscences of Columbia.* Columbia, 1861.

Real Estate Report: Columbia, S. C. Columbia, 1990.

Report and Recommendations of the Richland County-City of Columbia Study Commission. Columbia, 1972.

Reports on the Free School System, to the General Assembly of South-Carolina. . . . Columbia, 1840.

Reynolds, John S. *Reconstruction in South Carolina, 1867–1877.* Columbia, 1905.

Rice, John Andrew. *I Came Out of the Eighteenth Century.* New York and London, 1942. Engaging insights into Columbia of the 1890s as seen by a small boy.

Richland County Board of Education. *Annual Reports.* Columbia, 1914–c. 1919.

Royall, Anne. *Mrs. Royall's Southern Tour; or, Second Series of the Black Book.* 3 vols. Washington, 1830–31.

Ruckstuhl, F. Wellington. *The Value of Beauty to a City.* Columbia, 1905.

Sass, Herbert Ravenel. *Outspoken: 150 Years of the News and Courier.* Columbia, 1953.

Scott, Edwin J. *Random Recollections of a Long Life: 1806 to 1876.* Columbia, 1884. Unusual account of business scene in both Columbia and Lexington. Reprinted in 1969 with index.

Seaboard Air Line Railroad. *Mercantile and Industrial Review of Columbia and Richland County.* n. p., 1908?

Selby, Julian A. *Memorabilia and Anecdotal Reminiscences of Columbia, S. C. . . .* Columbia, 1905.

Shand, Robert W. "Columbia from 1846 to 1866." *State* (10 June 1928): 15, 27. Reminiscences edited by Edwin L. Green.

Sharkey, John. "Columbia, the Gem of the Midlands—South Carolina, That Is." *Washington Post* (2 April 1989): E 1–2.

Simkins, Francis Butler, and Robert H. Woody. *South Carolina During Reconstruction.* Chapel Hill, 1932.

Simms, William Gilmore. *The Geography of South Carolina.* Charleston, 1843.

Smith, Alfred Glaze, Jr. *Economic Readjustment of an Old Cotton State: South Carolina, 1820–1860.* Columbia, 1958.

Smith, Wilbur, and Associates. *The Columbia Canal Study.* Columbia, 1979.

Smith, Wilbur, *et al. Columbia Area Transportation Study.* Columbia, 1972.

Smythe, Mrs. A. T., *et al. South Carolina Women in the Confederacy.* 2 vols. Columbia, 1907.

Snowden, Yates. *History of South Carolina.* 5 vols. Chicago and New York, 1920.

South Carolina Department of Archives and History. *A Guide to Local Government Records in the South Carolina Archives.* Columbia, 1988.

South Carolina Division of Research and Statistical Services. *South Carolina Statistical Abstract.* Columbia, 1990.

South Carolina Historical Records Survey Project. *Inventory of the County Archives of South Carolina: Richland County.* Columbia, 1940.

"South Carolina Manufactures." *De Bow's Review* (June 1853): 621–23. A survey of Richland County and vicinity.

Southern Christian Advocate (16 August–29 November 1850). Eight articles by "Champagnon du Voyage" on rides in Columbia area.

Southern Famine Relief Fund of Philadelphia. Philadelphia, 1867?

"Southerners After the Yankees Have Withdrawn." *Nation* (15 August 1867): 133–35.

Springs, Holmes B. *Selective Service in South Carolina, 1940–1947*. Columbia, 1948.

Sproat, John G. "Firm Flexibility: Perspectives on Desegregation in South Carolina." Abzug and Maizlish, eds., *New Perspectives on Race and Slavery in America* (Lexington, 1986): 164–84.

Stirling, James. *Letters from the Slave States*. London, 1857.

Stokes, Allen H., Jr. *A Guide to the Manuscript Collection of the South Caroliniana Library*. Columbia, 1982.

Street, Elwood. "When the Soldiers Come to Town." *Survey* (18 August 1917): 433–35.

Stroyer, Jacob. *My Life in the South*. Salem, Mass., 1885. Unusual account by ex-slave of life at "Kensington" in the 1850s.

Taylor, Alrutheus Ambush. *The Negro in South Carolina During the Reconstruction*. Washington, 1924.

Teal, Harvey S., and Robert J. Stets. *South Carolina Postal History and Illustrated Catalog of Postmarks, 1760–1860*. Lake Oswego, Ore., 1989.

Thomas, John P., Jr. *Columbia Graded Schools: First Year, 1883–84*. Columbia, 1883.

Townsend, Belton O'Neall. "The Political Condition in South Carolina." *Atlantic Monthly* (February 1877): 174–94.

———. "The Result in South Carolina." *Atlantic Monthly* (January 1878): 1–12.

———. "South Carolina Morals." *Atlantic Monthly* (April 1877): 467–75.

———. "South Carolina Society." *Atlantic Monthly* (June 1877): 670–84. This series of articles by a young Florence attorney provides unique insight into local conditions during a crucial period.

Underwood, James Lowell. *The Constitution of South Carolina*. 3 vols. Columbia, 1986, 1989, 1992.

United States. Bureau of the Census. *Heads of Families at the First Census of the United States Taken in the Year 1790. . . .* Washington, 1907–1908. Also, subsequent census returns (titles vary), 1800–1980.

Wade, Richard C. *Slavery in the Cities: The South 1820–1860*. New York, 1964.

Wallace, David Duncan. *The History of South Carolina*. 4 vols. New York, 1934.

Wallace, David Duncan, and J. A. Gamewell, eds. *Richland Almanac*. Spartanburg, c. 1904.

Webster, Laura Josephine. *The Operation of the Freedmen's Bureau in South Carolina*. Northampton, Mass., 1916.

"Weep No More, Columbia." *Newsweek* (3 May 1965): 27–34.

Weir, Robert M. *Colonial South Carolina*. Millwood, N. Y., 1983.

Wikramanayake, Marina. *A World in Shadow: The Free Blacks in Antebellum South Carolina*. Columbia, 1973.

Williams, J. F. *Old and New Columbia*. Columbia, 1929. Among the most reliable of local reminiscences.

Williamson, Joel. *After Slavery: The Negro in South Carolina During Recon-struction, 1861–1877.* Chapel Hill, 1965.

Winberry, John J. "Indigo in South Carolina: A Historical Geography." *Southeast-ern Geographer* (November 1979): 91–102.

Woodward, C. Vann, ed. *Mary Chesnut's Civil War.* New Haven and London, 1981.

Zagarri, Rosemarie. "Representation and the Removal of State Capitals, 1776–1812." *Journal of American History* (March 1988): 1,239–56.

Zimmerman, Christie Powers. *Receipts and Recollections.* Columbia, 1977.

Newspapers

Charleston newspapers (pre-1800) and the *News and Courier* in the late 19th century often contain Midlands material; however, Columbia's own press obvi-ously is more relevant to the local scene. The most important files are those of the *State* (1891 +) and especially the afternoon *Columbia Record* (1913–1988). An in-dex to both dailies beginning in November 1973 is available at the Richland County Public Library. Also, researchers may consult a printed index to early is-sues of the *State*, 1891–1901, 1903–1912. For a description of holdings in various depositories see John Hammond Moore, *South Carolina Newspapers* (Columbia, 1988). Other substantial files of area newspapers include:

Batesburg Advocate, 1901–1911
Carolina Free Press, 1930–1940
Chapin Times, 1976 +
Columbia Register, 1875–1898
Columbia Telescope, 1816–1839
Daily Phoenix, 1865–1875
Daily Record, 1897–1913.
Daily South Carolinian, 1849–1865
Daily Southern Guardian, 1858–1865
Daily Telegraph, 1847–1851
Dispatch-News [Lexington], 1919 +
Fort Jackson Journal, 1953–1960
Independent News of Irmo, 1980 +
Journal [West Columbia], 1955 +
Leader [Fort Jackson], 1962 +
Leesville Twin-County News, 1913–1921
Lexington Dispatch, 1894–1913
Osceola, 1972–1978
Palmetto Leader, 1925–1957
Richland Northeast, 1982 +
St. Andrews News, 1975–1985.
South Carolina Gazette, 1925–1930.

South-Carolinian, 1838–1849.
Southern Times and State Gazette, 1830–1838.
Star-Reporter, 1963 +
Tri-Weekly South Carolinian, 1849–1865.
Twin-City News [Batesburg], 1925 +

Dissertations and Theses

Barnwell, Robert W., Jr. "Loyalism in South Carolina, 1765–1785." Ph.D. diss., Duke University, 1941.

Bass, Robert Duncan. "The Autobiography of William J. Grayson." Ph.D. diss., University of South Carolina, 1933.

Bellardo, Lewis Joseph, Jr. "A Social and Economic History of Fairfield County, South Carolina, 1865–1871." Ph.D. diss., University of Kentucky, 1979.

Bridwell, Ronald E. "The South's Wealthiest Planter: Wade Hampton I of South Carolina, 1754–1835." Ph.D. diss., University of South Carolina, 1980. Massive study of an individual who did much to shape Columbia and Richland County.

Ford, Ralph Watson. "The Changing Pattern of South Carolina's Railroad System: 1860–1912." Master's thesis, University of South Carolina, 1986.

Harris, Herbert Richard. "The Confederate War Effort in Richland District, South Carolina." Master's thesis, University of South Carolina, 1976.

Hayes, Jack Irby, Jr. "South Carolina and the New Deal, 1932–1938." Ph.D. diss., University of South Carolina, 1972.

Hellams, Wilton. "A History of South Carolina State Hospital, 1821–1900." Ph.D. diss., University of South Carolina, 1985.

Holland, Davis Rutledge. "A History of the Desegregation Movement in the South Carolina Public Schools During the Period 1954–1976." Ph.D. diss., Florida State University, 1978.

Lofton, Paul Stroman, Jr. "A Social and Economic History of Columbia, South Carolina, During the Great Depression, 1929–1940." Ph.D. diss., University of Texas, 1977. Thorough study of a crucial decade.

McNeill, Paul Wesley. "School Desegregation in South Carolina, 1963–1970." Ph.D. diss., University of Kentucky, 1979.

McQuillan, David Charles. "The Street Railway and the Growth of Columbia, South Carolina, 1882–1936." Master's thesis, University of South Carolina, 1975. In-depth analysis of an important subject.

Mendenhall, Marjorie S. "A History of Agriculture in South Carolina, 1790 to 1860." Ph.D. diss., University of North Carolina, 1940.

Myers, Florence Bacher. "Columbia Court House and Post Office: The Building and Its Architect, 1870–1874." Master's thesis, University of South Carolina, 1977.

Peay, Mary Elizabeth. "W. H. Hand and His Influence Upon Public Education in South Carolina." Master's thesis, University of South Carolina, 1932.

Secrest, Andrew McDowd. "In Black and White: Press Opinion and Race Relations in South Carolina, 1954–1964." Ph.D. diss., Duke University, 1972.

Seman, Paul Frederick. "Structural and Spacial Distribution of Black Owned Businesses in Columbia, South Carolina, 1900 to 1976." Master's thesis, University of South Carolina, 1977.

Sherrill, William Howard, Jr. "The Columbia Industrial Park: Past, Present, and Future." Master's Thesis, University of South Carolina, 1977.

Smith, Fenelon DeVere. "The Economic Development of the Textile Industry in the Columbia, South Carolina, Area From 1790 Through 1916." Ph.D. diss., University of Kentucky, 1952. Important survey of regional mill growth.

Stokes, Allen H., Jr. "Black and White Labor in the Development of the Southern Textile Industry, 1800–1920." Ph.D. diss., University of South Carolina, 1977.

Stoudemire, Robert Harold. "The Organization and Administration of the City of Columbia." Master's thesis, University of South Carolina, 1948.

Swearingen, Mary Hough. "Poor Relief in Richland County." Master's thesis, University of South Carolina, 1936.

Thompson, Michael Edwin. "Blacks, Carpetbaggers, and Scalawags: A Study of the Membership of the South Carolina Legislature, 1868–1870." Ph.D. diss., Washington State University, 1975.

Van Orsdell, Consuelo. "The Carolina Orphan Home, With Addenda on the Richland County Children in the Carolina Orphan Home." Master's thesis, University of South Carolina, 1941.

Records of Governmental Bodies and Organizations

Some pertinent materials are, of course, available at Columbia's City Hall and Richland County's Judicial Center. In addition to specific items cited below, one should consult these publications: South Carolina Department of Archives and History, *A Guide to Local Government Records in the South Carolina Archives* (Columbia, 1988) and Allen H. Stokes, Jr., *A Guide to the Manuscript Collection of the South Caroliniana Library* (Columbia, 1982).

South Carolina Department of Archives and History

Bureau of Refugees, Freedmen, and Abandoned Lands, 1865–1870.
Petitions to the General Assembly, 1776–1862.
Reports of the Commissioners of Columbia, 1786–1819.
Richland County, Supervisors' Scrapbooks, 1912–1946.
State Parks Division, 1965–1966.
State Superintendent of Education, 1865–1871
Unpublished census schedules, 1790–1880, 1900–1910.

South Caroliniana Library

Broad River Bridge Company, 1870–1912.
Bureau of Refugees, Freedmen, and Abandoned Lands, 1866–1867.

Columbia Chamber of Commerce, 1904–1955.
First Baptist Church, Columbia, 1809–1840, 1876–1878.
First Presbyterian Church, Columbia, 1794–1952.
Richland County Citizens Committee, 1964–1976.
Richland County Committee for Conservative Government, 1962–1964.
Richland County Democratic Club, 1876–1880.
Richland County School Board, District One, 1949–1962.
South Carolina State Grange, 1873–1905.
WPA Records, 1934–1940.
Way Side [sic] Hospital, 1862–1865.

Unpublished Research Papers and Journals

South Carolina Department of Archives and History

Applied History Program, University of South Carolina. "Historical and Architectural Survey of Waverly: Columbia's First Suburb." Project coordinated by Michael C. Scardaville, 1987.
Elmore, B. T. "Journal of the Volunteer Company from Columbia." Describes activity relative to the Seminole War, 11 February–11 May 1836.

South Caroliniana Library

Carlton, David. "The Columbia Canal and Reconstruction: A Case Study."
Dickey, Gary C. "The LaVarre Hall Takeover of the *Columbia Record.*"
Edens, Jenny. "J. Drake Edens and the Modern Day Republican Party."
Gay, Charles E. "Historical and Field Research on Fort Congaree of 1718."
Giles, Doris B. "The Anti-War Movement in Columbia, South Carolina, 1965–1972." The library also has interviews relative to this subject taped in 1987 with Brett Bursey and Laughlin McDonald.
Holton, Elizabeth C., and Caroline L. Sherrill. "History of First Church of Christ, Scientist [Columbia]."
Kershaw, Joseph. "Account Book, 1774–1775." Copy of original at State Historical Society of Wisconsin, Madison, Wis.
Klugh, J. Eugene. "The Defeat of the Civic Center."
McKay, Robert. "South Carolina Redeemed, 1865–1887." A Reconstruction scrapbook.
McLeod, Daniel. "County Home Rule—Past, Present, and Future."
Moore, John Hammond. "South Carolina and the Southern Claims Commission, 1871–1880." Copy also available at the South Carolina Department of Archives and History.
Robinson, David W. "Columbia Academy."
Wheeland, Craig M. "The Policy Process in Columbia, South Carolina: A Case Study of Minority Representation on City Council."

University of South Carolina, Instructional Services Center

McFadden, Grace Jordan. "Quest for Human Rights: The Oral Recollections of Black South Carolinians." Tapes made c. 1980.

Personal Papers

South Carolina Department of Archives and History

Olin D. Johnston.

South Carolina Historical Society

James Simpson to Sir Henry Clinton, Miscellaneous Manuscripts.

South Caroliniana Library

Artemus Family, John M. Bateman, George A. Buchanan, Burn Family, Valentine B. Chamberlain, John A. Chase, Jr., Childs Family, Bettie J. Clarke, Conner Family, Thomas Cooper, William Couper, William A. Courtenay, Robert Means Davis, Edwin De Leon, Emily Caroline Ellis, Grace Brown Elmore, Gustavus A. Follin, Jr., Nancy Fox, James Heyward Gibbes, Wade Hampton Gibbes, William E. Gonzales, Samuel Green, Hampton Family, Heyward Family, Charles Woodward Hutson, Richard M. Jefferies, James Jones, Ellison Summerfield Keitt, Kincaid-Anderson Family, LaBorde Family, Francis Lieber, Samuel Leland, John McCray, Fitz William McMaster, Robert Whitehead McNeely, Mrs. J. A. Moore, Palmer Family, John B. Patrick, C. C. Platter, William Campbell Preston, Reedy-Beacham Family, William W. Renwick, Reynolds Family, Roberts Family, Seibels Family, Richard Singleton, Louisa McCord Smythe, Yates Snowden, John Taylor, Samuel Spencer Verner, Charles G. Ward, Patterson Wardlaw, LeRoy Franklin Youmans.

Interviews

Julian Adams, Daniel G. Boice, Ronald E. Bridwell, Dennis E. Daye, A. Mason Gibbes, Augustus T. Graydon, Fritz Hamer, Herbert Hartsook, James Hill, Daniel W. Hollis, Jane McDowell Hopkins, Laura Jervey Hopkins, Theodore J. Hopkins, Jr., Thomas L. Johnson, James C. Leventis, Heyward McDonald, John Middleton, Thomas S. Price, Nancy C. Rampey, Timothy D. Renick, Betty Jean Rhyne, Eleanor Richardson, Katherine Hurt Richardson, George C. Rogers, Jr., Timothy Rogers, Isabel Whaley Sloan, Allen H. Stokes, Jr., Harvey Teal, Reed Wilson, John H. Wright.

Index